ENGLISH PLACE-NAME SOCIETY

The English Place-Name Society was founded in 1924 to carry out the survey of English place-names. The annual subscription is 25*s*., and members receive the annual volume; in certain circumstances they may take in place of the current volume one for an earlier year if stocks allow. The Society has issued the following volumes:

    I. (Part 1) *Introduction to the Survey of English Place-Names* (out of print).
    (Part 2) *The Chief Elements used in English Place-Names* (out of print and discontinued).
    II. *The Place-Names of Buckinghamshire.*
    III. *The Place-Names of Bedfordshire and Huntingdonshire* (out of print).
    IV. *The Place-Names of Worcestershire* (out of print).
    V. *The Place-Names of the North Riding of Yorkshire* (out of print).
  VI, VII. *The Place-Names of Sussex*, Parts 1 and 2.
 VIII, IX. *The Place-Names of Devonshire*, Parts 1 and 2.
    X. *The Place-Names of Northamptonshire.*
    XI. *The Place-Names of Surrey.*
    XII. *The Place-Names of Essex* (out of print).
    XIII. *The Place-Names of Warwickshire.*
    XIV. *The Place-Names of the East Riding of Yorkshire and York.*
    XV. *The Place-Names of Hertfordshire.*
    XVI. *The Place-Names of Wiltshire.*
    XVII. *The Place-Names of Nottinghamshire.*
    XVIII. *The Place-Names of Middlesex (apart from the City of London).*
    XIX. *The Place-Names of Cambridgeshire and the Isle of Ely.*
XX, XXI, XXII. *The Place-Names of Cumberland*, Parts 1, 2 and 3.
XXIII, XXIV. *The Place-Names of Oxfordshire*, Parts 1 and 2.
XXV, XXVI. *English Place-Name Elements*, Parts 1 and 2.
XXVII, XXVIII, XXIX. *The Place-Names of Derbyshire*, Parts 1, 2 and 3.
XXX, XXXI, XXXII, XXXIII, XXXIV, XXXV, XXXVI, XXXVII. *The Place-Names of the West Riding of Yorkshire*, Parts 1–8.

All communications with regard to the Society should be addressed to:

THE HON. SECRETARY, English Place-Name Society, University College, Gower Street, London, W.C. 1.

ENGLISH PLACE-NAME SOCIETY. VOLUME XXXI
FOR 1953–54

GENERAL EDITOR
A. H. SMITH

THE PLACE-NAMES OF
THE WEST RIDING
OF YORKSHIRE

PART II

ENGLISH PLACE-NAME SOCIETY.   VOLUME XXXI

THE PLACE-NAMES OF THE WEST RIDING OF YORKSHIRE

By

A. H. SMITH

PART II

OSGOLDCROSS AND AGBRIGG

WAPENTAKES

CAMBRIDGE

AT THE UNIVERSITY PRESS

1961

PUBLISHED BY
THE SYNDICS OF THE CAMBRIDGE UNIVERSITY PRESS

Bentley House, 200 Euston Road, London, N.W. 1
American Branch: 32 East 57th Street, New York 22, N.Y.
West African Office: P.O. Box 33, Ibadan. Nigeria

©

CAMBRIDGE UNIVERSITY PRESS
1961

Printed in Great Britain at the University Press, Cambridge
(Brooke Crutchley, University Printer)

PREFACE

THE second part of the place-names of the West Riding of Yorkshire deals with the names in the wapentakes of Osgoldcross and Agbrigg. This region, which extends from the marshlands along the lower reaches of the Ouse to the mountains on the Cheshire and Lancashire borders in the west, largely comprises the southern watershed of the Aire on its eastern course and that of its chief affluent the Calder. The principal towns are Goole, Pontefract, Wakefield, Dewsbury and Huddersfield.

The list of abbreviations and sources will be included in Part vii. So too will the historical introduction, the linguistic survey, the road-names and the river-names (referred to as Introd., Phonol., Roads and RNs. respectively). An analysis of the elements and the personal names in the place-names will also be included. A complete index to the place-names of the three Ridings will also be issued. As far as possible cross-references are given to pages in the first three parts, but in cases where the page-reference to later parts is not available when these earlier parts are sent to press, reference is to the part and the township in which a name occurs. For that reason each part contains its own index of the townships dealt with, as well as a township map of the appropriate wapentakes. For information on the various elements (which are printed in bold type) reference should be made to *English Place-Name Elements* (vols. xxv and xxvi of the Society's publications).

Acknowledgments of the help I have received from many quarters will be made in Part vii.

A. H. SMITH

UNIVERSITY COLLEGE, LONDON
October 1958

CONTENTS

Addenda and Corrigenda . . . . . *page* xi

IV. Osgoldcross Wapentake 1

V. Agbrigg Wapentake 99

Index of Townships in Part II 320

Map of the townships in the Wapentakes of Osgoldcross and Agbrigg . . . . *at end*

ADDENDA AND CORRIGENDA

ii, 14. BALNE. It should be noted that the recorded meaning of e.ModE *balne* is 'a water-bath, a warm-water bath'; *balne* is not actually found with the meaning 'bathing-place'. But no other suggestion can be made to explain the forms of this difficult name.

ii, 83. TANSHELF. Ekwall, Studies[1] 12, thought this was from an OE pers.n. *Tata*, gen. *Tatan*, but the OE weak gen. ending *-an* is not usually found in YW p.ns. (one spelling *Tyken-* for Tickhill i, 52 from a Chancery document is a rare example), and the contraction of *Tatan-* to *Tan-* therefore improbable. Dr Feilitzen makes the interesting suggestion that the first el. is an older p.n. OE *tād-denu* 'toad valley'.

ii, 88. Diblands Close. The ME surname *Dibel* (Reaney 94) is also possible.

ii, 98. *Hulin.* On the surname *Hulin* cf. Reaney 163 (from 1275).

ii, 110, 111. St Mary, *Saynt Anne Close.* These may have been properties of guilds in the parish church, as Professor Dickins notes.

ii, 115. SHARLSTON. Professor Löfvenberg suggests that there might have been an OE pers.n. *Scearf* (corresponding to ON *Skarfr*, cf. Björkman NP 122), which would explain many of the spellings; but it assumes that all the *S(c)harn*-spellings are errors for *S(c)haru-*. But it is a possible explanation.

ii, 126. CLUMPCLIFFE. Professor Löfvenberg points out that ON *klubba* is not an assimilated form of *klumba* (cf. Jóhannesson 368ff): the first meaning suggested for the name is not therefore appropriate.

ii, 141. WOODLESFORD. The single form *Widles-* (if it is not an error) arises from loss of *-r-* by dissimilation, and the modern form as well as some earlier spellings could arise directly from this (cf. Phonol. §25), as suggested by Professor Löfvenberg.

ii, 150. HORBURY LIGHTS. Professor Löfvenberg reminds us of the phonological difficulty of derivation from **leaht** 'channel', which should locally have become *laght, laught* (we may compare the development of lēac-tūn to Laughton i, 141). He suggests an OE (Angl) **līhte* denoting something like 'clearing, glade' (connected with lēoht 'light' which is often used with tree-names); cf. Löfvenberg 122.

ii, 153. Strawbenzio. Professor Dickins compares the German *Straubenzee*.

ii, 174. ARDSLEY. Dr Feilitzen suggests that the pers.n. could be OE *Ēanrēd*, which through assimilation of *-nr-* to *-r(r)-* appears as *Earæd* (BCS 533–4), *Eared* (cf. NoB 33, 79 note 27). This would also be appropriate for Ardsley i, 290.

ii, 198. MIRFIELD. The first el. could be the related sb. OE *myrgen* 'joy, pleasure', and the name would mean 'open land where games or the like were held'; it would in that case be comparable in sense to Wakefield ii, 163.

ii, 226. THICKLES. An OE *þiccels* would of course be normally formed from a verb (cf. EPN i, 150 s.v. -els). It should therefore be derived directly from a verb like OE *þiccian* 'to thicken, crowd together' but its topographical sense would doubtless be associated with *þicce* 'thick, dense', 'thicket', as suggested.

ii, 227. PADANARUM. This, and Padanarum (iii, 52), may be, as Professor Dickins suggests, examples of someone showing off his knowledge of Hebrew; the name means 'tilled land of the highlands'.

ii, 292. SCARHOUSE. Cf. Skier's Hall i, 112 (Addenda).

IV. OSGOLDCROSS WAPENTAKE

> *Osgotcros wapentac* 1086 DB
>
> (*wap' de*) *Osgodecros* 1166 P, *Osegodecros* 1246 *Ass*, *Hosgodecross* 1295 YI
>
> *Osgodescros wap'* 1167 P, *Osegotescros* 1188 P
>
> *Osegotecros wap'* 1180, 1183 P, 1252 Cl, 1293 Kirkst, *-crosse* 1280 YI, *Osgotecros* 13 YD x, c. 1210 Pont, 1219 *Ass*, 1276 RH, 1286 YI
>
> (*wap', libert' de*) *Osgodcros(se)* 1284 Kirkst, 1322 Pat, 1323 *Ass* 11, 1362 Works *et freq* to 1638 SessnR
>
> (*wap', libert' de*) *Osgotcrosse* 1316 Vill, 1327 Ipm, 1360, 1413 Pat, 1428 FA
>
> *Osgoldcrosse* 1379 PT, 1641 Rates

This wapentake extends westward from the lower Ouse to Castleford and South Kirkby; it lies between Lower Strafforth Wapentake on the south and the Aire on the north; the Went is the principal river running through it from the low hills in the west across the Great North road towards the extensive marshlands (now drained by many dikes) south of the Ouse. The principal towns are Goole, Pontefract and Castleford. Osgoldcross Wapentake takes its name from *Osgold Cross* in Pontefract 79 *infra*, where the wapentake presumably assembled. It is not uncommon for a cross to mark the site of a hundred or wapentake meeting-place, as was the case also in Staincross i, 261, Ewcross pt. vi *infra*, Buckrose YE 119 or Norman Cross Hnt 180. Within Osgoldcross there were two ill-defined non-administrative districts, Balne and Marshland.

BALNE, which survives as the name of the township of Balne 14 *infra*, and enters into other local names like Balne Hall 15, Balne Croft 26, Balne Moor 15, Bone Lane 46 *infra* as well as a few minor f.ns. (Balne Close 33 *infra*, etc.), was also used, chiefly from the fourteenth century, as an affix in names like Thorpe in Balne (from 1339) i, 19 *supra* and similarly in the early spellings of Fishlake (from 1343) i, 15 *supra* and Heck (from 1246) 18, Pollington (from 1365) 21, Moss (from 1586), Moseley (from 1607) 48, and Carlton (from 1274) pt. iv *infra*. It thus appears to have been the name of a large district which included the whole of the parish of Snaith and extended a little further south to Thorpe in Balne and Fishlake (in Lower Strafforth Wapentake), that is, roughly the land between the lower reaches of the Don and the Aire. It may have come to be used as a district name by an extension of its use in the name of the extensive Balne Moor. On the name *v.* Balne 14 *infra*.

MARSHLAND, *Merskland(ia)* 1302 BM, 1315 Pat, 1357 Selby, 1362 Works, 1400, 1412 Pat, *Mersshland* 1413, 1455, 1461 ib, *-lond* 1435 ib, *Mersland* 1419, 1422, 1467 ib, *Marsshland* 1473 ib, *Marsland* 1535 VE, *Marsh(e)land* 1547 FF, 1590 Camd, 1621 *Comm*, 1696 Pryme. Reedness, Whitgift, Goole and Hook 9, 11, 16, 20 *infra* are described as *in Merskland*, etc. These references show that Marshland was once the large area of marshy land along the south side of the Ouse, chiefly the parish of Whitgift. *v.* mersc, land. The earliest spellings in *Mersk-* are due to substitution of ON *-sk* for ME *-sh*.

i. Adlingfleet

In this parish Eastoft township, which is partly in Lincolnshire, was formerly part of Haldenby township.

1. ADLINGFLEET (98–8321)

Adelingesfluet 1086 DB
Adelingfleoth 1154–63 BM, 1164–77 YCh 487, 1293 BM, *-flet* 1199–1209 YCh 488, 1245, 1305 Ebor
Athelingflet(e), *-yng-* 13 Selby, YD ix, 1226 FF, 1230 P, 1275 YI *et passim* to 1399 Pat, *Athlingflet* 1531 Test iv
Athelingeflet(e) 1223 Pat (p), 1256 FF, 1302 Pat, *-fled* 1250 Baild
Adlingflet(e), *-yng-* 1260 Ch, 1267 Ebor, 1305 YI, 1320 YD ix, 1379 PT *et freq* to 1590 FF
Adelingeflet 1268 Ebor   *Adthelingflet* 1316 Vill
Adhelingflet(h) 1291 Tax, 1428 FA
Addlenfflett 1574 *Dep*

'The prince's water-channel', *v.* flēot, one of several examples of this word in the district (cf. Ousefleet 7, Swinefleet 10 *infra*, and YE 313). From its use in p.ns. along the Ouse, it might denote 'the stretch of a river, a reach' or refer to small creeks or inlets along the shores of the river; Adlingfleet is some distance from the Ouse but stands on the bank of the old River Don. The first el. is OE æðeling 'a prince, a nobleman'; there is no evidence for the use of this word as a pers.n., as suggested by Goodall.

ADLINGFLEET COMMON, 1824 O.S., from ME *commun* 'common land'. ADLINGFLEET INGS, *Adlingflete Inge* 1649 *YAS* 178, *v.* eng 'meadow'. ADLINGFLEET MOOR, 1846 *TA*, *mora de Athelingflete* 1342 YD x, *v.* mōr. BRACKEN HILL, *v.* brakni, hyll. BROADMARSH WELL. COW LANE. DODD'S DIKE. EAST FIELD, 1769 *EnclA*, *v.* ēast, feld. ELLCROFT BRIDGE. FOURSTANGS LANE, (a ditch) *Fourestangeg* (sic) 13 YD ix, *Fourstanges* 1349 ib x, *Lefour Stanges* 1380 ib, 'four poles', *v.* fēower, stǫng, used to mark a boundary or the like. GARNER HILL. GILL'S CLOSES. MAINS, *Adlingfleet Main* 1842 *TA*, *v.* main 'demesne land'. PENTLANDS, *Penteland* 1344 YD x, *The Pentlands* 1698 *Glebe*; doubtless an early example of e.ModE *pent* 'a place where water is pent up, an enclosed pool' (first evidenced 1570, NED s.v.), *v.* land. SAND HILL, 1771 M, *v.* sand, hyll. STONECROSS CLOSES, *Stonehorse close* (sic) 1735 *Eastoft*, *v.* stān, cros; the site of the cross is still marked and it is no doubt *boscin crose* 'wiche standethe betwixt Adlingeflete and Vsflete' 1575 *Dep.* WARE HO. WEST FIELD, 1769 *EnclA*, *v.* west, feld. WHINS GATE, *Whyennes-gate* 1607 Hnt, cf. *Wins House* 1817 M, *v.* hvin 'whin, gorse', gata.

FIELD-NAMES

Spellings dated 1316–1321 are YD ix, 1322–1396 YD x

(*a*) Adlingfleet Clough 1824 O.S. (*v.* clōh), Adlingfleet Grange 1817 M, Ings Meadow 1846 *TA* 5 (*v.* eng), South Field 1769 *EnclA* (*le Southfeld* 1343, *v.* sūð, feld).

(*b*) *Aldbrek* 1316 (*v.* ald, bræc 'thicket', dial. *breck* 'uncultivated strip'), *Biornhilles* 1316 (probably the OE pers.n. *Beorn*, as in Barn Hill YE 251, hyll), *Castelandes* 1316 (possibly ME *cast* 'a cast', used like OE wearp to describe 'land thrown up, silt', land), *le Croftes* 1321, *Croft* 1343, *Crostdyk* (sic) 1322 (*v.* croft, dīc), *Gousfelan* (a lane) 1318 (*v.* lane), *Holandaile* 13 Selby (*v.* hol[1], land, deill 'a share of land'), *le Intakes* 1316, *Intackdyc* 1383 (*v.* intak 'land taken in from waste', dīc), *Kagathlande* 1366 (*v.* foll., gata, land), (*the*) *Keyhead(e)* 1575 *Dep* (*v.* kay 'a quay', hēafod), *Mideldaile* 1342 (*v.* middel, deill 'a share of land'), *Morecroft* 1320, *Morediklandes* 1316 (*v.* mōr, croft, dīc and Adlingfleet Moor *supra*), *Nudyck* 1380 (*v.* nīwe, dīc), *le Pergarth* 1396 ('pear orchard', *v.* peru, garðr), *le Radecance* (sic for -*cauce*) 1316 (*v.* rād 'fit for riding on', caucie 'a raised way across marshland'), *les Resshcroftlandes* 1342, *Ruskitlands* 1698 *Glebe* (*v.* risc 'rush', croft, land), *le Thwerlandes* 1344 ('cross lands', *v.* þverr, land), *Waterhyng* 1383 (*v.* wæter, eng), *Watertonhyng* 1383 (from a local *Waterton* family 14 YD x, 19–20, eng).

2. Eastoft (98–8016)

Eschetoft(h) 1164–77 YCh 487, 1293 BM, *Es(s)hetoft* 1276 RH,
　1323 *MinAcct* 45
Esketoft 1199–1209 YCh 488, 1304 Ebor
Estoft(e) 13 *et freq* Selby, 1252 Ch, 1293 QW, 1314 Pat, 1316 Vill,
　1342 Baild *et freq* to 1594 FF
Essetoft 1304 Selby
Esttoft 1327 *MinAcct* 48, 1331 FF
Eastoft(e) 1572 WillY, 1641 Rates, 1822 Langd

'Homestead near the ash-wood', *v.* eski (sometimes influenced by
OE æsc), topt.

Gowersyle Moor (lost), *Guuersile, Queresile* 13 Selby, *Gowerstyle
more* 1589 *Eastoft, Gowcell more* 1597 ib, *Gower-, Goarsyle more* 1642,
1649 ib, cf. also *novam silam, Newsile* 13 Selby. The first el. may well
be the ME pers.n. or surname *Gu(h)er, Go(h)er* (OFr *Gohier* from
OG *Godehar,* or, in the case of the surname, from the Fr district
name *Goelle,* OFr *Gohiere, v.* Reaney 143). The second el. is from
MLG *sīl* 'a drain, a canal', or an OE equivalent **sīl* (cf. *sēoluc* 'a
gulley', EPN ii, 119–120, *Sylecrosse,* Sile Bank 10, 12 *infra*).

Eastoft Carr, cf. *Aykercarr* 1527 *Eastoft, v.* kjarr 'marsh'; the
meaning of *Ayker-* is uncertain.　Eastoft Hall, 1824 O.S.
Eastoft Moor, *Eastoft-moor-dyke* 1539, 1559 Hnt, *v.* mōr, dīc.
Field Lane.　West Ings, *Cotchers West Ings* 17 *Eastoft, v.* west,
eng; *Cotcher* is probably a ME byname *Coccher* (Thuresson 94).

FIELD-NAMES

The principal forms in (*a*) are modern (1935, *ex inf.* Mr P. G. Tyler).
Spellings dated 13 are Selby, others dated without source are *Eastoft.*

(*a*) Blow Hole Close, Bolt Field (cf. Boltgate 6 *infra*), Booth Hill
(*Bouth hill* 17, *Boothill* 1634, *v.* bōth, hyll), Butcher Tailor, Carr Close (cf.
Eastoft Carr *supra*), Clay Close, Croft, Dun Side Close (*v.* R. Don), Horse
Close, Laithe Close (*v.* hlaða 'barn'), Paddock, Purgie, Shot Ends (dial.
shot 'a division of land'), Walk End close 1735, Warp Bush Close, Whin's
Common & Wood (*v.* hvin 'whin, gorse').

(*b*) *Aeregarth* 13 (*v.* eyrr 'sand bank', garðr 'enclosure'), *Blacksyke* 1539,
1559 Hnt (*v.* blæc, sīc), *Caluecroft* 13 (*v.* calf, croft), *Grafield Close, Greyfleet
close* 17, 1735, *Grenesteles* 1525 (*v.* grēne[1], stigel 'a stile'), *Le Gulley close*

1626, *Halsich* 13 (*v.* hall, sīc), *Hamestons closes* 1735, *Holfletdale* (*pratum*) 13 (*v.* hol[1], flēot, dāl), *Holmerdale* 13 (*v.* hol[1], mere, dāl), *Hudmore, the Houdmore* 1555, *Houndmore* 1589 (*v.* hund, mōr), *Luilandes* (sic for *Lin-*) 13 (*v.* līn 'flax', land), *Lembrig* 1412 SelbyOb (*v.* brycg, the first el. is probably ME leme 'an artificial watercourse'), *The Purples Rawe* 1588, *Purpols close* 17, *High & Low Purples* 1735 (from the ME surname *Purpel*, cf. Weekley 143, *v.* rāw 'row (of houses), etc.'), *le Redkerre* 1412 SelbyOb ('reed marsh' *v.* hrēod, kjarr), *Ryven butts* 1527 (*v.* butte 'an abutting strip', the first el. is *riven* 'riven, torn apart', perhaps in the NCy sense 'ploughed'), *Seaton close* 1639 (the surname *Seaton*, clos), *Stile bridge closes* 1624 (*v.* stigel 'stile', brycg, clos), *Trasmire closes* 1634, *Turfmeirs als. Trusmeirs* 1635, *Trusmire closes* 1735 (confusion in the writing of *-s-* and *-f-*, but probably OE *trūs* 'brushwood', *v.* mýrr, clos), *Warendic* 13, *Warrand Close* 17 (*v.* wareine 'warren', dīc, clos), *Yowl croft* 1555 (*v.* croft, *Yowl* is from the ON pers.n. *Jóli*, ODan *Iuli* or the ME surname *Youle*).

3. FOCKERBY (98–8419)

> *Fulcwardby*(e) 1164–77 YCh 487, 1293 BM
>
> *Folquard*(e)*by* 1194–1203 YCh 490, 1304 Selby, 1328 Banco *et freq* to 1422 YI
>
> *Folkwerdeby* 1199–1209 YCh 488   *Folcortheby* 1246 *Ass* 11d
>
> *Folc-, Folkwardeby* 1246 *Ass* 11d, 1293 BM, 1332 FF
>
> *Folkehuardeby* 1258 YI
>
> *Folk-, Folcard*(e)*by* 1241 FF, 1250 Fees, 1271 Baild, 1275 YI, 1304 Ebor
>
> *Fowquardby* 1316 YD ix   *Foquarby* 1537 *MinAcct*
>
> *Folquarby* 1352 FF
>
> *Folkerby* 1362 Works
>
> *Fockarby* 1549 YD ii, *Fockerbie, -by*(e) 1573 WillY, 1590, 1607 FF, *Fokerby* 1579 FF

'Folcward's farmstead', *v.* bȳ. The ON pers.n. *Folkvarðr* and the Dan *Folkward* are loans from OHG *Folcward* (DaGP s.n.). This p.n. is therefore probably from the latter and is of post-Conquest origin.

FOCKERBY HALL.   FOCKERBY NESS, *Great & Little Ness* 1847 *TA*, *v.* nes 'headland', here land within a bow of the old River Don. FOCKERBY PASTURE, cf. *Pasture Close* 1847 *TA*, *v.* pasture.   GARTH-END CLOSES.   HIGHFIELD BRIDGE, *High Fields* 1847 *TA*, cf. *Fockerby High-bridge* 1828 Hnt.   INTAKES, *Great & Little Intake* 1847 *TA*, *v.* intak.   MARMIRE BARN, *Marmiers* 1847 *TA*, *v.* mýrr 'mire', the first el. is possibly marr 'fen'.   MILL FIELDS, 1847 *TA*,

named from *Frockerby Mill* (sic) 1824 O.S., *v.* **myln, feld.** NESS
LANE, *Ness Lane Flatt* 1847 *TA*, cf. Fockerby Ness *supra*. SWARTH
ENDS, 1847 *TA*, from OE *swearð* 'sward' or **sweart** 'black', **ende.**
WARP CROFTS, 1847 *TA*, *v.* **wearp** 'silted land', **croft.** WILLOW
BANK.

FIELD-NAMES

The principal forms in (*a*) are 1847 *TA* 160.

(*a*) Bratts, Calf Close, Coney Garth (*v.* **coning-erth** 'rabbit warren'),
Cow Close, Curb Croft, Dike Close, Ox Croft, Rands (*v.* **rand** 'edge, border'),
Reed Hills, Rush Croft, Sawn Close, Town End Close (-*closez* 1537 *MinAcct*),
Upper Ings, West Croft, West Field.

4. HALDENBY (98–8217)

> *Haldanebi, -by* 1100–8 YCh 470, Hy 2 (1257) Ch, 1167–77 YCh
> 487, 1197 FF, 1199–1209 YCh 488, 1200 Cur, 1223 Pat, 1226 FF
> *et freq* to 1331 FF
> *Aldanebi* 1157 YCh 354, *Aldenebi, -by* 1189 (1308) Ch, 1219 FF,
> *Audeneby* 1218 FF
> *Haldenebi, -by* Hy 2 *MaryH* 6d, 1190, 1193 P (p), 1246 *Ass* 36,
> 1279–81 QW *et freq* to 1526 FF
> *Haldanby* 1304 Ebor, Selby, 1305 YI, 1316 Vill, 1379 PT,
> 1621 FF
> *Haldenby(e)* 1331 DodsN, 1362 Works, 1405 YI, 1526 FF
> *Hawdenby(e)* 1546 YChant, 1565 FF

'Haldan's farmstead', *v.* **bȳ.** The ON pers.n. *Hálfdan*, ODan
Hal(f)dan, is frequent in English usage. It was the name of the leader
of the great Danish army which settled in Yorkshire in 876 (cf.
Introd.); Feilitzen 283 notes the occurrences in DB, and Björkman
(NP 61, ZEN 43) records many other instances; it is also found in the
parallel p.n. Holdenby Nth 85.

BOLTGATE LANE, *Bought yait* 1542 *Eastoft*, *The Bolt gate* 1754 ib,
cf. also *Bolt close* 17 ib, 1842 *TA*, doubtless 'a gate that could be
bolted', from OE **bolt, geat.** BULLY FIELD, 1842 *TA*. EAST FIELD.
EAST GREEN, cf. *Far Green*, *West Green* 1842 *TA*, *v.* **grēne²**. THE
FLATS, *v.* **flat.** GREAT WOODS, 1842 *TA*. HALDENBY COMMON, 1842
TA. HALDENBY HALL, 1824 O.S. HALDENBY MOOR, cf. *High Moors*,
Moor Closes 1842 *TA*. HALDENBY NESS, *Hawdenby nesse* 1575 *Dep*,
v. **nes,** referring to a tract of ground in a bow of the Old River Don,

as in Fockerby Ness 5 *supra*. HALDENBY PARK, *Hawdenby(e) parke* 1557 WillY, 1575 *Dep*, *Haldanby Parke* 1621 FF, *v.* park. SAND Ho, formerly *Whins House* 1824 O.S., *v.* hvin 'whin, gorse'.

FIELD-NAMES

The principal forms in (*a*) are 1842 *TA* 186.

(*a*) Breaks (*v.* bræc[1] 'thicket, uncultivated piece of ground'), Burn Field, Coney Garth (*v.* coning-erth 'rabbit warren'), Croft, Crooken Flat, Crowby Hills, French Flat, Gales Garth (*v.* garðr), Hard Rush Close, Hop Garth, Mill Hill Flat, Moor Way, New Land, Old Garth, Pitts, Plum Greaves (*v.* plūme, græfe 'copse'), Pool Ness, Rimasike Hills, Sand Close, Seggs (*v.* secg 'sedge'), Shuttle Close (cf. Shuttleworth i, 49 *supra*), Stock Field (cf. Stock Field 10 *infra*), Well Ness.

ii. Whitgift

1. OUSEFLEET (98–8223)

> *Use-, Vseflet(e)* 1100–8 YCh 470, Hy 2 (1257) Ch, 1197 FF, 1198 DodsN, 1199–1209 YCh 488, 13 YD ix, 1218 FF, 1221 Cur *et passim* to 1336 Ch, *-fleth* 1157 YCh 354, 1189 (1308) Ch, *-fleoth* 1164–77 YCh 487, 1293 BM
> *Us-, Vsflet(e)* Hy 2 *MaryH* 6d, 1226 FF, 1304 Selby, 1331 DodsN *et freq* to 1558 FF
> *Huseflet* 1200 Cur, 1226 FF, *Husfliet* 1208 P
> *Ouseflet* 1304 Ebor, Selby, 1331 FF
> *Usseflet* 1336 Ch, 1362 Works, 1363 YD iv
> *Osseffleth'* 1379 PT
> *Uslytte* 1546 YChant, *Uslet* 1550 WillY, *Usflett als. Uslett* 1592 FF, *Usleete* 1638 SessnR

Ousefleet is on the south bank of the Ouse, not far from its confluence with the Trent, when it becomes the Humber. The rivername (*v.* Ouse in RNs.) is clearly the first el. The second el. is OE flēot 'a creek, inlet, estuary', as in nearby places, Adlingfleet 2 *supra*, Swinefleet 10 *infra*, or Yokefleet across the river (YE 255). There is now no 'clough', creek or inlet from the river here, other than a small drain some distance to the west, but the silting up of the shore at Ousefleet would certainly have changed the local topography. It might indeed have referred to a channel through which the river passed between the mainland and some sand-bank. The sense 'the

Ouse channel', that is, the one through which the main course of the river passed, would be reasonable.

COLMBRIGGS LANE, *Colmanrigges* 13 YD ix, *the Combriggs* 1649 *YAS* 178, from the ME pers.n. *Colman* (OIr *Colmán*), as in Commondale YN 148, etc. (cf. *Revue Celtique* xliv, 41, Feilitzen 218) and hryggr 'ridge'.

BOSOM CROSS, 1824 O.S. CAYTHORPE, *Cathropp* 1649 *YAS* 178, *Kaythorp* 1717 PRWst, *v.* þorp; the first el. is doubtful. COMMON PIECE LANE, *Common Piece* 1828 *EnclA.* HALL FIELDS. HALL GARTH, 1824 O.S., *v.* hall, garðr. HAVERLANDS, *Haverlands* (*Brecks & Longlands*) 1649 *YAS* 178, *v.* hafri 'oats', land; for *brecks*, *v.* bræc[1] 'thicket, uncultivated strip'. HOGGARD LANE. LONG-DIKE BANK, *le . . . klandik* 13 YD ix, *Long Dycke bancke* 1575 *Dep*, *the Longdike bancke* 1649 *YAS* 178, *v.* lang, dīc, banke. OUSEFLEET HALL, formerly *Ousefleet Grange* 1824 O.S., *v.* grange. OUSEFLEET INGS, *v.* eng 'meadow'. OUSEFLEET MOOR, 1824 O.S., *v.* mōr. OUSEFLEET NESS, *v.* nes, here land within the bend of the Ouse (cf. Fockerby Ness, Haldenby Ness 5, 6 *supra*). OUSEFLEET PASTURE, 1824 O.S., *v.* pasture. PARK GROUNDS, *Uslet Parke* 1593 FF, *v.* park. TOWNEND CAUSEWAY, *Townend feild* 1649 *YAS* 178, *v.* tūn, ende. WILF PARK (lost), *Wylffe parke* 1574 *Dep*, *Woulfe parke* 1575 ib, *Wolfe Parke* 1585 WillY, *Uslett als.* Willoughe Parke *als.* Wilfe Parke 1593 FF, 'willow park', dial. *wilf* (*v.* wilig with -*f* for ME -*gh*, as in the pronunciation of words like *laugh*, *clough*), park.

FIELD-NAMES

The forms in (*a*) are 1828, 1833 *EnclA* 15. Spellings dated 1218–1235 are FF, 1649 *YAS* Md 178, vi.

(*a*) Cow Lane, Flatts (*v.* flat), Sheep Fold.

(*b*) *Burricroft* 1314 YD ix (*v.* croft), *Cathropp west butts* 1649 (*v.* west, butte 'an abutting strip'), *Cottewalecroft* 1235 (*v.* cot 'cottage', walu 'ridge of earth', croft), *Grene* 1535 VE (*v.* grēne[2]), *the Heblane* 1649 (*v.* lane), *Horscroft* 1226 (*v.* hors, croft), *Lunde* 1535 VE (*v.* lúndr 'a wood'), *Meldecroft* 1226 (*v.* melde, a plant such as orach, croft), *Samsundayl* 1226 (the ME pers.n. *Samson*, deill 'a share of the common land'), *Swanbutts* 1649 (*v.* swan, butte), *Washail*, *Wessayl* 1226 (apparently a nickname for a piece of ground, ON *ves heill* 'be hale, wassail'), *Westheyk* 1218 (*v.* west, eik 'oak').

2. REEDNESS (97–7923)

> *Rednesse* 1164–77 YCh 487, 1196 P (p), 1199 FF, 1199–1209 YCh
> 488, 1200 DodsN, 13 YD ix, 1208 FF *et passim* to 1357 Selby,
> (-*in Merssheland*) 1456 Pat, -*nes* 1230 P (p), 1240, 1246 FF, 1540
> Test vi
> *Reddnesse* 1266 Baild
> *Redenesse* 1304, 1324 Selby, 1327 *MinAcct* 48, 1328 FF *et passim*
> to 1390 YD ix
> *Reidnesse* 1305 YI, *Reydnes* 1536 FF
> *Reedness* 1609 FF, (-*in Marshland*) 1626 PRCnt

'Reedy headland', *v.* hrēod, nes². The word *nes* is used of other
places in the district to denote a piece of land (not necessarily high)
around which a river flows in a semicircular sweep; cf. Cotness
YE 250, Fockerby Ness, Haldenby Ness, Ousefleet Ness 5, 6,
8 *supra*.

BANK FIELD, 1846 *TA*, named from *Gowlebancke* 1641 *MinAcct*, *v.*
Goole 16 *infra*, banke, feld.   CASTLE.   COW CLOSE, *Coweclose*
1574 *Dep*, *Kowe Close* 1575 ib, *Cow closes* 1649 *YAS* 178, *v.* cū,
clos.   CRABLEY STAITH.   CUCKOLD CROFT, 1846 *TA*, *Cukwaldcroft*
1421 SelbyOb, from ME *cukwald* 'a cuckold', croft.   EAST MOOR
FIELD, 1846 *TA*, *Estmorefeld* 1421 SelbyOb, *v.* ēast, mōr, feld.
FERRY STAITH, cf. *Ferry House Inn* 1846 *TA*, *v.* ferja, stæð.   HIGH-
FIELDS HO, *High Field* 1771 M.   LONG FIELD, 1846 *TA*, *Langfeld*
1356 YD ix, *v.* lang, feld.   MARGRAVE LANE (site of MAUGRE),
Maugre 1400 WillY, *Mawgre Haull* 1540 ib, *Mawgrey* 1552 ib, a
French p.n., 'bad place', from OFr *mal-gre* 'ill-favour' (*v.* mal²),
doubtless in reference to its situation in the marshes.   MARSH
FURLONG, 1846 *TA*, *v.* mersc, furlang.   MOOREND FM, 1824 O.S.,
v. mōr, ende.   MOOR FIELDS.   NORTH GARTHS, cf. South Garths
infra.   OLDLANE GATE, *le Oldlane* 1421 SelbyOb, *v.* ald, lane.
RAINSBUTT, 1634 *Eastoft*, 1817 M, probably identical with *Rauenes-
bosk* 1327 *MinAcct* 48, 'raven's bush', *v.* hrafn, buskr, the latter
replaced by *butte* 'an abutting strip of land'.   REEDNESS CLOUGH, *v.*
clōh, here denoting the small creek by which a stream or dike enters
the Ouse.   REEDNESS DRAIN, formerly *Runlet Drain* 1824 O.S.,
v. Runnel Drain 11 *infra*.   REEDNESS FIELD.   REEDNESS HALL.
ROYAL CROFT, 1846 *TA*, *Ryhyllcroft* 1356 YD ix, *v.* rȳge, hyll, croft.
RUSH CROFT, 1846 *TA*, *v.* risc, croft.   RYE FIELD, *Ryefeld* 1356 YD
ix, *v.* rȳge, feld.   SLACK WELL.   SOUTH GARTHS, *Rede[n]esgarth*

c. 1394 Works, *Reedness Garths* 1846 *TA*, v. garðr 'enclosure'.
STOCK FIELD, (*le*) *Stokfeld* 1356 YD ix, 1421 SelbyOb, v. stocc
'stock, stump', feld. THIMBLE HALL. WEST MOOR FIELD, 1846
TA, v. west, mōr.

FIELD-NAMES

The principal forms in (*a*) are 1846 *TA* 329. Spellings dated 1208 are FF,
1356 YD ix, 1421 SelbyOb.

(*a*) *Camill-*, *Camell Garth* 1713, 1714 *LdsRL* 135–6 (cf. Camblesforth pt. iv
infra), v. garðr, Dikes, East Field, Foreshore, Imming Croft (*Ymingcroft*
1421, probably a pers.n. *Imming*, formed from OE *Imma*, croft), Mill Garth,
New Breaks (*Newbrek* 1356, v. nīwe, bræc), Short Ings (v. eng), Thieves
Dale (ib 1764 *Glebe*, v. þēof, dæl), Wendings (v. wending 'a bend in a road'),
Woods Garth.

(*b*) *Croftdyk*, *-dike* 1324, 1325 Selby (v. croft, dīc), *Engbyk* 1356 (v. eng,
and possibly byht 'bend in a river'), *les Gruthes de Rednesse* 1421 (possibly
e.ModE *growth*, used in dial. of coarse grass growing at highwater mark on
the Humber, cf. NED s.v.), *les Gulles* 1421 (v. goule, gole 'a channel, a
drain', as in Goole 16 *infra*), *Kerdic* 1208 (v. kjarr 'marsh', dīc), *Rowaldecroft*
1208 (a pers.n. from ON *Hróaldr*, croft), *le Sylecrosse* 1421 (from MLG sīl
'a drain', cros, cf. *Gowersyle* 4 *supra*), *Stephenridding* 1421 (the ME pers.n.
Stephen, rydding 'clearing').

3. SWINEFLEET (97–7722)

> *Swynefleth* Hy 2 BM, c. 1190–1207 YCh 492, *Swine-*, *Swyneflet(e)*
> 1189–1207 YCh 493, 1190–1220 ib 494, 13 AD iii, 1246 *Ass* 35d,
> 1253 FF *et passim* to 1382 BM, *-flitt* 1618 PRRth
> *Swin-*, *Swynflet(e)* 1266 Baild, 1294 Ebor, 1304 Selby, 1305 Ch,
> 1316 Pat *et freq* to 1448 Pat, *-fleit* 1549 YD ii, *-flett* 1557 FF

The second el. is OE flēot, which on topographical grounds no
doubt refers to a reach of the Ouse or, if the river was divided by
sandbanks, to one of its channels; it can hardly mean 'inlet' here;
cf. Ousefleet 7 *supra*. It is difficult to see how *flēot* in this sense
could be connected with OE swīn 'swine',[1] and Ekwall is therefore
right in accepting the possibility of OE swin[2] 'creek, channel' as the
first el. Presumably this secondary channel was called 'the *Swin*',
to distinguish it from the main course of the Ouse. The term is found
chiefly in YE and L p.n.s

BETWEEN DIKES, *land between Dikes* 1846 *TA*, v. betwēonan, dīc.
BOG GATE. CROSSMOOR BANK. CROWTREE HO. DUNMIRES, 1764
Glebe, v. dunn, mýrr. FIELD HO. KING'S CAUSEWAY. LONG

INGS, *Long Ing* 1846 *TA*, v. lang, eng.   LONG SHORES, 1846 *TA*,
v. lang, scora.   MILL TROD, *Milne Trodd or litle trodd, Uppertrodd*
1641 *YAS* 178, from myln and OE *trod* 'a track, a footpath'.   NEW
CLOSE, 1641 *YAS* 178, v. nīwe, clos.   PADDOCK HO, 1824 O.S., v.
pearroc 'enclosure'.   PUDDINERS, 1846 *TA*.   QUAY FIELD, *Keyfield*
1612 *Cause* 708, 1846 *TA*, named from *le Kay* 1306 Selby, *kaya de
Swynflet* 1362 Works, *Quay* 1824 O.S., v. kay 'a quay, wharf'.
READING GATE, *Riddyngate* 1412 SelbyOb, *Ridingate* 1641 *YAS* 178,
v. rydding 'clearing', gata.   RUNNEL DRAIN, *Runlet Drain* 1824
O.S., ModE *runlet* 'a small stream, a runnel'.   MIDDLE & UPPER
SANDS, 1846 *TA*, *Vppersands* 1641 *YAS* 178, v. sand.   SWINEFLEET
MOOR.   UNDERWOODS, 1846 *TA*, v. under, wudu.

FIELD-NAMES

The principal forms in (a) are 1846 *TA* 390.   Spellings dated without
source are *YAS* Md 178, v, vi.

(a) Angeram Flatt (*Angramflatt(s)* 1591, 1650 WillS, *-flates* 1641, v. anger
'pasture', flat; it goes back to an old dat. plur. *Angrum* or a surname formed
from it), Butts Furlong, Landing Place (cf. Quay Field *supra*), Land Mill,
Long Field, New Brooks.

(b) *the Eshes* 1648 (v. æsc 'ash-tree'), *Ingsclose Lea* (v. eng, clos, lēah),
The Leaze 1648 (v. lǣs 'pasture'), *le Milneclose* 1641 (v. myln, clos).

4. WHITGIFT (98–8022)

> *Wite-, Wytegift, -gyft* c. 1070 Selby, 1078–85 YCh 468, 1104–6 ib
>   475, 1154 Selby, 1197 FF, 1200 Cur, 1230 Selby, 1304 Ebor,
>   *-gifth* 1164–1209 YCh 487–8, 1293 BM, *Wytgift* 1362 Works
> *Witesgift* 1204 ChR
> *Wigtset, Wigesech'* (sic) 1221 Cur
> *White-, Whytegift, -gyft* 1232 Ch, 1246 *Ass* 36, 1276 RH, 1304
>   Selby, 1316 Vill, 1331 FF *et passim* to 1372 BM, *-giftes* 1302 BM,
>   *-geft* 1314 YD ix, *-guift* 1370 DodsN, *Whythgift* 1362 Works
> *Whittegift* 1327 *MinAcct* 48
> *Whit-, Whytgift(e), -gyft* 1412 SelbyOb, 1415 Pat, 1434 Test ii
>   *et passim* to 1822 Langd, (*-in Marsland*) 1557 WillY, *-giffe* 1531
>   Test iv.
> *Witgiffe als. Widgiffe* 1552 FF, *Wydgyfte* 1557 WillY

Whitgift is named from its once having been dowryland, the second
el. being ON gipt 'gift, dowry' or a Scandinavianised form of OE

gift; cf. also **morgen-gifu** as in Morgay Sx 519. The first el. may be OE hwīt 'white', but as the implication of the word in this context is not clear, it is more satisfactory to take it as a pers.n. OE *Hwīta* (or possibly the fem. *Hwīte*) or indeed the ON byname *Hvíti*.

BEWTHORPE, *Great & Little Bowthorpe* 1846 *TA*, v. þorp; the first el. is uncertain.   BOON ROWS, 1846 *TA*, doubtless 'strips of land ploughed as a tenant's service to his lord' (ON *bón* 'boon', rāw). BOYNTON CLOSES, *Boynton's Closes* 1846 *TA*, from *Boynton* as a surname, clos.   BURN FIELD, 1846 *TA*.   CAUSEWAY HO, cf. *Causey Close* 1846 *TA*, v. caucie 'a raised track through marshland'. CHAPEL FIELD, 1846 *TA*, v. chapel, feld.   CHURCH LANE, *Church Lane Close* 1846 *TA*, v. cirice, lane.   COMMON HO.   GIBBET (site), formerly *Emanuels or Stump* 1824 O.S.   HIGH FIELDS, 1824 O.S. IN FIELDS, *Infield* 1846 *TA*.   LONG MARSH, 1846 *TA*, v. lang, mersc.   MILKING HILL.   MOXON CLOSE, 1846 *TA*, the surname *Moxon* (common in YW in the Wakefield area), clos.   NEW BREAKS, 1846 *TA*, v. nīwe, bræc.   QUART LANE.   WHITGIFT CLOUGH, v. clōh.   WHITGIFT HALL, 1824 O.S., cf. *le Hallclose* 1641 *MinAcct* 39, v. hall.   WHITGIFT MOOR.   WHITGIFT PASTURE, 1757 *EnclA*, v. pasture.   WHITGIFT WOOD.

FIELD-NAMES

The principal forms in (*a*) are 1846 *TA* 430. Spellings dated without source are *MinAcct* 25, 41, 51.

(*a*) Black Bank 1824 O.S. (*v.* blæc, banke), College Close (owned by Catharine Hall, Cambridge), High East Field, Hoyles Closes, Long Close, Niffield, Riddings (*v.* rydding), Rudds Close, Sile Bank (cf. *Gowersyle* 4 *supra*), Sotheron Close, Sparrow Croft, Thistley Close, High West Field (*le Westfeild* 1624, *v.* west, feld).

(*b*) *Bridsak* 1276 RH (*v.* bridd 'bird', āc 'oak'), *Foweracres close* 1624 (*v.* fēower, æcer, clos), *le Groues als. gruf(f)es* 1614, 1636 (*v.* gróf 'a stream, a pit'), *le Kiddinges* 1614 (*v.* kide, eng), *le Sheepcroftland* 1624 (*v.* scēap, croft), *le Subsiseclose* 1641.

iii. Snaith

Goole Fields was originally part of Goole township. Goole is now a municipal borough.

1. AIRMYN (97–7225)

> Ermenie, -ia 1086 DB, Ermine 1244 Ass 4, -minne, -y- 1254 Abbr, 1276 RH, Hermin 1276 RH
>
> Eyremin(ne), -myn(ne) 1100–8 YCh 470, 1257 ForP i, 173, Hy 3, 1416 YI
>
> Aire-, Ayreminna, -myn(ne) 1130–9 YCh vi, 1154–81 ib, 1189 (1308) Ch, 13 Selby, YD ii, 1247–55 YI et freq to 1448 Pat, -men 1287 YI
>
> Ayrmin(a), -myn(ne) Hy 1 Dugd vi, Hy 2 MaryH 6d, 1331 FF, c. 1348 Works, 1405 YI, -men 1430 YD vi
>
> Aereminne 1157 YCh 354   Eyrminne 1252 FF (p)
>
> Heyrmyn(ne) 13 Selby, c. 1362 Works
>
> Armyn(e), -mine 1495 lpm, 1553 WillY et freq to 1641 Rates

'Mouth of the R. Aire', v. R. Aire (RNs.), mynni (which also occurs in Wharfe's Mouth (Cawood) pt. iv, Nidd Mouths (Moor Monkton) pt. iv infra). On the later Armyn spellings cf. Phonol. §11.

AIRMYN BANK, Armin Bank 1824 O.S., v. banke.   AIRMYN BUTTS. AIRMYN GRANGE, Grange 1817 M, Armyn Grange 1824 O.S., v. grange.   BOOTH FERRY, Booth-ferry 1598 DoncCrt 169, -Ferrie 1621 PRSn, named from Booth YE 253, v. ferja; 'here is a good Inn and a Ferry across the Ouse' 1822 Langd; the ferry has been replaced by a bridge.   COBBLER HALL.   DECOY FM, New Decoy House 1817 M; ModE decoy sometimes occurs in marshland p.ns. to denote the narrow arms of water fitted up to snare wild duck (cf. the references in NED s.v.).   DOWNES GROUND.   HALL GARTH, 1824 O.S., v. hall, garðr.   HOOK CLOUGH, formerly Tealpit Clough 1824 O.S., from ME tele 'teal', pytt, clōh.   HOWPE FM.   NEW POTTER GRANGE, Potter Grange 1817 M.   OAKS HILL.   PARK FM.   PASTURES, Armin Pastures 1817 M, v. pasture.   PERCY LODGE, cf. Moram Willelmi de Percy c. 1250 Pont, named from the great Percy family. RIDDINGS FM, probably identical with Hookridding 1410 YD viii, v. Hook 20 infra, rydding 'clearing'.   STREET HEAD BRIDGE. TOFTS FM.

FIELD-NAMES

(a) Crane Lane 1824 O.S. (v. cran, lane), Ferry House 1822 Langd (cf. Booth Ferry supra), Goat House 1817 M.

(b) (le3) Englishe mo(o)re 1614, 1636 MinAcct 41, 35 (v. Englisc, mōr, to distinguish it from waste owned by Dutchmen, as in Dutch Flat 16 infra).

2. BALNE (103–5919) [bɔːn]

Balne(a), Baln(a) 12, 13 Selby (freq), 1180–90 YCh 495, 1185–1205
    ib 496, l. 12 Lewes 303, 13 YD i, 1200 Cur, 1230–40 Bodl 34,
    1241 AD v, 1285 Baild et passim to 1822 Langd, (Norh-) 13
    YD x, (North-) 1345 Ass, 1376 FF, (-juxta Snayt) 1280 Ass 7,
    (South-) 1408 YD vi
Baune 1167 P (p), 13 Selby
Beln' 1202–8 Ass
Balme 1530 YD i, 1546 YChant
Bawne 1559 PRSn, 1568 FF, 1571 Dep et freq to 1605 FF, (-Towne)
    1665 Visit, Bawen 1567 WillY

Balne was also the name of a district (v. 1 supra). Ekwall's interpretation of this name as a metathesised form of an OE bēan-lēah 'bean clearing' is unlikely on the grounds of such a common type of p.n. being replaced by a form so obscure, as well as the unusual type of metathesis. Goodall's suggestion of a PrCelt *baljos, surviving in Ir baile 'village' and many Ir p.ns. in Bally-, with a Celtic diminutive suffix -n, is doubtful, for baile occurs only in Ir and Gael and its use here could only be ascribed to Vikings from Ireland; this is not a locality where such influence is to be expected. The most likely explanation on phonetic grounds at least is Lat balneum 'a bath, a bathing place'; Pryme 55 (s.a. 1695) writes: 'Mr Horatio Cay . . . says that the Romans . . . seeing a part of the country for a huge way round about boggy and full of quagmires, they gave it the name of Balneum, which is now called Bawn.' This explanation of the name may be on the right lines, but if the name had been given by the Romans we should have expected it to have undergone OE i-mutation, giving a late OE *Belne. More probably it is a later creation, and in this name, as well as in Balne Beck (RNs.), Balm Rd iii, 221, Balne Bridge 169, Bawn f.n. 194, Bawn iii. 213, infra, we have evidence of an independent English borrowing of Lat balneum, not as early as Roman times but considerably earlier, in the case of Balne, than the first literary record of e.ModE *balne* (the earliest instance is from 1471, NED s.v. *balne*). It was probably used in most instances like OE bæð 'bath' to denote 'a stream or pool suitable for bathing'. In Balne also it probably denoted first a bathing place and then, from its use in the name of the extensive Balne Moor (*infra*), it came to be thought of as a district name. *v.* Addenda.

BALNE HALL, *Balneshale* 1166 P (p), *Balnehal(l)e* 1197 Selby, *-hal* 1276 RH, *-hall* 1733 YDr, *Bawn(e)hall(e)* 1563 PRSn, 1571 *Dep*, *v.* hall. BALNE HALL WOOD, 1841 O.S. BALNE LODGE, 1841 O.S. BALNE MANOR HO, *Manor House* 1841 O.S. BALNE MOOR, *Balne Moor(e)* 1750 YDr, 1771 M, *v.* mōr. BARN FALL WOOD, *Barnet Fall Wood* 1841 O.S., *v.* bærnet, (ge)fall. BLOWELL BRIDGE, 1841 O.S., cf. *Blosike* 1276 RH, *v.* blár 'dark, cheerless', sīc, wella. CAT LANE, 1841 O.S. CHAPEL GARTH, 1841 O.S., *v.* chapel, garðr. COCKSHOT WOOD, *Cockshutt Wood* 1841 O.S., *v.* cocc-scīete. CROSS HILL, 1841 O.S., *v.* cros, hyll. CROW WOOD, 1841 O.S., *v.* crāwe, wudu. GELDER WOOD. GORE WOOD, 1841 O.S., a narrow triangular wood, *v.* gāra, wudu. HAIGH END, *Hagg End* 1771 M, *v.* haga 'enclosure', ende. HAZING LANE. HIGHGATE, *le Hygh-*, *Highgate* 1340 YD x, 1588 FF, *v.* hēah, gata, cf. Lowgate *infra*. LOCK GATE. LONG WOOD, *Holland Wood or Longwood* 1841 O.S. LOWGATE, 1841 O.S., cf. Highgate *supra*. MARTIN WOOD, 1841 O.S. PARK LANE, 1841 O.S. PARKSHAW WOOD, 1841 O.S., *v.* park, sceaga 'copse'. SOUTH END, 1841 O.S. SWARDSHAW WOOD, *Sweetshaw Wood* 1841 O.S., OE sweard 'sward' or swēte 'sweet', sceaga 'copse'. THORNTREE LANE, 1841 O.S. TOADHAM LANE. WEST END, 1841 O.S. YEWTREE HO, 1841 O.S.

FIELD-NAMES

(a) Black-Carr green 1750 YDr (*v.* blæc, kjarr), Burns House 1784 PRBw, Folly Hall Wood 1824 O.S., Rushamore 1720 YDr (*v.* risc, mōr).

(b) *Batelis(e)twaite*, *-thwayt* 13 Selby (the ME surname *le Batel* (cf. Reaney 25), *v.* þveit), (*le*) *Grene in Balne* 1384, 1430 YD vi, *la Grene in Southbalne* 1408 ib (*v.* grēne²), *Holme in Balne* 1592 WillY (*v.* holmr 'water-meadow'), *Hopkynshawes* 1528 FF (the ME pers.n. *Hopkin*, sceaga 'copse'), *Hubert croft* 1340 YD x (the pers.n. *Hubert*, croft), *Milnecroft* 13 YD i (*v.* myln, croft), *Nortcroft* 13 YD i (*v.* norð, croft), *Holdpersonedich* 1253 AD v (*v.* ald, persone, dīc), *venellam . . . Owtlane* 13 Selby (*v.* ūt, lane), *Wehtwonge* 1253 AD v ('wet meadow', *v.* wēt, wang).

3. GOOLE (97–7423) [guːl]

Gulle in Houk' (a watercourse), aque Gulle 1362 Works
Gowle 1535 Dugd iv, 1546 YChant, 1553 FF, 1571 Dep et freq to
    1665 Visit
Goyll 1535 VE
Goole 1540 WillY, 1558 FF, 1682 Comm 66

v. goule 'a ditch, a stream', surviving as dial. gool 'a channel made by a stream'. Goole was originally a stream-name and in 1362 Works 331 reference is made to the building of a new bank to prevent flooding of the river Gulle; it is also referred to as gulla in Merskland 1356 Selby. The modern form is dialectal, since Goole, like Hook 20 infra, belongs to an area where formerly OE, ME ū remained [uː] (cf. Phonol. § 32).

CLOUGH.   OLD GOOLE, Goole 1824 O.S.   THE GROVES.   LOCK HILL.   MILLHOUSE LANE.   OLD POTTER GRANGE, 1824 O.S. SHUFFLETON.   SWANG CLOUGH.   TOMPITS HOLMES.   WEST HO.

FIELD-NAMES are included in Goole Fields infra.

4. GOOLE FIELDS (97–7520)

Goole Field Houses 1771 M, a modern township carved out of Goole. v. feld and cf. Field Ho infra.

BURYING HILL.   BUTTS.   EARNSHAWS WARPING DRAIN, 1824 O.S., a warping drain is one by which the flooding of low-lying land can be effected to deposit alluvium.   FIELD HO, Feildhouse(s) 1555, 1563 WillY, Field houses 1655 PRSn, v. feld, hūs and Goole Fields supra. GOOLE HALL, 1824 O.S.   GOOLE MOORS, 1824 O.S.   THE HILLS. HOOK MOOR, 1768 EnclA, Mora de Hu(c)k a.1227, c.1250 Pont, v. Hook 20 infra, mōr.   MOOR FIELDS, cf. Moor Tops, Moor Close 1844 TA.   PARK FM.   SAND HILLS, Sandhill Wood 1824 O.S., v. sand, hyll.   WARPING DRAIN, 1844 TA.   WHITE HO.

FIELD-NAMES

The following f.ns. belong to the townships of Goole and Goole Fields. The principal forms in (a) are 1844 TA 178. Spellings dated without source are YAS Md 178, v, x.

(a) Ash Tree Close, Bank Close, Crabtree Close, Dutch Flat (near Dutch River in RNs.), Homestead Close, Long Close, Long Lands, Pasture Close, Pump Close, Warped Close & Land.

(b) *Barker close* 1635 (v. barkere, perhaps as a surname, clos), *Cuddy close* 1635, *Darie house closes* 1673, *the Gayre close* 1635 (v. geiri 'a triangular plot', clos), *Goulle Lathes* 1412 SelbyOb (v. Goole *supra*, hlaða 'barn'), *the high Closes* 1635, *Laughton flatt* 1635 (v. lēac-tūn 'garden', flat), *Mangall alias Magnell growndes* 1612 Cause, *Well closes* 1635.

5. GOWDALL (97–6222)

> *Goldale* 12 Selby, 1258 YI (p), 1280, 1305 YI, 1328 Banco, 1359
>   FF *et freq* to 1543 WillY, *Goldal* 1307 YD ix, *Goldall(e)* 1409 ib,
>   1438 YD viii, 1472 MiscEngl
> *Goldahe* (sic) 1226 FF
> *Goldhale* 1353 DodsN
> *Gowdale* 1546 YChant, *Goudle* 1602 PRSn, *Gou-, Gowdall* 1641
>   Rates, 1822 Langd
> *Gouldale* 1558 FF, *Gouldall* 1571 *Dep*, *Gowldall* 1598 FF

'Nook of land where marigolds grow', v. golde, halh. The *halh* is a piece of ground within one of the loops of the Aire. On the later forms v. Phonol. § 27.

BLACK DRAIN, 1841 O.S. BUCK PIT. BUTT FIELDS. DORR LANE & PIT, *Dor* 12 Selby, 'the broad way, the road which leads to *Dor*' 1344, 1348 YD ix, v. dor 'a gate', doubtless one across the highway; cf. Heck 18 *infra*. FIELD LANE, formerly *Gowdall Lane* 1841 O.S. GOWDALL BROACH, 1822 Langd, probably identical with *le Brotis* 1307 YD ix, *le Brot*' 1318 ib, v. brot 'a small plot of ground'. GOWDALL FIELDS & HILL. GOWDALL REACH, 1841 O.S. PALMER CLOUGH, no doubt named from one of the several *Palmers* mentioned in PRSn from the sixteenth century. SEA BANK. TOM'S WELL.

FIELD-NAMES

Spellings dated without source are YD ix.

(a) *Dormer Green* 1750 YDr (cf. Dorr Lane *supra*), Eastmoor 1773 *EnclA*, Mucky Lane 1841 O.S.

(b) *Beghalltoft* 1409 (v. Beal 55 *infra*, topt), *le Bestmor* 1369 (ME beste 'a beast', mōr), *Brigkar* 1387, *Broggekar* 14 (v. brycg, kjarr), *Gowdall Garth* 1609 FF (v. garðr, probably here 'a fishery' as it is described as 'in the water of *Ayre*'), *le Kar* 1307, 1318 (v. kjarr 'marsh'), *Lundikke* 1369, *le Lundyke* 1409 (v. lúndr 'a wood', dīc), *le Midelfeld* 1307 (v. middel, feld), *Nagkyrakys* 1387 (cf. foll., -*kyrakys* is probably for -*skyrakys*, cf. *Schiraikchened infra*), *Naggetoft* 1395 YD x (probably, as in prec., ME nagge 'a nag, a horse', topt), *Schiraikchened* (sic for -*eheued*) 14 ('bright oak', v. scīr², āc, hēafod), *le Stonsike* 1307, 1318 (v. stān, sīc).

2

6. GREAT HECK (97–5920)

> *Hech* 1153–5 YCh 1497, 1177–93 ib 1516, *Heccha* 1194 P
> *Hecca* 1156 YCh 186, 1173 ib 197, 1196 P
> *Heck(e)* 13 Selby (*freq*), 1226 FF, 1225 DodsN, 1234 FF, 1243
> Fees (p), 1280 YI, 1323 *MinAcct* 45 *et freq* to 1587 FF, (*Suth-*)
> 13 Selby (*Balne-*) 1246 *Ass* 11d, 1341 YD ix, 1353 DodsN,
> 1362 YD ix, (*South-*) 1361 DodsN, (*Great-*) 1571 *Dep*, (*Bawn-*)
> 1573 FF, (*-Magna*) 1599 FF
> *Hek(k)* 13 Selby, 1316 Vill, 1344 YD x *et freq* to 1428 FA, (*Baln(e)-*)
> 1359 FF, 1381 YD xii, 257, 1498 Ipm, *Southek* 1374 FF, *Great*
> *Heke* 1538 FF

v. hæcc 'a hatch, a gate'. The topographical possibilities are in this case restricted and the likeliest interpretation is that Heck was simply a gate, perhaps on some road. The form *Heck* is northern, but in this area it might be from Merc *hecc* (with ON -*k* for ME -*ch*), cf. Phonol. § 1. The affixes Great, *Balne-* (from its proximity to Balne 14 *supra*) and *South-* distinguish it from Little Heck *infra*.

LITTLE HECK, with forms similar to prec., is distinguished as *Lytel-* 14 YD ix, *Ly-*, *Lit(t)le-* 1353 DodsN, 1538 FF *et freq* to 1589 FF, *Litil-*, *Lytyl-* 1381 YD xii, 257, 1498 Ipm, *North-* 1359, 1376 FF, 1392 YD ix, *-Parva* 1599 FF.

BOOTY LANE & WELL. COMMON DRAIN, formerly *New Drain* 1841 O.S. EARTH HILL. GREEN LANE, 1841 O.S. HECK BASIN, *The Basin* 1841 O.S., in the canal. HECK HALL, *Hæc Haull* 1608 PRSn, *Hall* 1817 M, v. hall. HECK HOLLANDS. INTAKE LANE, *Intakgate* 1397 YD ix, v. intak 'a piece of land taken in from waste', gata. LITTLE HECK WOOD, *Little Heck Covert* 1841 O.S. MILL BALK, 1841 O.S., v. myln, balca. MOOR LEE LANE, *Moor Leys Lane* 1841 O.S., v. mōr, lēah, lane. SHAW MOOR & WOOD. WINDMILL HO, named from *Heck Mill* 1841 O.S.

FIELD-NAMES

The principal forms in (*a*) are 1772, 1777 *EnclA* 38. Spellings dated without source are YD ix.

(*a*) Cockshutts Wood 1841 O.S. (*v.* cocc-scīete), Common Croft, East Field (*Estfeld* 1397, *v.* ēast, feld), (Heck) Ings (*v.* eng), The Intacks, Intake Pasture (cf. Intake Lane *supra*), Little Heck Common, Mill Field, Old & New (cf. Windmill Ho *supra*), Newfields (*Newfield Wood* 1841 O.S.).

(b) *Colmancroft* 1397 (the ME pers.n. *Colman*, from OIr *Colmán*, croft), *le Dufcotʒerd* 1399 YD x (*v.* dūfe, cot, geard), *Hekfalles* 1399 YD x (*v.* (ge)fall 'clearing'), *Lucok croft* 1397 (the ME pers.n. *Luuecok* (Reaney 206), *v.* croft), *Midilfeld* 1397 (*v.* middel, feld), *le Morecroft* 1392 (*v.* mōr, croft), *le Southangle* 1399 YD x (*v.* sūð, angel), *le Sprynges* 1392 (*v.* spring), *Wellsfall* 1397.

7. HENSALL (97–5923)

Edeshale 1086 DB   *Hetheneshale* 1305 Ch

Heþensale 12 Selby, *Hethensale* 13 YD x, 1280 YI, 1323 *MinAcct*, 1337 DodsN *et freq* to 1379 PT, -*all(e)* 1316 Vill, 1355 DodsN, 1381 YD xii, 257, 1621 PRSn, *Hechensale* (sic for *Heth-*) 1226 FF

Hedenessale 1180–1200 YCh 498

Heuensale 13, 1364 YD x, *Heuensall* 1361 DodsN, 1374 FF

Heynesale 1296 LacyComp

Heyneshale 1296 *MinAcct* 1

le Henssall 1406 TestLds, *Hensale* 1421 YI, *Hensall* 1444 Pat, 1531 Test v, 1541 WillY *et passim* to 1587 FF

'Hethin's nook of land', *v.* halh, here alluding to a piece of land partly surrounded by the Aire; this piece of land is now called Hensall Ings (*infra*). The first el. is the common ON pers.n. *Heðinn*, corresponding to ODan *Hithin* (cf. also Highley iii, 3 *infra*). The spellings *Heuen-* have the colloquial substitution of -*v*- for -*th*- (cf. Phonol. § 49).

BECK DRAIN, 1841 O.S., *v.* bekkr.   BROACH RD, cf. *Broath Field* 1824 *EnclA*, *v.* brot 'a small piece of land'.   BUTT LANE, *les Buttes* 1397 YD ix, *v.* butte 'an abutting strip'.   CHURCH LANE.   COMMON LANE & HECK COMMON.   HECK INGS, 1841 O.S., *v.* Heck 18 *supra*, eng.   HENSALL INGS, 1699 AireSurv, *v.* eng.   INGS LANE, 1841 O.S., *v.* prec.   NANPIE LONG REACH, 1841 O.S.   SEA BANK, 1841 O.S.   WEELAND, 1699 AireSurv, *v.* hwēol, land, cf. Weeland 74 *infra*.

FIELD-NAMES

The principal forms in (a) are 1824 *EnclA* 44.

(a) Elmhold Field, Hazel Hough Field, Mill Field (*Mill Field Lane* 1841 O.S.), New Field, North Field, Stodmore Lane 1841 O.S. (*v.* stōd, mōr), Town Field.

(b) *Bridtoft* 1365 YD ix (v. bridd (or a pers.n. from it), topt), *Caluecroft* 13 Selby (v. calf, croft), *Hensall Marsh* 1699 AireSurv, *Intack* 1699 ib (v. intak), *Kilkirode* 1180–1200 YCh 498 (v. rod[1] 'clearing'), *Lincroftum* 13 Selby (v. līn 'flax', croft).

8. Hook (97–7525) [hu:k, uk]

Hooc 1154–89 Riev   *Huuc* a.1227 Pont
Huck(e) 1164–96 YCh viii, 13 Selby, AD iii
Huch 13 Selby
Huc 13 BM, 1208 FF, 1314 Ch
Huk c. 1217 *RegAlb* ii, 98d, c. 1250 Pont, 1286 Ebor, 1294 Ch,
    14 AD iii, 1363 Ch, *Huke* 13 AD iii, 1519 Test v
Houk(e) Ed 1 *Nost* 11d (p), 1314 BM, 1316 Vill, 1318 Selby, 1327
    MinAcct 48 *et passim* to 1492 FF, (*-in Mersland*) 1409 YD ii,
    Howke 1402 YI, 1522 FF, 1525 AD iii *et passim* to 1571 *Dep*,
    (*-als. Hewke*) 1558 FF, (*-in Marshland*) 1621 ib
Hook(e) 1331 FF, 1535 VE, 1540 Selby *et passim* to 1822 Langd
Hok(e) 1379 PT, 1503 Ipm, 1546 YChant

The early spellings *Huke*, *Huuc* and *Houk(e)* indicate an original *hūc*; this has remained as dial. [hu:k], for Hook, like Goole 16 *supra*, is within the dialect area where OE *ū* remained (cf. Phonol. § 32); the modern *Hook* is a StdE representation of dial. [hu:k]. From time to time, however, the normal OE *hōc* has intruded, as shown by the occasional spellings *Hooc*, *Hoke*, and this is certainly the source of the alternative dial. spelling *Hewke* (cf. Phonol. § 30). The striking topography of Hook lying in a sharp bend of the Ouse leaves no doubt about the name being derived from an OE **hūc* related to the verbs ON *húka*, MLG *hūken*, MHG *hūchen* 'to crouch' as suggested by Ekwall (DEPN s.n.).

Balk Lane, *Balk Lane Close* 1844 *TA*, v. balca.   Carr Lane, 1844 *TA*, v. kjarr 'marsh', lane.   Ferry Lane, *Ferry Lane Close* 1844 *TA*, v. ferja (across the Ouse).   Halifax Lane, *Halifax Close & Lane* 1844 *TA*.   Hall Garths, 1844 *TA*, v. hall, garðr.   Hook Carr, *Far & Near Carr* 1844 *TA*, cf. *Kerdic* 13 AD iii, v. kjarr, dīc.   Hook Hall, 1844 *TA*, *Hall* 1824 O.S., v. hall.   Long Lane, 1844 *TA*.   New Close, 1844 *TA*.   Silverpit, *Silver Island* 1817 M, *Silverpit Bite* 1824 O.S., v. pytt, byht 'bend in a river'; *Silver* is of uncertain meaning here.   South Field, 1768 *EnclA*, v. sūð, feld.

SPRINGBALK LANE, 1844 O.S., *v.* spring, balca.   WEST FIELD, 1768
EnclA, *v.* west, feld.   WHIN CROFT, 1844 *TA*, *v.* hvin 'gorse', croft.

FIELD-NAMES

The principal forms in (*a*) are 1844 *TA* 215; spellings dated 1621 are
Comm 4908, 1768 *EnclA* 20.

(*a*) Bank End Close, Brigg Close (*v.* brycg), Chapel Acres (*v.* chapel,
æcer), Charter Lane, Follys (*v.* folie), Herd Close, Hobler Hill Close,
Holme Field 1768 (*v.* holmr), Marshall Close, Marsh Field (ib 1768, *v.*
mersc, feld), Mill Close & House (*Mill Field* 1768, *Hook Mill* 1824 O.S.,
v. myln), Moors Lane, Murham Clough & Lane, Nabb Acre, Nabbs (*v.*
nabbi 'a knoll'), North Field (ib 1768, *v.* norð, feld), Outshores (*v.* ūt,
scora), Pinfold (*v.* pynd-fald), Sand (*Le Sand* 1621, *v.* sand), Spring, Swine-
herd Hill, Tom Pit Holme, Town End Close, Warping Drain (cf. Earnshaws
Warping Drain 16 *supra*), Water Lane, West Close.

(*b*) *Eswineryding* 13 AD iii (probably the OE pers.n. *Æscwine*, rydding
'clearing'), *le Gates* 1621 (*v.* gata 'a road'), *Howkelathes* c. 1394 Works (*v.*
hlaða 'barn'), (*le*) *Landemere* 13 Selby, 1327 *MinAcct* 48 (*v.* land-gemǣre
'a boundary'), *the procter howse* 1575 *Dep* (ME *proctour* 'proctor, agent',
perhaps as a surname, hūs), *Roomes* (a fishery) 1621 (*v.* rūm 'an open space'),
le Sandike 13 AD iii (*v.* sand, dīc).

9. POLLINGTON (103–6119)

Pouilgleton 1154–60 Selby
Pouelington(*a*) 1180–90 YCh 495, 1185–1205 ib 496, 13 Selby,
    YD i, x, 1225 DodsN, 1232–7, c. 1262 Selby, *Poulin(g)ton* 1250
    YI, 1276 RH
Polington(*a*), -*yng*- 1154–89, c. 1219 Selby, 1219 FF, 1263 Selby,
    1305 Ch *et passim* to 1449 Pat, (-*in Balne*) 1263, 1365 FF, (-*in
    Northbalne*) 1345 *Ass* 16
Polinton, -*yn*- 1251 FF, 1315 Pat
Pollington, -*yng*- c. 1262 Selby, 1379 PT, 1540 NCWills

The name appears to go back to an OE *Pofelingtun*, *v.* tūn 'farmstead'. The connective -ing[4] usually, but not exclusively, points to a
pers.n. as the first el. in such compounds, but no such pers.n. as
Pofel is known in OE. Pollington must therefore be taken with Pool
pt. iv *infra*, where OE *pofel* can only be a significant word; *v.* pofel,
which is perhaps to be associated with Scots *poffle* 'plot of ground';
its origin and precise meaning is unknown. The only common
topographical features of Pollington and Pool are that they are both

low-lying and both have a good deal of sand; there is an old sand-pit at Pollington and there are extensive sand beds along the Wharfe to the west of Pool. It is possible therefore that OE *pofel* is in some way connected with OE **popel** 'a pebble' and that it denoted 'a plot of sandy or gravelly soil', but no proof is available for this. The most we can be certain about is that Pollington means 'farmstead associated with a piece of ground called *Pofel*'. On the affix in the early spellings, *v.* Balne 1, 14 *supra*.

RAMSHOLME (lost), *Ramesholm(e)* 13 Selby, 1207 OblR, 1209 DodsN, 1262 Selby, 1263 FF. 'Ram's water-meadow', from OE **ramm** 'a ram' or pers.n. from it, or possibly a later and common variant of the OE pers.n. *Hræfen*, ON *Hrafn*, and holmr.

BALK LANE, 1841 O.S., *v.* **balca**. BERRIDGE LANE. CROW CROFT, 1841 O.S., *v.* **crāwe**, **croft**. PINFOLD LANE. POLLINGTON CARR, 1772 *EnclA*, *v.* **kjarr** 'marsh'. POLLINGTON BRIDGE, formerly *Trundle Bridge* 1841 O.S., *v.* **trendel**, **brycg**. POLLINGTON GRANGE, 1841 O.S., *v.* **grange**. POLLINGTON HALL, 1841 O.S., *Low Hall* 1817 M, *v.* **hall**.

FIELD-NAMES

The principal forms in (*a*) are 1772 *EnclA* 38. Spellings dated 1263 are FF, 1386 YD ix.

(*a*) Butt Green, East Field (*Estfeld* 1386, *v.* **ēast**, **feld**), Little Field, Low Green, Mill Field, Pollington Whin 1841 O.S. (*v.* **hvin** 'gorse'), West Field (*Westfeld* 1386, *v.* **west**, **feld**).

(*b*) *Midelfeld* 1386 (*v.* **middel**, **feld**), *the Preyle* (a close) 1554 TestLds (OFr *praiel* 'meadow', cf. Vincent § 820), *Swaynis-*, *Swaine(s)croft* 12, 13 Selby, 1263 (the ON pers.n. *Sveinn*, **croft**), *le Thwayt* 1386 (*v.* **þveit** 'clearing'), *Vtting-*, *Uttingcroft* 1262 Selby, 1263 FF (the ME pers.n. *Utting*, formed from OE *Utta*, **croft**), *Wyte-*, *Whyteker* 1262 Selby, 1263 (*v.* **hwīt**, **kjarr** 'marsh').

10. RAWCLIFFE (97–6822) ['rɔ:klif]

   Rouþeclif 1078–85 YCh 468, *Routheclif(f)*, *-clyf* 1219 Selby, 1252 Ch, 1254–80, 1272 Selby, 1293 QW, *-clive*, *-cliue* 1238 Cl, 1272 YD iii, 1282 Dods N

   Rodecliff, *-clyf* l. 11, 1154 Selby, 1286 AddCh, *-cliua* 1104–6 YCh 475, *Rotheclive* 1260 Baild

   Roudecliuf 1126–35 YCh vi, *-cliue*, *-cliua* 1135 Selby, 1155–61 YCh 481, 1193 P, *-clif(e)* 1275 WCR, 1343 Selby

Rouclif(*f*), *-clyf*(*f*) 1189, c. 1200, 13 Selby (*freq*), 1316 Vill, 1334 FF,
(*-in Inclesmore*) 1344 YD ix, *-clyve* 1312 Selby
Rawclyff(*e*) 1379 PT, 1583 FF, *Rowclif* 1548 WillY, 1571 *Dep*
Roclif(*f*) 1535 VE, 1546 WillY

'The red bank', *v.* rauðr, clif, cf. Roecliffe pt. v *infra* and Rawcliffe
YN 15. The cliff is the bank of the R. Aire. For the affix *v.* Inkle
Moors i, 3 *supra*.

BELL LANE, probably named from a family called *Bell* in the parish
from the sixteenth century (PRSn *freq*).   BOTTOMS CLOUGH, cf.
Bottom Close, Clough Close 1845 *TA*, *v.* botm 'valley bottom', clōh.
BRIDGE LANE, 1841 O.S., *v.* brycg.   BRIER HILLS WOOD, *Brier Hill
Plant.* 1841 O.S., *v.* brēr, hyll.   COMMON FM.   CROW WOOD.
DOWBELLER FM, *Dobellers* 1611 PRSn, 1817 M, *Dowbellows Farm*
1824 O.S., doubtless a surname, which may be connected with MDu
dobbelare 'gambler'.   ELMS FM.   FIELD HO & LANE, *Field Lane Close*
1845 *TA*, *v.* feld.   FIRTH DRAIN, *Over-, le Netherfrith'* 13 Selby,
Little Firth 1845 *TA*, *v.* fyrhðe 'a wood'.   GOSSIPS MOOR.   HALES,
1844 *TA*, *v.* halh 'nook of land'.   KEY CLOUGH & LANE, *Key Close*
1845 *TA*, *v.* kay 'quay, wharf'.   KING'S MOOR, *the Kinges Moore*,
the Kinges Waist 1682 *Comm* 66, *v.* cyning, mōr, wēste.   LANGHAM,
Langholme 13 Selby, *Langholmgite* 1362 Works, *v.* lang, holmr 'water-
meadow', gyte 'drain'.   MARLPIT DRAIN, *Marlpit* 1841 O.S., *v.*
marle, pytt.   MILL HO & LANE, *Mill Close* 1845 *TA*, *Mill Lane*
1841 O.S., *v.* myln.   NEW LANE, 1841 O.S.   PEACHCLOSE PLANT.,
Peach Close 1845 *TA*, probably the surname *Peach*, clos.   PLUMTREE
FM.   RABBIT HILLS, 1841 O.S.   RAWCLIFFE BRIDGE, 1817 M, *v.*
brycg.   RAWCLIFFE GREEN, *le Grene* 13 Selby, *v.* grēne[2].   RAW-
CLIFFE MOORS, *moris de Rouclif* 1368 *MinAcct* 26, *v.* mōr.   RAW-
CLIFFE PASTURES, 1817 M, *v.* pasture.   RICKARD GYME, probably
the ME pers.n. *Ricard*, cf. Gyme i, 4 *supra*.   RIDDING LANE, *le
Riding* 13 Selby, *le Ruddyng* 1368 *MinAcct* 26, *v.* rydding 'clearing'.
THE SCALP, *Rawcliffe Scalp* 1841 O.S., dial. *scalp* 'a mud-bank'
(here of the R. Aire).   STOCK'S HOUSES, *Stokhousgarthe* 1403 YD x,
v. stocc 'stump', hūs, garðr.   THORNTREE CLOUGH.

FIELD-NAMES

The principal forms in (a) are 1845 *TA* 326. Spellings dated 13, 1219, 1251, 1254–8 are Selby.

(a) Almshouse Close, Apple Tree Garth (v. garðr), Barfit Close (*Barthwait, -thayth, Barthtwayt, Barthwath* 13, probably 'Barði's clearing', from the ON pers.n. *Barði* and þveit), Bastow Close, Bigley Shaw (ib 1841 O.S., v. bygg 'barley', lēah, sceaga 'copse'), Black Drain Close, Boarden Bridge Close, Boar Garth (v. bār, garðr), Bog Close, Bottle Close (possibly the surname *Bottle* (Reaney 41), clos), Brick Garth, Broad Field, Buffit Close, Bullace Tree Close (ME *bolace* 'wild plum'), Catforth Close, Causey End Close (v. caucie), Chequer Close (cf. Chequer Field 80 *infra*), Chester Close, Clough Close (v. clōh), Dam Close & Dike (*ripam de Dik* 13, *Dam Shaw* 1841 O.S., v. dammr, dīc, sceaga), Drew & Drewhouse, Dyse Croft, East Field (*le Estfeld* 13, v. ēast, feld), Eskham Field, Far Carr (v. kjarr), Far Garth (v. garðr), Ferry Close (v. ferja), Finglah Close, Foster Close, Gate Close, Guide Post Close, Guyme (cf. Gyme i, 4 *supra*), Hacks Close, Hagg (v. hǫgg), Hatter Close, Hazle Garth (v. hæsel, garðr), Hill Close, Hog Hill Close, Hollin Lane Close (v. holegn 'holly'), Hopwood Close, Huggermoor Hill, Hutch Croft, Ings & Ings Close (*le Hengtoft* 13, *Rawcliffe Ings* 1841 O.S., v. eng 'meadow'), Intake (v. intak), John Roe Top, Mangle Close & Garth, Mapplebed Close (v. mapel, bedd), High & Low Marrishes (v. mersc, merisc 'marsh'), Maurice Head, Far & Near Medium, Moor Close, New Lane Close, Normans Friend, Ossingham, Peak Close, Peat Moors, Pen Close, Queen Ing, Ramper Close, Reed Close, Reedholme Moors, River Garth, Saffron Garth (v. garðr), Sand Close, Sandhills (v. sand, clos, hyll), Sandwith Close (*le Sandwath* 13, v. sand, vað 'ford'), Seed Close, Smith Close, Stack Garth Close ('stack yard'), Stack Hill, Street Close, Sutton Close & Croft, Swinehill Close, Town End Close, Warped Moors or Warp Moor (v. wearp), Warping Drain & Clough (cf. Warping Drain 16 *supra*), Welberry Close, West Field (ib 1841 O.S., *le Westfeld* 13, v. west, feld), Wiggin Flatt, Willow Garth, Yole Head (*Yole* 13, *le Yole* 1316 YD x, *le Yoll dik* 1509 ib from ON hjól 'a wheel' in the sense 'river-bend' or 'mill-wheel'), Ysle.

(b) *Alstancroft* 13 (the OE pers.n. Ǣlfstān, croft), *Altunecroft* 13 (perhaps an error for prec.), *Braythwayth* 13 (v. breiðr, þveit), *Goduscroft* 13 (perhaps a ME fem. pers.n. *Godus* (cf. Alms Cliff pt. v *infra*), croft), *le Hay* 13 (v. (ge)hæg 'enclosure'), *Herholme* 13 (v. holmr 'water-meadow'), *le Kerdik* 13 (v. kjarr 'marsh', dīc), *Lauer(d)rid(d)ing* 13, 1219 (v. hlāford 'lord', rydding), *Ling, Leling* 13 (v. le, lyng 'heather'), *Mor(e)holm(e)* 13 (v. mōr, holmr), *Moshirst* 13 (v. mos 'swamp', hyrst 'wood'), *Nes, le Nesse* 13, 1219, 1254–8 Selby (v. nes 'a headland', the peninsula now called Rawcliffe Scalp), *le Neudig(g)ote* 13 (v. nīwe, dīc, gota 'drain'), *Newridding* 13 (v. nīwe, rydding), *Osbernefletker* 13 (the ME pers.n. *Osbern* (cf. Feilitzen 338), flēot, kjarr), *Rouclifwode* 1368 *MinAcct* 26, *Rowcliffwood* 1609 ib 17 (v. wudu), *Sturesber* 13 (v. beorg 'hill', the first el. is the ME pers.n. *Sture*, probably of Scandinavian origin, cf. OSwed *Sture*, Feilitzen 376), *Suthwelle' Croft* 1254–8 (owned by *Beatricia de Suthwell'* ib, *v.* croft), *Tendhaikes* 1251 (*v.* eik 'oak', *tend* may stand for tēn 'ten'), *Thikcroft* 13 (*v.* croft, the first el. may be from þicce[1] 'thicket' or possibly the ON byname *Þykkr*), *Wolgroholme, Wlgerholme* 13, 1254–8 (the OE pers.n. *Wulfgār*, holmr 'water-meadow'), *le Wetecroft* 13 (*v.* hwǣte 'wheat', croft).

11. SNAITH (97–6422)

Snaith, Snayth 1078–85 Selby (YCh 468), c. 1101 *et freq* Selby (YCh 43, 481), 1219 Fees, 1242 Pat, 1246 *Ass* 10, 1249 Ch, 1250 Fees, YI, 1275 WCR, 1280 Ebor *et passim* to 1538 FF, (*soka de-*) 1276 RH, c. 1300 Selby, (*the Soak of-*) 1536 YD x, *Snaythe* 1333 YD ix, 1365 BM, *Snayth als. Sneath* 1608 FF

Esneid, Esnoid, Esnoit 1086 DB, *Esneit* 1101 YCh 473, Hy 1 (1307) Pat

Snaid 1100–8, 1120–35, Hy 2 *RegAlb* i, 65, ii, 10, 1205 DodsN, 1250–8 YD i, 173, *Snayd* 1280 YI

Sned c. 1140 HCY

Sneid c. 1140 HCY, 1154 Selby, 1169, 1196 P, 1205 YCh 491, 1208 P, *Sneydh* 1230 P

Sneit, Sneyt 1156 RBE, 1190, 1193 P, 1210–2 RBE, 1226 FF, *Snait, Snayt* 1251 YI, 1252 Ch, 1258 YI, 1280 *Ass*, YI

Snehe 1166 RBE

Sneith, Sneyth 1189 Selby, 1169 P, 1199–1209 YCh 488, 1251 BM, 1275 Ebor, 1293 BM *et freq* to 1319 *AddCh*

Snecth 1204 ChR   *Snayht(e)* 13, 1307 YD ix

Snath 1403 YD x, 1535 VE, *Snathe* 1531 Test v, 1542 ib vi, 1552 WillY, 1599 PRSn

'Piece of land cut off', *v.* sneið, and cf. the cognate OE snǣd 'a detached piece of ground'. The precise meaning cannot be determined. Lindkvist 80 notes various Scandinavian usages (Norw *sneide* 'a slope', *sneid* 'the top of a gable wall', Swed dial. *sned* 'a gable', Dan *sned* 'slope') which point to some such general sense as 'slope'. Actually there is no slope to speak of at Snaith—there is a fall of only some 5 feet in the half-mile down to the Aire. The sense 'piece of land cut off from the rest by the Aire or some stream is more likely. Carlton (pt. iv *infra*), for example, was a detached part of Snaith parish across the Aire in Barkston Ash wapentake and it may well be that some such fact is to be assumed to explain Snaith. But the name is very old and the place had acquired considerable importance long before we have any precise knowledge of the disposition of the various boundaries; in earlier times Snaith is described as *Soca de Snayth* 1276 RH, c. 1300 Selby (*v.* sōcn 'estate'). The variant spellings *Sned, Snehe* may reflect the influence of OE *snǣd*, whilst the DB and other forms *Esneit* show French influence (cf. IPN 103).

STREET-NAMES: BEAST FAIR, LOW GATE, MARKET PLACE.

BALNE CROFT, *Baunecroft* 1246 *Ass* 11d, *Bouncroft* 1352 YD ix, *Balncrofte* 1558 FF, *Bawn(e)croft(e)* 1560 PRSn, 1571 *Dep*, 1606 FF. *v.* Balne 14 *supra*, croft.

COWICK, EAST & WEST, *Cuwic, -wik* 12 Selby, 13 YD x, 1221 Cur, 1223 FF, 1246 *Ass* 41d, *Cuwich* 1197 P (p), *Kuwic* 1246 *Ass* 12, -*wyke* 1251 YI, *Couwyk', -wik* 13 Selby, 1331 *MinAcct* 77, 1333 YD ix, 1364 FF, 1381 YD xii, 257, *Cowyk(e), -wik, -wick(e)* 1229 Selby, 1331 Pat *et freq* to 1531 Test *v.* 'Cow farm', *v.* cū, wīc, which often denoted 'a dairy farm'.

PHIPPIN PARKS, (*bosco de, wood of*) *Fippin'* 13 YD x, 1223 FF, 1232–7 Selby, (*bosco de*) *Pippin* (sic) 1225 Pat, (*park of*) *Fyppyn* 1383 YD ix, *Phipping Pk.* 1576 PRSn, *Fippinge Parke* 1571 *Dep, parci de Phipping* 1649 *MinAcct* 13. The first el. is doubtless the ME pers.n. *Phippen*, a diminutive of *Phip*, which is itself a short form of *Philip* (cf. Reaney 250); the second is wudu or park, usually Latinised in the earlier spellings.

SNAITH INGS, *Snaythynges* 13 Selby, *le Snaything'* 1262, 1263 ib, *Suaythyng* (sic) 1263 FF, *Snaytheng* 1377 *AddCh* 45830. Despite the last spelling, these thirteenth century forms can hardly contain ON eng 'a meadow'; *eng* does not become *ing* till later (cf. Phonol. § 13). *v.* sneiðing 'a piece of land cut off', and cf. Snaith *supra* and Ekwall, PN -*ing* 25.

TURN BRIDGE, *pontem turnatum* 13 Selby ii, 120, (*le*) *Turn(e)brigg(e)* -*brig, -bryg* 13 ib, 1392 Works, 1398 DodsN, 1418, 1431 Pat, 1442 DodsN, 1482 YD ix, 1588 FF, -*bridge* 1602 PRSn, 1688 SelbyW. This is now a bridge which carries the Snaith–Goole road over the old R. Don; in the sixteenth century the place is described as 'a port towne serueing indifferently for all the west parts'. The name simply means 'swing bridge' (the usual sense of Lat *pons turnatus*), *v.* trun, brycg.

ASHTON WOOD, 1840 *TA*, no doubt named from a member of a family of *Ashton* known in the parish from the sixteenth century (PRSn *freq*). BANK SIDE, 1841 O.S., -*Houses* 1822 Langd, *v.* banke, sīde. BARRIER BANK, *Bar Bank* 1841 O.S., denoting a flood-bank. BEEVER'S BRIDGE. BETWEEN RIVERS DIKE, *Between Rivers* 1840 O.S. BLACK DRAIN, 1840 *TA*. BOURN MILL BALK. BURDEN HO, 1840 *TA*, cf. *Burden Close* ib. BUTT LANE, *Butt Lane Close* 1840 *TA*, *v.* butte, lane. THE CARR, *Cowick Carr* 1841 O.S., *Carr Close* 1840 *TA*, *v.* kjarr 'marsh'. CARR LANE, 1840 *TA*, *v.* prec. COWICK HALL, *Hall* 1817 M. COWICK MOOR, *mora de Kuwyc* 1251 YI, cf. also *North(e)mor(e)* 1323, 1368 *MinAcct* 45, 26, *Southmor* 1368 ib, *Neather moore* 1682 *Comm* 66, *v.* mōr 'marshy moorland'. COW PASTURE, 1840 *TA*, *Cowpastour* 1368 *MinAcct* 26, *v.* cū, pasture. CROSS HILL, *Crossehill* 1609 *MinAcct* 77, *v.* cros, hyll. DOWSON'S LANE, from the surname *Dowson*, cf. *Margaret Dowson* of Airmyn 1600 PRSn 164. EASTFIELD HO, *Estfeld* 1345 YD ix, *v.* ēast, feld. FIELD HO, *Feildhowses* 1591 FF, cf. *Field Close* 1840 *TA*, *v.* feld, hūs. FISH BALK LANE, *Fish Balk* 1773 *EnclA*, *Fish Balk Close* 1840 *TA*, *v.* fisc as a surname, balca. GOATHEAD LANE. THE GODDARDS, perhaps identical with *Goldwelgarth* 1609 *MinAcct* 17, *v.* golde, wella, garðr. GREENLAND, 1822 Langd, *v.* grēne[1], land. HAGG LANE, 1840 *TA*, cf. *le Fremanhagge* 1380 YD ix, *Hagg Ho* 1771 M, *Hags and Parks* 1817 M, *v.* frēo-mann 'free man', hogg 'a clearing'. ING GOOLE (a pool), 1840 *TA*, 'meadow channel', *v.* eng, goule and cf. Goole 16 *supra*. INGS DRAIN & LANE, 1841 O.S., cf. *North-enge(s)* 1323, 1368 *MinAcct* 45, 26, *Far Ings, Ings Close, Little Ings* 1840 *TA*, *v.* eng 'meadow'. LADY GYME REACH, 1841 O.S., *v.* Gyme i, 4 *supra*. LITTLE LONDON, *Little London Close, London Grove* 1840 *TA*. LORD DOWNE'S CLOUGH, cf. *Downe Arms Inn* 1840 *TA*, both named from Viscount Downe. MANOR HILL, 1841 O.S. MARSH HO, cf. *Marsh Close* 1840 *TA*, *v.* Snaith Marsh *infra*. NORTH PARK, *Old Park* 1841 O.S., *v.* park. PARK HO, 1817 M, *Parkehouse* 1621 PRSn, *v.* park, hūs. THE PARKS, *(The) Parks* 1817 M, 1841 O.S., *v.* park. PICKHILL BANK, 1841 O.S., *v.* pightel 'enclosure'. PRIESTLEY'S CLOUGH, named from a member of a family of *Priestley* known in the parish from the sixteenth century (PRSn *freq*). SNAITH HALL, *Snaithall* 1615 PRSn, *Snayth hall* 1733 YDr, *v.* hall. SNAITH MARSH, 1841 O.S., *v.* mersc. SOAK DIKE, *Soak Drain* 1840 *TA*, *v.* soc 'drain', dīc. SOUTH FIELD, *Sudcampum* 13 YD x, *Sowthfeld* 1462 ib, (*le*) *South(e)feld* 1503 YD ix, 1509 ib x, *v.* sūð, feld. SOUTH

PARK, *New Park* 1841 O.S., cf. North Park *supra*.   SPA WELL.
WAD HOUSES, *Wodehouses* 1326 *Ass* 2, possibly OE *wād* 'woad'
as in *woad-house* 1829 (NED s.v.), hūs.   WENT BRIDGE, *Wentebrigge*
1368 *MinAcct* 26, *v.* R. Went (RNs.), brycg; there are three other
bridges across the Went which are so called, cf. 51 *infra*; they
cannot easily be distinguished in the early material.   WENT GREEN,
Went Green Close 1840 *TA*, *v.* grēne[2].   WENT MOUTH.

FIELD-NAMES

The principal forms in (*a*) are 1840 *TA* 365. Spellings dated 12, 13, 1252
are Selby, 1316 YD x, 1323 *MinAcct* 45, 1333–1403 YD ix, 1418–1509,
16 YD x, 1609 *MinAcct* 17, 1682 *Comm* 66, 1773 *EnclA*.

(*a*) Armstile Close, Bean Close, Bog Close, Brick Close, Bridge Close
(cf. *Estbrigg* 1323, *v.* ēast, brycg), Brogery Hill, Bryan Hills, Calf Garth (*v.*
calf, garðr), Cawthrons Garth, Coney Hills (*v.* coni, hyll), Cow Close Bank,
Cowick Field (ib 1773, cf. Field Ho *supra*), Cowick Green Close, Crabtree
Close, Cransells (*Cranhales* 1609, *v.* cran 'crane', halh), Crook Close (cf.
Croakes more 1682, *v.* krókr, mōr), Dor Close (*v.* dor 'a gate'), Duck Holes,
East Close (*Estclos* 1368, *v.* ēast, clos), Folly, Gomorrah Close, Grass Garth
(*v.* gærs, garðr), Gudger, Hales Close, Hallmires, Hazle Hurst Lane (*v.*
hæsel, hyrst), Holme Close (*Holme* 1252, *v.* holmr 'water-meadow'), Hunting
Green, Jack Croft, Jenny Garth, Lane Close, Langham, Laws Garth, Long
Lands, Low Bottoms, Moor Hills & Tops, Morkshaw (*v.* sceaga 'copse'),
Narrow Garths, The North Bank, Old Garth, Old Ings Close, Far, High,
Middle & Harrow Oxems (*Midel-*, *le Overoxnhaghe(dyk)* 1380, *Mydyl-*,
Mydiloxmay(dyke) 1462, 'oxen enclosure', *v.* oxa (gen.sg. oxan, gen.pl.
oxna), haga), Ox Pasture, Parkside Paddock (cf. Park Ho *supra*), Pashley
Close, Peat Moor, Pinder Piece, Pinfold Close, Red Hills, Rushey Close,
Saffron Garth, Sand Hill Close, Severance Garth, Slough Ings, Snaith Field
(ib 1773, *v.* feld), Sodom Close (cf. Gomorrah Close *supra*), Stack Yard
Close, Stile Close, Thornburgh Garth, Town End Close, Went Door close
(*v.* R. Went, dor 'gate'), Wessalls, West Close, Whin Beds (*v.* hvin 'gorse',
bedd), Wilsford Close, Wood Close (cf. *Cuwikwood* 1223 FF, *v.* wudu).

(*b*) *Almondhead* 1609, *Anabledykdoughter thynge* (a meadow) 1480
('Anabel Dyke's daughter's property', *v.* þing), *Babbeland* 1358 YD vii
(the OE pers.n. *Babba*, land), *Bents* 1682 (*v.* beonet 'bent-grass'), *Estbirdales*
13 ('the town's shares of common land', *v.* bȳ (gen.sg. bȳjar), dāl), *le*
Byrkshawe 16 (*v.* birki, sceaga), *le Bright* 1609 (perhaps an error for byht
'bight, bend of a river'), *Broadoake* 1682 (*v.* brād, āc), *Brocaithirne* 1381
(perhaps an error for *Brotaic*, *v.* prec., eik 'oak', hyrne 'corner of land'),
Brookehurst 1609 (*v.* brōc, hyrst), *Bruntcliffedge* 1682 (*v.* brant 'steep', clif,
ecg), *Bull croft* 1632 PRSn (*v.* bula, croft), *Burnelhouse* 1368 *MinAcct* 26
(the ME surname *Burnel*, hūs), *Carterknoll* 1682 (the surname *Carter*,
cnoll 'hillock'), *Cokepasture* 1323 (ME *coke* 'cook', perhaps as a surname,

pasture), *Coksty* 1351 (*v.* prec. or cocc[1] 'hill', stīg 'path'), *Coittes, Cottes* 1557, 1570 WillY (*v.* cot 'cottage'), *le Crosgate* 1403 (*v.* cros, gata), *Deercroft* 1609 (*v.* dēor, croft), *Dep(e)syk* 1462, 1503 YD ix, 1509 ('deep stream', *v.* dēop, sīc), *aque del Dik, Dyk* 1368 *MinAcct* 26, 1418, *Dyke juxta Cowyk* 1392 Works, and *Dykesmers(c)h* 1323, *Dikemerssh* 1368 *MinAcct* 26, *Dikesbaue* (sic for *-banc*) 13 (*v.* dīc, mersc, banke, cf. Dikes Marsh in Thorne i, 2 *supra*), *Dobenhill* 1682 (probably the pers.n. *Dobbin*, hyll), *Emycecroft* 1471 YD ix (doubtless a form of the OG fem. pers.n. *Amisa* (Forssner 28), croft), *Ermegarent Land* 1333 (probably the OG fem. pers.n. *Ermengard*, land), *Fylcok toft* 1503 YD ix (probably *Fillcock*, a nickname, topt 'enclosure'), *le Foodesehirlls* 16, *le Fordol(s)* 1316 YD x, 1345 (*v.* fore, dāl), *Foxhole banck* 1682 (*v.* fox-hol, banke), *Futriding'* 13 (*v.* rydding 'clearing'), *Legate* 1588 FF (*v.* le 'the', gata 'road'), *Gildestede* 13 ('the guild place', *v.* gild(i), stede), *le Gott* 1503 YD ix (*v.* gota 'channel'), *Gramoreses* 1403 YD x, *Gramerose* 1462, *Grymthorpe* 1609 (the ON pers.n. *Grímr*, þorp), *Harthillgrove* 1682 (*v.* heorot, hyll, perhaps as a surname *Harthill*, grāf), *le Heighes* 1368 *MinAcct* 26 (*v.* hēah[2] 'high place'), *Henclifmore* 1276 RH (*v.* henn, clif, mōr), *Hensall gate* 1609 (*v.* Hensall 19 *supra*, gata), *le Heuedland* 1316 YD x (*v.* hēafod-land), *le Hyghtdyk* 1503 YD ix (*v.* hēhðu 'height', dīc), *Ladymer* 1509 (*v.* mere 'pool'), *Littlecomon* 1682, *Longdoles* 1368 *MinAcct* 26 (*v.* lang, dāl), *Middelclos* 1368 ib (*v.* middel, clos), *Olderiddyng* 1323 (*v.* ald, rydding), *Peshedthyng* (a meadow) 1503 YD ix (perhaps a surname 'Peasehead', *v.* þing 'property'), *Phiteker* 13 ('grassland marsh', *v.* fit, kjarr), *Rauenesbogh'* 1323 (from the pers.n. OE *Hræfen* or ON *Hrafn*, boga 'arch, river-bend'), *Risshemershe* 1323 (*v.* risc 'rush', mersc), *Roehill* 1682 (*v.* rā[1] 'roe', hyll), *Roubanteldik* (sic for *-bances-*) 13 (*v.* rūh, banke, dīc), *Smaleng* 12, *le Smalheng* 13, 1316 YD x, *les Smalengges* 1418, *le Smayllynges* 16 ('narrow meadows', *v.* smæl, eng), *Sowthend* 1588 FF (*v.* sūð, ende), *Spikyng'* 1323 (this name, like similar names *Spikyng* 75 and *Do(u)ble-, Syngle spykynges* 74, (Tadcaster West) pt. iv, (Knaresborough) pt. v *infra*, is probably ME *spiking* 'a headless spike-nail', *duble spiking* 'a large spike-nail', though the particular application is unknown; it might denote a narrow strip of land shaped like a spike-nail, perhaps a long narrow triangular strip, cf. also Sparable Clough (Barwick) pt. iv), *Spring* 1368 *MinAcct* 26 (*v.* spring), *Stanhill'* 12 (*v.* stān, hyll), *Stathe* 1380 (*v.* stæð 'landing-place, shore'), *Tinteland* 1418, *Typpynghous* 1418, *Traystones* 1682, *Turpyncroft* 1609 (the surname *Turpin*, croft), *Whitebarnelands* 1463 (*v.* hwīt, bere-ærn, land), *Wilbymore or Dandsome mor* 1395, *Wri-, Wrymor(e)* 1347, 1392, 1418 (*v.* wrēo 'wry, twisted', mōr), *lez Wro* 1471 YD ix (*v.* vrá 'nook of land').

iv. Kirk Bramwith

Kᴵʀᴋ Bʀᴀᴍᴡɪᴛʜ (103–6211)

> *Branuuat, -uuet* 1086 DB   *Branwyth* 1200 Cur, 14 *Sawl* 193
> *Bramwik* 1154 Selby (YCh 480), *-wic* 1199–1213 ib, *Bramewich* 1169 P, *Brāwict* 1204 ChR, *Bramwich* 1291 Tax

Bramwit, -wyt 1155–61 YCh 481, 1252 Ebor
Bramwith, -wyth l. 12 *Lewes* 303, 1199 (1232) Ch, 1201, 1230,
 1251 FF *et passim* to 1525 Test vi, (*Kyrk-*, *Kirke-*) 1341 FF,
 1502 Ipm, 1548 WillY
Brampwyth 1316 Vill

This name should be taken with South Bramwith (i, 13 *supra*),
which is on the opposite bank of the Don. There is some hesitation
in the earlier spellings between *-with* (from ON **viðr** 'wood') and
-wic (from OE **wīc** 'dairy farm') and, if the DB spellings of both
names are taken into account, OE **wudu** 'wood'. This confusion
occurs also in Skipwith and some other YE p.ns. (*v.* YE 263); in view
of the greater abundance and antiquity of *-wic* spellings for Skipwith,
OE **wīc** would there seem to be original (with ON **viðr** as a later
replacement), but there is no such certainty with Bramwith. The DB
spelling with *-uuode* (for South Bramwith) points to an original OE
brōm-wudu 'broom wood' with ON **viðr** substituted later. The *-wic(h)*
spellings would then be due to the medieval graphical ambiguity of
c and *t*, and the single *-wik* could be an early scribal misreading. On
Bram- for OE *brōm*, *v.* EPN i, 52 and cf. Phonol. § 29. The church at
Kirk Bramwith is frequently mentioned from the thirteenth century
(*v.* **kirkja**, cf. Kirkhouse Green *infra*).

BRAITHWAITE, *Braytweyt* 1276 RH, *Brai-*, *Braythueyt*, *-thuayt*,
-thwait(e) 1281 YI, 1327 Ipm, 1383 Pat *et freq* to 1822 Langd,
Braitewaite 1422 IpmR, *Brathwayte* 1538 FF, *Brayffeith* 1549 WillY,
Brafit 1681 PRCnt, 1843 *TA*. 'Broad clearing or meadow', *v.* **breiðr**,
þveit. On the later forms *-fit*, etc., cf. Phonol. § 49.

KIRKHOUSE GREEN, *Kirkestgren* 1499 Ipm, *Ki-*, *Kyrkhousgrene* 1503
ib, 1594 FF, *Kyrckhurstgrene* 1581 WillY, *Kirk(e)hirstgrene* 1590,
1609 FF, *Kirkehurstgrove als. Kirkehowsegreene* 1604 ib. 'Church
wood green', *v.* **kirkja**, **hyrst**, **grēne**[2]. The confusion of *hyrst* and *hūs*
occurs also in the nearby Hawkehouse Green 48 *infra*.

ASHFIELD. CHURCH TOWN COMMON, 1843 *TA*. DOWBORN BANK,
Gobarn croft (sic) 1488 Ipm, *Dow(n)born Field* 1843 *TA*, *Gobarn*
(or *Dowborn*) is perhaps a surname, *v.* **croft**. GREAT GREEN HO,
formerly *Grene croft* 1606 FF, *Green Croft* 1771 M, 1841 O.S., *v.*
grēne[2], **croft**. OLD LANE. PALMER LANE, *Palmers Lane* 1841 O.S.,
ME *palmer* 'a pilgrim', perhaps as a surname, **lane**. RUSHY LANE,
1843 *TA*. WOOD END, *Le Wood End in Bramwith* 1617 SheffMan,

Woodend 1626 PRSn, *v.* **wudu, ende.** BRAMWITH WOODHOUSE, 1658 WillS, *Wodehous* 1338 FF, *Bramwithwodhouse* 1594 FF, *Woodhowse* 1606 FF, *v.* **wudu, hūs.** WOODHOUSE INGS, *Woodhouse-ing* 1559 Hnt i, 151, cf. *le Engedike* 1480 *MinAcct* 511, *Ings* (*Head*) 1843 *TA*, *v.* **eng** 'meadow'.

FIELD-NAMES

The principal forms in (*a*) are 1843 *TA* 240. Other spellings dated without source are *MinAcct*.

(*a*) Apple Garth, Applehurst (*v.* **æppel, garðr, hyrst**), Barley Hill, Bate Ridding (*v.* the ME pers.n. *Bate*, **rydding**), Bullatoft, Calf Close, Calling Croft, Calvers, Carr Close (*v.* **kjarr**), Cockshaw Close, Coney Garth (*v.* **coning-erth** 'warren'), Dikehouse Fall, Fall Close (*v.* **(ge)fall**), Farming Croft & Nooking, Fity Close, Hecklers Garth, Hop Yard, Lea Field, Leven Croft, Line Garth (*v.* **lin, garðr**), Long Rushes, Mill Close & Field, Moate Close, Moor Field, Neeson Hall 1771 M, Nettlewaite (*v.* **netele, þveit**), Neville Field, North Field, Nutting Croft, Obbity Hole Wood, Ox Close, Pighill (*v.* **pightel**), Pinching Ing, Pond Hill, Reynard Croft, Ritching Croft, Round Bank, Rumblehurst, Rushy Garth, Sand Hole, Scholars, School Garth, Shaw (*v.* **sceaga**), Smithfield, Stack Garth Close, Stockings, Suky Croft, Tallow Crofts, Tom Croft (*Thomasin Croft* 1662 *Glebe*, *v.* **croft**, with the fem. pers.n. *Thomasin* as first el.), Trimming Croft, Tundy Field, Water Croft, Well Garth, Wheat Croft, Wise Witch, Wood Croft, Wood Shaw.

(*b*) *Bridecroft* 1384, *Brydcroft* 1421, *Birdcroft* 1502 Ipm (*v.* **bridd** 'bird', no doubt as a byname, **croft**), *Bramwithfery* 1486 (*v.* **ferja**), *Fallthorowenook* 1559 Hnt ('fall-through nook'), *Kirkemore* 1538 (*v.* **kirkja, mōr**), *Moreherne* 1662 *Glebe* (*v.* **mōr, hyrne** 'nook, bend'), *Westhalff* 1535 VE (*v.* **west, half**), *Westyard* 1538, 1540 (*v.* **west, geard**), *Yhaldeholme* 1384, *Haldholme* 1424 *Rent* 255 (*v.* **jalda** 'a nag', **holmr** 'water-meadow').

v. Owston

Carcroft in Owston township together with Skellow are now in Adwick le Street Urban District (i, 68 *supra*).

1. OWSTON (103–5511)

Aust(h)un 1086 DB
Oustun, -ton(a) 12 YD i, c. 1150 Crawf (p), 1180–5 YCh 1585, 13
  Nost 55d, 1234 FF, 1254 Ebor *et passim* to 1525 Test vi
Houston 1336 FF
Auston 1371, 1384 YD vi, 1588 FF
Owston 1473 YD viii, 1540 MonRent, 1581 WillY

'East farmstead', *v.* **austr, tūn.**

CARCROFT

> *Kercroft, -kroft* 12 YD i (p), *Nost* 146, 1190–1210 YCh 823 (p), 13 *Nost* 55d *et freq* to 1366 FF
> *Kerecroft* c. 1170 Pont (p), 1203 DodsN, FF
> *Kar-, Carcroft(e)* 1365 DodsN, 1371 FF *et passim* to 1586 FF
> *Care Crofte* 1487 *MinAcct* 66

'Enclosure near the marsh', *v.* kjarr, croft.

SHIRLEY, *Scherlay* 1379 PT (p), *Sherlaye haull* 1552 NCWills, *Shirlaye* 1600 PRBw. 'Bright glade or clearing', *v.* scīr², lēah.

THORNHURST FM, *Tornhyrst* 12 *Nost* 146, *Thornhyrst* 13 *Nost* 145d, *Thornhurst(h)* 1280 Ch, 1323 *MinAcct* 16 (p), *Thornehirst* 1379 PT (p), 1380 Ch, 1390 *Nost* 67d. 'Thorn wood', *v.* þorn, hyrst.

BLACKER GREEN, 1719 PRBw, 1771 M, *v.* blæc, kjarr, grēne². BLACK SIKE WELL, *Black Syke Drain* 1843 *TA*, *v.* blæc, sīc. BREAKS PLANT., cf. *Breaks Close* 1843 *TA*, *v.* bræc. BRICK KILN PLANT., 1841 O.S. BRIERY COTTAGE, 1841 O.S., *Briarey Cottage* 1843 O.S., cf. *Briery Yard* 1631 *BWr* 5, *v.* brērig, geard. BURNT INGS, 1841 O.S., cf. also *le Brende* 13 *Nost* 147d, *Burnt Row & View* 1843 *TA*, *v.* brende 'burnt' (or 'place cleared by burning'), eng. BUSKEY PLANT., *Bushey Close Plantation* 1843 *TA*, *v.* buskr, clos. COCKSHAW DIKE, *Cokschaghe* 1379 PT (p), *Cockshaw Drain* 1843 *TA*, *v.* cocc² 'woodcock', sceaga 'copse'. CORPSE LANE. DICKEN FM, 1841 O.S. DUCK HOLT, *Duck Hole* 1843 *TA*, *v.* dūce, hol¹. EMILY WOOD, 1841 O.S. FELHURST BRIDGE, 1841 O.S., *litle felhurst* 1540 MonRent, *v.* fjǫl 'plank', hyrst 'wood'; *fjol* might itself have denoted a plank-bridge (cf. Fell Beck Bridge (Bishopside) pt. v *infra*). HAYWOOD, *Hey-, Haywood* 1558, 1583 WillY, 1725 PRBw, 1817 M, *Haywood or Rimer House* 1799 ib, *Rimor House* 1771 M, *v.* (ge)hæg, wudu; *Rimer* is a surname. HOLME, *Holm(e)* 13 *Nost* 147d, 1274 DodsN, 1293 QW, 1408 YD vi, *v.* holmr 'water-meadow'. JOAN CROFT, 1843 *TA*, *v.* croft. LADY WELL. MORLEY WELL, 1843 *TA*, cf. also *Morley Ing* ib, doubtless *Morley* (cf. 182 *infra*) as a surname, wella, eng. NORTH QUARRY, 1841 O.S. NORTH PARK. OWSTON COMMON, 1760 *EnclA*. OWSTON GRANGE, 1841 O.S. OWSTON HALL, 1841 O.S. PICKHILL LANE, *Pickhill* 1841 O.S., *Pighill* 1843 *TA*, *v.* pightel 'enclosure'. RANDALL CROFT WOOD, 1843 *TA*, *v.* croft. ROCKLEY, *Rookeley* 1379 PT (p), *Rokley Hall* 1542 WillY, *Rockeley* 1600 PRBw, probably 'rook clearing', *v.* hrōc, lēah.   Row Plant., 1841 O.S., *v.* rāw.   Rushy Moor, 1755 PRBw, *Rishemore* 1620 FF, *v.* risc, mōr.   Sixteen Acres Plant., 1841 O.S.   Shirley Pool, 1841 O.S., *v.* Shirley *supra*, pōl.   Sourpiece Wood, 1841 O.S., 1843 *TA*, *v.* sūr, pece.   South Quarry, 1841 O.S.   Stock Bridge, *Stockbridge Common* 1760 *EnclA*, *v.* stocc, brycg, cf. Stockbridge i, 25 *supra*.   Stoney Lands Lane. Stony Flat Plant., *Stoney Flatt* 1843 *TA*, *v.* stānig, flat.   Tumholme, *Tumbholm(e)* 1371 YD vi, 1379 PT (p), 'Tumbi's watermeadow', *v.* holmr; on the pers.n. *Tumbi* (DB), probably from an ODan *Tumbi*, *v.* Feilitzen 388.   Well Sike, *Well Syke Drain* 1843 *TA*, *v.* wella, sīc.   Wheat Holme, *Wet Holmes* 1843 *TA*, *v.* hwǣte, holmr.   White Hall, *Whte Hall* (sic) 1797 PRBw, *v.* hwīt, hall.

FIELD-NAMES

The principal forms in (*a*) are 1843 *TA* 313. Forms dated without source are *MinAcct*, those dated 1540 are MonRent.

(*a*) Abbess Close, Adam Butt (*v.* butte), Baggit Close & Toft, Laith & Middle Baggot (probably the ME surname *Bagot*, *v.* clos, topt, hlaða), Balne Close (cf. *Balnefeld* 1368, *v.* Balne 14 *supra*), Blanchard's Holme Field (the ME pers.n. *Blanchard*, holmr), Broom Close, Bun's House 1841 O.S., Bustard, Carr (*v.* kjarr, cf. Carcroft *supra*), College Close (belonging to University College, Oxford), Common Close & Croft, Cross Close, Diamond Ing, Eccols Close Drain, Eccolt's Close, Ellis Croft, Emery Wood, Far Park, Fat Field, Forest Flatt, Franchise Field (ME *fraunchise* in one of its various senses 'privilege, immunity, sanctuary'), Hall Ing, Harrott Field, Hay Field, Honey Lands (*Honylandes* 1591 WillY, *v.* hunig, land), Hoo Plantation (*v.* hōh), Ings Pot, Intake Wood (*v.* intak), Lane & Lane End Croft, Limperhurst & Crooked Limpers (*Lympothurst* 1430 YD vi, 'lime-pit wood', *v.* līm, potte, hyrst), Line Croft (*v.* lin 'flax', croft), Long Garth, Long Ing, Low Park, Marstell, Nor Croft, Old Wife Close, Ox Close, Rain Close (*v.* reinn 'boundary strip'), Sand Close, Shutt Close (dial. *shutt* 'a division of land'), Thistley Croft, Townfields 1743 *BWr* 14, Townsend Close, Vicar Ing, Well Close, West Croft, Whins (*v.* hvin 'gorse'), White Cross Close, White Flatt, Wikeham Field, Willow Garth, Wood Nooking.

(*b*) *Algarr-, Auger-Wroo* 1540 (*v.* vrá 'nook of land'), *Fullerhurst* 1480, 1486 (ME *fuller* 'a fuller of cloth', hyrst), *Godeshirn* 1368, *Godyuthirne* 1323, *Godewyfhirne* 1384, *Godewyueshern'* 1486 (probably 'good-wife nook', *v.* hyrne), *Gosehirne* 1384 ('goose nook', *v.* gōs, hyrne), *Harwarland* 1371 YD vi (probably a ME pers.n. *Herward* from OE *Hereweard*, ON *Hervarðr*, land), *Holmehirst* 1384 (*v.* Holme *supra*, hyrst), *Littilbrige yngs* 1540 (*v.* lytel, brycg, eng), *Milnehirste* 1323 (*v.* myln, hyrst), *Nad(e)oxgang(e)* 1384, 1480 (*v.* ox-gang), *Sharpelaypitt* 1384 (*v.* pytt, the first theme may be a local surname).

2. SKELLOW (103–1052)

Scanhalle, -a 1086 DB
Scalehale 1180–95 YCh 1585, 1200 DodsN, *Scal'* 1185 BM
Scelehal 12 *Nost* 146
Skelehall 1203 FF, *-hale* 1246 *Ass* 8d
Skelhal(e) 12 YD i, 1243 FF, 1246 *Ass* 38d, YI, 1336 FF, *-hall* 1371
  FF, 1473 YD viii
Schelhal(l) 1219, 1246 FF, 1246 *Ass* 38d, 1252 FF
Skelal(e) 1316 Vill, 1328 Banco *et freq* to 1402 FA
Skellall 1487 FF
Skellawe 1379 PT (p), *Skellow(e)* 1493 FF, 1546 YChant *et freq* to
  1641 Rates
Skelow 1499 lpm
Scelah 1730 PRCnt

Skellow and Skelbrooke (43 *infra*) are both near a small stream
which is now called The Skell, Skelbrooke doubtless being the
original stream-name; Skellow is some two miles downstream from
Skelbrooke village on a slope above the Skell stream; Wrangbrook
(37 *infra*) is at the head of the stream and was clearly once the name
of the upper part of it. The difficulty of interpretation lies in the
early variation between *Scale-*, *Schel-* and *Skel(e)-*; Skelbrooke itself
could simply be a compound of OE scēla 'shieling' (influenced by
the cognate ON skáli) and brōc, 'brook near the shieling or hut',
and Skellow could contain *Skell*, a back-formation from this stream-
name and halh 'nook of land'; *Skell* as an early reduced form of the
stream-name *Skelbrook* would be unusual but not impossible. The
first el. of Skelbrooke might also be ON skjallr 'resounding', as in
R. Skell (*v.* RNs.), but such a description of so small a stream would
be somewhat exaggerated; ODan skial 'boundary' is also formally
possible, for though the stream itself forms parish boundaries only at
intervals, it is very near the wapentake boundary which goes along
the Great North Road; the stream runs into Old Ea Beck along which
this boundary continues. On the whole, since there may be difficulties
with a derivation of Skelbrooke from *skial* in a hybrid of an OScand
word with brōc (when we might have expected ON bekkr 'stream'),
we should favour Ekwall's etymology from OE scēla, with ON sk-
replacing sh- and sometimes with the cognate ON skáli influencing
the earlier forms. As regards the *halh* in Skellow, the old village
stood on an exposed site on a hill some 30 ft. above the level of the

stream, but the *halh* would be the hollow between the hills through which the Skell flows. Skelbrooke would thus mean 'stream by the shieling', and Skellow 'nook of land or hollow near the Skell(brook)'. In Skellow the modern form *-ow* is due to dial. vocalisation of *-l* (cf. Phonol. § 6).

CRABGATE LANE. CROSS FIELD, 1801 *EnclA* 81, *v.* cros, feld. HOLMEROYD or HUMBER HEAD DIKE, *v.* i, 69 *supra.* HUMBER HEAD INGS, 1840 *TA*, *v.* prec., eng. SKELLOW CROSS, 1843 *TA*, *v.* cros. SKELLOW INGS, *Shellow Ings* 1764 *Glebe*, *the Ings* 1843 *TA*, *v.* eng 'meadow'. SKELLOW MILL, 1766 PRBw, *v.* myln.

FIELD-NAMES

The principal forms in (*a*) are 1840 *TA* 359. Spellings dated 1801 are *EnclA* 81.

(*a*) Cistern Field 1801, Citron Field, Cock Garth, Crabtree Close, Cuckoo Park, Field Dyke, Hob Croft, Ing Field Dyke, Mill Garth (cf. Skellow Mill *supra*, *v.* garðr), Sandy Field (ib 1801), Skellow Common 1801, West Field (ib 1801), Wood Close.

vi. Burghwallis

BURGHWALLIS (103–5312)

> *Burg* 1086 DB, 1170–83 YCh 1554, 1555, 1243 FF, (-*waleys*) 1272 Ebor, *Burgo* 1137–9 YCh 1492, *Burgum* 1185 Templar
> *Burc* 13 (1310) Ch
> *Burgh* 13 RegAlb ii, 64d, 1246 *Ass* 22d, 1316 Vill, (-*Waleys, -eis, -ays*) 13 YD i, 1283 Ch, 1287 Ebor, 1291 Tax *et passim* to 1606 FF, (-*wales*) 1376 FF, 1384 YD vi, 1432 YD iv, (-*Waleʒ*) 1402 FA, (-*Walas*) 1409 DiocV, (-*walles*) 1487 FF, (-*wallis*) 1736 PRHtnP
> *Bourgh Walleys* 1300 Ebor
> *Brughwalles* 1531 Test iv
> *Borowallys* 1541 FF
> *Burche Walles* 1552 NCWills
> *Burgewalles* 1571 WillY
> *Broughwales, -wallis* 1571, 1586 WillY

v. burh 'fortification'. The affix *Wallis* is the name (*le Waleys,* etc.) of an important family here from the twelfth century and after

(1185 Templar 134, 1246 *Ass* 22d, 1283 Ch, 1328 FF 209, etc.). Their name occurs also in some of the early forms of Newton (Ledsham) pt. iv *infra*.

ROBIN HOOD'S WELL, *Robbinhood-well* 16 DodsN, *Robin Hood(s) Well* 1622 Hnt, 1675 Og, 1771 M, cf. also 'the stone of *Robert Hode*' 1422 Brett. The reference is to the Robin Hood of the ballads; cf. Robin Hood's Bower i, 226 *supra*, Little John's Well 44 *infra*. This well is in Barnsdale (37 *infra*). The editor of Brett dates the deed with 'the stone of *Robert Hode*' 1322 and this would antedate the earliest mention of Robin Hood (in *Piers Plowman* B. v, 402) by some fifty years (cf. my note in MLR xxviii, 484); on checking this the correct date is certainly a century later; but it is still a very early reference.

ABBESS DIKE.   BURGHWALLIS COMMON, 1851 *TA*.   MILL DAM, *Dam* 1841 O.S., *v.* dammr.   SCORCHER HILLS, *Scotchin Hill* 1764 *Glebe*, *Scorching Hill* 1841 O.S.   SIXROOD LANE.   SKELLOW GRANGE, 1771 M, *v.* Skellow 34 *supra*, grange.   STONYCROFT LANE, *Stoney Cross Lane* 1851 *TA*.

FIELD-NAMES

Spellings dated 17, 1764 are *Glebe*.

(a) Bekinfield dry close 1764, Burgwallis Wood 1851 *TA* 76, Middle Field Close 1818 *EnclA* 175.

(b) *The Hullett acre* 17, *Rawson balk* 17 (the surname *Rawson*, balca), *the Reine* 17 (*v.* reinn 'boundary strip'), *Skellow Ings* 17 (*v.* Skellow 34 *supra*, eng), *Wikehamfeld* 1502 Ipm.

vii. South Kirkby

Skelbrooke and Hamphall Stubbs townships are now in Hampole (i, 70 *supra*).

1. NORTH ELMSALL (103–4812)

    Ermeshala, -hale 1086 DB
    Helmeshal 1251 Ch, 1258 YI
    Elmesale 1264 YI, 1428 FA, (*North-*) 1320 YD viii, 1341 *Surv et*
        freq to 1365 FF, *Elmesall* 1316 Vill, (*North-*) 1379 PT, 1402 FA
        et passim to 1459 Calv, *North Elmesaull* 1522 Test v
    Elmsale 1296 LacyComp
    Northemsale 1341 *Surv*

'Nook of land by the elm', *v.* elm, halh, and for the use of the gen.sg. *elmes*, cf. EPN i, 158 (-es²). 'North' to distinguish it from South Elmsall 39 *infra*. On the DB spelling *Ermes*, cf. IPN 106.

BARNSDALE, the *merry Barnisdale* of the Robin Hood ballads, *Barnysdale* c. 1420 Wyntoun's *Chronicle*, *Barnysdale ryg* 1468 Brett, *Barnesdale* 1543 Leland, 1609 *Bright* 521. 'Beorn's valley', *v.* dæl. The OE pers.n. *Beorn* occurs also in Barnsley i, 302 *supra*.

MINSTHORPE

> *Manestorp* 1086 DB, 12 Brett, *Manethorpp'* 1379 PT (p), *Mansthorp* 1436 DodsN, 1495 FF
> *Menethorp* 1166 P (p), *-torp* 1219 FF (p)
> *Mensthorp(e)* 1320 YD vii, 1552 FF, *-trop(e)* 1590 WillY, 1603 FF
> *Menesthorp* 1365 FF
> *Menthorpe* 1375 FF
> *Minsthorpe* 1817 M

The variation between *Mane-*, *Mene-* and *Manes-*, *Menes-* is best accounted for by taking the first el. to be either OE (ge)mǣne 'common, owned communally', 'common land', or OE (ge)mǣnnes 'community', with *Manes-* as normal development of a shortened vowel æ or an AN spelling; the modern form is paralleled by the development of Minskip pt. v *infra*. The name would mean 'outlying farm held by community or on the common land', *v.* þorp. Ekwall (DEPN 306) would take Menthorpe YE 261 to be from (ge)mǣne and to have a similar meaning.

SLEEP HILL, *Slepehill* 1175–85 Pont (YCh 1550), 1323 *MinAcct* 45, 1540 MonRent, 1542 Dugd v, *Sleiphil* 13 Pont, *Slephil(l)* 1230 Ebor, 1322 Brett, *-hull* 1311 Ch, *Slepill* 1322 Brett, 1379 PT (p), *Sclephill* 1420 Brett, *Sleepehill* 1608 FF. 'Slippery or muddy hill', *v.* slǣpe, hyll.

WRANGBROOK

> *Wrangebroc*, *-brok(e)* 12 Brett, 1177–85 YCh 1510, 1180–98 ib
> 1677, 1186 Brett, 1190–1200 YCh 1751, 13 Brett, 1347 Baild
> *Warangebroc* 1158–72, 1190–1220 YCh 1676, 1750
> *Wrainbroc* 1200 Brett, *Wraynebrok* 1379 PT
> *Wrangbroc*, *-brok(e)* 13 *Nost* 24d, 1230 Ebor, 1276 RH, 1320 YD
> viii *et passim* to 1539 Bodl 72, *-brooke* 1540 MonRent
> *Wrambrughe* 1570 WillY

'Twisted, crooked stream', v. **wrang, brōc**. The stream makes a right-angled turn here; cf. *the croke acre* f.n. *infra*. On the AN spelling *Warange-* cf. IPN 104.

COLLY WELL WOOD.   DALE LANE, *le Dale* 1392 YD viii, cf. *Dale Close & Field* 1842 *TA*, v. **dæl** 'valley'.   GREAT BREAKS, (*Far*) *Breaks* 1842 *TA*, v. **bræc** 'strip of uncultivated land'.   GREY COCKS, *Growcoke* 1525 WillY, *Far Grey Cock* 1842 *TA*, 'grey hillock', v. **græg, cocc**[1]; *Grow-* is perhaps an analogical spelling from ME *grewhound* 'greyhound' (cf. NED s.v.).   HAGUE HALL BECK, 1841 O.S., v. **haga** 'enclosure'.   INCH LANE, cf. *Inch Croft* 1842 *TA*.   MANOR FM.   MILL LANE, cf. *Mylneflate* 1341 *Surv*, *Mill Croft*, *Mill Hill* 1842 *TA*, v. **myln**.   MOSLEY MIRES, *Mosley Myers* 1841 O.S., *Musley Miers* 1842 *TA*, 'clearing in the marsh', v. **mos, lēah, mýrr**.   MUTTON FLATT, *Moutonflatte* 1437 *Surv*, *Multen Flatts* 1771 M, *Mutton Flatts* 1841 O.S., from OFr *motoun, molton*, ME *moltoun* 'a sheep', and *flat*; cf. Mutton Hall 52, *Motonkarre* 42, -*kerre* 82 *infra*.   NORTH ELMSALL HALL.   SHEEPWALK LANE, *Sheep Walks* 1842 *TA*, from e.ModE *sheep-walk* 'pasture for sheep'.   STONE PIT WOOD, 1841 O.S., v. **stān, pytt**.   THORN TREE WELL.   WILBY WOOD, 1841 O.S.

FIELD-NAMES

The principal forms in (*a*) are 1842 *TA* 145. Spellings dated c. 1175 are YCh 1782, c. 1200 YCh 1750–1, 12, 13, 1322 Brett, 1323 *MinAcct* 45, 1341 *Surv*, 1345, 1368, 1486 *MinAcct* 26, 45, 66.

(*a*) Allums, Barn Garth, Bright Riddings (v. **rydding**), Brockholes (*Brockhold* 1563 *BWr* 26, v. **brocc-hol**), Calf Close, Carr & Carr Hill (v. **kjarr** 'marsh'), Cawthornes, Chapel Garth, Clay Cliff, Crabtree Close, Dove Cote Garth, Far Royd Hill (v. **rod**[1]), Foal Garth, Green Balk, Gurroyds, Harewood (Hill), Harper Steels (v. **stigel** 'stile'), Haver Lands (*Haverland(e)s* c. 1200, 1322, v. **hafri** 'oats', *land*), Hay Riddings (v. **hēg, rydding**), Hop Riddings (v. **hoppe, rydding**), Hunger Hills (*Hungyrhill* 1392 YD viii, v. **hungor, hyll**), Intake (v. **intak**), Leys Close (v. **lēah**), Lings (v. **lyng** 'heather'), Long Lairs, Marl Pits, Low & Upper Newsam (*Newsam Grange* 1592 WillY, doubtless from *Neu-husum*, v. **nīwe, hūs, -um**), Oak Flats, Ormery, Ox Pasture (*Oxpasture* 1323, -*past'* 1341, -*pastour* 1368, v. **oxa, pasture**), Pack Close, Pine Belly (a derogatory name for poor land), Pudding Pie Close, Pudding Poke, Rails, Road Hill Leys (*Rodehill* 1563 *BWr* 26, v. **rod**[1], **hyll**), Rushley Close & Carr, Rye Riddings (v. **rȳge, rydding**), Sloe Land Field, Smear Lands (v. **smeoru** 'fat', *land*), Smeator, Stoney Holes, Stripe (ib 13 *Nost* 24d, v. **strīp**, an early example of the word), Little Thicks (*v.* þicce[1] 'thicket'), Walk Close, Weet Lands, Well Close, Willow Garth, Winn Close, Wood Close & Field, Yard End Flats.

(*b*) *le Appellgang* 1392 YD viii (*v.* æppel, gang 'way'), *Brodenge* 1368 (*v.* brād, eng 'meadow'), *Cheverilriding* c. 1200 (OFr *chevrele* 'a kid', rydding), *Clifurelang* 13 (*v.* clif, furlang), *Cotey(h)erd(e)* 1323, 1368 (*v.* cot, geard), *the Croke acre* 1468 Brett (*v.* krókr 'crook, bend', æcer, cf. Wrangbrook *supra*), *Ellerkere* 1345, *Erlescarres* 1480, *Erlestarres* 1468 (*v.* elri 'alder' with metathesis to erle, kjarr), *le Erle Acre* 1480, 1486 (*v.* prec., æcer), *Flaskedales*, -*doles* 13 (*v.* flask 'swamp', dāl 'share of the common land'), *Franerocsic* c. 1175 (*v.* sīc), *Halmote* 1323 (*v.* halimote), *the howle or hollowe of Barnesdale* 1609 Bright 521 (*v.* hol[1]), *Langdene* 12 (*v.* lang, denu 'valley'), *Latheflat* 1341 (*v.* hlaða 'barn', flat), *Meneland* 13 Brett ('common land', *v.* (ge)mǣne, land, cf. Minsthorpe *supra*), *Mide-*, *Middelfurlang* c. 1200 (*v.* middel, fur-lang), *Moderles halfaker* c. 1200, *Munkeflat* 13 (*v.* munuc, flat, from the monks of Bretton who had land here), *Raven(e)scroft* 13 (named from *Osegote Raven* 13 Brett 187, *v.* croft), *Rydinges* 13, *Ridding* 1535 VE, *Ridynglande* 1486 (*v.* rydding 'clearing'), *le Rig* 13 (*v.* hrycg), (*prati super*) *le Ryne* 1368 (OE *ryne* 'flow, run of water', cf. rynel 'runnel'), *Rodeland* 1323, *Roid-*, *le Ridland* 1341 (*v.* rod[1] 'clearing', (ge)rydd 'cleared', land), *Sowthcrofteflatte* (*v.* sūð, croft, flat), *Swalh* 13 (*v.* swalg 'pit, pool'), *Ulsebern* 13 (the OE pers.n. *Wulfsige*, bere-ærn 'barn'), *Waiouroxgang* 1414 YD viii, 1418 ib vi (cf. *Robert le Waiur* 1320 YD viii, *Richard Waiour* 1418 ib vi, 71, both of this parish, *v.* ox-gang).

2. SOUTH ELMSALL (103–4811)

Ermeshale 1086 DB, *Emsala* 1137–9 YCh 1492, *Elmeshale* 1170–80 ib 1782, 1243 Fees, and other forms and meaning as for North Elmsall 36 *supra*, *Suthelmeshal(e)* 1230, 1268 Ebor, *Southelmesale* 1253 ib, 1327 FF, 1328 Banco *et freq* to 1366 FF, *Suthelmessale* 1254 Nost 74, *South Elmishall* 1285 KI, *Southelmesall* 1378 YD viii, 1522 Test v.

BALK LANE. THE BECK, *Beck* 1852 *TA*, *v.* bekkr. BRADLE CARR LANE, *Bradley Car Lane* 1841 O.S., *v.* brād, lēah, kjarr. BROAD LANE FM, *Broad Lane House* 1771, 1817 M, named from Broad Lane 42 *infra*. BULLSYKE WELL. COAL PIT FIELD, *Coleputtes* l. 12 Nost 29, *v.* col[1], pytt. COMMON END, *Common Side* 1817 M, *v.* Elmsall Common *infra*. CRAB TREE LATHE, 1841 O.S., cf. *Crabtree Barn & Shutt* 1852 *TA*, *v.* crabbe, trēow (or as a surname), hlaða. ELMSALL COMMON, 1841 O.S., cf. *super Communam* 1461 *MinAcct* 509, ME *commun* 'common land'. FIELD LANE, cf. *Field House* 1841 O.S., *v.* feld, hūs. GOOSEHOLE LANE, *Goose Holes* 1852 *TA*, *v.* gōs, hol[1]. GRIMSING PLANT. HACKING HILL. HOLLINS

LANE, cf. *Little Hollins, Hollings Lane* 1852 *TA*, *v.* Top Hollins 43 *infra*.   MORK ROYD LANE, *Munthroyde* (sic) 1771 M, cf. *Murrok-thyng* (*messuag'*) 1414 YD viii, 1418 ib vi, *v.* rod[1] 'clearing', þing 'property'; the first el. is a surname *Murrok*.   RISE HILL, *Rise Hill Close* 1684 *Glebe*, *v.* hrīs 'brushwood', hyll.   SPRING LANE, 1852 *TA*, *v.* spring.   TROUGH LANE, cf. *Trough Close* 1852 *TA*, *v.* trōg 'a trough'.   WATERFIELD, 1852 *TA*, *Waterfall* (a field) 13 Brett, *v.* wæter, (ge)fall 'clearing'; there is no stream here to account for a derivation from wæter-gefall 'waterfall'.   WEST FIELD, 1813 *EnclA* 22, *v.* west, feld.

FIELD-NAMES

The principal forms in (*a*) are 1852 *TA* 146. It is difficult to decide whether medieval f.ns. should be in North Elmsall (38 *supra*) or South Elmsall.

(*a*) Barrow Croft, Burned Close, Busky Close, Butt Close, Cloven Balk Close, Deeps, Dodge Hill Gap, Far Crofts, Flacking, Gate Saddles (ME *gate-shadel* 'a cross roads'), Gleadle Ing, Green Field, Hall Hill, Hards, Far & Near Ing, Laithe Close (*v.* hlaða), Langleys (*v.* lang, lēah), Long Croft, Mill Close (cf. *Mill Field* 1813 *EnclA*), Moor Croft, Moorhouse, Nether Croft 1718 *WYEnr* 156, North Croft (*Northcroft(e)* 1323, 1368 *MinAcct* 45, 26, 1341 *Surv*, 1718 *WYEnr*, *v.* norð, croft), Ox Pasture, The Penny Closes, Rail Close, Quarry Field (ib 1813 *EnclA*, *v.* quarrelle, feld), Street Close, Turn Ing (*v.* trun, eng), Wareham Croft, Windmillfield (ib 1813 *EnclA*).

(*b*) *Camelhul* 1230 Ebor (cf. Camblesforth pt. iv *infra*, *v.* hyll), *the Pasture-feild* 1684 *Glebe* (*v.* pasture, feld), *Skytrykhill* 1480, 1486 *MinAcct* 511, 66 (*v.* scitere 'sewer', ric, hyll and cf. *Skitterick* ii, 168 *infra*), *Smythous* 1461, 1486 *MinAcct* (cf. *Willelm' Smyth edificabit super communam vnam Smythous* ib, *v.* smiðð, hūs 'a smithy').

3. SOUTH KIRKBY (103–4510)

Cherche-, Chirchebi 1086 DB
Sudkirkebi 1119–29 *Nost* 14, 1188–1205 YCh viii
Suthkerchebi 1121 YCh 1428
Sukirbia 1127 *Nost* 7d, *Sukirkebi* 1177–93 YCh 1516, *-kyrkebi* 1251 FF, *Sukirkbi* 1257 *Nost* 20d
Suthkirkebi, -kyrke-, -by c. 1130–40 YCh 1467, 1153–5 ib 1497, e. 13 *RegAlb* ii, 19, 1226 FF, 1230 Ebor, 1246 *Ass* 4, 1249 *RegAlb* ii, 6d, 1253 Ebor *et passim* to 1314 Pat, *Sud-* 1295 YI, *South-* 1309 *Nost* 23d, 1322 YD xii, 292 *et freq* to 1437 *Surv*, *Sowthe-* 1586 WillY

Sutkirkeby 1229 FF
Suthkerkeby 1230 FF
Suthkyrkby, -kirk- 1237 *Nost* 136, 1316 Vill, *South(e)-* 1407 YD
viii, 1467 Brett, 1590 WillY, *Sowth(e)-* 1525 FF
Kirby 1292 *Nost* 63d, *South-* 1407 YD viii, *Sowth Kyrbie* 1564
Visit
Ki-, Kyrkeby 1296 LacyComp, 1350 BM, 1368 *MinAcct* 26, (-*by*
Elmesall) 1439 Pat

'Farmstead or village with a church', *v.* **kirkju-bý**. There was a
church here at the time of the DB survey. 'South' in relation to the
lost *Kirkby* in Pontefract (79 *infra*), six miles to the north. The
village was obviously called 'south' before the name of *Kirkby* in
Pontefract fell into disuse in the twelfth century.

DUNSLEY, *Dunnesleye in territorio de Suthkirby* l. 13 *Nost* 21d,
Dunesley 1341 *Surv*, 'Dunn's clearing', from the OE pers.n. *Dun(n)*
and **lēah**.

HAGUE HALL, *le Heye* l. 12 *Nost* 28d, *Haye* 1240 FF, *Esthaghe* 1424
Rent, *Westhaydike* 1516 *Surv*, *Eastheage* 1649 WillS, *Hague Hall*
1822 Langd. *v.* (ge)**hæg** 'an enclosure', replaced by **haga** (as in other
p.ns. like Haigh Hall 177 *infra*).

LANGTHWAITE GRANGE, *Langthwayt(e)* 1341 *Surv*, 1368, 1486 *Min-*
Acct, *Langfitt* 1684 *Glebe*. 'Long clearing', *v.* **lang, þveit**. On the
spelling -*fitt* cf. Phonol. § 49.

MOORTHORPE, *Torp* 1086 DB, *Morthorp(pe)* 1246 *Ass* 34, 1316 Linds,
1322 YD xii, 292, *Morethorpe* 1540, 1561, 1605 FF. 'Outlying farm
on the moor', *v.* **mōr, þorp**. As often, this p.n. was originally a
simplex *thorp*, with *mōr* added after the Conquest.

SHERBARROW (lost)
Syrebaru(e) l. 12, c. 1260 *Nost* 21, 29
Cherebarue l. 12 *Nost* 28d, *Cherbarwe* 1390 Works
Schirebarue 13 *Nost* 25d, -*bar'* c. 1260 ib 21, *Schyrebarwe* Ed 1 ib
11d, *Shireberewe* 1280 Ch, *Schirbarwe* 1292 *Nost* 63
Chirebarue, -we 13 *Nost* 25d, 1276 RH
Scherbarwe 1309 *Nost* 23d
Skirbarow 1310 Ebor
Shearborowe 1625 Crewe 402

'The bright grove', v. scīr² (with *Skir-* from the cognate ON skírr), bearu. Spellings with initial *Ch-* for *Sh-* are paralleled by Chevet i, 278 *supra* and Chevin (Otley) pt. iv *infra*.

BALL PARK WOOD, 1841 O.S. BRIERLEY GAP, 1841 O.S., v. Brierley i, 268 *supra*, gap; this is the eastern approach to Brierley township. BRIGG FLATT. BROAD LANE, v. brād, lane, cf. Broad Lane Fm 39 *supra*. BULL LANE. BURNT WOOD LANE. CARR LANE, cf. *Litel-, Mikelkar* 1437 *Surv, Kirby Carr Close* 1842 *TA*, v. kjarr 'marsh'. COBB CARR, *Cobker* 1516 *Surv*, e.ModE *cob* in one of its various senses, 'a great man', 'a male swan', 'a horse' or the like, and kjarr 'marsh'. COBLER OR ST ANDREW'S HILL. GALLON CROFT FIELD, 1813 *EnclA* 22, v. croft; *Gallon* is probably from the ME surname *Galon* (OFr *Galon*). HOB HO. HOMSLEY LANE. KIRKBRIDGE, 1813 *EnclA*, v. kirkja, brycg. LIDGATE, 1841 O.S., *atte Lytheyate* 1379 PT, v. hlið-geat 'swing-gate'. LIMPHILL. MELLWOOD LANE, *Mellwood Field* 1813 *EnclA*. NANNY WOOD, 1841 O.S. NORTH FIELD, 1813 *EnclA*, v. norð, feld. NOR WOOD, 1841 O.S., v. norð, wudu. THE RIDDINGS, cf. *le Northryddyng* 1378 YD viii, v. norð, rydding 'clearing'. SAXON CAMP (site), *Camp* 1841 O.S., an old rectangular earthwork. SOUTH KIRKBY COMMON, cf. *Common Side* 1841 O.S. STOCKING GATE, cf. *Adam de Stockyng* 1378 YD viii, *Stocking Street* 1841 O.S., v. stoccing 'clearing', gata, strǣt. WATER LANE. WHITE APRON ST.

FIELD-NAMES

The forms in (*a*) are 1813 *EnclA* 22. Spellings dated 1309 are *Nost* 23d, 1368, 1486 *MinAcct* 26, 66, 1437, 1516 *Surv*.

(*a*) Dean Holme Field (*v*. denu, holmr), Easter Field, Flatts 1750 YDr (*v*. flat), Winness Field.

(*b*) *Aysbriggemor* 1309 (*v*. brycg, mōr), *Atkin Crofte* 1615 *Crewe* 395 (the surname *Atkin*, croft), *Bolsters* (a close) 1684 *Glebe*, *Brodynge* 1486 (*v*. brād, eng 'meadow'), *Hayward land* 1571 Hnt (the surname *Hayward*, land), *Moloncarre* 1424 Rent, *Motonkarre* 1426 Ramsd (cf. Mutton Flatt 38 *supra*, ME *moltoun, moulton* 'sheep', *v*. kjarr 'marsh'), *Morehede* 1486 (*v*. mōr, hēafod), *Morthorpker* 1368 (*v*. Moorthorpe *supra*, kjarr), *Nedirgrene* 1486 (*v*. neoðera, grēne²), *leʒ Prestynges* 1437 (*v*. prēost, eng), *le Rod* 1413 YD vi (*v*. rod¹ 'clearing'), *Roley* 1296 LacyComp ('rough clearing', *v*. rūh, lēah), *le Schayebrigge* 1309 (*v*. sceaga 'copse', brycg), *le Wrooriddynges* 1437 (*v*. vrá 'nook', rydding 'clearing').

4. SKELBROOKE (103–5012)

Scalebre, -bro 1086 DB, *-broc* 1161 Pont, 1163 ff P (p), 1170 Pont, 1170–84 YCh 1549, c. 1219 YD i, 1221 Cur, *Schalebrok* 13 Brett

Scelebroch 1160–75 YCh 1548, *Schelebrok* 1230 Ebor

Skelebroc, -brok(e) 1220 Cur (p), 1253 Ebor, 1286 YI, *-brockes* 1296 LacyComp

Skelbrok(e), -brook(e) 1298 YI, 1311 Ch *et passim* to 1598 FF, *-broughe* 1573 WillY, *-browke* 1588 FF

Skeldebrok 1315 Pat

'Stream near the shieling', *v.* Skellow 34 *supra*, brōc.

HILL FM, cf. *Hillside Close* 1848 *TA, v.* hyll.   LOW HOLLINS, 1848 *TA*, TOP HOLLINS, SKELBROOKE HOLLINS, *Hulin* 13 Brett, cf. *Hollineflat* 1684 *Glebe, v.* holegn 'holly'.   LOW MOOR, 1848 *TA*. MUCKEY LANE, *Mackhill Lane* 1841 O.S., *Muck Lane Close* 1848 *TA, v.* muk, hyll, lane.   SKELBROOKE HALL, *Hall* 1841 O.S.   SKELBROOKE REIN, 1841 O.S., *v.* reinn 'boundary strip'.   TONGUE END, *The Tongue* 1848 *TA, v.* tunge 'tongue of land'.

FIELD-NAMES

The principal forms in (*a*) are 1848 *TA* 357.

(*a*) Little & Long Aukland, Bannister Platt (*v.* plat² 'a plot of ground'), Barnsdale Close & Tongue (cf. Barnsdale 37 *supra*, clos, tunge), Bridle Close, Brier Carr (*v.* brēr, kjarr), Carr Close, Crabtree Close, Cross Lands, Dale Flat, Doncaster Close & Field (near the Great North Road to Doncaster), Goss Hill, Grunt Hill, Hanger Hill, Horn Close, Horse Close, Ing Close, Lawn Bridge Close (*v.* launde), Ling Leys (cf. *Lynges of Skelbrok, le Lynges* 1422 Brett, *v.* lyng 'heather'), Little Intake (*v.* intak), Little Moor, Long Field Close, Miln Flatt (*v.* myln, flat), Oak Tree Close, Ox Close, Roe Close, Sainfoin Close (ModE *sainfoin*, a forage herb), Skelbrooke Park, Stubbs Close, Walnut Garth, Water-fall (cf. Waterfield 40 *supra*), White Gate, Wilderness, Willow Garth, Wood Nooking.

(*b*) Fellers (*claus*') 1541 MinAcct 23.

5. HAMPHALL STUBBS or STUBBS HALL (103–4911)

Hanepol 1086 DB

Stubbes 1230 Ebor, 1254 *Nost* 74, (*-Lacy*) 1285 KI, (*-juxta Hampoll*) 1428 FA, *Stubbys* 1540 MonRent

Stobbes 1253 Ebor, *Stobes* 1379 PT, (*Hampall-*) 1556 FF

Hampall Stubs 1612 FF, 1698 PRHick, *Hampull Stubbs* 1641 Rates

'The tree-stumps', *v.* stubb. In the DB survey Ilbert de Lacy's part of Hampole (i, 70 *supra*) apparently included Stubbs, which was simply called *Hanepol* to distinguish it from Stubbs Walden (53 *infra*), which he also held. In 1285 (KI 7) it was held by Robert de Pontefract of Henry de Lacy, Earl of Lincoln. A local stream was called *Stubbisike* 12 *Nost* 29 (*v.* sīc).

CRAG CLOSE, *Craggs Close* 1838 *TA*.   HAZEL CLOSE.   HOLLINS LANE, 1841 O.S., *v.* holegn 'holly'.   LITTLE JOHNS WELL, *Little Johns Cave & Well* 1838 *TA*, *L*ᵗ. *Johns Well* 1841 O.S., named from Little John of the Robin Hood Ballads (cf. Robin Hood's Well 36). PIG GARTH, 1838 *TA*, *v.* pigga, garðr.   STUBBS HALL, 1822 Langd, *v.* Hamphall Stubbs *supra*.   TOP INGS, cf. *Upper & Nether towne ynge* 1540 MonRent, *v.* eng 'meadow'.   WELL CLOSE, 1838 *TA*, *v.* wella, clos.

FIELD-NAMES

The principal forms in (*a*) are 1838 *TA* 190, those in (*b*) are 1540 MonRent.

(*a*) Bridge Close & Ings (*Brigge ynges* 1540 MonRent, *v.* brycg, clos, eng), Crossland Close, Garth (*v.* garðr), Hampole Field, Great Hollings (*v.* holegn 'holly'), Kay Close, Laith Close (*v.* hlaða), Low Ings, Sheep Walks, Skelbrooke High Field, Smiths Ings ('occupied by *George Smith*', *v.* eng), Spring Close, Willow Garth.

(*b*) *Cowe close* (*v.* cū, clos), *farder felde* ('further field'), *fenye yarde* (*v.* fennig, geard), *Graunge ynge* (*v.* grange, eng), *Ympyarde* (*v.* impa 'sapling', geard), *Maltehouse crofte*, *Myddelfeld*, *Myre carre grounde* (*v.* mýrr, kjarr), *Upper myre ynge* (*v.* mýrr, eng), *New close*, *le Orchard*, *Oxe pasture*, *Shepe leys* (*v.* scēap, lēah), *Spittell ynge* (*v.* spitel, eng), *Upper Crofte* (*v.* croft), *Wadcrofte ynge als. Wheat croft ynges* (*v.* hwǣte, croft, eng), *Westfelde*.

viii. Campsall

Campsall and Sutton townships are now included in Norton; Sutton was formerly partly in Burghwallis parish.

1. ASKERN (103–5613)

Askern(e) c. 1170 Pont (p), 1192–1210 P, 1201 OblR, 1218 FF, Kirkst, 1268 FF, 1286 Abbr *et passim* to 1428 FA, *Haskerne* 1196 P, *Askarn(e)* 1488 Ipm, 1538, 1598 FF. 'House near the ash-tree', *v.* askr (perhaps replacing OE æsc), ærn.

ASKERN COMMON, 1841 O.S.   ASKERN FIELD & HILL.   ASKERN
LAKE.   ASKERN MATHER, MATHER DIKE & PITS, perhaps e.ModE
mathers 'stinking camomile' or maðra 'madder'.   CHAPEL HILL.
HIGHFIELD HO.   MILL HO.   NORTHFIELD HO.   SPA WELL.
THISTLE GOIT.

FIELD-NAMES

The forms in (*a*) are 1818 *EnclA* 136 and those dated 1841 are O.S.

(*a*) Church Field, Graycliffe 1841, High Balk Field, Long Acre 1841,
Middle Field, Moor House 1841.

(*b*) *Ashcarr* 1623 FF (*v.* æsc, kjarr), *Riss(h)ingthorpe* 1317 Ch, DodsN
v. þorp, the first el. may be a derivative of risc 'rush'), *Scales, Askernescales*
1534, 1550 FF (*v.* skáli 'a shieling').

2. CAMPSALL (103–5413)

Cansale 1086 DB, 1196 Abbr, 1207 Cur
Camasella 1137–9 (16) YCh 1492   *Camscila* 1173 ib 197
Camshale 1142–86 *RegAlb* i, 71
Camsala, Camsal(e) 1150–75 YCh 1551, 1155–70 ib 1502, 1156 ib
    186, 1208, 1218 FF, 1218 Kirkst, 1230, 1287 Ebor *et passim* to
    1368 *MinAcct* 26, *Camsall* 14 *Sawl* 193d, 1441 DiocV, 1535 FF
Campshale 1158–67 YCh vi
Kamishalla c. 1225 Pont (p), *K-, Cameshal* 1227 Ebor, 1230 P,
    1244 Pat, 1252 FF, -*hale* 1323 Cl
Camesale 1264 YI, 1291 Tax, 1296 LacyComp, 1299 YI, 1335 FF,
    Camesall 1316 Vill
Campsale 1294 Ch, 1335 *RegAlb* iv, 91d, 1336 FF *et freq* to 1428
    FA, *Campsall* 1402 FA, 1409 DiocV *et passim* to 1534 FF
Kempsall 1547 FF

The great majority of spellings points to an OE *Cames-hale*. The
second el. is OE halh 'nook of land', which doubtless refers to the
ground below Campsall village where the small valley of Stream Dike
widens between the hills; there are two small streams flowing through
this opening. The first element is difficult to interpret; but it would
appear to be either a PrWelsh p.n. *Cambeis* or an OE pers.n.
Cam, both of which are derived from Brit cambo- 'crooked'. For
Kempston Bd 75–6 Ekwall has proposed PrWelsh *cambeis* with OE
tūn added and he thinks (DEPN) that this PrWelsh p.n. is also found
in Campsall (with OE *halh* added); from its use in Welsh p.ns. it

would appear to mean 'bend of a river' or 'a bay'. From a topographical point of view it can hardly denote 'bend of a river' in Campsall, though if the sense 'bay' could be extended to include an inland topographical feature such as was later denoted by OE *halh*, it would be formally possible in Campsall. But there is uncertainty in this extension of meaning and Campsall is perhaps better interpreted as 'Cam's nook of land'; such an OE pers.n., recorded only in Exon DB as *Cammi* and in the patronymic *Cameson* (Feilitzen 213), is doubtless of Celtic origin; Förster, *Keltisches Wortgut* 213, notes the MWelsh byname *Cam* (from Brit **cambo-**, OWelsh *cam* 'crooked'). Whether the p.n. contains the Brit p.n. *Cambeis* or a pers.n. from *Cambo-*, the early spellings of Campsall show that here Brit *mb* was assimilated to *mm*, later *-m-* (cf. Jackson 509–11).

BAR PLANT., 1841 O.S.   BARNSDALE BAR & WOOD, cf. *Barnsdale Lodge* 1822 Langd; *v.* Barnsdale 37 *supra*; the wood was formerly *Oak Wood* 1841 O.S.; the 'bar' is on the Great North Road (*v.* **barre**).   BEEVERS HOLT.   BONE LANE, cf. *Balneyng* 1341 *Surv*, *Balne(h)eng* 1345 *MinAcct* 45, *Balnyng* 1368, 1486 ib 26, 66, *v.* Balne 14 *supra*, **eng, lane**.   CAMPSALL COMMON & HALL, 1841 O.S. CAMPSMOUNT, 1771 M, cf. *Mountgarth* 1608 *MinAcct* 12, *v.* **mont** 'a hill'; the first el. appears to be a back-formation from Campsall. CHURCH FIELD.   LITTLE MOOR COMMON, *Litelmor(e)* 1368, 1486 *MinAcct* 26, 66, *v.* **lytel, mōr**.   LONGLAND FIELD.   OLD WHIN FOX COVERT, formerly *Barnsdale Whin* 1841 O.S., *v.* Barnsdale 37 *supra*, **hvin** 'gorse'.   PARKNOOK QUARRY.   STONY HILLS.   TRAINLANDS. WHINBED.   WOOD FIELD, 1817 M, *v.* **wudu, feld**.

FIELD-NAMES

Spellings dated 1341 are *Surv* 10, 5, others dated 1345–1608 without source are *MinAcct* 12, 26, 45, 66, 509, 511.

(b) *Braderode* 1341 (*v.* **brād, rod**[1] 'clearing'), *Brek* 1341 (probably dial. *breck* 'uncultivated strip', *v.* **bræc** 'brake'), *Brondehes* 1486 (possibly 'clearings made by burning', *v.* **brand, (ge)hæg**), *Bulmerings* 1608 (probably a surname *Bulmer*, **eng** 'meadow'), *Dalegate* 1341 (*v.* **dæl, gata**), *Drykerrode* 1341 ('dry marsh clearing', *v.* **drȳge, kjarr, rod**[1]), *Euereseldford* 1341 (if the first theme is not a pers.n. *Ever(h)ild* (cf. Everhill Shaw iii, 191 *infra*), it is a local name meaning 'wild-boar's slope', *v.* **eofor, helde, ford**), *Foxhols* 1341 (*v.* **fox-hol**), *Gaucrofte* 1341 (*v.* **gaukr** 'cuckoo' or the ON pers.n. *Gaukr*, **croft**), *Goldyngoxgang* 1461 (the surname *Golding* (cf. Feilitzen 273), ox-gang), *Gonnylde Croft* 1341 (the ON fem. pers.n. *Gunnhildr*, croft), *Harstonlay* (*v.* lēah, the first theme is probably 'boundary stone', *v.* hār², stān), *Hemeryoxgange* 1461 (the surname *Emery*, ox-gang), *Hergyn-*, *Harging-*, *Harkincrofte* 1341, *Hargincroft* 1368, *Herkyngcroft* 1480, *Harkyng crofts* 1608 (the first el. is probably an ON pers.n. *Herkingr*, a supposed derivative of the by-name *Herkia* from *herki* 'a lazy person', which may be the source of the DB pers.n. *Herch* (Feilitzen 289), *v.* croft), *Ladygarth* 1608 (*v.* garðr), *le Mylneflatte* 1341 (*v.* myln, flat), *Neuhuse, Neuuose* 1086 DB (*v.* nīwe, hūs), *Northeforth* 1341 (*v.* norð, ford), *Portyngbusk* 1341 (*v.* buskr), *Quarrelflat* 1341 (*v.* quarrelle 'quarry', flat), *Saltflat* 1486 (*v.* salt, flat), *Scateflattes* 1608 (probably from s(c)late 'slate', flat), *Shakalalenge* (sic) 1341 (*v.* sceacol 'shackle' in one of its senses, eng), *Smythrode* 1341 (*v.* smið, rod¹), *Stokyng(ges)* 1341 (*v.* stoccing 'clearing'), *Thomascroftes* 1341 (the pers.n. *Thomas*, croft), *Westyerd(e)* 1461, 1486 (*v.* west, geard).

3. FENWICK (103–5916)

Fenwic 1166 P (p), 1185 Templar, 1206, 1208, 1226 FF, -*wyc* J
   (1249) Ch, -*wyk(e)* 13 YD i, 1252 Ch, 1374 FF *et freq* to 1496 FF
Fennewick 13 YD i, *Fenewyke* 1299 YI
Fennicke 1622 PRSn

'Dairy farm in the fen' *v.* fenn, wīc.

BOX WOOD. CLOUGH BRIDGE & LANE, *Clough Lane* 1841 O.S., *v.* clōh 'a dell'. ELL WOOD. FENWICK COMMON, 1841 O.S. FENWICK HALL, 1618 PRSn, 1817 M, *v.* hall. FENWICK LONDON HILL, *Land Hearn* 1539 Hnt i, 150, -*herne* 1559 ib 151, *London Hill* 1841 O.S., 'corner of land', *v.* land, hyrne; cf. London Hill i, 16, Moss London Hill 49 *infra*. FLEET DRAIN, cf. *Fletdyke* 1559 Hnt, *v.* flēot, dīc. HAGGS FM, *Hagg House & Wood* 1841 O.S., *v.* hǫgg 'clearing'. LADY THORPE, *Ladythorp(e)* 1503 Ipm, 1580, 1606 FF, *v.* hlǣfdige, þorp. LAWN, *Great & Little Lawn* 1846 *TA*, *v.* launde 'a forest glade'. MOAT HILL, *v.* mote. NEAR WOOD, 1841 O.S. SHAW WOOD, *v.* sceaga 'copse'. WENT LOWS, cf. *Fenwick Lows* 1841 O.S., dial. *low* 'low-lying ground by a river' (the R. Went).

FIELD-NAMES

The principal forms in (*a*) are 1846 *TA* 155. Spellings dated 1488 are Ipm, 1539, 1559 Hnt i, 150–1.

(*a*) Doughty Close, Fenwick Close, High Springs, Kirby Close (cf. *Kyrkeby feldes* 1488), Middle Close, Pickhill (*v.* pightel 'enclosure'), Suet Pit.

(b) *Bladworth-field-dyke* 1539, 1559, *Felyhalfeld* 1488 Ipm (*Felyhal-* may be an error for *foly-hall*, v. folie, hall, feld), *Lynt-dyke* 1539 (probably ME *lynt* 'flax', later also 'a fishing net', dīc), *Oldcote croft* 1488 (v. ald, cot, croft), *Park-dyke* 1539, 1559 (v. park, dīc), *Pocok Croft* 1488 (the surname *Pocock* 'Peacock', croft), *Saint or Seate syke*, *Saint-pit*, *the Saint or Seate layne* 1539 (probably sænget 'a clearing made by burning', v. sīc, lane or leyne 'piece of arable land', pytt), *Tarne-bracke or Torne-hagge* 1539, *Thorne Haige* 1559 (v. þorn, bræc[1] 'a brake, thicket', hǫgg 'clearing' or haga 'enclosure').

4. Moss (103–5914)

del Mose 1416 Brett (p), *Moss(e)* 1446 Pat, 1496 FF, 1546 YChant, (*-in Balne*) 1586 FF, (*-alias Moseley*) 1605 FF, 1771 M, *The Moss* 1636 WillY, *yᵉ Moss* 1683 PRDr; v. mos 'swamp, bog', here, as in Moseley *infra*, referring to the great tract of marsh land between the Aire and the Don. v. Balne 1, 14 *supra* for the affix.

FLASHLEY CARR, *Flaxcleyker* 1241 AD v, *Flaxley Carr-end* 1539, 1559 Hnt. 'Clearing in the swamp', v. flask (with *Flax-* as a metathesised variant, later replaced by flasshe), lēah, and kjarr 'marsh'.

HAWKEHOUSE GREEN, *Hawk(e)house-grene*, *-Green* 1541 WillY, 1771 M, *Haukhurst grene* 1588 WillY; v. hafoc 'hawk', hyrst 'wood', grēne[2]. As with the nearby Kirkhouse Green 30 *supra*, hyrst is replaced by hūs.

MOSELEY GRANGE, *Moselay*, *-ley* 1276 RH (p), 1344, 1376 FF, 1402 FA, 1605 FF, (*-in Bawne*) 1607 FF, *Moslay(e)* 1345 Ass 14, 1428 FA, *Mosselay*, *-ley* 1482 Test iii, 1488 Ipm *et freq* to 1586 FF, (*-in the Mosse*) 1573 FF. 'Clearing in the swamp', v. mos, lēah and Moss *supra*. For the affix *in Bawne*, v. Balne 1, 14 *supra*.

ALDER WOOD. ASH CARR DRAIN, *Ash Car(r)* 1841 O.S., 1843 *TA*, v. æsc, kjarr 'marsh'. BARCROFT GATES, *Bear Croft* 1843 *TA*, v. bere 'barley', croft. CARRS, cf. *Carr Close* 1846 *TA*, v. kjarr 'marsh'. CAUSEWAY BANK, v. caucie. CLAY BANK. COPLEY SPRING WOOD. CROOKED HOLE BRIDGE. DORMER GREEN, 1841 O.S., *Dormoor Green* 1843 *TA*, v. dor 'gate', mōr, grēne[2]. ELM FIELD FM. GILL LANE, 1841 O.S., probably the surname *Gill*. HEYWORTH LANE, 1841 O.S. JETT HALL. MANOR FM. MILL DIKE (1), 1841 O.S., *Milne-dyke* 1539, 1559 Hnt, v. myln, dīc. MILL DIKE (2), *Mill Goight* 1841 O.S., v. myln, gota. MOSS CARR, v.

Carrs *supra*. Moss Common, 1841 O.S. Moss London Hill, *London Hill* 1841 O.S., cf. Fenwick London Hill 47 *infra*. Noble Thorpe Lane, cf. Thorpe Grange *infra*. Old Green Lane, *Green Lane* 1841 O.S., *v.* grēne[1], lane. Old Lane, 1841 O.S. Paitfield Lane. Pinfold Lane, cf. *Pinfold Close* 1846 *TA*, *v.* pyndfald. Thorpe Grange, 1817 M, *v.* þorp, grange; the þorp would seem to have been known as Noble Thorpe (*supra*). The Willows, Willow Bridge, cf. *Willow Tree Close* 1846 *TA*, *v.* wilig. Wrancarr, *Wrang Car* 1841 O.S., *v.* wrang 'crooked', kjarr 'marsh'.

FIELD-NAMES

The principal forms in (*a*) are 1846 *TA* 292.

(*a*) Allam Field, Boucher Close, Bramwith Acre, Burn Close, Carter Close, Crow Croft, Dagger Field, East End 1841 O.S., Frier Closes, Hatchet Head, Hill Close, Kettle, Kettle Bottom (*v.* ketill), Knowles Spring, Lady Croft, Laithe Close (*v.* hlaða), Mill (Hill) Close, Old Wife's Smock, Ox Close, Parish Close, Parker Close, Pighill (*v.* pightel), Pigman Croft, Pinder Close, Randleshaw, Redfield, Rein Close (*v.* reinn 'boundary'), Smeaton Garth, Tang Close, Vicars Close, Yate Close, Yonders Croft.

(*b*) *Edmondtoft* 1488 Ipm (the OE pers.n. *Ēadmund*, topt), *Grav(e)ingclose-side*, *Grange-close-syde* 1539, 1559 Hnt, *Hankirfeld* 1482 Test iii, *Newyng* 1488 Ipm (*v.* nīwe, eng), *Richardfeld* 1488 Ipm, *Scruthill*, *-dyke*, *Scrutt-lane*, *Scruitt-pit* 1559 Hnt (possibly a metathesised form of ON skurðr 'a cut, canal'), *Starr-hill* 1539 Hnt (*v.* storr 'sedge', hyll).

5. Norton (103–5415)

Norton(e), *-tun(a)* 1086 DB, 1119–35 *Nost* 7d, 1121–7 YCh 1428, 1159, c. 1160 Pont, 1160–70 Templar, c. 1170 Pont, 13 *Nost* 62d, 1215 ChR *et passim* to 1596 FF. 'North farmstead', *v.* norð, tūn, from its position in the north of the parish; cf. Sutton 50 *infra*.

Black Clump, 1841 O.S. Bradley's Well, *Bradley Well* 1841 O.S. Cliff Hill, 1841 O.S., *the Cliff* 1729 YDr, *v.* clif, hyll. Common End, cf. Norton Common *infra*. Dryhurst Closes, *v.* drȳge, hyrst. Ings Dike, *v.* eng, dīc. Low Field, 1818 *EnclA* 136. Norton Common, 1841 O.S., ME *commun* 'common land'. Norton Priory, 1817 M, *Norton Priorie* 1610 FF. Norton Windmill, 1841 O.S. Old Acre Rd. Park Closes. Rye Croft Field. Sheep Cote Quarry, *Sheep-coats*, *Sheep-coat layth* 1729 YDr, *Sheep-cote Field* 1818 *EnclA*, *v.* scēap, cot. South Field, 1818 *EnclA*, *the South Field of Norton* 1734 YDr, *v.* sūð, feld.

SPITTLERUSH LANE, *Spittle-rush-lane-end* 1731 YDr, *spittle-rush* may be an old plant-name from *spittle* 'saliva' and risc. STYGATE LANE, *v.* stīg 'path', gata. WEST FIELD, 1818 *EnclA, the Westffield* 1709 *WYEnr* 34, *Norton West Field* 1739 YDr, *v.* west, feld. WHITELEY PLANT., *v.* hwīt, lēah. WILLOW BRIDGE, 1817 M, *v.* wilig, brycg. WILLOW GARTH, *v.* prec., garðr.

FIELD-NAMES

The forms in (*a*) are YDr, those in (*b*) 1535 VE.

(*a*) the East Field of Norton 1731 (*v.* ēast, feld, cf. South & West Field *supra*), Newhill Close 1739, Orms Ing 1752 (probably the ON pers.n. *Ormr*, eng), the Smithy lane 1741 (*v.* smiððe, lane), Stepping-Stone Ing 1752 (*v.* eng), the Upper field 1731 (cf. Low Field *supra*), the Wainhouse garth 1735 (*v.* wægn 'wagon', hūs, *or* the surname *Wainhouse*, garðr).

(*b*) *claus' voc' Bustard* (probably ME *bustard* as a surname, cf. *Bustard-thorpe* (Dringhouses) pt. iv *infra*), *Housegarth* (*v.* hūs, garðr), *Prioryerde* (*v.* prior, geard, cf. Norton Priory *supra*).

6. SUTTON (103–5512)

Sutone 1086 DB, *Sutton(a)* 1170–80 YCh 1554–5, 1336 FF, 1402 FA *et passim* to 1658 WillS, (*-neer Owston*) 1666 Test. 'South farmstead', *v.* sūð, tūn, from its position in the south of the parish in contrast to Norton 49 *supra*.

CAMP, ancient earthworks. LADY GAP, 1839 *TA, v.* gap. SUTTON COMMON, 1841 O.S. SUTTON FIELDS, *Sutton Field* 1817 M, *v.* feld. TOWN'S WELL. WETFLAT PLANT., *v.* wēt, flat.

FIELD-NAMES

The principal forms in (*a*) are 1839 *TA* 387.

(*a*) Barley Close, Little Benby, Bottoms, Burbutts, Common Pound, Folly Lane, Hard Bottoms, Huntsman's Close, The Ings (*Sutton enges* 1341 *Surv, v.* eng), Kettleflat Close (*v.* ketill, flat), Long Close, Mill Field, Parson Close, Pease Close (*v.* pise, clos), Potter Close, Rape Close.

(*b*) *Prestedales* 1175–83 YCh 1555, cf. *partes sacerdotis* ib 1554 (*v.* prēost, dāl 'share'), *Sutton toft(e)* 1341 *Surv* (*v.* topt), *Wynstombe lands* (sic) 1424 Rent, *Wynescomlandes* 1426 *Ramsd* (*v.* land, the first el. is probably a surname).

ix. Kirk Smeaton

KIRK SMEATON (103–5116)

> *Smedetone* 1086 DB
> *Smyde-*, *Smidetona* 1147–55 YCh 1494 (p), 1170–80 YCh 1589,
> *Smidhetone* 1242 YD ii
> *Smithetun*, *Smi-*, *Smytheton(e)* 12 YD i (p), 1170–80 YCh 1782,
> l. 12 Kirkst, c. 1200, c. 1220 Pont, 1239 Ebor *et freq* to 1303
> Ebor, (*Kyrke-*) 1311 NCWills, 1313 Dunelm, 1328 Banco,
> (*Magna-*) 1316 Vill
> *Smetheton* 1276 RH, 1286 YI, 1293 Kirkst, 1374 FF, 1382 BM,
> 1480 MinAcct 511, *Kirksmethton* 1379 PT
> *Smeton* 1409 DiocV, 1413 YI, 1428 FA *et freq* to 1496 FF,
> (*Kyrk(e)-*, *Kirk-*) 14 Sawl 193, 1506 WillY, 1535 VE
> *Kyrk-*, *Kirkesmeaton* 1564, 1587, 1605 FF

'The smiths' farmstead', *v.* smið, tūn, cf. Smeaton YN 211, 281, and Little Smeaton 53 *infra*, from which it is distinguished by the affix (*v.* kirkja); the church, which is first mentioned in DB, is referred to in many of the sources cited (1239 Ebor, etc.). In all these names the form *Smethe-* arises from ME lengthening and lowering of OE -*i*- in an open syllable (*v.* Phonol. § 23).

WENT BRIDGE, *pontem de Wente* 1190 YCh 1641, *ponte(m) de Wenet* 1190–1210 YCh 1642, 1194–1211 Kirkst, *Wentbrig(g)*, *-bryg* 1302 Ebor, 1335, 1375 FF *et freq* to 1638 SessnR, *-bridge* 1545 TestLds, 1597 SessnR, 1616 PRDr, *Wentebrigg(e)* 1307, 1316 WCR, 1327 Baild (p), 1368 MinAcct. 'Bridge across the Went', *v.* R. Went (RNs.), brycg; it carried the Roman road from Doncaster to Tadcaster. It is not always easy to distinguish early references for the various Went Bridges (in Snaith 28 *supra*, in Walden Stubbs 53, and in Purston Jaglin 88 *infra*), but this was the principal one.

BLACK MIRES, 1764 Glebe, *Blakmire* 1688 ib, 'black marsh', *v.* blæc, mýrr.   BROOMFIELD PLANT., cf. *the Broome* 1688 Glebe, *v.* brōm.
CASTLE HILL, 1841 O.S., an ancient earthwork off the Great North Road on the south bank of the R. Went, *v.* castel, hyll.   CRAB TREE LANE, 1841 O.S.   CUSWORTH HILL, cf. Cusworth i, 65 *supra*.
FORD.   LONG LANE, 1841 O.S.   MIDDLE FIELD, *the middle feild* 1688 Glebe, *v.* middel, feld.   MILL DAM.   MUTTON HALL, 1817 M,

cf. Mutton Flatt 38 *supra*.   PACKSADDLE PLANT., 1841 O.S.   PIN-
FOLD CROSS, *v.* pynd-fald, cros.   SHOOTERS HILL, 1841 O.S.
SMEATON CRAGS, 1841 O.S., *v.* cragge.   UPPER WELLS LAIR.
WENT EDGE, *Wenthedge* 1609 *Bright* 521, 1688 *Glebe*, *Went Edge
Field* 1812 *EnclA* 152, *v.* R. Went, ecg.   WINDHILL PLANT., *Winde
hill stye* 1609 *Bright* 521, 'exposed hill', *v.* wind, hyll, stīg 'path'.
WOODLE HOLE LANE, 1841 O.S., *v.* wudu, hol[1].

FIELD-NAMES

The principal forms in (*a*) are 1764 *Glebe*. Spellings dated l. 12 are Kirkst,
1609, 1661 *Bright* 521, 1688 *Glebe*, 1709 *WYEnr* 34, 1812 *EnclA* 152.

(*a*) Above Street Field 1812 (*v.* strǣt, here referring to the Great North
Road), Coalpit Gate (*v.* col[1], pytt, gata), Cob Croft (cf. Cob Carr 42), Dogbush
(*Dogbuske* 1609, *-hedge* 1688, *v.* dogga, buskr), Holme bush (*Hollin busk*
1688, *v.* holegn 'holly', buskr), Middle Field 1812, the Pighell 1709, the
Poggy Pighell 1709 (dial. *poggy* 'swampy', pightel), Ratingpitt (*v.* raton
'rat', pytt), Ropp (*Ropepit* l. 12, probably OE rāp 'rope', pytt, possibly one
where ropes were made), Willowbridge Ing 1709, Wood Field 1812 (*the
wood feild* 1609, *v.* wudu, feld).

(*b*) *Allerthorp* 1517 FF (*v.* þorp), *Bakestanes* l. 12 (*v.* bæc-stān 'baking
stone'), *Cerswist* 1139 YCh 1492 (*v.* cærs 'cress', possibly wisce 'marshy
meadow'), Clay Close 1688 (*v.* clǣg, clos), *Dykeside* 1661 (*v.* dīc, sīde),
Drakehov c. 1220 Pont ('dragon mound', *v.* draca, haugr), 'a place called
the fryeing pans' 1609 (ME *fryinge panne* 'frying pan', but the allusion is
obscure unless it referred to the shape of a piece of ground), *Gaite Shaddles*
1609 (ME *gate-shadel* 'cross roads'), *Godinerode* l. 12 (possibly for *Godiue-*,
the OE fem. pers.n. *Godgifu*, rod[1] 'clearing'), *Lairpiteflait* l. 12 ('clay pit',
v. leirr, pytt, flat), *Marecroftes* l. 12 (*v.* croft), *New hedge* 1609 (*v.* nīwe,
hecg), *the quarrel* 1688 (*v.* quarrelle 'quarry'), *Reedidale* 1688 (*v.* hrēodig,
dæl 'valley' or dāl 'share'), *the Sailes* 1688 (*v.* salh 'willow'), *farr Shortrakes*
1609 (*v.* hraca 'path'), *Somervileland* 1424 Rent, 1426 Ramsd, *Somervillesland*
1480 *MinAcct* 511 (the ME surname *Somerville*, land), *Wanegap* 1688
('wagon opening', *v.* wægn, gap).

x. Womersley

1. LITTLE SMEATON (103–5316)

Smedetone 1086 DB, *Smithe-*, *Smytheton*(*a*) 1339 FF, (*-Minori*)
12 Pont, (*parva-*) 13 YD ii, 1311 NCyWills, 1313 Dunelm *et freq*,
(*litle-*) 1315 DodsN, *Smetheton* 1339, 1369, 1374 FF, *Smeton* 1413
YI, (*Parva-*) 1402 FA, (*Lit(t)le-*) 1504 FF, 1572 YD xiii, 68, *Little*

Smeaton 1584, 1608 FF, *Smeaton parva* 1638 SessnR, with the same meaning as Kirk Smeaton 51 *supra*, from which it is distinguished by the affix (*v.* lȳtel).

Brockadale Houses, *Broken Dale* 1841 O.S., *v.* brocen 'broken', dæl 'valley'.   Church Field.   Long Crag, 1841 O.S., *v.* lang, cragge.   Smeatley's Lane.   Smeaton Leys, *The Leys* 1786 *EnclA* 34, *v.* lēah.   Smeaton Windmill, 1841 O.S.   Willow Bridge, 1841 O.S., *v.* wilig, brycg.

FIELD-NAMES

The forms in (*a*) are 1786 *EnclA* 34.

(*a*) Ings (*v.* eng 'meadow'), Low Field, Mill Field (*v.* myln), West Field.

2. Walden Stubbs (103–5516)

Eistop, Istop 1086 DB   *Stobis* 1264 YI
Stubbis, -ys 1175–83 YCh 1555, c. 1240 Pont, 1276 RH, (-*waldyng*) 1452 YD i, 1501 Ipm
Stubbes c. 1210 Pont, 1240–8 YCh viii (p), 1244 YI, 1251 Ass (p) *et passim* to 1504 FF, (-*Walding, -yng*) 1280 *Ass*, 1327 FF, 1413 YI, 1418 YD vi, 1605 FF, (-*woldyng*) 1429 YD vi, (-*Walden*) 1572 YD xiii, 68, (*Waldinge-*) 1607 FF
Stubbs 1281 DodsN, (-*Walden*) 1822 Langd, *Walden Stubes* 1587 WillY

'The tree-stumps', *v.* stubb. On the DB spellings with initial AN (*e*)*is-* for *s-*, cf. IPN 103. Cf. Hamphall Stubbs 43 *supra*, Cridling Stubbs 62 *infra*, from which it is distinguished by the name of a twelfth century local man *Walding* (OG *Waldin*, cf. Feilitzen 408, or an OE *Walding*, a patronymic formed from OE *Walda*); *Willelmus filius Walding* was witness to the charter 1175–83 YCh 1555.

Badger Lane, 1841 O.S.   Birka, *Birka Drain* 1841 O.S.   Boisters Bridge.   Common Lane, 1841 O.S., named from Stubbs Common *infra*.   Long Rain, *v.* reinn 'boundary strip'.   Old Lake Drain, *Lake Drain* 1841 O.S.   Stubbs Common, 1786 *EnclA* 34.   Stubbs Grange & Hall, 1841 O.S.   Stubbs Hollins, *v.* holegn 'holly'.   Swimpit Wood.   Tanpit Lane.   Wentbank Ho.   Went Bridge, 1841 O.S., cf. Went Bridge 51 *supra*.

FIELD-NAMES

(a) Near Field, North Field, West Field 1786 *EnclA* 34.

(b) *Harbarr Intack* 1629 *Bright* 524 (*v.* here-beorg, intak), *Stubbrigg*(e) 1636, 1641 *MinAcct* 35, 39 (*v.* stubb, hrycg).

3. WOMERSLEY (103–5219) [ˈwuməzlə]

> *Wilmereslege* 1086 DB, *-ley* 1286 YI, *Wilmerisley* l. Hy 3 BM, 1276 RH
> *Wilmeresleia* 1086 DB
> *Wulmerslee* 1137–9 YCh 1492
> *Wilmerlay, -ley* 1250, 1288 Ebor
> *Wil-, Wylmersley*(e), *-lay* 1286 Ebor, 1306 DodsN, 1316 Vill, 1317 Ch, 1327 FF *et passim* to 1428 FA
> *Wolmer*(s)*ley* 1311 NCyWills, 1313 Dunelm
> *Wymersley* 1316 Vill, *Wymmersley* 1441 DiocV
> *Wymbursley als. Wymbrisley* 1426 Pat, *Wymbersley* 1504 FF
> *Wommersley* 1501 Ipm, *Womerslay, -ley* 1556 WillY, 1590 FF, 1638 SessnR, *Woomersley* 1557 FF
> *Wembersley* 1530 FF
> *Wombresley* 1556 FF

'Wilmer's forest-clearing', *v.* lēah. An OE pers.n. *Wilmǣr* is not recorded independently, but the two themes *Wil-* and *-mǣr* are common in other dithematic pers.ns., whilst the particular combination is paralleled by OG *Willamer*. The modern form with *Wom-* [wum] is of recent development, as in Wombleton YN 67 (cf. Phonol. § 25), whilst the two early spellings *Wlmer-* and *Wulmer-* are due to association with the common OE *Wulfmǣr*.

BELL LANDS. BELT PLANT., *The Belt* 1841 O.S. BIRDSPRING WOOD, *Bird Spring* (a spring wood) 1739 YDr, *v.* bridd, spring 'a plantation'. BOOTY LANE. BRADLEY DRAIN, 1841 O.S. BROAD OAK SPRING, 1739 YDr, *v.* brād, āc. BROWN INGS. BUSKY WOOD. CHURCH FIELD, 1805 *EnclA* 38. CLIPSALL WOOD, 1841 O.S. COW-CLOSE WOOD, 1841 O.S. DAFFODIL WOOD, *Dilly Wood* 1841 O.S. DALE HILL. DAWLAND HO, *Dorland House* 1841 O.S. FOX WOOD, 1841 O.S. FULHAM HO, *Fullum* 1556, 1572 WillY, *Fullhum* 1572 ib, *Fullam* 1590 FF, *Fulham* 1606 FF, *Fullome* 1614 FF, 'dirty pool or meadow', *v.* fūl, lumm, holmr. GALE COMMON & LANE, 1841 O.S. GRANT SPRING, 1841 O.S., *v.* spring. GREAT LAWN REIN & WOOD,

1841 O.S., *v.* launde 'glade', reinn 'boundary strip'.   GREEN LANE,
1841 O.S.   GROVE WOOD, *Grove* 1817 M, *v.* grāf 'grove'.   HARE-
SPRING HO, 1841 O.S., *v.* hara, spring.   HIGHFIELD HO, 1841 O.S.
HOLLINGWORTH SPRING.   KELSEYCROFT WOOD, 1841 O.S.   LADY
ING WOOD.   LINECROFT WOOD, 1805 *EnclA* 38, *v.* līn 'flax', croft.
LONGCROFT WOOD, 1841 O.S., *v.* lang, croft.   NEW SPRING, 1841
O.S.   NORTH FIELD, 1805 *EnclA*.   OX STOCKING WOOD, *v.* oxa,
stoccing.   ROWS WOOD, *Rose Wood* 1841 O.S.   SAULCROFT WOOD,
1841 O.S.   SHACKLETON SPRING, 1841 O.S.   SPRING LODGE, 1841
O.S.   STEEL SPRING, 1841 O.S.   STOCKING GREEN, *Stocking
Spring* 1841 O.S., *v.* stoccing 'clearing'.   WHEATCROFT WOOD, 1841
O.S., *v.* hwǣte, croft.   WOMERSLEY BECK (*Beck Side* 1841 O.S.),
GRANGE (1817 M) & PARK (1841 O.S.).   WOOD HALL, 1658 WillS,
v. wudu, hall.

FIELD-NAMES

(*a*) West Roads Field 1805 *EnclA*.

(*b*) *Mersed lande* 1574 WillY (probably an error for marled 'marled').

xi. Kellington

1. BEAL (97–5325)

Begale 1086 DB, *Begala*(*m*) 1147–54, 1154 YCh 1475, 1501
Bechala 1121–7 *Nost* 4d, *Bekhala* 1154–8 YCh 1499
Bexalam c. 1154 Pont
Begehal Hy 2 (1230) Ch (YCh 1451)
Becchehale 1215 ChR
Beghal(*e*) 1234 FF, 1296 LacyComp, 1317, 1323 *MinAcct*, 1341
    Surv, 1343 *Ass*, -*heale* 1337 FF, -*halle* 1379 PT, *Beghhall* 1316
    Vill
Beighale 1368 *MinAcct* 26, *Beighall* 1555 TestLds
Beal(*l*) 1529 TestLds, 1535 VE *et freq*, (-*als. Beghall*) 1584 FF
Beagh(*h*)*all* 1641 Rates, 1822 Langd

'Nook of land in the bend of a river', *v.* bēag, halh. The reference
may be to the land across the Aire from Beal village; this oval
stretch of land is completely surrounded by the Aire itself and Old
Eye (which is doubtless an old course of the Aire and which formed
the *bēag*).

KELLINGLEY

> *Kellinglaia(m)*, *-ley(am)* 1144–7, c. 1154 Pont, Hy 2 (1230) Ch,
>   1155–8 YCh 1451, c. 1160 Pont
> *Kelinglai(am)*, *-ley*, *-yng-* 1147–54 *et freq* Pont, 1467 Ch
> *Kellingeleia* c. 1185–93 YCh 1624
> *Kelyngeley* 1541 *MinAcct* 84

If the one *Kellinge-* spelling can be relied on, the first el. is an
elliptical local folk-name *Ceollingas*, and Kellingley would denote
'the forest-clearing of the folk of Kellington', *v.* Kellington 59
infra, *-ingas* (esp. EPN i, 302 §*d*), lēah. Otherwise, it means 'Ceolla's
forest-clearing', *v.* *-ing*[4]; the OE pers.n. *Ceol(l)a* would doubtless be
that of the man who also gave his name to Kellington.

BEAL BRIDGE, *Beighall brig* 1555 TestLds, *v.* brycg.   BEAL DAM, *v.*
dammr.   BEAL WOOD, 1841 O.S., *v.* wudu.   COMMON LANE,
Common Road 1841 O.S., ME *commun* 'common land'.   EAST INGS,
le Estenge 1341 *Surv*, *the easte ynge* 1548 TestLds, *East Ing Close*
1699 AireSurv, *v.* ēast, eng 'meadow'.   HOLLINS FM.   HUMBLE
HOLME, *Humble holms* 1699 AireSurv, 'hop water-meadow', *v.*
humele, holmr.   KELLINGLEY SCALP, *Kellingley Scoop* 1841 O.S.,
probably dial. *scalp* 'a mud-bank, a bare place in a pasture-field';
dial. *scope* is a form of *scalp* (EDD s.v.); cf. The Scalp 23 *supra*.
KEMP BANK, 1844 *TA*.   KEMP FIELD.   LUNN HILL, *Beghalelund*
1323 *MinAcct* 45, *Beallonde* 1341 *Surv*, *Beighalelond* 1368 *MinAcct*
26, *Beghallound* 1424 Rent, *v.* lúndr 'wood'.   NEW LANE, 1841 O.S.
SPRING GARDENS, 1841 O.S.   STUBBS BRIDGE.   SUDFORTH LANE,
Sutforth Lane 1841 O.S., *Sudfurth Close* 1842 *TA*, 'south ford', *v.*
sūð, ford.   THORNFIELD HO, 1771 M, *v.* þorn, feld.   TURVER'S
LANE, *Turver Lane* 1841 O.S.   WILLOW GARTHS, 1842 *TA*, *v.* wilig,
garðr.

FIELD-NAMES

The principal forms in (*a*) are 1842 *TA* 36. Spellings dated 1323 are
MinAcct 45, 1341 *Surv* 10. 5, 1368–1614 *MinAcct*, 1699 *AireSurv*, 1791
EnclA 7.

(*a*) Ash Tree Close, Battle Garth, Berry Croft, Bog Piece (*v.* bog), Break-
ing Croft, Breck Close, Broad Ing (*Brode enge* 1341, *Beale broad Ing* 1699,
v. brād, eng), Broad Ings Bite 1841 O.S. (*v.* prec., byht 'bend in a river'),
Broom Croft (*v.* brōm, croft), Buckroyd (*Buckroyd Field* 1791, *v.* bucc, rod[1]),
Butcher Garth, Carr Close (*Beghaleker(r)* 1323, 1341, *Bealcar* 1480, *v.* kjarr
'marsh'), Chapel Close, Clow Close, Common Close & Hill (cf. Common
Lane *supra*), Coney Garth (*v.* coning-erth 'warren'), Crabtree Close, Dilly

Close, Drysis Close (*Dryhirste* 1541, *v.* drȳge, hyrst), East Field 1791, Elbow Close (doubtless *elbow* used of a sharp river-bend), Elm Close, Elmers Close (*Ellmires* 1699, *Ellmer Ness* 1841 O.S., 'eel marsh', *v.* ǣl, mȳrr, nes), Ferry Stead (*v.* ferja, stede), Fold Close, Gallandine Close, Gravel Hole Hill, Guide Post Close, Hab Ings, Hollam Bank (*Hoole Bank* 1699), House Close & Field, Ilm Royd, Ing Close (*v.* eng), Intack Close (*v.* intak), Jany Field 1791, Justipips, High & Low Loan, Loan Hill (probably identical with Lunn Hill *supra*), Low Field (ib 1791), Middle Field 1791, Mill Close, Moor Field (*Moor Lane Field* 1791), Morass Close, Mown Flatt, Narrow Garth, New Crofts, Oak Tree Close, Old Eye 1841 O.S. (*v.* ald, ēa, an old course of R. Aire, cf. Hawday (Drax) pt. iv), Old Field 1791, Padgate Close, Paget Close (cf. *Pag(g)et garth(e)* 1559, 1614, the surname *Paget*, garðr), Pillow Croft, Pinfold Croft, Piper Field & Thorn, Pond Hill, Rushy Carr, Sand Hill Dike 1841 O.S., Scholey Close, Stack Garth, Street Close, Thick Holme, Thorn Close, Total Hill (probably tōt-hyll 'look-out hill'), Town Field 1791, West Field (ib 1791, *v.* west, feld), West Holme (*Bighalholme* 1486, *the West holme of Beall* 1549 TestLds, *Beale Westholm* 1699, *v.* west, holmr 'water-meadow'), Woodholme.

(*b*) *Allen Bank* 1699 (the surname *Allen*, banke), *Beghallyng(es)* 1486, 1507 TestLds, cf. also *prati de Beighale* 1368 (*v.* eng, cf. East Ings *supra*), *Brodmede* 1368 (*v.* brād, mǣd), *Burry croft* 1699 (*v.* croft, the first el. may be a surname), *Edmonson thing* 1559 (the surname *Edmondson*, þing 'property'), *le Gore* 1341 (*v.* gāra, 'a triangular piece of ground'), *Grene* 1368 (*v.* grēne[2]), *Harecroft* 1699 (*v.* hara, croft), *Kitchingthing(e)* 1559, 1614 (the surname *Kitching*, þing 'property'), *Litelcarre* 1486 (*v.* lytel, kjarr 'marsh'), *vasta voc' Littelheued* 1368, *Litelhed* 1486 (*v.* lytel, hēafod), *Mappeldole* 1486 (*v.* mapel, dāl), *Mekylmarsh* 1341 (*v.* micel, mersc), *Northstubkyrdoles* 1384 (*v.* stubb, kjarr, dāl), (*fossatam que Anglice vocatur*) *Poste-Leiesic* 1154 Pont (*v.* post, lēah, sīc), *Rainor 2 closes* 1699, *Sowenge* 1341 (*v.* sugu, eng), *Thorpething(e)* 1559, 1614 (*Thorpe* as a surname, þing 'property').

2. EGGBOROUGH (97–5623)

Eg(e)-, E-, Acheburg 1086 DB, *Egeburgh* 1180–90 YCh 1630, 1234 FF

Egburc 1155–70 YCh 1502, 1161–77 Templar, 1175–7 YCh 1626, -*burg(h)* 1156 YCh 186, 1173 ib 197, 1190–1210 ib 1625, 1202 FF *et passim* to 1593 FF, -*browghe* 1552 WillY

Eggeburg(h) 1194 Kirkst, 1249 Ch, 1316 Vill

Ekburgh 1416 YI

Hekburgh 1488 WillY

'Ecga's fortification', from the OE pers.n. *Ecga* and burh.

SHERWOOD HALL, *Sirewud(e)* 1175–7 YCh 1627, 1202 FF, -*uuode* 1175–7 Templar, *Sir-, Syrwud* 1202 FF, 1203 DodsN, *Shirwode* 1352

YD ix, *Shyrwo(o)d* 1379 PT (p), 1573 FF, *Sherewood(e)* 1577 FF, 1601 PRSn, *Sher(e)wood hall* 1605 FF, 1666 Visit. 'Bright wood', *v.* scīr², wudu.

TRANMORE, *Tranemore* 1305 Ch, *Tranmore* 1601 FF. 'Moor frequented by cranes', *v.* trani, mōr, cf. Tranmoor (Burn) pt. iv *infra.*

ARAM BRIDGE, cf. *Haram Acre* 1789 *EnclA*, *Haram Lane* 1842 *TA* 236. CROW WOOD. EGGBOROUGH INGS, *prati in Eggeburgh'* 1323 *MinAcct* 45, *Egbrough Ings* 1699 AireSurv, *v.* eng 'meadow'. EGGBOROUGH NESS, *v.* nes. EGGBOROUGH SLEIGHTS, *Sleights* 1839 *TA*, *v.* slétta 'level field'. FALLS WOODS, *Falls Closes* 1839 *TA*, *v.* (ge)fall 'a forest clearing'. GALLOWS HILL, 1839 *TA*, cf. *Gally Ho.* 1771 M, *v.* galga, hyll. GOOSE HILL REACH. HAZEL OLD LANE. HIGHFIELD HO, *High Fields Lane* 1817 M, cf. *High Egbrough Field* 1839 *TA*. HUT GREEN, *Hud Green* 1771 M, *Hut Green* 1800 *EnclA*, 1817 M, probably e.ModE *hut* 'a hut, a mean dwelling', grēne². SAND HALL, 1822 Langd, *v.* sand, hall. WATER LANE. WHITLEY BRIDGE, 1841 O.S., cf. Whitley 60 *infra*, *v.* brycg.

FIELD-NAMES

The principal forms in (*a*) are 1839 *TA* 142. Spellings dated 1305 are Ch, 1352 YD ix, 1541, 1554 *MinAcct* 84, 319.

(*a*) Balk Close, Bartle Garth, Bennett Lands, Blunett Garth, Bogs, Broom Closes, Buck Pond Close, Clay Croft (*le Claycroft* 1352, *v.* clǣg, croft), Clough Close (*v.* clōh), Coat Garth (*v.* cot, garðr), Corner Close (ib 1699 AireSurv), Crabtree Close, Crow Croft, Dogshaw (*v.* dogga, sceaga 'copse'), Elbow, Fern Close, Fleet Closes (*v.* flēot), Foot Gate Close, Fox Cover Close, Gill Croft, Great Garth, Grimshaw Garth, Half Garth, Hensal Town End Close (cf. Hensall 19 *supra*), Hesp Flatt, House Garth, Ingmire (*v.* eng, mýrr), Ley Close, Leys (*v.* lēah), Little Garth, Long Croft, Lund Crofts (*v.* lúndr 'wood'), Mettam Flatts, Middle Field (ib 1800 *EnclA*), Middle Moor, Mill Hill Close, Morritt Garth, Oaks Close, Old Croft, Ox Close, Pinder Flatt, Potter Leys, Royds (*v.* rod¹), Rush Close, Rye Croft, Scorr Falls (*v.* skor 'ditch', (ge)fall 'clearing'), Shaw (*v.* sceaga 'copse'), Stoney Garths, Tilling Croft, Tuffling Moor, Unclough Close, Walling Crofts, Warren Closes, West Garth, White Moor Closes, Winter Close, Worm Close, Worrimans (*Warrimans* 1699 *AireSurv*, doubtless a surname).

(*b*) *Bailycroft* 1352 (*v.* baillie 'bailiff', croft), *Brodhold* 1175–7 Templar (*v.* brād, hald 'shelter'), *Elmtre* 1305 (*v.* elm, trēow), *le Flaske* 1352 (*v.* flask 'swamp'), *Fordales* 1305 (*v.* fore, dāl 'share'), *He(c)ksall* 1541, 1554 (probably 'nook of land belonging to Heck' (18 *supra*), *v.* halh), *Punfaldthorn*

1305 (*v.* pynd-fald, þorn), *Pwytemore* 1305 ('pewit moor', an early example of *pewit*, first noted for 1529 in NED), *Skirdis* 1305 (probably 'bright, clear ditch', *v.* skírr, dīc, with AN -*s* for -*ch*, cf. IPN 102), *Schireflet* 1161–77 Templar, 1175–7 YCh 1626 ('bright, clear stream', *v.* scīr[2], flēot, cf. prec.), *Wadworthcroft* 1352 (cf. Wadworth i, 59 *supra*, probably here used as a surname, croft), *Westdik* 1305 (*v.* west, dīc), *Wichiglund* 1175–89 YCh 1631, *Wykynglund* 1305 (*v.* víkingr, lúndr 'wood').

3. KELLINGTON (97–5524)

Chelin(c)-, Chellinc-, Ghelintune, -tone 1086 DB

Kelington(a), -yng- 12, 1202 Selby, 1190 P (p), c. 1190 Pont, 1240
   Bodl 169, 1290 Ebor, 1296 *MinAcct* 1 *et freq* to 1428 FA,
   Kelinton, -tun 1185 Templar, 1202 FF

Kellingtun, -ton(a) 12 YD i (p), 1185–1210, 1189 YCh 1603, 1632,
   1202 FF, c. 1220 Pont (p), 1531 Test iv, *Kellinton* 1202 FF

Killington 1191 P (p)

Kellingley (56 *supra*), with similar forms for the first el., is two miles away in the neighbouring township of Beal, and both p.ns. have a similar origin for the first el. They are from the OE pers.n. *Ceol(l)a* (Redin 46) with initial *K*- due to Scandinavian influence. As the vowel in *Kel(l)-* appears to have been short, the pers.n. in these p.ns. may be a hypocoristic form of some pers.n. in *Ceol-* (*Ceolrǣd*, etc.) rather than the simple theme *Cēol*. 'Ceolla's farm-stead', *v.* ing[4], tūn.

ROALL HALL

Ruhal(e), Ruhala 1086 DB, 1161–77 Templar (p), 1190–1210 YCh
   1625, 1208 ff P (p), *Ruala* 1166 RBE (p), *Ruhall* 1202 FF

Rughala, -hale 1154–8 YCh 1499, 1159 DodsN, Pont

Rohal(a) Hy 2 (1230) Ch, 1155–8 YCh 1451, 1202–8 Ass (p)

Rouhal(e) 1276 RH, 1300 Abbr, 1331 FF, -*hall* 1331 ib, 1379 PT,
   1428 FA

Rowelle 1313 Pat, *Rowell Hall* 1658 WillS

Rowale 1352 YD ix, *Rouall* 1402 FA, *Rowall* 1490 FF, 1491 YD
   xvii, 98 *et freq* to 1604 FF, *Rowalhaull* 1550 WillY

Roll 1573 FF, *Rowle-Hall* 1822 Langd

'Rough nook of land', *v.* rūh, halh, referring to the level land almost entirely surrounded by streams flowing into the Aire.

ALL ASH, *Hall Ash* 1841 O.S., *v.* hall, æsc.   CARR LANE, 1841 O.S.
THE CARRS, *Ker* 1296 LacyComp, *Carr* 1842 *TA*, *v.* kjarr 'marsh'.

CHURCH LANE, 1841 O.S., cf. *Church Field* 1793 *EnclA*, *v.* cirice, feld. EAST FIELD, 1793 *EnclA*, *v.* ēast, feld. GREEN LANE. INGS LANE, *Killington Ings* 1699 AireSurv, *Ings* 1793 *EnclA*, *v.* eng 'meadow'. LONG MARSH, 1842 *TA*, *v.* lang, mersc. MARSH DRAIN, 1841 O.S., *Kellington Marsh* 1699 AireSurv, *Marsh* 1841 O.S., *v.* mersc. ROALL INGS, cf. Ings Lane *supra*. SOUTH FIELD, 1841 O.S., *v.* sūð, feld. TEASEL HALL, 1841 O.S. UPPER COMMON, *Over Common* 1841 O.S. WHALES LANE. WIDE ARCH.

FIELD-NAMES

The principal forms in (*a*) are 1842 *TA* 236, which includes some f.ns. for Whitley 61 *infra*. Spellings dated 1296 are LacyComp xiii, 415, 1699 AireSurv, 1793 *EnclA*.

(*a*) Allams, Allanson Garth (*v.* garðr), Andrew Field, Arneroyd Close (*v.* rod[1]), Baker Garth, Bog (*v.* bog 'marsh'), Bottoms, Brig Syke (*v.* brycg, sīc), Broach (possibly ME *brotes* 'small plots of land', *v.* brot), Broath Field 1793, Bustard Garth, Coal Croft, East Carr, East Croft, East Toft (*v.* topt), Falls (*v.* (ge)fall 'clearing'), Far Park, Flatts Garth, Foulds Garth, Fox Marsh, the Green, Hall Garth, Lair Close, Lascelles Garth, Middle Field, New Close, Old Ea, Old Eye (a water-course, *v.* ald, ēa, cf. Hawday (Drax) pt. iv *infra*), Ox Close, Pick Haver Garth, Sand Pit, Shift, Short Ends, South Moor, Spoil Bank, Stones Close, The Swamp, Tarn Field, Temple Carr (probably from the Knights Templars, cf. 1185 Templar), Water Garth Close, West Carr, West Ings, Wheat Marsh, Whin Close (*v.* hvin 'gorse').

(*b*) *avenames de Kellingtona* c. 1208 Pont (*v.* af-nám 'land newly taken into use'), *Longcroft* 1699 (*v.* lang, croft), *Long roid* 1699 (*v.* lang, rod[1]), *Lound* 1296 (*v.* lúndr 'wood'), *Pinfalda* 1296 (*v.* pynd-fald), *Renting* 1699, *le Stoch* 1296 (*v.* stocc).

3. WHITLEY (97–5621)

Wite-, *Wytelai(e)*, *-lay*, *-legh* 1086 DB, 12, 1202 Selby, 1251 Ass (p), 1276 RH, 1280 YI
Wittelay 1194 P   *Wetelegh* 1251 Ass
Withelai 1202 FF, *Wytheley* 1279–81 QW
Whitley, *-lay* 1316 Vill, 1355 DodsN *et passim* to 1591 FF
Whiteley 1323 *MinAcct* 45, *Whitte-*, *Qwytlay* 1379 PT
'Bright forest-glade or clearing', *v.* hwīt, lēah.

WHITLEY THORPE, *Witlaithorp* 1535 VE, *Whitleythorp(p)*, *-thorpe*, *-lay* 1540 FF, 1571 *Dep*, 1591 FF *et freq* to 1817 M. *v.* þorp 'an outlying farmstead'.

GRAVEHILL LANE, cf. *Gravel Pit Lane* 1841 O.S., *Gravel Pit* 1842 *TA*.
HORSECLOSE WOOD, *Horse Close* 1842 *TA*, v. hors, clos.   KELLING-
TON COMMON, *Commons* 1793 *EnclA*.   LEE LANE, 1841 O.S., v.
Whitley Lee *infra*.   SHEEPWASH LANE.   WHITE FIELD, 1772 *EnclA*.
WHITLEY LEE, *Low & Over Lee* 1772 *EnclA*, v. lēah 'clearing'.
WHITLEY WOOD, *Whytley Wood* 1588 WillY, v. wudu.   WILLOW
GARTH, 1842 *TA*, v. wilig, garðr.

FIELD-NAMES

The principal forms in (a) are 1772 *EnclA* 38; cf. also Kellington f.ns. 60
supra.

(a) the Breaks (v. bræc[1]), Bult Lane (v. bulut 'ragged robin'), Middle
Field, Mill Field, South Moor (ib 1817 M).

(b) *Hethe* 1276 RH (v. hǣð), *Westdale* 1279–81 QW (v. west, dāl).

xii. Darrington

1. CRIDLING STUBBS (97–5121)

Cred(e)ling, *-yng* 1155–77 YCh 1455, 1229 PatR (p), 1316 Vill,
1341 *Surv*, (*-stubbes*) 1480 *MinAcct*, 1557, 1607 FF, *Credelinge*
1210 P (p)
Crid(e)linc 1156 YCh 186, 1173 ib 197
Cri-, *Cryd(e)ling*, *-yng* 1202 FF (p), c. 1220 Pont, 1296 LacyComp,
1313 Pat, 1323, 1368 *MinAcct*, (*-Stubes*) 1614 PRDr, (*-Stubbs*)
1675 Comm 53
Cridelinge 1229 FF, 1296 LacyComp, *Cridlinge Stubbes* 1598 FF

Two p.ns. are involved in this name, Cridling itself (now represented by Cridling Park *infra*) and Stubbs (*infra*); the township
name Cridling Stubbs denotes 'Stubbs near Cridling', and is so
described to distinguish it from Hamphall Stubbs and Walden
Stubbs 43, 53 *supra*. Cridling is probably an old singular formation of a pers.n. with -ing[2], 'Cridela's or Creodela's place'; this type
of p.n. is not common but is clearly established, and in cases like
Cridling (where no trace of the OE plur. ending remains in ME) is
preferable to an old folk-name in *-ingas*; v. EPN i, 288 § 6, 289 (vii).
The OE pers.n. *Cridela* is not on record but is a normal *-el* derivative
of *Crida* (*Creoda* with back-mutation). Ekwall (DEPN s.n.) has
suggested that Cridling is a compound of this pers.n. *Creoda* and

OE hlinc 'ridge, bank', which is formally possible but unlikely, partly on topographical grounds, and partly because *hlinc* does not appear with certainty in Yorkshire p.ns.

CRIDLING PARK, *parco de Cridlyng* 1368 *MinAcct* 26, *parkes of Crydelinge* 1544 *Surv*, *Credling Park(e)* 1551, 1591 WillY, 1616 PRDr, *Cri-*, *Crydling Park(e)* 1629 TN(Kn), 1665 Visit, 1817 M, *v.* Cridling Stubbs *supra*, **park**; Cridling Park probably represents that part of the manor which was originally called Cridling.

STUBBS, *Stobbes* 1296 LacyComp (p), *Stubbes*, *-ez* 1368, 1486 *MinAcct* 26, 66, cf. also the spellings of Cridling Stubbs *supra*. *v.* **stubb** 'stump', Stubbs no doubt denoting 'a clearing where the tree-stumps were left'; cf. Hamphall Stubbs, Walden Stubbs 43, 53 *supra*.

COBCROFT FM, *Cobcrofte* 1533 WillY, 1541 *MinAcct* 84, 1557 Test-Lds, from e.ModE *cob* 'a cob, a horse' (cf. Cobb Carr 42 *supra*), **croft**.   KING'S STANDARD HILL, *King's Standard* 1847 *TA*, *v.* **standard** 'a tree-stump' and cf. f.n. Corn Ings Standard *infra*; Cridling was formerly part of the king's estates (1544 *Surv* 10. 23). LEYS WOOD.   LOW BALK LANE, cf. *Balk Field* 1847 *TA*, *v.* **balca**. NORTHFIELD HO, *North Field Close* 1847 *TA*, *v.* **norð**, **feld**.   PARK FM & WOOD, cf. *Parke enge* 1341 *Surv*, *Park* 1817 M, *v.* Cridling Park *supra*.   SANDY DIKE.   SCRATCH LANE, *Serates* (sic) 1847 *TA*, probably from ON **skratti** 'goblin', dial. *Scrat*, *Scratch* 'the Devil'. STUBBS COMMON, *Common* 1847 *TA*.

FIELD-NAMES

The principal forms in (*a*) are modern (1935), a 1902 agreement of Sidney Sussex College Cambridge (marked *SS*), or 1847 *TA* (marked *TA*). Spellings dated 1341 are *Surv* 10. 5, 1323, 1368, 1480, 1486 *MinAcct*.

(*a*) Barley Land Ings *SS*, Bowbrigg Field ('arch bridge', *v.* **boga**, **brycg**), Bridle Field, Busky Close *SS* (*v.* **buskr**), Calf Garth *SS* (*v.* **calf**, **garðr**), Catley Close *TA*, Clay Field (ib 1764 *Glebe*, *v.* **clæg**, **feld**), Clayton Close *SS*, Corn Ings Standard (cf. King's Standard Hill *supra*, *v.* **corn**[1], **eng**), Crabtree *TA* (*v.* **crabbe**, **trēow**), Grass Garth *TA* (*v.* **gærs**, **garðr**), Green Close, Hague Field Close *TA* (*v.* **haga** 'enclosure'), Hollar Close *SS*, How Garth, Joe Hall, Long Nooking *SS*, Marshall Close, Middle Green *TA*, New Close *TA*, Paddock, Plaster Pits *SS*, The Pond (The pound *TA*, *v.* **pund**), Quarry Field (ib *TA*), Rampa Field, Red Hill Field, Long & Short Rift, Rough Sale Field, Sod Horse Field, Sparrow Castle Field, Stackgarth Close *SS* ('stackyard'), Upper Crofts *TA*, Varasour Field (sic).

(b) *Bourehill* 1480 (v. būr[1] 'cottage', hyll), *Clai-*, *Clayrode* 1323, 1368 (v. clǣg, rod[1]), *Cokyl* 1341 (v. cocc[1], hyll), *Daly-*, *Dailflat* 1480, 1486 (v. deill, flat), *Digasland* 1480, *Forstersyerd* 1480 (v. forestier, geard), *le Greve* 1341 (v. grǣfe 'copse'), *Grymdoleʒ* 1480 (the ON pers.n. *Grímr*, dāl), *Mappledole* 1480 (v. mapel, dāl), *le Oxe enge* 1341 (v. oxa, eng), *Pierot Crofte* 1341 (probably the Fr pers.n. *Pierot*, a diminutive of *Pierre*, croft), *South-eng(e)* 1323, 1368 (v. sūð, eng), *Southwode* 1368, 1486 (v. sūð, wudu), *Stockyng* 1323 (v. stoccing), *Storthes* 1323 (v. storð 'plantation').

2. DARRINGTON (97–4820)

> *Darni(n)tone* 1086 DB   *Dernington* 1307 Ch
> *Dardinton(a)*, *-tun(a)* c. 1090, 1122 *et freq* Pont (YCh 1486, etc.), 1148 YCh 179, 1155–8 ib 1451, Hy 2 (1230) Ch, 1193 P (p), 1229 Ebor, *Darditona* 1122 Pont, *Dardington(a)* 1135–42 *et freq* to 1235 Pont (YCh 1469, 1493, etc.), 1251 FF, 1286 Ebor, *Dardinctun(a)* 1155–70 YCh 1502, 1173 ib 197, *Dardigtuna* 1156 ib 186, *Dardhinton'* 1208 FF
> *Darthin(g)ton(a)*, *-yng-* c. 1170 Kirkst, 1204 FF (p), 1226 ib, 1282 Ebor, 1290 Baild, 1293 Kirkst *et passim* to 1445 *Bodl* 142a
> *Derthington*, *-yng-* 1364 Kirkst, 1379 PT, 1402 FA, 1410 Pat *et freq* to 1495 Ipm
> *Derlingtone* 1279–81 QW, *Darlyngton* 14 *Sawl* 194
> *Darington'*, *-yng-* 1243 Fees, 1270–80 *Bodl* 23, 1495 Ipm *et freq* to 1615 FF
> *Darrington(e)* 1558 WillY, 1612 NCWills, 1638 SessnR

Almost all spellings in *Darn-*, *Dard-*, *Darth-* up to the fourteenth century point to a late OE *Dearðing-*, *Darðingtūn*, apart from the occasional *Derth-* (from 1364). Moorman 57 derives the name from OE *Dēornōðingtūn* 'Dēornōð's farmstead' (v. -ing[4], tūn), and Karlström 91 supposes that the early *Darth-*, *Darn-* spellings are either AN (cf. Barnby Dun i, 17 *supra*) or are 'a reflection of the development of ONb *ēa* (= WSax *eo*) into *ǣ* (later *a*) in front of *r*', cf. Luick § 357, n. 4. Darlington (Du 60), *Dearthingtun* 1002–16 YCh 923, *Dearningtun* c. 1130 SD, appears to be a parallel, though medieval *Dar-* spellings are far less common. In the case of Darrington, Ekwall meets the difficulty by supposing the ultimate base of the first el. is the OE pers.n. *Dægheard* (presumably reduced to *Dærd-*), but the *Darn-* spellings, and those in *Darl-* which are due to AN influence (Zachrisson, ANInfl 138 ff), presuppose an *-n-* in the OE form. On the whole, the better interpretation seems to be 'farmstead associated with Dēornōð'.

WENT HILL, *Weneteshil* 1180–1200 *Nost* 19, *Wenteshill* c. 1200, 14 ib 17, 18d. 'Hill by the Went', *v.* R. Went (RNs.), hyll. The hill is a steep-sided lofty ridge running along the Little Went for about a mile.

BICKERING WOOD, *Pickering Wood* 1841 O.S.   DALE FIELD, 1817 *EnclA*, *v.* dæl, feld.   DARRINGTON HALL, 1841 O.S.   DARRINGTON LEYS, *Darrington Leas* 1797 PRDr, *Leys Close* 1841 *TA*, *v.* lēah 'clearing'.   GREAT CLUMP, *Clump* 1841 *TA*.   GROVE HALL & WOOD, *Greave Hall* 1771 M, *Grove Hall* 1795 PRDr, *Grove Wood* 1841 O.S., *v.* grāf 'grove'; *Greave* is from the related grǣfe, as in the nearby Greavefield 67 *infra*.   HALL FLATS.   HAVERCROFT LANE, *Havercroft Field* 1817 *EnclA* 170, 'oat enclosure', *v.* hafri, croft. HODGE WOOD, 1841 O.S., cf. *John Hodge* (of this parish) 1682 PRDr 52.   HOLDGATE HILL, *Holgate Hill* 1841 O.S., 'hollow way', *v.* hol[2], gata.   HUNTER'S WOOD.   MARLPIT LANE, 1841 O.S., *v.* marle, pytt.   MOOR HILL FIELDS, cf. *Darrington Moore* 1618 FF, *v.* mōr. OLD WOOD, 1841 O.S.   SPITAL GAP, 1841 O.S., *v.* spitel, gap. THORNTREE CLOSES.   WENT BRIDGE INGS, *v.* Went Bridge 51 *supra*, eng.   WEST FIELD, 1817 *EnclA*, *Westfeld* 1208 FF, *v.* west, feld.   WEST PARK, 1841 O.S., *v.* west, park.

FIELD-NAMES

The principal forms in (*a*) are 1841 *TA* 125, and include f.ns. from Stapleton 65 *infra*. Spellings dated c. 1190, c. 1200 are Pont, 1208 FF, 1487, 1541, 1636 *MinAcct* 66, 35, 84, Chas 1 *Surv* 10. 1, 1712 *WYEnr* 68, 1817 *EnclA* 170.

(*a*) Barley Garth, Brachia land 1764 *Glebe*, Butcher Bile, Calf Garth, Clay Field 1817, Fish Pond Wood, Hollin Hill (*v.* holegn 'holly'), Horse Pasture, Horse Race Field 1817, Laverack Stone Field 1817 (*v.* lāwerce 'lark', stān), Long Lands, Mill Close (cf. *Mill Hill Field* 1817), the North ffield 1712 (*Nortfeld* 1208, *v.* norð, feld), Ox Pasture, Pear Tree Close, Peas Stubble Close, Ponds Close, Pudding Poke Close, Quarry Hill, Rand (*v.* rand 'border'), Ravinsall 1712, Sainfoin Close, Shoulder of Mutton, Smeaton Craggs, Sod Wall, Street Furlong (cf. *Stree Field* (sic) 1817), Tippet Leys, Wall Close, Willing Royd (*v.* rod[1]), Yellow Close.

(*b*) *Arnelsland* 1487 (probably the ME pers.n. *Arnold* from OG *Arnald*), le *Flatt* 1636 (*v.* flat), *Heueplandas*, -*es* (sic) c. 1190, c. 1200 (*v.* hænep 'hemp', land), *Musewelles* c. 1190, c. 1200 (a common type of p.n. usually derived from mos 'moss' or mūs 'mouse', **wella**), *Northlande* Chas 1 (*v.* norð, land), *Osebne-*, *Hosbernerode* c. 1190, c. 1200 (the ME pers.n. *Osbern* (ON *Ásbjǫrn*), rod[1] 'clearing'), *le Parson garth* 1541 (*v.* persone, garðr), *Quar(r)efurs* c. 1190, c. 1200 (*v.* carrefors 'cross-roads'), *le Rise* 1636 (*v.* hrīs 'brushwood'), *Spronesdale* (sic) c. 1190, c. 1200 (the OE pers.n. *Sprow*, dæl), *Sudfeld* 1208 (*v.* sūð, feld).

3. STAPLETON (103–5018)

Stapleton(e) 1086 DB, 1255 Ch, *Stapilton(a)* 1136–40 *et freq* Pont (YCh 1469, etc.), 1368 *MinAcct* 26, 1379 PT, *Stapelton(a)*, *-tun* 1135–40 Pont, Hy 2 (1230) Ch, 1155–8 YCh 1451, 1166 RBE (p), c. 1170 Kirkst, 1220–40 *Bodl* 74 *et passim* to 1428 FA, *Stepelton* 1276 RH, *Stappleton* 1558 WillY, 1612, 1624 PRDr. This oft-repeated p.n. is from OE **stapol** 'pillar, post' and **tūn** 'farmstead'. Its precise significance is not certain but it could mean simply 'farmstead by a pole' or possibly 'a farm built with or on poles' (*v.* EPN ii, 146).

BANK WOOD, 1841 *TA*, *v.* **banke**, **wudu**. BRIERY FIELD WOOD, *Briery Wood* 1841 O.S., *v.* **brērig**, **wudu**. BROCKADALE. CASTLE FM, 1817 M, *v.* **castel**. FROZEN WELL. HEPWORTH WOOD, 1841 O.S. HOME FM, 1841 O.S. KINGSLAND WOOD. KIRKDIKE PLANT., *v.* **kirkja**, **dīc**. MILL WOOD, named from *Stapleton Wind Mill* 1781 PRDr. SCROMBECK FM, *Schrombeck* 1841 O.S. STAPLETON HALL & PARK, *Stapleton Park* 1771 M, 1806 PRDr, *v.* **park**. WAKE WOOD, 1841 *TA*.

FIELD-NAMES

For modern f.ns. *v.* Darrington 64 *supra*.

(*b*) *Stapelton Wode* 1368 *MinAcct* (*v.* **wudu**), *Wulfpuittedale* 12 Kirkst (*v.* **wulf**, **pytt**, **dæl**).

xiii. Ferry Fryston

The township was later called Ferrybridge (97–4724); part of it (Water Fryston) is transferred to Castleford (69 *infra*), part to Pontefract Municipal Borough, and the rest to Knottingley Urban District (73 *infra*).

FERRY FRYSTON

Friston(e), *-tona*, *Fryston* 1086 DB, 1154 YCh 1475, c. 1160 Pont, 1166 RBE (p), 1204 ChR, c. 1215 Pont, 1246 FF, 1246 YI *et passim* to 1522 Test vi, (*Fere-*) 1542 FF, (*Ferrie-*) 1605 FF, *Freston* 1300 Ebor, *Ferry Freiston* 1535 VE, *Freyston* 1538 FF, *Ferefrieston* 1597

FF, *Ferry Freeston* 1654 *ParlSurv* 25. The compound recurs in Water Fryston *infra* and Monk Fryston pt. iv *infra*. For the latter there are two OE spellings; one (*Fryyetune*) is in an unreliable thirteenth century copy and is a mis-transcription of OE *Frysetune* or *Frygetune* (or possibly *Fryþetune*, which is adopted in BCS 1112 and by Ekwall, DEPN s.n.); the second (*Fristun*) is from a reliable eleventh-century document. Since all other spellings point to an OE *Frīstun*, Birch's reading *Fryþetune* should be rejected. Although a pers.n., OE *Frisa* or ON *Frisi*, might be thought of for the first el., the fact that there are these three YW examples and others in L and Sf points rather to the name meaning 'farmstead of the Frisian(s)', *v.* **Frīsa**, **tūn**. The regular absence of a medial *-e-* in the spellings of the YW names is paralleled by many other compounds with racial-names like OE *Fresland*, etc. (cf. EPN ii, 116, s.v. **Seaxe**); cf. also the uninflected forms in Bretton 99 *supra*, Normanton 121 *infra*. It may be noted that most p.ns. containing *Frīsa* seem to belong to the Viking period (cf. Introd.). For the affix in Ferry Fryston, *v.* Ferrybridge *infra*.

FERRYBRIDGE, *Ferie* 1086 DB, *Fereia* 1086 DB, c. 1212 Pont, *Feria* 12 (*freq*) ib, 1137–9 YCh 1492, *Feri* c. 1192 Pont, 1247 YI, *Fery* 1290 AD vi, 1296 LacyComp, 1303 KF, 1329 FF, 1469 BM, 1541 *MinAcct*, *Ponte(m) ferie* 12 Font, 1226 FF, 1229 Pat, 1320 Abbr, 1349 Ch, *pontis de Feria* 1227 ib, *Pontefereye* 1246 FF, *pontem de Fery* 1271, l. 13 *RegAlb* iv, 30d, 31, *Fery-, Feribrig(ge), -bryg(g)* 1198 Fount, 1314 Dunelm, 1317 Pat, 1328 Banco *et passim* to 1597 SessnR, *-bridge* 1545 TestLds, *Ferebrig(ge)* 1433 Pat, 1521 Test vi, *Ferrybrigge* 1584 FF, *-Bridge* 1654 *ParlSurv* 25. *v.* ON **ferja** 'ferry'. This name carries the use of the word *ferry* back some three and a half centuries. The ferry, which carried the traffic of the Great North Road across the Aire, was replaced by a bridge by the end of the twelfth century (*v.* **brycg**).

WATER FRYSTON, *Friston(a)*, *Fryston* 1155–8 YCh 1451, c. 1220 Pont, 1255 Ch *et passim*, (*-on Ayr(e)*, *-upon Aire*) 1289 Ebor, 1415 YI, 1533 WillY, (*-be, -by the Water*) 1354, 1374 FF, 1397 TestLds, 1483 NCWills, (*-juxta, -super aquam*) 1428 FA, 1521 WillY, 1555 BM, (*-Bywater*) 1524 NCWills, 1532 Test vi, 1534 WillY, (*Water-*) 1532 Test vi, 1563 PRLed, *Watter Freiston* 1535 VE, *Water Freston* 1546 YChant, *Waterfrieston* 1594 WillY. *v.* Ferry Fryston *supra*. For the affixes *v.* R. Aire (RNs.), **wæter** 'water' (cf. Allerton Bywater pt. iv *infra*, also on the Aire).

WHELDALE

> *Weldale* 1086 DB, 1252 Ipm   *Wluedale* (sic) c. 1192 Pont
> *Queldale, -dal(am)* 1086 DB, c. 1090 Pont, 1220 Cur, 1246 *Ass* 4,
>   1316 Vill *et passim* to 1604 FF
> *Quendale* 1226 FF
> *Quelledale* 1243 Fees (p)
> *Wheldale* 1419 Test i, 1489 WillY, 1522 Test vi, 1547 FF

'Wheel valley', *v.* hwēol, dæl, referring to a bend in the course of the R. Aire here. Cf. also Wheldon Wood *infra*. On the *Qu-*, *Wh-* spellings *v.* Phonol. § 39.

BECK HOUSES, cf. *Beck Pasture* 1841 *TA*, *v.* bekkr 'stream'. BUB-WITH HO, 1771 M, *Bubwyth houses* 1407 TestLds, named from the family of *Bubwith* (cf. *John Bubwith* of Pontefract 1437 TestLds xxvi, 181); cf. the nearby Bubwith Bridge 80 *infra*. BULLHILL, 1841 *TA*, *v.* bula, hyll. CATTLELAITH LANE, cf. *Laith Garth* 1841 *TA*, *v.* cattel, hlaða 'barn'. CROW CROWNS, 1841 *TA*. ENDLESS FLAT, 1841 O.S. NEW FRYSTON, *Newton Fryston* 1522 Test vi, *v.* Ferry Fryston *supra*, 'Newton' from Newton (Ledsham) pt. iv on the opposite side of the Aire, renamed 'New' with the growth of the present village. FRYSTON HALL, 1841 O.S. FRYSTON PARK, *Low Park Ho* 1771 M, *Top Park* 1841 O.S., *v.* park. GREAVEFIELD LANE, cf. *Greave Close & Nooking* 1841 *TA*, *v.* græfe 'copse'. GREEN QUARRY, 1841 O.S., *TA*. HEALD WOOD, 1841 O.S., *TA*, *v.* helde 'slope'. HIGH ROYDS WOOD, 1841 O.S., *TA*, *v.* hēah, rod[1] 'clearing'. HOLMEFIELD FM, 1841 O.S., *TA*, *Home Field* 1817 M, cf. *Holmeland* 1421 *MinAcct*, 1424 Rent, named from *Friston Holm* 1699 AireSurv, *v.* holmr 'water-meadow'. KIRKHAW LANE, *Kirk Haw(e) Close* 1841 *TA*, *v.* kirkja, haga 'enclosure'. LONG DALES, *Long Dale* 1841 *TA*, *v.* lang, dāl 'share of land'; they are long, very narrow fields. OLD FIELD PLANT., *Old Field* 1813 EnclA 23, *v.* ald, feld. PARK PLANT., 1841 O.S., *TA*, *v.* Fryston Park *supra*. RED HILL, 1841 *TA*. ROUND HILL, *Roundhillfeild(e)*, *-field* 1636 *MinAcct* 35, an Anglian tumulus (cf. Introd.) *v.* rond, hyll. SAND PIT. SHILLING HILL, cf. *Shilling Ings* 1841 *TA*, 'meadows paying a shilling rent', *v.* scilling, eng, hyll. SKEW BRIDGE. SOWGATE LANE, *Sowgate* 1841 *TA*, possibly sūð, gata, from its position towards the south of the parish. STANILANDS HO. STRANGLAND LANE, *Stranglands* 1841 *TA*, *v.* strang 'firm', land. STUMP CROSS, 1841 O.S., cf. *novam crucem* 'new cross' 1235 Pont, *le Stub crosse* 1475

TestLds, *v.* stubb, cros, a boundary cross between Ferrybridge and Pontefract, of which the stump remains (cf. Pont i, 199, n. 3). TAYTHES LANE, 1841 O.S., *le Tathes* 1421 *MinAcct* 507, *the myddle taythx* 1555 TestLds, *Low Tays* 1841 *TA*, ON *taða* 'a manured field' (cf. dial. *tathe*, NED s.v., and Taythes (Sedbergh) pt. vi *infra*). WELL WOOD, cf. *Welleclif* c. 1216 Pont, *v.* wella, clif. WENTCLIFF HILL, 1841 *TA*, possibly from wente 'a path, track' and clif, but since this is a prominent hill with a windmill, the first el. may have been wind, subsequently changed to *Went-* by analogy from R. Went, Wentbridge, etc.; the place itself is not near the river Went. WHELDALE INGS, *Wheldale Ing* 1699 AireSurv, *v.* Wheldale *supra*, eng 'meadow'. WHELDON WOOD, *Whelden* 1587 WillY, *Wheldon-Hall* 1822 Langd, *Weldon* 1841 O.S., near Wheldale *supra*; this name is also from hwēol 'wheel', with dūn 'hill' (since it stands on the hillside above Wheldale). WHIN COVERT, 1841 O.S., *v.* hvin 'gorse'. WILLOW GARTH, 1841 *TA*, *v.* wilig, garðr.

FIELD-NAMES

The principal forms in (*a*) are 1841 *TA* 157. Spellings dated 12 are Font, c. 1160–c. 1216 Pont, 1532, 1533 Test vi, 1541 *MinAcct* 84, 1552, 1555 TestLds, 1654 *ParlSurv* Y. 25, 1699 AireSurv.

(*a*) Ash Rein (*v.* æsc, reinn 'boundary strip'), Bacon Close, Brand Hill (*v.* brand, hyll), Brocher Row, Brock Holes (*v.* brocc-hol), Burrows, Bushes, Butt Hill, Church Ings (*Friston church ing* 1699, *v.* eng), Clay Banks, Coney Garth (*v.* coning-erth 'warren'), Cow Becks, Dale Close, Dog Pits, Dove Coat Garth, Dove Royds (*v.* rod¹), Green Hill Plantation, Hardistys, Hart Close, Hollin Bush 1841 O.S. (*v.* holegn 'holly'), Horse Becks, Hoyster Close, Hunters Close, Ings (*Friston Ing* 1699, *v.* eng), John O' Gaunt, Leys Croft, Liquorice Close & Garth (the Pontefract district has long been a noted centre of liquorice cultivation, *v.* clos, garðr), Long Croft, Long Holme (*v.* holmr), Long Lands, Long Moor, Make me Rich, Marsh (*Ferrybridg Marsh* 1699, *v.* mersc), Mirey Butts, Myson Chair, Narrow Beck, New Lathes 1771 M (*v.* hlaða 'barn'), North Ings (*Friston North Ing* 1699, *v.* norð, eng), Owl Holes, Pinfold Close (*v.* pynd-fald), Quarry Hole, Ram Close, Red Laith Garth (*v.* hlaða, garðr), Settings, Short Moors, Shuttle Bank Close, Silver Pits, Skinfield Lane Close, Slough Close (*v.* slōh 'mire'), Small Tails, Sow Hill Close, Stack Hills, Stinting, Stone Bridge, Stoney Flatt, Stoops, Swithen (*v.* sviðinn), Thin Hills, Throstle Rood, Tithe Laith Garth, Toad Hole, Toft Close, Two Gules, Vicar Bank, West Lawn (*v.* launde), Whin Hill Close (*v.* hvin 'gorse'), Woodhalls.

(*b*) *Feribrigge causaye* 1552, *Cowsyeway Close* 1654 (*v.* caucie 'a raised way in marshland'), *the churche bryge* 1532, *the Church way* 1654 (*v.* cirice, brycg, weg), *the cowe close* 1555 (*v.* cū, clos), *Dikeslandes* 12 (*v.* dīc, land), *Fery Felde(s)* 1437 *Surv*, 1541 (*v.* Ferrybridge *supra*, feld), *Gate* 1533 (*v.* gata), *Hamelinmilne* c. 1160 (*Hamelin* was tenant of Knottingley, DB, *v.* myln), *Herneshil* c. 1192, *Limpit(h)* c. 1212, 1215 (*v.* līm, pytt), *Malederie* 12 (OFr *maladerie* 'a hospital, esp. one for lepers', first recorded in English from the fifteenth century, NED s.v.), *Puthale* c. 1216 (*v.* pytt, halh), *The Saffron garth* 17 *Glebe*, *Towne ynge* 1541 (*v.* tūn, eng), *Wheldale Carr* 1699 (*v.* Wheldale *supra*, kjarr 'marsh').

xiv. Castleford

The townships of Castleford and Glass Houghton (70 *infra*), with that of Whitwood (124 *infra*) and part of Ferry Fryston (65 *supra*), are united to form Castleford Urban District.

1. CASTLEFORD (97-4325)

> *æt Ceaster forda* 948 (l. 11) ASC (D)
> *Casterford* c. 1130 SD, 1226 FF, *Castreford* Hy 2 (1230) Ch, 1155–8 YCh 1451, 1241 Lib
> *Castelford(e)* 12, 13 (*freq*) Pont (YCh 1475, 1486, etc.), 1155–8 YCh 1451, 1178–84 (1328) Ch, 1216–56 *RegAlb* iii, 12d, 1220 Cur, 1251 Ch *et passim* to 1528 FF, *-forth* 1276 RH, 1435 Baild, *et freq* to 1506 WillY, *-fourthe* 1584 FF
> *Castleford* 1290 Ebor, 1579 *Dep et freq* to 1817 Langd, *-forthe* 1529 TestLds
> *Castilford* 1399 Pat, 1530 Test v, *Castyllforth* 1419 Test i

'Ford near the fortification', *v.* ceaster, ford. On the identification of OE *Ceasterforda* in ASC with Castleford, cf. Mawer, *Brandl Festschrift* 47. The *ceaster* or fortification is generally accepted as being that of the Roman station *Legeolio* mentioned in AntIt. At this place Ermine Street from Doncaster to the north crosses the Aire and traces of an ancient ford remain; in medieval times reference is made to the *passagium* or ferry of Castleford (as in 1159 Pont). In the ME period OE *ceaster* was replaced by OFr castel. The fact that *castel* replaces *ceaster* and the evidence of the occasional later spellings in *Castre-* show that Castleford, as we should expect, had the typical northern OE form *cæster* (*caster*), as in Doncaster i, 29 *supra*, etc. (cf. EPN i, 86 § 3).

BEANCROFT ST, *Beancroft Field* 1822 *EnclA*, *v.* bēan, croft.   CASTLE-FORD BRIDGE, *pontem de Castilforth* 1507 TestLds, *Castilforth brigge*

1545 ib, *Castleforde Brigge* 1579 *Dep*, *v.* **brycg.**   Castleford Ings, *Castilford Ing* 1342 Ext 147, *Castleforth ynges*, *-Ing* 1554 TestLds, 1699 AireSurv, *Castlefurthe Inges* 1623 FF, *v.* **eng** 'meadow'. Half Acres, *the halfe acre* 1592 Meth 124, *v.* **half**, **æcer.**   Heald Field, 1822 *EnclA*, *v.* **helde** 'slope'.   Longacre, *les Longacres* 1384 *MinAcct*, *v.* **lang**, **æcer.**   Red Hill, cf. Red Hill 71 *infra*.   Round Hill, 1822 *EnclA*, *v.* **rond, hyll.**   Ryebread.   Snawthorne Hill.

FIELD-NAMES

The principal forms in (*a*) are 1846 *TA*.   Spellings dated 1764 are *Glebe*, and 1822 *EnclA* 49.

(*a*) Averay Sike roods 1764, Bent acre 1764 (*v.* **beonet, æcer**), Broken Cross, Castle Hill 1771 M (*v.* **Castleford** *supra*, **hyll**), Church Field 1822, Dimpledale (*v.* **dympel** 'hole, pit', **dæl**), Fothering roods 1764 (*v.* **fōdring** 'grazing', **rōd**), Gill Croft 1764 (probably ME pers.n. *Gille* or the surname *Gill*, **croft**), Hardwick Roods (cf. East Hardwick 72 *infra*, **rōd**), Jane Ridge 1822, Limepit Close (*v.* **līm, pytt**), Mire Field 1822 (*v.* **mȳrr**), Old Field Close, Passforth Row, the Shuffle 1764, Stony Flatt.

(*b*) *le Brode Enge* 1413 YD x (*v.* **brād, eng**), (*le*) *Haghouse* 1424 Rent, 1426 *Ramsd* (*v.* **hogg, hūs**), *le Mere* 1413 YD x, *lez Meyr* 1461 YD xii, 234 (*v.* **mere** 'pool'), *leʒ Oldtowne* 1461 ib (*v.* **ald, tūn**), *Thilloles* 1258 YI (*v.* **þille** 'plank', **hol**[1]).

2. Glass Houghton (97–4424)

> *Hoctun* 1086 DB   *Hogton* 1366 DodsN
> *Hoghton* 1251 Ch, 1304 Ebor, 1316 Vill, 1323 *MinAcct* 45 *et passim*
>   to 1523 TestLds
> *Hoytton* 1263 Hem ii, 26
> *Houghton* 1503 FF, 1530 Test v, 1578 *Dep et freq* to 1740 LdsM,
>   (*Glass-*) 1817 M, 1822 Langd
> *Hooghton* 1535 VE
> *Glass Houton* 1793 PRRth

'Farmstead on the spur of land', *v.* **hōh, tūn**; the place is on the edge of a hill. 'Glass' from the glassworks here; cf. 'at the Glass-house at Houghton near Pontefract is made . . . all sorts of Window Glass' (1740 LdsM 84).

Cutsyke, *Cutthesik* c. 1235 Pont, *Cutsik* 14 *Nost* 124d.   A compound of ME **cut** 'a cut, a cut water-channel' and **sīc** 'a stream'; *cut* is usually associated with *mill* in p.ns. and so refers generally to a mill-conduit.

HOLY WELL, *Heliwelle* 12 Pont, *Hali-*, *Halywell(e)*, 1263 Hem ii, 26, c. 1280 BM, 1309, 1360 Calv, 1415 BM, (*-in Hoghton*) 1384 Calv, 1517 WillY, *Helewell* 1401 BM, *Helywell* 1496 Calv, *Hallywell* 1506 WillY, 1612 FF, *Halleywell* 1556 FF, *Haylywell* 1557 TestLds. 'Holy spring', *v.* hālig, wella. The secondary form *Hely-* represents the ONb mutated form hǽlig, as also in the forms of Holywell Green iii, 50 *infra*.

CARR BECK, GATES & WOOD, named from Houghton Carr *infra*, *v.* bekkr, gata, wudu. CHURCH FIELD LANE, *Church Field* 1822 *EnclA* 49. FERN HILL. FLASS LANE, *v.* flasshe 'swamp'. HOLE HILL, *Hoile Hill* 1841 O.S., *v.* hol[1], hyll. HOLYWELL WOOD, 1841 O.S., *v.* Holy Well *supra*, wudu. HOUGHTON CARR, *Houghton Carr(e)* 1589, 1606, 1613 FF, *v.* kjarr 'marsh'. MICKLE HILL, 1841 O.S., *v.* micel, hyll. PARK FIELDS. RED HILL, 1579 *Dep*, 1841 O.S., *v.* rēad, hyll. WEETWORTH.

FIELD-NAMES

The forms in (*a*) are 1822 *EnclA* 49.

(*a*) Highbridge Field, High Field, Near Field, Ruscroft Field, Spawnd Hill Field, West Field.

(*b*) *Sutcliff* 1337 YD x (*v.* sūð, clif), *the Towne gaite* 1540 TestLds (*v.* tūn, gata).

xv. Pontefract

All the townships of this parish except East Hardwick, which remains a separate civil parish, now form the Municipal Borough of Pontefract. Knottingley with much of the township of Ferry Fryston 65 *supra* now forms an urban district.

1. CARLETON (97–4620)

Carleton(am) 1155–8 YCh 1451, Hy 2 (1230) Ch, c. 1200 Pont, 1258 YI, 1296 LacyComp, 1323 *MinAcct* 45, 1341 *Surv et passim*, *Karleton* c. 1212 Pont, 1258 YI. This is a common type of p.n. in YW and in all probability a Scandinavian form of the common OE *ceorla-tūn* 'farmstead of the churls or ordinary freemen', *v.* ceorl, karl, tūn (cf. EPN i, 89, ii, 2).

BATES HILL. CARLETON GREEN, 1841 O.S., v. grēne[2]. FURLONG
LANE. GREEN LANE, 1841 O.S., v. Carleton Green supra. LONG
LANE, 1841 O.S. MOOR LANE, cf. les, lee Mores 1424 Rent, v. le,
mōr. MOVERLEY FLATS. SWAN HILL, 1697 PontCD 194, v. swan,
hyll. WESTHAUGH. WHITE HO.

FIELD-NAMES

Spellings dated 1341 are Surv 10. 5.

(b) les Brekkes 1384 MinAcct, 1437 Surv (v. bræc[1]), crucem de Carlton
1505 TestLds (v. cros), Carleton Hall 1666 Visit, Dores 1341 (v. dor 'a gate'),
Larreputtez 1341 ('clay pits', v. leirr, pytt), Milnhulle 1341 (v. myln, hyll),
Scolyngraues 1341, Stayngraues 1341 ('stone pits', v. steinn, græf), Thorgram
Well 1341 (perhaps from the ON pers.n. Þorgrímr, wella), Westflatte 1341 (v.
west, flat), Wodegreue 1341 (v. wudu, græfe 'copse').

2. EAST HARDWICK (103–4618)

Herdewica 1120–2 YCh 1430, -wyk 1296 LacyComp
Herthewic, -wyk(e) 1121–7 YCh 1428, 1258 YI, 1328 Ch
Herdwik, -wyk(e) 1243 Fees, 1258 YI, 1368 MinAcct, 1402 FA
Hardwic(ke), -wyk(e), -wik(e) 1215 ChR, 1535 VE, (Est-) 1424
     Rent, 1437 Surv, 1456 WillY et freq, (East(e)-) 1558 WillY,
     1568 FF
Easthardwicke als. South(e)hardwicke 1608, 1614 FF

'Herd farm', v. heorde-wīc, in reference to that part of a manor
devoted to livestock as distinct from a bere-tūn or arable farm. The
spellings with Herthe- may be due to ON influence (cf. IPN 65).
'East' and 'South' in relation to West Hardwick and Blind Hardwick
79, 88 infra.

FIELD-NAMES

The principal forms in (a) are 1743 WYEnr 353 and in (b) 1437 Surv 11. 9.

(a) The Barr Crofts (v. bere 'barley', croft), Black hall acres, the Bull
Ing, the Low ffield, the Low Moor, Narrow Gate close, Oldfield Gap (v.
gap 'opening'), Water Ings (v. wæter, eng), the Wrang Lands (v. wrang
'twisted', land).

(b) Cokys hedland (the surname Cook, hēafod-land), Depehedebuttez, le
Dephedynge (v. dēop, hēafod, butte 'an abutting strip', eng 'meadow'),
le Hedeland (v. hēafod-land), le Lynghill (v. lyng 'heather', hyll), le Litelynge
(v. lytel, eng), Mideldyke (v. middel, dīc), Rygrodesyke (v. hrycg, rod[1]
'clearing', sīc), Southill (Syke) (v. sūð, hyll, sīc), Stankersted (v. stān, kjarr,
stede), Swynesyke (v. swīn, sīc), Wodwardthyng (the surname Woodward,
þing 'property').

3. KNOTTINGLEY (97–5023)

Notingelai, -leia 1086 DB, *Nottingl', -le(ya), -laia* 1147–54 YCh 1501,
c. 1154 Pont, Hy 2 (1230) Ch, 1155–8 YCh 1451, c. 1200 Pont
Cnottingel(e), -leg 12 Font, 1205 ChR, 1226, 1241 FF, 1241 Lib,
1254 Pat, *Cnottingaleia* 1155–70 YCh 1502, *Chnottingele* 1244
Lib, *Cnotingele* 1349 Ch
Knottingley(e), -lay, -yng- 1119–21, 1135–40 Pont, 1137–9 YCh
1492, Hy 3 *Heal* 159d, c. 1219 Selby, 1232 *Heal* 134, 1258 YI,
1294 Ch, 1296 LacyComp *et passim* to 1597 FF, *Cnottinglai, -leg*
Hy 2 *RegAlb* i, 66, 1202 FF, 1225 *RegAlb* i, 74d
Cnotneleia 1156 YCh 186, *Cnotinleia, -leg* 1173 YCh 197, 1230
RegAlb iii, 31d
Cnotinglai, -leg 1164–6 *RegAlb* i, 66, 1230 ib iii, 31d, *Knotinglay,
-yngley* 1280 *Ass*, 1502 Ipm

'The forest-clearing of Cnotta's people', *v.* -ingas, lēah. The first
el. is an OE pers.n. *Cnotta* suggested for Knotting Bd 15 and OE
Cnottinga hamm BCS 895 (Brk). Any connexion with OE **cnotta**
'hillock' (as proposed by Zachrisson, *Some English Place-Name
Etymologies* 30) must be rejected on topographical grounds; Knottingley lies low on the Aire bank. On the DB and other early spellings
with AN loss of initial *C-,* cf. Zachrisson, ANInfl 50, IPN 104.

BANK DOLE, 1844 *TA, Bankedale* 1675 *Comm* 53, *v.* banke, dāl
'share of the common land'. BANKS GARTH, 1844 *TA, v.* garðr,
Banks doubtless the surname. BENDLES, 1844 *TA.* THE CROFT,
v. croft. DOVEROYD HO. EAST INGS, 1793 *EnclA, v.* eng 'meadow'.
ENGLAND LANE, 1844 *TA.* FERNLEY GREEN. FERRYBRIDGE
POTTERY, *Pottery* 1841 O.S. GAGGS WARREN. GANDER HAVEN,
1841 O.S. THE GRANGE. THE HALL, *Old Hall* 1841 O.S. HEALD
LANE. HILL TOP, 1841 O.S. KERSHAW HO, 1817 M, a surname
Kershaw (cf. Kershaw iii, 132 *infra*). LEYS LANE, cf. *Leys Close
& Quarry* 1841 O.S., *v.* lēah. MARSH END, cf. *Beale Marsh* 1699
AireSurv, *v.* Beal 55 *supra*, mersc. MILL BRIDGE, cf. *Milnhill*
1530 *TN(Kn)*, named from *le Flete Milln* 1535 VE, *v.* flēot, myln.
MOOR HO, cf. *Moor Close* 1844 *TA* and Moor Dyke *infra, v.* mōr.
PARK BALK, 1844 *TA, v.* park, balca. PICKHILL GARTH, *Pighill* 1699
AireSurv, *v.* pightel 'a small enclosure'. THE RAMPART. ROPE
WALK, 1844 *TA.* ROUND HO. SIMPSON'S HILL, 1844 *TA.* SKEW
BRIDGE. SOUTH MOOR, 1771 M, *v.* sūð, mōr. SPAWD BONE,

Spawd House 1771 M, *Spaldbone Close* 1844 *TA*, from ME *spald-bone* 'shoulder bone', no doubt in allusion to the similarity in shape of the piece of ground. SPURRIER HOUSES, 1817 M, 1841 O.S., from the surname *Spurrier* (ME *sporier* 'spur-maker'), hūs. STOCKING LANE, *le Stockyng* 1341 *Surv*, *Stokyng* 1368 *MinAcct*, *Stockinge* 1586 *TN(Kn)*, *v*. stoccing 'clearing'. THORNTREE FLATS, *Thorntree Close & Flatt* 1844 *TA*, *v*. þorn, trēow, flat. THROSTLE ROW, 1844 *TA*, *v*. þrostle, rāw. TRUNDLES LANE, *Trendell'* (*loco vasto voc'*) 1368, 1480, 1486 *MinAcct*, *v*. trendel 'something of circular shape', here probably referring to a circular sweep of the Aire or the land enclosed by it. WEELAND, 1607 Hnt, *Wealand* 1694 PRClt, *v*. hwēol, land, denoting land enclosed in a turn of the Aire. WEST INGS, *Westenge* 1341 *Surv*, *the West(e)ynge* 1548 TestLds, *v*. west, eng. WILLOW GARTHS, 1844 *TA*, *v*. wilig, garðr. WILLOW ISLAND, 1841 O.S.

FIELD-NAMES

The principal forms in (*a*) are 1844 *TA* 250. Spellings dated 1341 are *Surv* 10. 5, 1368–1624 *MinAcct*, 1675, 1682 *Comm*, 1699 AireSurv, 1793 *EnclA*, 1841 O.S.

(*a*) Avie Pasture, Barncastle Close, Beck Close (ib 1675, *v*. bekkr, clos), Bone Mill Garth, Brockholes Close (*v*. brocc-hol 'badger hole'), Broom Hill (*v*. brōm, hyll), Bull Horn Close, Burdles, Butts Close, Cathill Layer 1771 M (*v*. catt, hyll), Clay pit Close, Clayton Garth (*v*. garðr), Claywick (*Claywicke* 1675, *v*. clǣg, wīc), Cock Garth, Cockholes Close, Crooked Far Street, Dogtail Flatt, East Ings (ib 1793, *v*. ēast, eng, cf. West Ings *supra*), Forge Hill, Goose Island, Greenhouse Close (*Green House* 1817 M), Greenwood Close, Hales 1841 (*v*. halh), Hazle Close, High Cross Close, Holes, Hugget Close, Ings Close (*v*. eng), Kinshaw Holes Close, Kitchen Chair, Little Marsh 1793, Long Lands, Low Green 1793, Marsh Close, Middle Field, Mill Close, Moor Dyke (*Moordyke Close* 1675, *v*. mōr, dīc, clos), Moorway Close, Park Gate, Penny Hill Close & Garth (*v*. pening, hyll), Pittage, Ploughedshot (dial. *shot* 'a division of land'), Pudding Bank, Quarry Holes, Racca & Racca Close (*Racca Field* 1841, *Racca Green* 1793), Racca Crabtree (cf. *Crabetres* 1368, *v*. crabbe, trēow), Rail Close, Royds Close (*v*. rod[1]), Ruddings Close (*v*. rydding), Set Cocks, Set Headland, Skipton Close (*five acres called Skipton* 1712 *WYEnr* 68), Stack Garth ('stack yard'), Stocking Close (cf. Stocking Lane *supra*), Stoney Lands, Swineholes Garth, Tanners Bar 1841, Tempest Garth, Tenter Balk Garth, Waithwheatfield, Wall Close, Warrens, Watchhouse Close, Waterfield Hill, Well Close, Willgoose or Wildgooseleyes 1712 *WYEnr* 68, Windmill Croft, Womens.

(*b*) *Bullockclose* 1675, *Buttlebank* 1530 *TN(Kn)*, *Cloghes* 1368 (*v*. clōh 'a dell'), *lez Dereinges* 1624 (*v*. dēor, eng), *doublespykynge(s)* 1384, 1421 (from e.ModE *duble-spiking* 'a large spike-nail', *v. Spikyng* 29 *supra*), *Flodmilne*

1368 (v. flōde 'gutter', **myln**), *Hadge Close* 1699, *Haghous* 1368, *le Hemp-garth* 1541 (v. **hænep**, garðr), *Lathegarthe* 1540 (v. hlaða, garðr), *Midelhurst* 1486 (v. **middel**, **hyrst**), *Rawcroft* 1682 (v. rāw, croft), *Roghstorth* 1368 (v. rūh 'rough', storð 'plantation'), *Spikyng* 1368 (v. *Doublespykynges supra*), *Thorncroft* 1461, 1486 (v. þorn, croft).

4. PONTEFRACT (97–4622) [ˈpɔmfrat, ˈpoumfrət]

In most early documents the name is in its Latin form: nom. *Ponsfractus* 1258 YI; acc. (*apud, ad*) *Pontemfractum* c. 1160 Pont, 1217 Pat, 1231 FF, 1412 SelbyOb; gen. *ad Fracti-pontis aquam* 1141 Ordericus (s.a. 1069), (*villa, castrum*) *Pontisfracti* p. 1122, 1159, 1258 Pont, 1166 RBE, 1272 Ebor, 1409 DiocV, *Pontefracti* 1215 ChR, 1428 FA; dat., abl. (*in*) *Pontefracto* 1090 *et freq* Pont (YCh 1418, etc.), 1120–2 *et freq Nost* (YCh 1429, etc.), 1156 YCh 186, l. 12 *Bodl* 2, Hy 2 (1230) Ch, 1194 P, 1234 FF, 1243 Fees *et passim* to 1452 Test ii. English and French forms are as follows:

Pontefratch 1100–35 Selby, *-frayth* 1297 YI, *-freyt* 1375 FF, *-fret* 1459 KirkstRent, *-fract(e)* 1340 *Ass* 1d, 1342 Calv, 1344 *Bodl* 26 *et freq* to 1817 M, *-frack* 1672 SelbyW

Pumfrate c. 1185–93 YCh 1624

Puntfreit 1226 FF, *Punfred* 1234 FF, *-frayt* 1295 YI

Pontfreit, -freyt 1303, 1402 Pat, *-frauit* 1352–62 Kirkst, *-ffrayt* 1374 BM, *-fret(t)* 1392 Brett, 1495 Ipm, 1611 PRDr

Pountfreyt, -frayt, freit 1323, 1340 *Ass*, 1388 Baild, 1398 YD i, 1399 Pat *et freq* to 1458 Pat, *-fret(t)* 1410 Pat, 1424 Baild, 1436 Test ii *et passim* to 1583 FF, *-fryt* 1555 BM

Pountifreit 1365 FF, *Pontifract(e)* 1415 Fabr, 1546 Test vi, 1547 WillY, *Pountefrett* 1544 *Surv*, *Pontyfrett* 1614, 1619 *Comm* 246

Pounfre(i)t 1409 YI, 1497 FF, *Pownfrett* 1454 Test ii, *Powmfrett* 1475 Linds

Pomfracch 1443 YD vi, *-fret(e), -frett(e)* 1472 Test iii, 1524 NCWills, 1529 TestLds, 1535 FF *et passim* to 1638 PRLds, *-frit(t)* 1500 YD iii, 1695 Pryme

The name of Pontefract arose on the foundation of the Priory of Cluniac monks and the establishment of the vill as the seat and castle of Ilbert de Lacy, a great Norman landowner in the district, whose estates formed the Honour of Pontefract. At the time of the DB survey the manor was known as *Tateshale, -halla* (v. Tanshelf 83 *infra*), and Symeon of Durham records that '*Taddenesscylf erat tunc villa regia quae nunc vocatur Puntfraite Romane, Anglice vero Kirkebi*'.

A place having two or three names is analogous to the case of Whitby (YN 126–7), which was variously known as *Streoneshalh*, *Prestebi* and *Witebi*; *Prestebi* was certainly a name for that part of the manor where Whitby Abbey was situated. Similarly *Kirkebi* (*v. Kirkby* 79 *infra*), which gave place to Pontefract by the twelfth century, doubtless bore reference to the Cluniac monastery, and Tanshelf remained the name of the more westerly part of the manor.

The name Pontefract means 'broken bridge' (Lat *pons fractus*, OFr *pont freit*); Holmes, *Pontefract, its Name, Lords and Castle*, identifies the site of the bridge as that of the present Bubwith Bridge (80 *infra*) which carries the road from Pontefract to Ferrybridge across a small stream called Wash Dike. This bridge, though providing an important communication with the Great North Road, is some distance from the centre of Pontefract.

The various forms of the name reflect both Latin and French origins. Pontefract is a survival of the documentary Latin form *pontem fractum*, etc., and the current StdE pronunciation ['pɔntifrækt] is a spelling pronunciation; a few spellings like *Pontifract(e)*, etc. carry this usage back to the fifteenth century. Other early spellings *Puntfreit*, *Pontfreit*, *Pountfreit*, etc., are from OFr, AN *pont(e)freit*, which was doubtless the regular form in the vernacular in early times. The later spellings *Pom-*, *Pown-*, *Powmfret*, as well as more recent local pronunciations ['pɔm-, 'pɔumfrət] are developments of this, with assimilation of the dental *-n-* to *-m-* before the labiodental *-f-*.

PONTEFRACT STREET-NAMES

BAILEY GATE, *vico voc' le Bayley* 1631 *MinAcct* 30, *Bayleygate* 1650 *ParlSurv* 46, named from *ballium* c. 1220 Pont, *le Baille* 1384, 1421 *MinAcct* 507, *le Bayl* 1475 Linds, *le Baylly* 1541 *MinAcct* 84, *the Balye* 1546 YChant, *the Bayly* 1555 TestLds, from OFr *bail* 'a palisade, the wall of an outer court of a castle' (here Pontefract Castle), *v.* gata.   BAXTER GATE (lost), *Baxtergate* 1421 *MinAcct* 507, 1690 *PontCD* 191, *Ba(c)kstergate* 1426 Ramsd, 1546 YChant, 1650 *ParlSurv* 46, *v.* bæcestre 'baker', gata, cf. Baxter Gate (Doncaster) i, 30 *supra*.   BEAST FAIR, 1782 *PontCD*, cf. *Nawtmerkette* (*infra*).   BOND GATE, *Bondegate* 13, c. 1220, 1253 Pont, 1296 LacyComp, 1368 *MinAcct* 26 *et freq* to 1541 ib 84, *Bondgate* 1421 ib 507, 1421 Rent, 1521 Test vi, *-gayte* 1546 YChant, *Bongate closes* 1658 WillS, *v.* bondi 'a peasant landowner', gata; this st.n. occurs elsewhere in YW, We, etc.   BOOTHS, *les bothes* 1384, 1421 *MinAcct* 507, 1424 Rent, *the boothes* 1519 TestLds, *v.* bōth 'a booth, a stall'.   CORN MARKET.   FINKLE ST, cf. i, 299 *supra*.   GILLY GATE, *vico Sancti Egidii* c. 1240 Pont, *Geli-*, *Gelygate* 1424 *Rent*, 1486 *MinAcct* 66, 1564 YChant, named from St Giles' church (*the*

chapell of St Gyles 1652 *ParlSurv* 47), *v.* **gata**. HALFPENNY LANE, formerly
PENNY LANE *infra*. HORSE FAIR, *the Horse-Fair* 1759 YDr, *v.* hors, feire,
cf. Horse Fair (Ripon) pt. v *infra*. LOVE LANE, *v.* lufu, lane. MARKET
PLACE, *the markett stede* 1528 TestLds, *Market-steide* 1546 YChant, *v.*
market, stede, place, cf. also (*the*) *Market cros*(*s*) 1651 PontCD 522, 1652
ParlSurv 47 (*v.* cros), which was another name for *Osgold Cross* 79 *infra*;
cf. also *Newmarket*, *North Markett* (*infra*). MICKLEGATE, *magno vico*
c. 1190, c. 1225 Pont, 1368 *MinAcct* 26, 1384 ib 507, 1424 Rent, *Mikilgate*
1461 *MinAcct* 509, 1486 ib 66, *Mikkylgate* 1519 TestLds, *Mi-*, *Mycklegate*
1546 YChant, 1649 WillS, 'the great street', *v.* mikill, gata. MILL DAM,
le Mylne dame 1541 *MinAcct* 84, cf. *le Southdame* (*infra*), *v.* myln, dammr.
NEWGATE, *Neugate* 1368 *MinAcct* 26, 1421 ib 507, *Newegate* 1384 ib, (*le*)
Newgate 1424 Rent, 1447 YD vii, 'new street', *v.* nīwe, gata. NORTHGATE,
Northgate c. 1215 Pont, 1379 PT (p), 1384 *MinAcct* 507 *et freq* to 1650
ParlSurv 46, *vico boriali Pontisfracti* 1324 Calv, *North Gaite* 1522 TestLds,
-*gayte* 1546 YChant, 'north street', *v.* norð, gata. PENNY LANE (now
HALFPENNY LANE), *Penilayn* 1406 TestLds, *Penny Lane* 1640 PontCD (this
was the road to Wakefield, for the upkeep of which the people of Feather-
stone were responsible; probably OE pening 'penny' (perhaps in allusion to a
penny-rate or toll for its maintenance), lane; it was also called *Yᵉ Street Way*
1675 Og. ROPER GATE, *Ropergate* 1323 *MinAcct* 45, 1341 *Surv*, 1384
MinAcct 507 *et passim* to 1658 WillS, -*gatte* 1515 TestLds, -*gaite* 1521 Test
vi, ME ropere 'a rope-maker', gata. SALTER ROW, *Salterrowe* 1368
MinAcct 26, 1384, 1421 ib 507, 1650 *ParlSurv* 46, *Saltrawe* 1424 Rent,
Saltrowe 1424 ib, 1461 *MinAcct* 509, *Salterawe* 1546 YChant, 'salt-makers'
or salt-merchants' street', *v.* saltere, rāw; cf. also *Saltergate* 1649 WillS
(*v.* gata). SOUTHGATE, *Suthgata*, -*gate* 1155 Pont, 1180–1200 YCh 1577,
c. 1180, c. 1228 Pont, *Sutgata*, -*gate* 1180–1200 YCh 1575, 13 *Nost* 98, *vico*
Australi 1384 *MinAcct* 507, *South*(*e*)*gate* 1495, 1540 TestLds, 1546 YChant,
Soughtgait 1551 TestLds, 'south street', *v.* sūð, gata. SPINK LANE.
WALKER GATE, (*le*) *Walkergate* 1322 YD xii, 302, 1368 *MinAcct* 26 *et passim*
to 1546 YChant, *Walkerstret* 1480 *MinAcct* 11, 'cloth-dressers' street', *v.*
walcere, gata.

Lost street-names include: *regiam stratam vocatam le Brig* 1495 TestLds
(*v.* brycg), *la Castelane* 1100–2 YCh 1418 (*v.* Pontefract Castle *infra*, lane),
Cokelon 1424 Rent (*v.* cocc², lane), *Cok*(*e*)*wel*(*le*)*gate* 1368 *MinAcct* 26, 1421
ib 507, 1424 Rent (*v.* cocc², wella, gata), *Coppergate* 1519 TestLds (probably
ON *koppari* 'joiner', gata, cf. Coppergate YE 285), *Cotelerrawe* 1384
MinAcct 507, *le Kolilerrowe* (sic) 1384 YD xii, 302, *Cotler-*, *Cottelerrowe* 1421
MinAcct 507 ('cutlers' street', from ME *coteler*, rāw), *Estgate* 1440
MinAcct 507 ('east street', *v.* ēast, gata), (*les*) *flesshebothe*(*s*) 1384 *MinAcct*
507, 1486 ib 66, -*boothes* 1426 Ramsd, *the fleshbothes* 1424 Rent (OE *flǣsc*
'flesh', bōth 'booth, stall'), *Fridaymarket* 1368 *MinAcct* 26, 1424 Rent
(*v.* Frigedæg, market), *Frystongate* 1437 *Surv* ('the road to Ferry Fryston
(65 *supra*)', *v.* gata), *Hemp Cross* 1716 PontCD 205 (*v.* hænep, cros),
Jordanlane 1486 *MinAcct* 66 (probably the ME pers.n. *Jordan*, lane),
Lether-, *the Leather Market* 1650 *ParlSurv* 46, 1734 PontCD 240 (*v.* market),
Little Lane 1753 PontCD 289 (*v.* lytel, lane), *London-gate* 1685 Bright 545

('the London road', *v.* gata), *Malfeigate, -fay-* c. 1220 Pont, 1413, 1496 YD xii, 302–3, *Malefaygate* 1344 *Bodl* 26 (OFr *malfei* 'ill-fated', used as a surname (cf. Reaney 225), gata), *Le Nawtmerkette* 1426 *Ramsd, Nawt-, Nautmarket(t)* 1546 YChant, 1685 *Bright* 545, 1711 *PontCD* 201 ('cattle market', *v.* naut, market, cf. Beast Fair *supra*), *Novo Mercato* c. 1210 Pont, *novo foro* 13 YD xii, 301, c. 1223 Pont, *Newmerket* 1487 *MinAcct, New(e) Market* 1546 YChant, 1607 *PontCD* 525 (*v.* nīwe, market, cf. Market Place *supra* and Pont i, 163 n. 3), *Northmarketplace* 1559, 1587 *MinAcct* 45, 72, *the North Markett* 1650 *ParlSurv* 46 (*v.* norð, market, place, cf. Market Place *supra*), *Hossegatelane* 1384 *MinAcct* 507, *Osgatelayne* 1421 ib ('Osgot's lane', *v.* lane, probably to be associated with *Osgold Cross* 79 *infra*), *Pinfoldlane* 1650 *ParlSurv* 46 (*v.* pynd-fald, lane), *Purston Row* 1708 *PontCD* 553 (*v.* Purston Jaglin 87 *infra*, rāw 'row of houses, street'), *Shepemerket* 1424 Rent (*v.* scēap, market), *le Sheperawe* 1437 *Surv* (*v.* scēap, rāw 'street'), *Shoe market* 1711 *PontCD* 199 (*v.* market), *Slutwell lane* 1686 *Bright* 550 (ME *slutte* 'a slut, a slattern', wella, lane, perhaps a name for a ducking-pool), *Stokwelgat* 1480 *MinAcct* 511 ('well with a pole', *v.* stocc, wella, gata, a common type of name), *Swinemarket* 1724 *PontCD* 211 (*v.* swin, market), *the Worth-gate* 1686 *Bright* 550 (*v.* gata, the first el. is possibly worð 'enclosure', perhaps shortened from Ackworth 93 *infra*, cf. *Ackworthzate* (sic) 1424 Rent).

Old buildings included 'a prison called *the Kidcott*' 1535 Star (a common NCy name for a town lock-up, *v.* NED s.v.), *the Motehall* 1484 Ch, *the Moitt Hall* 1535 Star, *the Moot Hall* 1799 *PontCD* 344 ('the moot-hall').

BAG HILL, *Baghil* 1159–70, c. 1170–83 YCh 1528, 1588 (Pont), 13 Pont, *-hull* 1368 *MinAcct* 26, *-hill* 1384 ib 507, 1424 Rent, 1473 YD xii, 302, 1541 *MinAcct* 84, *Baggahil* c. 1210 Pont, c. 1219 YD i (p), *Baggehil* 1222 Pont, *Bagehill* 1559 FF. The origin of *Bag-* in this and other p.ns. like Bag Hill ii, 177, Bagley i, 53 *supra* is not certain, but would appear to be an OE bagga 'bag', either as a topographical word 'bag-like hill' or as the name of some animal, possibly 'badger' (the problem is discussed in EPN i, 17 s.n.). *v.* hyll.

BRACKENHILL (lost), *Brakenhil(l)* c. 1090, c. 1160 Pont, Hy 2 (1230) Ch, *Brackanhil* 1119–2 Pont, *Brachehel* 1122 ib, *Brackeneil* 1135–6 ib, *Brakenehil* c. 1220 ib. This appears to be a different place from Brackenhill in Ackworth (94 *infra*) and to have been near Penny Lane on the borders of Purston Jaglin (cf. 1220 Pont). *v.* brakni, hyll.

FOULSNAPE (lost), *Fulsnaph* 12 Pont, *Fulsnap(e)* c. 1210, c. 1216, 1235 ib, 1546 YChant, *-snaape* 1475 TestLds, *Foul(e)snape* 1464 DodsN, *-snapp* 1566 FF. 'Foul poor pasture', *v.* fūl, snap or snæp 'boggy ground'.

GROVE TOWN, *Greve* c. 1200, c. 1210 Pont, *Grove Cottage* 1841 O.S. *v.* grǣfe 'a copse', replaced by ModE *grove* (from grāf), cf. Greavefield Closes 80 *infra*.

BLIND or SPITTAL HARDWICK, *Herd(e)wic* 12, c. 1196, 1251 Pont, *Spitle Hardwick(e)* 1294 DodsN, 1556 WillY, *Spittell Herdwike* 1535 VE, *Blynd-*, *Blind(e) Hardwick(e)* 1584 WillY, 1631 *Ramsd*, 1722 *PontCD* 664, *Hardwick, Blind*, or *Spital* 1822 Langd. 'Herd farm', *v.* heorde-wīc, cf. East Hardwick 72 *supra*, from which it is distinguished as *Spittal* (*v.* spitel) since it belonged to the Hospital of St Nicholas in Pontefract (called *Spitle* 1294 DodsN xi, 48, *le Spitill* 1384 *MinAcct* 507, *the Spitell* 1424 Rent, *Spitle Hedge* 1712 *WYEnr* 68, cf. YAJ xi, 48, Pont ii, 502), and also as *Blind* (*v.* blind) because there is no thoroughfare through the hamlet.

KIRKBY (lost), *Ki-*, *Kyrkebi, -by* c. 1090, 1122 Pont, c. 1137 SD, 1440 *MinAcct* 507. 'Church farm', *v.* kirkju-býr. There was a church in Tanshelf at the time of the DB survey, but this name may refer to the site of the monastery (cf. Pontefract 75, South Kirkby 40 *supra*).

MONK HILL, *monte(m) monachorum* c. 1190 Pont, *Munkhill* 1323 *MinAcct* 45, *Monkhull* 1368 ib 26, *-hill* 1384 ib 507 *et freq* to 1658 WillS. This was the site of the monastery. *v.* munuc, hyll.

OSGOLD CROSS (lost), 'a messuage over against *Osgodcross alias Pontefract Market Cross* adioyning the Chapell of St Gyles' 1652 *ParlSurv* (E. 317, Yorks 47). This is undoubtedly the cross from which Osgoldcross Wapentake was named (*v.* 1 *supra*); it was near Market Place 77 *supra*. The name means 'Osgot's cross', *v.* cros. The pers.n. *Osgot*, which also appears in the local street-name *Osgatelayn* 78 *supra*, is an anglicised form of ON *Āsgautr* (as in Osgodby YN 104, Horse Godly iii, 58 *infra*, cf. Feilitzen 164–6).

ST THOMAS'S HILL, *Sancte Thomas hill* 1558 TestLds 206. This hill was named after Thomas Earl of Lancaster who was beheaded here on 22 March 1322; a guild in Pontefract was also named after him (*Gilda B. Thomae Loncastr'* 1401 Test i, *Capelle sancti Thome* 1541 *MinAcct* 84), and a bequest to this guild in 1401 included the cost of constructing a stone cross instead of the wooden cross then standing *versus Montem Beati Thomae juxta viam ducentem versus Bongate* (Test i).

WATERFALL (lost), (*the*) *Waterfal*(*l*) c. 1204, c. 1230, 1235 Pont, 1480
MinAcct, 1552 TestLds, (-*field*) 1800 *EnclA* 146, *Watrefal* c. 1220
Pont, *le Watyrfall* 1437 *Surv*, *Waterfalle closes* 1541 *MinAcct* 84.
v. water-(ge)fall 'waterfall'; the original topography is obscured in
the built-up area near the monastery, but there are still springs in the
neighbourhood.

BUBWITH BRIDGE, crossing 'the beke that goos fro *Baghill brige* to
*Bubw*ᵗ *house* oppon the northe' 1521 Test vi; cf. Bubwith Ho 67
supra. Both are named from the family of *Bubwith* known in Pontefract from the fifteenth century (TestLds xxvi, 181, etc.), *v.* brycg.
BUTTON PARK, probably identical with *le Bothom*(*e*) 1384, 1421
MinAcct 507, *v.* botm, bōðm 'bottom'.   THE BUTTS (now a street),
1738 *PontCD* 253, *butte* c. 1200 Pont, *v.* butte 'an abutting strip in
the common field'.   CARR HILL, *v.* kjarr, hyll.   CHEQUER FIELD,
the Chekers 1526 Test v, *Chequer field*(*s*) 1658 WillS, 1664 *PontCD*
439, 1716 ib 207, *the Chequer-feild* 1686 *Bright* 550, 'chequered
field', cf. Chequer Close 24 *supra*, *Chakbord*, f.ns. 121 *infra*.
CHURCH BALK LANE, *v.* balca 'boundary ridge'.   COBBLER'S HILL &
QUARRY, cf. *Cobler Quarry* 1841 O.S.   DANDY WINDMILL.   DARK-
FIELD LANE.   DUNHILL'S HILL.   FAIRY HILL, 1817 M.   FRIAR
WOOD, *Fryer*(*s*) *Wood* 1686 *Bright* 550, 1705 *PontCD* 474, named
from the Black Friars of Pontefract (cf. YAJ xxxii, 397); *v.* frere,
wudu.   GALLOWS HILL, *ad furcas latronum* ('thieves' gallows')
c. 1190 Pont, *Gal*(*l*)*owhill-close* 1541 *MinAcct* 84, -*Crofte* 1578, 1587
ib 62, 72, *the gallowe hill* 1555 TestLds, *v.* galga, hyll.   GOSPEL
THORN (lost), *majori spina* 1235 Pont *v.* þorn; the successor of this
old thorn tree existed in 1892 at the point where the bounds of
Pontefract, Knottingley and Ferrybridge met; called *Gospel Thorn* in
the eighteenth century (Pont i, 199 n), because the Gospel was read
there when the parish bounds were beaten.   GREAVEFIELD CLOSES,
the Greave Closes 1685 *Bright* 545, *Greave field* 1709 *PontCD* 198,
Grave Field 1800 *EnclA* 146, *v.* græfe 'copse', feld; it is near Grove
Town 79 *supra*.   HARPER WELL (local, cf. Pont i, 150n), *Harpere
Welle* c. 1175 Pont, 'harper well', *v.* hearpere, wella; *le harper* is a
common byname in WCR.   LADY BALK.   NEW HALL (now OLD
HALL, in ruins), 1822 Langd, *Neuhala* c. 1160 Pont, 1234 FF, *v.*
nīwe, hall.   ORCHARD HEAD.   PONTEFRACT CASTLE, *Castello Pont'*-
fractis, -*Pontis*- 1119–35 Nost 7d, 1189 ib 4, *Castrum Pontefracti* Hy 3
BM, *castri Pontisfracti* 1296 LacyComp, *Pounfrete Castle* 1473 YD

xii, 302, *Pomefret Castle* 1561 *Dep*, founded by Ilbert de Lacy as his chief seat in the Honour of Pontefract, *v.* castel. PRAIL LANE, *Preall* 1684 *Glebe*, OFr *praiel* 'meadow'. RIDGLEY HILL. ST IVES WELL, cf. *St Ives Closes* 1716 *PontCD* 206, a well named probably from *St Ivo* (as in St Ives, Hu 221), *v.* wella. SHEEPWALK. SHOOLABOARDS LANE, *Shooell broodes* 1555 TestLds, 'narrow strips', *v.* scofl 'shovel', brǣdu 'breadth', a fairly common f.n. STREET FURLONG, 1712 *WYEnr* 68, 1757 *PontCD* 299, 'upon the streit toward Wentbrige called *the streit furlong*' 1407 TestLds, *v.* strǣt, furlang; the 'street' is Watling Street. TOLL HILL, *vico dicto tullonum* 13 *Nost* 116d, cf. *Gatelow Toll* 1707 *PontCD* 197, *v.* toln, hyll.

FIELD-NAMES

The principal forms (dated without source) in (*a*) are *PontCD*. Spellings dated without source are 1200–1253 Pont, 1384 *MinAcct* 507, 1406 TestLds, 1421 *MinAcct* 507, 1424 Rent, 1426 *Ramsd*, 1437 *Surv* 11, 9, 1440 *MinAcct* 507, 1472–1484 TestLds, 1486 *MinAcct* 66, 1495–1519 TestLds, 1521 Test vi, 1539, 1541 *MinAcct* 71, 84, 1548–1558 TestLds, 1554–1608 *MinAcct* 12, 19, 62, 72, 1615 *PontCD*, Chas 1 *Surv* 10, 1, 1650 *ParlSurv* Y. 46, 1685, 1686 *Bright* 545–50, 1690–1772 *PontCD*, 1800 *EnclA* 146.

(*a*) Broad Garth 1753, Broad Lane Garth 1707 (*v.* brād, lane, garðr), Cattle-Laithe 1822 Langd (*v.* cattel, hlaða 'barn'), Hemp or Hide Closes 1744, Highlands 1841 O.S., Hirst Garth 1713 ('a liquorice garth', *v.* garðr, *Hirst* may be the common YW surname *Hirst* from hyrst 'wood'), Lady Close 1733, Mapper Noul Hill 1737 (*Knaperknolle* 1541, *v.* cnoll 'hillock'), North Field 1737 (ib 1800, *the Northe feilde* 1555, *v.* norð, feld), Rankle Pits 1771 M (*v.* pytt, the first el. may be ME *rankle* 'a sore', perhaps simply a derogatory name), South ffield 1712 *WYEnr* 68, Town Fields 1727, Town's Close 1744 (*v.* tūn, feld, clos), Well Close 1717 (*Well close head* 1555, *v.* wella, clos), West Field 1711 (ib 1800, *v.* west, feld).

(*b*) *Abbay flat* 1424, *thabbay flaite* 1521 (named from the monastery, *v.* flat), *le Ancorhouse* 1608 (*v.* ancra 'recluse', hūs, doubtless an alternative name for *Hermitage infra*), *Auntlynhous* 1421.
Baclif 1541 (*v.* bæc, clif), *Baghill brige* 1521, *Baggill Brigges* 1558 (*v.* Bag Hill *supra*, brycg), *Baghill felde* 1541 (*v.* prec., feld), *le Balze* 1484 (*v.* balg 'rounded', applied to 'a rounded hill'), *Bateclose* 1505 (the pers.n. *Bate*, clos), *Beneflat, -pighull* 1424 (*v.* bēan, flat, pightel 'enclosure'), *Benetenges* 1384, 1421, 1424, *-ynge, -ings* 1424, *Bennet ynges* 1521, *-Ings* 1691, cf. also *Benets* 1424 (possibly beonet 'bent grass', but more probably the ME pers.n. *Benet* (from *Benedict*), and eng 'meadow'; *beonet* is usually reduced to *bent* in p.ns.), *Blackstonflat* 1424 (*v.* blæc, stān, perhaps as a surname, flat), *Bondegatcroftes* 1348 Baild (*v.* Bond Gate *supra*, croft), (*heremitag*', *hermatagü voc*') *le Bordell* 1384, 1421 (ME *bordel* 'a brothel', cf. *le Hermitage*

infra), *Bransill* 1437, *Brandisthill* 1505 (possibly from brant, stīg, hyll 'steep path hill'), *Branthill* 1384, 1421 (*v.* brant 'steep', hyll), *Bull hall* 1547.

Carter closes 1541, *le Casteldyke* 1437 (*v.* castel, dīc, cf. Pontefract Castle *supra*), *Catelyngplace* 1486, *Chapelgarthe* 1554, *Chaplegarth als. Connygarth* 1587 (cf. *Chapel* 1690 *PontCD* 192, *v.* chapel, garðr, *v.* also *Conyngarth infra*), *Cokcliff Turffmore* 1539 (*v.* cocc[2], clif, turf, mōr), *le Conyngarth* 1421, *Conygarth(e)* 1541, 1554 (*v.* coning-erth 'warren').

Dalebanke 1424 (*v.* dæl, banke), *Deadman grave* 1424, *Denvell* (a close) 1555, *les-*, *the Doles* 1384, 1421, 1424 (*v.* dāl 'share of the common land').

the feldes of Pontefract 1519 (*v.* feld), *Felterrode* 1200 (ME *felter* 'felt-maker', first recorded in 1605 (NED), rod[1] 'clearing'), *lez Ferrers* 1486 (probably ME *ferrer* 'blacksmith, farrier'), *Flaghil* 1214, *Flaggehill* 1541 (probably ON *flaga* 'flagstone' or *flag* 'turf', cf. flage, hyll), *Flatholme* 1424 (*v.* flat, holmr), *Foxesike* 1384 (*v.* fox, sīc), *le Frayre* 1406, *Les Freres* 1424, 1426, *lez Fratur* 1495, *le Fratour gardyn* 1539 (ME *frari*, e.ModE *fratrye* from OFr *frerie* 'fraternity, friary', cf. frère 'friar', cf. Friar Wood 80 *supra*).

Gilcroft(e)-sike, -syke 1424, 1437 (probably the ME pers.n. *Gille*, croft, sīc), *Grevelathes* 1424 (belonging to *Thomas Greves* ib, *v.* hlaða 'barn').

the headelande 1552 (*v.* hēafod-land), *le Hermitage* 1496 YD xii, 303 (cf. *gardinio vocato Reclus* 1421, *le Ancorhouse*, *le Bordel* (*v.* 81 *supra*), *v.* ermitage), *Heselclif* 1253 (*v.* hæsel, clif), *the hie garthe* 1528 (*v.* hēah, garðr), *Holle-, Holsyke* 1384, 1421, *Holksike* (sic) 1424 (*v.* hol[1], sīc), *Hudcroftegarth* 1424 (the ME pers.n. *Hudde*, croft, garðr), *Hundell* 1472 (possibly hund, hyll).

Impecroft 1215 (*v.* impa 'a sapling', croft), *Jouet acre* 1424 (the ME fem. pers.n. *Juet*, æcer, cf. Jowitt Ho i, 199 *supra*).

Keteldike 1424 (the ON pers.n. *Ketill*, dīc), *Knollesalmeshous* 1406 Pat, 1447 ib (the surname of *Robert Knolles* 1406 Pat, l.ME *almes-hous* 'almshouse').

the Lanes 1665 Visit (*v.* lane), *Langelayrode* 13 Nost 137d (*v.* lang, lēah, rod[1]), *les Leghes* 1384, 1421, 1424 (*v.* lēah 'clearing'), *Leverica acra* 1220 (*v.* lāwerce 'lark', æcer).

Malinsonȝerd 1424 (the surname *Malinson*, geard, here 'a garden'), *the Marle pitts close* 1685 (*v.* marle, pytt, clos), *Mylner well* 1505 (ME *milner* 'miller', perhaps as a surname, wella), *lez Moris* 1421 (*v.* mōr), *Mosylee* 1421 (*v.* mos, -ig, lēah), *Motonkerre* 1440 (cf. Mutton Flatt, *Motonkarre* 38, 42 *supra*, ME *moulton* 'sheep', kjarr).

Nethirferlong 1437 (*v.* neoðera, furlang), *le Newe close* 1541 (*v.* nīwe, clos), *Neucroft* 1421, *New(e)croft(e)* 1424, 1437 (*v.* nīwe, croft), *Northdame* (*stagni molend'*) 1486 (*v.* norð, dammr, cf. Mill Dam 77 *supra*, *Southdame infra*), *Nuttingwell* 1482.

lez Oldefeld 1484 (*v.* ald, feld), *Orgin Well* 1437, *Orgramwell* (*leys*) 1505, 1548, 1615, *Organ Well Leys* 1615 (probably OE *organa* (Lat *origanum*) 'penny-royal', wella, lēah).

a garden called Paradise 1424, *Parkerclose* 1578 (ME *parker* 'park keeper', clos, cf. Pontefract Park 83 *infra*), *the peele* 1521 (*v.* pēl 'a palisade'), *Pikles* 1535 VE (*v.* pightel 'small enclosure'), *Pynfold* 1424 (*v.* pynd-fald), *Potter-*

well 1421 (*v.* pottere, wella), *Preistbrigg close* 1686 (*v.* preōst, brycg, clos), *Puddinge Mittanes* 1650, *Puldale* 1424 (*v.* pōl, dæl).

le Quenecrosse 1437 (*v.* cwēn, cros).

(*le*) *Ris* 1215, 1216 (*v.* hrīs 'brushwood'), *Rotterclos* 1521 (*v.* clos).

Saddleholme 1608 (*v.* sadol, holmr), *Selware-, Scheldwarhil* 1210, 1216 (possibly an anglicised form of the ON pers.n. *Skialdvǫr, v.* hyll), *Seman-flates, -ynges* 1424, 1437 (ME *seman* 'seaman', probably as a surname, flat, eng), *Settery close* 1541, *Smithy Place* 1587 WillY (*v.* smið ðe, place), *Soure-land* 1424 (*v.* sūr, land), *le Southdame* 1384, *Suthtdam* 1473 YD xii, 302 (cf. *Northdame supra*), *le Spicerclose* 1475 (cf. 'the essart lately *Alice Spicer'* 1424, *v.* clos), *the Stulpe* 1424 (*v.* stólpi 'a stake, post'), *Sudfeld* 1216 (*v.* sūð, feld).

the Taverne 1521, *le Tenturgerde* 1322 YD xii, 302 ('tenter yard', *v.* geard), *Tenterland howse* 1424 (*v.* prec.).

Wekes 1201, 1216, *Welhouse* 1588 (*v.* wella, hūs), *Westrode* 1253 (*v.* west, rod[1]), *le Wyleghes* 1384, *leʒ Wylloghes* 1421 (*v.* wilig 'willow'), *mess' voc' Wyndston'* Chas 1, *Wollewell* 1384, 1421 (*v.* wella, the first el. may be wull 'wool'), *le Wood* 1539, 1541, *Wood in Pountfret* Chas 1 (*v.* wudu).

Yaldholme 1608 (*v.* jalda 'a nag', holmr).

5. PONTEFRACT PARK (97–4422)

parco Pontisfracti c. 1220 Pont, 1446 TestLds, *parco de Pontefracto* 1608 *MinAcct* 12, *Pontefreit Parke* 1294 DodsN, *the parke of Pomfrett* 1552 TestLds, *Pontefract Park(e)* 1659 WillS, 1822 Langd. *v.* Ponte-fract 75 *supra*, **park**.

PARKGATE HO, *Park Gate Farm* 1841 O.S., *v.* Pontefract Park *supra*, **geat**. PARK GRANGE, *Park House* 1817 M, *v.* prec. STRAWBERRY HILL.

FIELD-NAMES

(*a*) Monk Road 1771 M, Park Closes 1742 *PontCD* 263 (*Parke close* 1541 *MinAcct* 84, 1555 TestLds, *v.* Pontefract Park *supra*, clos).

(*b*) *Penyclose* 1480, 1486 *MinAcct* 511, 66, *Pennyclose* 1608 ib 12 (*v.* pening 'penny', clos, cf. Penny Lane 77 *supra*).

6. TANSHELF (97–4422)

Taddenesscylf 947 (11) ASC(D), *-sclyf* c. 1137 SD
Tatessella, Tateshal(l)e, -halla 1086 DB
Tanessolf 1165–75 YCh 1598, *Tanesolf(e)* 1258 YI
Tan(e)self 1255–8 YD i, 170, 1353 YD xvi, 99
Thanschelf 1296 LacyComp

Tans(c)helf(e) 1256 DodsN, 1257 Ch, 1296 LacyComp, 1335 FF, 1341 *Surv et passim* to 1619 DodsN
Tamschelf 1368 *MinAcct* 26
Tanshall 1535 VE, *Tanshill* 1546 YChant

'Tædden's shelf of land', *v.* scelf; the OE spelling with *scylf* (as well as the erratic form *-sclyf* in SD) is WSax (*v.* EPN ii, 106, 5). The OE pers.n. *Tædden* is not on independent record, but it could be a derivative with an *-en* suffix (cf. IPN 171) of the pers.n. *Tad(d)a* (as in Tadcaster pt. iv *infra*). The late OE spelling may not be reliable, cf. Ekwall, Studies[1] 12. The contraction to *Tan-* is noteworthy. *v.* Addenda.

AVERLANDS FM.   MARLPIT HILL, *Marlepittes* 1486 *MinAcct* 66, *Marl Pit House* 1817 M, *v.* marle, pytt.   MILL HILL, 1841 O.S., *Miln' hill* 1486 *MinAcct* 66, *the mylne Hill* 1515 TestLds, named from the windmill or *molend' ventr' de Tanshelf* 1486 *MinAcct* 66, *v.* myln, hyll.   PRIORY WOOD.

FIELD-NAMES

Spellings dated 1341 are *Surv* 10, 5, 1424 Rent; others dated without source are *MinAcct*.

(b) *Ap(p)ulyerd(e)* 1368, 1486 ('orchard', *v.* æppel, geard), *Cliflands* 1608 (*v.* clif, land), *Colmesholm* 1368, *North-*, *Southcolm(e)holme(s)* 1461, 1480, 1608 (possibly from the OE pers.n. *Culm*, for which *v.* Colmworth Bd 53, holmr), *Crulleshull'* 1368 (possibly ME *crull* 'curly', used as a nickname, hyll), *Flat(t)hom* 1341, 1486 (*v.* flat, the second el. may be OE hamm 'meadow', but it would be a unique example in YW and is therefore to be taken as a reduced form of holmr), *le Gores* 1296 (*v.* gāra 'a triangular piece of land'), *Grewlet* 1486, *Halgarth* 1486 (*v.* hall, garðr), *Kingsclose* 1608, *Ladynge* 1486 (*v.* ladda, eng), *Ledestonethorn* 1461 (*v.* Ledston pt. iv *infra*, þorn), *Legehurst* 1461 (*v.* hyrst), *Lindhull* 1341 (*v.* lind 'lime-tree', hyll), *Longacres* 1486 (*v.* lang, æcer), *Newchep* 1461 (*v.* nīwe, cēap 'market'), *North-*, *Southolm(e) holme(ʒ)* 1486 (*v.* holmr), *Stanescrosse* 1486 (*v.* cros, the first el. is probably stān, cf. Stansfield iii, 177 *infra*), *Stongroues* 1608 (*v.* stān, græf 'a pit' or grāf 'copse'), *Swaloghgreue* 1384, *Swalgrave* 1480 (*v.* swalwe[1] 'swallow', grāf, græfe 'copse'), *Tanshelfebarres* 1424 (*v.* barre), *Tamschelfgrene* 1368 (*v.* grēne[2]), *le Tengacres* 1461 (*v.* æcer), *Vikerclos* 1368 ('vicar's enclosure', *v.* clos), *Westchep* 1255–8 YD i, 170 (*v.* west, cēap 'market', cf. *Newchep supra*), *Westclos* 1368, *Westhag* 1368 (*v.* west, haga), *Westhorne* 1486 (*v.* west, þorn), *Wodegrene* 1486 (*v.* wudu, grēne[2]), *le Wrok* 1486.

xvi. Featherstone

The townships of Featherstone and Purston Jaglin now form Featherstone Urban District.

1. ACKTON (97–4122)

Aitone 1086 DB
Haiketon 12 Kirkst, *Haikton* 1379 PT
Aike-, *Ayketon*(*a*) 12 *Nost* 102, 13 Kirkst, 1243 Fees (p), 1297 LS, 1317 DodsN *et passim* to 1497 FF
Aicton c. 1166 Kirkst, 1614 FF, *Aykton* 1290 DodsN
Acton 1537 Test vi, 1564 WillY, 1638 SessnR, *Ackton* 1585 WillY

'Oak-tree farmstead', v. eik (possibly replacing OE āc), tūn, cf. Aketon (Follifoot) pt. v *infra*.

LOSCOE, *Loft Scoh* 12 Kirkst, *Loschou* 1459 KirkstRent, *Loschoo* 1537 TestLds, *Losco Grange* 1586 WillY, *Lost Cough* 1624 FF. 'Wood with a loft(house)', v. lopt, skógr, cf. Loscoe Wood i, 82, Loscar Wood i, 152 *supra*, Loskey House YN 62.

ACKTON HALL, 1841 O.S. ACKTON PASTURE, 1841 O.S., 1843 *TA*, v. pasture. CARR BECK, cf. *Carr Ing* 1843 *TA*, v. kjarr, bekkr, eng. FROBISHER WOOD. HAVERTOP LANE. STEPPING STONES. WEST END FM. WOOD HO, *Wodhouslayne* 1480 YD xii, 303, v. wudu, hūs, lane.

FIELD-NAMES

The principal forms in (*a*) are 1843 *TA*.

(*a*) Acre, Adams Royd (v. rod[1]), Balk Close (v. balca), Bean Close & Lands, Bloom Garth, Broom Close, Brown Leys End, Butcher(s) Close, Coal Pit Close, Coney Garth (v. coning-erth), Cutsyke Close (v. Cutsyke 70 *supra*), Dog Pit Close, Far Garth, Farthing Nook, Footgate Close, Gosslips, Hare Park Wood, Hell Hole Close, Hill Close, Intake (v. intak), Kiln Hill, Laith Close, Langfield Lands, Long Garth, Moor Close, Myers Close, Nearburn, Nether Field, North Moors, Pickard Ing (v. eng), Sough Close, Syke Ley Close, Top Green, West Croft, Willow Garth.

(*b*) *the Cawsey in Pomfrete Layne* 1537 Test vi (v. caucie, Pontefract 75 *supra*, lane), *Tachwait* 12 Kirkst (v. þak, þveit), *Waghemundesmire* 12 ib (possibly an OE pers.n. *Wægmund* which is, however, recorded only in the patronymic *Wægmunding* in *Beowulf*, but the form is difficult).

2. FEATHERSTONE (97–4221)

Fredestan 1086 DB　　*Friestane* 1166 RBE (p)

Ferestan(e) 1086 DB, 13 YD vii (p), 1292 *Nost* 63d

Federstan(a) 1108–14, 1119–28, 1120–2, 1121–7 *et freq* YCh 1428–
　　1601, 12 *Nost* (*freq*), 1270 ib 168, 14 *Sawl* 194, 1487 Ipm,
　　Federston 1458 DodsN, 1487 Ipm, 1535 VE, *Fedarstan* 1367 FF,
　　Fedyrstan 1392 WillY

Fedrestan(a) 1119–35 *et freq* Nost, 1124 Pont, 1167 P (p), *Federe-*
　　stan' 1190 P (p)

Fetherestan 1119–29 YCh 1488, 1244 YI

Fetherstan(a), -*stane* 12 *Nost* (*freq*) (YCh 1466, etc.), 1166 P (p),
　　1215 ChR, c. 1240, c. 1244 Pont, Ed 1 *Nost* 11d, 1280 Ch, 1286
　　Ebor, 1316 Vill *et passim* to 1428 FA, -*ston(e)* 1344 FF, 1428
　　FA, 1441 DiocV *et freq* to 1562 FF, *Fethirstan(a)* c. 1244 Pont,
　　1324 YD v, 1371 FF, 1431 Pat, -*ston* 1409 DiocV

Fethestain c. 1130–40 YCh 1466

Fedherstan e. 13 BM

Fedderstone 1562 FF

Featherston 1591 FF

The most satisfactory explanation of this name and of Featherstone
Nb, St, is that they are compounds of OE feoðer- 'four' (found only
in compounds) and stān, denoting 'four stones' and doubtless
referring in each case to a cromlech or a tetralith with three standing
stones surmounted by a fourth. But no trace of any such tetralith
has survived; cf. Introd. The numerous early spellings with -*d*- are
due to AN influence (cf. IPN 109) and the single form with -*stain* to
the substitution of ON steinn.

CHURCH LANE, cf. *Church Close & Garth* 1842 *TA*, v. clos, garðr.
COMMON SIDE, cf. *Common Close* 1842 *TA*.　　FEATHERSTONE
COMMON, 1841 O.S.　　FEATHERSTONE GREEN, 1841 O.S., v. grēne[2].
HEPRON WOOD, *Hipron Wood* 1842 *TA*, perhaps from Hipperholme
iii, 79 *infra*, as a surname.　　MANOR HO.　　PARK LANE, cf. *Park Field*
1795 EnclA 45, 1842 *TA*, v. park.　　SAND PIT, cf. *Sand Hole Close*
1842 *TA*, v. sand, hol[1], pytt.　　SEWER BRIDGE, *Sough Bridge* 1841
O.S., v. sogh 'bog', brycg.　　SPRINGFIELD FM.　　WARREN FM,
Warren House 1841 O.S., *Warren Hill* 1842 *TA*, v. wareine.　　WILLOW
LANE, cf. *Willows* 1842 *TA*, v. wilig.

FIELD-NAMES

The principal forms in (a) are 1842 *TA* 2. Spellings dated 12 are *Nost* 102, 1530–1545 TestLds, 1795 *EnclA* 45.

(a) Great & Little Anthem, Arnold Close, Balk Close (*v.* balca), Brig Ing (*v.* brycg, eng), Broomhill (*Bromehill* 1641 *MinAcct* 39, *v.* brōm, hyll), Burl Ings (*v.* eng), Calf Garth, Coal Pit Close, Cutt Ing (*v.* cut, eng), Darley Close & Little Moor, Flask Close (*Flaskes* 12, *v.* flask 'swamp'), Great & Little Moor, Flask Close (*Flaskes* 12, *v.* flask 'swamp'), Great & Little Folly (*v.* folie), Gilly Garth, Goit Ing (*v.* gota, eng), Hanging Close (*v.* hangende 'steep', clos), Harps, Hoblass Close, Hungerhill Close (*Hungriha* (sic) 12, *v.* hungor, hyll), Jub Garth, Kelham Close, Long Ing, Middle Field (ib 1795), Mill Field & Hill (*Mill Field* 1795), Moor Field (ib 1795, cf. *Moreland* 1487 *MinAcct* 66, *Fethirstone More* 1530, *v.* mōr, feld), North Garth, Pickhill Close (*v.* pightel), Pit Close (*Pittclosse* 1635 *YAS* 78, 7, *v.* pytt, clos, cf. Coal Pit Close *supra*), Priss Garth, Rail Close, Red House Close, Round Hill, Shillit Close, Sour Ing (*v.* sūr, eng), South Garth, Spetch Garth, Swine Acre, Sybil Close, Toftons, Washing Stand Ing, West Ings (*Westenge* 12, *v.* west, eng), White Flatts, Wood Close.

(b) *Birdales* 12 (*v.* bȳ, gen.sg. bȳjar, dāl 'town shares in the common land'), *Birkflat, Brek(e)flat* c. 1244 Pont (*v.* bræc[1] or brekka, flat), *Langlandes* 1531 (*v.* lang, land), *Newhall* 1665 Visit (*v.* nīwe, hall), *the Scotfold* (sic) 1531 (*v.* fald), *Woderode* c. 1240 Pont (*v.* wudu, rod[1]).

3. PURSTON JAGLIN (103–4319)

Preston(e), -*tona* 1086 DB, 1120–2 YCh 1430, 1159–70 ib 1595–6,
  1166 RBE (p), 1200–20 YCh 1599, 1201 Cur (p), 1219 FF *et passim* to 1605 FF, (-*Jakelin*, -*Jakelyn*) 1269, 1334, 1340 FF, 1371 Baild *et passim* to 1497 FF, (-*Jacklinge*) 1605 FF
Pruston Jackling(e), -*lynge* 1581–1583 FF, 1597 SessnR *et freq* to 1641 Rates, -*Jacklyn* 1650 ParlSurv 48
Pruston Jackling 1658 WillS

'Priests' farmstead', *v.* prēost, tūn. *Jakelyn*, a diminutive of OFr *Jacques*, is probably the name of some feudal tenant who has not yet been identified. On the form *Purston* cf. Phonol. § 16.

COMMON LANE, named from *Purston Common* 1771 M, *Common Side* 1817 M. FIELD HO, named from *campis de Preston* 1437 *Surv*, *Preston feild* 1641 *MinAcct*, *v.* feld. GIRNHILL LANE, *Grenehill* 12 *Nost* 101d, *Gernill Field* 1843 *TA*, 'green hill', *v.* grēne[1], hyll. HOUND HILL LANE, *Hound Hill Field* 1811 *EnclA* 21, *v.* Hundhill

Hall 94 *infra*. MONKROYD FM, *Monkred* (sic for *-rod*) 1524 NCWills, *Monckroade* 1644 WillY, *Monkrode* 1666 Visit, 'monks' clearing', *v.* munuc, rod[1]. RAVENSKNOWLE FM. SHEEP BRIDGE, 1841 O.S., *v.* scēap, brycg. LITTLE WENT BRIDGE, 1841 O.S., *v.* Went Bridge 51 *supra*, brycg.

FIELD-NAMES

The principal forms in (*a*) are 1843 *TA* 323. Spellings dated 1437 are *Surv* 11, 9, 1480 YD xii, 303, 1641 *MinAcct* 39, 1811 *EnclA* 21.

(*a*) Apple Tree Flatt, Ash Croft, Baxter Hill, Broad Ing, Calf Croft & Garth, Castle Syke, Chappel Close, Coney Close, Crabtree Flatt, Diblands Close & Field (*Dibbelland* 1437, *Diblands* 1811, perhaps connected with ModE *dibble* (*v.* dibbing), land), Docking (*v.* docce, eng), Dymond Close, Ell Close, Gods House Close, Gooding Leys, Goose Croft, Gores (*v.* gāra), Half Acres, Hall Slacks, Holgate Close (*v.* hol[1], gata), Ings (*v.* eng), Martin Close, Moat Close, Moor Close, Mosley Field (ib 1811 *EnclA*, *v.* mos, lēah), Nooking, Outgang Close (*v.* ūt-gang), Park Close, Pasture Hill Field (ib 1811), Pease Roods, Pick Hill, Pindfold, Slaning Close, Spring well Balks, Syke Close (*Preston Syke* 1437, *Syke Field* 1811, *v.* sīc 'stream'), Toad Hole, Went Close (*v.* Little Went Bridge *supra*), Willow Garth & Holes, Wood Slacks, Wranglands (*v.* wrang, land).

(*b*) *Cobgraveflatt* 1480, *Killingcrofte als. Gillingcrofte* 1641 (*v.* croft, the first el. is probably a surname), *Kirkfurlang* 1480 (*v.* kirkja, furlang), *Nethyrfeld* 1480 (*v.* neoðera, feld), *Whitehouse* 1658 WillS (*v.* hwīt, hūs), *Woodfield* 1630 PontCD.

xvii. Wragby

Huntwick was formerly part of Purston Jaglin township. Foulby (now in Huntwick township), though always in Wragby parish, was formerly in Sharlston township (114 *infra*).

1. WEST HARDWICK (103–4118)

Harduic, Arduwic 1086 DB

Hardewic(h) 1108–14 YCh 1465, 1189 *Nost* 4, *Hartwic* c. 1156 Pont

Herdewic(a), -wyk(e) 1119–35 *Nost* 7d, 1227 ib 5d, 1251, 1280 Ch, 1334 FF, (*West-*) 1390 *Nost* 67d, 1400 Pat, *Erdewyk* 1400 YD i

Herdvic, -wic 1159–70 YCh 1595–6, e. 13 *Nost* 106

Herthewyke, -wic(k) 13 YD i, l. 13, 1343 *Nost* 66d, 172

West Hardwike, -wick(e) 1559 YD i, 1585 WillY, 1615 FF

v. East Hardwick 72 *supra*.

THE BUSHES, *Hardwick Bushes* 1841 O.S., *v.* busc.   HARDWICK
BECK, *v.* bekkr.   RIGLET LANE.   SOUTH INGS FIELD, 1843 *TA*, *v.*
sūð, eng.

FIELD-NAMES

The principal forms in (*a*) are 1843 *TA* 191. Spellings dated e. 13 are
Nost 106, 1641 *MinAcct* 39.

(*a*) Butland Field, High Shutt Field (dial. *shut* 'a division of land'), Hill
Top, Low Field.

(*b*) *Brodheng* 13 YD i (*v.* brād, eng), *Fayrewell laine* 1641 (*v.* fæger, wella,
lane), *le forkedetre* e. 13 ('the forked tree', *v.* trēow), *Hesthilles* e. 13 (*v.*
hestr 'horse', hyll), *Magge flatts* 1641 (the fem. pers.n. *Mag*, flat), *le Slacks*
1641 (*v.* slakki 'a hollow'), *Westrodes* 1641 (*v.* west, rod[1] 'clearing'), *Wood-
inge* 1641 (*v.* wudu, eng).

2. HESSLE (103–4317)

Hasele, Asele 1086 DB
Hesal 1119–35 *Nost* 7d
Hesel(a) 12 *Nost* (*freq*) (YCh 1428, etc.), 1215 ChR, 1255–77 *Nost*
   103, *Hesella* 1189 *Nost* 4
Hesil(l), -*yl* 1277–91 *Nost* 168d, 1370 Baild, 1397 TestLds *et freq*
   to 1577 DodsN
Hassell 1527 FF
Heysyll 1532 FF
Hesle 1558 WillY
Hessell 1587 WillY, 1665 Visit

'The hazel-tree', *v.* hæsel, cf. Hessle YE. The predominant *Hesel*
form doubtless represents the substitution of the cognate ON hesli
(cf. Phonol. § 1).

WRAGBY

Wraggebi, -*by* 1160–70 YCh 1597, 13 *Nost* 65d, 103d, 104, 1308,
   1315 WCR (p)
Wragheby 1332 Ipm
Wragby(e) 1343 *Ass* 7, 1400 Pat, 1533 FF, 1652 PRRth
Wrauby 1360 *Ass* 1
Wraweby 1375 FF (p)

'Wraghi's farmstead', from the ODan pers.n. *Wraghi* and bȳ. The
pers.n. is distinctively East Scand (cf. Introd.).

HANGING BANK, 1843 *TA*, *v.* hangende 'steep', banke.   HESSLE
BECK.   HESSLE COMMON, 1841 O.S.   HESSLE HALL, 1817 M.
HILL TOP, 1817 M.   KING ROYD LANE, *East-*, *Westkingroids* 1615
YAS 78. 1, *v.* rod[1] 'clearing', the first el. may be cyning or the
surname *King*.   LONGLEY WOOD, *Langeleye* 13 *Nost* 34, *v.* lang,
lēah.   OFFLEY BRIDGE, 1841 O.S.   OWLET HALL, 1817 M, a
common type of name in which *hall* is combined with a bird-name,
cf. Gawthorpe 102 *infra*.   ROEBUCK WOOD, 1841 O.S.   TAYLOR
WOOD, 1841 O.S.   WENT LANE, cf. Went (RNs.).

FIELD-NAMES

The principal forms in (*a*) are 1843 *TA* 208. Spellings dated 1277–91,
l. 13, 1347 are *Nost* 107d, 168d, 172, 177, 1554, 1578, 1605 *MinAcct*.

(*a*) Bason Green 1841 O.S. (*Basinge grene* 1554, 1578, on the pers.n.
Basing cf. Bassingthorpe i, 182 *supra*, *v.* grēne[2]), Black Butts, The Flatt (*v.*
flat), Hessle Green 1841 O.S. (*v.* grēne[2]), The Ing (*v.* eng), Jennett Pighill
(*v.* pightel 'enclosure'), Ox Close, Rob Royd (the pers.n. *Rob*, from *Robert*,
rod[1]), Wood Close.

(*b*) *Birkclif* 1277–91 (*v.* birki, clif), *Cauwisrodo* 1277–91 (*v.* rod[1]), *Dede-*
mangraue 1347 (*v.* dēad, mann, græf 'pit'), *Douuedale* 1277–91, *Dowdalefeild*
1605 (*v.* dūfe 'dove', dæl), *Hamund croft* 1277–91 (the ON pers.n. *Hámundr*,
croft), *Heseker* 1277–91, *Hesilker* 1341 *Surv* ('Hessle marsh', *v.* kjarr), *Hesel-*
scathe, *Hesilschaye* l. 13 ('Hessle wood', *v.* sceaga), *Mukescroft* 1277–91
(probably ODan *Mukke* or a strong form of OE *Muca*, croft), *le Nue Rydinge*
1347 (*v.* nīwe, rydding 'clearing'), *New Roydes* 1605 (*v.* nīwe, rod[1] 'clearing'),
Pristflatte 1554, *Prestes flatte* 1578 (*v.* prēost, flat).

3. HUNTWICK (103–4019)

Huntwic, *-wyk*, *-wick*(*e*) 1166–93 YCh 1610, 1193–1210 ib 1611,
     1203 *Nost* 9, 1371 DodsN, 1402 FA *et passim* to 1608 FF
Huntewik, *-wic*(*h*), *-wy*(*c*)*k* 13 *Nost* 105d, 108d, 1202 DodsN, FF,
     l. 13 *Nost* 172, 1314 Pat, 1573 WillY, (*Heye-*, *Hauer-*, *Hare-*)
     13 *Nost* 172, 175–6, *Huntewykes* 1280 Ch

This may denote 'the hunter's dwelling' or contain the OE pers.n.
Hunta, *v.* wīc. In the thirteenth century there appear to have been
two parts of the manor called *Huntewykes*, each part distinguished as
Heye- (from (ge)hæg 'hunting enclosure') and *Hauer-*, *Hare-*
(probably from hafri 'oats', denoting the arable part of the
manor).

FOULBY

> *Folebi*, *-by* 1166–93 *Nost* 105, 109, 13 ib 107, YD x, 1291–1312 *Nost* 170d, 1326 *Ass* 1, 1407 YD vii
>
> *Folleby* 13 *Nost* 107
>
> *Folby*(*e*) 1390 *Nost* 67d, 1400 Pat, 1415 *Bodl* 71 *et freq* to 1585 FF
>
> *Foulby* 1437 Baild, 1555 FF, 1634 WillY
>
> *Fouldbie*, *-by* 1591 WillY, 1607 FF   *ffowbye* 1598 SessnR

'Foli's farmstead', from the ON byname *Foli* (LindBN) or ODan *Foli* (DaGP), *v.* bȳ.

NOSTELL PRIORY

> *Osele* 1086 DB   *St Oswald del Ostell* 1424 Rent 258
>
> *Nostlec* 1108–14 YCh 1465 (*Nost*)
>
> *Nostla* a. 1114 Dugd vi, 1121–9 YCh x, 1126–1180 YCh 1012–32 (*freq*), 12 *Nost* (*freq*)
>
> *Nostleighe* a. 1114 (15) Tockw, *Nostlai*, *-lay* 1121–7 YCh 1428, 1189 *Nost* 4, 1215 ChR, *Nosteleia* 1130–40 YCh 1466
>
> *Nostel* 1115–20, 1135–9, 1156–9, 1160–80 YCh 1034, 1433, etc. (*Nost*), e. 13 *MaryY* ii, 70d, 1249, 1300 Ebor
>
> *Nostlad* 1147–53 YCh 1017, 1154–9 ib viii, *Nostlath* 1148–52 ib, p. 1153 YCh vi, 1154–69 Tockw, 1189 *Nost* 4d, *Nostleth* 12 YCh vi, 1189 *Nost* 4d, *Nostlat* 1188–1202 YCh viii, e. 13 Tockw, *Nothlathes* 1331 *Ass* 5
>
> *Nosthle* 1147–53 YCh vi, *Nostle* 1175–90 YCh 1591, l. 12 ib vi, e. 13 *RegAlb* ii, 19, 1219 FF, 1220 Cur, 1240–50 *Bodl* 69, 1247, 1249 *RegAlb* ii, 6d, iii, 93
>
> *Nostele* 1237 Ebor, 1379 *Bodl*
>
> *Nostelle* 1280, 1282 Ebor
>
> *Nostell* 1300 Ebor, 1380 Ch, 1400 Pat, 1409 DiocV *et passim* to 1624 FF, (*-Abby*) 1666 Visit
>
> *Nostall* 1654 PRHtnP

Nostell was the site of an important Augustine priory dedicated to St Oswald, King and Martyr, and founded in 1121; the appearance of the name in DB would therefore rule out any connexion with the name of St Oswald (which was one of Moorman's suggestions). Goodall 72 rejects the DB spelling *Osele* without initial *N-* on the grounds of the later spellings which have it regularly, and he supposes that Nostell is an *-el* derivative of some word connected with

OFris *nōst*, MLG *nöste*, which mean 'water-trough'. Ekwall (DEPN), following another of Moorman's suggestions, accepts the DB form and takes the name as a compound of OE ōsle 'blackbird' and lēah 'glade'. Whilst there is ample evidence elsewhere to illustrate the prefixing of initial *N-* from the old def.art. *atten* through wrong analysis, as in Nosterfield YN 223, etc. (*v.* EPN i, 13–14 s.v. **atten**), the very early and persistent spellings with *-t-* in *Nost-* do not support Moorman's proposal, especially as other YW p.ns. which probably contain OE ōsle (Ouslethwaite i, 293, Ossett 188 *infra*) provide no parallel to this development of an intrusive *-t-*. In addition, none of these suggestions satisfactorily explains the various early spellings with *-lad*, *-lath*, *-leth* (which are not cited by these authorities). Such spellings as *-lath*, *-lad* could be derived from ON hlaða 'a barn', but *-leth* is an unusual variant of this. In any case the final element must have been a rare word to have lost its etymological significance early enough to give rise to these variants, as well as to confusion with lēah (in *Nostleighe*, etc.) and its ultimate disappearance (in *Nostle, Nostel*, etc.). The most likely source seems to be OE lǣd or lād 'water-course', with *-th* through ON influence or confusion with *hlaða* 'barn', and with *-leighe* (and subsequently *-le*, *-el*), due in the first place to AN variants of *-th* (cf. IPN 109). The first el. could be an OE *nōst* cognate with OFris *nōst* 'cattle-trough', MLG *noest* 'bucket', OHG *nuosc* 'conduit' (as suggested by Goodall), assuming that the DB spelling is erratic; a similar word appears in Nost Ing (Hawksworth) pt. iv *infra*. But if initial *N-* is not original, the first el. should be from OE ōst 'a knob, protuberance, a knot', probably used topographically of a hillock or protuberance in the ground (cf. Ekwall, Studies[1] 75); such a description might well apply to what is now called Planetree Hill by which Nostell Priory stood. On the whole, amongst these speculative suggestions, an OE *nōst-lǣd* 'water-course used as a conduit or providing a drinking-place for cattle' seems most likely on formal as well as topographical grounds.

COLCAR ING WOOD, *Cot(e)carreflatte* (sic) 1554, 1578, 1587 *MinAcct*, *Conquering Wood* (sic) 1841 O.S., *v.* cot 'cottage', kjarr 'marsh', flat; *Col-* for dial. [kɔu] is an inverted spelling after *Cotecarre* was reduced to *Cocar*. GARMIL LANE. HUNTWICK GRANGE, 1841 O.S., *Hunwick(e) gra(u)nge* 1554, 1578 *MinAcct*, *v.* grange. HUNT-WICK LANE, *Huntewic lane* 13 *Nost* 176d, *v.* lane. HUNTWICK

WHIN, 1841 O.S., *v.* hvin 'gorse'.   SWINE LANE, *Swyne Lane* 1650
ParlSurv, Swine-Lane-House 1822 Langd, *v.* swīn, lane.   UPPER
LAKE, 1841 O.S., one of three lakes in Nostell Park.   THE WILLOWS.

FIELD-NAMES

Spellings dated 13 are Nost 108d, 172–177, 1554–1641 *MinAcct.*

(*a*) Eighteen pounds close 1840 *TA* 305.

(*b*) *Barkerroodes* 1559, 1578, *Berk'roodes* 1641 (*v.* barkere 'a tanner',
rod[1] 'clearing'), *Bonderodes* 13 (*v.* bondi 'yeoman', rod[1]), *Brakenlay, -leye* 13
(possibly identical with Brackenhill 94 *infra, v.* brakni, lēah), *Depker* 13
('deep marsh', *v.* dēop, kjarr), *Goselingbanc* 13 ('gosling bank', *v.* banke),
Huntewichille 13 (*v.* hyll), *Huntewicslac* 13 (*v.* slakki 'a hollow'), *Mickebrode*
13 (*v.* micel, brǣdu), *Neubrec, Huntewicbreck'* 13 (*v.* brǣc), *Olde-, le Holde-*
mor 13 (*v.* ald, mōr), *Orgraueker* 13 (*v.* ōra[2] 'ore', grǣf 'pit', cf. Orgreave
i, 184 *supra*), *Robinsic* 13 (the pers.n. *Robin*, sīc 'stream'), *Rodeyerd* 13 (*v.*
rod[1] 'clearing', geard), *Whinney close* 1641 (*v.* hvin 'gorse', clos).

xviii. Ackworth

ACKWORTH (103–4417)

   Ac-, Aceuurde 1086 DB
   Hacwrda 1119–35 *Nost* 7d, *Hachewrda* 1119–47 ib 73, *Hackewrthe,*
      -a 1119–29 ib 14 (YCh 1488), c. 1130–40 ib 73 (YCh 1467), 1215
      ChR, *Hachaworda, -wrtha* 1121–7 *Nost* 130, 1189 ib 4, *Hake-*
      word', -wurda 1190–1193 P
   Akeworth, -w(u)rth 1201 Cur, 1240 Ebor, 1291 Tax, 1428 FA
   Ackew(o)rth(e) 1227 *Nost* 6, 1296 LacyComp, *MinAcct* 1, 1307
      Pat, 1366 YD i, 1369 FF, 1379 PT, 1551 YD viii, *Akkeword* 1302
      Ebor
   Akeswrthe 1286 Ebor
   Acworght 14 *Sawl* 194
   Akword 1300 Ebor, *Ac-, Akworth(e)* 1316 Vill, 1341 *Surv*, 1368
      MinAcct 26, 1402 Pat *et passim* to 1638 BM
   Aickworth 1619 DodsN
   Ackworth 1771 M

Apart from the 1190–1193 P spellings and that in 1215 ChR, all
the early forms with initial *H-* are from a single manuscript (*Nost*),
and too much stress need not be laid upon them. There is ample
evidence for inorganic *H-* in the early ME forms of YW p.ns. (such as

Adwick i, 79 *supra*, Addingham pt. vi, Ainsty pt. iv, Aismonderby (Ripon) pt. v, Ilkley pt. iv, etc., *infra*), but none occurs for the loss of OE initial *h*-. Ackworth, therefore, is 'Acca's enclosure', from the well-evidenced OE pers.n. *Acca*, and worð. The early spellings with -*ck*- favour this rather than OE āc 'oak-tree', which occurs in Oakworth pt. vi *infra*.

BRACKENHILL, *Brakanhill* Ed 1 BM, 1557 WillY, *Brakenhyll*, -*hil*(*l*) 1384 *MinAcct* 507, 1567 WillY, (-*cliff*) 1486 *MinAcct* 66, *Braknyll* 1402 Pat, *Brakynynghilcliff* (sic) 1461 *MinAcct* 509, *Brackenclyff* (sic) 1608 ib 12. *v.* **brakni, hyll, clif**, and cf. *Brackenhill* 78 *supra*.

HUNDHILL HALL, *Hundehill'* 1200 Cur, *Hunhill* 1379 PT (p), *Hunsdell* 1472 Test iii, *Hundyll* 1562 FF, *Hundill-Hall* 1822 Langd. 'Hounds' hill', *v.* **hund, hyll**, doubtless referring to a hill where dogs were kept; cf. *Bitch Hill* 186, Hungate (Ripon) pt. v, Hund Hill (Newton on Hodder) pt. vi *infra*.

ACKWORTH CARR BRIDGE, *Carr Bridge* 1841 O.S., *v.* **kjarr, brycg**. ACKWORTH GRANGE, 1841 O.S., *v.* **grange**.   HIGH & LOW ACKWORTH, 1771, 1817 M, the two villages in the township.   ACKWORTH MOOR TOP, 1771 M, 1841 O.S., named from *Ackworth Moore* 1658 WillS, cf. also *Morhull* 1341 *Surv*, *Moorhillfield* 1712 *WYEnr* 68, *Moorside* 1368 *MinAcct* 26, *Moreside* 1384 ib 507, *v.* **mōr, hyll, sīde, topp**.   ACKWORTH PARK, *his* [*the king's*] *parkes of* . . . *Akworthe* 1544 *Surv*, *Ackworth Park*(*e*) 1658 WillS, 1775 *WB* 75, *v.* **park**.   BERRIL FM, *Burnil Closes or Burnil houses* 1656 *Bright* 531, probably the surname *Burnel* (cf. Burnhill 96 *infra*), *v.* **clos, hūs**; the form of the name has been influenced by that of Burial Field *infra*, near which it lies.   BROOMHILL PLANT.   BURIAL FIELD, *Bennit Ings or Burial field* 1685 *Glebe*, *Berrill field* 1712 *WYEnr* 68; the older name is from the surname *Bennet* and eng 'meadow'; the current name probably originated in the ground being a burial place of victims of the Plague; on the main road a little west of the site is the Plague Stone (grid 446190).   CASTLE SYKE HILL, 1841 O.S., *v.* **castel, sīc, hyll**.   DICKY SIKES.   GREEN LANE.   THE GROVE, 1841 O.S., *v.* **grāf** 'copse'. HOLT SPRING, *Holt* 1841 O.S., *v.* **holt** 'a wood'.   LEE LANE. LEMON ROYD.   LONG LANE, 1841 O.S.   LOW GRANGE, 1841 O.S., *v.* **grange**.   MILL LANE, cf. *Milneker* 1323 *MinAcct* 45, *Mulnkarr*, -*flatt* 1341 *Surv*, *Milnecarre* 1461 *MinAcct* 509, *Milnacre* 1608 ib 12, *v.* **myln, kjarr, flat, æcer**.   MOOR TOP, *v.* Ackworth Moor Top

supra. OUTGANG, 1771 M, *v.* ūt-gang 'exit' (from the village).
PLAGUE STONE, *v.* Burial Ground *supra.* POTWELLS FM, *Potwells*
1817 M. RIDDINGS, 1841 O.S., *le Riddyng by Akworth* 1408 Pat,
Riddinge 1544 *MinAcct, the Riddinges* 1598 HAS 16, 285, *v.* rydding
'clearing'. RIGG LANE, *Ridge Lane* 1841 O.S., *v.* hrycg, lane.
ROSE LANE. SANDY GATE LANE, *v.* sandig, gata. SOUTH FIELD,
Southfeld' 1323 *MinAcct* 45, *v.* sūð, feld. STANDING FLAT BRIDGE,
cf. Standing Flat 98 *infra.* TAN HOUSE SPA. TOWN SHORE
DIKE, *v.* scora 'a bank, a slope'. TOWNS WELL. WENT HO,
possibly identical with *villa de Went* 1276 RH, *v.* R. Went (RNs.).
WHITEGATE HILL, a Roman road, *v.* hwīt, gata.

FIELD-NAMES

The principal forms in (*a*) are 1712 *WYEnr* 68. Spellings dated 1323 are
MinAcct 45, 1341 *Surv* 10, 5, 1368–1608 *MinAcct* 12, 26, 66, 507, 509, 511,
1685, 1764 *Glebe.*

(*a*) Breadcroft, the Cow Pasture 1772 *EnclA* 101 (*v.* cū, pasture), Grime
Ing (the ON pers.n. *Grímr*, eng), Hundell syke (*v.* Hundhill *supra*, sīc
'stream'), the Midle field, Midlestocks (*v.* stocc 'tree-stump'), Old Taile
close 1764 (*v.* ald, tægl 'tail of land'), Parkin Leyes close 1764 (*Perkinleyes*
1685, the pers.n. or surname *Perkin*, lēah), Pudding Bush 1764.

(*b*) *Aklynges* 1368 (an early example of *oakling* 'young oak'), *leʒ Bankeʒ*
1461, 1486, *le Banke* 1608 (*v.* banke), *Beneragaynestak* (sic) 1486, *Beneringtacke*
1608 (*v.* intak, the first el. may be some surname like *Bever* or *Beverage*),
Brigtree de Akworth' 1368 (*v.* brycg, trēow), *Caldwellyng* 1341 (*v.* cald,
wella, eng), *Conybank* 1608 (*v.* coni 'rabbit', banke), *Conyngarth* 1461, 1486
(*v.* coning-erth 'warren'), *Coteyhard* 1341 (*v.* cot, geard), *Detflatt* 1341 (*v.*
flat), *Elmetyherd* 1341 (*v.* geard, the first el. may be a surname derived from
Elmet pt. iv *infra*), *le Estfe(e)ld* 1323, 1341 (*v.* ēast, feld), *Fordelande* 1486 (*v.*
ford, perhaps as a surname, land), *Garbrige* 1486 (*v.* gāra, brycg), *Hallyley*
1598 HAS 16, 285, *Horsyng* 1341 (*v.* hors, eng), *Kyrkcrofteng* 1341, *Kirke-*
croft 1486 (*v.* kirkja, croft, eng), *Lityllmoryng* 1341 (*v.* lytel, mōr, eng),
Lokendam 1341 (*v.* dammr), *Lyndrik* 1341 *Surv* (*v.* lind, ric, and cf. Lindrick
i, 54 *supra*), *Meresyde* 1529 TestLds (*v.* mere 'pool', sīde), *Mykelwell Flatt*
1341 (*v.* micel, wella, flat), *North Feld* 1341 (*v.* norð, feld), *leʒ Raileʒ* 1486
(*v.* Rail Gap i, 117 *supra*), *Slyterleyhill'* 1486 (*v.* hyll, the first el. may be an
error for ME *slitheri* 'slippery', as in Slippery Ford (Oakworth) pt. vi *infra*),
Smythynge 1461, *Smethyng* 1480 (*v.* smið, eng), (*le*) *Southwod(e)* 1384, 1486
(*v.* sūð, wudu), *Stanbecks Close* 1685 (*v.* clos), *Stone stiel acre* 1685 (*v.* stān,
stigel, æcer), *Suthynge* 1486, *Swithing* 1608 (*v.* sviðnungr 'a place cleared by
burning'), *Thwayte* 1486 (*v.* þveit), *Waltonrodes* 1384 (*Walton* as a surname,
rod[1] 'clearing'), *Wodesyde* 1384 (*v.* wudu, sīde).

xix. Badsworth

1. BADSWORTH (103–4615)

Badesuu(o)rde 1086 DB, *-w(u)rth, -worde, -worth* 1226 FF, 1255
Pat, 1267 Ebor, 1316 Vill, 1366 Test i, 1433 YD x, *Badisworth*
1555 TC
Baddewrd' 1170–80 YCh 1582   *Badeworde* 1279 Ebor
Baddeswrd', -uurda 1170–80 YCh 1582, l. 12 *Nost* 18d, *-wurth* 1226
FF, *-wrhe* c. 1250–8 YD iii, *-worth* 1267 Ebor, 14 *Nost* 17, *Sawl*
193, 1335 FF *et passim* to 1432 Test ii

'Bæddi's enclosure', *v.* **worð**. On the OE pers.n. *Bæddi* cf. Badsey
Wo 260.

BADSWORTH COMMON, 1841 O.S.   BADSWORTH HALL, 1841 O.S.
BADSWORTH WHIN, 1841 O.S., *v.* hvin 'gorse'.   BARRS DRAIN, cf.
Barr Close 1840 *TA, v.* **barre**.   BEACONSFIELD RD, *Beacon Close &*
Field 1840 *TA, v.* (ge)bēacon 'beacon'.   BURNHILL BRIDGE, *Burnhill*
Bridges, Burn Close & Ing 1840 *TA*, probably **bruni** 'place cleared
by burning', hyll.   CARR WOOD, *Carr Woods, Car Field* 1840 *TA,*
v. **kjarr** 'marsh'.   FIRTH FIELD, 1814 *EnclA* 23, *The furthe* 1629
Glebe, the firthfield 1764 ib, *Frith Field, Flatt & Hall,* 1840 *TA*, cf.
le Comunfryth 14 *Nost* 17, *v.* fyrhðe 'wood'.   MOOR HO, 1822
Langd, *Moor Houses* 1817 M, *v.* mōr, hūs.   OAKTREE LANE, cf.
Oak Tree Close & Lane 1840 *TA*.   SHEPHERD'S HILL, 1841 O.S.

FIELD-NAMES

The principal forms in (*a*) are 1840 *TA* 26, and these include f.ns. for
Upton 98 *infra*. Spellings dated 14 are *Nost* 17, 1510 Hnt ii, 442, 1629,
1764 *Glebe*.

(*a*) Bean Knowl, Beckett Hole, Blackstock (*Black stocks* 1764, *v.* blæc,
stocc 'stump'), Bottoms, Broad Ings (*v.* eng 'meadow'), Bromade, Broom
Close, Calder Flatt (*Northcaldewelleflat* 14, *Little Calderflat* 1764, *v.* cald,
wella), Coal Pit Close, Cow Close, Crabtree Close, Craven Close, Far &
Near Ellers, Elms Close, The Field, Foal Garth, Fox Hills, Frith Stoop Flatt
(*Firth Stoop Gate flat* 1764, *v.* Firth Field *supra*, stólpi 'stake', gata), Fystill
flat 1764 (*v.* þistel, flat), Goose Bait (*v.* gōs, ON beit 'pasture'), Green Gate
Close, Grey Cock, Hall Close & Flatt, Harewood Hill, Holme Field (*v.*
holmr), Holywell Ing, Housewifedale Close, Hoyle (*v.* hol[1]), Hutterhill (*le*
Hoterel 14, *Huttrellynge* 1431 YD x), Inglands (*v.* eng, land), Intake (*v.*

intak), Kilnhirst Ing, Kirkem Briggs, Laithe Close (v. hlaða 'barn'), Leys, Lunland, Lunn Orchard, Mesne Frith (v. main, cf. Firth Field supra), Mill Close, Field & Hill (Mill Field 1814 EnclA 23, v. myln), Moledikes, Moor Close & Leys (v. mōr, clos, lēah), Owler Holt (v. alor, holt), Owlers (v. alor), Parson Gap, Pearl Close, Peats Close, Pick Hill, Pighill (v. pightel), Pinfold (Garth) (v. pynd-fald), Pog Close, Pond Close, Pot Hill, Low Pot, Potter Lane, Pottil Field, Prickfirth 1764 (cf. le Prykefurlanges 14, v. pricca, fyrhðe, furlang), Rail Close, Raw Yards, Rein Close, Sharp Garth, Stack Garth, Stocking Close, Street Lands, Thief Lane Close, Tom Wood Ash, Top Hill, Topin, Tops, Topwith, Tub Close, Warren Burrow, Well Head, Wenthill (Ing), West Field, Wetlands, Wheatlands, White Cross, Willey closes, Willow Bridge & Garth, Winter Firth, Wood close.

(b) Bolemers 1226 FF (v. bula, mersc), Bukler Ing 1510 (v. eng), Clayforthe-lands 1629 (v. clǣg, ford), The Lyncolne thorne 1629 (Lincl'ewytethorn 14, v. hwīt, þorn), le Longpit 14 (v. lang, pytt), New Close 1510, Skirskites 14.

2. THORPE AUDLIN (103–4715)

Torp(e) 1086 DB, 1121–7 YCh 1428, 1135–42, 1154–8 ib 1493, 1499, 1190 ib 1641, 1215 ChR, 1216 Nost 5, Torph c. 1160 Pont
Thorp(e) 1154–9, 1190 YCh 1503, 1641–2, 1226 FF, 1316 Vill et passim to 1530 WillY, (-Aud-, Awd(e)lyn(e), -lin) 13 YD xiii, 47, 14 Linds, 1343 DodsN et freq 1605 FF, (-Audelun) 1428 FA, (-aldlay) 1419 Test i, (-Audeley) 1490 Test iv, (-Awdlay) 1509 Test v, (-Awdle(y)n) 1543 WillY, 1566 FF, (-Awdlyn) 1597 FF, (-Audlin) 1641 Rates

'Outlying farmstead', v. þorp. The affix Audlin (OG Aldelin) from Aldelin, whose son William was tenant in 1190 (YCh 1641).

ROGERTHORPE

Rogar-, Rugartorp 1086 DB
Thorp 1177–93 YCh 1643
Torp Rogeri 1121–7 YCh 1428, 1215 ChR, 1216 Nost 5
Rogertorpe 1121 Tockw, Rogerthorp(e) 1195–1215 YCh 1644, 13, 1329 YD xiii, 47, 1431 YD x et freq to 1619 FF, Rogertrope 1579 WillY

v. þorp 'outlying farmstead'. The first el. is probably the ContG pers.n. Roger (cf. Forssner 217), possibly here replacing an earlier ON Hróðgeirr.

BROOM HILL, cf. le Brom 14 Nost 17, v. brōm, hyll. DARNING LANE. HILLTHORPE. MORNING FIELD LANE, Mourning Field 1814 EnclA

62.   PEARTREE FIELD, 1814 *EnclA*.   SALLIWELL FIELD, 1814 *EnclA*,
v. salh 'willow', wella.   SCHOLES FIELD LANE, 1814 *EnclA*, *Scales*
1307 Pat, *v.* skáli 'a shieling'.   STANDING FLAT, 1841 O.S.   THORPE
GATE, 1841 O.S.   THORPE MARSH.   WATCHIT HOLE LANE.

FIELD-NAMES

Spellings dated without source are FF.

(*a*) Bull Piece 1814 *EnclA* 62.

(*b*) *le Clos* 1226, *la Crofte* 1226, (*parci de*) *Hulin, Hulinstanes* 1226 (ME
surn. *Hulin,* stān), *Mabbezorde* 1431 YD x (the fem. pers.n. *Mab,* geard),
Round about close 1655 Bright 530, *Thorpe Hamell* 1619 (*v.* þorp), *Wacel* 1226.

3. UPTON (103–4713)

Uptun, -ton 1086 DB, 1245 Lib, 1272 Ebor, 1337 FF *et passim* to
1598 FF, *Opton* 1218 FF, Kirkst, *Hupton* 1244 Fees, *Upton* 1295 YI,
Uppeton 1316 Vill. 'Upper farmstead', *v.* upp, tūn.

BEARDSHAW WELLS.   BULLCAR PLANT., *Bulker* 1295 YI, *Bulcarre*
1546 YChant, 'bull marsh', *v.* bula, kjarr.   ELM LEYS, *Hemleys*
1771 M, *Elm Lees* 1840 *TA*, *v.* elm, lēah.   EWE BANK GATE, *Ewe
Bank* 1840 *TA*, *v.* eowu, banke.   FIELD LANE, 1840 *TA*.   GREEN
LANE, 1840 *TA*.   MOOR LANE, 1840 *TA*, *v.* mōr.   SANDALL ING,
1840 *TA*, *v.* eng 'meadow'; the first el. is probably a surname (from
Sandal Magna 107 *infra*).   SAND LANE, 1840 *TA*.   SPOUT HOLE,
cf. *Spout Lane* 1840 *TA*, *v.* spoute 'a spout, gutter'.   UPTON
BEACON, 1841 O.S., 'there was formerly a beacon on the high ground
at Upton' 1828 Hnt ii, 444, *v.* (ge)bēacon.   UPTON MOOR TOP,
Moor Top 1817 M, *v.* mōr, topp.   WAGGON LANE, 1840 *TA*.
WALTON WOOD, 1817 M, probably a surname (from Walton 112
infra), wudu.

FIELD-NAMES.   Cf. Badsworth f.ns. 96 *supra*.

V. AGBRIGG WAPENTAKE

AGBRIGG WAPENTAKE

Agebrvge, Hagebrige Wapentac 1086 DB, *Agebrig(a), -brigg* 1181, 1197 P

(*wap' de*) *Aggebrig(e), -brigg(e), -bryg* 1166, 1180, 1188 P, 1219 *Ass* 1, 1246 ib 6d, 1276 RH, 1286 YI, 1297 LS, 1303 Aid, 1316 Vill, 1330 YD v, 1345 Pat, *-brugg* 1246 *Ass* 4

(*wap' de*) *Akebrygg* 1293 *Ass* 28, *Akbrigg* 1322 Pat

(*wap' de*) *Agbrig(e), -brigg* 1357 *MinAcct*, 1428 FA, 1545 LS

This wapentake takes its name from Agbrigg 117 *infra* in the extreme east of the district; it presumably met at the bridge there. The wapentake comprises lower and middle Calderdale and the mountainous country which lies south of Huddersfield towards the Lancashire border, including Saddleworth and Springhead, two townships which belong topographically to Lancashire and were in fact in the Lancashire parish of Rochdale. The prominent towns are Wakefield, Dewsbury and Huddersfield, and the area in the Calder valley is much industrialised. From about the seventeenth century it was combined with Morley Wapentake iii, 1 *infra* to form *the Wap(p)entake of Agbrigg(e) & Morley* (1620 Skyr, 1638 SessnR), *Agbridgge & Morley* (1649 *MinAcct* 13). The township of Morley (182 *infra*) was transferred to the Agbrigg division some time after 1610 M, when it was shown to be in the Morley Wapentake; *v.* also Wakefield 163 *infra*.

i. Sandal Magna

1. WEST BRETTON (102–2913)

Bretone 1086 DB

Bretton(a), -tun 1155 Pont, 1180–90 *Bodl* 43, 1190–1220 YD v, YCh 1792, 1196 P, 1202 FF, 1202–8 *Ass*, 1216 ClR, 1219 FF, 1243 Fees *et passim* to 1428 FA, (*West-*) 1193–1211 YCh 1525, 13 YD iii, 1304 Ch, 1308 WCR *et passim* to 1666 Visit, (*Lytul-*) 1430 YD viii

Brecton 1256 Pap

Breton 1256 Pap, (*West-*) 1508 WillY

Westbritton 1433 Hall

Westberton 1529 YD vi

'Farmstead of the Britons', v. Brettas, tūn, and Monk Bretton i, 273 *supra*. The single *Brecton* spelling is not significant, as it is probably a misreading of *Bretton*; c and t are often indistinguishable in the court hand. The affixes are from west and lȳtel 'little'.

BULLCLIFF, *Bulclif(e)*, *-cliff(e)*, *-clyff(e)* 1404–1443 YD vi, 1433 Hall, 1457, 1470 YD viii, 1525 YD vi, *Boultcliffe* 1575 WillY, *Boulcliffe* 1656 PRThl, 1822 Langd, *Bull Cliff* 1817 M. The later spellings suggest that this is from OE bult 'heap, hillock' and clif 'steep bank', but it may be OE bula 'bull'.

BENTLEY DIKE & SPRING, named from the nearby Bentley Grange 218 *infra*. BOWER HILL, cf. *Bower House* 1622 *Bretton* 84, *Sterlyngbowere* (a tenement) 1557 YD viii, from the surname *Sterling* and būr[1] 'a cottage, a dwelling'. BRAMLEY LANE, *Bram-*, *Bromley* 13 Hnt ii, 240, *Bromelay* 1383 YD vi, 'broom glade', v. brōm, lēah. BRETTON HALL, *aulam* 13 Hnt, *Bretton hall* 1545 Test vi, 1553 YD viii, 1642 WillY, *-haull* 1545 TestLds, v. hall. BRETTON PARK, 1822 Langd, v. park. BRICK BANK. BRIDGE ROYD WOOD, 1841 O.S., v. brycg, rod[1]. BROAD CARR. BULLCLIFF WOOD, 1841 O.S., v. Bullcliff *supra*, wudu. BURN BANK, *Burnebanke* 1557 YD viii, probably 'burnt bank', v. bruni, banke; OE burna 'stream' does not appear in p.ns. of this locality. CLAP HO & WOOD. COMMON END, 1841 O.S. DEER PARK. HAIGH LODGE, *del Haygh* 1383 YD vi, v. haga 'enclosure'. HIGH ROYD WOOD, *Heghrode* 1321 Hnt ii, 241, v. hēah, rod[1] 'clearing'. LOWER & UPPER LAKE, *Bretton Lake*, *Lower-*, *Upper Lake* 1845 *TA* 224, ME *lake* 'lake'. JENKIN WOOD, 1841 O.S. KAYE SPRING, 1841 O.S. PIKELEY HILL. POT HO, 1817 M. REDDIE CARR ING. SMITHY RIDGE, cf. *Smith(e)rode* 1190–1220 YCh 1791, e. 13 YD v, *Smidiroda* 1190–1220 ib, v. smiððe 'a smithy', rod[1] 'clearing', hrycg. TOCKHILL. TOWN END, 1841 O.S. TOWN WELL.

FIELD-NAMES

Spellings dated c. 1200 are YCh 1792, 13, 1344 Hnt ii, 240–1, 1346–1511 YD vi.

(a) Dog Pond Ing 1849 *TA* 69, Sun Wood 1849 ib.

(b) *Abbott flatt* 1557 YD viii (v. abbat, flat), *le Balghgrene* 13 YD iii (v. balg 'rounded', grēne[2]), *Brerirode* 13, *le Brererode* 1346 (v. brēr(ig) 'briar', rod[1] 'clearing'), *Broderode* 13, 1383 (v. brād, rod[1]), *Edw(a)n Royd*, *-Rode* 1510, 1511 (the pers.n. *Edwin*, rod[1]), *Falenge* 13, 13 YD iii, *le Falange* 1383 (*v.* (ge)fall 'clearing', eng 'meadow'), *Fitchfield* (sic) 13, *Nether-, Overgate-rode* 1383 (*v.* gata 'road', rod[1]), *Godynacre* 1383 (from the OFr pers.n. *Godin,* æcer), *Gotrode* 1383 (probably gāt 'goat', rod[1]), *Grescroft* 13 (*v.* gærs 'grass', croft), *le Hawe Stubbyng* 1383 (*v.* haga 'enclosure', stubbing 'clearing'), *Kerlandes* 1345 YD viii (*v.* kjarr 'marsh', land), *Laterode* 13 (*v.* rod[1]), *Littelmore* 1383 (*v.* lytel, rod[1]), *Malinrode* 13 (the ME pers.n. *Malin,* rod[1]), *Mapilhurst* 13, *Mapelhirstes* 1383 (*v.* mapel, hyrst 'wood'), *Mariotrode* 1344, 1383 (the ME fem. pers.n. *Mariot,* rod[1]), *le Northfeld* 1352, 1383 (*v.* norð, feld), *Okinshaglandes* 13 YD iii, 'oaken copse', *v.* ācen, sceaga, cf. Oakenshaw 113 *infra*; here it might be a surname derived from the latter p.n.), *Riutchclive* c. 1200, *Rauth-, Ruchclive* 13 YD vi (the ME surname *Ruth* (Reaney, 137), *v.* clif), *Russellerode* 1383 (the ME surname *Russel,* rod[1]), *Scrikhurst* 13 (*v.* scrīc 'missel-thrush, shrike', hyrst 'wood'), *Sougurnrode* 1383 (*v.* rod[1], the first el. is possibly ME *sogorner* 'temporary resident', used as a surname), *le Southefeld* 1383 (*v.* sūð, feld), *Trunclive* c. 1200, 13 YD vi, *Trumclyf* 1383 ('round cliff', *v.* trun, clif), *Walterode* 13 (the ME pers.n. *Walter,* rod[1]), *Westfield* 13 (*v.* west, feld).

2. CRIGGLESTONE (102–311b)

Crigest', -tone 1086 DB   *Crichelest'* 1166 P (p)

Crikeleston' 1164–96 YCh viii (p), l. 12 *Nost* 33d, 1202 FF, 1208 P (p), 1243 Fees (p), 1246 *Ass* 5d, 1462 *MinAcct* 99, *Crikleston* c. 1250 Heal 51, *Crikeliston* 1274, 1275 WCR

Crideleston' 1196 P (p)

Crigleston 1188–1202 YCh viii, 13 YD xii, 259, 1304 YI, 1313 WCR, 1396 YD iii, 1605 FF, 1641 Rates, *-toun* 1331 WCR, *Crigliston* 13 *Heal* 49d, *Grigleston* 1371 FF

Cri-, Crygeleston 1202, 1249 FF, 1251 *Ass* (p), 1308, 1315 WCR, 1323 *MinAcct* 45 *et freq* to 1377 AD i, *Crigeliston* 1234 FF, 1274, 1297, 1307 WCR, *Crigileston* 1275 WCR, *Crigheleston* 1316 Vill

Crykelston 1382 YD viii   *Kirkeleston'* 1492 *MinAcct* 02

Crigelston 1323 WCR, *Cry-, Crigilston* 1412 YD i, 1468 Pat, 1546 WillY

Cregilston, -yl- 1382 YD viii, 1440 Brett, 1513 FF, 1552 WillY

Ekwall is undoubtedly right in taking the first el. of Crigglestone as an older place-name, OE *Crȳc-hyll*, which contains OWelsh **cruc** 'a hill', with OE **hyll** added tautologically; this type of hybrid is repeated in such p.ns. as Churchill So, Wo 106, Crichel Do. *Crȳc-hyll* would appear to refer to the hill on which Crigglestone stands overlooking the Calder, now called Crigglestone Cliff, and Crigglestone itself means 'the farmstead of *Cryc-hyll*' (*v.* tūn), being paralleled by Crudgington Sa (*Crugetone* 1086 DB, *Crugelton* 12, 13 DEPN); for the gen. compound in Crigglestone cf. Penistone i, 336 *supra* and *v.* EPN i, 158–9 s.v. -es² (§ iii). The early ME -*k*- (for ME -*ch*- which would be normal in this type of p.n.) is due to ON influence and the voicing of ME intervocalic -*k*- to -*g*- is common in such p.ns. as Wigginton or Wiganthorpe YN 14, 35 (from *Víkingr*).

BLACKER HALL, 1672 *Bretton* 71, *Blacker* 1316 WCR, 1323 *MinAcct* 45, 1371 YD viii, (-*Hall*) 1552, 1642 WillY, *Blakkare, Blackare* 1394, 1395 YD vi, *Blakkerhall* 1516 YD viii. 'Black marsh', *v.* blæc, kjarr; this p.n. has been suggested (YAJ xxxv, 235) to have originated in the name of the *Blacker* family (cf. Blacker i, 292 *supra*), but this is a common YW p.n. and may well be a spontaneous and descriptive p.n.

CHAPELTHORPE, *Schapelthorpe* 1285 WCR, *Chapel Thorp* 1393 *Grant* 7, *Chapelthorp(e)* 1396 YD iii, 1397 TestLds, 1447 DodsN, 1709 WMB, *Chappelthorp(e)* 1585 WillY, 1599 FF, *Cappelthorpe* 1610 FF. *v.* þorp 'outlying dependent farmstead'. *Chapel-* is probably an affix added to an original simplex *Thorp* and refers to the chapel which was a chapel of ease and perpetual curacy of the parish church of Sandal Magna. On this and other local p.ns. in þorp (Gawthorpe, Hollingthorpe, Kettlethorpe, and Painthorpe) *v.* Introd.

DAW LANE, 1841 O.S., leading to DAW GREEN (lost), *Dawgrene* 1454 YD vi, 1576 WillY, 1609 *Grant* 9, *Dowgrene* 1576 ib, *Dawgreen(e)* 1649 WillS, 1656 *WB* 144, 1709 WMB, 1817 M, cf. also the f.ns. Daw Pit Close, *Dawroide* (*infra*). The site was near Painthorpe. The name is, like Daw Green in Dewsbury 186 *infra*, from l.ME *dawe* (OE *dawe) 'a jackdaw', and then also 'a fool, a sluggard, a slut' (cf. NED s.v. *daw*), possibly used as a nickname. 'Jackdaw green', *v.* grēne².

DIRTCAR, DURKAR HO, *Drit-, Drytker* 1285, 1307, 1314 WCR, *Dirkar* 1377–99 DodsN, -*ker* 1522 YD vi, 1587 WillY, 1695 *Sand* 2, -*car* 1605 FF, *Dricar* 1447 DodsN, *Dirtcarr(e)* 1514 FF, 1688 *YAS* 97, 1709 WMB, *Durcker* 1614 FF. 'Dirt marsh', *v.* drit, kjarr.

GAWTHORPE HALL, *Guketorp* (sic) 1252 Ebor. There are six other examples of this p.n. in YW (188, 230, (Bingley), (Harewood) pt. iv, (Carleton), and (Dent) pt. vi *infra*), and it occurs elsewhere as

Gowthorpe Nf, La 83, YE 176, 244. These names are usually interpreted as compounds of the ON pers.n. *Gaukr* (a byname from
gaukr 'cuckoo') and **þorp** 'outlying farmstead'; this is certainly the
case in Gowthorpe (Selby) pt. iv. Whilst there is no doubt about the
use of ON *Gaukr* as a by-name in England (Björkman, NP 49, ZEN
37), the frequent repetition of this p.n. compound rather suggests
that the first el. is **gaukr** itself, and the p.n. means 'cuckoo farmstead'. The true significance is uncertain, but bird-names are
frequently used in the names of houses (such as Spink Hall i, 259,
Owlet Hall ii, 90, 190, Laverock Hall ii, 279, and many others *passim*,
as well as Gawk Hall (Blubberhouses) pt. v, or the lost *Gauke-
house* i, 220, also containing **gaukr**), and may signify no more than
places which such birds frequented; but dial. *gowk* (like the ON
pers.n.) means also 'a simpleton, a fool', and it seems at least a
possibility that the numerous Gawthorpes denote 'a fool's house'
and have much the same significance as the numerous Folly Halls
(*v.* **folie**).

HOLLINGTHORPE, *Holynthorp, -in-* 1297, 1307, 1316 WCR, *Hollin-
thorpe, -yn-* 1548 WillY, Jas 1 *Surv, Hollingthorp(e)* 1567 WillY, 1709
WMB. *v.* **þorp** 'outlying dependent farmstead'. The first el. is
holegn 'holly'.

KETTLETHORPE HALL, *Ketelesthorp* 1242 DodsN, 1275 WCR (p),
1310 *Surv, -torp* 1246 *Ass* 30d (p), *Ketelisthorp(e)* 1307, 1323 WCR,
Ketilthorp(e) 1297 LS (p), 1331 WCR, 1377 YD viii, 1448 Pat,
Kettlethorpe 1505 *WB* 69, 1653 *Sand* 79. 'Ketil's outlying farmstead', from the ON pers.n. *Ketill* and **þorp**. The late ME loss of the
gen. inflexion is to be noted.

NEWMILLERDAM, *le Newmyldame* 1462 *MinAcct* 99, (*le) Newmylne-
dam(m)e, -miln(e), -dam* 1492 *MinAcct* 02, Jas 1 *Surv*, 1651 WillS,
1659 Pick, *New(e) Milner Dam(m)e, -Mylner-* 1558 WillY, 1577
Holinshed, 1584, 1592 WillY, *Nu-, Newmillerdam(e), -damm* 1612
NCWills, 1647 YDr, 1709 WMB. *v.* **nīwe, myln, dammr**. The water-
driven cornmill for which the dam was made was *le Newmylns* 1405
WCR 1d, *molend' aquatic' voc' Newmylls* 1461 *MinAcct* 99, *Newe-
mylne of the dam* 1486 *WCR* 1, *molen' aquatic' et blad' voc' Newmylne*
1492 *MinAcct* 02, *Newmylne* 1591 WillY, and the dam is also referred
to in the f.ns. Dam Close and *Damstede* (*infra*).

NEWSHOLME LANE, *Newsome* Jas 1 Surv, 1709 WMB, 1844 *TA*, *Newsome feild* 1613 *Cause* 908, 1688 *YAS* 97, *Newsam Ing* 1709 WMB. Probably OE *æt nīwan hūsum* 'at the new houses', *v.* nīwe, hūs, -um, as in Newsome 258, Temple Newsam pt. iv, Newsholme pt. vi, etc. *infra*.

PAINTHORPE, *Paynesthorp* 1203 DodsN, *Penyesthorp* 1353 Dugd vi, *Pain-*, *Paynthorp(e)* 1448 YD vii, 1564 FF, 1650 *YAS* 97, 1709 WMB, *Paynethorp(e)* 1525 WCR 6d, 1610 FF, *Painethirpe* 1688 *YAS* 97, *Panthorpe* 1579 WillY. *v.* þorp 'outlying dependent farmstead'. The first el. is the ME pers.n. *Pain* from OFr *Paien*, MedLat *Paganus* (Feilitzen 343), as in Painsthorpe YE 131.

BIRCH LATHE, -*Laith* 1841 O.S., *Birk Laith* 1817 M, cf. *the Birkes* 1649 *Bretton* 40, *Birkecloses* 1626 ib, *v.* birki, hlaða 'barn'. BOAT HOUSE FM, *Boat House* 1841 O.S., cf. *Boat Close* 1844 *TA*; it is on the bank of the R. Calder. BOYNE HILL, 1640 WillY, 1709 WMB, *Boynhill* 1577 Tayl, cf. also *Boynefirth(s)* 1709 WMB, 1713 *Sand* 17, from the surname *Boyne* (cf. '*Hassacke* formerly *Boynes*' 1709 WMB); *v.* hyll, fyrhðe 'wood', hassuc. BRICE HILL, 1844 *TA*, from the surname *Brice*, hyll. BROADLANDS FM. BROWN WOOD, 1844 *TA*. CALDER BRIDGE, CALDER GROVE, 1841 O.S., *v.* Calder (RNs.), brycg, grāf. CLEW BRIDGE. CLIFF HO, 1817 M, 1841 O.S., cf. also *Cliffe Close* 1844 *TA* and Crigglestone Cliff *infra*. THE CLOUGH, 1841 O.S., *v.* clōh 'a dell'. CRIGGLESTONE CLIFF, *Chriglestone Cliffe* 1699 *WCR* 7d, *Crig(g)leston Cliff* 1709 WMB, *v.* clif, here a steep bank to the west of the village (cf. Crigglestone *supra*). DENNINGTON, 1771 M, *Denton Lodge* Jas 1 *Surv*; it stands in a small valley (The Clough *supra*) and probably contains denu 'valley' as in the f.ns. Dane Royd *infra*, *v.* tūn; but earlier material is needed. FOX ROW. GREAT CLIFF, 1844 *TA*, *v.* Crigglestone Cliff *supra*. GREENFIELD FM. HALL GREEN, *Hall green(e)* Jas 1 *Surv*, 1709 WMB, *v.* hall (probably here Gawthorpe Hall), grēne². HAVERROID PLANT. THE HOLE, *the Hole Ing* 1688 *YAS* 97, *Hoyle Farme* 1709 WMB, *Hole* 1817 M, *Hoyle Ings* 1844 *TA*, *v.* hol¹ 'hole, hollow'. HOLLING HALL, *Hollin Hall* 1841 O.S., *v.* holegn 'holly', hall. HOLMES PLANT., *(the) Holmes* 1314 WCR, 1688 *YAS* 97, *v.* holmr 'water-meadow'. HUMLEY HILL, 1844 *TA*, *Humley* 1486 *WCR* 1, 1695 *Grant* 50, 1709 WMB, (*The common called-*) 1716 *Glebe*, (-*royd*) 1709 WMB, *Humbley Side* 1709 ib, cf. also Slack *infra*; this may be appropriately derived from OE humol 'a rounded hill' and lēah 'clearing', as the spelling of Slack (*infra*) suggests the first el. is *hum(b)le-* rather than *hum-*. KING'S WOOD, 1844 *TA*. LAWNS DIKE, cf. *Lands Frees* 1844 *TA*, *v.* launde 'a forest glade'. LOW FM, 1841 O.S. LOW MOOR, 1844 *TA*, *Woolley Low Moor* 1799 *EnclA* 87, the lower part of Woolley Moor i, 288 *supra*. OWLERS BECK, cf. *Oler Close* 1844 *TA*, *Oulerbrigg* 1709 WMB, *v.* alor 'alder', bekkr, brycg; there are still alders here. OWLET LATHE, *Owlet Laith Close* 1844 *TA*, *v.* hlaða 'barn'. PATCH WOOD, 1844 *TA*, *Little Patch* 1844 *TA*, probably *patch* in the sense 'patch of ground'. PRIESTLEY LODGE, 1841 O.S., perhaps *Priestley* as a surname (cf. Priestley Green iii, 80 *infra*). SLACK, *Humble Slack* 1638 WillY, *the Slack* 1709 WMB, *v.* slakki 'hollow in a hillside', and Humley Hill *supra*. SPA HO, *Carter Spa(w)* 1817 M, 1841 O.S., *Spa Close* 1844 *TA*, e.ModE *spa(w)* 'mineral spring'; *Carters Spaw* is described as a public bath on Low Moor (1799 *EnclA* 87). STONY LANE, *Stone lane Close*, *le Stonie lane* Jas 1 *Surv*, *Stonylaneclose* 1650 *WCR* 8d, *v.* stānig, lane, clos. STOWE HO. WADHOUSE LANE, *Wad House* 1817 M, 1844 *TA*, cf. *Wade Crofte, -Inge* Jas 1, probably the surname *Wade*, *v.* hūs, croft, eng. WOOD MOOR, 1817 M, 1844 *TA*, -side 1709 WMB, *Woodmore* 1666 PRThl, *v.* wudu, mōr. WOODMOOR HILL, 1841 O.S.

FIELD-NAMES

The principal forms in (*a*) are 1844 *TA* 119. Spellings dated 12 are *WB* 90, c. 1190 YCh viii, 1297–1331 WCR, 1452, 1525, 1699 *WCR*, 1462, 1492 *MinAcct* 99, 02, Jas 1 *Surv* 11, 19, 1646, 1648, 1695 *Sand*, 1650, 1688 *YAS* 97, 1709 WMB, 1799 *EnclA* 87; others dated without source are *Bretton*.

(*a*) Top Abbot, Adam Royds (*v.* rod[1] 'clearing'), Allott Acre, Balk Field 1799 (*v.* balca 'boundary ridge'), Barker Ing (*v.* barkere 'tanner', probably as a surname, eng 'meadow'), Birching Ing (*v.* bircen, eng), Birk Close (*v.* birki, clos), Bottom Field (ib 1799, *the Bothome Close* 1708, *v.* botm), The Bottoms (*Great & Little Bothome* 1688, *v.* botm), Briery Close (*Bryery Close* 1709, *v.* brērig, clos), Brimshaw, Broad Stone (*le Brodestone* Jas 1, *v.* brād, stān), Broom Close, Buss Hill, Long, Old & Short Calder (*Coulders, Shortecoldearse* Jas 1, *Short Gowlders, Long Calders* 1613 *Cause* 908, *v.* cald, ears 'rounded hill', a name obviously not to be confused with Calder Grove *supra*), Calfcroft 1771 (*v.* calf, croft), Calf Royds (*Calfrod* 1371 YD viii, *v.* calf, rod[1] 'clearing'), Callinger, Chantry Close, Chapel close 1709, Cinder Hill (*v.* sinder, hyll), (Great) Claim, Coal Pit Close, Cockglode 1721 Tayl (*v.* cocc[2] 'woodcock', glād 'glade'), Common Side 1841 O.S., Crabtree Close, Croft Head, Crompt Close, Cross Lands, Cuckoo, Dam Close (*v.* Newmillerdam *supra*), Dane Royd (ib 1699, *le Deyneroide* Jas 1, *Deanroyd* 1709, *v.* denu 'valley', rod[1], cf. Dennington *supra*, Dean Syke *infra*), Daw Dike Close (ib 1684 Tayl), Daw Pit Close (*the Daw Pitts* 1695, *v.* Daw Lane *supra*, dīc, pytt), Dearnley Ing, Dentcliffe (*Dentley Oake Shutt* Jas 1, *Daynecliffe* 1613 *Cause* 908, *Dencliffe Okes* 1665 *YAS* 82, *Dentcliffe Oakes* 1709, *v.* clif; the first el. appears to be *dent-* but its origin is obscure unless it is a shortened form of Dennington *supra*), Devil Garden, Dirtcar Green 1799 (*v.* Dirtcar *supra*, grēne[2]), Disherts, Duck Royd (probably identical with *Dockrey Roydes & Holes* 1709, *v.* docce 'dock', vrá, rod[1], otherwise *v.* dūce 'duck'), Ellen Tree (*Ellyntree shutt* Jas 1, *Ellintree Field* 1799, *v.* ellern 'elder-tree', dial. *shut* 'division of land'), Eve Royds, Feather Ing, Felkers, Finny Royd (*Fenay Royd* 1709, *v.* fennig 'marshy' rod[1], or a surname derived from Fenay 258 *infra*), Firths (*Overfirthe* Jas 1, *the Firth* 1693, *the Firth Close* 1695, *Firths Field* 1799, *v.* fyrhðe 'wood'), Frostles, Gallas Field 1709 (probably galga 'gallows'), Garlick Wells (ib 1613 *Cause* 908, OE gārlēac 'garlick', wella), Gate Close (*the Gates* 1688, *v.* gata), Glead Royd (*v.* gleoda 'kite', rod[1]), Goit Close (*v.* gota 'water-channel'), Goldthorpe Close, Green Close (ib 1709), Green Croft, Haslewells 1709 (*v.* hæsel, wella), Hassocks (*Hassacks* 1709, *v.* hassuc 'clump of coarse grass'), Headland, Hearne Royd, Heave(s) Royd, Great Hendle & Little Hindle (*ij closes called Hendalls* 1663 *Glebe*, *v.* halh), Horn Close, Hunger Hill (ib 1771, *v.* hungor, hyll), The Ing (ib 1688, *v.* eng 'meadow'), Jep Royd (*Jeproid* Jas 1, 1650, cf. *Ieppefeld* 1323 *MinAcct* 45, the ME pers.n. *Jeppe*, rod[1], feld), Joan Ing, Kirk Balk (*v.* kirkja, balca 'boundary ridge'), Kirkhill (ib 1341 YD vii, *Kirkhill Shutt* 1609 *Grant* 9, *v.* kirkja, hyll), Knowle Close (ib 1663 *Glebe*, 1709, *v.* cnoll 'hillock'), Lancar Smithy (*le Longecarsmethe* Jas 1, *v.* lang, kjarr 'marsh', smiððe), Leitch Land, Lindleys, Line Butts, Long Close (*the Long Close* 1695), Low Green 1841 O.S. (now Broadlands Fm), Long Lands, Lumb Close (*v.* lumm 'pool'), Market Stead, Mill Brook (*Myllnebrooke shutt* Jas 1, *v.* myln, brōc, dial. *shut* 'division of land'), Mold Royd (*Moldroide* Jas 1, *v.* molde 'soil', rod[1]), Nether Royds, Netherton Lane, New Close (ib 1646, 1652), North Field (*Northfeld* 1425 YD vii, *v.* norð, feld), Below Orchard (*le Orcherd* 1462, *-ard* Jas 1, *v.* orceard), Overking's Wood 1721 Tayl, Ox Close, Oxley Close, Pease Close, Pickard Croft, Pig Hill (*the Pighell* 1688, *v.* pightel), Pinfold Close (*v.* pynd-fald), Pit Close (ib 1771, *le Pitt close* Jas 1, *v.* pytt), Pith Hill, Pond Close (cf. *Ponde Inge* 1650, *v.* ponde, eng), Quarry Close (*Quarell Close* 1709, *v.* quarrelle 'quarry'), Ridings (*v.* rydding 'clearing'), Riley Royd (*Ryley Roides* 1699, *-Royds* 1709, from the surname *Riley* (cf. Riley 246 *infra*), rod[1]), Rockley Royd, Rought or Waste (*v.* rūhet 'rough ground'), Rough Close, Round Ing, Shay Shutt (cf. *Shagheforlange* 1408 *WCR* 1, *Shawshutt* Jas 1, *the Shayclose or Shayshutt* 1648, *Shaw(e)feild* Jas 1, *v.* sceaga 'copse', dial. *shut* 'division of land'), Short Leys, Shrog (*v.* scrogge 'brushwood'), Smithfield, South Field (*campo australi* 1310 Surv), Stubbings (*v.* stubbing), Swine Croft, Tanyard Ing, Thistle Close & Stubbing, Thorn Tree Close (ib 1709), Far & Near Tithe Free, Toad Hoyle (*v.* tādige, hol[1]), Tom Royd, Waterside, West Crofts (*Westcrofte* 1462, 1492, *v.* west, croft), Whitels, White Stocks (*Wytestock* 1308, *Whitestock* (*close*) Jas 1, *the White Stocks* 1695, *v.* hwīt, stocc 'stump'), Willow Garth, Wood Ing, Woollin Well (*Wluinewellk'* 12, *Woollen Well Flatt* 1716 *Glebe*, the OE pers.n. *Wulfwine*, wella, kjarr, flat).

(b) *Armel-, Armyl-, Armorecrofte(s)* 1525, Jas i (*v.* croft), *Bluntbancke, -ing* Jas i (the surname *Bl(o)unt,* banke, eng), *Bradleia rode* c. 1190 (*v.* brād, lēah, rod¹), *Carr Close* 1672 *Grant* 92, *-yngge* Jas i, *le Carr pasture* Jas i (*v.* kjarr, eng), *Criglestone Towne feild* Jas i (*v.* tūn, feld), *le Croke mores* (*v.* krókr 'bend', mōr), *Dammestede* 1342 Tayl, *Damsted(e)* 1462, 1492 (*v.* dammr, stede, cf. Newmillerdam *supra*), *Dawroid* 1625 (*v.* Daw Lane *supra*), *Dockfourth* Jas i (*v.* docce, ford), *Dosynerode* 1297 (*v.* rod¹), *Drakerre* 1452 (*v.* kjarr), *Emmott Roides* Jas i (the surname *Emmot*, rod¹), *Hayflatt* 1652, *the Hay Royde* 1688 (*v.* hēg, flat, rod¹), *John Well-head* 1684 *Glebe, Jony Well head* 1688 ('John's spring', *v.* wella), *Ketelberne croft* 12 (the ON pers.n. *Ketilbjǫrn*, croft), *Langfurley, Long furtheleʒ* Jas i (*v.* lang, ford, lēah), *Leuenad Crofteng* 1242 DodsN (the OE pers.n. *Lēofnōð*, croft, eng), *Leueceflat* 12 *Nost* 33d, *Leveteflat* c. 1190 (probably the OE pers.n. *Lēofgeat*, flat), *Lirkhill* 1688 (*v.* hyll, the first el. may be connected with dial. *lirk* 'a wrinkle'), *Long Hage* 1652 (*v.* haga), *Midleshutt* Jas i (dial. *shut* 'division of land'), *Norreskerre* 1452 (the ME surname *Norreis*, kjarr 'marsh'), *Pearesroid* 1652 (the ME pers.n. *Per*, rod¹), *Rye Close* 1699 (*v.* rȳge, clos), *Rourode, Westrowerode* 1331 (*v.* rūh 'rough', rod¹), *Serigge* 1308 (*v.* hrycg), *the Spring Royde* 1650 (*v.* spring 'plantation', rod¹), *Through Roides* 1650, *Westenges* 1314 (*v.* west, eng), *Whynimores, Shorte Whynny More* Jas i (*v.* hvin 'gorse', mōr).

3. SANDAL MAGNA (102–3418), now in the County Borough of Wakefield

> *Sandal(a), -dale* 1086 DB, 1164–81 YCh viii, 1188–1202 ib, l. 12 *Nost* 33d, 13 *Lewes* 298d, 1203 Cur (p), 1230 FF, 1239 Ebor, 1241 Lib, 1274 WCR *et passim* to 1428 FA, (*Maiori-*) 1091–7, 1147 YCh viii, (-*Major*) 1247 Ebor, (*Magna-*) 1324 *Lewes* 299d
>
> *Sandhale* 1402 YI   *Sandehall'* 1492 *MinAcct* 02
>
> *Sandall* 1409 DiocV, 1452 Brett, 1454 Test ii, 1515 FF, (*Grete-*) 1546 YChant, (-*Magna*) 1563 FF, 1649 WYD
>
> *Sondall* 1448 Pat
>
> *Saundall* 1531 Test iv, (-*Magna*) 1550 WillY

'Sandy nook of land', *v.* sand, halh; cf. Kirk Sandall i, 21 *supra*, from which it is distinguished as 'Magna' or *Grete* because of its important castle (*v.* magna).

MILNTHORPE, *Milne-, Mylnethorp(e)* 1297 LS (p), WCR, 1303 Pat, 1323 WCR (p), 1341 YD vii, 1400 Pat *et freq* to 1643 YD i, *Millynthorp* 1324 WCR, *Miln-, Mylnthorp(e)* 1373, 1526 FF, 1587 WillY, *Milthorpe* 1574 ib, 1659 Pick. 'Outlying farmstead with a mill', *v.* myln, þorp. Cf. Introd. Similar names occur in Thurnscoe and Worsborough i, 92, i, 297 *supra*.

NEW BIGGIN HILL, *le Neubiging* 13 YD vii, *-bigg'* 1298 ib, *the New-biggeing* 1286 ib, *-bigging* 1315 ib, *Newbyggin* 1274 ib, *Newbyghing* 1314 YD vii, *-bygyng*, *-i-* 1405 *WCR* 4d, 1527 WillY, 1535 VE, (*-hill*) 1647 WillY, *le Nubigging* 1331 WCR, *Newbygginhill, -y-* 1575 FF, Jas 1 *Surv*, 1709 WMB. 'The new building', *v.* nīwe, bigging, a common type of p.n. in the north.

PLEDWICK

> *Plegwic, -wik, -wyc, -wyk(e)* 13 YD vii (p), 1246 *Ass* 30d, 1252 FF (p), 1285, 1327 WCR
> *Plegewyc* 1252 YD x (p), *-wykes* 1315 WCR
> *Pleggewyk* 1284 WCR (p), 1310 *Surv* 11, 17
> *Pleghwyk* 1379 PT (p)
> *Pledwick(e), -weycke, -wyk, -wike* 1479 DodsN, 16 YD vii, 1534 FF, 1535 VE *et freq* to 1709 WMB

This is probably a compound of OE plega 'play, sports, game' and wīc 'a hamlet, a dependent farmstead, a building', corresponding to OE pleg-stede or pleg-stōw 'sport place, place where games were held'. But the OE pers.n. *Plecga* is also possible, but less likely because of the absence of medial *-e-* in most of the earlier spellings. In either case medial *-g-* is due to ON influence. The later *Pled-* is merely a substitution for *Pleg-*.

PUGNEYS, *Pukenhale* 1310 *Surv*, 1312 Cl, *Pokenhale* 1323 *MinAcct* 45, *Pugnall* Jas 1 *Surv*, 1699 *WCR* 4, *Pignall* 1709 WMB, (*Low*) *Pugnals* 1845 *TA*. 'Goblins' nook of land', *v.* pūca (gen. pl. *pūcna*), halh, the latter denoting a piece of flat low-lying water-meadow within a loop of the R. Calder.

ROUGHLEY HILLS (local), *Rughlawesc'* 1310 *Surv*, *Rou(g)hloweshawe* 1323 *MinAcct* 45, 1342 Tayl, *Roughley hill* Jas 1 *Surv*, *-Hills* 1845 *TA*. 'Rough mound on a hill', *v.* rūh, hlāw, hyll, and sceaga 'copse'.

STAND BRIDGE, *Stanbrigsyk* 1330 WCR, *Stainbriggbeck* 1530 DodsN, *Stanbrigg(e)* 1565 WillY, 1699 *WCR* 4, 1709 WMB, (*-Inge*) Jas 1 *Surv, -bridge* 1709 WMB, *le Standbrigg* Jas 1 ib, *Standbrig(e)* 1651 *Grant* 75, 1686 *Sand* 1. 'Stone bridge', *v.* stān (replaced by ON steinn in the *Stain-* spelling), brycg. The intrusive *-d-* after *-n-* occurs also in several p.ns. in *Hand-* (from hana), cf. Phonol. § 46.

THURSTONHAUGH (lost), *Thurstanhaye* 1274 WCR, *-hawe* 1307, 1309 ib, *-hagh(e)* 1310 *Surv*, 1316 WCR, 1323 *MinAcct* 45, (*-in Sandale*)

1327 WCR, *Thorstanhahe* 1277 ib, *-hagh* 1313 ib, *Thurstonhagh* 1319
YD viii, *-hawe* 1492 *MinAcct* 02, *Thornstanhagh* 1405 *WCR* 1d,
Thrustanhaghe 1452 ib 1. 'Thurstan's enclosure', *v.* haga. The
pers.n. is an anglicised form of ON *Þorsteinn* (Feilitzen 396).

WOODTHORPE, (*le*) *Wodethorp*(*e*) 13 YD vii, 1252 FF, YD x (p), 1277,
1307 WCR, 1297 LS (p), *Woodthorp*(*e*) 1330 DodsN, 1582, 1588
WillY, (*-field*) 1533 *Grant* 73, *Wodthorpe* 1511 YD viii. 'Outlying
farmstead by the wood', *v.* wudu, þorp.

BEECHFIELD. BELLEFIELD. BELLE VUE, 1817 M. CARR LANE,
Sandalker 1298 WCR, *Sandall Carr, le Carr pasture, le great Carr
Yng* Jas 1 *Surv, v.* kjarr 'marsh', cf. Carsom f.n. *infra.* CASTLE
HILL, 1817 M, *v.* Sandal Castle *infra.* CASTLE LODGE, 1817 M.
CLEEVETHORPE. GALLOWS HILL, cf. *Gallows Flatt* 1845 *TA, v.*
galga, hyll, flat. HIGHFIELD. HILL TOP, 1709 WMB, *v.* hyll,
topp. MANYGATES HO, *Manygates* 1617 Tayl, 1709 WMB, *Manni-
gates Close* 1650 *WCR* 1, 'many gates' *v.* manig, geat (pl. gatu).
MILNTHORPE GREEN, 1799 *EnclA* 87, *Milnethorp Green* 1709 WMB,
cf. *Adam atte Grene* 1326 WCR, *v.* Milnthorpe *supra,* grēne². PIN-
FOLD LANE, *Sandall Pinfold* 1709 WMB, *v.* pynd-fald. PORTO-
BELLO HO, *Portobello* 1841 O.S. POUNT. SANDAL CASTLE,
Castrum, Castri, etc., *de Sandale* 13 Dugd vi, 1413 Pat, *Castrum de
Sandall* 1462 *MinAcct* 99, 1471 Pat, *Sandall Castle* 1637 Tayl, cf.
also *Castellflate* 1415 YD vii, and Castle Field f.n. *infra, v.* castel,
hyll, feld; the castle, of which there are remains, was a stronghold of
the Earls of Warren on the prominent Castle Hill, and the Battle of
Wakefield 1460 was fought near here. SANDAL CLIFF, probably
identical with *Hecliffes* 1310 *Surv,* 'high banks', *v.* hēah, clif.
SANDAL COMMON, 1845 *TA,* formerly *le Mur'* 1425 YD vii, *Sandall
Moore* Jas 1 *Surv, v.* mōr. SHOOTER HILL (lost), *Schytarhille* 1275
WCR, *Shit*(*t*)*erhill* 1558 Tayl, 1650 *YAS* 97, *Shooterhill* Jas 1 *Surv,*
1709 WMB, (*-alias Litle Oldfeild*) 1600 WCR 3d, *Shotterhill* 1612
MinAcct 21, *Shoterhills* 1682 Tayl, cf. Shooter Close 1845 *TA, v.*
scēotere 'a shooter, archer', hyll, most likely where archery was
practised. SUGAR LANE, cf. *Sugar Closes* 1709 WMB, ME *sugre*
'sugar', probably denoting 'sweet land'. THREE HOUSES INN,
Sandal-Three-Houses 1822 Langd. WHEATCROFT, 1845 *TA, v.*
hwǣte, croft. WOOLGREAVES, *Wulfgrene* (sic for *-greue*) 1307 WCR,
Woolgraves 1709 WMB, 'wolf wood', *v.* wulf, grǣfe.

FIELD-NAMES

The principal forms in (*a*) are 1845 *TA* 343. Spellings dated 1298–1309
are WCR, 1310 *Surv* 11, 17, 1314, 1316, 1324 WCR, 1323 *MinAcct* 45,
1407–1452 *WCR*, 1461, 1462, 1492 *MinAcct* 60, 99, 02, 1485, 1499, 1551,
1600 *WCR*, Jas 1 *Surv* 11, 19, 1612 *MinAcct* 21, 1650, 1699 WCR, 1709
WMB, 1799 *EnclA* 87.

(*a*) Bigland(s), Binns Close 1709, Black Banks (ib 1699, *le black banke
feild* Jas 1, *Black bancks* 1709, *v.* blæc, banke), Bridge End, Briery Close,
Broad Croft, Brook Close (cf. *le Brooke* Jas 1, *v.* brōc), Brooks Smithy 1841
O.S., Broom Close (*le Brome Close* 1699, *v.* brōm, clos), Little Burnett
(probably bærnet 'place cleared by burning'), Butterwells (*Buterwell* 1310,
v. butere, wella), Butts Field (*v.* butte 'abutting strip of land'), Campy Close
& Lands (*Compylands* Jas 1), (Great & Hall) Carsom (*Carsome shutt, -sam*
Jas 1, 1650, *le Carsum Close* 1699, probably from a ME *ker-hūsum* 'at the
houses in the marsh', *v.* kjarr, hūs, -um, Great Carr *infra*, and for the reduction cf. Newsholme 104 *supra*), Castle Field (*le Castell Felde* 1415 YD vii
Castelfeld 1551, (*le*) *Castlefeild* Jas 1, 1709, *v.* castel, feld, Sandal Castle
supra), Chevet Close (cf. *Cheyfteoxgang* 1341 YD vii, named from the nearby
Chevet i, 278 *supra*, *v.* ox-gang), Cross (*Crosse Close* 1637 Tayl, doubtless
named from *crucem ad finem pontis de Wakefeld* 1638 Tayl 312–13, *v.* cros),
Denkin Close, Dickencross (*Dicconcrosse* Jas 1, the ME pers.n. *Diccon* (a
derivative of *Richard*), cros, cf. *Diconcroft* 172 *infra*), Dove Croft, Fence
Hills, Flower Croft, Fowlwell (*Fowlewells* Jas 1, *v.* fugol 'bird' or fūl 'foul',
wella), Foxes (cf. *Foxfrythe* Jas 1, *le Foxfirthes* 1699, 'fox wood', *v.* fox,
fyrhð̄e), Great Carr (*v.* kjarr 'marsh', Carsom f.n. *supra*), Hanging Acres
(*v.* hangende 'steep', æcer), Hazlewells (*Haslewell* 1639 WB 21, *v.* hæsel,
wella), Hell Croft, Hoblands (cf. *Hobbinleyroide* 1551, from *Hobbin*, a variant
of *Robin*, lēah, rod[1], land), Hooton Bridge, The Ing (*v.* eng 'meadow'),
Jonas Acre, Kiln Croft (*Kiln Croft Close* 1765 *Grant*[2] 193, *v.* cyln, croft),
Kiln Hill (*Kilnehill feild* Jas 1, *le Kilne Hill* 1699, *v.* prec., hyll), The Leys
(*v.* lēah), Little Field Close (*littlefeild* Jas 1, *v.* lytel, feld), Long Floor (*Long
Flower* Jas 1, 'long pavement or floor', *v.* lang, flōr(r)), Long Ing, Long Tofts
1709 (*le Longtofte feild* Jas 1, *Long-*, *Shorte-Tofts* 1666 *Sand* 3, *v.* lang, topt
'enclosure'), March Lane, Meeting Close, Far & Near Mutton, Pease Close,
Peter Field (ib 1799), Pighill (*leȝ Pighilles* Jas 1, *v.* pightel 'enclosure'),
Quarry Close & Hill (cf. *le Quarrel(l)feild* Jas 1, *-close* 1699, *v.* quarrelle
'quarry', clos, feld), Rat Hole Close (*Rathoile* Jas 1, *v.* ræt 'rat', hol[1]),
Riddle Close, Low & Upper Ridings (*le Rideings* 1699, *Ridings* 1709, *v.*
rydding 'clearing'), Low & Top Rods (*v.* rod[1] 'clearing'), Round Ing, St.
Mary (*St. Mary Close* Jas 1, *le Sct' Marys Closes* 1699, doubtless land
devoted to the service of the Virgin Mary; the parish church is dedicated to
St Helen), Sandal Grove 1841 O.S., Silverwood Beck Close, Smithy Croft,
Stand Flatts, Stony Royd, Sykes Close, Tenter Croft ('croft with tenters for
stretching cloth'), Thickheads (*Lit(t)le Thick(e)head(e) Close* Jas 1, 1600,
v. þicce 'thicket', hēafod, or from a nickname *Thickhead*), The Tongue (*v.*
tunge), Town End Close (ib 1653 *Grant* 82), Town Ing (*le Touneng* 1342

Tayl, *Pledwick Towne Ing* Jas 1, *le Towne Ings* 1699, *v.* tūn, eng), Town Row 1709 (*v.* prec., rāw), Washing Nook, Waterside Close, Watery Lane Close, Well Ing 1709, Willow Garth & Holt, Winn Close, Woodthorpe Green 1799.

(b) *le Asshe Yng* Jas 1 (*v.* æsc, eng), *le Neare barrowe royde* Jas 1 (*v.* beorg 'hill, barrow', rod[1]), *Bysmarerowe* 1307 (OE, ME *bismer* 'shame', rāw 'row of houses', possibly 'houses of ill-repute or fame'), *Bleasers* 1613 *Cause* 908, *Bluntcloise* 1407 (cf. *Bluntbancke* 107 *supra*), *Broadbalke* 1612 (*v.* brād, balca 'boundary ridge'), *Brodeollers* 1600, Jas 1 (*v.* brād, alor 'alder-tree'), *le Fer-, Nerbrowne Roid, -royd* Jas 1 (doubtless the surname *Brown*, rod[1] 'clearing'), *Burghes* 1314, *Burgleve* Jas 1 (*v.* burh, possibly a reference to the Castle Hill), *Clayton Close* Jas 1, *Cloghes forlange* 1408 (*v.* clōh 'dell', furlang), *Le Cryngles* Jas 1 (*v.* kringla 'a circle, the circular sweep of a river', no doubt describing the loops in the course of the R. Calder), *Crosse-shutt* 1650 (*v.* cros, dial. *shut* 'a division of land'), *le Erleroide* 1452 (*v.* eorl, here referring to one of the Earls of Warren, rod[1] 'clearing'), *le Fleches* 1324 (possibly OFr *fleche* 'an arrow', here used probably to denote 'a place where archery was practised', cf. EPN i, 176 s.v. fleinn), *le Freehold Close* 1699, *Gesthous* 1342 Tayl (ME *gest* 'guest', hūs), *Gyecliff* 1445 (possibly an allusion to the famous Guy of Warwick of ME romance; Guy's Cliffe Wa 264 replaces an older p.n. only in the sixteenth century), *Gytynereng* 1407 (probably ME *gyternere* 'a gittern player', as a byname, eng), *le Grene dike* Jas 1 (*v.* grēne[1], dīc), *Halflordeland* 1485, *le Halling* Jas 1, the *hallestede* 1298 (*v.* hall, eng, stede), *peruen' de Heronsell'* 1492, *Hoggecrofte* Jas 1 (*v.* hogg 'hog', croft), *Hoyleynge* Jas 1 (*v.* hol[1], eng), *le Intac* 1425 YD vii, *Great, Little Intack* 1684 Tayl (*v.* intak), *le Jeffery Closes* 1699 (the pers.n. *Geoffrey*, clos), *le Kykeeng* 1342 Tayl (*v.* eng, cf. Keighley pt. vi *infra*), *Kil(l)nefeild* Jas 1, *-grenes* 1314 (cf. Kiln Croft f.n. *supra* feld, grēne[2]), *Langacres* 1310 (*v.* lang, æcer), *Le longe Orchard* Jas 1 (*v.* orceard), *Longrode* Jas 1 (*v.* rod[1] 'clearing'), *Malynroide* 1499 (the ME pers.n. *Mal(l)in*, rod[1]), *le Myredoles* 1650 (*v.* mýrr, dāl 'share of the common land'), *Nelcrofte, Nellson Crofte* Jas 1 (the fem. pers.n. *Nell* and the surname *Nelson* derived from it, croft), *le Overend* Jas 1, *le Overfurlong* Jas 1, *Parrockes* Jas 1 (*v.* pearroc 'a paddock'), *Pyecroft* (*Close*) 1650, 1651 *Grant* 75 (*v.* pie[2] 'magpie', croft), *Pitt Close* 1638 Tayl (*v.* pytt), *Prustons Crofte* Jas 1 (a croft occupied by *Ric' Purston* ib), *Ravennes-acre* 1425 YD vii (the ON pers.n. *Hrafn*, æcer), *Ryssches* 1310, *le Rishes* 1323, 1342 Tayl (*v.* risc 'a rush'), *Robbinroyde* Jas 1 (the pers.n. *Robin*, rod[1]), *Rothellclose* 1650, *Rodland* 1462 (*v.* rod[1] 'clearing', land), *Round Ing* 1679 Tayl (*v.* rond, eng), *Saynt Anne Close* Jas 1, *Southill* 1310, *Southhillfeild* 1650 (*v.* sūð, hyll), *Southwode* 1316 (*v.* sūð, wudu), *Standrawing, -eynge* Jas 1, 1650 (*v.* stān, rāw 'row of houses', eng), *Stoneacre* 1407 (*v.* stān, æcer), *le Townefeild* 1612, *le Turneng* 1323, 1342 Tayl (*v.* trun 'round', eng), *le Vrchynlaine* Jas 1 (ME *urchon* 'hedgehog', lane), *Welleferme* 1323 (*v.* wella), *le Westhay* Jas 1 (*v.* west, (ge)hæg 'enclosure'), *Westwod(e)* 1307, *-side* 1316 (*v.* west, wudu), *le Yate(steed)* Jas 1 (*v.* geat 'gate', stede).

4. WALTON (102–3517)

Waleton, -tun(a), -t' 1086 DB, 1159–80 YCh 1681, 1166 P (p) 13
YD vii, p. 1229 *Nost* 35d, 1243 Fees, 1298, 1307 WCR, *Walton* 1252
FF, 1275 WCR, 1297 LS, 1305 DodsN *et passim* to 1515 FF, (*Midle-*)
1594 FF. 'Farmstead of the Welshmen or serfs', *v.* Walh (gen. plur.
Wala), tūn; cf. Introd.

THE BALK, cf. *Great Balk Close* 1844 *TA, v.* balca 'boundary ridge'.
BULL BRIDGE, cf. *Bull Groves* 1844 *TA.*   CLAY ROYD BRIDGE.
ELMWOOD HO.   FAIRHOLME.   FOX WELL.   HARE PARK, 1706
PRCrf, 1771 M, *v.* hara, park.   HAW PARK, 1841 O.S., *Hou* 1159–
72 *Nost* 34, *v.* haugr 'mound', park.   LOWER TOWN, 1841 O.S.,
Netherwalton 1594 FF, & OVERTOWN, *Ouer-, Overwalton* 1314 YD
vii, 1594 FF, *Walton, Upper* 1822 Langd, *v.* neoðera, uferra, Walton
supra.   SIKE LANE.   SOAP HOUSE BRIDGE, *Soap House* 1841 O.S.,
OE *sāp*, ME *sope* 'soap', hūs.   STONE HEAPS.   STUBBS FM, cf.
Stub(s) Piece 1811 PRCrf, 1817 M, *v.* stubb 'stump'.   THORNTREE
HILL.   WALTON COMMON, 1799 *EnclA.*   WALTON HALL, 1763
Grant[2].   WALTON PARK, 1841 O.S., *v.* park.

FIELD-NAMES

The principal forms in (*a*) are 1844 *TA* 421. Spellings dated 1314 are
YD vii, and 1317 YD vi.

(*a*) Beck Close (*v.* bekkr 'stream'), Far Carr (*v.* kjarr 'marsh'), Near
Carson (cf. Carsom f.n. 110 *supra*), Cut Close (*v.* cut 'water-channel'),
Far Dikes, Far Moors, Gate Shackles (probably for ME *gate-shadel* 'cross-
roads'), Hall Ing (*v.* Walton Hall *supra*, eng 'meadow'), High Field, Far &
Near Ings (*v.* eng), Law Close, Loack House Close, Lord Ing, Marsh Ing,
North Field (ib 1684 Tayl), North Royd (*litle North Royds* 1684 Tayl, *v.*
rod[1] 'clearing'), Old Moor, Pellett Croft, Rick Close, Rye Croft, Snary
Wells, Swine Dikes, Town Croft, Tween Towns (cf. Lower-, Overtown
supra), Well Close.

(*b*) *Aylmerod* 1314 (the ME pers.n. *Ailmer* (OE *Æþelmǣr*), rod[1] 'clearing'), *le Deneheued* 1317 (*v.* denu 'valley', hēafod), *le fal* 1314 (*v.* (ge)fall
'clearing'), *le faurteneoxgang* 1314 (*v.* oxgang 'a measure of land'), *Hughrod*
1314 (the ME pers.n. *Hugh*, rod[1]), *Hugthorn* 1314 (*v.* prec., þorn), *le long-
drihalges* 1314 (*v.* drȳge 'dry', halh 'nook of land'), *le longmore* 1314 (*v.* lang,
mōr), *Mirfeldacre* 1314 (Mirfield 197 *infra* as a surname, æcer), *le Schortun-
enge* 1314 (*v.* sceort, tūn, eng), *le Thorngrene* 1317 (*v.* þorn, grēne[2]).

ii. Crofton

CROFTON (102–3817)

Scroftune, Scrotone 1086 DB, *Croftun(e)*, *-ton(a)* 12 *Nost* 7d, 32–3 (YCh 1428, 1430, 1672 etc.), 1121 Tockw, 1154–77 YCh 1459, 1673, 1201 Cur, 1215 ChR, 1219 FF, 1280 Ch, 1286 WCR *et passim* to 1634 PRCrf, *Croffeton* 1316 Vill. 'Farmstead with a croft', *v.* croft, tūn.

BIRKWOOD HO, *Bi-*, *Byrkewood* 1554 *MinAcct* 19, 1641 ib 39, (*-bothom(e)*)) 1557 *Surv*, 1641 *MinAcct* 39, *Berkwood* 1614 *MinAcct* 41, *Birkwood* 1608 FF, 1639 WillY, *Burkwood* 1650 PRCrf. 'Birch wood', *v.* birki, wudu.

OAKENSHAW FM

Akensache 1133–53 YCh 1672, *-shag* 12 *Nost* 32, *-schae* l. 12 ib 15, *-s(c)hawe* Ed 1 ib 11d, 1280 Ch

Akeneschage 1153–5, 1177–93 YCh, 1497, 1516

Okinschawe 1292 *Nost* 63, *Okynshaa*, *-shaw* 1522, 1529 WillY

Okenshaw(e) 1554 *MinAcct* 19, 1555 FF, 1639 PRCrf

'Oaken wood', *v.* ācen, sceaga, cf. Oakenshaw iii, 17 *infra*.

THE BALK. BRACKEN HILL, 1844 *TA*, *Broken hill* (sic) 1663 *Glebe*, *v.* brakni, hyll, cf. *Brackenhill* 78 *supra*, 119 *infra*. BRAND HILL, 1663 *Glebe*, *v.* brand 'place cleared by burning', hyll. BURCROFT FM. CHURCH HILL, cf. *pontem ecclesiæ* l. 12 *Nost* 33, *Church Close & Croft* 1844 *TA*. COCK LANE, cf. *Cocke-cole hill* 1663 *Glebe*, *Cock Close* 1844 *TA*. CROFTON HALL, 1649 PRCrf, *Hall* 1817 M. MANOR HO. OAKENSHAW BECK, *Okenechauebrok* 1310 *Surv*, *v.* Oakenshaw *supra*, bekkr, brōc. OLD HALL, 1841 O.S. RED BECK. SHAY HILL, *Croftonsahe* 1286 WCR, *The Shay* 1802 EnclA 118, *Shay Hill Close* 1844 *TA*, *v.* sceaga 'copse', hyll. SLACK LANE, cf. *Slack Hill Close* 1844 *TA*, *v.* slakki 'hollow in a hillside'. SPRING HILL, 1841 O.S., *v.* spring 'well-spring', hyll. WINDMILL HILL, cf. *the Windmill house* 1725 PRCrf, *v.* wind, myln.

FIELD-NAMES

The principal forms in (*a*) are 1844 *TA* 120. Spellings dated 12 are *Nost* 32–3, 1219 FF, 1323 *Nost* 60d, 1554–1641 *MinAcct* 19, 39, 45, 1663, 1764 *Glebe*, 1802 EnclA 118.

8

(*a*) Agbrigg Bottoms (*v.* Agbrigg 117 *infra*, botm), Barber Close & Royd, Barbles, Bare Croft, Great Bollands, Bollands Close, Boulby Croft, Brook Side Close, Broom Close (*Brome close* 1641, *v.* brōm, clos), Brown Croft, Bull Croft, Burgess Royd, Carr Lane Close (*le Ker* 12, *Ker* 1219, *v.* kjarr 'marsh'), Coal Pit Field 1802, Crab Tree Close, Crofton Green 1802 (*v.* grēne²), Doddish Close (ib 1764, *The Doddish* 1663), Easam Close, Emroyd Close, Fat Hills (*Farthill* 1554, 1559), Friday Flatt, Green End Shutt (dial. *shut* 'division of land'), Grey Croft, Halstead Close (*Hallstead* 1841 O.S., *v.* hall, stede), Harrot Hills (*The Harrot hills* 1663), Hawksworth Hill Field, High Croft, Home Croft (*Holmescrot* (sic) 12, *v.* holmr 'water-meadow', croft), Horse Close, The Ings (*v.* eng 'meadow'), Laith Close (*v.* hlaða 'barn'), Lidget 1841 O.S. (*v.* hlid-geat 'swing-gate'), Little Royd (*v.* rod¹ 'clearing'), Mill Close (*clusam molendini* 12, *v.* myln, clos), Nelson Close, Noble Bitt, Old Field, Ox Close, Ox Hill Close, The Park, Pease Croft, Pighill Close (*v.* pightel 'enclosure'), Pinfold (*v.* pynd-fald), Quarry Hill Close, The Ring, Smithy Close, Stack garth ('stack yard'), Steel Ings (*v.* stigel 'stile', eng), Tan Pit Croft, Thorn Close, Town End Close, Turn Royd (*v.* trun 'round', rod¹), Washbeck Close, Well Close & Croft, West Beck 1841 O.S. (*Westbec* 1219, *v.* west, bekkr 'stream'), Willow Garth, Wood Close.

(*b*) *Archeclose* 1554, *Bromerode* 1641 (*v.* brōm, rod¹), *Castelgate* 12 (*v.* castel, gata), *Crumelandis* 1219 (*v.* crumb 'crooked', land), *The Culers* 1663, *Cumberland* 12, *Doodley* 1614, *Dooles* 1559, 1578 (*v.* dāl 'share of the common land'), *Estaldefeld* 12, *Estolddefeld* 1219 (possibly an OE pers.n. *Ēastwald*, not recorded, but it may be a compound of ēast, ald 'old' and feld), *Faukesoxgand'* (sic) 1323 (the ME surname *Faukes*, oxgang), *Flaskedale* 1219 (*v.* flask 'swamp', dāl), *Forbyland* 1641, *Holewell* 1554 (*v.* hol¹, wella), *Ladyhouse* 1641, *Lycherood* 1641 (*v.* līc 'corpse', rod¹, doubtless 'clearing where a body was found'), *Lytster-*, *Lister-close* 1554, 1559 (ME *litester* 'dyer', clos), *Maceon Oxengang* 1323 (*v.* oxgang, *Maceon* is a surname from OFr *macon* 'mason'), *Maldrode* 12 (the ME fem. pers.n. *Mald* 'Maud', rod¹), *None fosse* 12, *Petecuppehull* 1219 (possibly an error for set-copp 'flat-topped hill', otherwise pete 'peat', copp 'hill-top', hyll), *Queteclif* 1219 (probably for hwīt, clif), *Rawegrenes* 12 (*v.* rāw 'row (of trees or houses)', grǣfe 'copse'), *Redker* 12 ('red marsh' or 'reed marsh', *v.* rēad, hrēod, kjarr), *Stokewelle* 12 (*v.* stocc, wella), *Surdeualeng* 12 (*v.* eng 'meadow', cf. *Walter de Surdeuall* 12 *Nost* 32d), *Wallesland* 1424 Rent, *Walterode* 1383 YD vi (the pers.n. *Walter*, rod¹), *The Wilks* 1663.

iii. Warmfield

1. SHARLSTON (102–3918)

Scharuest(on)' 12 *Nost* 109, 1173–93 YCh 1516, 13 *Nost* 108d, 1296 Lacy Comp (p), *Scharvestona* 1180–5 YCh 1542, *Shareueston* 1304 YI

Scharneston(e) c. 1160 *Nost* 14d, e. 13 ib 109, 1276 YI, 1286 WCR
  Sharneston 1254 FF, 1303 Aid, 1316 Vill, 1344 DodsN, 1360
  FF, 1380 Ch, 1390 *Nost* 67, 1400 Pat, *Scarneston* 1276 RH
Sashtunia c. 1173 Pont
Sarneston 1243 Fees
S(c)harweston 1291–1312 *Nost* 170d, 1297 LS, *Scarweston* l. 12
  Nost 170d, 172
Sharston' 1379 PT, *S(c)hareston* 1428 WillY, 1447 Pat, *Sherston*
  1695 M
S(c)harleston(e) 1428, 1453 WillY, 1532, 1574 FF *et passim* to
  1591 FF, *Sharlston* 1633 PRCrf, 1641 Rates
Shyrleston 1555 BM
Sharleton 1587 FF

The few spellings with *Scharwes-* make it certain that the correct
earlier form is *Scharues-*, for which some at least of the *Scharnes-*
spellings are misreadings, due to the ambiguity of *u* and *n* in the
court hand. The interpretation is difficult; Goodall and Moorman
connect the first el. with OE *scearn* 'dung' and *scearn-wifel* 'dung-
beetle', but these suggestions are based upon the assumption that
the early *Scharnes-* spelling is the correct form. Ekwall (DEPN
s.n.) associates the name with Shareshill St, which has similar
spellings for the first el. (*Servesed* 1086 DB, *Sarneshull* 1213, *Share-
weshulf* 1252) and derives both from OE *scræf* 'cavern, pit, hovel',
Sharlston from OE *Scræfes-tūn* '*tun* by a *scræf* or narrow valley';
the sense 'narrow valley' is not appropriate here and if the name is
from *scræf* it must be used in one of its normal senses 'cave, hole, pit,
hovel'. But the use of the gen.sg. form in this compound would be
unusual, whilst the supposed metathesis to *Sharf-* occurs only in
these two p.ns., which have in fact none of the normal spellings of
scræf as in other p.ns. like Shrawley Wo 78 (*Scraue-*, *Shraue-*, etc.).
Similar objections would also apply to an OE pers.n. connected with
OE *scrēawa* 'shrew, rascal', since a derivative corresponding
to some such word as MHG *schröuwel* 'devil' would have produced OE (Angl) *scrēwel*, and even if it were metathesised we should
have expected ME *Scher-* forms. The best suggestion therefore,
for Sharlston at least, is Moorman's. OE *scearn-wifel* could have
been used as an appellative in a compound of this kind, but it
could also have been a nickname in the same way as OE *wifel*
'beetle' was in names like Wilsill (Bishopside) pt. v *infra*. It is
obviously in a much reduced form in the ME spellings, but it easily

8-2

accounts for the variation between *Scharues-*, *Scharnes-* and *Scharwes-*, possibly also the later *Scharles-*, though that has probably developed through the influence of the common pers.n. *Charles*. *v.* tūn and Addenda.

Burcroft Fm, *Burcroft Shutt* 1842 *TA*, *v.* būr[1] 'cottage', croft. Coalpit Field, *le Colepittes* 1323 WCR, *v.* col[1], pytt. Damhead Wood, 1841 O.S., *Dam Wood* 1842 *TA*, *v.* dammr; the dam is northeast of the village. Dean Field, 1841 O.S., cf. *Dean or Piper Close* 1842 *TA*, *v.* denu 'valley' (a small valley about 1 mile west of the village). Fleming Hall (lost), *Flemynge hall* 1564 Visit, named from the *Fleming* family (15 YD vi, 196, 1564 Visit), *v.* hall. Grime Lane, *Grime Lane Shutt* 1842 *TA*, possibly ON gríma 'a mark on tree' which is well-evidenced in road-names (cf. Legrams iii, 246 *infra*), lane, dial. *shut* 'division of land'. High St, 1841 O.S., part of the Roman road from Agbrigg and Wakefield to Pontefract (cf. Streethouse 123 *infra*). Lidget Lane, *v.* hlid-geat 'swing-gate'. Netheroyd Wood. Sharlston Common (1841 O.S.), Green, & Hall (*Hall* 1841 O.S.). Westend Ho.

FIELD-NAMES

The principal forms in (*a*) are 1842 *TA* 350. Spellings dated 12, e. 13 are *Nost* 109.

(*a*) Bernard Royd Leys, Bloom Croft, (Beck, Hollytree & Pit) Broomhill (*v.* brōm, hyll), Burrels Croft, Calf Croft, Carr Close & Lane (*v.* kjarr 'marsh'), Cross Dykes, Cuthbert Close & Shutt (dial. *shut* 'division of land'), Doles (*v.* dāl), East Field Pighill (*v.* pightel 'enclosure'), Edward Royd (ib 1841 O.S., *v.* rod[1] 'clearing'), Elm Close, Hammer Shutt, Holt Close, Ing Close (*v.* eng), Lady Close, Long Hedge Shutt, Mill Close, Nutton Close, Outen Gate End Shutt, Park Side Shutt, Piper Close, Raw Royd, Ruddings Close & Shutt (*v.* rydding 'clearing'), East & West Sands (*v.* sand), Sands Gate Shutt (*v.* prec., gata), Shillitoes Close (the surname *Shillitoe*), Short Butts, Smythy Close (cf. *Red Smithy* 1841 O.S., *v.* smiðöe), Steads Close, Wet Rushes Shutt, White Close, Willow Garth Shutt, Wood Shutt.

(*b*) *Borygthorpgrene* 12 (*v.* þorp, grēne[2]), *Gamelgrene* 12 (the ON pers.n. *Gamall*, grēne[2]), *Grefwellefurlang* 12, *Grifwellesic* 1180–5 YCh 1542 (*v.* gryfja 'hole, pit', wella, sīc), *Kirketoftes* e. 13 (*v.* kirkja, topt 'enclosure'), *Miccledale* 12 (*v.* micel, dāl 'share of common land'), *Polche* 12 (probably OFr *poulce* 'dust', surviving as dial. *powce* 'dust, rubbish', possibly here 'a heap of coal-dust'), *Staneswellesic* 12 (*v.* stān, wella, sīc).

2. WARMFIELD (102–3721)

Warnesfeld 1086 DB

Warnefeld(e) 1119–1292 Nost (*freq*) (YCh 1428–1542 *freq*) 1121
Tockw, 1201 Cur, 1215 ChR, 1252–1290 Ebor (*freq*), 1297 LS,
14 *Sawl* 194 *et passim* to 1486 MinAcct 66, *-feud* 1280 Ch, 1296
LacyComp, *MinAcct* 1, *-feild* 1624 FF

Warenfeld 1180–90 YCh 226   *Warnfeld* 1389 BM

Wernefeld 1201 Cur, 1340 *Ass* 1d

Warmefeld(e) 12 Nost 73, 1441 DiocV, 1495 Test iv, 1509 Test v
et freq to 1562 FF, *-feyld* 1603 NCWills, *-feild* 1624 FF

Warmfeld 1532 FF, *-field* 1641 Rates

Possibly 'stallion open country', *v.* **wrǣna** (**wǣrna**), **feld**; cf.
Ekwall, Studies[2] 67–8, but the first el. might well be OE *wærna*, a
metathesised form of **wrenna** 'wren', *Warm(e)-* is due to the labialisation of *-n-* to *-m-* by the following *-f-*.

AGBRIGG, *Aggebrigg(e)* 1277 WCR, 1286 YI, (*-brook*) 1327 WCR,
Agbrig(g) 1324 WCR, 1601 FF, 1697 *Grant*[2] 185, (*-broke*) 1331 ib,
1462 *MinAcct* 99. 'Aggi's bridge', from the ON byname *Aggi* or
ODan *Aggi* and **brycg**. The bridge (which was repaired in 1572 YD
iii) crossed a stream called *Aggebriggbrook*, etc. (which is a continuation of Oakenshaw Beck 113 *supra* to the Calder); it runs alongside
the canal, forming the Wakefield boundary. The bridge, which is at
the foot of the extensive Heath Common near the junction of the
roads from Pontefract (cf. High Street 116 *supra*, Hell Lane *infra*)
and Doncaster, was the meeting place of the wapentake (*v.* 99
supra); in 1286 (YI) an inquisition was held there and in 1324 WCR
40 it is reported as a place of execution.

HEATH, *Heth(e)* 1153–60 Nost 14, 1297 LS, 1379 PT, 1516 WillY,
1532 FF, *le Heth'* 1486 MinAcct 66, Bruera 1252 Ebor, *Heyth* 1565
FF, *Heath(e)* 1568 Arm, 1587 FF *et passim* to 1741 PRCrf. *v.* **hǣð**
'heathland' (Lat. *brueria*); it is still heathland.

KIRKTHORPE, *Torp* 1135–40 Pont, *Kirketorp* c. 1254 *Nost* 75, *Ki-*,
Kyrkethorp(e) 1461, 1486 MinAcct 09, 66, 1529 NCWills, 1547 FF,
Kirkthorpe 1591 WillY, *Kirthorpe* 1607 FF. *v.* **þorp** 'outlying farmstead'. The affix *Kirk-* (*v.* **kirkja**) alludes to the fact that the hamlet
belonged to Warmfield church for tithes (13 *Nost* 75).

BLACK HILL, 1841 *TA*, *v*. blæc, hyll.   BOUNDARY LANE, 1841 O.S.,
Boundary Close 1841 *TA*, the lane leads across the parish boundary to
Normanton.   CHURCH FIELD, 1841 *TA*.   COBBLERS HALL.   DAME
MARY BOLLES WELL.   ELSICKER LANE.   FRIESTON'S HOSPITAL
(almshouses), cf. *Hospital Croft* 1841 *TA*, and *the Hospital garth* 1764
Glebe (which belonged to Sagar's Hospital), *v*. garðr.   GLED HILL.
GOOSEHILL.   GRAVEL ASH.   GREEN LANE, 1841 O.S.   HEATH
COMMON, formerly *Hethegrene* 1486 *MinAcct* 66, *Greenheath Moore*
1675 Og, *v*. Heath *supra*, grēne[2].   HEATH HALL, 1695 *Sand* 2, 1817
M, *v*. Heath *supra*, hall.   HEATH OLD HALL, *the Oldhaull* 1539
WillY, *Old Hall* 1817 M, *v*. ald, hall and prec.   HELL LANE, 1841
O.S., named from *Hell-hole* 1728 LdsM, *v*. hell, hol[1]; this is a con-
tinuation of the Roman road from Pontefract called High Street 116
supra.   HILL TOP FM.   HORSE RACE END, *Race End Close* 1841
TA, doubtless a reference to the use of Hell Lane as a race-course
across Heath Common.   KIRKTHORPE WOOD, 1841 O.S. *v*. Kirk-
thorpe *supra*.   MARSHALL HILL.   MOUNT TARRY BY IT.   PEAS
HILL, *Pesehil* e. 13 *Nost* 109, *v*. pise 'pease', hyll.   PENHILL FIELD,
1841 O.S., *TA*, possibly a further example of the common hill-name
Penhill, Pendle (*v*. Brit penno- 'hill', hyll).   PLUMP HILL.   WARM-
FIELD COMMON, formerly *The Green* 1841 O.S., *le Grene* 1486
MinAcct 66, *v*. grēne[2].   WILLOW LANE, 1841 *TA*, *v*. wilig, lane.

FIELD-NAMES

The principal forms in (*a*) are 1841 *TA* 422 with some modern ones (1935)
marked (mod). Spellings dated c. 1196 are *Nost* 109d, 1292 *MinAcct* 26,
1325–1331 WCR, 1341 *Surv* 10, 5, 1461, 1486 *MinAcct* 09, 66, 1642, 1714
TN(F) 14, 15.

(*a*) Broomhill(s) close (*v*. the nearby Broomhill 116 *supra*), Bull Croft,
Burnt Heath, Cangle Ing, Cart Brigg *&* Royd (*v*. cræt, brycg, rod[1]), Chappel
Ing, Charley Close, Coal Pit Close, Conduit Close, Crabtree Close, The
Croft (*mod*), Dam Close, Dead Hills, Dean Close *&* Field (cf. Dean Field
116 *supra*), Fall, Followings (*mod*), Gregory, Holt Close, Lady Jane, Ledge-
hill 1714, Long Acre (*mod*), Long Royd, Low *&* Top Marsh(es) (*March
Lane* 1841 O.S., *v*. mersc), Middle Field (ib 1841 O.S.), Middle Leys (*v*.
lēah), Middup, Ox Close, The Park 1841 O.S., Patterdale (ib 1714, a
detached piece of land across the Calder in an old loop of the river), Pepper
Croft, Quarry Close, Raw Croft, Rodicar (*Rataker* c. 1196, *v*. æcer), Royds
Close (*Rodes* c. 1196, *v*. rod[1] 'clearing'), Rushmore (*mod*) (*Rissemoreflatte*
1461, *Rushy Moor* 1841 *TA*, *v*. risc, mōr), Sandy Ford, Secker Close, Sheep
Heads, Shrogg (*v*. scrogge 'bush'), Simmons (cf. *Symhousflatte* 1461, the

ME pers.n. *Sim* (from *Simon*), hūs), Smyth's Wood, Little Sours, Springs (*mod*) (ib 1841), Staincross Close, Sunburns (*mod*) (ib 1841 *TA*), Tanners (*mod*) (*Tanhouse Close* 1841 *TA*), Town Pitts, The Vineyard 1841 O.S., Walker Close, West Lands, Well Gate (*mod*), Well Royd, Willow Garth, Windmill Close (*Lowmylne, molend' ventric'* 1461, 1486, *v.* myln), Wood Close.

(*b*) *Asshewelhull* 1461, 1486, *Esche-, Esshewell* 1486 ('ash well', *v.* æsc, wella), *Brockhells als. Brockholes* 1642 (*v.* brocc-hol 'badger hole'), *Brodyng-(ebank)* 1486 (*v.* brād, eng 'meadow'), *Dedehusflate* 1461 (*v.* dēad, hūs, flat), *Ellerscawe* c. 1196, *Allerschagh* 1292, *Allrenschah* 1341, *Allershaghwode* 1461 (*v.* alor 'alder', alren, elri, sceaga 'copse'), *leʒ Flatteʒ* 1461 (*v.* flat), *cot' voc' Holhout* 1486, *Inecroft* 1292, *Kingesflatte* 1461, *Kyngesflat* 1486, *Kyrkethorp' Grene* 1486 (*v.* Kirkthorpe *supra*, grēne[2]), *Middelmora* c. 1196 (*v.* middel, mōr), *Mylndam* 1341 (*v.* myln, dammr), *Southcroft* 1461, 1486, *pastur' voc' Stonour* 1486 (*v.* Stennard Well 151 *infra*), *Westhesthille* c. 1196 (*v.* hestr 'horse', hyll), *Whytewrynge* 1486 (the ME surn. *Whyttewere* 'white-leather dresser' (Reaney 352), eng).

iv. Normanton

Of the townships in this parish Altofts and Normanton now form Normanton Urban District, and Snydale (122 *infra*) is united with Ackton (85 *supra*) to form a single civil parish. Newland was formerly in Normanton township.

1. ALTOFTS (102–3724)

Altoftes c. 1090, 12 Pont *freq* (YCh 1492–3, etc.), 1207 FF, 1276 RH, 1296 LacyComp, *MinAcct* 1, 1313 Pat, 1323 Calv, 1332 Kirkst *et passim* to 1606 FF, *-tofte* 1135–40 Pont, 1294 Ch, *-toftis* Hy 2 (1230) Ch, 1155–8 YCh 1451, *-toftys* 1297 LS, 1401 Calv, 1509 FF, *-tofts* 1359 BM, 1384 *MinAcct* 07, 1586 FF. Probably 'the old building-sites', *v.* ald, topt. On DB *Toftes*, identified with Altofts, *v. Toftes* i, 106 *supra*.

BRACKENHILL (lost), *Brakanhill* (*in Altoft(e)s*) 1323, 1342 Calv, 1337 Kirkst, 1338 DodsN, *Brakenhill* 1360, 1384 Calv, *Brakinhill* 1366 DodsN, *Brackon hill* 1656 PRMth, *v.* brakni, hyll, cf. *Brackenhill* 78 *supra*.

FERNLEY HILL, *Fernleighdikes* 1371 MethMR 146, *Fernelees* 1541 ib 204, *Fernley dike* 1544 ib 207, *Fernyleies* 1592 Meth 129, *Fearnley Hill* 1840 *TA*. *v.* fearn, lēah, hyll.

FOXHOLES FM, *Foxoles* 1122 Pont, 1484 MethMR, *Foxholeford* 1202 FF, *Foxholes* 1323 *MinAcct* 45, 1411 MethMR 169, 1766 LdsM,

Foxoleforth 1353 MethMR 135, *Foxehool bankes* 1546 TestLds, *Foxholles* 1567 FF. *v.* fox-hol 'fox's earth'; the ford was presumably across the Calder.

GILCAR, 1840 *TA*, *Gildeker* 1296 LacyComp, *MinAcct* 1, 1323 ib 45, *Kildeker* 1323 ib, *Gylker* 1341 *Surv*, *Gillekerre* 1384 *MinAcct* 07, *Gilleacre* 1486 ib 66. 'Marshland belonging to a guild', *v.* gildi, kjarr.

ALTOFTS HALL, 1771 M, *Old Hall* 1841 O.S. ALTOFTS INGS, *Ings* 1812 *EnclA* 47, *Ings Close* 1840 *TA*, *v.* eng 'meadow'. BIRKWOOD FM, 1841 O.S., *Burkewood* 1638 TN(*No*), *v.* birki 'birch', wudu. CALVERLEY GREEN, 1840 *TA*, the Calverley family owned land here (cf. Calv), *v.* grēne². CHOKE CHURL BRIDGE, *Choak Churl Bridge* 1840 *TA*. CLAY PIT. CROWCROFT HO, *Crow Croft* 1840 *TA*. ELLENTREES, 1841 *TA*, *Ellingtrees* 1694 TN(*Ho*), *Ellen Tree Field* 1812 *EnclA*, *v.* ellern 'elder-tree'. FOXHOLES BIGHT, *v.* Foxholes *supra*, byht 'river-bend'. HIGH GREEN RD, *High Green* 1840 *TA*. LEE BRIGG. LOW COMMON. LOW HO, 1841 O.S. PEN BANK, 1840 *TA*, *Penbanke* Hy 6 MethMR, *v.* penn 'a pen, fold', banke. RUDDINGS WOOD, *Ruddyng* 1341 *Surv*, *Riddings* 1840 *TA*, *Ruddings Whin* 1841 O.S., *v.* rydding 'clearing', hvin 'gorse'. WOOD NOOK.

FIELD-NAMES

The principal forms in (*a*) are 1840 *TA* 11. Spellings dated 1341 are *Surv* 10, 5, 1812 *EnclA* 47; others dated without source are *MinAcct*.

(*a*) Ashrows, Beckmouth Close, Between Towns Close (*Between Towns Field* 1812), Bog Close, Brackenhirst (*v.* *Brackenhill supra*, hyrst 'wood'), Breary Butts (*v.* brērig, butte), Butcher Garth, Carr Hill (*v.* kjarr, hyll), Cern Bank, Church Close, Coblers Acre, Cowsly Close, Crooked Royd, Cross Close (cf. *Cross Field* 1812), Dean Close, Great Cross, Green Gate Close, Habit Royd, Great & Little Haggs, Hales (Garth) (*v.* halh, garðr), Hartstonley (*Harstingley* 1694 TN(*Ho*), *Harthstonley* 1812, probably 'hearth-stone', lēah), Hemp yards, Howler Close, Huggen Royd, Kiln Garth, Lang Wood (*Langwood Field* 1812, *v.* lang, wudu), Launder Lane, Far & Near Lawners, Lawns (*Highlaund* 1608, *v.* launde), Little Broom, Long Garth, Mears (*Midilmer* 1341, *Mikkilmere* 1323, *v.* mere 'pool', middel, micel), Middle Park, Padding Mere (probably *Perinmer* 1296 LacyComp, 1341, from the surname *Perrin*, mere 'pool'; for the change cf. *paddock* from pearruc 'park'), Parson Cliff (*Personclif* 1323, *Parsonclyff* 1608, *v.* persone, clif), Pinfold Close (*v.* pynd-fald), Potterford Close, Great & Little Pringle (probably from dial. *pringle* 'a small silver coin' or the surname), Sand Beds

& Holes, Little Shrog (v. scrogge 'bush'), Slid Close, Sough Ing (Southenge 1323, Sowthynge 1341, v. sūð, eng), Tilley Hall Garth, Tom Croft, Town Ings, Turn Greaves (v. trun 'round', grǣfe 'copse'), Washfield Close, Whinny Close (v. hvin 'gorse'), White Gate Close.

(b) Belleslaghton 1323 (probably the surname Bell, lēac-tūn 'garden') Callschlaghton 1341 (possibly an error for prec.), bordis de Chakborde 1323 (named from its resemblance to a chess-board, cf. Chequer Close f.n., Chequer Field 24, 80 supra), Coteyerde 1486 (v. cot 'cottage', geard), Damsted 1341 (v. dammr, stede), Elcarre 1608 (v. kjarr), Elyncroftflatt 1341 (v. ellern 'elder-tree', croft), feldes of Altoftes 1530 TestLds (v. feld), Flattraitte 1341 (v. flat), Hallseland 1341, Longstanenge 1341 (v. lang, stān, eng), Myln-, Milneflat(t)e 1341, 1384, 1486 (v. myln, flat), (le) Miln(e)holm(e) 1323, 1384, 1486 (v. prec., holmr 'water-meadow'), aqua' Rudhill 1486, Sandes 1323 (v. sand), Standlidgatt 1341 (v. hlid-geat 'swing-gate'), Swa(y)n-, Sweynescroft 1292, 1323, 1341 (the ME pers.n. Swain (ON Sveinn), croft), Westflat 1323, Westrebi 1086 DB (v. vestr, bȳ), le Wylugh-, Willoughferme 1384, 1461 (v. wilig 'willow').

2. NEWLAND (102–3622)

Noua terra 1240–50 Bodl 101, Neuland 1357 YD i, New(e)land(e) 1547 FF, 1577 Holinshed, 1638 SessnR. 'Land newly reclaimed from waste', v. nīwe, land. As with Newland pt. iv infra, the wasteland was low-lying ground along the river. There are many references in WCR to the reclaiming of the lord's waste in the late thirteenth and the fourteenth centuries.

NEWLAND HALL, 1771 M.   NEWLAND PARK, Park 1771 M.   ST JOHN'S FIELDS, 1841 O.S.   WOODHOUSE MOOR, 1840 TA, v. Woodhouse 122 infra.

3. NORMANTON (102–3822)

Norme-, Normatune, Normantone 1086 DB
Normantun, -ton(a) 1177–86 YCh viii, 1190–1215 ib 1573, 13
    Lewes 303, 1225 Pat, 1235 FF, 1244 Ebor et passim to 1542
    Test vi
Northmanton(e) 1275–1298 WCR (freq)
'Farmstead of the Norwegians', v. Norðman, tūn, Introd.

MALLET HALL (lost), the Maletes hall 1570 NCWills, Mally Hall Close 1840 TA, cf. also Malleting 1543 Leland; it was owned by Fraunces Mallett, dean of Lincoln (NCWills ii, 62), v. hall, eng 'meadow'.

Woodhouse, 1587, 1605 FF, *Wodehuse* 1256 DodsN, *-house* 1547 FF, *Wodhous* 1379 PT (p). *v.* wudu, hūs.

Ashfield, 1804 *EnclA* 72, *v.* æsc, feld.   Ashfield Beck, 1841 O.S., *v.* prec., bekkr.   Ashgap Lane.   Beck Bridge, cf. *Beck Butts Lane* 1841 O.S., Beck Field *infra*, *v.* bekkr.   Chapel Row.   Dodsworth Hill.   The Garth.   Hall Croft.   Havertop Lane, 1841 O.S., *Havertoft(s)* Chas 1 *Rent*, 1684 *Glebe*, *v.* hafri 'oats', topt 'enclosure'. Haw Hill, 1840 *TA*, cf. *Hawgate* 1698 *Glebe*, *v.* haga 'enclosure', hyll, gata.   Hopetown.   Normanton Common, 1840 *TA*. Normanton Whin, 1841 O.S., *v.* hvin 'gorse'.   The Orchard. Wain Dike Beck.

FIELD-NAMES

The principal forms in (*a*) are 1840 *TA* 303. Spellings dated 1407–1409 are *WCR*, Chas 1 *Rent*, 1684, 1698 *Glebe*, 1804 *EnclA* 72.

(*a*) Beck Close (ib 1689 WYD, *v.* foll.), Beck Field (ib 1804, *v.* Beck Bridge *supra*), Breaks Close (*v.* bræc), Broad Ing (*Broadyngefeild* 1635 *YAS*, *v.* brād, eng), Burn Tree Shutt, Burton Cliff (*Burton Clift Knowle* 1698, *v.* clif, cnoll), Coal Pit Close, Cramlands (ib 1698, *v.* cramb 'bend', land), Dale Field (ib 1804, *v.* dæl, land), Great Dunstall (*Dunstall* 1698, *v.* tūnstall), Eel Pits (*Eelpitt Close* 1686 WYD, *v.* æl, pytt), Grease Croft, Grimeroyds, Intack Ends (*v.* intak), Little Hole, Longlands, Marsh Close, Mill Close & Flat, Orlidge Close & Shutt (*the Orledge Shutt* 1684, probably ME *orloge* 'clock', dial. *shut* 'division of land', doubtless one set aside for the maintenance of a public clock), Pinfold Shutt (*v.* pynd-fald), Pippin (Close) (*Pippin Field* 1804), Pog Close (cf. Pog Moor i, 304 *supra*), Pond Close, Quarry Close, Stockwell Ing, Twin Close, Twistleton Close, Wall Close, Well Close, West Field 1804, Wheat Butts (*les Whetebuttes* 1408, *Whetebutlegges* 1409, *v.* hwǣte, butte), Woodall Close, Woodhouse Whin 1841 O.S. (*v.* hvin 'gorse'), Wry Flatt.

(*b*) *Holmings* 1302 DodsN (*v.* holmr, eng).

4. Snydale (97–4020)

Snitehal(a), *-hale* 1086 DB, 1201 Cur, *-hall* 1364 DodsN, *Snytehall* 1428 FA

Slithale 1190 P, *Selichal(a)* 1191–1193 P

Snit-, Snythal(a), *-hale* 12 Kirkst, 1166 RBE, 1175–1200 YCh 1605–6, 13 DodsN, 1219 FF *et freq* to 1370 Kirkst

Snytall 1303 KF, 1316 Vill, 1369 FF, 1395 YD vii *et freq* to 1558 TestLds

Snytale 1323 *MinAcct* 45, 1357 BM, 1486 *MinAcct* 66

Sni-, Snydall 1357 BM, 1379 PT, 1509 Test v *et passim* to 1686
WYD
Snydale 1361 *Ass* 5, 1523 TestLds, 1641 Rates

'Nook of land frequented by snipe', *v.* snīte, halh, here probably
'hollow on a hillside'. The forms with *S(e)l-* for *Sn-* are AN.

WENTWELL FM, *Wench(e)well(feild)* 1635 *YAS* 78, 7, *Wentwell Close*
1844 *TA*, also nearby are *Wenthill, Went Dike* 1635 *YAS*, 'a furlong
called *Went*' 1641 ib 9; this is the source (*v.* wella) of the R. Went or
Went Beck (RNs.); *Wench-* probably represents an older gen.sg.
Wentes-.

BIRDHOUSE COTTAGES.   BUTCHER'S GAP LANE, 1841 O.S., *Butcher-*
gapps 1635 *YAS* 78, 7, *v.* gap.   CHURCH LANE, 1844 *TA*.   MILL
HILL, MILL HOUSES, cf. *the Millfeild* 1686 WYD, *v.* myln.   MILL
LANE, 1841 O.S.   SNYDALE HALL, *Snydall Hall* 1817 M.   STREET-
HOUSE, 1817 M, on the Roman road to Pontefract (*v.* High Street 116
supra).   TOWN'S WELL.   WHINNY LANE, part of the Roman road
to Pontefract (cf. Streethouse *supra*).

FIELD-NAMES

The principal forms in (*a*) are 1844 *TA* 366. Spellings dated c. 1166 are
Kirkst, 1328 YD xiii, 53, 1635, 1641 *YAS* 78, 79, 1686 WYD.

(*a*) Bell Close, Biles Mire (*The Bylesmyre* 1698 *Glebe*, the pers.n. *Bil(l)*,
mýrr 'mire'), Bottom Field (*le Bothomfeild* 1635, *the bottom feild* 1686, *v.*
botm, feld), Bridge Close & Ing, Bull Yard, Crabtree Close (cf. *Crabtreeflatt*
1635, *v.* crabbe, or the surname *Crabtree*, flat), Cross Close (ib 1686),
Demesne Lands, Epwith Garth, Field Leys, Hart Close, Hold Plough
(*Hold-, The Holtplough* 1684, 1698 *Glebe*), Holling Bush Close, Long Garth,
Long Pits, Moorlands Close, Mutton Yard (*Motton yeards* 1641, ME
mo(l)toun 'mutton, sheep', geard), New Leys, Old Pit Close, Ox Close,
Pinder Close, Quarry Close, Shaw Close (*les Schaghes* 1328, *v.* sceaga
'copse'), Shut Close (dial. *shut* 'division of land'), Thistle Hill Close
(*Thistlehillflatt* 1635, *v.* pistel, hyll), Town Croft, Tughill Park, Well Garth,
West Close (*Westclosse* 1635, *v.* west, clos), Willow Garth.

(*b*) *Brerelandes* 1328 (*v.* brēr 'briar'), *le Churchebalke* 1635 (*v.* balca
'boundary ridge'), *the Cross lane* 1641, *Drakylgate* 1328 ('dragon hill road',
v. draca, hyll, gata), *Eastcrofts* 1641, *Fachhil* c. 1166, *Fohildyck* 1328 (probably OE fāg 'variegated, bright', hyll), *Gallowlands* 1641 (*v.* galga, land),
narr, farr goodroyd hill 1635 (probably the surname *Good* or gōd, rod[1]),
the Goose crofts 1641 (*v.* gōs, croft), *Lesewelle* c. 1166 (*v.* wella), *Levitts half
acre* 1641 (the surname *Levitt*, as in Hooton Levitt i, 136 *supra*), *Newyate*

furlong 1635 (*v.* nīwe, geat), *le Northtoft* 1328 (*v.* norð, topt), *the Pittcarr close* 1641 (*v.* pytt, kjarr), *Robincroft* 1686, *Seaven leas* 1635 (*v.* seofon, lēah), *the Tentergarth* 1641 (ME *tentour* 'tenter', garðr), *the towne gate* 1545 Test Lds (*v.* tūn, gata), *the Towne pitts* 1641 (*v.* prec., pytt), (*le*) *Water-doles* 1328, 1641 (*v.* wæter, dāl), *le Wyndmillfeild* 1635.

v. Featherstone

The township of Whitwood in this detached part of Featherstone parish (85 *supra*) is now united with Castleford (69 *supra*).

WHITWOOD (97–4024)

> *Witeuude, -wde* 1086 DB, *-wde* c. 1090, 1135–40, c. 1160, 1240 Pont (YCh 1493, 1504, etc.), *Wi-, Wytewodam, -wod(e)* 1122 Pont, c. 1143 *Nost* 101d, 1281 Ebor, 1297 LS, *Wytewud* Hy 2 (1230) Ch, *Wytwode* 1363 YD vii
> *Withewdam, -w(o)de* 1136–40 YCh 1469, 1154–8 ib 1499, 1189 ib 1603
> *Wittewude* 1196 P (p)
> *White-, Whytew(u)d(e), -wode* 1211 P (p), 1230 Ebor, 14 *Nost* 124d, 1301 Ch, 1303 DodsN, 1344 *Ass* 28d *et passim* to 1497 FF, *-wood* 1230 Pont, 1316 Vill, 1588 FF
> *Qwittewode* 1337 YD x
> *Whittewood* 1364 MethMR

'The white bright wood', *v.* hwīt, wudu. The sense is probably that of thinly growing, and therefore bright, woodland.

WHITWOOD MERE, *Mara(m)* c. 1090, 1135–40, 1222 Pont (YCh 1493, etc.), (*-de Witewode*) c. 1235 ib, *Lamar* 1220, 1246 Pont, (*le, the*) *Mere* 14 *Nost* 124d, 1528 FF, TestLds, *Whit-, Whytwod Mere* 1467 Calv, 1550 FF, (*le, the*) *Meare* 1585, 1593 WillY, (*Whitwood-*) 1608 FF. 'The pool', *v.* le, mere. The pool may be the one formed by an old loop of the R. Calder.

CHOAK CHURL BECK, cf. *Chalk Churl Close* 1843 *TA*, cf. Choke Churl Bridge 120 *supra*.   FAIRIES HILL.   FOUR LANE ENDS.   FOX BRIDGE, 1841 O.S.   THE ISLAND, *Whitwood Island* 1804 *EnclA*, the land within an old loop of the Calder now detached from the township.   LUMLEY ST, cf. *Lumley Hill* 1843 *TA*.   MANOR HO, 1841 O.S.   METHLEY BRIDGE FM, 1841 O.S., *v.* Methley Bridge 128 *infra*. MILL HO, MILL ST, cf. *Mill Dam & Garths* 1843 *TA*, *v.* myln,

dammr, garðr.   WAINDIKE BRIDGE, 1841 O.S., *Wain Dyke* 1843 *TA*,
v. wægn, dīc.   WHIN COVERT, 1841 O.S., *v.* hvin 'gorse'.   WHIT-
WOOD COMMON, 1804 *EnclA* 47.   WILLOW BRIDGE, 1841 O.S.
WOOD LANE, cf. *Wood Close* 1843 *TA*.

FIELD-NAMES

The principal forms in (*a*) are 1843 *TA* 432. Spellings dated 1222, 1235
are Pont, 14 *Nost* 124d, 1541 *MinAcct*.

(*a*) Black Flatt (*Blakeflat* 1222, *v.* blæc, flat), Black Heath, Bridge Ing
(*v.* eng), Castle Hill, Church Beck, Cow Close, Cutsyke Close (*v.* cut 'cut,
channel', sīc), Damsteads (cf. Mill Ho *supra*), Dick Bank (*Dicbankeeng* 14,
Digbank 1541, probably dīc, banke, though the pers.n. *Dick* is possible),
Ear Croft, Fox Garth, Goose Acre, Grimesmoor (*Grymesmere* 14, the ON
pers.n. *Grímr* or grim in one of its senses 'goblin' or the like, *v.* mere 'pool'),
Hall Flatt, Holme (Pond) (*v.* holmr 'water-meadow'), Kiln Garth, Leylands
(*v.* lǣge 'fallow', land), Long Hamel, Long Lands (*les Longelandes* 14, *v.*
lang, land), Luck Garth, Mire Ings (*v.* mýrr 'bog', eng), Moor Croft (*Morecroft* 14, *v.* mōr, croft), Old River (an old course of the Calder), Ox Close,
Pottery (Close & Croft), Rush Intack (*v.* risc, intak), Spoil Bank, Stottfold
(probably stōd-fald 'stud fold'), Thief Lane Close, Thrush Close, Toad
Hole, T'other Garth, Well Brigg Close, West Field, Wicker Close, Widdens
(*les Wythens* 14, *v.* wīðign 'willow-copse'), Willow Garth (*v.* wilig, garðr).

(*b*) *Belleflat* 14 (*v.* belle, perhaps as a surname, flat), *Birkeflat* 14 (*v.* birki,
flat), *le Breck*' 14 (*v.* bræc 'uncultivated strip'), *Crosseflat* 14, *Fulfort* 1235,
Folford 14 ('dirty ford', *v.* fūl, ford), *Hirst* 1235 (*v.* hyrst 'wood'), *le Mere-
gate* 14 (*v.* Whitwood Mere *supra*, gata), *Osolvepit* 1235 (the OE pers.n.
Ōswulf, pytt), *Otresford Brig*' 14, 1357 MethMR 137 (*v.* oter 'otter', ford,
brycg), *Oulaygate* 14 (*v.* gata), *Prescroft* 14 (*v.* prēost, croft), *le Rawebrigsiche*
14 (*v.* rāw 'row (of houses)', brycg, sīc), *Rawson landes* 1541, *Sandbed(eeng)*
1222, 14 (*v.* sand, bedd, eng), *les Sandeforwonges* 14 (*v.* sand, fore, wang
'meadow'), *Stanwalrawe* 1235 ('stone wall row (of houses)', *v.* stān, wall,
rāw), *les Stubbings* 14 (*v.* stubbing), *Trowebrigge* 1235 ('tree-trunk bridge',
v. trēow, brycg).

vi. Methley

The township of Methley is now in Rothwell Urban District (*v.* 136
infra).

METHLEY (102–3926)

> *Medelai*, -*lei*(*a*), -*lay*, -*ley* 1086 DB, 1180–1200 YCh 1576, 1578,
> 1226, 1251 FF, 1246 Pont, 1275 WCR, 1427 Pat
> *Methelei*(*a*), -*le*(*y*), -*lay* 1155–62 YCh 1452, c. 1200 BM, 1251 Ch,
> 1283 Ebor, 1285 WCR *et passim* to 1486 *MinAcct* 66

Meydlay 1379 PT
Metelay 1415 Fabr
Medlay, -ley 1439 Baild, 1521 WillY *et freq* to 1608 FF
Meithley 1522, 1530 TestLds
Meethley 1522 ib
Myedleye 1578 PRLds
Meathley 1584, 1587 WillY, 1588 LS
Methley 1541 WillY, 1608 FF

There is some ambiguity in the significance of these early spellings, but some of the later ones, notably *Meyd-*, *Myed-*, *Meithe-*, *Meeth-*, denote a long vowel, which could be original or which could have arisen in the fourteenth century from the lengthening of a short -ĕ- in an open syllable. Formally the els. could be ON meðal 'middle' (perhaps replacing an earlier OE middel) with OE lēah 'forest-clearing' or ēg 'island, land partly surrounded by water', or they could be OE mǣð 'mowing, mowing grass' with lēah. The greater part of the township is low-lying ground, which must have been marsh rather than woodland, and its name is therefore more likely to contain ēg than lēah; it occupies the angle formed by the confluence of the Calder and the Aire. Topographically a compound of meðal and ēg seems most probable in the sense 'middle water-land'; that is, 'land between the two rivers'.

CARR HALL (lost), CARR HOUSES, denoting different places, Carr Hall (1841 O.S.) being near the Aire at Mickleton and Carr Houses on the Calder near Methley Junction; the earlier material, which may refer to either, includes *Midel-*, *Ouercar* 1373 MethMR, *Kerres* 1374 ib, *the Carr* 1496, 1578 ib, 1592 Meth, *Ker(r)banck, -dike, -loine* 1367, 1394 MethMR, *Carheed* 1493 ib, v. kjarr 'marsh'.

CLUMPCLIFFE, *Clubclifrowe* 1380 MethMR, *-cliff(e)* 1592, 1601 Meth, 1630 PRMth, 1817 M, *Clubecliffe* 1469 MethMR, *Clobeclyfe* 1532 TestLds, *Clump cliffe* 1841 O.S. The first el. is ME *clobe, clubbe* 'a club, a thick stick' (ON *klubba* from earlier *klumba*, which is related to e.ModE *clump* 'heap, mass, lump', 'a clump of trees'), but its meaning in this p.n. is uncertain; the house stands at the top of a bank and topographically the root meaning 'heap' or 'lump' would be adequate, as would 'stump' or the like, v. clif. v. Addenda.

CRINGLESWORTH, *Crybelforth* (sic) 1351 MethMR, *Cringlesforth, -ford* 1366, 1399 ib, *Grimelford* Hy 6 ib, *Crynylsforth* 1532 TestLds,

Crynglesfurthe pasture 1559 ib, *Cringleforde* 1592 Meth. *v.* **kringla** 'circle', here referring to a loop of the R. Calder, **ford**.

EAR MOITS (local), 1809 *TA*, *the Eymotes* 1527 MethMR, 'pasture called *Finotes* (sic for *Emotes*) at the meetinge of the waters' 1592 Meth, *Upper & lower erits* (sic) 1699 AireSurv. *v.* **ēa-mōt** 'rivers' meet', that is, the confluence of the Calder and the Aire.

HUNGATE, HUNGATE LANE, *Hungait* 1363, 1598 Meth, 1588 PRMth, -*gate* 1817 M, *Herngat Lone* (sic) 1410 Pat, *Hundegate* 1411 Meth. 'Hounds' road', probably one where hounds were kept, *v.* **hund**, **gata**, cf. Hungate (Yk) YE 290.

METHLEY MIRES, *Mires* 1339 Meth, (*the*) *Myers* 1373, 1386 MethMR, *the town Mires* 1516 ib, cf. also *The Miers comon* 1592 Meth, *Myredike* 1460 MethMR, *Miringdikes* Hy 6 ib, *Myreside* 1386 ib. *v.* **mýrr** 'swamp, mire', **dīc**, **eng**, **sīde**.

MICKLETOWN, *Magna villa de Metheley* 1354 Meth, (*the*) *Mickle-town(e)* 1405 MethMR, 1561 PRMth, 1644 WillY, *the Mykletowne* 1522 TestLds. *v.* **micel**, **tūn**; the use of ME *toun* to denote a part of a village, a second village of the same name, or a new hamlet within the township, is common in YW, as in Old Town i, 303 *supra*, Westerton 176, Middlestown 206, Hightown iii, 28, Chapeltown and Moor Town (Chapel Allerton) pt. iv, etc. *infra*; it is also used when combined with township names to denote the village proper as in Soyland Town iii, 69, Sowerby Town iii, 149, Warley Town iii, 126 *infra*. Some of these names were alternative to older names and consist of the original affix with *to(w)n*, as in Old Town, Westerton, Middlestown, Littletown iii, 28, etc.

MOOR HO, *Morehous(e)* 1405, 1544 MethMR, c. 1600 Meth, -*laine* 1364 MethMR, -*feildes* 1592 Meth, named from *the More* c. 1600 ib, cf. also *Low Moor* 1682 PRMth, *Southmore(side)* 1465, 1590 MethMR, 1600 Meth, *Moore side* 1682 PRMth, *v.* **mōr**, **hūs**.

THORPE (lost), *Sowthorp* 1351 MethMR, *the Thorpe by Kelder* 1410 ib, *Thorpe* 1592, 1600 Meth, cf. also *Thorpedikes* 1371, *Thorpgrene-side* 1371 MethMR, *Thorplidyate* 1473 ib. *v.* **þorp** 'outlying farm-stead'; it has not been identified, but it was obviously near the Calder and near Pinder Green 129 *infra*, probably where Methley Junction is. 'Sowth' to distinguish it from Thorpe on the Hill 149 *infra* or because it was south in the township.

WOOD ROW, 1771 M, *Woodrawe* (*Lidyate*) 1375, 1404 MethMR, 1592, 1602 Meth, *-rowe* 1612 PRMth, 1646 WillY. *v.* **wudu, rāw,** 'row (of houses) near the wood'.

ALLERTON FERRY, *the Ferie* 1592 Meth, *Boate* 1666 PRMth, *Boatstake* 1726 ib. *Ollerton Boat, Boatstake* 1759 LdsM, *v.* **ferja** 'ferry'; a ferry was also called 'a boat' (as in Bottom Boat 159 *infra*); *Boatstake* was doubtless 'the stake to which the ferry-boat was moored'.   ALMS-HOUSES, 1817 M.   ASTLEY COAL STAITH, *Methley Staith* 1841 O.S.; *Jo: Astley* held a close in Methley in 1564 MethMR 215; Astley is across the Aire in Swillington (pt. iv *infra*), *v.* **stæð** 'landing-place'. BOAT LANE, *Boat laine* 1699 AireSurv, *Boat Street* 1817 M, the lane leads to Allerton Ferry *supra*.   BOND HO, cf. *Bond Garth* 1809, probably the surname *Bond*, *v.* **garðr**.   CHURCH SIDE, 1812 PRMth, *Kirkside* 1368, 1570 MethMR, *v.* **kirkja, sīde,** cf. Church Field, etc. f.n. *infra, Churchgrene* 1406 MethMR (*v.* **grēne²**). COMMON SIDE, 1817 M, *le Comons* 1590 MethMR, ME *commun* 'common land'.   CONEY MOOR, *Methley Cony Moor* 1723 LdsM, *v.* **coni** 'rabbit', **mōr,** Coney Borrows f.n. 130 *infra*.   CROOKED PARK, *Parke Crooke* 1541 MethMR, *Crooke Parke* 1580 MethMR, *Crockeparke* 1590 ib, *The Cruke* 1592 Meth, *v.* **krókr** 'bend' (perhaps here referring to the crooked road to Methley Lanes, cf. *Crooklainend* 1509 MethMR), **park;** cf. Crooks Close f.n. *infra*. DUNFORD HO, 1817 M, *Dunsforth(e) house, place* 1592, 1600 Meth, 'Dunn's ford', from the OE pers.n. *Dun(n)*, **ford.**   GREEN LANE, *Greneloinedikes* Hy 6 MethMR, *v.* **grēne, lane, dīc.**   GREEN ROW. HAZEL FM, *Hesil-, Hasillplace* 1409, 1448 MethMR, *Hasill house* 1592 Meth, *the hessill house* 1600 ib, *Hazel Hall* 1841 O.S., *v.* **hæsel** (ON **hesli**) 'hazel'.   HIGH TOWN.   HOLME FM, *Holme* 1373 MethMR, *the holmes* 1592 Meth, cf. *Holmdike* 1490 MethMR, *v.* **holmr** 'water-meadow', **dīc.**   LEMON ROYD, 1809, *Lemanroide* 1550 MethMR, *-roides, the Leaman roide* 1592 Meth, *v.* **rod¹** 'clearing', the first el. is doubtless ME *lemman* 'lover' used as a surname.   LONG ROW. MELWOOD HO.   METHLEY BRIDGE, 1778 Meth, *Meth(e)ley brig(e)* 1536 MethMR, 1547, 1557 TestLds, *New bridge* 1549 ib, *the newe brige* 1557 ib, cf. *ye bridge end* 1605 PRMth, *v.* **brycg;** the bridge carries the Castleford road over the Calder.   METHLEY GRANGE, 1841 O.S.   METHLEY HALL, 1817 M, cf. *Robert atte Hall* 1357 MethMR 137, *Walter del Halle* 1396 Meth 95, *v.* **hall.**   METHLEY LANES, 1817 M, *the laine(s)* 1592, 1600 Meth, *v.* **leyne.**   METHLEY

PARK, 1765 LdsM, *le, the Parke* 1414, 1592 Meth, 1427 MethMR, *Oldparke* 1415 Meth, *v.* park; it was a new enclosure in 1414 Meth 97. MIDDLE ROW. MILL MOOR, cf. *the Milnedame* 1482 MethMR, *v.* myln, dammr, cf. f.ns. *infra.* MOSS CARR, *Mossekerr* 1380 MethMR, *Mosker comon* 1592 Meth, *-lane* 1661 PRMth, *Moscow* 1817 M, *v.* mos 'moss, bog', kjarr 'marsh'. OAKSFIELD, *the Okefeilde* 1592 Meth, *the Okes feld* 1618 ib, *Oakes Field* 1786 *EnclA* 24, named from *le Okes* 1590 MethMR, *v.* āc, feld. PARKIN FM, *Richard Parkin's house and crofte* 1592 Meth, named from the family of *Parkin* settled here from the sixteenth century (PRMth 6 *et freq.*). PINDER GREEN, 1817 M, *Pindergrene* 1541, 1628 MethMR, also *Pinderplace* 1592, 1600 Meth, *Pindarplace in Thorpe quondam Pinders* 1615 Meth 81, ME *pyndere* (cf. pundere) 'pinder', used as a surname, *v.* grēne[2], place; cf. *Thorpe* 127 *supra*. PINFOLD LANE, *Pinfold* 1497 MethMR, *the Pinfoulde* 1572 ib, *v.* pynd-fald. PIT LANE, cf. *Pit close (-leies, -wood)* 1592, 1611 Meth, *v.* pytt, clos. SAND HOLD HILL. SCHOLEY HILL, 1841 O.S., *Scholes Hill* 1817 M, *v.* skáli 'shieling' (or a surname derived from it). SHAN HALL, *Willm. Shan house* 1592 Meth, named from the local family of *Shan* (1453 MethMR 179, 1592 Meth 79, 118, PRMth *passim*). SILVER ROW. SMIRTHWAITE HO, from a family of *Smirthwaite* well known locally in the seventeenth century (PRMth *freq*). STONEY LANE, *Stonyloine* 1368 MethMR, *Stonilone* 1372 ib, *-lane* 1525 ib, *v.* stānig, lane. WATERGATE, 1726 PRMth, *Watergait* 1569 MethMR, *v.* wæter, gata, here a road leading to the Calder. WEST HALL, 1817 M, *the Westhouse* 1537 MethMR, 1592, 1600 Meth, *v.* west, hūs. WHITE CROSS FIELD, 1786 *EnclA* 24, *Whitecrosse* 1373 MethMR, *v.* hwīt, cros. WHITE HOUSE FM. WILLOW GROVE, cf. *Willow Holt* 1809. WINDMILL MOOR, 1786 *EnclA* 24. WINTER WOOD, *West Winterwood (closes)* 1691 Meth, cf. also (*the East-, West*) *Winter close(s)* 1592, 1601 Meth, *v.* winter, wudu, clos.

FIELD-NAMES

The principal forms in (*a*) are modern (1935), with some, dated 1809, from a local valuation (Meth 108–9). Spellings dated 1592, 1600–1680 are Meth, 1786 *EnclA*. Others dated without source are MethMR.

(*a*) Adam Croft & Gale (cf. *Addam Laithes* 1592, *East-, West- Ad(d)am Lath close* 1618, *Glover Adamleyes* 1671, the pers.n. *Adam*, hlaða 'barn'), Alderman Ground, Allerton Banks 1809 (*Allerton Water banck* 1367, *Ollertonbanke* 1555, *-banckes* 1592, *v.* Allerton Bywater (across the Aire) pt. iv *infra*, banke), Asholt Ing 1809 (*Asholl Ing* 1618, *Esh-, Ashall Ing*(*e*) 1592, 1680, 'ash wood', *v.* æsc, holt, eng).

Becks Close 1809 ((*the Greate, Litle*) *beck*(*e*) *close* 1592, 1611, 1614, *v.* bekkr 'stream'), Bell Close 1809, Bracken Close 1809 (cf. *Brackenflat*(*t*) 1373, 1618, *v.* brakni, flat), Bradford Close 1809, Brecks 1809 (*v.* bræc), Bridge Ing, Broad Royd (*Brodrode* 1348 Meth, *Broderoide* 1424, 1466, *Broade Royde* 1591 Arm, *v.* brād, rod[1]), Brooms (*The Bromes* 1592, *v.* brōm).

Carlton Royds (*Carleton roide* 1592, probably the common p.n. Carlton as a surname, rod[1]), Chadwick 1809, Church Field (ib 1786, *-feilde* 1592, *Kirkfield* 1622, *v.* kirkja, feld), Church Ing 1809, *Church Syke* 1809 (*Kirksike, -syke* 1339 *et freq* Meth, *v.* kirkja, sīc 'stream'), Clump Close (olim *The Cliffeclose* 1592, *v.* Clumpcliffe *supra*), Coney Borrows 1809 (*v.* coni 'rabbit', burg 'burrow', Coney Moor *supra*), Cow Shutt Fen 1809 (*Cowshotfen*(*n*) 1526, 1592, named from *Cowshutt* 1603, *v.* cū, dial. *shut* 'division of land', fenn), The Croft (cf. *Croftsike* 1366, 1541, *v.* croft, sīc), Crooks Close (*Crokes* 1367, *le Crookes* 1590, *v.* krókr, perhaps here a river-bend).

Damstone Royds (probably identical with *Damatisrode* 1402, *damisill roide* 1592), Doctor Close 1809.

Eaden Close 1809.

Fallow Close (cf. *Falghfields* 1544, *v.* falh 'fallow', feld), Fine Lands (*Fenlandike* 1364, *v.* fenn, land, dīc), Great & Little Firth 1809 (*the Firth* 1413, (*the*) *Firthwood* 1592, 1611, *v.* fyrhðe 'wood'), Fleet Lane Side 1809, Frickley Flat 1809 (from the name of a local tenant).

Gait Close, Gamskar (Ings) (*Gamelcarr* 1473, *Gamleskargappe* 1541, *Gamelscar* 1592, cf. *Gamblebancke* f.n. *infra*, a surname from the ON pers.n. *Gamall*, kjarr 'marsh'), Garth, Gib Hills 1809 (*Gibehill* 1380, *Gib*(*b*)*hill* (*close*) 1386, 1592, 1624, the ME pers.n. *Gibbe* (from *Gilbert*), hyll), Gilkers Close 1809 (*Gilkar* 1367, *Gillcarr* 1592, *v.* kjarr, the first el. may be the ME pers.n. or surname *Gille*, but cf. Gilcar 120 *supra*), Gotts Garth 1809, Grainge Field (*Grange field* 1611, *v.* Methley Grange *supra*), Green Sykes 1809 (*Grenesike Lane* 1465, (*-close*) 1592, *v.* grēne[1], sīc), Gregg Royds 1809 (*Gregroide* 1377, 1592, the ME surname *Grege*, rod[1]), Grime Royd Close (*Grimrode* 1369, *Grym-, Grimeroide* 1473, 1592, the ME pers.n. *Grime* (ON *Grímr*), rod[1]), Grime Slack (*Grimslake* (a close) 1574, *Grimeslak*(*e*), *-slack* 1592, *v.* prec., slakki 'a depression, hollow').

Hall Ings 1778 PRMth (ib 1592, (*The*) *Hall Inges* 1428, 1592, *v.* hall, eng), Hanging Close, Hard Ing (*Hardenge* 1373, *-inge* 1382, *-inges* 1504, *v.* heard, eng), Great & Little Hasps (*Hespes* 1542, *Hie-, Highespes* 1578, 1592, *v.* hēah 'tall', æspe 'aspen tree'), Haver Croft 1809 (*v.* hafri 'oats', croft), Haw Ing 1809, Healds (*the Hildes* 1416, *the heldes* 1543, *v.* helde 'slope'), Hemp yards (*the Hempyeard*(*e*) 1592, 1684 *Glebe, v.* hænep, geard), High Leys 1809 (*Heghleies* 1453, *Hie leis* 1578, *le Heigheleyes* 1590, *v.* hēah, lēah), Hop Gap (*Hobgaips* 1522 TestLds, *-gap* 1592, *Southehoppegappe* 1590, probably hob 'goblin', gap 'opening, gap in a fence'), Great & Little Hyron 1809 (*Hirn* 1371, *the Hirun* 1550, *Hirnedike* 1377, *the Hiron pasture close* 1592, *v.* hyrne 'corner of land').

Ings (*the Ing*(*e*) 1592, 1680, *Ynge Croftes* 1550, *v.* eng, croft), Intake (*the Intak* 1592, *Intackyate* 1515, *v.* intak, geat).

Jep Ing 1809 (*Geppeinge* 1367, *Jeping(e)* 1432, 1592, cf. *Jeppebuttes* 1382, *Jeppedingdike* 1460, the ME pers.n. *Jeppe*, eng), Jowall Close 1809.
Kiln Close 1809 (cf. *Kilnhouse* 1411, *v.* cyln, hūs).
Lady Close 1809, Leatherforth 1809 (*Letherford(e)* 1356, 1592, *Ledderfurth* 1469, probably OE *leaðor* 'soap, lather', OE *leðer* 'leather' or OE *hlæddre* 'ladder', ford, though the sense of the compound is uncertain), Leycroft Leys (*Lacok-*, *Locockeleies* 1592, lacuc 'small stream' or a surname from it, lēah, cf. Laycock (Oakworth) pt. vi *infra*, Leys Hills ((*le*) *Leighes* 1353, 1373, *v.* lēah), Line Garth 1809 (*v.* lin 'flax', garðr), Ling Croft 1809 (*Lincroftedike* 1406, *v.* lin 'flax', croft), Lord Ing 1809 (ib 1592, *v.* eng), Low Field (ib 1786).
Middup 1809, Middups (*Medope* 1369, *Meddopp* 1557 TestLds, *Medhop*, *Midhop Yate* 1592, *v.* midd, hop, cf. Midhope i, 225 *supra*), Milner Close 1809, Low Milner (*Molnerbalkes*, *Milnebalke* 1550–1, *Milneloine* 1372, *-laine* 1471, *Milner lane* Hy 6, *Milnerroide* 1376, 1592, ME *milnere* 'miller', balca, lane, rod[1]), Moor Ing Croft 1809.
Nauch Firth, Little Nautsforth 1809 (*Lit(t)le Knottesforth(e)* 1592, probably naut 'beast' or the ME surname *Knotte*, ford), Nether Close (ib 1592), New Laithe, New Royds (*Nurode* 1357 Meth, *Newroide* 1542, *Neweroydes* 1647, *v.* nīwe, rod[1]), North Ings 1786 (*the Northing(e)s* 1531, 1542, 1592, *v.* norð, eng), North Royd (*Northroide(s)* 1592, *v.* norð, rod[1]).
Oaker Syke Close 1809, Oatfield, Old Mires, Ox Close (*Ox(e)close* 1590, *v.* oxa, clos).
Pease Royd 1809 (*v.* pise, rod[1]), Peigh Hill 1809 (*v.* Pighill *infra*), Pen Bank (*Panbanke* 1592, *Storrs Penbanke* 1671 Bright 626, cf. *Penland* 134 *infra*, *v.* penn 'fold', banke), Pighill 1809 (*Pighill* Hy 6, 1541, *le Pighell* 1590, *v.* pightel 'enclosure'), Pillow Close 1809 (cf. *Pyletcroft* f.n. *infra*), Poppie Hole (*Popla(ie)hole* 1542, 1592, probably Popeley iii, 15 *infra* as a surname, hol[1]), Pulleine Close (from a tenant called *Pullen* 1809).
Quarry Hill (*The Quarrel hill Close* 1592, cf. *Querrelcliffe* Hy 6, *Warell Close* 1490, *the Querlez* 1409, *v.* quarrelle 'quarry').
Rails Close 1809 (ME *raile* 'fence'), Red Gate Close 1809, Rhodes Close, Ridings 1809 (*the Rydinge(s)* 1371, 1411, *Rydinglonend* 1367, *v.* rydding 'clearing', lane), Rotherma Dyke 1809, Round Ing, Rudds Close (*the Ridde* 1382, *Ridd* 1411, *Rud* 1545, *the Riddend* 1367, *Highridend* 1382, *v.* ryd(e) 'clearing', ende), Rushley Close 1809.
Salmon Close (ib 1592, cf. *Samondokgange* (sic) 1590, the pers.n. *Sal(o)-man*, *v.* ox-gang), Sand Beds (*le Sandbed(des)* 1353, 1570, 1592, *v.* sand, bedd), Sandholes, Seven Acres (*the 7 acre close* 1592), Shan Close 1809 (*v.* Shan Hall *supra*), Smith Close (cf. *Smythihalf* 1391, *Smeðiehalfe close* 1592, *v.* smiððe, half, clos), Snydale Bank (*Snitallbancke* 1411, *v.* Snydale 122 *supra*, banke), South Land (ib 1367, *-lond* 1448, *le Southelandes* 1590, *v.* sūð, land), Stanniford Close (*Stenerfurth* 1539, *Stanerford* 1592, cf. *Stener* 1517, *v.* stæner, ford, Stennard Well 151 *infra*), Steward Ing (*Steward Inge(s)* 1375, 1428, *v.* stigweard 'steward', eng), Swarth Lands 1809, Sweet Bit 1809 (*Sweetbitt* 1473, *Swetebit* 1592, *v.* swēte, bita), Syke House 1809 (*Sike* 1369, *Sikehousecrofte*, *-dike* 1400, 1491, *v.* sīc 'stream', hūs).

Thorpe Ing (*Thorpe Inges* 1592, 1622, *-Inggs* 1671 *Bright* 626, *v. Thorpe supra*, eng), Thursker 1809 (*Thirskerr* 1382, *Thurskerdike* 1424, *Thrusker* 1592, *v.* þyrs 'giant, demon', kjarr 'marsh'), Tom Royd 1809 (*Tomroide* 1364, 1592, *Tomerode* 1590, the pers.n. *Tom*, rod[1]).

Wakefield Gap 1809 (*Wakefe(i)ldgap(pe)* 1392, 1592, *v.* Wakefield 163 *supra*, gap 'opening, gap'), Wall Flat 1809 (ib 1373, 1618, *v.* wall, flat), Warren Close 1809, Water Close, Webster Close (a tenant *Webster* 1809), Well Garth 1809, Whinny Close (cf. *Whinneparke* f.n. *infra*), White Yard (*Whitgarth* 1453, *the Whit(t)yeards* 1464, 1659 PRMth, *White-yeard(es)* 1497, 1592, the surname *White*, geard), Willows (*Wyleighs* 1369, *v.* wilig), Windhill Close (*Windhilland* 1371, *Windhill(e)* 1592, 1600, *v.* wind, hyll).

(*b*) *Abbaycrofte, -end* 1367, 1407 (ME *abbaye* 'abbey' (probably Ponte-fract), croft), *Acre-end* 1382, *-lone* 1374 (*v.* æcer), *Ailsilon* 1371 (the ME pers.n. *Ailsi* (OE *Æþelsige*), lane), *Aierbanck* 1592 (*v.* R. Aire (RNs.), banke), *the Akkes syed* 1558 TestLds.

le, the Bayl(l)e grene 1361 YD vii, 1551, *Bayliegrene* 1552, 1600 (ME baillie 'bailiff', grēne[2]), *the balke ende* 1656 PRMth (*v.* balca 'boundary ridge'), *Barbiyerde* 1397 (*v.* geard), *Barleycroft(e), -li-* 1472, 1516 (*v.* bærlic, croft), *Barleke sike closes* 1592 (*v.* prec., síc 'stream'), *Barmebie place* 1592 (from the family name of *John Barnbie* 1433 MethMR 175, place), *Beck-crooke* 1585 (where 'the Kelder lately encroached and won half a rood of land' ib 222, *v.* bekkr, krókr 'bend in a river'), *Belhallidaie* 1592, *Benetcrofte* 1368 (the surname *Bennett*, croft), *a little ditch called Betyr* 1397, *Bierbanke Ings* 1556 (*v.* foll.), *Byrdolls Ings* 1498 ('town shares of common land', *v.* bȳ (gen.sg. bȳjar), dāl, eng), *East-, Westbotham* 1373, *Bothomlaine* 1404, 1474, *Bothomleydike* Hy 6 (*v.* botm (bōðm), lane, lēah), *Briglanend* 1508, *-laine* 1536 (*v.* brycg, lane), *le Brodlaine* 1366 (*v.* brād, lane), *the Brooke* 1592, *Brokeclose* 1466, *Brokdikes* 1408 (*v.* brōc, lane, dīc), *Brownefeilde* 1542 (the surname *Brown*, feld), *Broninghalueacre* 1374, *Browningroides* 1550 (the surname *Browning*, rod[1]), *Burton's Hawe* 1611 (*v.* haga), *Busselgarth* 1464 (*v.* garðr), *Buttes* 1369, *the buts* 1600 (*v.* butte), *Butlerland* 1352, *le Buttle Oxgange* 1590.

Causedikes 1374 (*v.* caucie 'causeway', dīc), *Chamberlaingarth* 1364 (*v.* garðr), *Chauntre-, Chaunteryland, -place* 1406–1409, 1592 (named from *The Chauntre* 1592), *Che(e)tland* 1347, 1363 ('escheated land', that is, land which reverted to the lord when there was no qualified heir), *Chippindale house* 1592, *Chrisfordlane* 1364 (*v.* ford), *Claycrofte* 1550 (*v.* clǣg, croft), *Cochill* 1575 (*v.* cocc[1] 'hill, heap', hyll), *Coitgrene, -yerde* (*v.* cot 'cottage', grēne[2], geard), *Cokhouse* 1367 ('cook house'), *Cole pitt* 1378, *the Cole delfes* 1380 (*v.* col[1] 'coal', pytt, (ge)delf), *Colinplace* 1367, *Colnland* 1364, *Colt Flatte* 1575 (*v.* colt, flat), *le Commonspott* (a parcel of land) 1590 (*v.* spot), (*West)coum(e)garth* 1426, 1458 (probably ME *colm* 'coal-dust', cf. Combs 211 *infra*, garðr), *Cow close* 1592, *Crosse Flate* 1618, *Cutler laine* 1600.

Daniel Crosse 1527 (*v.* cros), *Dannaldplace* 1592, *Deynealdedikes* Hy 6 (probably a pers.n. or surname from OE *Denewald*), *Dewson-, the Dewsome-*

feild(e) 1522, 1592, *Dighton Crookes* 1590 (*v.* krókr), *Dobynacre* 1373 (the ME pers.n. *Dobin*, æcer), *Dodmanslak* 1592 (the surname *Dodman* 'Dodde's servant', slakki), *Dumesell* 1590.

le, the Eastfeilde 1590, 1592, (*the*) *Eastmore* 1458, 1600, *Eastroiddike* 1351, *Eastrode* 1358 (*v.* ēast, mōr, rod[1]), *Elyncroflatt* (sic for -*tre*-), *Ellintree or Ellinflatt* 1618, -*or Elintreflat* 1627 (*v.* ellern 'elder-tree'), *Elmflatt* 1373 (*v.* elm, flat), *Encliffbrooke* 1397, *Eshenge* 1369, -*inge* 1504 (*v.* æsc, eng).

the feilde 1592 (also *magnus campus* 1354 Meth, *v.* feld), *Foulelone* 1373 (*v.* fūl, lane), *Frerecrofte* 1367, -*land(es)* 1350, 1373, -*oxegange* 1374, -*rode* 1367, -*yate* 1385 (*v.* frere 'friar', croft, land, oxgang, rod[1], geat).

Gagacre 1592 (*v.* æcer, the first el. is possibly the nickname *Gage*, cf. Weekley 171), *Gamblebancke(s)* 1464, 1592, *Gamle-* 1447 (named from the family of *William Gamble* or *Thomas Gamill* (ON *Gamall*) who were responsible for repairing the banks of the R. Calder here, cf. MethMR 178, 181, cf. Gamskar f.n. 130 *supra*, *v.* banke), *Gamilbrigge* 1426 (*v.* prec., brycg), *Gawkethorpe close* 1529 (probably a surname from one of the YW Gawthorpes, *v.* 102 *supra*), *Geffrayrode* 1348 (possibly identical with *Geffreyrode* f.n. 148 *infra*, from the ME pers.n. *Geoffrey*, *v.* rod[1]), *Grasscroft* (*v.* gærs, croft), *Great Roodes* 1590 (*v.* rod[1]), *the Grene* 1385 (*v.* grēne[2]), *Grenebalkes* 1550 (*v.* grēne[1], balca 'boundary ridge'), *Grenecroftes* 1592, *Grenfordlaine* 1336 (*v.* grēne[1], ford), *Greneside* 1371, *le Grishall* 1361 YD vii, *Gunnessonenge* 1367 (a patronymic *Gunneson*, from ON *Gunni*, *v.* eng), *Gutterlaine* 1576 (ME goter, OFr *gutiere* 'gutter', lane).

Hallifax als. Hall place in Thorpe 1601 (doubtless a surname from Halifax iii, 104 *infra*, *v.* place), *Hallegarth* 1396 (*v.* hall, garðr), *Hawsingdike* 1351, 1367, 1497, *Awisingdikes* 1371 (the ME fem. pers.n. *Hawisa, Hatherwisa*, from OG *Hadwid* (Forssner 144), eng, dīc), *Hec(c)lecerdike* 1488, Hy 6, -*car(r)* 1536, 1592 (*v.* kjarr 'marsh', dīc; if the first el. is e.ModE *heckel* 'heckle, flax-comb', the use here is obscure), *Herdwikeloke* 1398 (probably *Hardwick* as a surname, loc 'fold', possibly also in the later sense 'river-barrier'), (*le*) *Hewyn-, Hewenclif(f)bro(o)ke* 1327 WCR, 1331 ib, 1374, *Hewyncle-* 1374 (ME *hewen* 'hewn, excavated', clif, brōc), *le Hill* 1590, *The Hilles, the hilles close* 1592, *le Hilhous(e)* 1363, 1388 (*v.* hyll, hūs), *Hiperom Carr* 1473, *Hyperon Car* 1592, *Hiperoxgange* 1433 (a surname from Hipperholme iii, 79 *infra* (cf. *John Hiperom* of Methley 1473 MethMR 184), kjarr, ox-gang), *Hoion close* 1592, *Hollyn-, Hollingehirste* (*pitt*) 1406, 1555 (*v.* holegn 'holly', hyrst 'wood'), *Holingloine(end)* 1358, 1367, *Holinlonside* 1371 (*v.* prec., lane), *Holynrode* 1373 (*v.* prec., rod[1]), *Hollings* 1499 (*v.* holegn 'holly'), a piece of land called *Holtbitt* 1371 (deforced by *Robert del Holte* ib 145, *v.* holt 'wood', bita 'small piece of land'), *Hormere* 1358, *Hormiredike* 1377 (*v.* horu 'filth', mýrr 'bog', dīc), *Horeson greave(s)* 1592 (ME *horeson* 'whoreson', probably as a nickname, grǣfe 'copse'), *Hoghrode* 1373, *the Howroide* 1592 (*v.* hōh 'spur of land', rod[1]), *Hows(e) ing(e)* 1364, 1592 (*v.* hūs, eng), *Hughroid* 1413, *Heughroiddike* 1462, *Hewroide* 1571 (the ME pers.n. *Hugh, Hew*, rod[1]), *Hungenhill* (sic) 1373, *Hungerhill* 1550, 1618 (*v.* hungor, hyll).

Iblone 1373, *Ibbeloneend* 1371, *Liblaine* 1474 (the ME pers.n. *Ibbe* (from *Isabel*), lane), *Illeroide* (*v.* rod[1]), *Lehimpeyeard* 1377, *Impeyarde* 1472 (*v.*

impa 'sapling', geard; 1413 MethMR 171 speaks of 'wood, to wit, young oaks, carried from *the Impeyeards'*), *Inwalle* 1367 (*v.* in, wall).

Jakcroftend 1572, *Jack Hurn* 1699 AireSurv (the ME pers.n. *Jakke*, croft, hyrne 'corner of land'), *Johnyeardbrigge* 1487 (*v.* geard, brycg).

Laciehouse 1400, *Lascie Carr* 1459 (cf. *William Lacie* 1491 MethMR 188, *v.* hūs, kjarr), *the Layses* 1428 (*v.* læs 'meadow'), *The Landes* 1592 (*v.* land), *The launde* 1592 (*v.* launde 'glade'), *Leighenges* 1375, *le leighous* 1428, *Leighyherd* 1367, *Leghgarth* 1414 (*v.* lēah and Leigh Close f.n. *supra*, eng, hūs, geard, garðr), *Lenaibittes* 1374, *Lenaycrofte* 1377 (probably a pers.n. from OE *Lēofnōð*, bita (cf. *Holtbitt* f.n. *supra*), croft), *Leperdike* 1491, *Leaper flat(tes)* 1592 (named from the local family of *Le(e)per*, cf. *Thomas Leeper* 1361 MethMR 138, *v.* dīc, flat), *Lidyate* 1367, 1596, -*gate* 1413 (*v.* hlid-geat 'swing-gate'), *Lillerode(dike)* 1371, 1372, -*roide* 1380 (the ME pers.n. *Lille*, rod[1]), *the Lingybit stile* 1530 (*v.* lyng 'heather', bita (cf. *Holtbitt supra*), stigel 'stile'), *Littlecliffe* 1537, *the little Crofte* 1578, *Littleroid* 1366 (*v.* lytel, rod[1]), *Longbusteile* (a stile) 1512 (*v.* stigel), *Lonkerdike* Hy 6, *the Longcarre* 1592 (*v.* lang, kjarr, dīc), *the longe Crofte* 1578, *Longepasture* 1564, *Lousacre* 1627.

Malinge acre 1592, *Mapelwellchill* (sic) 1313 (*v.* mapel, wella, hyll), *Marshallcrofte* 1372, -*enge* 1385, -*house* 1592, *Marchelldike* 1400 (named from a local family of *Marshall* (cf. *Isabella Marshall* 1372 MethMR 147, *Thomas Marshall* 1411 ib 169), *v.* croft, eng, dīc), *Meindike(s)* 1366, 1372, *Meandike* 1458, *Meanland* 1592, *Meinrodelone* 1367, *Menerodgappe* 1373, *the Manroide* 1585 (*v.* (ge)mǣne 'common', dīc, land, rod[1], gap), *Meriwell Ing* 1592 (*v.* myrig 'pleasant', wella, eng), *Micclegate* 1497 (*v.* micel, gata), *Midelgaite* (*v.* middel, gata), *Moldcrosse* 1373 (perhaps molda 'hill', cros), *Munkcrofte* 1371, *Monklaghton* 1373 (*v.* munuc, perhaps here as a surname, croft, lēac-tūn 'garden'), *Morneside Close* 1590.

A Neck of Ing 1699 AireSurv, *the Newhedge* 1524, *Nibbehous* 1370, *Nibbells end*, *Niblone* Hy 6 (a pers.n., perhaps from the ON byname *Nibbr*, unless this is a variant of *Iblone* (*supra*), *v.* lane), *Norman house* 1505 (the surname *Norman*, hūs), *Northcroft* 1294, 1311 Meth, *Northfeilde dike* 1514, *North-forth* 1373, -*ford* 1411, *Northloine* 1367, 1382, -*lone* 1371, -*laine* 1592, *Nundicrofte* 1367 (cf. *Agnes Nundie* ib 142, *v.* croft).

Okalkerr 1385, *Okelcar* 1394 (a pers.n., possibly from ON *Auðkell*, kjarr), *Okebanke* 1577, *the Okecroftsike* 1592, *Okeforth* 1419, *Ok(e)ing(e)* 1516, 1542, 1592, *Okespringe* 1554 (*v.* āc 'oak', banke, croft, ford, eng, spring 'plantation'), *Oldhes* 1351 (*v.* ald, ēa, probably denoting one of the old courses of the Calder; it stood between Methley and Altofts), *Ouldhous(s)ike* 1367 (*v.* ald, hūs, sīc), *Oldrode(gapp)* 1365, 1385, -*roides* 1592 (*v.* ald, rod[1], gap), *Outgange* 1376 (*v.* ūt-gang 'exit'), *Oxinhedge* 1485.

the pale 1592 (ME *pale* 'fence, enclosure'), *Penland* 1374 (*v.* penn 'fold', land, Pen Bank 131 *supra*), *Person acre* 1381, *the Persons cottage* 1592, *Parsondike* 1479 (John Lancaster, the Rector, being presented for default in repair of this ditch, ib 185), 'a gate at' *Parsongapend* 1492, *Parson Gapp* 1541, *Personyate* 1516 (*v.* persone 'parson', æcer, dīc, gap 'opening', geat 'gate'), *Pyletcroft* 1354 Meth, *Pilatcrofte* 1394, *pillet Croftes* 1415, *Pillocroftes* 1592 (possibly identical with Pillow Close f.n. *supra*, *v.* pil-āte 'pill-oats', croft),

Pingell 1590, *the pingle* 1592 (*v.* pingel 'enclosure'), *Pyper place* 1592, *Peyper place* 1599 (the surname *Piper*, place), *Placedike* 1395, *Pocockeing* 1516, *the pocock Ing* 1592 (the surname *Pocock*, eng), *Pokerrid* 1366 (*v.* ryde 'clearing'), *Porterclaies* 1474, *-close* 1492, *-ford* 1473, *-house* 1389, *-place* 1491, 1765 LdsM, (*-in Thorpe*) 1592 (from the surname *Porter*, *v.* clǣg, etc.), *Pranbrigge* 1431, *-land* 1505 (perhaps e.ModE *pra(y)ne* 'prawn' as a nickname, brycg, land), *Pr(e)istpighill* 1397, 1525, *Preistplace* 1596, *Preist-*, *Purstroide* 1505, 1592 (*v.* prēost, pightel 'enclosure', place, rod[1]).

Rainolderoides 1592, *Reynoldyerde* 1367 (the ME pers.n. *Rainold*, rod[1], geard), *the Rakes* 1406 (*v.* hraca, dial. *rake* 'a rough path'), *Ravenroide* 1592 (the pers.n. *Raven* (ON *Hrafn*), rod[1]), *Rawingdike*, *-inge* 1428, 1497, *Rawland(e)* (*-laine*, *-Winn*) 1428, 1465, 1479 (*v.* rāw 'row', eng, land, hvin 'gorse'), *Redi-*, *Redymer(e)dike* 1403, Hy 6, *Riddimere dike* 1592 ('reedy pool', *v.* hrēodig, mere, dīc), *Remelaine* 1415, *Riderlaine* 1364, *Ryderloine* 1382 (the ME byname *Ridere*, lane), *Rymerdikes* 1371 (the e.ModE byname *Rimer* 'rhymer', dīc), *the Rise bobb* 1600 (doubtless 'brushwood clump', *v.* hrīs, ME *bobbe* 'cluster', cf. Hollin Bob Close 138 *infra*), *Rissehous* 1400, *the Rode* 1372, *the Roide(s)* 1485, 1592 (*v.* rod[1] 'clearing'), *Rodeland(e)* 1349, 1366, *Roideland* 1402, *Roxland* (sic for *Roþ-*) 1505 (*v.* rod[1], land, cf. *Rodeland* 148 *infra*), *Russelhouses*, *-roodend* 1371, 1397 (from the surname *Russel*, hūs, rod[1]).

Saverei landes 1592 (the surname *Savory*, ME *Saveric*, *Savari* (Reaney 284), land), *Saxton place* 1598 (named from the family of the cartographer Christopher Saxton, who made the 1592 survey of Methley (Meth), cf. Thoresby xxviii), (*the*) *Scarth* 1377, 1414, 1428, *Scarthdike(s)* 1370, 1394 (*v.* skarð 'opening, pass', dīc), *Scryvenroide* 1592, *Screvenroyd* 1684 *Glebe* (a surname from Scriven pt. v *infra*, rod[1]), *Selbrig* 1367 (*v.* selja 'willow', as in Selby pt. iv *infra*, brycg), *Shortflat(tes)* 1373, 1618, *Shorthalueacres* 1374 (*v.* half, æcer), *Shortrawe* 1420 (*v.* sceort, rāw 'row of houses'), *Shrogge* 1611 (*v.* scrogge 'brushwood'), *Sycroftside* 1366, *the Six acre close* 1564, *Six Acres* 1671 *Bright* 626, *Skyers* 1386, *Skiersgrene* 1592, *-loine* Hy 6, *-yait* 1559 (the surname *Skiers*, cf. Skier's Hall i, 112 *supra*, *v.* grēne[2], lane, geat), *Skilmilndike* 1370, *Skynnergrene* 1415 (the surname *Skinner*, grēne[2]), *the Slaughterhouse Wood* 1592, *Slo-*, *Slethorncarr*, *-karr* 1376, Hy 6 (*v.* slāh-þorn 'sloe thorn', kjarr), *Smithwillaker* 1473, *Snitalleine*, *-laine* 1379, 1394 (*v.* Snydale 122 *supra*, lane), *Soterbuttes* 1494, *Sowterbutes* 1545, *-butts* 1592 (*v.* sūtere 'shoemaker', probably as a surname, butte), *Southcroft* 1294, 1311 Meth, *Southlund* 1522 TestLds, *the South Lound* 1592 (*v.* sūð, lúndr 'small wood'), *Southroide* 1402 (*v.* rod[1]), *Suthslades* 1339 (*v.* slæd 'valley'), *Sparlingbancke* 1539 (the surname *Sparling*, from ME *sperling* 'a smelt', banke), *Spenhous(e)* 1562, 1592, *Spen place* 1600, (*the*) *Spenroid(e)* 1465, 1592 (*v.* Spen iii, 21 *infra*), *Spitilrode* 1371, *Spittleroide* 1389, 1472 (*v.* spitel 'hospital', rod[1]), *Spivehurst* 1592 (cf. Spivie Holme iii, 253 *infra*, *v.* hyrst), *Spring Close* 1680, *Staiesrode* 1367, *Stainplegis* (a piece of flat ground) 1347 (*v.* steinn, *-plegis* may stand for plek 'a small plot of ground'), *Stanawleighe* 1371, *Stan(i)leighs* 1366, *Stanleis* 1473, *the Stanilies* 1592 (*v.* stānig 'stony', lēah), *Stanrode* 1344 (*v.* stān, rod[1]), *Stokerloine* 1386 (the surname *Stoker*, unless a mistake for *Strakerlaine infra*, lane), *Stokeshill* 1600, *yᵉ Stockes Hill* 1605

PRMth (*v.* stocc 'stump', hyll), *Stock(w)ellflat(t)* 1373, 1618 (*v.* stocc, wella), *the Stonebrige* 1543 (*v.* stān, brycg), *Stonnigarth* 1423 (*v.* stānig, garðr), *Storr Scarr end* 1556 (*v.* storð 'plantation', kjarr), *Strakerlaine* 1447, *Strokerloindikes* Hy 6, *Strandike* 1364, 1385, 1526, *Strondike* 1540 (*v.* strand 'shore, river bank', dīc), *Stubbil* 1497 (ME *stuble* 'stubble'), *Swampe* 1550 (*v.* sumpe), *Swincote* 1577 ('pigsty', *v.* swīn, cot).

    Thewlesoxegange 1472, *-house* 1592 (the YW surname *Theules* (Reaney 318), ox-gang, hūs), *Todehole* 1370 (*v.* tādige 'toad' or todd 'fox', hol[1]), *Towngrene* 1381 (*v.* tūn, grēne[2]), *Turmaningdike* Hy 6, *Turner lane* 1499.

    Walkarbanck 1544, *Walkerhouse* 1458, *-land(e)* 1415, 1467, *-royde* 1611 (*v.* walcere 'cloth-dresser' used as a surname), *The Walles* 1592 (*v.* wall), *Walshenrodend* 1367, *War(r)wykhenge, -inge* 1363, 1385 (*Warwick* as a surname, eng), *Weauer house* 1592 (the surname *Weaver*, hūs), *Wellhead* 1591 Meth, *-place* 1592, *-sike* 1382 (*v.* wella), *Wesheforde banke* 1590 (*v.* wæsce 'washing-place', ford), *the Westfeilde* 1590, *Westforthtele* 1502 (*v.* west, ford, probably stigel 'stile'), *Westroid* 1460, 1542 (*v.* rod[1]), *Wetfores* 1550 (*v.* wēt 'wet', furh 'furrow'), *the Whaige* 1592 (possibly wagen 'quagmire'), *Whilewright garthes* 1496 (the surname *Wheelwright*, garðr), *Whinn(i)eparke* 1541, 1592 (described as 'whinnie grounde', *v.* hvin 'gorse', park), *Whitedike(s)* 1351, 1371 (*v.* hwīt, used as a surname *White*, dīc), *Whitleygarthe* 1590 (*Whitley* as a surname, garðr), *Wikwood* 1533, *Willerode* 1367, *Wilroide* 1516 (the pers.n. *Will*, rod[1]), *Williamkarrgappe* 1374 (*v.* kjarr, gap), *William crofte* 1367, *Wilsoncroftes* 1505, 1592, *Wynkerr* 1411, *the Wythin Carr* 1592 (*v.* wiðign 'willow copse', kjarr), *Wodhall* 1410 (*v.* wudu, hall), *Worstall* 1543, *Wormestalles* 1592 (*v.* wurm, stall, dial. *worm-stall* 'a shelter for cattle against flies, etc.', cf. Wormstall(s) i, 305, iii, 122, (Arthington, Ledsham) pt iv, *Wrmestalhirst* iii, 46, *Wormstall* (Birkin) pt. iv, Worstall Crags (Norwood) pt. v), *Worthery Lidyaite* 1547 (*v.* hlid-geat), *the Wrekland* 1465 (perhaps wrecca 'outlaw', land), *Wroho(i)le* 1521, 1597, *Wrohouslaine* 1367, *Wroosloine* 1385 (*v.* vrá 'nook of land', hol[1], hūs).

    Yeomand lande 1592.

vii.   Rothwell

    Rothwell is now an urban district and includes the old township of Methley (125 *supra*) and the townships of Oulton (141 *infra*) and Rothwell; Lofthouse is a separate civil parish in the Urban District of Rothwell and includes Lofthouse and Thorpe on the Hill (149 *infra*); Middleton township (139 *infra*) is now in the City Borough of Leeds (*v.* pt. iv *infra*).

1.   LOFTHOUSE (102–3325) ['lɔftəs]

    Locthuse, Loftose 1086 DB

    Lofthusũ 1166 P (p) 1235 *Bodl* 8, *Lofthushum* c. 1180–93 YCh 1818

    Lofthus(e) c. 1200 YD i, 13 Kirkst, *Nost* 137d, 1202 FF, 1235 YD i, 1243 Fees *et passim* to 1292 YI, *-hous(e)* 1303 Aid, 1315 WCR, 1342 *Surv*, 1388 YD vii *et passim* to 1606 FF

    Loftus 1250 DodsN, 1277 WCR   *Loftas* 1649 PRRth

Lofthouses 1323 WCR
Loftehouse 1379 PT *et freq* to 1547 FF, *-howse* 1596 FF

'House with a loft or upper chamber', *v.* lopt-hús. This compound occurs several times in Y as Lofthouse (Harewood) pt. iv, (Fountains Earth) pt. v, (Sedbergh) pt. vi, Loftus (Staveley) pt. v *infra*, YN 140, Loftsome YE 243, and it was often originally a plur. name, sometimes as here in the dat.plur. (*v.* -um).

CARLTON, *Carlentone* 1086 DB, *Carleton* 1243 Fees (p), 1251 Ch, 1258 YI, 1342 *Surv et passim* to 1606 FF, (*-juxta Rothewell*) 1486 TestLds, *Carrleton* 1597 SessnR. 'The churls' farmstead', *v.* ceorl, karl, tūn, and Carleton pt. iv *infra*.

LANGLEY, *Langeleigate* 1292 *MinAcct* 26, *Langleyat* 1341 *Surv*, *Langeldyate* 1341 Chapt 89, *Langalyate* 1342 *Surv*, *Longley gate* 1425 Rent, *Langley ,-laie* 1590, 1601 WYD, (*-Green*) 1817 M. 'The long clearing', *v.* lang, lēah, geat 'gate', a common type of p.n. in YW.

OUZELWELL GREEN, 1817 M, *Owsellwell greene* 1620 PRRth, *Ouslewell grene* 1651 ib, *Ousawell-*, *Owswelgreen(e)* 1664, 1673 PRRth, *v.* ōsle 'blackbird', wella, grēne[2]; *wella* is often combined with bird-names, as in Pinchwell i, 171, Birdwell i, 294 *supra*, *Spynkwell* 154, Spinkwell 177, 187, *Spinkeswell* 291, Ouzelwell 214 *infra*, etc.

BECKET LANE, 1841 *TA*, named from the *Beckett* family common in the parish from the seventeenth century (PRRth *passim*). BRIGHT-EYES ROW, *Upper & Lower Bright Eye* 1841 *TA*. BUSHY CLIFFE WOOD, 1841 *TA*, *v.* busc, clif. CARLTON CARR, 1841 O.S., *v.* kjarr 'marsh'. CARLTON FIELDS, *Carlton Field Close* 1841 *TA*. CASTLE GATE & HEAD, 1841 *TA*, *v.* castel, gata, hēafod; the site of a Roman camp is noted on 6″ O.S. CONEY WARREN, *Coney Close, Coney Warrant Close* 1841 *TA*, *v.* coni, wareine. DEALTRY PLANT., cf. *Ben Dealtry* of this parish, 1804 PRRth 973. GREEN END FM, *Green End Close* 1841 *TA*, *v.* grēne[2] (here Ouzelwell Green), ende. HILL HO. HOLLY HO, cf. *Hollings* 1841 *TA*, *v.* holegn 'holly'. HOWLET CROSS. JUMBLES LANE, *Jumble Lane* 1841 *TA*, cf. Jumples Ho iii, 115 *infra*. LANGLEY WOOD, 1841 O.S., *v.* Langley *supra*, wudu. LEADWELL LANE. LEDGER LANE, cf. *Joshua Ledger of Carleton* 1701 PRRth 401. LEE MOOR, *Lee Mo(o)re* 1680 PRRth, 1709 WMB, *v.* lēah, mōr. LEE MOOR GATE, *Lee Mo(o)re Gate* 1709 WMB, 1712 PRRth, *v.* prec., geat. LOFTHOUSE HILL, 1841 O.S. MATTY

LANE. MILNER LANE, doubtless named from the *Milner* family, very common in the parish from the seventeenth century (PRRth *passim*). NEW CLOSE WELL, *New Close* 1841 *TA*. NORTHFIELD, 1709 WMB, *the Northe felde* 1545 TestLds, *Carleton North feild* 1659 Pick, *v.* norð, feld. PITFIELD, 1837 *EnclA* 3, cf. *Pitt Close* 1612 Surv 421, *v.* pytt, feld. PYMONT HO. ROBIN HOOD, 1841 O.S., *TA*, *v.* Robin Hood's Bower i, 226 *supra*. ROPERY HO. ROTHWELL HAIGH, partly in Rothwell 144 *infra*. ROYDS GREEN, 1841 *TA*, part of Royds Green 146 *infra*. SHAYFIELD LANE, *Shay Field* 1837 *EnclA*, *v.* sceaga 'copse', feld. SHOP LANE. SPRINGWELL, cf. *Spring Close* 1841 *TA*, *v.* spring. STAINTON LANE. SWITHINS WELL, *Swithens Well* 1841 *TA*, *v.* the adjoining Swithins Fm 145 *infra*; there may have been some confusion with St Swithin (cf. St Swithin's Chantry 161 *infra*). TOWN END, 1841 *TA*. WELL CLOSE, 1841 *TA*. WEST BECK & BRIDGE. WESTFIELD, 1837 *TA*, *v.* west, feld. WESTGATE, 1542 *AOMB*, 1617 PRRth, *v.* west, gata.

FIELD-NAMES

The principal forms in (*a*) are 1841 *TA* 268. Spellings dated 1323 are *MinAcct* 45, 1342 *Surv* 756, 1425 Rent 298–301, 1542 *AOMB*, 1584–1611 WYD, 1837 *EnclA* 3.

(*a*) Alum Carr (*Allanker* 1601, the pers.n. or surname *Allen*, kjarr 'marsh'), Aumphrey Lane, Barley Close, Bean Close, Beck Close & Ing (*v.* bekkr, clos, eng), Beets (*v.* bete 'rough sods'), Birks Close, Borewell, Bottoms, Broad Oak, Brook Garth, Broom Close (*Broome Close* 1601, *v.* brōm, clos), Buck Garth, Burnel Close, Carr Ing (*v.* kjarr, eng), Charlie Royds, Clay Furrows or Furs, Coal Pit Close, Crimbles (*Crymylrode* 1342, *Crymbilrode* 1425, *v.* crymel 'small plot of land', rod[1]), Denbrook, Doll Close (cf. *Dowlerode* 1425, possibly connected with e.ModE *dowl* 'boundary mark' (cf. NED s.v. *dool*), *v.* rod[1]), Fallow Field, The Flatt, Footgate Close, Fox Close, Gambol Garth (cf. *Gamblebancke* 133 *supra*, garðr), Great Intake (*v.* intak), Grove Pit Close, Gulyard, Gussett, Hanging Royd (*Hengenderode* 1270 *Nost* 44, *v.* hengjandi 'steep', rod[1]), Hardacre Close (*v.* heard, æcer), Hemp Royd (*v.* hænep, rod[1]), Hollin Bob Close (cf. ME *a holyn bobbe* 'a cluster of holly' in *Sir Gawain* 206, cf. *the Rise bobb* 135 *supra*, Collen Bob iii, 164, Ling Bob iii, 206, etc. *infra*), Hough Hill, Kiln Garth, Knowle (Ing) (*v.* cnoll 'hillock', eng), Laith Close (*v.* hlaða), Broad & Narrow Lindley, Lofthouse Lane End 1841 O.S., Long Acre, Long Tofts, Marsh Close, Moat Close, Moor Close, Nether Field, Oakfield Close, Old Field 1837, Orgrave Field (ib 1837, 'ore pit', *v.* ōra[2], grafa, cf. Orgreave i, 184 *supra*, Orgrave Field 147 *infra*), Ox Close, Pighill (*v.* pightel 'enclosure'), Pond Close, Priest Leys (*v.* prēost, lēah), Proud Garth, Quarry Hill (*Quarrel Hill*

1601, v. quarrelle 'quarry', hyll), Scott Close, Slack Hill (v. slakki 'hollow'), Smithy Garth, Stone Bridge Close & Green, Stone Stocks, Swain Royds (*Swaynrod(e)* 1342, 1425, the ME pers.n. *Swain* (ON *Sveinn*), rod[1]), Sweet Bit (v. swēte, bita), Great & Little Swindell, Swindell Tree (ME *swingel-tree* 'the cross tow-bar of a plough' with *swindle* as a dial. variant, cf. NED s.v.), Tannergarth, Tenter Croft, Toad Moor Carrs, Toft Ings (v. topt, eng), Tofts Garth, Tumbles, Waggon Way, Water Slacks (v. wæter, slakki 'hollow'), West Croft, Wheat Close & Croft, Willow Holt, Wood Side.

(b) *Acre-end* 1601 (v. æcer, ende), *Dabelrode* (*assart' voc'*) 1342 (the surname *Dabell*, v. rod[1]), *Derlingrode* 1425 (ME *derling* 'darling' as a surname, rod[1]), *Dyker Rode* 1542 (ME *dikere* 'ditcher', probably as a surname), *Edyth- Edithrod(e)* 1323, 1342, 1425 (the fem. pers.n. *Edith*), *Elerode* 1342, *Fordland* 1425, *Jackrode* 1425, *Jonrodewodward* (an assart) 1425, *Lawe rode*, *Roods* 1590, *Lofthouse hall* 1584, 1611, *Menro(i)de* 1342, *Mene-*, *Maynrode* 1425 (v. (ge)mæne 'common', rod[1]), *Netherode* 1425 (v. neoðera, rod[1]), *Oldrode* 1425, *Randolf(f) Crofte* 1342, 1425 (the ME pers.n. *Randolf*, croft), *Southrode* 1425, *Tythe Laithe garthe* 1590 (v. hlaða 'barn', garðr 'yard'), (*le*) *West Rode* 1425, 1542.

2. MIDDLETON (102–3127)

Milde(n)tone 1086 DB
Middelton(e) Hy 2 (1230) Ch, 1155–8 YCh 1451, 1207 OblR, 1208
    FF, 1303 KF *et freq* to 1329 FF, (*-by Rothewell*) 1400 Pat
Mideltun, -ton' 1185 Templar (p), 1198–1208 YCh 1648, 1305
    YD v, 1402 FA, 1434 Calv, *Midilton, -y-* 13 Nost 138d, 1285
    KI, 1379 PT
Middleton juxta Rothwell 1621 FF

'Middle farm', v. middel, tūn.

BALKCLIFFE, *Baycliffe Hilly* (sic) 1841 *TA*, v. balca 'ridge', clif; it is a steep declivity at the end of a ridge. BELLE ISLE, 1763 PRRth, *Newbell-ile* 1762 ib. CLAPGATE, 1841 *TA*, cf. *Clap Farm* 1817 M, dial. *clapgate* 'a self-closing gate, a small hunting gate wide enough for a horse to pass' (EDD s.v.), cf. Clap Gate (Kearby) pt. v. CONYERS SPRING, *Colliers Spring Wood* 1841 *TA*, from the family name of *Fra. Coniers* of Middleton (1672 PRRth 313), changed to *Collier* through association with local coal mining. COPLEY FM, from the family of *Copley* frequent in the parish from the seventeenth century (PRRth *passim*). DAY HOLE END, *Day Hole* 1841 *TA*, v. Day Hole 189 *infra*. EBOR HO, *Aber House* 1779 PRRth, 1817 M. GLASSHOUSE FM, 1841 O.S., cf. also Glass Houghton 70 *supra*, Glasshouses 145 *infra* for references to glassworks locally, cf. glæs, hūs.   HOLME WELL, cf. *Holmes Close*, 1841 *TA*, *v.* holmr 'water-meadow'.   INTAKE LANE.   LINGWELL SYKE, *Lingwell* 1651 PRRth, cf. Lingwell Gate 158 *infra*, *v.* lyng 'heather', wella.   LOW GRANGE.   MAJOR FM, 1841 O.S.   MIDDLETON GRANGE, *The Grange* 1841 O.S., *v.* grange.   MIDDLETON WOOD, *Mid(d)leton Wood(e)* 1594, 1641 PRRth, *v.* wudu.   MILL FM, cf. *Mill Hill & Ing* 1841 *TA*, named from *Middleton Millne* 1657 Pick, *v.* myln.   NABBS END, 1841 O.S., *v.* nabbi 'a knoll'.   NEWHALL, 1822 Langd, *Neuhale* 13 Kirkst, 1296 YI, *Midleton new hall* 1651 PRRth, *v.* nīwe, hall, New Hall i, 95 *supra*.   NEW LANE FM, 1841 O.S.   SHARP HO, 1841 O.S., *Sharphous* 1770 PRRth, named from the *Sharp* family common in the parish from the sixteenth century (PRRth *passim*).   SISSONS FM & WOOD, cf. *Sissons House* 1757 PRRth, 1817 M, named from the Y family of *Sisson(s)*, living locally in the eighteenth century (PRRth).   THROSTLE CARR BECK, *Throstle Carr* 1841 *TA*, *v.* þrostle 'thrush', kjarr 'marsh'.   WEST FM, 1841 O.S., *West Hall* 1763 PRRth.   WEST WOOD, 1841 *TA*.   WINDMILL FM, *Winmiln feild* 1648 PRRth, *Winde Milne felde* 1651 ib, *Midleton Wynd mil feild* 1654 ib, *Winman Field* (sic) 1817 M, *Windmill* 1841 O.S., *v.* wind, myln, cf. foll.   WINDY HILL, *Midleton windey Hill* 1787 PRGf, *v.* wind, hyll, cf. Windhill Gate i, 287 *supra*.

FIELD-NAMES

The principal forms in (*a*) are 1841 *TA* 287; spellings dated 1708 are *WYEnr* 20.

(*a*) Lower Aires, Bean Close, High & Low Birks, Bottoms, Boulton Hill, Broad Butts (*v.* butte), Broom Close, Calf Garth, Cinder Hill, Coal Hill, Coal Pit Close, Combstock Close, Coney Garth (ib 1708, *Le Conyger* 1425 Rent, *v.* coning-erth 'warren'), Dam Close, Dukesbery Horn, Flaws Hill, Garnet Croft, Hall Flatt, Hanging Ing (*v.* hangende 'steep', eng), Hill Hole Woods, Hobroyd, Hole Ing, Hoyle Close, Hurn Close, Joffling(s), Kersey Lands, Laith Close (*v.* hlaða 'barn'), Low & Upper Leys (possibly identical with *Leighes* 1292 *MinAcct* 26, *le Leghes* 1323 ib 45, *v.* lēah), Messling Carrs, Middleton Hall 1708 (ib 1539), Moor Close, Moor Flats 1708, Mosley End (*v.* mos, lēah), the Northfields 1708, Old Field, Oven Close, New & Old Park (*the Parkes* 1546 TestLds, *Nether & Upper Parke* 1708, *v.* park), Pick Hill, Pit Close & Hill, Rein Wood (*v.* reinn 'boundary strip'), Rushey Close & Flatt, Sampson Royd 1708, Sheep Coat Close 1708, Shrogg (*v.* scrogge 'brushwood'), Slip, Smithy Close, Sour Lands, Spoil Bank, Sprutts, Stail, Stoney Bank, Watergate Close, Well Hole, Well Pit Close, White Cross Close, Whiteley Garth, Wolt Royds, Worlds End Close.

(*b*) The *Rydings* 1636 WillY (*v.* rydding 'clearing').

3. OULTON (102–3628)

Aleton 1180 P (p) (possibly identical)
Olton 1251 Ch, 1252 Skyr, 1334–7 SR (p), 1425 Rent *et freq* to
1594 FF, *Holton* 1548 PRRth
Oldton 1297 WCR (p), 1425 Rent, 1586 FF, *Oldeton* 1323, 1487
MinAcct 45, 66
Owlton 1598 SessnR, *Oulton* 1651 PRRth, 1658 WillS

'Old farmstead', *v.* ald, tūn.

WATER HAIGH FM, *Waterhagh(e)* 1292 *MinAcct* 26, 1425 Rent, 1487
MinAcct 66, 1547 *WB* 105, *-haigue* 1716 PRRth, *Wathehagh*' (sic)
1487 *MinAcct* 66. 'Enclosure near the water', *v.* wæter, haga; it is
near the R. Aire.

WOODLESFORD

Wri-, *Wryd(e)lesford(e)* 12 *WB* 1 (p), 1185–1202 YCh viii (p),
1201 Cur (p), c. 1204 Pont (p), 1243 Fees, 1246 *Ass* 3d, 1250 FF
(p), 1251 Ch, 1254 YI *et freq* to 1425 Rent, *-forth* Hy 3 Calv (p)
Wrīslesfordia c. 1150 Crawf
Widlesford 1188–1202 YCh viii (p)
Writeleford l. 12 *Lewes* 300d (p), *Writhelesford* 1270 *Nost* 44
Wrilesford 1201 Kirkst (p)
Wriddlisford' 1202 FF (p)
Wirdlesford c. 1250–8 YD iii
Wrideleford 1276 RH, *Wridelford*' 1487 *MinAcct*
Wodelesford 1252 (17) Skyr, *Wudelesford* 1425 Rent, *Wo(o)dlesworth*
(sic) 1618, 1620 PRRth, *Woodlesford*, *-forth* 1626 ib, 1638
SessnR, 1667 PRRth, *Woodesforth* 1682 SelbyW
Wreddelsforthe 1548 PRRth
Wordleworthe 1572 PRLds, *Wordlesford* 1651 PRRth
Wriglesforth 1596, 1599 PRRth, *-worth* 1620, 1744 ib

The oldest form of the name is certainly *Wridelesford*, with an
occasional *Writel-* through AN influence and *Writhel-* through ON
influence or that of the OE variant wrīð for wrīd. In the later spellings
Wrigles- arises from *Wrideles-* through a rationalising substitution
(from ModE *wriggle*), and the second series, which culminates in the
current form *Woodlesford*, begins with such metathesised spellings
Wirdles-, *Wordles-* and follows the normal dial. development (with
loss of *-r-*) to *Wo(o)dles-*. The name means, as Ekwall suggests, 'ford
near a thicket', from an OE wrīdels (a derivative of wrīd 'a bush'

with the suffix -*els*) and ford. The ford was presumably one which carried the Wakefield–Tadcaster road across the Aire where Swillington Bridge now stands. *v.* Addenda.

APPLEGARTH, 1841 *TA*, 'orchard', *v.* æppel, garðr, cf. apaldrs-garðr. CROFT BRIDGE. ESHALD HO & WELL, *Eshald* 1710 PRRth, *Ashelwell* 1841 *TA*, doubtless named from a family called *Eshald* (cf. Esholt pt. iv *infra*), known here from the sixteenth century (PRRth *freq*). FLEET BRIDGE & LANE, *Flete* 1292 *MinAcct* 26, *Fleet(e)* 1342 Ext, 1649 *MinAcct* 13, *v.* flēot, here probably a stretch of the R. Aire or a secondary channel, which forms a mill stream. FLEET MILLS, 'the mills of *Flete*' 1425 Rent 303, *Fletemylneȝ* 1487 *MinAcct* 66, *Fleet Mill* 1736 PRRth, *v.* prec., mўln. GREENLAND FM. HESP LANE, 1841 O.S., *Hespes* 1323 *MinAcct* 45, *Les Espes* 1425 Rent, *Little & Mean Hesps* 1841 *TA*, *v.* æspe 'aspen-tree'. HIGHFIELD HO. THE HOLLINS, *Holin hall* 1735 PRRth, *v.* holegn 'holly'. HOLMSLEY FIELD, 1845 *TA*, *Hamesleye* 1270 *Nost* 44, *Holmesley* 1841 *TA*; the modern form suggests that *Hames-* must have had a long vowel, and the first el. may therefore be an OE pers.n. *Hām* (a strong form of OE *Hāma*, probably cognate with OHG *Haimo*, cf. Redin 97), *v.* lēah; this p.n. was also used as a local surname in *Jos. Holmsley* (PRRth 756). HOME CROFTS. MILL HO, cf. *Mill Field* 1841 *TA*. OULTON BECK, *aque voc' Altonbec* 1487 *MinAcct* 66, *v.* bekkr. OULTON GREEN, *Oldton Grene* 1425 Rent, *v.* grēne². OULTON HALL, 1817 M, cf. Hall Carrs, etc. *infra*. OULTON PARK, *the Park* 1342 Ext, *v.* park. POTTERY LANE, cf. *Pothouse* 1770 PRRth, an old pottery. SUGAR HILL, 1841 *TA*. WOODLANDS.

FIELD-NAMES

The principal forms in (*a*) are 1841 *TA* 312. Spellings dated 1341 are Surv 756, 1342 Ext, 1425 Rent 291–303, 1752–1756 PRRth.

(*a*) Barley Banks, Bridge End, Brigg Ing (cf. *Briggrene* 1425, *v.* brycg, grēne², eng), Broad Royd (*le Brode Rode* 1425, *v.* brād, rod¹ 'clearing'), Brook Croft, Brow, Coats Close, Cock Pit Close, Cowling Garth, Davy Royds (*Dauyrode* 1425, the ME pers.n. *Davy* (from *David*), rod¹), Dub Laith (*v.* dubb 'pool', hlaða 'barn'), Dye Syke, Ellar Close (*v.* elri 'alder-tree'), Fordingworth (*Faldingwoth* (sic), -*yng*- 1425, -*worth* 1461 *MinAcct* 09, 1608 ib 12, *Faleyngworth* 1487 ib 66, *v.* falding, worð, cf. Fallingworth iii, 54 *infra*), Gamble Royd (*Gamylrod* 1342, *Gamolrod* 1425, the ME pers.n. *Gamel* (ON *Gamall*), or the surname formed from it (cf. *Gamblebancke* 133 *supra*), rod¹), Haigh Mill (cf. *Haighflatt* 1342, *v.* haga 'enclosure'), Hall Carrs (cf. *Le Hall*

Crofte 1425 Rent, *v.* Oulton Hall *supra*, kjarr, croft), Hannah Royd, Lang Close, Low Ings, Low Laiths, Lund Close, Mankin Pits, Mold Roe (*The Mould Roo* 1764 *Glebe, v.* molde, vrá), Neal Royd (*Nelerode* 1323 *MinAcct* 45, *Nelroid* 1341 *Surv* 10, 5, *Neilrode* 1341 Chapt 93, *Nielrode* 1425, the ME pers.n. *Nele* (OIr *Niáll*), rod[1]), Ormond Top, Oulton Ing (*The Oulton Ings* 1764 *Glebe, v.* eng), Oven Croft (cf. Pottery Lane *supra*), Pick Pocket, Quarry Close & Field (*Oulton Quaries* 1752, *-Quarils* 1756, *v.* quarrelle 'quarry'), Ratten Royds, Rye Royd, Shoulder of Mutton, Sinking Ing (ib 1764 *Glebe*), Smiths Farm (*le Smythe* 1341 *Surv* 10, 5 (a cottage called), *the Smyth* 1341 Chapt, 1342, *Le Smythes* 1425, *v.* smiðð̄e), Stockings (*v.* stoccing), Stye Bank (*v.* stīg, banke, cf. Stye Bank Lane 146 *infra*), Thorny Lands (*Thorniland* 1292 *MinAcct* 26, *Thornigland* 1425, *Thorneland* 1487 *MinAcct* 66, *v.* þornig, land), Toberans, Wallow Field, Water Flatts, Well Close, Wheat Royd (*le Wete Royd* 1341 *Surv* 10, 5, *le Whetrod* 1342 ib 756, *v.* hwǣte, rod[1]).

(*b*) *Alisacre* 1425 (the fem. pers.n. *Alice*, æcer), *Asherode* 1425 (*v.* æsc, rod[1]), *Bolhill, -hull* 1425 (possibly to be identified with Bell Hill 144 *infra, v.* bol 'round hill', hyll), *Douecoteyerd* 1292 *MinAcct* 26, *Dovescote yard* 1425 (*v.* dūfe, cot, geard), *Forrestrode* 1425 (*v.* forest, rod[1]), *Gyleszerd* 1425 (the ME pers.n. *Giles*, geard), *Les Leghes* 1425 (*v.* lēah), *Le oldhous* 1425 (*v.* ald, hūs), *Olton Cross(e)* 1342, 1425 (*v.* cros), *Olton dam* 1341 Chapt 89, 1342, *le Damme*, *Oldton Damme* 1425, *Altondamme* 1608 *MinAcct* 12 (*v.* dammr), *Slepland* 1425 (*v.* slǣp 'slippery place, a slip-way', land), *Le Splene* 1425, *Les Willoghes* 1425 (*v.* wilig 'willow').

4. ROTHWELL (102–3428)

Rodouuelle, Rodewelle 1086 DB

Rowelle, -well(a) 12 YCh 1439, 1480, 1497, 1516 (*Nost* 14, etc.),
   c. 1212 Pont, 1215 ChR, 1241 Pat, 1242 Ebor, Lib, 1249 *RegAlb*
   ii, 6d, 1251 Ch *et passim* to 1313 Pat

Rouell(a) 1130–40 YCh 1466, 1316 Vill, *Rueliam* 1180–93 YCh
   1818, *Rouuelle* 1255–77 *Nost* 20, *Rouwell(e)* 1249 *RegAlb* iii, 92d,
   1253, 1290 Ebor, 1298 *Nost* 40d

Rothenwella 1121–7 YCh 1428

Rothewell(a), -welle 1189 *Nost* 4, 1255–77 ib 183, 1259 *Ass* (p),
   1270 *Nost* 44, 1284, 1286 Ebor, 1291 Tax, 1292 *Nost* 63d, 1297,
   1324 WCR, 1328 FF *et passim* to 1531 AD i

Rodwell(a) 1137–9 (16) YCh 1492, 1588 FF

Routhewele 1235 DodsN   *Rowthwell* 1550 TestLds

Rothwell 1280 Ch, 1409 DiocV, 1505 AD i *et freq* to 1641 Rates

Roithwell 1545 LS, *Roythewell* 1554 TestLds

The persistent early *Rowell* spellings, with AN loss of medial *-th-*, show that we have to start with late OE *Roð(a)-wella*, and the frequent *Rothewell* spellings with a medial *-e-* and the later dialect spellings

Roith- (which arise from short *o* in an open syllable, cf. Phonol. § 28) point rather to an OE *Rōða-wella.* The single *Rod-* and the single *Routhe-* spellings are from late transcripts and because of their uniqueness have no significance; Goodall's suggested derivation from ON **rauðr** 'red' must therefore be rejected, as indeed it must be for Rothwell Nth 118–19, which, according to Ekwall, is from an OE **roð** 'clearing', a word found in an OE p.n. form *Rōðe* (BCS 737) for Roe Green Hrt 165 and in other p.ns. Rothwell means 'well by the clearing(s)' (*v.* lēah), and if Royds Hall *infra* is in fact an old name it may be the name of the clearings referred to.

BANKS HO (lost), *le Bankez* 1341 *Surv, Bankes* 1341 Chapt, 1342 Ext, *le Banke* 1342 *Surv, Bank(s)house* 1735, 1738 PRRth, *v.* **banke.**

BELL HILL, *Bulchill* (sic) 1270 *Nost* 44, *Balghulflat* 1292 *MinAcct* 26, *Belle hill Layn* 1735 PRRth, possibly identical with *Bolhull* 1342 *Surv* and also *Bolhill* 143 *supra.* Despite the variations, this is no doubt 'rounded, smooth hill', *v.* **balg, hyll,** with **bol** of similar meaning and **belle** 'bell-shaped hill' as variants.

HALY PASTURE (lost), *Hali-, Halypastur(e)* 1323 *MinAcct* 45, 1341 *Surv,* 1425 Rent 289, *-pastour* 1341 Chapt, 1342 Ext, *Haileghpasture* 1341, 1342 *Surv, Hailepastur* 1342 Ext. Rather uncertain, but it is either 'holy pasture' (*v.* **hālig, pasture**) or possibly 'pasture at *Hailey*' (*v.* **hēah, lēah**).

THE HEATH (lost), *Hed* 1270 *Nost* 44, *Heth* 1341 Chapt, *le Heth(e)* 1425 Rent, 1461, 1487 MinAcct 09, 66, *Rothewell Heathe* 1552 WillY, *le Heath* 1608 *MinAcct* 12, *v.* **hǣð** 'heath'.

ROTHWELL HAIGH, *Roth(e)wel(l) Hawght* 1285 KI, *-Hagh* 1327 FF, 1328 Banco, 1448 *MinAcct* 66, 1597 PRRth, *-haught* 1461 *MinAcct* 09, *-Hay(e)* 1531 AD i, 1537 Roundhay, 1606 FF, *-Hagg* 1557 WillY, *-Haige* 1620 PRRth, *-Hague* 1654 ib, *-Haigh* 1754 LdsInt, *Roithewellhaie* 1557 TestLds, *the Haigue* 1652 PRRth, *v.* **haga** 'enclosure'; this was an ancient park of the Lacies (Whitaker 140).

ROYDS HALL, 1817 M, *Rodes* 1283, 1311, 1328 Ch, 1632 PRRth, (*-Hall*) 1651 ib, *Roodes* 1556 WillY, 1649 PRRth, (*le*) *Roydes* 1592 WillY, 1611 FF, 1618 PRRth, *Roades hall* 1654 ib. *v.* **rod**[1] 'a clearing' and cf. Rothwell *supra.*

Stainer (lost), *le Steenre, Damheuedsteenre* 1292 *MinAcct* 26, *Stener* 1323 ib 45, 1425 Rent, *Stenre* 1342 Ext, *Rothwelsten* (sic) 1425 Rent, *Rothewell Stayuener* (sic) 1461 *MinAcct* 09, *-Styner* 1546 TestLds, *Steyner* 1480 *MinAcct* 11, (*Roithewell-*) 1564 TestLds, *Stanore, Steynerhill* 1487 *MinAcct* 66, *Rothwellstoner* 1608 *MinAcct* 12, *v.* stæner 'rocky ground', and cf. Stennard Well 151 *infra*.

Swithins Fm, *Swythene* 1270 *Nost* 44, *Swi-, Swythen* 1341 Chapt, 1342 Ext, *Surv*, 1425 Rent, *Le Swithen* 1425 ib, *Swi-, Swythyn* 1461 *MinAcct* 09, 1487 ib 66, *Swithens* 1841 O.S., from ON sviðinn 'land cleared by burning', dial. *swithin* 'moor cleared by burning', an el. which recurs in YW p.ns.

Thwaite Ho, *Rothewelletwayt* 1276 RH, *le Twait* 1292 *MinAcct* 26, *le Thuayt(e)* 1323 ib 45, *Twhait, -y-* 1341 Chapt, 1342 Ext, 1487 *MinAcct* 66, *Thweit(e), -ai-* 1341 Chapt, 1342 *Surv*, (*the-, le-*) 1546 TestLds, 1608 *MinAcct* 12, *Le Thwate* 1425 Rent, *Thwaites* 1673 PRRth. *v.* þveit 'a clearing, a meadow'.

Bridgefield Terrace, cf. *Bridge Close* 1840 *TA*. Bullough Lane, *Bullock Lane* 1841 O.S., probably named from the *Bullough* family (18 PRRth *freq*). Butcher Lane. Carr Lane, *the car(re)* 1557, 1558 TestLds, *Carre house* 1587 WillY, *Care laine* 1692 PRRth, *Car Lane* 1817 M, *v.* kjarr 'marsh', lane. Church Field, 1845 *TA*. Church Well. Colley Well, *Caldewelle* 1255–77 *Nost* 20, *Caudewell* 1809 PRRth, 'cold well', *v.* cald, wella. Crier Cut (lost), *v.* The Goit *infra*. Dandy Row. Dungeon Lane, 1845 *TA, Dungon laine* 1747, 1766 PRRth, ME *dongeon* 'dungeon', but the context is uncertain. Gillet Bridge, 1845 *TA*. Glasshouses (lost, near Stourton Chemical Works on the R. Aire), *Fenton Glass House* 1752 PRRth, *Hague Glasshouse* 1758 ib, *Glasshouses* 1817 M; these are glass-factories; cf. also *John Walton, glassmaker* of Rothwell (1754 PRRth), Glass Houghton 70 *supra*. The Goit, formerly a by-pass to the R. Aire and now running alongside the canal (*v.* gota 'water-course'), which was called *Cryer(s) Cut(t)*, 1758 PRRth, 1761 LdsM, *Crier Cut* 1817 M, *v.* cut 'a cut water-channel'; a family called *Cryer* was frequent in the parish from the seventeenth century (PRRth). Goslem, *Gosling, Goz-lam, Gozallem* 1746, 1748, 1763 PRRth, perhaps representing an older *Gōs-lum* 'goose pool' (*v.* gōs, lumm). Haigh Fm & Ho, *Haigh* 1817 M, *Haigh House* 1840 *TA, v.* Rothwell Haigh *supra*. Haigh Park, 1840 *TA, v.* prec.,

park.   Hopefield Fm, 1845 *TA*, cf. *Hope Close* 1840 *TA*, *v.* foll.,
feld.   Hope's Fm, *Hope* 1270 *Nost* 44, *v.* hop, here 'a small side-
valley', Hope's Fm being at the top; but Hope's Fm and Hopefield
may contain a local surname *Hope* derived from the p.n.   Ingram
Parade, cf. *Ingram Place* 1841 O.S.   Iveridge Hall, 1770 PRRth,
1817 M, a house called *Iverrysshe* 1542 *AOMB*, *Iverush Hall* 1709
PRRth, *-rish-* 1769 ib, *v.* īfig 'ivy' (which has an e.ModE variant *ive*),
risc 'rush'; in this compound with *ivy*, the second el. may rather
be the northern dial. *rush* 'a thick growth of plants or shrubs, a
brake' (*v.* NED s.v. *rush* sb.[2]).   Manor Ho, cf. *Mannorgarth* 1608
MinAcct 12, *Manor Pasture* 1845 *TA*, ME *maner* 'manor', *v.* garðr,
pasture.   Marsh St, *Marshelane* 1480 *MinAcct* 11, cf. Marsh Close
1845 *TA*, *v.* mersc, lane.   Mill Hill, *Rothwell iuxta molendin'm*
1594 PRRth, cf. also *Mill Dam, Mill Goit* 1845 *TA*, *v.* myln, dammr,
gota (which denotes a different mill-stream from The Goit *supra*).
Newmarket Haigh, *Newmarkit, -et* 1742 PRRth, 1771 M, *v.* nīwe,
market, haga; the allusion is obscure.   The Paddock.   Patrick
Green, 1770 PRRth, named from the *Patrick* family frequent in the
parish in the seventeenth century (PRRth *freq*).   Pickpocket Lane.
Pindars Screed.   Rothwell Beck, *Rodwel becke* 1577 Holinshed,
v. bekkr.   Rothwell Castle.   Royds Green, 1817 M, *Rhod(e)s
Green* 1742, 1756 PRRth, *v.* Royds Hall *supra*, grēne[2].   Spring
Head, cf. *Spring Close* 1845 *TA*, *v.* spring 'spring'.   Springs Wood,
Spring Wood 1845 *TA*, *v.* spring 'plantation'.   Sterroid Well,
Starrod 1292 *MinAcct* 26, *Sterroyd Well Close* 1845 *TA*, *v.* stēor
'steer', rod[1].   Stone Bridge, *Stone Bridge Garth* 1845 *TA*, *v.*
stān, brycg, garðr.   Stourton.   Stye Bank Lane, *Stie Banks* 1775
PRRth, *v.* stīg 'path', banke, distinct from Stye Bank 143 *supra*.
Thwaite Mills, 1822 M, *v.* Thwaite Ho *supra*.   Urn Ho, *Horne,
below Horn* 1731, 1737 PRRth, *Horn Ho* 1841 O.S., *v.* horn, doubtless
used here to describe the end of the ridge on which Urn Ho stands.
Valley Fm, 1840 *TA*.   West Fm, *West Hall* 1841 O.S.   Wood
End Fm.

FIELD-NAMES

The principal forms in (*a*) are 1839 Gouthwaite, *Plan and Record of the
Hamlet of Rothwell Haigh*, 1840 *TA* 339 (Rothwell Haigh), and 1845 *TA*
338 (Rothwell cum Royds). Spellings dated c. 1260, 1270 are *Nost* 20, 44,
1292, 1323 *MinAcct* 26, 45, 1341 *Surv* 10, 5, 1342 ib 756, 1360 YD vii, 1461,
1480, 1487 *MinAcct* 09, 11, 66, 1505–1558 TestLds, 1608 *MinAcct* 12, 1672–
1800 PRRth, 1809 *EnclA* 33. Some of the f.ns. in (*b*) may belong to neighbouring townships (esp. those in Rothwell parish).

(a) Acre Garth, Ashwell Field 1809 (v. æsc, wella), Banderhouse Close 1839, Bankside (cf. *Banks Ho supra*), Bell Bushes, Bentcliff, Bog Close, Bone Tree Close, Braishy Close, Briers Close, Broad Dyke Spring, Broomhills, Butts 1839 (v. butte), Cabin Well 1748, Calf Pasture (*Calfpastur(e)* 1341, 1342 Ext, v. calf, pasture), Cinder Over Hills, Clap Gate Close (v. Clapgate 139 *supra*), Cleats Pasture (*Cletes* 1425, v. clǣte 'burdock'), Coalpit Close (*the Coalpit* 1764), Cock Hill (v. cocc[1], hyll), Coney Hills (v. coni, hyll), Cow Stand, Crabtree Close, Cramp Garth, Croft Close, Dams (cf. *Damforland* 1270, *Olton dam* 143 *supra*, v. dammr), Dubb Close (v. dubb 'pool'), Eller Royd (v. elri 'alder-tree', rod[1]), Elm Close, Far Ing 1839 (v. eng), Five Stiles Close, Foot Garth, Gaol Croft (named from *yᵉ Goale* 1690, *yᵉ Gaole* 1696, *Rothwell Gole* 1699, ME *gayhole* 'jail', cf. *Kidcote infra*), Garlick Close, Gill, Gladdow Close, The Glover Ing 1764 *Glebe* (the surname *Glover*, eng), Great Ing, Green Dykes, Handley Close & Pasture, Hansom Close, Hardcastle Close, Hearse House, Heaton Close (cf. *Heaton Lodge* 1817 M), Hen Croft, Hill Top (ib 1817 M), High Pole Close, Hobby Royd, Hollow Back, Holmes (*Holm(e)* c. 1260, 1341, 1342 Ext, v. holmr 'water-meadow'), Ings 1839 (v. eng), Intake 1839 (v. intak), Iron Hills, Laith Close (cf. *Lathegarthe* 1292, v. hlaða 'barn', garðr), The Lawyers Ing 1764 *Glebe*, Lightnings, Limekiln Close, Line Close (v. lín 'flax'), Little Ing, Long Leys (v. lēah), Madge Pits, Martin Close, Massey Close, Milestone Close, Millstone Close, Far & Near Nabs (v. nabbi 'knoll'), North Field 1809, Oldgate Lane, yᵉ Old River 1778, Oral Royd, Orgrave Field (ib 1809, *Orgreues* c. 1260, v. ōra[2] 'ore', græf 'pit', cf. Orgreave i, 184 *supra*), Ox Close, The Pain Ing 1764 *Glebe* (the surname *Pain*, eng), Parnaby Sheepclose, Pea Hill, Pig Minster, Pinfold Close (*Pinfold(e)* 1552, v. pynd-fald), Pithill 1839 (*le Pighull* 1292, v. pightel 'enclosure'), Quarry Close (*Quarry Field* 1809, *le quarelcloghes* 1323, v. quarrelle 'quarry', clos, clōh 'dell'), Raw Royd (*Roherdrode* 1341 Chapt, 1342 Ext, the ME pers.n. *Rohard, Ruard* (OG *Rothard*), rod[1]), Savile Croft, Saw layne 1732 (*Sowlane head* 1672, *Sow Laine* 1700), Saxon Close, Sheep Close, Shoulder of Mutton, Sill Croft, Small Tailed Acre, Sour Ing, Spice Royd, Spivey Row (cf. Spivie Holme iii, 253 *infra*), Stand Close, Steward Ing, Stripcot Hill 1839, Tan House Close, Temple ford 1793, Tinkers Acre, Tom Bottoms, Town End garth, Waggon Way, Well garth, White Hall garth, Wood Yard close.

(b) *Akerode graue* 1270 (v. āc 'oak', rod[1], grāf 'grove'), *Assheredynge* 1487 (v. æsc, rydding 'clearing'), *Balgrene* c. 1260 (this is possibly an early use of *ball-green* 'a bowling green', which recurs in YW minor names), *Birkenabe* 1558 (v. birki, nabbi 'knoll', but perhaps an error for *Kyrkenabbe infra*), *Bowkerode* 1341, 1342, 1425 (probably dial. *bowk* 'a milk pail', 'a bucket or tub in coal-mining' (from OE *būc* 'pitcher' or the surname *Bowker* (Fransson 109), rod[1], most likely a reference to a clearing with a coal-pit), *Briggesgroue* 1487 (v. brycg, grāf 'grove'), *Brode-eng(e)* 1323, 1341, 1425, -*yng(e)* 1341 Chapt, 1342 (v. brād, eng), *Brodstremer* 1342 (perhaps an error for stǣner 'rocky place', v. brād, *Stainer* 145 *supra*), *Brokynge* 1342 (v. brōc, eng), *Chapman house* 1505 (the surname *Chapman*), *Rothwell church stele* 1505 (v. stigel 'stile'), *Cokpighill* 1341, -*hull* 1341 Chapt (v. cocc[2], pightel 'enclosure'), *the Connyng* 1341 Chapt, 1342 Ext (*v.* coni, eng), *Count(e)nayroid* 1342 Ext, *-rode* 1425, *Crokenge* 1341, 1342 Ext (*v.* krókr, eng), *le Esterne-leeghe* 1360 (*v.* ēasterra, lēah), *Ewelynge* 1342 (*v.* ǣwell 'spring', eng), *le Faltrogh* 1292, *Flascrogh* (sic) 1487 (*v.* (ge)fall, trōg 'trough, depression'), *Flodemylne* 1487 (*v.* flōde 'channel, gutter', myln), *Forsterchambr'* 1292 (*v.* forestier 'forester', ME (OFr) *chambre* 'chamber', probably used here as elsewhere in YW (Higgin Chamber iii, 147 *infra*) of a dwelling of some kind), *the Garthinge* 1552 (*v.* garðr, eng), *Geffreyrode* 1341 Chapt, 1342 Ext, *Jaffreyrode* 1425 (cf. *Geffrayrode* 133 *supra*), *Grenewood* 1552, *Haggeston-cliffe* 1557 (*v.* hǫgg (or *hag* 'a witch'), stān, clif), *Halgarth* 1487 (*v.* hall, garðr), *Hallache* 1425 (*v.* hall, læcc 'stream, bog'), *Hallenge(s)* 1292, 1425, *-ynge* 1487 (*v.* hall, eng), *Hardul(u)esflat(e)* 1270 (the OE pers.n. *Heardwulf*, ME *Hardulf*, flat), *Harestan* 1270 ('grey, boundary stone', *v.* hār², stān), *Hye Longe* 1558, *Kenyngschagh'* 1292 (*v.* sceaga 'copse'), *Ketelrode* c. 1260 (the ON pers.n. *Ketill*, ME *Ketel*, rod¹), *Kidcote* 1487 (lit. 'kid shed', *v.* kide, cot, a common name for a prison, *v.* NED s.v., cf. Gaol Croft 147 *supra*), *Kyrkenabbe* 1557 (*v.* kirkja, nabbi 'knoll'), *Knousthorptoftes* 1292 (named from Knowsthorpe (Leeds) across the R. Aire (pt. iv *infra*), *v.* topt 'enclosure'), *Merescal* c. 1260 (*v.* mere 'pool', skáli 'shieling'), *Mikelenge* 1292 (*v.* micel, eng), *Monkepit* 1292, *Munekewelle* c. 1260, *fonte monachi* 1270 (named from the monks of Nostell, who owned land here, *v.* munuc, pytt, wella), *the new launde* 1557 (*v.* launde 'glade'), *le Newparke* 1538 *MinAcct* (*v.* nīwe, park), *Normanroid* 1341, 1342 Ext, *-rod* 1425 (the pers.n. or surname *Norman*, rod¹), *Okewell(eng)* 1292, 1323 (*v.* āc, wella, eng), *the old lawnd* 1558 (*v.* launde 'glade'), *Owncroft* 1425, (*le*) *Oxpast(o)ur* 1292, 1341, 1342 (*v.* oxa, pasture), *Pernelpyt* 1480 (the ME fem. pers.n. *Pernel*, later used as a term for a wanton, pytt), *Pillerode* 1360 (probably an OE pers.n. *Pila* or ON *píll* 'willow', rod¹), *Quencroft* 1341, 1342 (*v.* cwene, croft), *pastur' voc' Rewles* 1461, *le Rules* 1538 *MinAcct*, *the olde Riveles grave wodde* 1557 (apparently ME *rivel* 'wrinkle', which is doubtless connected with rare ModE *rivel* 'rivulet' and ME *riveling*, cf. R. Rivelin), *le Ryne* 1292 (probably a ME *ryne* 'a run', possibly used as its derivative rynel is of 'a small stream'), *Rode-, Rotheland* 1292, 1487 (perhaps identical with *Rodeland* 135 *supra*, the form *Rothe-* being as in Rothwell *supra* from OE roð 'clearing'), *Roth-wellyngston'* 1487, *le Skynners* 1480 ('the Skinner's (place)', *v.* skinnari), *Smething* 1608 (*v.* smēðe 'smooth', eng), *Stanrode Enge* 1341, *Stanrodyng* 1341 Chapt, 1342 Ext (*v.* stān, rod¹, eng), *Stokyngrow* 1487 (*v.* stoccing, rāw), *Sumerwelle* 13 Kirkst (*v.* sumor, wella 'spring which flows in summer'), *aqua de Thymelbek* 1480 (probably an ON pers.n. *Þymill* or an OE *Þymel* (cf. Thimbleby YN 214), bekkr 'stream'), *Tommanker* 1341 Chapt, 1342 Ext ('Tom's man's marsh', *v.* kjarr), *le Trendle* 1292 (*v.* trendel 'something circular'), *Turneeng* 1323, *Turnenge* 1425, *-ynge* 1461, *-yngs* 1608 ('round meadows', *v.* trun, eng), *Turnholm* 1270 (*v.* prec., holmr 'water-meadow'), *Wnetherederode, Auenethrode* 1270, *Walleflat* 1292 (*v.* wall, flat), *Walleker-schagh* 1292 (*v.* walcere 'fuller', sceaga 'copse'; there was a *molend' fuller'* 'a fulling mill' here 1480), *Watyrhall* 1505 AD i (*v.* wæter, hall), *Westfor-langh* 1270 (*v.* west, furlang), *Wilkokrode* c. 1260 (the ME pers.n. *Wilcok*, rod¹), *Wranglandsike* 1292 (*v.* wrang 'twisted', land, sīc).

5. THORPE ON THE HILL (102–3126)

Torp 1086 DB, *Thorp(e)* 1328 Ch, 1592 WillY, (*-othe Hull*) 1309 Ch, (*-super leȝ Hill*) 1501 *Nost* 44d, (*-on the Hill*) 1542 WillY, (*-of t'Hill*) 1545 LS, (*-of the hill*) 1554 TestLds, (*-super Montem*) 1558 LS, (*-iuxta, under Rothewelhagh*) 1327 FF, 1448 Pat. *v.* þorp ' outlying farmstead'. For the affixes *v.* hyll, Rothwell Haigh 144 *supra*.

BOWLING HALL, *Bowlin(g) house* 1742, 1766 PRRth, probably named from the *Bowling* family, no doubt originating in Bowling iii, 244 *infra*, who were here from at least the sixteenth century (PRRth *freq*); they may have been there much longer since the local p.n. *Bollingthorp'* 1292 MinAcct 26 contains the same surname; the latter is probably an early alternative name for Thorpe on the Hill. CASTLE PIT. DOLPHIN BECK, 1840 *TA*, cf. also *Dolphin Lane* ib. KIDDOW SPRING, *Kidholt* 1501 *Nost* 44d, *v.* kide, holt 'wood'; the spring or 'plantation' was called *Thorpspring* 1501 ib, *v.* spring. THORPE HALL, *Thorp Hall* 1738 PRRth, *Thorp-House* 1797 ib. THORPE WOOD, 1840 *TA*. WHIN HILL, 1840 *TA*, *v.* hvin 'gorse', hyll.

FIELD-NAMES

The principal forms in (*a*) are 1840 *TA* 402.

(*a*) Black Field, Bottoms, Briar close, Browside, Butticars, Buttocks, Croft, Dunnil Field, Eight Acres, Five Acres, garth (*v.* garðr), Great Broom (*v.* brōm), Halfway House (ib 1783 PRRth), Hay Close, Low Carr, Marl Croft, Mile Garth, Near Carr, Near Intake (*v.* intak), Neplers, North Park, Pick Hill, Pinfold Croft, Pound, Pit Close & Hill, Plague Croft, Far & Low Plague (allusions to burial places during the Plague), Quarry Close, The Ring (cf. *Ryngbank* 1292 MinAcct 26, *v.* hring, banke), Roods, St James Park, Seven Lands, Shoulder of Mutton, Smithy Close, South Park, Stack's Garth, Sun Side, Thornhill(s), The Trees, Wood Ing, Wrigglesworth Close.

(*b*) *Hirstdike* (*at Thorpe*) 1397 MethMR, 1479 ib (*v.* hyrst, dīc), *Thorpe-yate* 1341 *Surv* 10, 5, *-yaite* 1342 Ext (*v.* geat 'gate'), *Threap Laine end* 1734 PRRth (*v.* þrēap 'dispute', lane, end).

viii. Wakefield

Wakefield is now a County Borough and includes the townships of Wakefield and Lupset from the old parish of Wakefield and the township of Sandal Magna (107 *supra*). The townships of Kirkhamgate, Outwood and Stanley now form Stanley Urban District. Alverthorpe with Thorns (in Wakefield township) was originally a separate township. Kirkhamgate, Lupset and Outwood townships were originally part of Stanley township.

1. HORBURY (102–3018)

Horberie, Orberie 1086 DB

Horebir', -biri, -y- 12 Fount (p), 1164–85, 1196–1202 YCh viii,
13 AD i, YD i, ib viii (p), 1233–40 YCh viii, 1238–54 AD i

Horbir', -byr' 1147 YCh viii, l. 12 *Lewes* 300d (p), 1206 FF, 1208
P (p), 1243 Fees (p), 1297 LS, *-beria* 1176 P (p), *-biri, -y, -byry*
12 Riev, 1189 Pont (p), 13 YD viii (p), a. 1218 YCh viii (p), 1251
Ass (p), 1269 FF (p), 1275 WCR *et passim* to 1577 Holinshed,
-bery 1301 DodsN, *-bero* 1379 PT

Orib'a 1164–96 YCh viii   *Hordbir'* 1204 Ass (p)

Horbury 1329 AD i, 1366 FF, 1416–1479 DodsN, 1510 Test v

Horubury 1316 Vill

'Fortification on the dirty land', *v.* horu, burh. The present town
stands on a hill, but the name may have described some fortification
nearer the river Calder; there is a Castle Hill on the lower ground
near an old ford which crosses the Calder. This is one of the few
YW examples of *burh* used in the dat.sg. *byrig*, as in Dewsbury 184,
Stanbury iii, 269 *infra*; it is a use more characteristic of the midlands
than the north (cf. EPN i, 58, Introd.).

CASTINGLEY (lost), *Caskinglay* 13 YD xii, 259, *High Castingley* 1653,
1676 Tayl, *Cassingley* 1572, 1650 *WCR, -close* 1775 (*Tythe Book*).
The first el. is obscure but it could be an adaptation of ME *kasteyne*,
ONFr *castaine* 'chestnut'. *v.* lēah.

HORBURY LIGHTS (lost), (*carbonum in*) *Horburylightes* 1461, 1462
MinAcct 60, 99, *-lyght* 1492 ib 02, *-Leights* 1696 PRHrb, *Horbery
lightes* 1635 *Comm, Great & Little Lights* 1849 *TA*, cf. also the *Lights
side* 1661 PRHrb, *Light Side Close(s)* 1775 (in a local *Tythe Book*),
1849 *TA*, and *Lights Colepits* 1718 PRHrb. The location of this place
and of *Ossett Lights* in the neighbouring township of Ossett (188
infra) is fixed by the *TA* map: Great Lights (grid 96–292190), Little
Lights (292192) and Light Side Close (295193) are just south of
Ossett Spa and on the bank south of the stream that forms the
boundary between the two townships. The Ossett fields are half a
mile north at Low Common; Common Lights (291203) and Lights
Bottom (293202) are on the west bank of the stream which is the
boundary between Ossett and Lupset. Phonologically these names
could be from OE *leoht* 'light' (cf. leoht adj.), but this does not easily
account for them, unless the allusions to *carbonum* and the *Colepits*

imply some kind of regular burning of coal for some purpose such as iron-smelting. Topographically, however, OE leaht 'water-channel' is preferable; in each case it would be used of the streams by which these fields stand. *v.* Addenda.

STENNARD WELL, *le Litle Steaner* 1600 *WCR* 4, *Vpper Stennard* 1709 WMB, 1799 (*Tythe Book*), *Stennard* (*Well*) 1849 *TA*; cf. *Littilstonyr* 172, *Stonour* 119, Stanniford f.n. 131, Steanard 187, 201, Steannard iii, 25, *Stainersike* ii, 163, *Stainer* 145, *Stener* iii, 57, 79, Stainer (Selby) pt. iv *infra*. These names are probably OE stæner 'stony, rocky ground', in some cases influenced by ON steinn 'stone' (plur. *steinar*); it no doubt survives as Scots dial. *stanners* (from 1508 NED) 'small stones and gravel on the margin of a river, or those in the bed of a river which are occasionally exposed and dry'.

ADDINGFORD HILL, 1849 *TA*, *Adinfforth* 1688 PRHrb, cf. also *Addington-Hill, -Pasture* 1841 O.S., 1849 *TA*, *v.* ford, tūn; the first el. is doubtful but could be from the OE pers.n. *Adding*. ASH-LEIGH. BENTON HILL, probably named from the family of *Benton* known here in the early nineteenth century (PRHrb 299, etc.). BERRY LANE. BULLING BALK LANE, *Bull Inge* 1709 WMB, *Bull Ing Balk* 1799 (*Tythe Book*), *v.* bula, eng 'meadow', balca 'boundary ridge'. CARR LODGE, 1817 M, *v.* kjarr 'marsh'. CASTLE HILL, 1849 *TA*, *Shanking Castle* 1709 WMB, cf. *Castlehouse* 1710 Tayl, *v.* castel, hyll, and for *Shanking* cf. *Shonkin* 1775 (*Tythe Book*). CLIFF Ho. CLUNTER GATE, cf. Clunters iii, 146 *infra*. THE CROFTS, *the Croft* 1653 Tayl, *Upper Croft* 1709 WMB, *yͤ Near & Far Croft* 1764 PRHrb, *v.* croft. CROSSFIELD HO. DOVE COTE HO, *Dove Coat Crofts* 1775 (*Tythe Book*), *Near & Upper Dove Cote* 1849 *TA*. DUDFLEET LANE & MILLS, *Dudfleete als. Dudfield* 1650 *WCR* 12, *Dud Fleet* 1849 *TA*, probably 'Dudda's reach', from the OE pers.n. *Dud(d)a*, flēot; it is on the R. Calder. DYEHOUSE MILLS, *Dyehouse Close* 1775 (*Tythe Book*), *Horbury Dye House* 1841 O.S. FAIRFIELD. GROVE HO. HALL CLIFFE, *le Hall Cliff Close* 1699 *WCR* 9, *Hall Cliff* 1701 PRHrb, 1709 WMB, cf. also *Halle-flat* 1308 WCR, named from *Horbury Hall* (*infra*), *v.* clif, flat. HALL CROFT, 1775 (*Tythe Book*), *v.* prec., croft. HIGHFIELDS. HILL CLIFFE HO, cf. *Hill Side* 1849 *TA*. HORBURY BRIDGE, 1616 PRThl, *Horbery breg* 1499 Test iv, *-brigge* 1635 Comm, *v.* brycg; this bridge carries the Wakefield–Huddersfield road over the Calder. HORBURY HALL (lost), 1709 WMB, *the Old Hall* 1666 PRHrb, *Ould Hall* 1697 ib, *v.* hall, cf. Hall Cliffe *supra*.   HUMBER PLACE.   JENKIN HO, 1841 O.S., *Jenkin (Bank)* 1849 *TA*.   LITTLE COMMON, *litle Common* 1653 Tayl, ME *commun* 'common land'.   LYDGATE VILLAS.   MILLFIELD 1668 BfdAnt i, 259, *(le) Milnefeild* 1650 *WCR* 1d, 1682 Tayl, *-field* 1699 *WCR* 8, 1709 WMB, named from *Horbury Mill* 1841 O.S. (*the mylne of Horburie* 1538 TestLds, *Horburie Mills* 1660 PRHrb), *v.* myln, feld.   NORTHFIELD HO, *le Northfeld* 1572 *WCR* 1, *v.* norð, feld.   NORTHGATE, *Northgate Head* 1709 WMB, *v.* norð, gata. QUARRY HILL RD, *le Quarrell* 1572 *WCR* 1, *Quarel Hill* 1709 WMB, *Quarry Hill* 1800 PRHrb, *v.* quarrelle 'quarry', hyll.   ROCK HO. SHEPSTYE WOOD, *Shipstye* 1572 *WCR* 1, 'sheep path', *v.* scēap, stīg. SOUTHFIELD LANE, *le Sow Feild* 1699 *WCR* 7, *Southfield, -feild* 1709 WMB, *v.* sūð, feld.   SPRING END, 1773 PRHrb, *v.* spring 'well-spring', ende; a spring, *Springe well* (*infra*), is nearby, from which Spring Field (Ossett) 190 *infra* is also named.   STONEBRIDGE HO, (*le*) *Stonebriggfeild* 1650 *WCR* 1d, 1709 WMB, *-field* 1699 ib 9, *ye Stonebridgefeild* 1668 BfdAnt 1, 259, *v.* stān, brycg; the bridge carries the Horbury–Wakefield road over a small stream on the east of the township.   STRINGER LANE, named from the *Stringer* family, known here from the seventeenth century (PRHrb *freq*).   SUN ROYD FM, *Swynrodhill* 1572 *WCR* 1, *le Vpper Sunroydhill* 1699 ib 9, probably 'swine clearing', *v.* swīn, rod[1], hyll.   TANFIELD HO.   TITHEBARN ST.   TWITCH HILL ST, *Twitchill* 1849 *TA*, dial. *twitchel* 'a narrow passage' (*v.* twicene).   WESTFIELD HO, (*le*) *Westfeild* 1551 *WCR* 1, 1682 Tayl, *the West Field* 1764 PRHrb, *v.* west, feld.

FIELD-NAMES

The principal forms in (*a*) are 1849 *TA*. Spellings dated 13, 14, 1307 are YD xii, 259–60, 1322 YD xvi, 93, 1323, 1461, 1492 *MinAcct* 45, 60, 99, 1405, 1452, 1456, 1485, 1525–1600, 1650, 1699 *WCR*, 1635 *Comm*, 1709 WMB, 1775, 1799 a local *Tythe Book* (*ex inf.* the late A. W. Brooke).

(*a*) Alm Royd, Audsley Flats (ib 1775), Armroyds 1775, Bank Furnace 1720 PRHrb, Far *&* Little Bensal (*Benshall* 1572, (*litle-*) 1709 WMB, *Bensill* 1709 ib, *Little Bensal* 1799, probably the pers.n. *Ben*, hall), Blunt Ing (ib 1775, *blunt ing* 1709, the surname *Bl(o)unt*, eng 'meadow'), Boat Ing 1709 (cf. Bottom Boat 159 *infra*), Bracken Hill Shut (*Bracken Hill* 1775, *v.* brakni, hyll), Bridge Close (ib 1775, *les Brigg closes* 1699, *v.* brycg, clos), Bridge Nook (*Little Brigg Nook Shutt* 1709, *Little Brig Nook* 1775, *v.* prec., nōk), Broad Cut (*v.* cut 'channel'), Broad Head Croft (ib 1775), Broad Leys (ib 1775, *v.* brād, lēah), Brook Mouth (ib 1775), Broom Close 1775, Burdett

Close, le Calf Croft 1726 Tayl (*v.* calf, croft), Cinderhill Close 1775 (*v.* sinder, hyll), Cold Royd (*le Colleroide* 1551, 1572, 'clearing where coal was got', *v.* col[1], rod[1]), Courses (ib 1775, *le Course* 1729 Tayl), Crimbles 1799 (*v.* crymel 'a small piece of land'), Crooked Royd (ib 1775), Crook Mire (ib 1799, *Crook Myre* 1635, *v.* krókr 'bend', mýrr), Crow Nest 1767 LdsM (*ye Crovnest* 1307, *v.* cráwe, nest, Crow Nest 186 *infra*), Dam Close 1775 (*v.* dammr), Denton Lane Close (ib 1775), Doyhams (ib 1775, *Doyam* 1650), Little & Old Ea 1799 (*v.* éa 'stream, river'), Earning Croft 1775, the Eastfeild 1709, East Royds 1709 (*v.* éast, feld, rod[1]), Ely Wife Nook 1775, Fisher Butts (ib 1799, *Fisherbutt* 1572, *v.* fiscere, perhaps as a surname, butte 'an abutting strip of land'), Flowery Holme, Gadge Well (*Gagewell, Gadgewell shutt* 1572, *Gadswell shutt* 1650, *Gadge Well Close* 1775, *v.* wella, dial. shut 'division of land', the first el. is doubtful), Gallows Close (ib 1775, *v.* galga), Gill Shutt, Goodall Ings 1775 (*ye Goodalling hedge* 1668 BfdAnt i, 259, cf. *Goodale crofte* 1572, from the local surname *Goodall*, eng, croft), Green Lane Shutt (*Greene Lane Close* 1670 Tayl, *le Greene lane* 1682 ib, *v.* grēne, lane), Harding (*le Hard Inge* 1572, *Hardings* 1650, 1775, *v.* heard, eng), Hawking Croft (ib 1709, 1764 *Glebe, Hawkin Croft* 1764 PRHrb, the surname *Hawkin*, croft), Heaton Field, Holme Shut (*v.* holmr, dial. shut 'division of land'), Hurtchin Royd (*Urchin Royd* 1775, ME urchon 'hedgehog', rod[1]), Knowles Close, Great & Round Langmires 1775 (*Longmere* 1323, *Lang(e)mar, -mer* 1525, *Langmyre* 1572, 'long pool', *v.* lang, mere), Langwell Nook, Lidy Load Close 1775, Longcroft 1709, Mary Banks, Mean Close (*v.* (ge)mǣne 'common'), Medley Inge 1709 (a surname from Methley 125 *supra*, eng), Michel Close 1709 (the surname *Mitchell*), Middlefield 1709, Middups 1799 (*Middoppe* 1635, *le Over Middups* 1699, 'middle valley', *v.* midd, hop), Middupford Close 1799 (*Middupfo(o)re* 1674 PRHrb, *le Middupford shutt* 1699, *v.* prec., ford), Mossy Acre, Near Croft, Near Intake (*v.* intak), Nine Penny, North Ing 1775 (*v.* norð, eng), North Park, North Town Carr (ib 1775, *v.* kjarr 'marsh'), Offloes (*Little Offerley* 1650), Orchard Croft 1775, Parish Flatts 1775 (*Parris flatt* 1572, *v.* paroche, flat), Parson Croft, Pickings (ib 1775), Pighills 1775 (*v.* pightel 'enclosure'), Pinder Field (cf. *Pinder Leys* 1799, ME pindere 'a pinder'), Pond Croft(e) 1775 (ib 1653 Tayl, *v.* ponde, croft), Prick Acre, Prick Arse 1775 (*Prickharse* 1572, *v.* pricca, ears), Priestwell Close (ib 1775, *Preistwell Shutt* 1709, *v.* prēost, wella), Renald Ing 1705 (*Raynoldynge* 1485, OG *Rainald*, eng), Robin Royd(s) (ib 1775, *ye Robin royd close* 1668 BfdAnt i, 259, the pers.n. *Robin*, rod[1]), Rough Ing 1775, Sallad Royd (*Sallott Royd* 1775, 'willow clearing', *v.* saliht, rod[1]), Sand Mary Banks 1775 (*St Marye bancke* 1572, *v.* banke), Savile Town Carr 1775 (cf. *Savile balke* 1572, in the lands of *George Savile*), Smithingley Leys (*Great & Little Smithingley* 1775, *v.* smiððe, lēah, but cf. *Snellynglaydike* f.n. *infra*), South Park, Spoil Bank, Stors Hill 1809 EnclA (*v.* storð), Strawbenzie, Summer Town Carr (ib 1775, *Sun(n)e Town(e) Car(r)* 1618, 1714 Tayl), Tallard Royd 1709, Tenters, Thornes Close 1775, Through Royd 1775, Thurwood (Wells) (*Thorodwells* 1699, possibly the ON pers.n. *Þóroddr*, wella), Tom Royd 1775, Walker Croft, West Lawgrave 1710 Tayl (ib 1659 ib, *v.* west, hlāw 'hill, mound', grǣfe 'copse'), Wheel Pit Close (ib 1730 Tayl), Willow Garth.

(b) *Belhous headeland* 1572 (v. bell-hūs 'belfry', hēafod-land), *le fore-shutt voc' Berfitcrofte* 1600, *Blend pitt* 1572, *ye Clarkwell grave* 1668 BfdAnt i, 259, *Caramland tre* 1572, *le Cramblingtree* 1650 (e.ModE *crambling* 'having many twists' (esp. of trees), v. NED s.v. *cramble*, trēow), *Cawseyleyse* 1572 (v. caucie 'causeway', lēah), *Conypitt* 1572 (v. coni 'rabbit', pytt), *le Crab-treeshutt* 1650 (v. crabbe, or the surname *Crabtree*, dial. *shut* 'a division of land'), *the crokyd thorne* e. 15 Towneley xiii, 504, *le New Crosseshoute* 1572 (v. cros, dial. *shut*), *Elinrod* 14 (v. ellen 'elder-tree', rod[1]), *Ellingtregrave* 1572 ('elder-tree grove', v. ellen, trēow, grāf), *Fairbancke Close & pingle* 1650 (*Fairbank* as a surname, v. pingel 'enclosure'), *Frierdore shoutt* 1572, *Great Riding* 1650 (v. rydding 'clearing'), *Halhe* 1307 (v. halh 'nook of land'), *le Holleforth* 1405, *le howe fores* 1572 (v. hol[1], ford), *Horbery Feild* 1635, *Horbery shrogys* e. 15 Towneley xiii, 455, *Hugmer'* 1303 Calv (v. mere 'pool'), *Inghagge* 1456 (v. eng, hǫgg), *Keysars Close* 1650, *Hye-, Lowkirstye* 1572 (v. stīg 'path'), *Leyswell Shutt* 1682 Tayl, *Lightstye* 1572 (v. Horbury *Lights supra*, stīg), *Longheshe* 1572 (v. lang, æsc 'ash-tree'), *Longrode* 1307 (v. lang, rod[1]), *the Meare* 1635 (v. mere 'pool'), *ye Millgate* 1668 BfdAnt i, 259, *le Mylnegote, le Milneholme* 13, 1322 (v. Millfield *supra*, gata, gota 'channel', holmr 'water-meadow'), *Mille-, Myllewell* 1461, 1462 (v. prec., wella), *Molebrist* 1327 WCR ('landslip', v. molde 'earth', (ge)byrst), *the Netherpasture* 1650, *Northbrok* 1323, *le Oldewaterstide* 13 (v. wæter, styde), *le Rish Fores* 1572 (v. risc, furh 'furrow'), (*le*) *Sandholm* 13, 1322, *Santhalm* (sic) c. 1210 YCh viii (v. sand, holmr), *Snellynglaydike* 1452, *Swillingley mouth* 1572 (possibly swelgend 'whirl-pool', or OE *swiling* 'swilling' (cf. Swillington iii, 168 *infra*), lēah), *Spynkwell* 1405 (ME *spynke* 'finch', wella), *Springe well* 1572 (v. spring, wella, Spring End *supra*), *Stonyfurlonge* 1572 (v. stānig, furlang), *le Swamp* 1699 (cf. sumpe 'swamp'), *le Welclosys* 1307 (v. wella, clos), *Westlane greave* 1618 Tayl, *White dike* 1572 (v. hwīt, dīc), *Whittakers* 1650 (v. hwīt, æcer), *le Willynges* 1551 (probably the pers.n. *Will*, eng 'meadow').

2. KIRKHAMGATE (102–2922)

Kirkhamgate 1709 WMB, 1817 M. The church (v. kirkja) may well be Woodkirk, as the hamlet is on the road from Wakefield to Wood-kirk, v. gata 'road'. The second el. is doubtful.

BATTY'S FOLD, *Battye farme* 1709 WMB, *Batty Fold* 1817 M, named from *Samuel Batty* who had closes here 1709 WMB 85; the same surname is found in Battye Ford 198 *infra*; v. fald.   BECK BOTTOM, 1841 O.S., v. bekkr, botm.   BRANDY CARR, *Brandicarr* 1709 WMB, v. kjarr 'marsh, brushwood' or possibly æcer; the first el. may be connected with the dial. word *brandy* 'smutty, blighted', etc. (EDD s.v.).   BUSHY BECK.   FOSTER FORD BECK.   THE HAUGH, *the Halkes* 1316 WCR, v. halh 'nook of land'.   LINDALE HILL, *Lindle Hill* 1841 O.S.   LOW HOD.   LOW PARK FM.   NOOK ING.

SILCOATES, 1822 Langd, *Silcotes* 1561 TestLds, *Sil-*, *Silkcoats* 1709 WMB, *v.* cot 'cottage, shed'; the first el. is doubtful.   TYPE WELL. WARREN HO, 1841 O.S., *v.* **wareine**.

FIELD-NAMES

(*a*) Bull Pit 1841 O.S., Bunny Hill (oth Back oth Laith) 1709 WMB (cf. *Bunny Springe, bosc*' 1600 *WCR* 6d, *Bunny Hall* 1607 *Surv*, *v.* hlaða, spring, the first el. is doubtless a surname, cf. Bunny Close 156 *infra*), *Longgrave head* 1709 WMB, *Woodside* 1841 O.S.

3. LUPSET (102–3119)

> *Lupesheved, -heued* 1275, WCR (p), 1297 LS (p), 1297 WCR,
>   *Lupishede* 1379 PT
> *Luppesheved* 1307, 1323 WCR   *Loppeshed* 1379 PT (p)
> *Lopishevedfeld* 1316 WCR, *-hed* 1505 WillY
> *Lupsetheued* 1321 DodsN, *Lupshead* 1362, 1363 ib, *Lupsed* 1415 ib
> *Lupset*(*t*) 1467 DodsN, 1497 Ipm, 1528 YD vi *et passim* to 1638
>   PRHrb, *-sitt* 1709 WMB, *Luppsett* 1650 Arm

The strong form *Hlupp* of an OE pers.n. *Hluppa* proposed for Lupridge D 303 would be possible in Lupset, but the origin of this pers.n. is uncertain, as there are no parallels, unless it be connected with the root of OE *hlīepan* (pa.t. *hlupon*) 'to leap'. But Lupset may well contain the ME byname *Lupe* (from OFr *loup* 'wolf'). *v.* hēafod 'headland', which here refers to a rounded eminence called The Mount overlooking the Calder valley.

SNAPETHORPE

> *Sneip*(*e*)*torp* 1156, 1173 YCh 186, 197
> *Snaipe-*, *Snaypethorp*(*e*) 1155–70 YCh 1502, 1297 *et freq* to 1324
>   WCR, 1572 *WCR* 2
> *Snaip-*, *Snaypthorp* 1315, 1323, 1329 WCR, 1362 DodsN, 1374,
>   1376 FF, 1391 YD vi, 1392 *MinAcct* 88 *et freq* to 1512 *Nost* 72d
> *Snapethorp*(*e*) 1434 Pat, 1578 Test iii, 1492 *MinAcct* 02 *et freq* to
>   1709 WMB, *Snapthorp* 1550 Test vi

'Sneypi's outlying farmstead', *v.* þorp, doubtless one belonging to Wakefield. The first el. is the ON byname *Sneypir* (LindBN), which denotes 'one who pinches' (from ON *sneypa* 'to disgrace'). On the later spellings *Snape-* cf. Phonol. § 11.

DOG HO, 1727 PRHrb.   GILL SIKE.   GORING HO.   LUPSET HALL,
1817 M, *Lubsit Hall* 1770 PRRth, *v.* hall.   THE MOUNT, *Mount
Sorrel* 1841 O.S.   SNAPETHORPE HALL, *the old haule* 1538 TestLds,
Oldhall 1650 *WCR* 1d, 1841 O.S.   THORNES COMMON, formerly
Thorner moer (sic) 1544 TestLds 163, *Thornes more*, a common 1607
Surv, *-Moor* 1709 WMB, *v.* Thornes 168 *infra*, mōr.   THORNES
PARK, 1841 O.S., *v.* prec., **park**.   WHINNEY MOOR, *Whi-*, *Whynny
more* 1607 *Surv*, 1709 WMB, *-Rodes* 1608 *Surv*, *v.* hvin 'gorse',
mōr, rod[1].

FIELD-NAMES

The principal forms in (*a*) are 1799 Tayl 242. Spellings dated 1325–1329
are *WCR*, 1392, 1492 *MinAcct* 88, 02, 1406, 1572 *WCR*, 1709 WMB.

(*a*) the Batts, the Boat Ing (cf. Bottom Boat 159 *infra*), Bob Close, Brook
Mouths, Bunny Close 1709 (*Bunny Cloase* 1608 *Surv*, cf. Bunny Hill 155
supra), East Royds, the Hall Green, Jack Inge 1709, the Laith Ing (*v.* hlaða,
eng), Great Langwells, the Ring Hedge, Stables Close 1709, Stocks Close,
Swaiths (*v.* swæð 'strip of grassland'), Thorns Mire (*the thornes myres* 1556
WfdBurg, 1608 *Surv*, *v.* Thornes 168 *infra*, mýrr), Thorntree close, Towler
Royds or Tallord Royds (*Tollard Roid* 1631 *Bretton*, *v.* rod[1]).

(*b*) *Alan grayve* 1572 (the pers.n. *Alan*, græfe 'copse'), *Alderrydynge* 1392
(*v.* alor, rydding 'clearing'), *Dykbankes* 1325 (*v.* dīc, banke), *Euerode* 1331
(the fem pers.n. *Eve*, rod[1]), *le Haghefeld* 1392, *le Haughfeld*' 1492 (*v.* haga
'enclosure', feld), *the Longe Carre* 1550 Test vi (*v.* lang, kjarr 'marsh'), *le
Lupsed Well* 1406 (*v.* wella), *Nicoll cloases* 1608 *Surv* (the surname *Nichol*,
clos), *Norman boithes* 1572, *Normanboith* Chas 1 *Rent* (the pers.n. or surname
Norman, bōth 'booth'), *le Westfeld* 1406 (*v.* west, feld), *Wheterode* 1329 (*v.*
hwæte, rod[1]).

4. OUTWOOD (102–3224)

bosco forinseco 1305 WCR iii, 184, (*les*) *Outewode* (*boscum*) 1436,
1438 Test ii, 1492 *MinAcct* 02, *Owtewoode* 1543 WillY, *the Outwood*
1587 FF, 1771 M, (*-side*) 1644 PRHrb, (*Wakefeild-*) 1656 Pick, *the
Oute Woode of Wakefelde* 1592 WillY, *le Owtwoodside* 1600 *WCR* 5,
Wakefield Owtwood 1607 *Surv*. 'The outlying wood', *v.* ūt, **wudu**.
This was the great demesne wood of Wakefield manor lying north of
the town, mentioned in DB.

NEWTON, *Neweton* 1190–1192 P, *Niweton* 1193 P, *Neuton* 1275 WCR
(p), 1297–1313 WCR (*freq*), *Newtone on le Cliff* 1327 ib, *Newton nere
Wakefelde* 1534 Test vi. 'New farmstead', *v.* nīwe, tūn; for the affix
v. Newton Hill *infra* and clif.

OUCHTHORPE ['autʃþəp]

Uchethorp(e) 1274, 1298, 1307 WCR
Ouchethorp(e) 1284–1323 WCR (*freq*), 1392 *MinAcct* 88, 1471 Pat,
   -*thrope* 1558 TestLds, *Owchethorp* 1404 WillY, 1547 FF
Ochethorp(e) 1492 *MinAcct* 02, 1544 WillY
Outchthorpe 1600, 1606 FF
Ouchthorpe 1597 SessnR, 1612 NCWills, 1623 FF

The first el. has been connected with the ME pers.n. *Uche* quoted
by Goodall 222 from Ch. This pers.n. is probably a short form of ON
Úlfketill, ME *Ulkel*, etc. and would not produce first el. of Ouchthorpe. The most probable explanation of Ouchthorpe is that the
first el. is OFr (*h*)*ouche* 'garden' (from MedLat *olca* 'arable land'),
which is common in Fr p.ns. (cf. Vincent § 815, Gröhler 129 ff).
The second el. is þorp 'outlying farmstead'; it is one of the many
thorpes in this district, some of which are distinguished by OFr
themes as in Chapelthorpe 102 or Painthorpe 104 *supra*.

WRENTHORPE

Wirintorp 1221 YCh viii (p), *Wyrinthorp* 1324 Arm (p), 1368 BM,
   Wyrenthorp 1342 DodsN
Wyfrunthorp 1260 Font, *Wyverin-* 1276 RH, *Wyverun-* 1284 AD
   iii, *Wyverom-* 1309 WCR, *Wyuerum-* 1323 ib
Wyrunthorp(e) 1285–1327 WCR (*freq*), *Wyrum-* 1286 ib (p)
Wyrnthorp(e) 1309 YD i (p), 1325 WCR, 1350 BM, 1351 DodsN,
   1362 BM, *Wi-*, *Wyrnethorp(e)* 1353, 1363 FF, 1406 Pat, 1425
   DodsN
Wern(e)thorpe 1309 YDi, 1359 BM
Wrenthorp(e) 1407 Pat, 1458 DodsN, 1499 *WCR*, 1518 FF *et
   passim* to 1709 WMB

'Wifrun's outlying farmstead', *v.* þorp. An OE fem. pers.n. *Wífrún*
is not recorded, but Searle cites an early ME *Wiverona uxor Eueracri
de Gipeswic* 1130 P. The rare theme *Wíf-* is known from such OHG
names as *Wifhildis*, and -*rún* is common in OE fem. pers.ns. like
Ælfrún, *Leofrún* or ON *Gúðrún*. The later contraction to *Wirne-*,
Werne- and metathesis to *Wren-* is to be noted (cf. Warrengate 165
infra).

WOODHALL (lost), (*la*) *Wodehall(e)* 1297, 1307, 1323 WCR, 1316 Pat,
Wodhall 1327 WCR, 1392 *MinAcct* 88, (-*yhate*) 1407 *WCR*, *Woodhall*

prope Wrenthorp 1617 Tayl, *-in Newton* 1653 ib. *v.* **wudu** (here Out-wood), **hall**; the references make it clear that the hall was in Outwood.

BLACKER LODGE.   BOARDMAN HILL.   BOLUS LANE.   BOOTH HILL. BRAG LANE END, 1841 O.S.   BROOM HALL, 1709 WMB, 1727 LdsM, named from the *Broome* family (cf. 1559 TestLds 324 and note); formerly *Wrenthorpe Hall* 1559 TestLds 325.   CARR GATE, 1808 Tayl, *Carryate* 1709 WMB, 1778 PRRth, *v.* **kjarr** 'marsh', **geat** 'gate' (to the wood of Outwood).   CHURCH HILL.   CROSSLAND PLACE.   CUT BECK, cf. *Cutt Close* 1847 *TA*, *v.* **cut** 'water-channel'. FOLLY HALL, *v.* **folie.**   FOX HALL, *Foxhole* 1587 WillY, *v.* **fox-hol.** LAWNS, LAWNS HO, *le Launde Yate* 1600 WCR 8d, *the Lawns* 1808 Tayl, *v.* **launde** 'forest-glade'.   LEDGER FOLD.   LINGWELL GATE, 1763 LdsM, 1817 M, *Lingwell yate* 1651 PRRth, 1709 WMB, *v.* Lingwell Syke 140 *supra*, **geat** 'gate' (to the wood of Outwood). LOFTHOUSE GATE, 1771 M, *Lofthouse Yate* 1709 WMB, *v.* Lofthouse 136 *supra*, **geat** (cf. prec.).   LOW FOLD.   THE MOUNT.   NEWTON HILL, formerly *Newtonclif* 1406 WCR 1, *the Cliff* 1558 Tayl, *v.* Newton *supra*, **clif.**   NEWTON LANE END, *Newton Lain End* 1709 WMB, *v.* prec., **lane**, **ende.**   OUCHTHORPE LANE, 1771 Arm, *Owchethorpelane* 1406 WCR i, *Ouchthorpe Laine* 1709 WMB, *v.* Ouchthorpe *supra*, **lane.**   POTOVENS, 1709 WMB, 1749 PRHrb, *Pottoums* 1657 Pick; this refers to a factory for earthenware and 'a poor cottage & an oven house' were rented in 1709 WMB 179, 184. RED HALL LANE, *Red Hall* 'a convenient brick house built by John Greenwood' 1715 Tayl 290; it was formerly Wrenthorpe Hall. ROBIN HOOD HILL, *Robinhoodstreteclose* 1650 WCR 3d, *Robbin Hood hill* 1657 Pick, on Robin Hood in YW p.ns. cf. Robin Hood's Bower i, 226 *supra*.   ROOK'S NEST, *Rook Nest* 1841 O.S., *v.* **hrōc**, **nest**, cf. Crow Nest 186 *infra*.   SNOW HILL, 1645 WillY, 1659 Pick, 1709 WMB, *v.* **snāw**, **hyll.**   SPRINGFIELD HO, *Spring Field* 1817 M. SPRING HILL, *Springwell Hill* 1808 Tayl, *v.* **spring** 'well-spring', **wella**, **hyll.**   TROUGH WELL, cf. *Trowgh Steele* 1607 *Surv*, *v.* **trōg** 'a trough', **wella**, **stigel** 'stile'.   WHITE HALL FM, *White Hall* 1841 O.S.   WILSON HILL.

FIELD-NAMES

Some modern f.ns. in Stanley belong to this township but cannot be separated. The principal forms in (*a*) are 1709 WMB. Spellings dated 1607 are *Surv* 10, 3, 1703–1770 Tayl 333, 328; others without source are *WCR.*

(*a*) Bane String Ing 1740, Bothome Inge (*v.* botm, eng), Brackin Closes, Breck Close (*v.* brekka), Broad Close (ib 1849 *TA*), burnt Close, But Lane 1733 (*Butlayne* 1617 Tayl, *v.* butte, lane), Calf croft 1770, Cockshutt (*Cok(e)shote*, *-shott* 1462, 1492, *v.* cocc-scīete), Coldholme (*v.* cald, holmr), Dennis Yard 1703, Great Inge (*v.* eng), Green Hill 1841 O.S., Gun Croft, Hartley Croft 1816 Tayl 296 (ib *1660* ib, formerly *Campyons* Eliz ib), Holdstring Close 1740, the Homestead 1770, the House close 1770, Howroid Feild (*v.* hol[1], rod[1]), Ingroade close, Little Inge Royd (*v.* eng, rod[1]), Long Tongue 1847 *TA* (*le Longtongue* 1650, *v.* lang, tunge 'tongue of land'), the Middlefeild, Midleflatts, Netherfield, New Intack (*v.* intak), Newton Rhodes 1740 (*v.* rod[1]), North Fields, the Parson Flats 1770 (*Parson(s) flat(e)*, *-flatt* 1461 *MinAcct* 60, 1499, *Persons-flat* 1462 *MinAcct* 99, *v.* persone, flat), the Pit Close 1770, Ruddings (*v.* rydding 'clearing'), Sladley Laine, Sweetercliff, Waterside, (Ouchthorp) Westfeild (*the West field* 1623 Tayl), Woodside (*the Wood syde* 1558 TestLds, *le Woodside* 1610 *Surv*, *Wakefeild woodside* 1658 Pick, *v.* Outwood *supra*).

(*b*) *Cleek lane* 1607, *Cleke lane* 1610 *Surv*, *le Corner Camp'* 1406 (*v.* camp 'field'), *Coteyerd* 1489, 1499 (*v.* cot, geard), *Dodge croft* 1607 (the pers.n. *Dodge*, croft), *Edishclose* 1650 (*v.* edisc 'enclosure'), *Goody(e) Green in Wood(d)all* 1617, 1653 Tayl, *-in Stanley* 1707 ib (cf. *Goody Bower* 167 *infra*, grēne[2]), *Moorecrofte* 1617 Tayl (*v.* mōr, croft), *Newton bridge* 1679 PontCD 650, *Neutonengs*, *-feld* 1380 AD iv (*v.* Newton *supra*, brycg, eng, feld), *Pollardhouses* 1392 ib 88 (the ME surname *Pollard*, hūs), *Sagar Close* 1607 (the land of *William Sagar* ib 10, 3), *Sandall crofte* 1544 TestLds, *Windy Well* 1558 Tayl.

5. STANLEY (102–3423)

> *Stanlei(e)* 1086 DB, 1202 FF, *-le* 1274 WCR, *-ley(e)*, *-lay* 1274–1321 ib (*freq*), 1284 AD i, 1295 *Bodl* 305, 1297 LS, 1336 FF *et passim* to 1822 Langd, (*Upper-*) 1606 FF
> *Stanneley* 1313 WCR, 1332 YD x
> *Taneley* 1316 Vill
> *Staneley* 1438 DodsN, 1469 Pat
> *Stand(e)ley*, *-lay* 1537 FF, 1545 TestLds, 1557 WillY

'Stony clearing', *v.* stān, lēah, cf. Stainley pt. v *infra*. The 1316 spelling *Taneley* is due to AN loss of initial *s-* (cf. IPN 103). The later spellings in *Stand-* are paralleled by several YW p.ns. in *Hand-* (from *Han-*), cf. Phonol. § 46.

BOTTOM BOAT, *Stanleiebothum* 1202 FF, *Stanliebothom* 1203 DodsN, *Bothem* 1286 WCR, (*le*) *Bothom* 1298, 1327 WCR, 1365 DodsN, *Bottome house* 1558 TestLds, *Bothom House* 1640 WillY, *The Bottomes* 1649 ib, *Bottoms* 1709 WMB, *Bottom Boat* 1709 ib, 1812

PRRth, *Bottom house als. Bottomford* 1712 *WYEnr* 67, *Bottom Boat Fery* 1817 M, *v.* botm (booᴍ) 'valley bottom'. *Boat* refers to the ferry across the R. Calder, and the word is used similarly of Allerton Ferry 128 *supra*; cf. also Boat Ing f.n. 152, 156 *supra*.

DEFFORD (lost), *Desford* (sic for *Def-*) 1338 DodsN, *Defford* 1392 *MinAcct* 88, *Depford* 1462, 1492 ib, 1500 Pat, *Disforth, -ford* 1709 WMB, *Deffers* 1764 *Glebe*. 'Deep ford', *v.* dēop, ford, cf. Defford Wo 194 for a similar development of form. The ford across the Calder was opposite Kirkthorpe in Warmfield; it was still marked as an ancient ford in 1841 O.S. (grid 102–358213).

HATFIELD HALL, *le Heth(e)felde* 1406, 1499 *WCR, Heathfeild* 1600 ib 8d, *the Heathfield* 1709 WMB, *Hatfield Hall* 1766 PRLds, 1771 M. 'Open field near the heath', *v.* hǣð, feld. The form has been influenced by that of Hatfield i, 7 *supra* or the surname formed from it, which occurs locally as in *clausum . . . ad opus et usum Joh'is Hatfeild* 1705 Tayl 157.

KIRK FIELD PLACE, *le (the) Kirkefe(i)ld(e)* 1324 WCR, 1332 YD x, 1499 *WCR* 1, 1545 TestLds, 1709 WMB, *le (the) Church(e)feild(e)* 1600 *WCR* 8d, 1709 WMB. *v.* kirkja, feld.

NORTHEY (lost), *le Northe(e)* 1391 Tayl, 1392 *MinAcct* 88, *Northey* 1545 TestLds, 1709 WMB, *(-cryme, -Lane)* 1600 *WCR* 8d, *North hey Laine* 1709 WMB. 'North island', *v.* norð, ēg ; the *ēg* may have been an island in the R. Calder (there is one near Lake Lock) or the land in one of the loops of the river.

WELBECK, *Willewebyth* 1274 WCR, *Wilbright* (sic) 1325 ib, *Wilbight* 1326 ib, 1392 *MinAcct* 88, 1461 ib 60, 1462 ib 99, *Welbright* (sic) 1363 DodsN, *Wilbycht* 1392 *MinAcct*, *le Willebygh* 1405 *WCR* 1d, *Wilbygh* 1492 *MinAcct*, *Wilbeck* 1751 LdsM, 1817 M. 'Willow bight', *v.* wilig, byht. The name refers to a loop in the course of the R. Calder.

BALK LANE, 1841 O.S., *v.* balca 'boundary ridge'.   CLARK HALL, 1841 O.S.   COCKPIT HOUSES, *Coalpit Houses* 1841 O.S.   FINKING LANE.   GLEBE FM.   THE HOLLIES.   LAKE LOCK, 1778 PRRth, 1808 Tayl.   LONG CAUSEWAY.   MOOR HO, 1841 O.S.   NEW MARKET GATE, 1817 M, *v.* Newmarket 146 *supra*, gata or geat.   NEW PARK, 'the new park' 1327 WCR 131, *New Park(e)* 1338 DodsN,

1817 M, *v.* nīwe, park.   OLD PARK, 1817 M, 'the old park' 1307
WCR 117, 1327 ib 113, *veteris Parci domini* 1499 *WCR* 1d, (*the*) *Olde
Parke* 1524 Test v, 1558 TestLds, 1597 SessnR, *v.* prec.   PARK
LODGE, *the Lodge* 1709 WMB, *v.* prec., loge.   PARK SIDE, cf. *Parke
pale* 1682 Tayl, *v.* prec.   ROOK'S NEST HO.   ST SWITHIN'S
CHANTRY & WELL, *the Close at Sainct Swythins* 1600 *WCR* 2, *Old &
Little St Swithens* 1709 WMB, *St. Swithins Well* 1817 M, from the
dedication to St Swithin, the ninth-century bishop of Winchester.
SMALLEY BIGHT, *Smalley* 1323 *MinAcct* 45, 1608 ib, 1841 O.S.,
'narrow clearing', *v.* smæl, lēah; *Bight* is OE byht 'bend in a river'
(here the Calder, as in Welbeck *supra*).   SPA FOLD.   STANLEY
FERRY, 1771 M, *v.* ferja (across the R. Calder).   STANLEY HALL,
1841 O.S., *Midgley als. Stanley Hall* 1771 M.   STANLEY LANE
ENDS, 1841 O.S.   STORY HO.   WEST FM, *Westhouse Yate* 1709
WMB, *West Hall* 1771 M, *v.* west, hūs, geat.

FIELD-NAMES

It is not possible to decide whether some of the f.ns. which follow belong
to Stanley or neighbouring townships; some in (*a*) certainly belong to Outwood (158 *supra*) but cannot be separated; cf. also Wakefield f.ns. 170 *infra*.
The principal forms in (*a*) are 1847 *TA* 374. Spellings dated 1292 are
MinAcct 26, 1297–1314 WCR, 1323 *MinAcct* 45, 1324–1331 WCR, 1392–
1492 *MinAcct* 60, 99, 02, 1554, 1558 TestLds, 1607, 1608 *Surv* 10, 3, 12, 4,
1612 *MinAcct* 21, 1709 WMB, 1793 *EnclA* 11; others dated without source
are *WCR*.

(*a*) Armitage Close, Ball Acre, Barley Close & Garth, Belhouse 1709 (cf.
Belhous 154 *supra*, the two may be identical), Bottom Acre (cf. Bottom Boat
supra, æcer), Boxhall 1709 (ib 1551, *v.* box 'box-tree', hall), Bradford Hall
1771 M (possibly the same as *Broadford* 166 *infra*, *v.* brād, ford), Bradley
Close, Brandy House Close (cf. Brandy Carr 154 *supra*), a Shutt called
Broadarse 1709 (*v.* brād, ears, dial. *shut* 'a division of land'), Broad Lane
Gaps, Broom Close, Calf Croft, Carr Pasture (*le Ker* 1407, *v.* kjarr 'marsh'),
Coal Staith, Codlings (cf. *Codlingcroft, -yng-* 1331, 1490, 1551, ME *codling*
'codling' as a nickname (Bardsley 497), croft), Colly hall Closes 1709 (*Coly-
hall* 1324, perhaps an early instance of e.ModE *colly* (OE **colig*) 'begrimed
with coal', but cf. *Colingholme* 171 *infra*, hall), Crabtree Close, Dean Croft,
Dent Croft, Dewsbury Hill (probably connected with *Doyseroide* 1489,
Dewsy-, Dewceroyd(s) 1709, which no doubt stands for ME *dey-house* 'dairy
house', *v.* dey, influenced by Dewsbury 184 *infra*), Dilly Close (*dilly*
'daffodil'), Doles 1709 (*v.* dāl 'share of the common land'), Evers Close,
Flagg Close 1709 (*v.* flagge 'reed'), the Flat 1709 (*le Flattes* 1331, *v.* flat),
Goslin Croft, the great Intack 1709 (*v.* intak), Gregson, Hackin Hills 1709,
Hanging Close (*v.* hangende 'steep'), Harrod Field (ib 1793, *Harwood field*

1709, *v.* hara, wudu, but cf. *Haweroidefelde* f.n. *infra*, with which it may be identical), Hartley Close, Hell Hole Close, Humbers & Little Humbers, Laith Close (*v.* hlaða 'barn'), Laverack Hall 1709 (cf. *Lerykroide* 1525, *Laueroke royde end* 1545, *v.* lāwerce 'lark', rod[1]), Lawfield 1709, Long Close (*longe cl003e* 1545), Longfield 1709, Low Field 1793, Marr Close, Martin Close, Medley Close (ib 1600, probably a surname from Methley 125 *supra*), Mellard, Mitchell Croft, Newell Close, New Ing, Nockett house & Lands 1709, Nooking, Old Royd, Oxe Close 1709 (*le Ox(e)close* 1607, 1650), the Paddock 1709, Paradice Close 1709, Pard Croft, Great & Little Penhill, Pinfold Croft, Pit Hill, Pog Close (cf. Pog Moor i, 304 *supra*), Pond Close, Quarry Close (*le Wharrel close* 1489, *v.* quarrelle 'quarry'), Queen Gates, Raven Royd, Royston Bank (possibly identical with *Rustanes* 1392, *le Rustans* 1406, *(the) Rustance* 1600, 1650, *Rustansforde* 1499, probably 'rough stones', *v.* rūh, stān, with the modern form influenced by Royston i, 284 *supra*), Shoulder of Mutton, Sour Ing, South Cliff, Spinke Farme 1709 (probably the surname *Spink* as in *Spinkrode* 173 *infra*), Stanley Green 1735 LdsM (*v.* grēne[2]), Stripe of Land (*v.* strip), Three Cornered Close (*Three nooked Close* 1709), Tom Croft 1709 (ib 1486, 1650, *Thomcroft* 1492, cf. *Tomroid* 1407, the pers.n. *Tom*, croft, rod[1]), Twitter Cliff 1709, Vaux Close, Watery Lane Close, Well Close, Willow Closes 1709, Windhills.

(b) *Aliceclose* 1489, *Ashmar Roydes* 1600 (*v.* rod[1]), *Blynd Well* 1600 ('hidden well', *v.* blind, wella), *Breckwyn(close)* 1600, *Butlerkerre* 1454 (the surname *Butler*, kjarr 'marsh'), *Cadeyerde* 1489 (*v.* geard), *le Cloggeclose* 1650, *le Cloos* 1392, *Colmanhustedherne* 1410 (the ME pers.n. *Colman*, hūs, stede, hyrne 'nook'), *Colwell Inge* 1600 (*v.* wella, eng), *le Croked Oldestyle* 1492 (*v.* stigel 'stile'), *Crolleweloyne* 1408 ('curlew lane', from ME *corlewe*, lane), *Fivianbrigge* 1314 Bodl 306 (the pers.n. *Vivian*, brycg), *Flaggerdroide* 1489 (*v.* rod[1]), *le Frerecroft* 1332 (*v.* frere 'friar', croft), *Galyroide* 1499 (*v.* the ME surn. *Galye*, rod[1]), *Gelyerde* 1525 (*v.* geard), *Gybun-, Gibboncroft(e)* 1409, 1600 (the surname *Gibbon*, croft), *les Gogges* 1392 (*v.* cogge), *Goldiflat* 1295 Bodl 305, *Goodall Close* 1600 (the local surname *Goodall*, cf. Goodall Ings 153 *supra*), *le Gote* 1392 (*v.* gota 'water-channel'), *Haldykebutts* 1600 (*v.* hall, dīc, butte), *Hary Carr* 1545, *Herryecarclose als. Henry Crofte* 1600, *Henrycrofte* 1409, *Herrycroft* 1499 ('Henry's marsh and croft', *v.* kjarr, croft), *Haw(e)roidefeld(e)* 1499, 1525, *Hawroyd(e)fe(i)lde* 1545, 1650 (*v.* haga 'enclosure', rod[1], feld), *le Heys* 1331 (*v.* (ge)hæg 'enclosure'), *Heley in Stanley* 1497 Ipm (*v.* hēah, lēah), *Northelay* 1525 (*v.* norð, prec.), *le Helme* 1462 (*v.* helm '(cattle) shelter'), *Howeflat* 1307 (*v.* haugr, flat), *Kylne pitts* 1600 (*v.* cyln, pytt), *le Kingesoke* 1406 (*v.* cyning, āc 'oak'), *Lindhou* 1325 (*v.* lind 'lime-tree', haugr 'hill'), *Lundslade* 1331 (*v.* lúndr 'wood', slæd 'valley'), *Magcrofte* 1600 (the fem. pers.n. *Mag*, croft), *Mikkelenge* 1323 (*v.* mikill, eng), *Moldroyde* 1410 (*v.* molde 'earth', rod[1]), *le Netherpooles* 1600, *les Poyles* 1650 (*v.* neoðera, pōl), *Netherstonbrigge* 1409, *le Ouerston-brigges* 1406 (*v.* stān, brycg), *Newclose* 1600, *Northhaghe* 1499 (*v.* norð, haga 'enclosure'), *Oliver Inge* 1638 Tayl (*v.* eng), *le Ressyforthlange* 1406 (*v.* risc, furlang), *Robbinroyd* 1699 (the pers.n. *Robin*, rod[1]), *Sakelwellbanke* 1410 (cf. Shackleton iii, 201 *infra*), *Shaye-, le Shawsike* 1600 (*v.* sceaga 'copse', sīc

'stream'), *Shovelbrode-Inge*, *-Royde* 1600 (*v.* scofl, brǣdu, eng, rod[1]), *Sladley
Lone yate* 1558, *Sladley Lane end* 1600 (*v.* slæd 'valley', lēah, lane, geat),
Stainersike 1600 (*v.* Stennard Well 151 *supra*, sīc), *Standelay feildes* 1545,
Stanleylideyate 1292, *-lidghate* 1323 (*v.* hlid-geat 'swing-gate'), *Stanley
Woodsyd* 1591 WillY, *Stavenmere* 1314 (*v.* stafn 'pole', mere 'pool'), *Stone-
hawe* 1461, *-halle* 1462 (*v.* stān, hall), *le Stoneylane* 1612, *Street cloase* 1608
(*v.* strǣt 'road'), *le Swyercrofte* 1407 (the surname *Swire*, croft), *Tippetynge*
1488 (*v.* eng, the first el. may be the ME surn. *Typet* (Reaney 322) or denote a
piece of land shaped like a tippet), *Trendles* 1392 (*v.* trendel 'a circle, ring',
describing something like a wood, a piece of ground, etc. of that shape),
Wayteroide 1489 (probably the surname *Waite*, rod[1]), *le Well yeard* 1600 (*v.*
wella, geard), *le Were* 1392 (*v.* wer 'weir'), *Wokeley* 1492, *Yarewelhill* 1454,
Yarwelyate 1461, *Yorwelgate* 1492 (*v.* gear 'a yair, fishing enclosure', wella,
geat 'gate').

6. WAKEFIELD (102–3320) (*v.* 149 *supra*)

> *Wachefeld*, *-felt* 1086 DB, *Wachefeld(a)* 1121 YCh viii, a. 1127
> Dugd vi, 1138–47, 1147 YCh viii
>
> *Wakefeld(a)* 1091–7 YCh viii, 12 *Lewes* 21d, *Nost* 32, 1106–1202
> YCh viii (*freq*), 1197 (1301) Ebor, 1204 DodsN, 1209 P, 1217
> Pat, 1219, 1226 FF, 1237 Ebor, 1267 AD v, 1274 WCR, 1276
> RH *et passim* to 1489 FF, *-fyld* 1461 Pat, *-fild* 1556 FF, *-field*
> 1509 HCY, 1641 Rates, *-feild* 1597 SessnR
>
> *Wakfeld* 1180–1202 YCh viii, 13 *Lewes* 23d, 1210–12 RBE, 1335 FF,
> 1428 FA
>
> *Wakefeud* 13 AD v, 1231 FF, 1233–40 YCh viii, 1238–54 AD i,
> 1240, 1250 FF, 1251 Pat, 1258 Ch *et freq* to 1323 WCR
>
> *Wackefeud* 1246 *Ass* 4, *-fild* 1583 NCWills
>
> *Waik(e)-*, *Waykefeld(e)* 1486, 1531 Test iv, 1534 WillY, 1545
> TestLds, YD viii *et freq* to 1643 YD i

Like Wakefield Nth 105, the name of this important place could
be 'Waca's stretch of open country', from an OE pers.n. *Waca*
suggested for certain p.ns. such as Wakeham Sx 43, Wakeley Hrt 210,
etc. and recorded as e.ME *Wache* (1155); this otherwise unrecorded
pers.n. would correspond to the common OHG *Wacho*. But Ekwall
(Studies[2] 189) makes the interesting and likely suggestion that the
first el. is OE wacu 'a watch, a wake' and in this p.n. it would refer
to some great annual wake or festival, during which in later times the
well-known cycle of mystery plays (the Towneley plays) was regularly
presented. Wakefield itself is the traditional capital of the West
Riding and it was certainly the centre of the very extensive manor
which extended some 30 miles through the whole of Calderdale to

the Lancashire border; as Goodall notes, it was within 10 miles of the meeting-places of five wapentakes: Osgoldcross (9 miles away at Pontefract 79 *supra*), Staincross (near Darton 6 miles away i, 317 *supra*), Agbrigg (1 mile away in Warmfield 117 *supra*), Morley (6 miles away at Tingley 175 *infra*), and Skyrack (10 miles away at Headingley pt. iv *infra*). Even Strafforth Wapentake met only 15 miles away (i, 78 *supra*). This concentration of wapentake meeting-places so close to Wakefield also suggests that from very early times it was a convenient place of assembly for the southern half of the Riding (that is, the part which lies south of the R. Wharfe); its location indicates at least a pre-Conquest importance, which the name itself would explain and which is partly supported by its standing as a post-Conquest centre of administrative and popular affairs; *v.* Introd. 'Open country where the annual wake or festival took place' is the most likely interpretation. *v.* feld, which here refers to the open country which formerly lay between the R. Calder on the south and the great wood of Outwood (156 *supra*) to the north of the old town. The numerous spellings with *-feud* for *-feld* are due to AN influence (IPN 113).

WAKEFIELD STREET-NAMES

BREAD ST, *le Breydbothes* 1354 YD i, (*le, leʒ*) *Bred(e)bothes* 1382 YD viii, 1452 Brett, 1461, 1462, 1492 *MinAcct*, 1551 *WCR* 4d, *-boethes* 1452 ib 1, (*vico vocato*) (*the*) *Breadebothes* 1545 TestLds, 1572 *WCR*, from OE *brēad* 'bread' and *bōth* 'booth'; in this street where bread was sold was *le Newe-bakehous* 1391 Tayl, *le Comenbakehous* 1492 *MinAcct*, *le Bakhous* 1525 *WCR* 2, *le Olde Bakhouse in le Bredebothes* 1551 ib 4d (*v.* bæc-hūs 'bake-house').

KIRKGATE, (*le*) *Kergate* 1275, 1308, 1313 WCR, 1313, 1317 YD x, 1322 YD iii, 1327, 1328 WCR, (*le*) *Kyrke-, Kirkegate* 1298 WCR, 1392, 1461, 1492 *MinAcct*, 1406 *WCR* 1 *et freq* to 1603 NCWills, *-gaite* 1533 WfdBurg, *Kirkgate* (*End*) 1456, 1504 Brett, 1540 TestLds *et freq* to 1709 WMB, *Kyrkgait Streit* 1537 TestLds. The name was originally 'road to the marsh', *v.* kjarr (here doubtless marshy land at the foot of the street on the Calder bank), gata. But by the fourteenth century *Ker-* was replaced by *Kirke-* (*v.* kirkja 'church'), presumably because not far from the top of the street stood the parish church (now the Cathedral), though the church is actually in Westgate.

MARKET PLACE, *le Markethstede* 1324 WCR, *market steide* 1545 TestLds, *the Market place* 1709 WMB, 1725 LdsM, *v.* market, stede, place; here was *the Market Cross* (*infra*).

NORTHGATE, (*le*) *North(e)gate* 1210–25 YCh viii, 1275 WCR, 1392, 1462, 1492 *MinAcct*, 1582, 1584 FF, 1597 SessnR *et freq* to 1709 WMB, (*-croftes*)

1278 YD x, -*gaite* 1548 TestLds, *Wakefelde Northgate* 1588 LS, *Norgate* 1597
SessnR. 'Street to the north', *v.* norð, gata.

SPRINGS (the lane leading from Warrengate to the Cathedral, cf. WfdBurg
22n), (*cursum aque voc'*) *le ʒ Spryngeʒ, -i-* 1456 *WCR* 1, 1600 ib 5, *aque voc'*
Spryng' 1462, 1492 *MinAcct, v.* spring 'well-spring'.

WARRENGATE, *Wrennegate* 1314, 1315 WCR, *Wrengate* 1461, 1492 *MinAcct*,
1597 SessnR, (*-end*) 1558 TestLds, *Rengate* (*head*) 1709 WMB, 1729 LdsM.
This name is not connected with Wrenthorpe 157 *supra*; it would appear to
be from OE wrenna 'a wren' and gata, but it is an unusual compound for
gata, and it may therefore be, as the modern form suggests, the name of the
Earls of Warren or from OFr wareine 'warren', 'road leading to the warren'
(it leads to Parkgate and Park ill *infra*), with *warren-* reduced to *Wren-* at an
early period as *Wifrun* was in Wrenthorpe.

WESTGATE, (*le*) *Westgate* 13 YD x, 1297, 1309, 1327 WCR, 1303 Calv, 1410,
1447 Brett *et freq* to 1650 *WCR* 2d, -*gait*(*e*) 1525 ib 2, 1560 YD i, *Westagate*
1296 WCR, *vico occidentali* 1405 *WCR* 4d, 1461 *MinAcct*. 'Street to the
west', *v.* west, gata.

Other street-names include: BOND ST. BULL RING. CHEAPSIDE.
CROSS LANE, *the crosse gate* 1608 *Surv*. HARDY CROFT. INGWELL ST, cf.
Ingwell Croft 1618 Tayl (*v.* eng, wella). LEGH ST, cf. *George John Legh* who
bought land here 1812 Tayl 302. NEW ST, *Newgate* 1524 Test v, *v.* nīwe,
gata. PINCHEON ST, cf. *Pinchen well Close* 1709 WMB, from the surname
Pincheon. SILVER ST, (*the*) *Silver street* 1709 WMB, 1736 LdsM, *v.* seolfor,
strǣt. SOUTHGATE. WESTGATE END, 1540 TestLds, 1652 Tayl, *v.* Westgate *supra*, ende.

Lost street-names include: *the Apple Market* 1740 LdsM, *les Bothes* 1350
YD x (*v.* bōth), *Butcher Row* 1679 Tayl, 1709 WMB, *le Fissh*(*e*)*bothes* 1461,
1462, 1492 *MinAcct* (*v.* fisc, bōth), *the Fish Shambles* 1709 WMB (*v.* fisc,
sceamol 'a shamble'), (*les*) *Flessh*(*e*)*bothes* 1358 YD x, 1392 *MinAcct* (OE
flǣsc 'flesh', bōth), *the hie strete of Westgate* 1556 WfdBurg, *the high street
leading . . . towardes Dewsbury* 1607 *Surv*, *the market crosse* 1559 WfdBurg,
the Cross 1725 LdsM (on the decision to rebuild the cross in 1707 *v.* Tayl
216 ff, Market Place *supra*, cros), *New Shambles* 1709 WMB (*v.* nīwe,
sceamol), *the oute layne in Westgate* 1556 WfdBurg (*v.* ūt, lane), *Ratton Row*
1709 WMB (*v.* raton 'rat', rāw 'row (of houses)', *Schamells* 1382 YD viii (*v.*
sceamol), *ye Stray lane* 1556 WfdBurg (*v.* stray, lane), *ye Suane lane* 1553 ib.

Amongst buildings in the town were: *le Almes Houses* 1689 Tayl, *Chaun-
tery Howse, Capell' B'te Marie sup' Ponte'* 1535 VE, *the chapell of oure ladie
of Wakefeilde Bridge* 1555 TestLds, *the chauntre* 1579 WfdBurg (the chantry
on Wakefield Bridge founded by Edward IV in memory of the Battle of
Wakefield 1470), *Co*(*o*)*keplace* 1461, 1462, 1492 *MinAcct* (a tenement, from
the surname *Cook*, place), *the Crowne Inne* 1684 Tayl, *Gaole* 1391 Tayl,
Godeswalles 1524 Test v (an almshouse, *v.* God, wall 'wall'), *the Golden Cock*
1709 WMB (an inn), *le Motehall* 1462, 1492 *MinAcct* ('assembly hall', *v.*

(ge)mōt, hall), *Newhall* Chas I *Rent* (*v.* nīwe, hall), *Six chimneys* 1722 Tayl (a former fine timbered house in Kirkgate, *v.* Tayl 184 ff), *Tollebothe* 1551 *WCR* 4d ('booth where tolls and market dues were paid', *v.* bōth), *the Whyte Horse* 1558 TestLds (an inn).

ALVERTHORPE

Alvelthorp 1199 (1232) Ch
Alvirthorp(e) 1274–1313 WCR (*freq*)
Aluer-, Alverthorp(e) 1285 WCR, 1291 DodsN, 1321 WCR, 1452
  Brett, 1596 AD i, *Alluerthorpe* 1498 FF
Allerthorp(e) 1467, 1468 DodsN, 1543 FF, 1551 TestLds, 1560
  WillY
Allathrope 1520 WillY
Alerthorpe 1590 NCWills
Ollerthorpe 1589 FF, 1603 NCWills

'Ælfhere's outlying farmstead', from the OE pers.n. *Ælfhere* (in the uninflected gen. as in Allerton pt. iv *infra* or Northallerton YN 210) and þorp. On the form *Oller-* cf. Phonol. § 5.

BITCH HILL (lost), *Bi-, Bychehil(l)* 1314, 1327 WCR, 1492 *MinAcct* 02, *-hull* 1461, 1462 ib 60, 99, *Bichull'* 1392 ib 88, *Bicchill* 1392 ib, 1408 *WCR* 1, *Bechehill* 1551 ib 4d, *the Bitchill* 1650 ib 9d, 1709 WMB. 'Bitch hill', *v.* bicce, hyll. Like Beech Hill (Knaresborough) pt. v, Hound Hill (Newton on Hodder) pt. vi *infra*, Hundhill 94 *supra*, the name refers to a hill frequented by bitches or where hounds were bred.

BROADFORD (lost), *the brode fore* 1558 TestLds, *Broad foard* (*beck*) 1607 *Surv*, 1709 WMB, *Brodfurre* 1610 *Surv. v.* brād, ford. From the earlier references it appears to have been near Alverthorpe; cf. Bradford Hall 161 *supra*.

BURMANTOFTS (lost), (*leʒ*) *Burghmantoftes* 1309 WCR, 1409 *WCR* 1, 1546 YChant, *Borwemantoftes* 1316 WCR, *Burmantoftes* 1546 YChant, 1560, 1583 YD i, (a close called, two closes of meadow called) *Burnitofts* 1731 LdsM. Of the same origin as Burmantofts (Leeds) pt. iv *infra*. From OE, ME *burh-man* 'a townsman, a burgess' and later in Y 'a burgage tenant' (*v.* NED s.v. *borough-man*) and ON topt, ME *toft* 'an enclosure, a curtilage'. The word *burhman* is also found as a surname as in *Willelmus Burghman* (13 Selby i, 191).

FALL INGS, *Fallyng(e)* als. *Falbank* 1461, 1492 *MinAcct*, *Fallynge* 1600 *WCR* 12d, *Fall Ing* 1709 WMB, *The Fallings* 1822 Langd. These meadows on the south side of the Calder (*v.* eng) are named from *le Fal(l)* 1285, 1296 WCR, 1406 *WCR* 1, *le Falles* 1323 *MinAcct*, which also gave name to *Fallebanck* 1309 WCR, *Falleloyneende* 1525 *WCR* 3, *ye falle layne* 1554 WfdBurg, *the Fall lane* 1607 *Surv*, and *pontem voc' Fallydyhate brig* 1456 *WCR* 1 (*v.* hlid-geat 'swing-bridge'). The name is derived from OE (*ge*)*fall*, which in p.ns. usually denotes 'a place where trees have been felled', but here it may well have been used of a waterfall in the river.

FLANSHAW

> *Flanshowe* 1274, 1307 WCR, 1399 Pat, -*hou* 1323 WCR
> *Flansowe* 1307 WCR, *Flanso* 1570 WillY
> *Flanshagh* 1391 Tayl (p)
> *Flansawe* 1497 Ipm, 1525 *WCR* 2d, 1562 FF *et freq* to 1616 FF, (-*grene*) 1525 *WCR* 2d, (-*loyne*) 1596 AD i, *Flanshaw* 1610 *Surv*
> *Flansall* 1527 BM, 1588 WillY, 1624 PRHrb, *Flanshall Lane* 1607 *Surv*, *Flancell* 1656 Pick

The first el. *Flans*- is from its form probably a pers.n. *Flan* with the ON gen.sg. -*s*; this could be a byname from ON *flan* 'a rushing about' which is the source of Scots dial. *flan* 'a gust of wind' (NED s.v.), of Icel. *flanni* 'a giddy person', and perhaps the ON byname *Flana* suggested for the Norw p.n. *Flanestad* (NG ix, 41). But in view of the doubtful existence of such a name, it is preferable to accept Goodall's suggestion that it is the well-evidenced OIr pers.n. *Flann* (from Ir *flann* 'red'). 'Flan's mound or hill', *v.* haugr; the hill is now Flanshaw Hill. The spellings in -*all* are inversions which could take place when original -*all* developed to -*aw* in the dialect; cf. also *Ravenshowe* 173 *infra* for a similar substitution.

GOODY BOWER (lost), *le Godeybowr* 1409 *WCR* 1, *Godeborestyle*, -*stile* 1461, 1462, 1492 *MinAcct*. The first el. is probably the surname *Goody* (probably from the OE fem. pers.n. *Godgifu* or the like), as in Goody Cross (Preston) pt. iv; *v.* būr 'a cottage, dwelling', stigel 'stile'. This is the *Gudeboure at the quarell hede* referred to in e.15 Towneley ii, 367, and the land in *Goodybower called Quarrell Pits* 1558 Tayl (app. x); it seems to have been near St Johns in the north of the town, as it is clearly to be associated with *Goody Green* in Outwood 159 *supra*, just north of this.

PINDERS FIELDS, *Pinderfield* 1709 WMB, *Pindar Cross & Middle Field* 1793 *EnclA* 11, *Pinder's Field* 1822 Langd. Pinders Fields lie to the north of the town. In 1556 the householders of Westgate were by custom to make a 'pyndefolde' at the end of Westgate (WfdBurg 23) and 1579 the pinder was to 'take all swine that cometh into the churche yeard & impound theym' (ib 26). This pinfold in Westgate End was obviously not connected with Pinders Fields; doubtless it was the Westgate one which is associated with the Pinder of Wakefield.

ROBERTHORPE (lost), *Roberthorp(e)* 1277 WCR, 1323 *MinAcct* 45, 1435 DodsN, 1497 Ipm, *Rodberthorp(e)* 1286, 1327 WCR, 1328 Banco, *Roberdethorp* 1410 *WCR* 1, *Robertthorp* 1435 DodsN, 1512 *Nost* 72d. 'Robert's outlying farmstead', *v.* þorp. The pers.n. is ME *Ro(d)bert* from OG *Rodbert*. The place was in the neighbourhood of Thornes.

SKITTERICK (lost), 1812 Tayl 302, *Schiterike* 1313 WCR, (*riuulum voc'*) *Skytryk* 1489 *WCR* 1, *Skyttyryge* 1533 WfdBurg 17, *Skittericke* (*Bridge*) 1579 ib, (*rivulum*) 1617 Tayl. This name occurs several times in YW, *Skyterick* i, 120, *Skytrykhill* 40, Broad & Long Skitrick i, 271 *supra*, Sluttering Hill ii, 189, Skitterick ii, 220, *Skittrick* (Thorner) pt. iv, *Skiterik* (Otley) pt. iv, *Skittricks* (Middleton) pt. v, Skittergate Gutter (Ripon) pt. v, as well as in YN 6; they are all doubtless 'open sewers'; *Skitterick* in Wakefield was a small stream that ran down Kirkgate from Wrengate (Tayl 109) and was a drain which was to be kept clear (WfdBurg 17). The name is from OE scite 'dung', cf. OE *scitere* 'sewer' with ON sk- substituted for sh-, and OE ric in the sense 'ditch' (cf. Ekwall, RN 365).

THORNES, *Spinetum, in Spineto* 13 AD iv, v, 1274–1298 WCR (*freq*), 1348 AD iv, *Thornes* 1316 Pat, 1323 WCR, 1449 Pat, 1452 Brett *et passim* to 1709 WMB, *Thurnes* 1558 TestLds, *Thorns* 1665 Visit. 'The thorn-trees', *v.* þorn (Lat *spinetum* 'thorn thicket, spinney').

WIND HILL, *Wyndochill* 1313 WCR, *Windothill* 1349 YD x, *Wi-*, *Wyndehull* 1392 *MinAcct* 88, -*hill* 1533 TestLds, *Wyndill* 1522 ib, -*hill* 1546 YChant, 1557 TestLds, *Windowhill* Chas 1 *Rent* 29, 34. The first el. is probably ON adj. *vindugr* 'windy, exposed to the wind', but its form has been somewhat confused with *windok*, a development of ON *vind-augi* 'window' recorded in early Scots dial. 'Windy hill', *v.* hyll.

ALVERTHORPE RD, *Aluerthorpe layne* 1610 *Surv*, *v.* Alverthorpe *supra*, lane. BALNE BRIDGE & MILLS, *Balne* 1274 WCR, *Balne Mills* 1841 O.S., ME *balne* 'bath', *v.* Balne Beck (RNs.), Balne 14 *supra*. BOROUGH CORNER. BROOKS BANK, *Brookebanke Close* 1617 *Comm*, *Brooke Banke* 1637 WillY, *Broksbank att Westgate End* 1709 WMB, *v.* brōc, banke; the brook is Balne Beck (RNs.) *supra*. CHALD LANE, *v.* Chald Beck (RNs.). CLIFFHILL HO, *le Clyff felde* 1525 *WCR* 4d, *the Cliffe feild* 1579 WfdBurg, *(the) Clyff-, Cliffe(i)ld, -field* 1551, 1600 *WCR*, 1607 *Surv*, *Cliff Field* 1682 *Grant*[2] 228, *Cliff Hill* 1709 WMB, *v.* clif, feld (replaced by hyll), named from *Cliff* 1342 YD x (p), 1573 ib viii, *le Clyff* 1525 *WCR* 4d, *the Cliffe* 1597 NCWills, 1729 LdsM. THE DAM, *the Milnedame* 1579 WfdBurg, *Wakefield Dam* 1709 WMB, *v.* myln, dammr; cf. *the mylne of Wakfeld* 172 *infra*; this is distinct from Mill Dam *infra* and was apparently where Ings Beck ran into the Calder which is dammed at this place. EAST MOOR, *(le) Eastmore* 1607 *Surv*, 1639 WillY, 1678 Tayl, *-moor* 1709 WMB, *v.* ēast, mōr; it lies east of the town. FLANSHAW HILL, 1841 O.S., *v.* Flanshaw *supra*, a prominent hill on Westgate Common. GREEN END, *Greenend hous* 1709 WMB. GREENHILL RD. GROVE FM (Westgate Common), *Grove Ho.* 1841 O.S., distinct from GROVE HALL, named from St John's Grove. HIGHFIELD HO. HOLME FM (Thornes), *le Thornesholme* 1406 *WCR* 1, *Thornes farder holme*, *the narr holme*, *the holme lane* 1608 *Surv*, *v.* holmr 'water-meadow' (near the R. Calder); *farder, narr* are dial. forms of 'farther', 'near'. HUMBLE JUMBLE ROW, *loc' voc' Humbleomble* 1392 *MinAcct* 88, *Humble Jumble feild* 1572 *WCR* 8, *-bridge* 1607 *Surv* 10, 3, *-closes* 1709 WMB, *Jumbelfield* 1607 *Surv*; this is doubtless e.ModE *jumble* 'a disorderly muddle' (first recorded c. 1529 as a vb., NED), with *humble* as an onomatopaeic intensifier; *humble-jumble* is once recorded in 1550 (NED s.v., 'an humble iomble or hotch potch'), cf. Jumples iii, 115. THE INGS, *le Erlesenge* 1407 *WCR*, *Erlesyng* 1461, 1462 *MinAcct*, *-yenge* 1492 ib, *ereyles heynges* 1533 WfdBurg, *the earles yngs* 1556 ib, *Wakefield Ings formerly called Earls Ings* 1709 WMB, *Le Ings* 1699 Tayl, *Ings* 1793 *EnclA* 11, *v.* eorl (here the Earl of Warren), eng 'meadow'; it was described in 1407 *WCR* as *prat' domini* 'the lord's meadow'. JACOBS WELL LANE. LAMBKIN WELL. LAWEFIELD RD (Thornes), *le Lawfelde* 1410 *WCR* 1, *the lawe Felde* 1544 TestLds, *Thornes Law feild* 1608 *Surv*, *Lawfield* (*Yate*) 1709 WMB; the road runs along the north of Thornes Park, not far from Lowe Hill (*infra*); 'open land near the mound', *v.* hlāw,

feld. LONG CAUSEWAY, *le Cawsey* 1485 *WCR* i, *v.* caucie 'a causeway, a raised way across marshy ground' (it runs through Pinders Fields). LOWE HILL, *Law Hill* 1709 WMB, 1771 M, named from (*the great*) *Nether law* 1608 *Surv* 12, 4, 1709 WMB, *v.* hlāw 'mound', hyll; it refers to a great castle mound in Thornes Park which Leland describes as 'an hille of erth caste up, wher sum say that one of the Erles Warines began to build, and as fast as he builded, violence of winde defacid the work . . . sum say that it was nothing but a windmille hille. The place is now caullid Lohille' (cf. Lawefield Rd *supra*). MANOR HAIGH, probably identical with *leӡ Hawes* 1410 *WCR* i, *v.* haga 'enclosure'. MILL DAM (Alverthorpe), possibly identical with *Brokmylndam* 1286 WCR, (*le*) *Bro(o)kemyln(e)dam(m)e* 1406, 1525 *WCR*, 1610 *Surv*, *Brook miln damme* 1607 ib (which all refer to the Alverthorpe district) and distinct from The Dam *supra*; *v.* brōc, myln, dammr; the brook is Alverthorpe Beck. MONCKTON FM. MOORCROFT (lost), 1709 WMB, MOOR HO, *Morcroft* 1275, 1286, 1298 WCR, (*le*) *Morecroft*, 1313 ib, 1380 AD iv, 1607 *Surv*, named from the old name of Westgate Common *infra*. NEW BRIGHTON. NEW SCARBRO'. PARKGATE FM, *Park Gate* 1808 Tayl. PARK HILL, 1841 O.S., *v.* park, geat, hyll; the park (on the east of the town) was partly in Stanley (*v.* New Park, Old Park 160–1 *supra*). PEASE HO, 1841 O.S. ST JOHNS, ST JOHN'S GROVE, *campus Sancti Johannis* 1406 *WCR* i, *Seynt John felde* 1499 ib 1d, *St John field* 1607 *Surv*, 1793 *EnclA* 11, *St. Johns Place* 1817 M. SNOW HILL VIEW, *Snowhill* 1743 *Grant*[2] 1, named from Snow Hill in Outwood 158 *supra*. SPRINGFIELD HO, SPRINGS (Flanshaw), distinct from Springs 165 *supra*; these are from spring 'plantation'. TURNER'S LANE. WAKEFIELD BRIDGE, 1607 *Surv*, 1705 Hrg, *ye brege* 1554 WfdBurg, *Wakefeld brydge* 1558 TestLds, *pontis de Wakefeild* 1610 *Surv*, *v.* brycg. WESTFIELD HO, *West Field* 1793 *EnclA* 11, *v.* west, feld. WESTGATE COMMON, (common called) *Westgate more* 1607, 1608 *Surv*, *Westgate Moor* (*side*) 1673 Tayl, 1709 WMB, *v.* Westgate 165 *supra*, mōr. WILLOW LANE, cf. *the Willow cloase* 1608 *Surv*, *v.* wilig.

FIELD-NAMES

The principal forms in (*a*) are 1709 WMB. Spellings dated 13 are AD v, 1392, 1461, 1462, 1492 *MinAcct*, 1538–1545, 1555–1560 TestLds, 1608–1610 *Surv*, Chas 1 *Rent* 29, 34, 1709 WMB, 1804 Tayl, 1813 *EnclA*. Others dated without source are *WCR*.

(a) Band Walk 1845 *TA* 418, Base Flatt (ib 1572, an OE pers.n. *Basa*
(cf. Bassingthorpe i, 182 *supra*), flat), Basings Close 1741 *Grant*[2] 230 (*Base-
heyng* 1307, *le Baseynge(s)* 1327, 1551, 'Basa's meadows', v. prec., eng),
Beck close 1813, Bottle Flat 1804, Church Steel (v. stigel 'stile'), Cliff Tree
Hill, Cockroyd 1804 (*the great Cockroyde* 1608, v. cocc[2], rod[1]), Crabtree
Close (cf. *les Crabtrees* 1650, v. crabbe), Crimbles (*Crymbells* 1608, possibly
identical with Crimbles in Horbury 153 *supra*, v. crymel 'a small plot'),
Dog Croft, the Eastfeild Close, Fidling Croft 1753 *Grant*[2] 2, The Flat 1813,
Hale Ing (v. halh, eng), Hall Ing (v. hall, eng), Horncastle Close, Horsefield
Close, Houndroyd (*le Houndroyde* 1409, v. hund 'hound' or the ON pers.n.
Hundi, rod[1] 'clearing'), Kelshaw Ing (*Kel-*, *Kilshay Inge* 1607, 1610, v.
sceaga 'copse', eng), Laine Close, Lindle Hill 1813 (*Lyndhill* 1607, v. lind
'lime-tree', hyll), the Milneroyds (*Millerodes* 1316, *Milnerod(e)* 1392, 1462,
1492, *-roides* 1499, v. myln, rod[1] and *the Mylne* 172 *infra*), Mirewell Inge
1707 Tayl (*Myrewellynge* 1650, v. mýrr, wella, eng), Mount Close 1841 O.S.,
Narway Lane Close, Nathan Deans 1813, Old Field 1793 *EnclA* (*Holdfeld*
Chas 1, v. ald, feld), Oliver Ing, Pale Close, Pickhill 1804 ('*the Peke hilles
whereon Wakefield standeth*' 1577 Holinshed, v. pēac, hyll), The Pinfold (*le
Punfold* 1391 Tayl, cf. Pinders Fields 168 *supra*, v. pynd-fald), Pryorhous
(the surname *Prior*, hūs), the Ryecroft (ib 1608, v. rȳge, croft), Shawfield
(ib 1607 (*le*) *Shayfe(i)ld* 1551, 1572, 1610, v. sceaga 'copse', feld), Siddall
Close (*le Siddalls* 1600, v. sīd 'large', halh 'nook of land'), Sour Ing 1813,
Spent, Stock Inge (*Stork Inge* 1607, v. eng), Toft-Shough, -Shove (*Toft shooe*
1607, v. topt 'enclosure', sceaga 'copse'), Wallit Close (*Walley cloase* 1607), The
Well Close (*the Wellcloase* 1607, v. wella), Wheat Close, Wood Yard 1845 TA.

(b) *Aluerthorpefeild* 1610 (v. Alverthorpe *supra*, feld).

Baynes Bridge 1673 Tayl, *Banister ynge* 1560 (the surname *Banister*, eng),
Bathehill' 1461, 1462 (v. bæð 'bath', hyll), *the Beggerbuttes* 1607, 1610,
Begger Lane 1607, *Le Begger layne* 1610 (ME beggare 'beggar', butte, lane),
Beiston Reanes 1650 (probably a surname from Beeston iii, 217 *infra*, reinn
'boundary strip'), *Beskroyde* 1328 (v. bēosuc 'bent grass', rod[1] 'clearing'),
le Bordland 1315 (ME bord-land 'land held by a bordar'), *Bright(e)hall* 1462,
1492 (possibly the surname *Bright*, hall), *Brodeclose* 1551, *le Brodole* 1323
(v. brād, clos, dāl), *Brooke* 1615 Comm, *le Brokfeld* Chas 1 *Surv*, *Brokeside*
1541 *MinAcct*, *Brookside (cloase)* 1607 (v. brōc, sīde, cf. Brooks Bank 169
supra), *Brounrode* 1325, *litle Browne-roade*, *-roide* 1607 (v. brūn, probably as
a surname, rod[1]).

Calferoide 1456 (v. calf, rod[1]), (*Narr*) *Karley* 1607, *Careley* 1610 (v. kjarr
'marsh', lēah), (*leȝ*) *Clayflattes* 1410, 1608, *the Clay greue* 1608 (v. clǣg,
flat, grǣfe 'copse'), *Claver landes* 1608 (v. clāfer 'clover', land), *Clyfford*
1462 (v. clif, ford), *Codenelcroft*, *-il-* 1298, 1314 (v. croft), *les Coytes* 1409
(v. cot 'cottage'), *Cokworthloyne* 1408 (v. lane), *Coling-*, *Collyholme* 1608,
1650 (the ME pers.n. *Coling*, holmr, but cf. Collyhall 161 *supra*), *Conyscroft*
1286, *Cunscroft* 1328 (the ME surn. *Cony*, croft), *Cortelyngthwaite* 1407 (v.
þveit), *Cow(e)cloase* 1607, 1608, *Coushotedole* 1324, *Cowshotesgreyff* 1551,
the Cow shott greave 1607 (v. cūscote 'wood pigeon', dāl, grǣfe 'copse'),
Crakoobroke 1456, *Crawe-*, *Crowmylne(hill)* 1610 (v. crāwe, myln).

Dicarynge 1572 (probably ME *dikere* 'ditcher', eng), *Diconcroft* 1406, *Dyconynge* 1551, *Dickon Inge* 1607 (ME *Diccon*, as in Dickencross 110 *supra*, croft, eng), *Dun cloase* 1607.

Elymcroft 1410, *Ellynroide* 1499, *Ellyntree cloase* 1608 (*v.* ellern 'elder-tree', rod[1], clos), *Erleyfeld* 1525, *Evepighill* 1331 (the ME fem. pers.n. *Eve*, pightel 'enclosure').

Flaxonfeld Chas 1 (*v.* fleax, feld), *le Fordole* 1406 (*v.* fore, dāl).

Gamersley lane 1608, *Gisburne Leyes* 1607 (a surname from Gisburn pt. vi *infra*, lēah), *Godmanroide* 1525 (the ME surname *Godman*, rod[1]), *God(e)wyn-rode* 1315, 1358 (the ME pers.n. *Godwin* (OE *Godwine*), rod[1]), *le Gote* 1391 ib (*v.* gota), *Gouleroide* 1456 (*v.* goule 'ditch', rod[1]), *Grisbiglee* 1331.

Haggs 1659 WillS (*v.* hǫgg), *the Great & litle Hawkes* 1607, *Hedalescrosse* 1485, *the headlesse crosse Lane* 1608 (*v.* cros), *Helaystones* 1407 (*v.* hēah, lēah, stān), *Herbertpygel, Herberdpykel* 1286 (the ME pers.n. *Herbert* (from OG), *v.* pightel 'enclosure'), *Hesperode* 1313 (*v.* æspe 'aspen', rod[1]), *le Hevedland* 13, *le Headland* 1610 (*v.* hēafod-land), *le Hillefeld* 1405, *the Hilfield* 1607 (*v.* hyll, feld), *Hodcrimbels* 13 AD iv (cf. Crimbles 171 *supra*), *Holywell* 1607 (*v.* hālig, wella), *Holotrydyng* 1410 (the ME pers.n. *Hulot*, rydding 'clearing'), *the hopgarth* 1544 ('hopyard', *v.* hoppe, garðr), *Hopperoide* 1456 (*v.* prec., rod[1]), *Horse cloase* 1607, *the North horsfall gate* 1608 (*v.* hors, (ge)fall, gata, cf. Horsefall iii, 182 *infra*).

Inetrode 1329.

Jaketquarter 1650 *YAS* 97, *Jack ynge* 1556, *Jacke ynge* 1608 (the pers.n. *Jack*, eng), *Jameslegh* 1409, *Jameslees* 1488 (the pers.n. *James*, lēah), *Janetroide* 1408 (the fem. pers.n. *Janet*, rod[1]), *Javell lane* 1607, *Jepoxgange* Chas 1 (the ME pers.n. *Jeppe*, cf. Jep Royd 106 *supra*, *v.* ox-gang), *Jowethous, Jewetroide* 1456, *Jowet Royd* 1607 (the surname *Jowett* (cf. Jowitt Ho i, 199 *supra*), hūs, rod[1]), *Joyous Willows* 1608, *Joyce Willows* 1650 (the fem. pers.n. *Joyce*, wilig), *Julianroide* 1405 (*v.* rod[1]), *Justing furlong* 1607 (ME *iusting* 'jousting').

Katerynlees 1488, *Katherine Lees* 1607 (*v.* lēah), *Kirk(e)gate landes* 1608, 1650 (*v.* Kirkgate 164 *supra*, land), *Kirkmanynge* 1618 Tayl (the surname *Kirkman*, eng), *Kirktwhaitt* 1535 VE (*v.* kirkja, þveit), *le Knolbuttes* 1406, *Knowlbuts* Eliz Tayl (*v.* cnoll, butte).

Lachilandes 1308 (*v.* læcc, land), *Lady brigge Inge* 1608 (named from *Isabell Brigges*, *v.* eng), *Langlayyherde* 1408 (*v.* geard), *le Lathegreue* 1410 (*v.* hlaða 'barn', grǣfe 'copse'), *les Leghes* 1325, *the Leys* 1652 Tayl (*v.* lēah), *Leveneth-eng* 1308 (the OE pers.n. *Lēofnōð*, eng), *Lyneyerde* 1525 (*v.* līn 'flax', geard), *Lit(t)le Hole Inge* 1608, 1650 (*v.* hol[1], eng), *the litle Indge* 1544 Test-Lds, *Littilstonyr* 1490, *Litilstener* 1492 (near *Milnerodes infra*, *v.* stæner, cf. Stennard Well 151 *supra*), *le Loneendeland* 13 (*v.* lane, ende), *le Longefeld* 13, *Longerawe* 1499, *Longrow head* 1607 (*v.* lang, rāw).

Magyherdwynt 1409 (the fem. pers.n. *Mag*, geard, wente 'path'), *close called Megg in Wintr* 1607 (doubtless an adaptation of prec.), *le Merow* 13, *Mikkelenge* 1342 Tayl (*v.* mikill, eng), *Mickilridyng* 1328 (*v.* mikill, rydding), *the mylne of Wakfeld* 1538 (*molendini de Wakefeld* c. 1225 YCh viii, *v.* myln and foll.), *le Mulnecroft* 1392, *le Millecroft* 1461, 1492 (*v.* prec., croft), *le Milneholm* 1297 (*v.* prec., holmr 'water-meadow'), *Moldyerd* 1331 (*v.* molde, geard), *Moseley Hay* 1315 (*v.* mos, lēah, (ge)hæg), *Mugg Sykes* 1608 (*v.* sīc 'stream').

le Nuecroft 1328 (*v.* nīwe, croft), *Neweroide* 1610 (*v.* nīwe, rod[1]), *Nykroid* 1406 (the pers.n. *Nikke* (from *Nicholas*), rod[1]), *le Northfelde* 1286, *the North feilde* 1555 (*v.* norð, feld).

the Orchard end 1607, *Orpytts, -pitt(e)s* 1546 YChant, 1608, 1699 ('ore pits', *v.* ōra[2], pytt), *Orrerode* 1308 (*v.* orri 'black-cock', rod[1]).

Papilyonholm, -lion- 1310 Surv, 1323, *Pampellion Holm* 1316 Pat, *Pamplyonholme* 1323 MinAcct, *-lioun-* 1342 Tayl (in Thornes, OFr *papilion* 'butterfly' or e.ModE *pampilion* 'a kind of fur', either used as a nickname, holmr), *le Parson Wall* 1600 (*v.* persone, wall), *Partehedge* 1610, *Pollard great close* 1607 (cf. *Pollardhouses* 159 *supra*), *le Prickehedge* 1689 Tayl (*v.* pricca 'prickle', hecg).

the quarell hede e. 15 Towneley ii, 367 (cf. *Quarrell Pits* 1558 Tayl, *v.* quarrelle 'quarry', hēafod), *Quene acr'* 1607.

Ray-, Reynoldpighill 1486, 1610 (the ME pers.n. *Rainald*, pightel 'enclosure'), *Raniesyke* 1557 (*v.* sīc 'stream'), *Ravenshow* 1329, *Rauynsall* 1499, *Ravensall* 1572, 1608 ('Raven's mound', from the ON pers.n. *Hrafn*, haugr, for the *-all* spellings cf. Flanshaw 167 *supra*), *le Ryerodeheued* 1329 (*v.* rȳge, rod[1], hēafod), *le Rodes* 1297, *the Roodes* 1557 (*v.* rod[1] 'clearing'), *Rowgh cloase* 1608, *v.* rūh), *Rownd Inge* 1608, *Rushielandes* 1650 (*v.* risc, land).

le Samonde-, le(з) Samon hekkes 1462, 1492 ('salmon traps', from ME, OFr *samoun*, hæcc, an interesting comment on the then state of the Calder), *Salman ryddyng* 1410 (the ME pers.n. *Sal(o)man*, rydding), *Sa(u)ndergeard(e)* 1600, 1610 (the ME surname *Saunder*, geard), *Scrathetwhaite* 1454 (perhaps ON skreið 'landslide', þveit), *the Shaw gappe* 1607 (*v.* Shawfield 171 *supra*, gap 'opening, gate'), *Sheprote land* 1608 ('sheep-rot land'), *Sherrefforth* 1327 ('sheriff ford', *v.* scīr-gerēfa, ford), *Shirelokroide* 1490 (the OE byname *Scīrloc* (ME *Shirlok*) 'bright-lock', rod[1]), *Sommer cloase* 1608, *Spinkrode* 1331 (named from *Adam Spink* ib 198, cf. Spinke Farme 162 *supra*), *Steelecootes* 1610 (*v.* stigel 'stile', cot), *le Steghill* 1410 (*v.* prec.), *Stokynge* 1406 (*v.* stoccing), *Stonyrode* 1275 (*v.* stānig, rod[1]), *Stringer Inge* 1607 (the surname *Stringer*, eng), *Swannildene* 1329 (the ME fem. pers.n. *Swanhild* (ON *Svanhildr*), denu 'valley'), *Swanroideyng* 1445 (*v.* swān 'herdsman', rod[1], eng), *Swylyngstones* 1407 (perhaps from *swilling*, stān, cf. Swillington iii, 168 *infra*).

Taverne Inge 1699 Tayl, *Thornesrydyng* 1325 (*v.* Thornes 168 *supra*, rydding), *Thornewellfeld* 1408, *Thornwell* 1607 (*v.* þorn, wella), *Twyseldene* 1316 (*v.* twisla 'fork of a river', denu 'valley').

Vswelroide 1454 (*v.* rod[1]), *le Uvergatelone* 1297 (*v.* uferra, gata, lane).

le Whan' 1406, (*vast' in Wrengate iuxta) le Wayne* 1461, 1462, 1492 (probably a tenement called 'the wagon'), *Wall cloase* 1607, *the Waver* ('a public watering trough in the springs') 1556 WfdBurg (probably, as in Waver Ing 228, *Waver ditch* iii, 255, and Waver Spring (Collingham) pt iv, from OE wæfre, in the sense of dial. *waver* 'a common pool', *v.* EPN ii, 236), *le Wellehous* 1410 (*v.* wella, hūs), *Wheterode* 1596 AD i, *Wheateroyd* 1610 (*v.* hwǣte, rod[1]), *Wildhaverlande* 1406, *-furlonge* 1607 ('wild oat land', *v.* hafri[1], land, *Wildhaver* is also a nickname), *Willefelde* 1410, *Wilfeildes* 1608, *le*

Windywell 1525, *Wyndywell* 1607 (*v.* wind, wella), *Wolmerrode* 1331, *Woll-merroide* 1499 (a pers.n. from OE *Wulfmǣr*, rod[1]), *the wood yate* 1558 (*v.* wudu, geat).

ix. East and West Ardsley

East and West Ardsley were originally separate townships, East Ardsley being also an ecclesiastical parish, and West Ardsley being in the parish of Woodkirk (176 *infra*). The two townships are now in the Municipal Borough of Morley (182 *infra*).

EAST ARDSLEY (102–3025)

> *Erdeslau, -lauue* 1086 DB
>
> *Erdeslaw(e), -lawa* a. 1127 Dugd vi, 1154–91 *Nost* 73d, 1194, 1196 P, c. 1200 Selby, 1208 FF, Hy 3 BM, 1234 FF, 1246 *Ass* 12, 1252 *Nost* 45d, 1288 YI, 1298 WCR *et freq* to 1411 YD x, *-lowe* 1219 FF, 1286, 1314 WCR, 1300 Baild, 1316 Vill, 1359 BM, 1402 Selby, *-loue* c. 1235 Puds, *-louwe* 1324 WCR, *Erdis-lowe* 1284 WCR
>
> *Herdeslau* 12 Brett, 1185 Templar, *-loue* 1166 P (p), *-lawe* 13 AD iv, 1251 *Ass* (p), *-lauwe* 1208 Cur, *Herdislaw* 12 Dugd, *-laue* Hy 3 BM, *Herdelaw(e)* 1226 FF, 1303 KF
>
> *Ardeslaw(e)* 1155–62 (16) YCh 1452, 1285 KI, 1402 BM, 1418 YI, (*Est-*) 1459 BM, *-lowe* 1383 YD i, 1535 FF, (*Easte-*) 1558 TestLds, *Ardislaw(e), -ys-* 1202 FF, 1552 WillY, 1605 FF, (*East-*) 1606 FF, *-low* 1577 DodsN
>
> *Ardesley, -lay* 1366 Test, 1510 FF, 1527 TestLds, *Ardyslay* 1552 YD i
>
> *Ards(e)ley east* 1641 Rates, 1651 PRRth
>
> *Adgeleye* 1614 PRHrb

'Erd's mound', *v.* hlāw. *Erd* is a pers.n. which represents an OE *Eard* or the OE *Eorēd* which appears to be the first el. of Ardsley i, 290 *supra*. Here, as in the latter, the spellings in *Ardes-* are late or from late manuscripts and no doubt represent the normal development of ME *er* to *ar*. The last spelling *Adge-* has an assimilation of *-ds-* to [dʒ] (cf. Phonol. § 52). *v.* Addenda.

WEST ARDSLEY, *Erdislaw* 1138–47 YCh viii, *Erdes-, Herdislaw(e)* 13 ib and other spellings similar to those of East Ardsley, *Westardeslawe, -lowe* 1400 Pat, 1459 BM, 1587, 1614 FF, *West Ardislawe, -ys-* 1540 FF, 1637 *Bodl* 113, *Ardsley west* 1641 Rates. West Ardsley village was also known as Westerton (*infra*) from an early date and West Ardsley remained the name of a township.

DUNNINGLEY

Duninglau(e) 1190–1210, e. 13 YCh viii (p), *Dunynglawe* 1581 FF,
    Duningley 1616 FF
Donnynglawe 1286 WCR (p), *Donynglawe* 1379 PT (p)
Donig(e)lawe 1297, 1298 WCR
Donislaw 1321 YD vi
Dunnynglaw 1559 FF, *Dunningley* 1822 Langd

Probably 'Duning's mound', from the OE pers.n. *Dun(n)ing* and hlāw, with a not uncommon uninflected genitive, but it could also be 'Dun's mound' from the OE pers.n. *Dun(n)* and the connective -ing[4].

LEE FAIR GREEN, also called LEE GAP (cf. Gap Ho *infra*), *Wodekirke-legh* 1358 WCR 2, *Lee Croft* 1708 *WYEnr* 9, *Lee Green* 1771 M, *Lee Fair* 1817 M, *Lee Fair or Green* 1822 Langd. *v.* Woodkirk *infra*, lēah, feire, grēne[2]. A fair at Woodkirk was granted by Henry 1 and confirmed by Stephen to be held on the Feast of the Assumption and on the Nativity (YCh 1442); in 1306 a servant of Henry de Swynlington was to be arrested for stealing a hide at 'Wodekirk fair'. The famous Lee Fairs or Lee Gap Fairs are held here on 24 August and 17 September.

TINGLEY, *Thing(e)-, Thynglau, -law(e)* e. 13 YCh viii (p), c. 1220 Calv (p), 1316 WCR (p), 1411 YD x, *-lowe* 1297 WCR, *Tynge-, Thingeslawe* 1208 FF, *Tinglawe* 1608 FF. 'Mound where the *thing* or council met', *v.* þing, hlāw. The place is at the crossing of the Wakefield–Bradford and Leeds–Huddersfield roads, and there are traces of a mound (marked on 6″ O.S. grid 281261) on the top of the hill just south of the cross-roads. There is no evidence that this was ever the meeting-place of the freemen of the West Riding, for that was held, in medieval times at least, at Wingate Hill (Stutton) pt. iv *infra*, but it was no doubt the meeting-place of Morley Wapentake, Morley itself being just over a mile away. The OE and ON word þing could certainly be used of a shire assembly as it was in Fingay Hill YN 213, but it was also used of a smaller assembly as in Morthen i, 168 *supra* or *Thingwall* YN 128, the meeting-place of Whitby Strand wapentake. This parish was undoubtedly an important one for assemblies, for Woodkirk (*infra*) has associations with Lee Fair Green (*supra*) which is the site of the great Lee Fair, *v.* further Wakefield 168, and Towneley xvii.

TOPCLIFFE, *Toftecliue, -clive* 1190–1210, e. 13 YCh viii (p), 1296 WCR, *-clyf* 1321 YD vi (p), *Toftclyf* 1297 WCR, *Topcliff, -clyff, -clyf(e)* 1454 WillY, 1510 FF, 1589 PRLds, 1616 FF, *Toplyfe* 1583 WillY, *-liff* 1603 FF. 'Steep bank by the enclosure', *v.* topt, clif. The modern form has arisen from association with Topcliffe YN 186 or popular etymology (because of the 'cliff').

WESTERTON, 1379 PT (p), 1459, 1462 Test ii, 1539 WillY, 1546 YChant *et freq* to 1614 FF. 'More westerly village', *v.* westerra, tūn. This was doubtless originally an alternative name for West Ardsley *supra* which survived only as the name of a township. On this kind of name substitution cf. Mickletown 127 *supra*.

WOODKIRK (originally an ecclesiastical parish, *v.* 174 *supra*)

   Wdekirk(a) 12 Dugd vi, 1121–7 YCh 1616, 1154–91 *Nost* 73d, 1215 ChR, Hy 3 BM, c. 1220 Calv

   Wudechirch(a) 1121–7 YCh 1428, 1202 FF, *-kyrce* c. 1150 Crawf, *-kirke* l. 12 YCh viii, *-kircha* 13 YD ix

   Wodechirch(ia) 12 *Nost*, 1121 Tockw, 14 YD i, *-chirk(e)* 1130–40 YCh 1466 (*Nost* 73), *-churche* a. 1127 Dugd vi, 1138–47 YCh viii, *-kircha* 12 *Nost* 4d, *-kirk(e)*, *-kyrk* 1135–9, 1180–1200 YCh 1442, 1617 (*Nost* 40), 1284 WCR, 1286 Ebor, 1291 Tax, 1292 *Nost* 63, 1293 DodsN, 1297 WCR *et freq* to 1504 FF

   Wodkirk(e), *-kyrk* 12 Dugd vi, e. 13 YCh viii, 1343 *Ass* 5, 1428 FA *et freq* to 1535 VE, *-chirche* 1288 YI

   Woddekerk 1321 YD vi

   Woodkyrke, *-kirk(e)* 1539 WillY, 1587, 1605 FF, *-church* 1605 FF, 1642 PRRth

'Church in the wood', *v.* wudu, cirice (replaced generally by ON kirkja). Like Skewkirk (Tockwith) pt. iv *infra*, which has the same meaning, it was a cell of St Oswald's priory of Nostell (1535 VE). There was a church here t. Hy 1 (Dugd vi, 99 'terram in qua prefata ecclesia sita est'); this was given by William Earl of Warren to Nostell Priory, and a number of Black Canons were sent out to found the cell (ib). Woodkirk has no associations with the Towneley plays, cf. M. H. Peacock, *Anglia* xxiv, 509–24.

ALBERTON HO. ARDSLEY COMMON, *the Common* 1708 *WYEnr* 9.
BAG HILL, 1534 WillY, possibly 'badger hill', *v.* bagga, hyll, Bag
Hill 78 *supra.* BEAVER'S HO. BEGGARINGTON HILL, 1817 M, a
name repeated elsewhere in YW (iii, 7, 88 *infra*), all seemingly
modern and probably imitative formations from ModE *beggar* and
the common ending *-ington*, denoting places which beggars haunted
or where they could stay; this place is near to Lee Fair Green *supra*
which was doubtless a haunt of beggars at fair-time. BLACK GATES,
1817 M, *v.* blæc, gata. BLIND LANE, 1841 O.S., *v.* blind, lane.
BOTTOMS WOOD, *The Bothams* 1841 O.S., *v.* botm (boðm). BOWLING
BECK, *v.* Bowling Hall 149 *supra.* BOYLE HALL. BROOM WELL.
BUSHY BECK. CARR GATE FM, *Car House* 1841 O.S., *v.* kjarr
'marsh' and the nearby Carr Gate 158 *supra.* CAVE LANE. CHURCH
FM. COGLANDS. COMMON SIDE. DENSHAW BECK & WELL.
THE FALL, *Fall* 1841 O.S., *v.* (ge)fall 'felling of trees, clearing'.
FAN PIT. FOLLY HALL. GAP HO, *v.* gap 'opening'. GRIFF HO,
(*le*) *Griff* 1348 YD i, 1726 LdsM, *v.* gryfja 'hole, pit'. HAIGH
HALL, 1817 M, *la, le Haye* 13, 1402 Selby, 14 YD i, *Haya* 1383 ib,
Nethir-, (*leʒ*) *Overhagh* 1462 ib, *Haigh* 1577 Tayl, 1658 WillS, *v.*
(ge)hæg, replaced by haga (as in Hague Hall 41 *supra*), both meaning
'enclosure'. HAIGH MOOR & WOOD, *The Hague Moor* 1764 *Glebe*,
Haigue Moor 1771 M, *Haigh Wood* 1841 O.S., *v.* prec., mōr, wudu.
HANGING ROYD WELL, cf. Hanging Royd 138 *supra.* HEALEY
CROFT, *Hily-, Hilicroft* Ed 1 BM, 1348 YD i (possibly identical with
or influenced by *leʒ Helay* 1462 YD i), 'hilly croft', *v.* hyll, -ig, croft.
HESKETH HO, 'horse race-course', *v.* hestr, skeið. HOPEFIELD HO.
IVY ROYD. JAW HILL. LOWFOLD. MANOR HO. MILL LANE.
MOOR GRANGE. MOOR KNOLL, *knol* Ed 1 BM, *v.* cnoll 'hillock'.
NOOK. OLD HALL. PILDEN LANE, 1841 O.S., *Pil(e)dhill(e)* Ed 1
BM, 1348 YD i, 'bare poor hill' from ME *piled* 'bare, poor (of
pasture)', hyll; the modern form is due to dissimilation of *-l*. RED
PIT. REIN RD, *v.* reinn 'boundary strip'. ROYSTON HILL.
SMITHY LANE, 1841 O.S., *v.* smiððe. SPINK WELL LANE, 1841
O.S., ME *spynke* 'finch', wella, cf. *Spynkwell* 154, Ouzelwell 137
supra; in some instances of this common p.n. we may have dial.
spink 'a bog hole'. SPRING BOTTOM. SPRING WOOD, 1841 O.S.,
v. spring 'plantation'. LOWER & UPPER STREET, 1841 O.S.,
Lower Street is the road to Rothwell, Upper Street that to Wakefield.
STUBBS WOOD. SYKE BECK, *v.* sīc 'stream'. TINGLEY COMMON,
1841 O.S., *v.* Tingley *supra*, ME *commun* 'common land'. TOP-

CLIFFE GRANGE & HILL, cf. *Topcliffe Hall, Moor* 1817 M, *v.* Topcliffe *supra.* TOP FOLD FM. UPPER GREEN, 1841 O.S., *Owrgrene* 1577 Tayl, *v.* uferra, grēne². WATERING LANE. WHITE ROW. WHITTINGLEY QUARRY. WHO COULD HAVE THOUGHT IT (a tavern). WINDMILL HILL. WOODHOUSE HALL, *Wodehusknol* 1297 WCR, *Wodhous(e) (Crofte)* 1552 YD i, *Woodas hill* 1736 PRRth, *v.* wudu, hūs, cnoll 'hillock'. WOODHOUSE LANE, *Wodhous layn* 1552 YD i, *v.* prec., lane. WOODKIRK BECK, *Woodkirke becke* 1637 DodsN, *v.* Woodkirk *supra,* bekkr.

FIELD-NAMES

The principal forms in (*a*) are 1708 *WYEnr* 9. Spellings dated 1208, 1234 are FF, Hy 3, Ed 1, 1317 BM, 1298 WCR, 14, 1309, 1348 YD i, 1321 YD vi, 1358 *WCR* 2, 1411 YD x.

(*a*) Broom Close, Calf Close, Dunningley Piece 1764 *Glebe* (*v.* Dunningley *supra,* pece), Ingffields, Pasture House 1817 M, Sparling croft & house, Spring Ing, Streethey Close (*v.* Street *supra*), Tenterlaw.

(*b*) *Habraham hoxegange* 14 (the pers.n. *Abraham, v.* ox-gang), *Alkeltoft'* 1348 (the ODan pers.n. *Alfkil,* topt 'enclosure'), *le Balk* 1348 (*v.* balca 'boundary ridge'), *Barweforlangges, le Est-, le Westbarforlang'* 1348 (*v.* bearu 'wood', furlang), *le Benebites* 1348 (*v.* bēan, bita 'piece of land'), *le Beneyerde* Hy 3 (*v.* bēan, geard), *Birkeleygrene* 1298 (*v.* birki, lēah, grēne²), *Borisuttslem* 14, *Brumalfrode* Hy 3 (probably the ON pers.n. *Brynjólfr, Brunólfr,* rod¹), *Caluecroft* 1208 (*v.* calf, croft), *Cardinelsal* (a wood), *Cardinalrode* 1234 (held by *Richard Cardinal, v.* (ge)fall (-*sal* is no doubt a misreading of -*fal*), rod¹), *Caulwelcroft* 1411 (*v.* cawel 'cole, cabbage', croft), *Chumpewelle* Ed 1 (cf. ModE *chump* 'a thick lump of wood', *v.* wella, the name may mean much the same as the common Stockwell), *Crossefurlangs* 1348 (*v.* cros, furlang), *Ed(e)wardrode* 1309, 1348 (the ME pers.n. *Edward* (OE *Ēadweard*), rod¹), *le Forlang'* 1348 (*v.* furlang), *Forms wood* 1414 Brett, *Frilay* 1348, *le Ganstedes* 1348 (*v.* gagn-staðr 'meeting place, place of a trial'), *Geffraycroft* 1411 (the ME pers.n. *Geoffrey,* croft), *Gossacre* 1411 (*v.* æcer), *le Hedland* 1411 (*v.* hēafod-land), *le Hille* 1348 (*v.* hyll), *le Hold Halb'* 1321, *Ingflat* 1208, *Yngetherd* 1321, *les Justynglandes* 1358 (ME *iusting* 'jousting', land), *Kirketh* (a path) 13 YD ix, *Langemeregrene* 1234 (*v.* lang, mere 'pool', grēne²), *Longcarr'* 1411 (*v.* lang, kjarr 'marsh'), *Longsnype* 1348, -*suyp* 1411 (e.ModE *snip* 'a small piece', probably 'a small piece of ground'), *Mapelwelflate* 1317 (*v.* mapel, wella, flat), *le Mathoureng* 1411 (ON maðra 'madder', eng), *the Merebrigge* 1298 (*v.* mere 'pool', brycg), *Mooredoles* 1637 *Bodl* 113 (*v.* mōr, dāl), *Nikcroft* (the pers.n. *Nick,* croft), *Northend* 1411 (*v.* norð, ende), *le Northsyde* 1411 (*v.* sīde), *le Orpittes* 1348 (*v.* ōra² 'ore', pytt), *Pasmaracre* 1411 (*v.* æcer), *Pichel* 1309 (*v.* pightel 'enclosure'), *Ricardengge* 1411 (the ME pers.n. *Ricard,* eng), *Robcroft* 1411 (the

ME pers.n. *Robbe*, croft), *Scorflat* 1208 (*v.* skor 'a rift, a ditch', flat), *pontem Selde* 1138–47 YCh viii, *les Shaghenges* 1358 (*v.* sceaga 'copse', eng), *Symhallroyde* 1411 (the ME pers.n. *Simme* (from *Simon*), hall, rod[1]), *le Stanynis* 1348, *Ticheboyacre* 1348 (*v.* æcer), *Tillewelle toftes* Ed 1, 1411, *Tilwelhille*, *-toft* 1348 (*v.* til 'useful', wella, topt, hyll), *Tingleyligeyate* 1627 WillY (*v.* hlid-geat 'swing-gate'), *Welleyherd* 1411 (*v.* wella, geard), *Westharfurlang*' 1411, *le Westrod* 1414 Brett (*v.* west, rod[1]), *Westeroxgang* 13 AD iv (*v.* westerra, ox-gang), *le Wetends* 1348 (*v.* wēt 'wet', ende), *Wetemerssh* 1411 (*v.* wēt 'wet', mersc), *le Wildehauerlandes* 1358 ('wild oat lands', *v.* hafri, land ; cf. a similar f.n. 173 *supra*; they may be identical), *le Wytflat* 1321 (*v.* hwīt, flat).

x. Batley

Batley is now a separate municipal borough and includes the old townships of Batley, Birstall (from Birstall parish in Morley Wapentake) and part of Upper Soothill (from Dewsbury parish 196 *infra*). Morley is now a separate municipal borough and includes the old townships of Morley (182 *infra*) from the parish of Batley, Ardsley (174 *supra*), Churwell (iii, 222 *infra*) and Gildersome (iii, 223 *infra*) (both from the part of Batley parish in Morley Wapentake), and Drighlington (from Birstall parish iii, 19 *infra*).

1. BATLEY (102–2324)

> *Bathelie* 1086 DB, *-leia*, *-lay* 13 YD ix, 1270 Ebor, *Bathaleia* 1216 Nost 5
> *Batelei(a)*, *-ley(a)*, *-lai(a)*, *-lay*, *-l'* 12 Nost 7d, 14, 73 (YCh 1435, etc.), 1188–1202 YCh viii, 1191 P (p), 1208–37 Nost 40, 1226 FF, 1248 Nost 41, 43, 1252, 1276 Ebor, 1280 Ass 6, Ch *et passim* to 1448 YD ix
> *Batteleg'*, *-lai*, *-le(y)* 1202 FF (p), 1215 ChR, 1246 Ass 3, 1286 Ebor, 1401 Calv, 1533 WillY
> *Batley*, *-lay* 1315 YD i, 1322 Abbr, 1362 Nost 27, 1401 BM *et passim* to 1533 WillY, (*Upper-*) 1817 M

'Bata's forest-glade', *v.* lēah. OE *Bata* is once recorded as the byname of a Winchester monk, *Ælfric qui Bata cognominabatur*, and once as *Bate* on a burial pyramid at Winchester. *Bate* occurs as a pers.n. in 1313 WCR iii, 3 (Ossett), and (*le*) *Bat* was a common nickname in ME, but the names are not necessarily identical; their origin is obscure (*v.* Redin 131, Reaney 24–5, Tengvik 287). OE *Bata* appears in certain other p.ns. like Badcombe So (*æt Batancumbræ* c. 965–71 BCS 1174), Batcombe Do 222, Battenhall Wo 162, etc. 'Upper' refers to Upper Batley.

CARLINGHOW, *Kerlinghow(e)* 1303 KF, 1315 YD i, 1427 YD xii, 234, *-hawe* 1379 PT (p), *Carlinghou, -yng-* 1303 Aid, *-how(e)* 1361 *Ass* 2, 1363 DodsN, 1612 FF, *-hawe* 1552 FF, *-all* 1558 TestLds, *Kerlynghawe* 1348 YD vi (p), *-howe* 1372 FF. 'Old woman mound', *v.* kerling, haugr, cf. Carling Howe YN 151.

HEALEY, *Helei, -lay(e)* 12 YCh 1820, 1246 *Ass* 4 (p), 1348 YD vi, 1375 YD xii, 255 *et freq* to 1557 TestLds, *Heylees* 1284 WCR (p), *Healey* 1582 WillY, 1677 Misc ii. 'High lofty clearing', *v.* hēah, lēah. This p.n. is common in this wapentake and the spellings cannot always be certainly identified, esp. as it is also a frequent local f.n. (*Heley*, etc. 162, 172 *supra*, 188, 249, etc. *infra*).

PURLWELL LANE, *Pirlewelle* 1246–55 *Nost* 41, *Purlwell Hall* 1822 Langd, cf. also *Pirlwelle* 229 *infra*, both early references to e.ModE *purl*, also dial. *pirl, prill*, sb. 'a small agitated rill' (from 1552), *purl* vb. (of water) 'to flow with whirling motion' (from 1586, NED s.v.), cf. Norw *purla* 'to bubble up, gush out', Swed dial. *porla* 'to murmur'. Ekwall (RN 333), who also notes *le Pirle* 1301 (Sa) and *Pirlewallsiche* c. 1300 (St), discusses these words (which seem to have an echoic origin) in relation to the r.n. Prill He; it is possible that Purlpit W 116 (*Purlepittes* 1634) and Purl Ing 210, etc. *infra* have a similar source. It is not unlikely that the various Purwells (Hrt 4, 10, O 253), and *Perwell* 217 *infra* etc., contain the root word *pire* (cf. Norw *pira* 'trickle') as does Pur Brook St (OE *Pire broc* BCS 890, cf. RN 333) rather than the OE *pirige* 'pear-tree' which is usually proposed, and would be equivalent in sense to Purlwell, 'bubbling spring or stream', *v.* wella. Although the cognates are Scandinavian, the distribution of the English examples points rather to an OE **pyrle* or **pirle*.

WOODSOME (lost), *Wo(u)dusme* (*infra diuis' de Batel'*) 1248 *Nost* 41, 43, *Wodesum* 1249 ib 43, *-om* 1542 FF, *Batel' Wodehus'* l. 13 *Nost* 42d, *Wodoson* 1379 PT (p), *Woodsome* 1545 *WB* 101, *Woddersome* 1548 WillY, *Wothersome* 1558 TestLds, *Woodowsome* 1689 Misc ii. '(At) the houses in the wood', *v.* wudu, hūs, -um, cf. Woodsome 268, Wothersome pt. iv *infra*.

BANK FOOT, cf. *the Middlebancke* 1675 Misc ii, *v.* banke.   BATLEY BECK, *v.* bekkr.   BATLEY CARR, 1765 PREm, *Batley Carre* 1631, 1635 Comm, *v.* kjarr 'marsh'.   BATLEY HALL, 1676 *Grant* 133, *-Halle*

1564 Visit, *v.* hall.   BLAKERIDGE LANE.   BOGGARD FIELDS & Ho.
BROOKROYD, *Brokerodes* 1448 YD ix, *Brookeroydes* 1620 FF, *Brook
Royde* 1656 Pick, *v.* brōc, rod[1] 'clearing'.   BROWN HILL.   CARLING-
HOW SHAW, *Carlinghow Chase* 1843 O.S.   CARLTON GRANGE.
CHAPEL FOLD, 1817 M, *v.* chapel, fald.   CLERK GREEN.   CLIFFE
Ho, cf. *Medylclyf* 1315 YD i, *v.* middel, clif.   COAL PIT LANE.
CROSS BANK.   DRYFIELD Ho.   EALAND Ho.   FIELD LANE, named
from *Batley Feild* 1695 WYD, *v.* feld.   GARFIELD Ho.   HICK
LANE.   HIGHFIELD MILL.   HILBEROYD RD, *Ilbertroyde Field* 1713
WYEnr 78, *the Ilbe Royd Field* 1803 *EnclA* 138, the ME pers.n.
Ilbert, rod[1].   HOLLIN BANK LANE, cf. *Holling Sike Ing* 1695 WYD,
v. holegn 'holly', sīc 'stream', eng 'meadow'.   HOWDEN CLOUGH
FM, *Holden Cloughe* 1546 FF, *v.* Howden Clough (Birstall) iii, 15
infra.   HOWLEY PARK, *Howley Parke* 1659 Pick, *v.* Howley Hall 182
infra.   HYRST Ho.   HYRSTLANDS.   INGS RD, *the Ing* 1689 Misc ii,
v. eng 'meadow'.   IVY BANK.   THE JAIL, *White Lee Goal* 1841
O.S., cf. Gaol Croft 147 *supra.*   KILPIN HILL, *Killpin Hill* 1843
O.S., possibly an old Celtic hill-name (*v.* cil 'nook', penno- 'hill'),
but Kilpin YE is of English origin ('calf pen', *v.* celf, penn).   LAMP-
LANDS, *Lump Lands* (sic) 1843 O.S.   LITTLE WOOD.   LONGLANDS
RD, *ye Long lands* 1689 Misc ii, *v.* lang, land.   LOW FOLD.   NOOK,
The Nook 1843 O.S., *v.* nōk.   OLD HALL.   RAMSILL Ho.   RIDING
MILLS.   RODS WOOD.   SHAY TERRACE, *v.* sceaga 'copse'.   SOUTH
FIELD.   SPRING MILL, 1843 O.S., *v.* spring 'plantation'.   SPY
FIELD Ho.   STAINCLIFFE, *Steynclif* 1342 Tayl, *Staneclif* 1548
TestLds, *Stainclife* 1587 WillY, *-cliffe* 1620 FF, 1695 WYD, *v.*
steinn 'stone', clif, cf. Stonecliff 207, Staincliffe pt. vi *infra.*   STAIN-
CLIFFE HALL, *Hall* 1843 O.S.   STILL Ho, 1843 O.S.   STOCKS
LANE.   STOCKWELL SHAY.   SUNNY BANK RD, *Sunny Bank* 1817 M.
THORNCLIFFE.   THROSTLE NEST.   UPLANDS.   WELLFIELD Ho.
WHITE LEE, 1677 *WB* 26, *v.* hwīt, lēah.   WIND HILL Ho.   WOOD
HALL.

FIELD-NAMES

Spellings dated 13 are *Nost* 41–3, 1315 YD i, 1653, 1675 Misc ii, 68, 75,
1695 WYD, 1713 *WYEnr* 78.

(*a*) Havercroft 1822 Langd (ib 1695, *v.* hafri 'oats', croft), the mean
Ing 1713 (*v.* (ge)mǣne 'common', eng), Mousecroft 1713 (ib 1695), New
Hall 1843 O.S. (*the New House* 1695, *v.* nīwe, hūs), the old house 1713 (cf.
prec.), Pighill Croft 1861 *Sav* (*the Pighell* 1713, *v.* pightel 'small enclosure'),
Staincliffe Commons 1803 *EnclA* 138 (cf. Staincliffe *supra*).

(b) *Alrychcroft* 1315 (the OE pers.n. *Ælfric*, ME *A(i)lrich*, croft), *Batley Height* 1694 *WB* 29 (v. hēhŏu 'height'), *Batelaykirk* 1367 (v. kirkja), *the Birkin Flatt* 1675 (v. bircen, flat), *the Bromebancke* 1675 (v. brōm, banke), *Cafurlang* 1315 (v. furlang), *the Conny Garth* 1675 (v. coning-erth 'warren'), *Cornewell* 1551 TestLds (v. cran 'crane', wella), *Gamelrode* 12 YCh 1820 (the ME pers.n. *Gamel* (ON *Gamall*), rod[1]), *Haterode* 13 (the ME byname *Hat(t)e* (Bardsley 144), rod[1]), *Helayschae* 13 (v. Healey *supra*, sceaga 'copse'), *Kirketoftes* 13 (v. *Batelaykirke* (*supra*), topt 'enclosure'), *the Longsyk* 1315 (v. lang, sīc 'stream'), *Lower Crofts* 1675, *Meaner Sike* 1695, ye *Milngate* 1315 (v. myln, gata), *Musholme* 1315 (v. mūs 'mouse', perhaps as a pers.n., holmr), *the Paddocke* 1675 (v. pearroc), *Rosefeild* 1653, 1655 WillS, *Schyle-fold* 1315 (v. fald), *Seven lands, Six land* 1695 ('seven, six lands of the common field', v. land), *Sudrode* 13, *Southroyde Feild* 1695 (v. sūð, rod[1]), *the Wheatcroft* 1675 (v. hwǣte, croft).

2. MORLEY (102–2627)

Morelei(a) 1086 DB, *Morlai, -lay, -lei, -ley, -leg(a)* 1121 Tockw, 1121–7 YCh 1428, 1189 *Nost* 4d, 1190–1210 YCh 1618, l. 12 *Nost* 40, 1199 ChR, 1202 FF, 13, c. 1207 Kirkst, 1208 FF, 1215 ChR, 1226 FF, 1280 Ch, 1285 KI *et passim* to 1504 FF. 'Glade or clearing on the moor', v. mōr, lēah. Morley, although itself in Agbrigg Wapentake, gave its name to Morley Wapentake iii, 1 *infra*. The actual wapentake meeting place may well have been at Tingley (175 *supra*) just over a mile from Morley.

FINSDALE PLANT., *Fi-, Fyncheden(e)* 1226 FF, 1347 Calv, 1379 PT (p), 1504 *WB*, FF, 1605 FF, *Finchesden(e)* 1246 *Ass* 26, 1252 Ebor, c. 1254 *Nost* 75, *Fy-, Finchden* 1612, 1618 FF. 'Finch valley' from OE *finc* 'finch' and denu (the latter being replaced by dalr in modern times, as in Arkendale pt. v, Lothersdale pt. vi *infra*). Finchley Mx 92 has a similar fluctuation in form between *Finche-* and *Finches-*; it may be noted that OE *Finc* is used as a byname in OE *Godric Finc* (Tengvik 362) and this pers.n. could in fact be the immediate source of the first el. of Finsdale.

HOWLEY HALL, *Honeley* (sic for *Houe-*) 1252 Ebor, *Houelai* c. 1254 *Nost* 75, *Hauleye* 1283 Ch, *Howley* 1425, 1461 DodsN, 1504, 1612 FF, (*-Hall*) 1546 WillY, *Holey* 1459, 1462 Test ii, 1537 FF, (*-als. Hough-ley*) 1564 FF, *Holly* 1504 *WB*, *Holley* 1520 WillY, *Hooley* 1595 SessnR. Probably 'woodland glade or clearing where ground-ivy grew', v. hōfe, lēah. The exact meaning of OE hōfe is not known, but it is once equated with *viola* 'violet' and in e.ModE with ground ivy

(NED s.v. *hove*), still called *ale-hoof*; ale-hoof was said to be used in brewing instead of hops. At an early date pre-consonantal *-f-* (ME *-v-*) was vocalised and resulted in ME *Howe-* (cf. Jordan § 216, 1) and other later spellings which show an inverted confusion with haugr 'mound' and hol[1] 'hollow'.

SCHOLECROFT, *Squalecroft* 1226 FF, *Scalecroft* 1252 Ebor, *Schalecroft* c. 1254 *Nost* 75, Ed 1 Arm, *Sk-, Scolecroft* 1261 YI, 1478 YD ii, 1563 YD iii, *Scholekroft* 1266 YI, *Scoylcroft* 1456 DodsN, *Scolescroft* 1463 YD iii, *Scolcroft* 1542 FF. 'Small enclosure with a shed', *v.* skáli, croft.

BANTAM GROVE, 1843 O.S.   BIRKBY BROW, *Buckley Brow* (sic) 1843 *TA*.   BIRKS, cf. *Birk Lane* 1843 *TA, v.* birki 'birch-tree'.   BROAD OAKS.   BRUNTCLIFFE, 1656 Pick, 1843 *TA, Borneclif* 1539 TestLds, *Brunclyffe, -cliff* 1545 WillY, 1675 Og, *Brancklift* 1643 ib, *Bruncliffe-Thorn* 1822 Langd, possibly OE burna or ON brunnr 'stream' clif, though the topography would rather suggest brant 'steep'; it refers to a steep bank overlooking Howley Beck; the *Thorn* is now Bruntcliffe Thorn.   BURN KNOLLS, *Burn Knowles* 1843 *TA*, possibly *burna* 'stream' but more probably bruni 'burnt place', cnoll 'hillock'.   CHAPEL HILL, cf. *Chapel Flatt & Lane* 1843 *TA*.   CLAY LANE, cf. *Clay Ings* 1843 *TA, v.* clæg, eng.   CLUBBED OAKS, 1843 *TA, Clubedhac* 13 Kirkst, 'massive or knobbed oaks', from ME *clubbed*, āc.   CROFT HO.   DAISY HILL, cf. *Daisy Close* 1843 *TA*. DEAN BECK, DEANFIELD, cf. *Dean Close* 1843 *TA, v.* foll.   DEAN HALL, 1843 O.S., *v.* denu 'valley'.   DEAN WOOD, 1843 *TA, v.* prec. DENSHAW HO.   FERNDALE.   GILLROYD, 1843 O.S., *TA, v.* rod[1]. HEMBRIGG QUARRY, *Embrigg Quarries* 1843 O.S., *Hembridge* 1843 *TA*.   HIGHFIELD.   HUGHENDEN.   LOW LAITHS, *Low Laithe* 1843 O.S., *v.* hlaða 'barn'.   LOW MOOR, cf. *Moor Plain* 1843 *TA*.   LOW TOWN END, 1843 O.S., *Town End Close* 1843 *TA*.   MORLEY SPRING WOOD, *Morley Spring* 1843 O.S., *v.* spring 'plantation'.   NEPSHAW LANE, *Nepesatherode* (sic for *-sache-*) c. 1207 Kirkst, *Nepshaw* 1555 TestLds, *Nipshaw* 1843 *TA*, probably from nēp 'turnip', sceaga 'copse', but cf. Nibshaw iii, 22.   NEW HO.   NEWLANDS.   OLD-ROYD, *Olderode* Ed 1 BM, 'old clearing', *v.* ald, rod[1].   OWLERS, OWLERS BECK, *v.* alor 'alder-tree'.   PARKFIELD MILLS.   ROOMS, 1817 M, *le Ruhm* 1202 FF, *Rowms Lane* 1843 *TA, v.* rūm 'an open space, a clearing'.   SCARTHINGWELL, cf. Scarthingwell pt. iv *infra*.

SCOTCHMAN LANE, 1843 *TA*.   SPRINGFIELD HO, cf. *Spring Close*
1843 *TA*, *v.* spring 'plantation'.   STREET FM, on the Wakefield–
Bradford road, called Upper Street 177 *supra*.   STUMP CROSS, 1822
Langd, *v.* cros.   SUMMERFIELD.   THORNFIELD, cf. *Thorn Close* 1843
TA.   WELL HILL, cf. *Well Cliffe* 1843 *TA*, *v.* wella, clif.   WINTER-
BOURNE.

FIELD-NAMES

The principal forms in (*a*) are 1843 *TA* 291.

(*a*) Asty Close, Upper & Low Barker, Barker Hill Shrogg, Bawhole,
Birket Garth, Botany Bay, Boyles, Broadland Balk, Brook Croft, Broom
Hill, Brown Royd, Bungate, Buntake, Calf Croft, Cinder Hills, Cliffe Wood,
Coal Pit Close, Colling Royd, Cross Hall 1843 O.S. (ib 1817 M), Dog Close,
Duffield, Fog Close (*v.* fogga 'aftermath, tall thin grass') Foul Syke,
Four Lanes End 1843 O.S., Four Royds, Gill Bottom, Gore Nook, Hacker,
Haigh Close, Hall Toft, Hard Flat, Hatchet, Hawk Stile, Hay Bottom, Helm
Croft (*v.* helm 'cattle shelter', croft), Hilly Rods, Hullar Bank & Flatt,
Hunger Hill (*Hungirhill* 1202 FF, *v.* hungor, hyll), Hunter Lands, Hurle-
butts, Joan Royd, Lady Ann Well, Lead House Croft, Lingy Close (*v.* lyng
'heather'), Little Half, Upper Mere, Mill Close & Lane, Milner Royd,
Nop Royd, Nutty Royd, The Paddock, Pales Bottom, Pease Croft (*v.*
pise, croft), Pickhill (*v.* pightel 'enclosure'), Pith Hill (*v.* prec.), Pond
Ings, Quarr Close, Round Brig, Rowan Bridge, Rowlands, The Ruins
(*Howley Hall in ruins* 1822 Langd), Salter Well Close, Smock, Sour Ing,
Spide Croft, Spot (*v.* spot 'bit of land'), Spout Croft (*v.* spoute), Steel
Gates (*v.* stigel, gata or geat), Swinehurst, Swine Park, Tenter Garth,
Ward Ing, Wheat Croft, Whetstone Well, Wilfrey, Windmill Close, Wood
Park.

(*b*) *The Newefeld* 1556 TestLds, *Nordhlane* l. 12 *Nost* 40 (*v.* norð, lane),
the Quakers Sepulture 1675 Og, *Schaes* 13 *Nost* 40d (*v.* sceaga 'copse'),
Wilmerecroft 1190–1210 YCh 1618, 13 Kirkst, *Wlmercroft* c. 1207 ib, ME
pers.n. *Wilmer* (OG *Uillimar*), croft).

xi. Dewsbury

Dewsbury is now a county borough which includes all the townships of
the parish (except Ossett, now a municipal borough, and part of Upper
Soothill 196 *infra*, which is now in the municipal borough of Batley 179
supra) as well as Thornhill 210 *infra*. Part of Dewsbury parish was in Morley
Wapentake iii, 3 *infra*.

1. DEWSBURY (102–2422) ['diuzbəri, 'dauzbəri]

Deusberia, -ie 1086 DB, *-burc* 1210–25 YCh viii, *-bury* 1293 DodsN,
    1689 Misc ii, *-bery* 1454 YD xii, 243

Dewesbiri, -y, -byry 1091–7 YCh viii, 1147 YCh viii, 13 YD xii,
  242, 1226 FF *et freq* to 1323 *Ass* 2, 1428 FA, *-beri, -y* 1147,
  1164–85, 1180–1202 YCh viii, l. 12 *Lewes* 23d, 1467 YD ii,
  1490, 1499 Test iv, *-bir(e)* 1230 Ebor, 1246 *Ass* 14, 1267 *Lewes*
  34d *et freq* to 1330 ib 38d, *-bury* 1316 Pat, 1348 FF, 1409
  DiocVisit

Deuhesbir' 12 Font   *Deuwythbiris* 1190 YCh 1748

Dawesberg (sic) 1164–81 YCh viii

Deuwesbyr(y) 1194–9 YCh viii, 1197 (1301) Ebor, 1314, 1323 YD i,
  Deuuesbury 1316 Vill

Deubir' 1202 FF   *Dewebire* 1233–40 YCh viii

Deaubir 1230 P, 1267 Ebor

Dyaubir 1267 Ebor

Dewysbir(y), -is-, -byry 1275–1323 WCR (*freq*), 1276 RH, *-bury*
  1323 WCR, 1597 SessnR, *-bery* 1401 Calv

Dowesbery, -is- 1324 *Lewes* 299d, 1564 FF

Dewsbury, -byry, -burie 1364 YD iv, 1379 PT, 1406 DodsN, 1494
  YD i *et freq* to 1605 FF

Deuse-, Dewsebery 1400 WillY, 1447 YD i, 1532 FF

Deuesbury 1466 WillY

Duesburie 1587 ib

The great majority of spellings points to *Dewesbiry* being the older
form, but there has been a certain amount of analogical transforma-
tion in such spellings as *Deau-, Dyaubir* with OE **dēaw** 'dew' and
in others like *Dawesberg, Dowesbery* and a recent pronunciation
[dauz-] with ME *dawe* 'jackdaw' (cf. Daw Green *infra*). But the
single spelling *Deuwythbiris* and perhaps also *Deuhesbir* make it quite
clear that the first el. is the Welsh pers.n. *Dewi*, which is from Lat
David-; the form *Deuwyth-* suggests that the pers. name was adopted
at a time when the OWelsh dental fricative *-ð* (from *-d*) was not
completely lost, but the date of this loss is not certain, as the loss
of final spirants in Welsh is rather fluctuating (cf. Jackson 426–7,
618–19). This Welsh pers.n. occurs in its OWelsh form *Dewi* in certain
p.ns. on the Welsh border, such as Dewchurch and Dewsall He ('St
David's church and well'). The burh 'fortification, fortified place',
was on the north side of the Calder as was Horbury, but no trace of
any such fort remains. On the midland form *-bury* cf. Horbury 150
supra.

BOOTHROYD, *Bouderode* 1274–1327 WCR (*freq*), *Buderode* 1296 ib (p), *Bowderode* 1379 PT (p), *Bowdroyd grene* 1525 *Surv*, -*roide* 1577 *WB* 51, 1590 WillY, *Bothrod* 1527 ib, *Bawdroid* 1592 ib, *Boothroyd* 1681 YD i, (-*Upper and Lower*) 1822 Langd, *Nether, Over Buth-, Bouthroyd* 1709 WMB. 'Clearing with a shed or booth', from OWScand **búð, rod**[1]. This p.n. occurs several times in YW, usually with the ODan form **bōth** (which has also in this name supplanted the ONorw form).

CROW NEST, 1771 M, *Crownest* 1636 WillY, 1712 WB. 'Crow nest', *v.* **crāwe**, **nest**. The name is repeated several times in YW, i, 294, ii, 153 *supra*, iii, 81, (Lawkland) pt. vi *infra*, Crow Nest Wood iii, 190, Crows Nest ii, 204 *infra*. Most of these places are well sited on the slopes of hillsides, sometimes on high ground, sometimes as at Crow Nest (Worsborough) or Crow Nest Wood (Hebden Bridge) iii, 190 on the lower part of steep banks near the valley bottom. In some cases therefore, the name probably signifies a place on higher ground with a good view (as in Crowneast Wo 91 in the highest part of the parish or as in e.ModE *crow's nest*); in some (like Crow Nest Wood) it means no more than 'rookery' or the like, and in others it is a p.n. type, containing *nest* in the figurative sense of 'residence, retreat' (evidenced from OE times); in YW this last type is very common, as in Eagle Nest, Glead Nest, Martin's Nest, Owl Nest, Rook's Nest, Swallow Nest, Throstle Nest, and was clearly in a fashionable mode of naming houses; the earliest YW reference to this usage is 1320 for *Haukenest* (Monk Fryston) pt. iv *infra*.

DAW GREEN, 1817 M, *Dawgreen(e)* 1658 WillS, 1709 WMB, 1740 *WB* 2006. The material for this name and *Daw Green* (Crigglestone) 102 *supra* is not easy to differentiate. Both names have the same origin, l.ME *dawe* 'jackdaw', **grēne**[2].

AMROYD HILL.   BECKET NOOK.   BROAD DAM.   BURGH MILLS, 1817 M.   CARR HO, *Batley Carre als. Dewsbury Carre* 1631 *Comm*, *v.* Batley Carr 180 *supra*.   CLEGGFORD BRIDGE, *Clegg Ford* 1771 M, a bridge carrying the Dewsbury–Thornhill road over the Calder, replacing a ford; the first el. is probably the common YW surname *Clegg* (cf. Battye Ford 198 *infra*) or ON **klegg* 'clay'.   DEWSBURY MOOR, 1817 M, *Dewsbury more* 1635 *Comm*, *Duesburymoor* 1800 PRHtsd, *v.* **mōr**, Moor End *infra*.   DEWSBURY MOOR HO, formerly *Moor Grove* 1843 O.S.   FALL LANE.   GRIMSTONE LODGE, 1843

O.S.   HEALD'S HO.   HILL HEAD FM.   KNOWLES HILL, 1843
O.S., *Knowls Lump* 1817 M, *v.* cnoll 'hillock'.   LIDGATE LANE, *le*
Lydtyatplat 1364 YD i, *Lyedeyhate* 1405 *WCR* 10, *the Lydyate* 1525
Surv, *v.* hlid-geat 'swing-gate'.   LIGHTHOUSE.   LONG CAUSEWAY.
MOOR BOTTOM, MOOR END, cf. *Dew(e)sbury Moor(e)side* 1639 WillY,
1771 M, *v.* Dewsbury Moor *supra*, botm, sīde.   PILGRIM FM, *Pilgrim*
Cottage 1843 O.S.   PINFOLD HILL.   PISMIRE HILL, *Pissmire-Hill*
1822 Langd, ME *pissemire* 'an ant', hyll; l.ME *pysmeryshylle* is
glossed *formicarium* 'ant-hill' (NED s.v.).   RAVENS WHARF, 1843
O.S., cf. Ravensthorpe 192 *infra*.   SANDS LANE, *the Sand*' 1525
Surv, *v.* sand; it is on the bank of the Calder.   SCARR END LANE,
v. Scarr End 194 *infra*.   SCHOLEFIELD BRIDGE.   SCOUT HILL, *v.*
skúti 'projecting cliff'.   STEANARD, 1803 *EnclA*, *Steuer* (sic for
Stener) 1364 YD iv, *v.* stæner 'rocky place', cf. Stennard Well 151
supra.   TATTERSFIELD BRIDGE.   WATERGATE.   WEBSTER HILL.
WESTBOROUGH.   WEST TOWN.

FIELD-NAMES

The principal forms in (*a*) are 1849 *TA* 131. Spellings dated 1525 are
Surv 10, 7, 1631, 1635 *Comm.*

(*a*) Balk Hill 1843 O.S. (ib 1822 Langd, *v.* balca 'boundary ridge', hyll),
Birking Bank, Britton Close, Brook Hole, Flatts, Four Lands, Great & Little
Ing (*v.* eng 'meadow'), Knowl Pighill (possibly identical with *Nell Pighell*
1525, *v.* Knowles Hill *supra*, pightel 'enclosure'), Longlands, Louse Croft,
Low Harts Hole, Ratcliffe Close, Rough Riding, Rye Close, Smithy Close,
Spink-well 1822 Langd (*Spinkewell houses* 1635, ME *spynke* 'finch', wella,
cf. Ouzelwell 137 *supra*), Tenter Croft, Waterside Close, Wood Croft.

(*b*) *Allebaildon-*, *Allabaydon-close* 1631, *Allabandon close* 1635 (obscure,
but perhaps a jocular name 'all abandon close'), *Barnardes landes* 1635 (the
ME pers.n. *Bernard*, land), *the Brome Feild* 1525 (*v.* brōm, feld), *Brookroyd*
1525 (*v.* brōc, rod[1]), *Crabtree Closse* 1525 (*v.* crabbe, perhaps *Crabtree* as a
surname as often in YW), *Crimbles* 1525 (*v.* crymel 'small plot'), *Deuwesbyr'*
brok 1323 YD i (*v.* brōc), *Dewesburi-*, *Deusbiriwode* 1323 *MinAcct* 45, 1329
WCR (*v.* wudu), *the Kettledge* 1525 (*v.* ketill 'kettle', ecg, or the ME pers.n.
Ketel, ON *Ketill*), *the kinges common* 1635 (the witness 'verily thinketh it is
the kinges inheritance', ib 5764, m. 6), *Lynlandes* 1635 (*v.* līn 'flax', land),
Makerode 13 YD xii, 242 (the ME pers.n. *Makke* (as in the Towneley Shepherd's Play), rod[1]), *The Sett* 1576 WillY (*v.* set 'dwelling, camp, fold', but
possibly here in one of its later senses like 'badger's earth or hole'), *Syke*
Close 1525 (*v.* sīc 'stream'), *Smal Royde* 1446 YD vii (*v.* smæl 'narrow',
rod[1]), *Southforth* 1364 YD iv (*v.* sūð, ford), *Westerwoode* 1588 WillY (*v.*
westerne, wudu), *Wulthanerod* 1226 FF (probably an OE *Wulfþegn*, rod[1]).

2. OSSETT (102–2820)

Osleset 1086 DB, *Oselesete* 13 DodsN, 1226 YD v, *Osseleset(e)*
1206–18 YCh viii, *Osolsete* 1221 ib, *Oselset* 1275 WCR
Osset(e) 1274–1321 WCR *(freq)*, 1284 AD iii, 1297 LS, 1316 Vill,
1336 FF *et passim* to 1590 NCWills, *Ossett(e)* 1346 DodsN,
1364 YD i, 1458 YD vi *et freq* to 1641 Rates
Awsett 1611, 1618 FF

The first el. is doubtless OE ōsle 'ouzel, thrush', although Ekwall
(DEPN) suggests an OE pers.n. *Ōsla* (a derivative of *Ōsa*, etc. and
equivalent to OHG *Ansila*) for this p.n. and Ozleworth Gl. Although
worð (as in Ozleworth) is mostly compounded with pers.ns. it is not
exclusively so, and OE (*ge*)*set* 'dwelling, camp, fold' seems to be
combined mostly with significant words, so that most probably
Ossett is 'fold frequented by thrushes' but could be 'Ōsla's fold'.

OSSETT STREET-NAME: HIGH ST, *the high Street* 1709 WMB.

GAWTHORPE, *Goukethorp(e)* 1274–1307 WCR *(freq)*, *Gouc-*, *Gouk-*
thorp(e) 1276 RH, 1325 WCR, *Gaukethorp* 1313, 1326 ib, *Gawk-*,
Gauthorp(e) 14 DodsN, 1588 WillY, 1590 NCWills, *Gawthrope* 1636
WillY, *-thorpe* 1709 WMB. 'Cuckoo farm', *v.* **gaukr**, **þorp**, and
Gawthorpe 102 *supra*.

HEALEY, *Heley*, *-lay* 1327 WCR (p), 1332 Arm (p), 1379 PT (p),
Healay, *-ley* 1525 Surv, 1683 YD i, *Mikil-*, *Littilheley* 1529 FF,
possibly the *Hely* in e. 15 Towneley xii, 244, but there are several
Healeys in this wapentake with which it could be identified (cf.
Index). 'High clearing', *v.* **hēah**, **lēah**; cf. Healey (Batley) 180 *supra*.

OSSETT LIGHTS (lost), *the Comon called the Lightes* 1525 *Surv* 10, 7,
Osset(t) L(e)ights 1709 WMB, 1757 PRHrb, cf. also *Lights Bottoms*
1846 *TA*. On this *v. Horbury Lights* 150 *supra*.

RUNTLINGS, *Runting(e)* 1525 *Surv*, 1572 WCR 6d, 1709 WMB,
-pyttes 1525 *Surv*, 1650 WCR 5d, *Runting (Park & Pighill)* 1846
TA, a compound of OE **hrunta** 'stump' (dial. *runt* 'the old stump of a
tree') and **eng** 'meadow', or an OE *hrunting* (from **hrunta** and -ing[1])
which would have much the same meaning as **stubbing** (from **stubb**
'a stump') or **stoccing** (from **stocc**); cf. OE *Hrunting*, the name of
Unferth's sword in Beowulf 1457.

SLUTTERING LANE, *Shuttering Hill* 1846 *TA*, probably identical with *Shirten crofte* (? sic for *Shitren*-) 1525 *Surv*, probably a derivative of scitere 'sewer' and hyll or even ric (as in the common *Skitterick* ii, 168 *supra*); the modern form is in error.

SOWOOD HO, *Southwood* 1301, 1364 DodsN, -*wod(e)* 1364 DodsN, 1461 *MinAcct* 60, 1492 ib 02, *Sowthwode* 1506 YD vi, -*wood* 1616 FF, *Sowod (wells)* 1525 *Surv*, 1535 VE, -*wood* 1656 PRHrb, (-*green*) 1709 WMB, *Sawwood* 1587 WillY, *Sow(e)wood* 1604 FF, (-*green(e)*)) 1639 WillY, 1665 PRHrb. 'South wood', *v.* sūð, wudu. For *green*, *v.* The Green *infra*.

BACK LANE, *Back Lane Croft* 1846 *TA*. BARMBY FOLD, possibly connected with *Northbarnebank* 1461, 1462, 1492 *MinAcct*, *v.* bere- ærn 'barn' or from the ON pers.n. *Bjarni* (*v.* Barnby Dun i 17 *supra*), banke. BOTTOM FIELD, *Bothom* 1600 WCR 9, *v.* botm (boðm). BRIDLE LANE, probably an adaptation of *Birdhill, Brid*-, *Birdleys* 1846 *TA*, *v.* bridd 'bird', hyll, lēah 'clearing'. CAVE'S WELL. CLOUGH WOOD, *v.* Holme Leas Clough *infra*. CROFT HO. CROWNLANDS, *Crowne Landes* 1600 WCR 5, cf. Crown Flatt 197 *infra*. DAY HOLE, possibly identical with *Deyhouse* 1709 WMB, 'dairy house', *v.* dey, hūs; but Day Hole is most probably dial. *day-hole* 'an adit or entry to a coalpit' (from *day* 'daylight', hence 'the outside of a mine') which occurs elsewhere in YW; there are old coal-workings here; there is an illustration of a seventeenth-century day-hole in HAS 30, 116. GREAT & LITTLE FIELD RD, cf. *Field Head* 1843 O.S. FLUSHDYKE, *the Dike* 1660 PRHrb, *v.* dīc; *Flush*- is from dial. *flush* ob. 'to clear a drain by holding back the water and releasing it suddenly' or *flush* sb. 'a stream from a mill-head' (EDD). GEDHAM MILL, *le Great, le little Geedon* 1679 WCR 5, *Geddam* 1846 *TA*. GIGGAL HILL, *Gigal Hill* 1817 M, probably named from a family called *Gigal* known in the district in the early nineteenth century (PRHrb *freq*). GILBERT DIKE. THE GREEN, *Sowood Green* 1709 WMB, *Green* 1817 M, *v.* Sowood Ho *supra*, grēne². GREEN HO. GREEN LEA. HAGGS HILL, 1817 M, *les Hagges* 1407 WCR 1, *Haggs* 1701 PRHrb, cf. *Hagbuttes* 1525 WCR 5, *Haggs butts* 1699 ib 7d, cf. *Street Haggs* (*infra*); *v.* hǫgg 'a felling of trees', dial. *hagg* 'a copse', hyll. HAGGS LANE END, 1841 O.S., *Haggs Lane* 1817 M, *v.* prec., lane, ende. HEADLANDS RD. HEALEY OLD MILL, 1843 O.S. *v.* Healey *supra*, myln. HEATH HO, named from Chickenley Heath 193 *infra*. HIGHFIELD HO. HOLME LEAS

CLOUGH, *Holm(s)ley* 1846 *TA*, *v.* holmr 'water-meadow', lēah, clōh 'dell'.   INGS MILL.   LODGE HILL, 1817 M, *v.* loge.   LONGLANDS, 1846 *TA*, *v.* lang, land.   LOW COMMON, 1841 O.S., cf. *Common End, Over Common* 1841 O.S., ME *commun* 'common land'.   LOW LAITHES, *Low Laiths* 1657 Pick, *v.* hlaða 'barn'.   MITCHELL LAITHES FM, *Mitchels-Barn* 1771 M, named from a family of *Mitchell*, common in the district from the early seventeenth century (PRHrb *freq*).   NEW PARK GRANGE, *le Newparke* 1364 YD i, *New Parke* 1591 WillY, *v.* nīwe, park, cf. Old Park *infra*.   NORTHFIELD MILLS, *le Northfeilde* 1600 *WCR* 5, *v.* norð, feld.   OLD PARK, 1817 M, *Gawthorpe Park* 1843 O.S., cf. *Parkeland(e)s* 1525 *Surv*, 1699 *WCR* 5d, *v.* New Park Grange, Gawthorpe *supra*.   OSSETT SPA, cf. *Spa Close* 1846 *TA*, a chalybeate spring.   OSSETT STREET SIDE, 1817 M, (*le, the*) *Streetside* 1638 WillY, 1650 *WCR* 5, 1665 PRHrb, cf. *Street Haggs* (*infra*), named from *the Kinges street* 1525 *Surv*, *Streete* 1649 WillY, *The Street* 1771 M, which is the Wakefield–Dewsbury road (*v.* strǣt); this is possibly the *Watlyn strete* mentioned in Towneley xxx, 126.   OWLERS, cf. *brood Oller* 1525 *Surv*, *v.* brād, alor 'alder-tree'.   OWLET HALL, 1817 M, on bird-names with hall cf. Gawthorpe 102 *supra*.   OWL HO, cf. prec.   OWL LANE, *Owl Lane Mills* 1843 O.S.   PALE SIDE, 1846 *TA*, ME *pale* 'a pale, a fence, an enclosure'.   PICKERSGILL ST, named from the family of *Pickersgill* well known here from the late seventeenth century (PRHrb 76 *et freq*).   PILDACRE HILL, 1843 O.S., *Pild ars Lane* (sic) 1709 WMB, *Lower & Upper Pildacre(s)* 1846 *TA*, probably a compound of ME *piled* 'bare, poor' (cf. Pilden 177 *supra*) and ears, and equivalent to the common f.n. Barearse; *-acre* is late substitution.   QUARRY HO, cf. *the Quarrel-, the Quarry-Feild, Quarrel flatt* 1525 *Surv* 10, 7, *Quarry Close* 1846 *TA*, *v.* quarrelle 'quarry'.   ROGER FM.   ROYDS HO, cf. *the Rode pyttes* 1525 *Surv*, *Royd Close* 1846 *TA*, *v.* rod[1] 'enclosure'.   RYECROFT VILLAS, *le Nether Rycroft* 1364 YD i, *Vpper Rye Croft* 1709 WMB, *Ryecroft Pighill & Royd* 1846 *TA*, *v.* rȳge, croft.   SHEPHERD HILL.   SPRING FIELD, cf. *Spring Close* 1846 *TA*, *v.* the nearby Spring End 152 *supra*; both are near Ossett Spa (*supra*).   STORRS HILL, 1802 PRHrb, *Storghill Close* (sic) 1699 *WCR* 7, *Storshill* 1709 WMB, *v.* storð 'plantation', hyll; *Storg-* is probably an error for *Story-* (i.e. *Storþ-*).   STREET HAGGS (lost), 1721 PRHrb, *Strethagh(es)* 1392 *MinAcct*, *Stretehages, -eȝ* 1462, 1492 ib, *-hagges* 1462 ib, 1600 *WCR* 10, *the street hagges* 1544 TestLds, *Street hagge* 1655 PRHrb, *v.* Ossett Street Side, Haggs Hill *supra*.

Town End, cf. *Town Knowl* 1846 *TA*, *Town Royd* 1709 WMB,
v. tūn, cnoll, rod[1].   Tufty Fm, *le Toftes* 1314 YD i, *Tuft* 1735
Tayl, *Tofts* 1841 O.S., *v.* topt 'enclosure'.   Westfield Mills, (*the*)
West Field 1650 WCR 10, 1807 *EnclA* 105, *v.* west, feld.   West-
wells Rd, *West Well Hill* 1846 *TA*.   Whinfield, cf. *Whynn Ginn*
1846 *TA*, *v.* hvin 'gorse', *ginn* is for *engine*.   Whitley Spring,
1846 *TA*.

FIELD-NAMES

The principal forms in (*a*) are 1846 *TA* 310. Spellings dated 1296–1327
are WCR, 1364 YD i, 1409, 1452 WCR, 1462, 1492 *MinAcct*, 1499 WCR,
1525 *Surv* 10, 7, 1551–1699 WCR, 1709 WMB, 1807 *EnclA* 105, and those
without date and source in (*b*) are 1525 *Surv* 10, 7.

(*a*) Adcock Royd (*Adkokroide* 1525 WCR, the ME surname *Adcok*, rod[1]
'enclosure'), Almond Royd (*Awmonroyde* 1525, *Hawmondroid* 1650 (the
first el. may be a form of ME *almoyn* 'alms, tenure by religious service', etc.,
but it has been confused later with ME *almande* 'almond', rod[1]), Bank End,
Bar Carrs, Barefoot Close (cf. *Barefootcrofte* 1452, the ME nickname *Barefoot* or an allusion to a poor plot of ground, *v.* croft), Barrow Cliffe (*Barracliff*
1600, *v.* beorg 'hill, barrow', clif), Batty Croft (cf. *Battye Ford* 198 *infra*,
croft), Beck Ing (*v.* bekkr, eng), Lower & Upper Bedley, Birchin Hill (ib
1525, *v.* bircen, hyll), Birchen Royd (*v.* prec., rod[1]), Blindwell Ing (*v.* blind,
wella), Brier Ing (*v.* brēr, eng), Broad Royd Pighill (*Brodroyd* 1525, *v.* brād,
rod[1], pightel 'enclosure'), Brown Lands, Burton Hagg, Low & Upper
Cherry Tree (*Cherrie tree flatt* 1600, *v.* chiri), Cold Wells, Cross Close
(*Crosseclose*, *Crosfeild* 1525, *v.* cros, feld), Dimple(well) Field (cf. *Dymple
Syke* 1525, *v.* dympel 'pool', sīc), Dobroyd (ib 1525, the ME pers.n. *Dobbe*
(from *Robert*), rod[1]), East Field 1807, Eddy Carr, Farthing Royd (ib 1807,
le Fardanrodesike 1364, *Farthingroyde* 1525, probably feorðing 'quarter,
farthing', rod[1], sīc), Fellowside, Fox Pighill (*v.* fox, pightel), Gallock Royd,
Gawthorpe Stoops (*v.* Gawthorpe *supra*, stólpi), Glead Wing (*v.* gleoda
'kite' with *wing*), Handroyd Head, Hanging Owler Pighill (*v.* hangende,
alor 'alder-tree', pightel), Haygate, Haygill Pighill, Healey Field 1807
(*Heitlay-Field*, -*closses* 1525, probably hǣð, lēah, but confused with Healey
supra), Hounley (*Longhowneley* 1600, *v.* hūne 'hoarhound', lēah), Howmires,
Great & Little Huntley (*v.* hunt(a), lēah), Issott Royd (*Issott-royde*, -*pighell*
1525, the ME fem. pers.n. *Isotte*, rod[1], pightel), Kirkbalks 1709 (*Kirkebalke*
1525, *v.* kirkja, balca 'boundary ridge'), Kirkstill (*Long-*, *Shortkirkstie*, -*stye*
1600, 1650, *v.* kirkja, stīg 'path', confused with stigel 'stile'), Laith Close &
Croft (*v.* hlaða 'barn'), Leak Stile, Lee Croft, Lower Lees (*v.* lēah), Mag-,
Megroyd (the ME fem. pers.n. *Magge*, rod[1]), Mapplewell (*Maplewelles* 1525,
v. mapel, wella), Marl Ing Royd (*v.* marle, eng, rod[1]), Moonstead, Moor
Croft, Mouling Yard, Mow Croft, Nan Jagger, Netherton 1817 M (cf. Mickletown 127 *supra*, it refers to the lower part of Ossett), Nook Ing, Oldfield,
Oldroyd Hill (*le Oldrode* 1364, *Ould royd hill* 1525, *Oldroid hill* 1650, *v.* ald,
rod[1]), Pailsmall Intake, Park Royds (cf. Old Park *supra*), Paupers Park, Pear

Tree Croft, Peaslands (*v.* pise 'pease'), Peathouse Mill 1817 M, Great &
Little Pighill (*le Pighel* 1327, *le Pichkel* 1364, *v.* pightel 'enclosure'), Priest
Pighill (*v.* prēost, pightel), Prior Ing, Raven Royd (1709, *Ravon roydes* 1525,
probably the pers.n. *Raven* (ON *Hrafn*), rod[1]), Rippling (*Riplinsyke* 1525,
Ryplyngesyke 1551, e.ModE *rippling* 'flowing in ripples', *v.* sīc), Run Butts,
The Shutts 1807 (dial. *shut* 'a division of land'), Skelman Royd, Slack Ing
(*v.* slakki 'a hollow', eng 'meadow'), Sour Close, South Dale (*Sowdill* 1525,
Over Sowdell 1699, *v.* sūð, dæl 'valley'), Staker Royd, Stony Pighill & Royd,
Swamp Pighill (*v.* sumpe 'swamp', pightel), Tail Small, Tan Pits, Tenter
Croft, Topling Butts, Warrant Close (*v.* wareine 'warren'), Wash Ings (*v.*
wæsce 'washing place', eng), Wasker Royd, Well Hole & Field, West Royd,
Wheatley, Wildman's Post (*Wyndmylnpost* 1525, *le Wilman Post* 1699,
probably 'windmill post' with metathesis, *v.* post), Winking Pighill, Wood-
head Close.

(b) *the birksteell close* (*v.* birki 'birch', stigel 'stile'), *le Byrode* 1364 ('the
town clearing', *v.* bȳ, rod[1]), *Bonderode* 1296, *-roide* 1499 (*v.* bondi 'peasant
landowner', rod[1]), *Chappell steide* 1525, *-stedes* 1600 (*v.* chapel, stede 'site'),
Clay Pitt(es) 1525, 1600, *Coolepitt closse* 1525, 1600 ('for Cole mynes there
have been diuers gotten within the graveshippe of Ossett' ib; there are still
old coal workings on the hillside above the Calder), *le Couschotcliff* 1364,
(*Hye*) *Cowshutlay* (doubtless e.ModE *cushat* 'dove', clif), *Crymbils* 1499 (*v.*
crymel 'small plot'), *Crockroodes*, *-roydes* (probably krókr 'crook, bend',
rod[1]), *Dickon royd* (the ME pers.n. *Dikkon*, rod[1]), *Dishforthe crofte* (probably
a surname from Dishforth YN 184, croft), *le Ellerschaghsik* 1364 (*v.* elri
'alder-tree', sceaga 'copse', sīc), *Fernlay close*, *Fyllie royde* (e.ModE *fillie*
'filly' (ON *fylja*), rod[1]), *the Flatt* (*v.* flat), *Fowden Landes*, *Gawkroide* 1409
(*v.* gaukr 'cuckoo', rod[1]), *Hardacres* (*v.* heard, æcer), *Haverroyde* 1525,
Havour roides 1600 (*v.* hæfer 'goat' or hafri 'oats', rod[1]), *le Heyclose, pastur*
1492, *Hobroide als. Robroide* 1572 (the ME pers.n. *Hobbe*, a variant of *Robbe*
(from *Robert*), rod[1]), *Jumble closse* (cf. Humble Jumble Row 169 *supra*), *Lee
Marled pighell* (*v.* marled, pightel), *the Meane closse* (*v.* (ge)mǣne 'common',
clos), *le Mellow Close* 1699, *Mouse pighell* 1699 (*v.* mūs, pightel), *Nelryddynge*
1525 WCR (the fem. pers.n. *Nell*, rydding 'clearing'), *Newcrofte* 1525, *le
Neu-*, *le Overneurode* 1364 (*v.* nīwe, rod[1], cf. Oldroyd f.n. *supra*), *Owld
Shawe* (*v.* ald, sceaga 'copse'), *the Rayle close* (probably *rail* in the sense
'fence'), *Reynaldgrafts* 1699 (the ME pers.n. *Rainald*, græf 'pit'), *Richard-
pyghel* 1313 (held by *Richard son of Bate* ib iii, 3, *v.* pightel), *the Nar Rye
royde* (*v.* rȳge, rod[1], *Nar* 'near'), *Sharphouse crofte*, *Stretbrode* 1462 (*v.*
Ossett Street Side *supra*, brǣdu), *the Tenn Landes* (*v.* tēn 'ten', land 'a strip
of the common field'), *le Walmeregaterode* 1364, *Walton Rydings* 1600 (*v.*
rydding), *Waltroyd* (the pers.n. *Walter*, rod[1]), *White royd well*, *Woddall Inge*.

3. RAVENSTHORPE (102–2120)

    This is a modern name, but the el. *Raven* occurs in some older
local names, *Ravensbrook* (*v.* foll.), *Ravinsall* 1544 TestLds (*v.* halh
'nook of land'), *Ravens Lodge* 1817 M, and Ravens Wharf 187 *supra*.

RAVENSBROOK (lost), *Ravenesbrok* 1296 WCR, *Ravensbrooke* 1525 *Surv*, *Ravenbrook* 1637 DodsN, probably an old name for Canker Dyke. 'Hræfn's brook' or 'raven's brook', *v.* hræfn, hrafn, brōc.

BRICKHOUSE (lost) 1843 O.S., *Red House* 1817 M.   RED LAITHS (lost), 1843 O.S., *v.* hlaða 'barn'.

4. NETHER SOOTHILL (6" O.S. 274NE)

> *Sothil(l)*, *hyll* e. 13 YCh viii (p), Hy 3 Arm (p), 1265 YI, 1274–1313 WCR (*freq*), 1276 RH, 1323 *MinAcct* 45, 1343 Baild, 1351 YD ii, 1485 WillY, -*hull* 1219 FF, 1251 YI
> *Sotil* 1243 Fees (p)
> *Sohill* 1276 RH
> *Suttehall'* 1297 LS, *Sutehill* 1376 YD xiii, 54, *Sudhill* 1695 M
> *Suthill*, -*hyll* 1373 YD i, 1377 ib xiii, 54, 1544 Arm, 1597 SessnR, *Sutill'* 1379 PT (p)
> *Sotehill* 1504, 1591, 1594 FF
> *Soothill* 1504 *WB*, 1641 Rates, (*Nether*) 1822 Langd

The spellings refer mostly to Lower Soothill (102–2524), a village in Upper Soothill township 197 *infra*. Nether and Upper Soothill are merely the names of townships. The els. are OE sōt 'soot' and hyll. There are collieries along this hillside and doubtless the allusion was to coal-dust and soot from coal-burning, cf. Sinder Hill f.n. *infra*. 'Nether' to distinguish it from Upper Soothill 196 *infra*.

CHICKENLEY HEATH

> *Chiken-*, *Chykenl'*, -*ley* 1196–1202 YCh viii, 1277, 1298 WCR (p), *Chykinley* 1297 WCR (p)
> *Chygenlay* 1230 P (p)   *Schkynlay* (sic) 1558 TestLds
> *Chikkinley* 1324 WCR (p), *Chickingley* 1525 *Surv*, 1563 WillY, 1617 PRBfd, *Chickynley*, -*in-* 1594 FF, 1665 PRHrb, *Chickenley* 1504 *WB*, 1715 Arm
> *Chekyngley*, -*ing-* 1435, 1461 DodsN, 1546 YChant, *Chekynley*, -*ley* 1435 DodsN, 1459, 1462 Test ii, 1504 FF

This is probably 'clearing used for chickens', *v.* cicen, lēah, but the first el. may be *chicken* used as a surname, as in the name of *John Chicken* (1309 WCR ii, 226) of Horbury. The heath (*v.* hǣð) is called *Middle & Upper Heath* 1814 *Surv*, 1843 *TA*.

EARLSHEATON, *Et(t)one* 1086 DB, *Hetun, -ton* e. 13 YCh viii (p),
1202–18 ib, 1316 Vill, (*Herles-*) 1284 WCR, (*-Comitis*) 1286 ib,
(*Erles-*) 1316, 1323 WCR, 1548 WillY, (*Erls-*) 1313 WCR, 1554 FF,
(*-juxta Dewesbyry*) 1361 *Ass* 4, *Earl(e)s Heaton* 1525 *Surv*, 1588 WillY
et freq to 1709 WMB, *Elersheaton* 1656 Pick. 'High, lofty farmstead',
v. hēah, tūn. *Earls-* is a feudal affix alluding to the Earls of Warren
in whose estates it was (WCR i, 211 *et freq*), to distinguish it from
Hanging Heaton 196 *infra*, *v.* eorl.

CHICKENLEY BECK, *the brooke of Chickinley, Chickenlay broke* 1525
Surv, *v.* Chickenley *supra*, brōc.   CLOUGH HO, *The Clough* 1843
O.S., *v.* clōh 'dell'.   GREENGATES MILLS, *Green gate close* 1814 *Surv*,
v. grēne[1], gata.   HEATH COTTAGE.   HIGH STREET, *the Heigh street*
1525 *Surv*, which doubtless refers to the Wakefield–Dewsbury road
(cf. Ossett Street Side 190 *supra*), rather than the High St in Earls-
heaton village, *v.* hēah, strǣt, cf. *Lower Street Close* 1814 *Surv*.
HILL END, named from *Erles Heaton Hill* 1709 WMB.   HOLLOW
BANK.   HOYLE HEAD, 1814 *Surv*, 1843 *TA*, cf. *Hoyle Milne* 1659
WillS, *v.* hol[1] 'hole, hollow'.   JILLING HILL MILLS, *Jaling Ing* 1814
Surv.   LITTLE ROYD, 1766 Arm, *le Lyttelrode* 1364 YD i, *Lytle royd*
1525 *Surv*, *v.* lytel, rod[1].   RIDINGS COLLIERIES, *the Rydinge* 1525
Surv, *Riding(s)* 1814 *Surv*, *v.* rydding 'clearing'.   SCARR END,
Heaton Scar 1771 M, *Scar End Mill* 1843 O.S., described as 'Earles
Heaton Laithe, Thirtye acres of Comon, it ys but a skarr and ys not
to be plowed and an evill pasture' (1525 *Surv* 10, 7), *v.* sker 'a rock,
rocky cliff'.   SYKE HO & ING, cf. *le Sikefield* 1650 *WCR* 5, *Great
Syke Field* 1709 WMB, *Syke Close*, 1814 *Surv*, *Syke Dyke Shutt*,
Syke Ing 1843 *TA*, *v.* sīc 'stream'.

FIELD-NAMES

The principal forms in (*a*) are 1843 *TA* 367 and 1814 *Surv*. Spellings
dated 1485, 1650 are *WCR*, 1525 *Surv* 10, 7, 1709 WMB, and those in (*b*)
without date are 1525 *Surv*. In (*b*) some f.ns. may belong to Upper Soothill
197 *infra*.

(*a*) Appleyard 1814 (*v.* æppel, geard), Ball Grave Ing, Bank 1814, (Little)
Bawn 1814 (*v.* Balne 14 *supra*), Beck Ing, Bogard Close (ib 1814), Bottoms
1814 (*Bothme* 1323 *MinAcct*, *v.* botm, boŏm), Bracken Hill (*v.* brakni, hyll),
Break Back 1814 (a field hard to till), Brear close 1814 (*v.* brēr), Broad Ing
(*v.* eng 'meadow'), Broad Royd 1814 (*v.* rod[1]), Broom Close (ib 1814),
Broom Croft 1814 (*Brome crofte* 1525, *v.* brōm, croft), Broom Hill 1814,

Butter Hill 1814 (v. butere, hyll), Butts, Calf Croft 1814, Car 1814 (*Car Mill* 1817 M, v. kjarr 'marsh'), Chapel Croft (ib 1814), Coat Croft 1814 (v. cot, croft), Common End Ridings 1814, Coney Croft 1814 (v. coni 'rabbit', croft), Cow Close, Crabtree Close 1814, Cross 1814 (v. cros), Cross Hill Ing 1814, Dipsey 1814, Dob Royd 1814, Eight & Eleven Lands 1814, Ellen Croft, Fen Lands 1814, Five Lands 1814, Fog Croft (v. fogga 'long grass', croft), Fold 1814, Godrismoor 1814, Green Ing, Half Acre 1814, Hall Yards 1814, Hallas Croft 1814, Hardings (v. heard, eng), Heasle Close 1814 (v. hæsel 'hazel'), High Briggs 1814 (*the heigh brigges* 1525, v. hēah, brycg), Horse Close (*Horse Croft* 1814), House Stead 1814 (v. hūs, stede), Ing Yard (*Ing* 1814, v. eng), Intack 1814 (v. intak), Kettle Edge, Kiln Croft, Laith Croft (*Layth Croft* 1814, v. hlaða 'barn', croft), Lamb Close 1814, Leigh Close 1814 (v. lēah), Long Croft & Ing 1814, Long Lands Ing (ib 1814), Mapplewell (v. mapel, wella), Marle close 1814 (v. marle), Mean Close 1814 (v. (ge)mæne 'common'), Mill Close (cf. *Mill Ing* 1814), Nether Shay 1814 (v. sceaga 'copse'), Old Field 1814, Oullers 1814 (v. alor 'alder'), Owlshaw (ib 1814, v. ūle, sceaga), Ox Close 1814, Paddock (*Lower & Upper Paddock* 1814, v. pearroc), Park 1814, Pease Close & Croft (ib 1814, v. pise 'pease'), Pighill (*Low Pickel, Great Pighill* 1814, v. pightel 'enclosure'), Pits 1814, Pond Croft 1814, Pool 1814, Rein 1814 (v. reinn 'boundary strip'), Round Heath, Rouse Mill 1843 O.S., Royd 1814 (v. rod[1]), Far & Near Royd Grave (ib 1814, *the Royd grave* 1525, v. prec., grāf 'grove'), Sands Close, Sinder Hill 1814 (v. sinder 'cinder', hyll, clearly spoil from coal-mining and smelting), Small Ing, Soothill Hall (*Sotehilhaul* 1535 WillY, *Sotell Hall* 1567 Visit), South Croft 1814, Sower Ing 1814, Springs 1814, Steel Croft 1814 (v. stigel 'stile'), Stoney Law (ib 1814, *Stonelaw* 1525, v. stān, hlāw 'mound, cairn'), Strumple 1814, Sunny Gate (*Sunegate rowe* 1525, *Sunnygatehedge, Sunnyate close* 1650, *Sunnigate Closes* 1709, *Suny Gate* 1814, v. geat), Sweet Park 1814, Swine Park, Tenter Field (*Tenter Croft* 1814), Thorpe Close 1814, Three Nook'd Heath (ib 1814), Throddle Croft (ib 1814, *Throddel(l)-crofte(s)* 1525, cf. dial. *throddle* 'fat, thriving' (a variant of *throdden*, which usually applies to cattle), v. croft), Tingle 1814, Toad Croft, Tungs Acre 1709 (*Tonguesacre* 1650, v. tunge, æcer), Warrand & Warrent Garth 1814 (v. wareine 'warren', garðr), Weaver Garth 1814, Well Close (*Well Close & Head* 1814), West Park 1814, Wheat Croft, Wheat Flatt & Royd 1814, Winny Close, Woodhead (ib 1814), Wood Nook 1814.

(b) le Kowehey 1377 YD xiii, 54 (v. cū, (ge)hæg 'enclosure'), *Crokte close, Gyll Inge* (the ME fem. pers.n. *Gille*, eng), *le Haylaythe* 1485 (v. hēg 'hay', hlaða 'barn'), *Hellycocke Inges* 1525, *Hellicockynge* 1650 (the first el. is uncertain but might be the ME surn. *Hellecok* (cf. Reaney 107, 160, s.n. *Elcock, Hellcat*), v. eng), *Hynchclyffe Crofte* (probably Hinchcliffe (237 *infra*) as a surname, croft), *Holdgate brigg* (v. ald, gata, brycg), *the Holme* (v. holmr 'water-meadow'), *Inge Sandes, Great Ingg-, Little Ingsandes* (v. eng, sand), *Laughton closse* (v. lēac-tūn 'garden'), *little Mylley, S(e)aveacres* 1525, *le saffeacres* 1650 (v. æcer), *Suthyll brwk* 1315 YD i (v. brōc), *Stockwell Laches* (v. stocc, wella, læcc 'stream, bog'), *Townknowle* (v. tūn, cnoll), *Whynny-sandes* (ib 1650, v. hvin 'gorse', sand).

5. UPPER SOOTHILL (6" O.S. 232 SE)

Soothill, Upper 1822 Langd, the name of a township, *v.* Soothill
193 *supra*.

CHIDSWELL

> Chides-, *Chydeshyll*, -*hill* 1275–1298 WCR (p), -*hull* 1343 *Ass* 1
> *Schydeshill* 1285 WCR (p)
> *Chudeshull* 1343 *Ass* 5
> *Chedishill* 1379 PT (p)
> *Chydssill* 1401 Calv, *Chidsill* 1556 WillY, *Chidchell* 1525 *Surv*,
>   *Chidsell* 1532 FF *et freq* to 1817 M, *Chidsall* 1657 Pick, 1695 M
> *Chedsell* 1558 DodsN
> *Chitsele* 1577 Tayl

The first el. is clearly an OE pers.n. *Cid(d)*; this is not independently evidenced, but a weak form *Cida* (possibly also *Cidda* in
the Calendar of St Willibrord) and a derivative *Cidding* are recorded
(Tengvik 141, 303), whilst the strong form *Cidd* appears in OE *on
Ciddesbeara* KCD 1318 (Do); Ekwall (DEPN s.n. Chiddingfold Sr)
supposes these to be WSax side-forms of OE *Cedd* and *Cedda* but in
view of the occurrence of *Cid* in this YW p.n. it is more likely to be
connected with OE *cīdan* 'to dispute, quarrel' as Tengvik suggests.
It certainly remains a byname in ME; Tengvik cites *Leowinus Chidde*
1131 P, and there is also a local example in *German Chidde* 1308 WCR
ii, 163 (Wakefield). 'C(h)id's hill', *v.* hyll.

HANGING HEATON

> *Etun* 1086 DB, *He(a)ton* 1315 YD i, 1402 FA, with the prefix
> *Hingand(e)-* 1266 YI, 1323 *MinAcct* 45, 1341 Baild, *Hyngyng-*, -*inge*
> 1490 YD i, 1582 WillY, *Hingyn*, -*in* 1565, 1593 ib, *Hengende-* 1276
> RH, *Hangand-* 1293 DodsN, *Hangyng-*, -*ing* 1557 WillY, 1567 FF *et
> freq* to 1822 Langd, *Hangenge-* 1558 DodsN, *Hangin-* 1659 Pick.

'High farmstead', *v.* hēah, tūn. The affix (to distinguish it from
Earlsheaton 194 *supra*) is northern ME *hengande* 'hanging, steep'
(*v.* hengjandi, pres. part. of ON *hengja*), which later becomes *hingande*
through the normal change of -*eng*- to -*ing*-, and was later replaced
by ME *hangande* (*v.* hangende). The village is at the top of a very steep
hillside.

BANK TOP, 1817 M, *Hetonbank* 1329 WCR, *v.* banke.   CAMROYD.
CAULMS WOOD, 1843 O.S.   COMMONSIDE, 1843 O.S., *Heaton*

Common Side 1817 M. CRACKENEDGE, 1849 *TA* 131. CROFT HO.
CROWN FLATT, 1814 *Surv*, cf. Crownlands 189 *supra*. DAY HOLE
cf. Day Hole 189 *supra*. DOGLOITCH WOOD, *Doggelache* 1377 YD
xiii, 54, *Dogloich (Wood)* 1814 *Surv*, 1841 O.S., *v.* dogga 'dog',
læcc 'stream, bog'. DUM WOOD, 1841 O.S. FIELD HEAD, *Field
(Wood)* 1814 *Surv*, *v.* feld. FOLLINGWORTH HO, 1814 *Surv*, *v.*
falding, worð, and Fallingworth iii, 54 *infra*. GREEN HILL. HEY
BECK, *Haighbecke* 1655 WillS, *Hayleck* (sic) 1658 Pick, *-Beck* 1817 M,
v. haga 'enclosure', bekkr. HILL TOP WELL, *the Hilltop* 1673 *YAS*
43, *v.* hyll, topp. HOLLINROYD, 1843 O.S., *Hollen Royd* 1814 *Surv*,
v. holegn 'holly', rod[1] 'clearing'. KIRKGATE. LAMBFIELD. LEES
HOUSE FM, cf. *Lees Field* 1814 *Surv*, *v.* lēah 'clearing'. LOW FIELD
HO. MILL LANE, cf. *Soothill millne* 1657 Pick, *v.* myln, cf. Damstead f.n. *infra*. OLD BANK. ONE ASH. ORCHARD HO, *Orchard*
1814 *Surv*, *v.* orceard. SCARGILL WOOD, 1841 O.S. SHAW CROSS,
1771 M, cf. *Shay* 1814 *Surv*, *v.* sceaga 'copse', cros. SOOTHILL
GRANGE, 1817 M. LOWER SOOTHILL, *v.* Soothill 193 *supra*. SOOT-
HILL WOOD, 1843 O.S., *Sutillwod* 1377 YD xiii, 54, *v.* wudu. TOWN
END, 1814 *Surv*.

FIELD-NAMES

The principal forms in (*a*) are 1849 *TA* 368. Spellings dated 1814 are
Surv. Some f.ns. for this township are included in Nether Soothill 194
supra.

(*a*) Annice (*Annice Ing* 1814), Bottom Ing, Bushe, Calf Close (ib 1814),
Damstead (ib 1814, *Suthyll mylndame* 1315 YD i, *v.* dammr, stede, cf. Mill
Lane *supra*), Day Croft (the surname *Day* or dey 'dairy', croft), Jumbles,
Knowles (*v.* cnoll 'hillock'), Micklefield (ib 1814), Naylor Wife Ing, Pan
Kiln, Pit Croft (*Pit Close* 1814), Quarry Close, Reachley, Street Close (ib,
Street Heath 1814, *v.* High Street 194 *supra*), Wood End (ib 1814).

xii. Mirfield

MIRFIELD (102–2020)

Mirefeld, -felt 1086 DB, *Mire-, Myrefeld* 1170–85 YCh 1692 (p),
1180–93 ib 1513 (p), l. 12 Font (p), 13 AD vi (p), 1245 Ebor,
1252 FF (p), 1297 WCR, 1329 FF, 1391 YD i, *-feud* 1219 FF
Mir-, Myrfeld(e) Hy 2 Dugd v, 13 YD i, 1202 FF, Hy 3 Arm (p),
1276 RH, 1285 KI, 1288 YI, 1303 Aid, 1309 YD iii, 1314 YD i,
1316 Vill, 1323 *Ass* 4 *et passim* to 1537 WillY, *-feud* 1297 WCR,
-fill 1558 NCWills, *-feild* 1605 FF

Mi-, *Myrifeud* 1195–1215 YCh viii (p), 1246 *Ass* 11d, *Mirifeld*, *-y-*
1246 *Ass* 5d, 1251 FF
Merefelde 1293 Ebor, 1486 *MinAcct* 66, *Merfeld* 1303 ib
Murfeld(*e*) 1531 Test iv, 1641 PRThl, *-feild* 1615 FF

'Pleasant stretch of open country', *v.* myrig, feld. The first el. is
hardly likely to be mýrr 'mire, swamp' on topographical grounds;
the name must have described the steep hillside on the north
side of the Calder and only one small piece of ground by the river
(the Lowlands) could have been swampy. As in other names (such
as Marley K 225, 558), *myrig* is here, perhaps more persistently,
reduced to ME *Mir*(*e*), but the *Miri-* spellings leave no doubt about
the interpretation. *v.* Addenda.

LOWER & UPPER HOPTON, *Hopton*(*e*), *-tun* 1086 DB, 13 Font, YD i,
1218 DodsN, 1219 FF, 1271 Font, 1274 WCR, 1303 YD i, 1328
Banco *et passim* to 1592 WillY, *Hopetune* 12 France. 'Farmstead in
the side-valley', *v.* hop, tūn, a common p.n. Upper Hopton, which is
the old village, is on the west side of the valley of Valance Beck,
which runs into the Calder.

NORTHORPE, *Northorp*(*p*), *-thorpe* 13 YD i, 1331 YD xii, 296, 1343
Nost 66d, 1379 PT, 1401 Calv, 1441 Arm (all p), 1517 ib, 1539
WillY *et passim* to 1822 Langd, *del Norththorpe* 1297 WCR, *North-
roppe* 1578 PRMrf. 'North outlying farmstead', *v.* norð, þorp.

BANK HO, 1843 O.S., (*y^e*) *Bank* 1737 PRMrf, 1817 M, *v.* banke.
BATTYE FORD, *ye Batty-ford* 1706 PRMrf, *Battie fore* ('which is very
dangerous') 1732 YDr, cf. *John Battee* and other members of the
family in the parish (1605 PRMrf 64, etc., cf. Batty's Fold 154 *supra*),
v. ford (across the Calder). THE BECK. BLAKE HALL, 1569
PRMrf, 1580 *WB* 54, 1594 FF, *Blackhall* 1605 FF, *the Blaike Hall*
1735 PRMrf, probably the surname *Blake*, hall. BOAT HO, 1595
PRMrf, *Boat-*, *Botehowse* 1596, 1600 ib, *the Boathouse in Mirfield*
1688 *WB* 54, from ME *bote* 'boat', hūs; it is by the R. Calder; cf.
also Bottom Boat 159 *supra*. BOLDERSTONE HALL, 1843 O.S., cf.
John Bolderston 1674 PRMrf 173, etc. BRACKEN HILL, *Brackan hill*
1748 PRMrf, *v.* brakni, hyll. BRIER KNOWL, *Brier Knowls* 1843
O.S., *v.* brēr, cnoll 'hillock'. BRIERY ROYD, *Breary Royd* 1720
WB 32, *v.* brērig, rod[1]. BROAD OAKS, 1843 O.S. BUTT END
MILL.

CALDER FM. CALF CROFT, *Crow Croft* (sic) 1843 O.S., *v.* calf, crāwe, croft. CANKER DIKE. CASTLE HALL HILL, *the Chastell* 1424 Rent (described as a third part of the vill of Mirfield), *Castle hall* 1583 PRMrf, 1593, 1636 *WB*, *v.* castel (the earliest spelling is OFr *chastel*), hall; the castle mound was called *Castle Hill* 1720 *WB* 32, *Mount* 1843 O.S. CHADWICK FOLD, 1843 O.S., cf. *Chadwick Ing* 1720 *WB* 32, both named from the *Chadwick* family, well-known here from the seventeenth century (PRMrf *freq*), *v.* fald, eng. CHAPEL FOLD. CHAPEL HILL, *Chaple Hill* 1817 M. CLOUGH, 1843 O.S., *v.* clōh 'dell'. COB ROW. COTEWALL. COVEY CLOUGH. CRIPPLE GATE, *Criplegate* 1763 PRMrf, -*gale* (sic) 1817 M, 1843 O.S., *v.* crypel-geat 'a cripple-gate, a hole in the wall to allow sheep but not bigger animals to pass'. CROSSLEY, CROSSLEY HILL, *Crosseley* 13 YD vi, *Crosley* 1678 Misc ii, 1762 PRMrf, *v.* cros, lēah; the family of *Cros(s)ley* was known here from the sixteenth century (PRMrf *freq*). CROW LEES, *Crow Leys* 1720 *WB* 32, *v.* crāwe, lēah.

DAISY HILL. DARK LANE, 1861 *Sav.* DOCTOR LANE. DRANS-FIELD HILL, 1822 Langd, *Dransfeild* 1598 SessnR; a family of *Drane-*, *Dra(u)nsfeld* was known in the district from the twelfth to the seventeenth centuries (*Dranefeld* 12 *WB* ix, 1, 1275 WCR, *Dronesfeld* 1307 ib, *Dronsfeld* 1315 ib, 1369 YD i, *Dransfeld* 1385 Brett, *Dra(u)ns-feld* 17 PRMrf), and it doubtless originated here; the p.n. is 'drone's open land', *v.* drān (as also in Dronfield Db 243), feld; OE *drān* may be here used as a nickname. DUN BOTTLE, *Dvn-*, *Dunbottell* 1602, 1605 PRMrf, a tavern, the name meaning 'the dun or dull brown bottle'.

EAST-THORPE, (*y*[e]) *Earthorp(pe)* 1590, 1745 PRMrf, *Earthop* (sic) 1817 M; *v.* þorp 'outlying farmstead'; the original first el. *Ear-* is obscure, but has been replaced by *East-* in recent times. ELMWOOD FM.

FIELD HEAD, *fieldhead* 1746 PRMrf. FINCHING DIKE. FLASH LANE. FOLD HEAD MILL, *Fold-head* 1708 PRMrf, *y*[e] *Foldehead* 1710 ib, *v.* fald (a common el. in this parish), hēafod. FOX ROYD, *Foxe royde* 1612 PRMrf, *v.* fox, rod[1] 'clearing'.

GILDER HALL. GOSLING HALL. GREEN HO, *the greenhowse* 1585 PRMrf, *v.* grēne[1], hūs. GREENSIDE, 1843 O.S. GREGORY SPRING, a wood called *Gregory springe* 1656 WB 45, named from Gregory 234 *infra*, *v.* spring 'plantation'.

HAGG, HAGG WOOD, 1843 O.S., *Esthage* 1219 FF, -*hagh(e)* 1346

DodsN, *le Hageheued* 13 YD i, *y* *hagg* 1726 PRMrf, *the Great Hagg* 1730 LdsM, *v.* hǫgg 'felling of trees, clearing', confused in some spellings with haga 'enclosure'.   HALL BANK, *Hawbancke* 1580 WillY, *v.* hall, bank.   HAND BANK, *Hanbanck(es)* 1598, 1600 PRMrf, *Handbancke* 1618 ib, *v.* hana 'cock', banke; the form may have been influenced by the local surname *Hand* (cf. *John Hande* 1659 PRMrf 144, etc.) but *hana* frequently becomes *Hand-* (as in Hand Bank i, 333 *supra*, etc., cf. Phonol. § 46).   HEPWORTH WOOD, 1843 O.S., probably a surname from Hepworth 242 *infra*.   HIGHFIELD HO. HIGHTHORPE.   HOLLIN HALL, 1667 *WB* 222, 1843 O.S., *Holynge* 1481 PrHosp, *v.* holegn 'holly', hall.   HOLME BANK, cf. *Lenethyrholme* 1314 YD i, 'the lower water-meadow', *v.* le, neoðera, holmr. HOPTON BROW & FOLD.   HOPTON GRANGE.   HOPTON HALL, 1485 *WB* 83, 1643 WillY, *v.* Hopton *supra*, hall.

INGS GROVE.   IVY HO.

JACK ROYD, 1771 M, the pers.n. *Jack*, rod[1] 'clearing'.   JORDAN WOOD.

KITSON HILL, named from the *Kitson* family (16 *et freq* PRMrf). KNOWL, *Knowle* (*lane*) 1593, 1614 PRMrf, *v.* cnoll 'hillock'.

THE LAWN.   LEE GREEN, *Lee grene* 1574 PRMrf, cf. also *Henry del Lee* 1332 Arm, *Richard Lee* 1574 PRMrf, *v.* lēah 'clearing', grēne[2].   LILEY HALL, *Li-*, *Lyley* 1589 WillY, 1649 PRMrf, 1656 Pick, 1666 Visit, 1696 *WB* 182, cf. *Lilley Bank toppe* 1639 WillY, probably 'flax clearing', *v.* līn, lēah, with a common loss of *-n-* as in Lillands iii, 39 *infra*.   LILEY WOOD, 1843 O.S., *v.* prec., wudu. LITTLE LONDON CITY, *Little London* 1726 PRMrf.   LITTLEMOOR, *y* *lyttle more* 1588 PRMrf, *Litellmore* 1669 ib, *v.* lytel, mōr.   LOWLANDS, low lying land by the Calder.

MADGE CROFT, *Matchcroft* 1761 PRMrf, doubtless the fem. pers.n. *Madge*, croft.   MANOR HO.   MAPPLEWELL LODGE.   MILL LANE. MIRFIELD BRIDGE, *the new brigge called Mirfeld brige* 1484 Test iii, *v.* brycg, cf. Jervoise 105.   MIRFIELD MOOR, 1796 *EnclA* 70, *Myrfield more* 1637 PRMrf, *v.* mōr, cf. Moor Top *infra*, High & Low Moor 1796 *EnclA*.   MOCK HALL, probably named from the f.n. *Mockbeggar* 1737 PRMrf, which occurs elsewhere in YW.   MOOR TOP, *More Top* 1746 PRMrf, cf. *y* *Moor-side* 1714 ib, *v.* Mirfield Moor *supra*.   MOUNT PLEASANT, 1843 O.S.   MOUSEHOLE LANE.

NAB, *the*, *y* *Nab* 1583, 1588 PRMrf, *v.* nabbi 'a knoll'.   NETTLETON RD, named from *Robert Nettleton* (1649 PRMrf 130) or some member of his family.   NEWHALL, 1652, 1656 *WB* 48, 1733 PRMrf,

v. nīwe, hall.   NEW HO, 1817 M, *Newhouse* 1646 WillY, *v.* nīwe, hūs.
NICK HO, *Nychous* 1554 WillY, *Nickhowse* 1640 Arm, *-house*
1649, 1690 PRMrf, the ME pers.n. *Nikke* (from *Nicholas*), hūs.
NORTHFIELD, *Little North Field* 1590 Arm, *v.* norð, feld.   NOR-
THORPE HALL, *Northropp Hall* 1564 Arm, named from the *Northorpe*
family (16 *et freq* PRMrf), or from Northorpe itself (*supra*), from
which the family also took its name.   NUN BROOK HO, *Nun-brook in
the Parish of Mirfield* 1776 PRHtsd, *Nunbrooke yate* 1623 Arm,
Nunbrooke 1625, 1686 PRMrf, 1700 YDr, *v.* Nun Brook iii, 5 *infra*,
geat 'gate'.

OVER HALL, 1817 M, (*y^e*) *Upper hall* 1648, 1732 PRMrf.   OWTON.
PAPER HALL.   THE PARK.   PARK FM.   PINFOLD LANE, *Pinfold*
1714 PRMrf, *v.* pynd-fald.   PUMP HO.

ROE HEAD, 1843 O.S., probably 'roe-buck head', *v.* rā, heafod,
cf. Hartshead, the adjoining township.   ROUND OAK.   LOWER,
MIDDLE & UPPER ROW, (*y^e*, *the*) *Row* 1725, 1729 PRMrf, 1789
PRHtsd, *Mirfield Upper Row* 1843 O.S., *v.* rāw 'row (of houses)'.
ROYD NOOK.   ROYDS HO, 1817 M, *Royds* 1662 PRMrf, *v.* rod[1]
'clearing'.

SANDS, SANDS HO, 1843 O.S., *v.* sand; it is near the Calder.
SHEEP INGS, *Shepeinges* 1605 PRMrf, *Sheepe Inges* 1608 ib, *v.* scēap,
eng 'meadow'.   SHILL BANK HO & LANE, *Shilbank* 1747 PRMrf,
Shillbank lane 1763 ib, *v.* banke; the first el. is doubtful.   SLIPPER
LANE.   SNAKE HILL, *the Snakehill* 1607 PRMrf, from OE *snaca* 'a
snake' and hyll.   SPRINGFIELD HO.   STEANARD LANE, cf. Stennard
Well 151 *supra*.   STOCKS BANK, *Stock-bancke* 1628 PRMrf,
probably named from the family of *Henry Stokkes* (1441 Arm 108),
Thomas Stokkes of Myrfeld (1474 ib 130) or *John Stocks of Stockbank*
(1768 PRMrf ii, 149), *v.* banke.   SUNNY BANK, 1843 O.S., *Sun
Banks* 1767 *WB* 43.

TAYLOR HALL, 1817 M, named from the *Taylor* family, well-
evidenced in Mirfield in the sixteenth and seventeenth centuries
(PRMrf *passim*).   THORNE GROVE.   TITHE LATHE, *v.* hlaða
'barn'.   TOMROYDS HO, *Tom Royd* 1720 *WB* 32, *Tomroyds Farm*
1843 O.S., the pers.n. *Tom*, rod[1] 'clearing'.   TOWNGATE, *Towne
gate* 1593 PRMrf, *v.* tūn, gata 'road' or geat 'gate'.

VALANCE BECK, *Ballance Wood* 1720 *WB* 32.

WARD'S END.   WARREN HO, 1753 PRMrf, *ye: warondehouse* 1680
PRHtsd, *Warant House* 1777 ib, *Warrand House* 1721 PRMrf, *v.*
wareine 'warren'.   WASP NEST.   THE WASTE, *Waste* 1817 M, *v.*

wēste 'waste-land'. WATER ROYD HO, *Le Wateroid* 1491 Arm, *Water royd* 1759 PRMrf, *v.* wæter, rod[1]; this place is on the hillside and so it may be from ME *Watte, Walter.* WELLHOUSE, 1629 PRMrf, *v.* wella, hūs. WESTFIELD HO, *le Westefeld* 1314 YD i, *Wesfeld* 1564 Arm, *v.* west, feld. WESTFIELDS, *Westfeilds yeat* 1775 PRMrf. WESTROYD, 1720 PRThl, (*lez*) *West roides* 1590 Arm, 1598 PRMrf, *v.* west, rod[1]. WHITLEY WOOD, 1843 O.S., *Whitleghes* 1406 WB 4, *v.* hwīt, lēah. WILLOW GROVE. WOODEND, cf. *Mirefeld Wude* 1246 FF, *v.* wudu, ende.

FIELD-NAMES

The principal forms in (*a*) are 1720, 1767 *WB* 32, 43. Spellings dated 13 are YD i, 1339 Arm, 1406 *WB*, 1507, 1519 Arm, 1560 YD i, 1590–1591 Arm, 1615 *WB*, 1626, 1630 Arm, 1643 YD i, 1675–1688 Arm, 1690 *WB*, 1713 Arm, 1739 *WB*, 1861 *Sav.* Others dated without source are PRMrf.

(*a*) Angrams 1861, Ball Yard, Birks (*v.* birki 'birch-tree'), Bondgate 1775 (*v.* bondi, gata), Chapel Well 1843 O.S. (ib 1767, *-wells* 1720), Cinderhill 1759 (*v.* sinder, hyll), the Common End 1735, Coney Garth (*v.* coning-erth 'warren'), Crow Wood 1843 O.S. (*v.* crāwe, wudu), Cookoo Hill 1843 O.S., Edish close (*v.* edisc), Gibhole 1760 (ME *gibbe* 'a gib, a cat', hol[1]), the Hall Miln 1734, Hemp Garth (*v.* hænep, garðr), Hive close, Hungerhill 1740 (*v.* hungor, hyll), Kem Croft, Kirk Flatt *&* Ing, Knowle-Ing 1739 (*v.* Knowl *supra*, eng), Ledgard Bridge 1736, 1775 (cf. PRMrf ii, 173, 'Rob't Ledgerd . . . 1627 did leye a paine on the Inhabitence of Mirefeild of £100 to repaire the said bridge'; the Ledgard family were numerous here, 18 PRMrf *freq*), Marle Peighill (*v.* marle, pightel), Mean Slack (*v.* (ge)mǣne 'common', slakki 'hollow'), Nant Ing (dial. *naunt* 'aunt', eng), Nether Field 1796 *EnclA* 70, Newthropp 1713 (*v.* nīwe, þorp), Pitt Ing, Quarry Hill 1822 Langd, Senior Slack (*Senier closes* 1686, the surname *Senior*), Sower Ing (*v.* sūr, eng), Spittle well (*v.* spitel, wella), Thewle's Intacke 1861 (the surname *Thewles*, ME *Theules* 1327 WCR, *Thewelesse* 1379 PT, 'mannerless', *v.* intak), the Upper End of yᵉ Towne 1732 (*the Overend of the towne* 1581), Water Hall 1739 (ib 1623), yᵉ Windy Bank 1735, (the) Yew Tree 1721, 1723.

(*b*) *Aldredilrode* (sic for *-redis-*) 1219 FF (the OE pers.n. *Aldrēd*, rod[1]), *Bayhall* 1569, *Brig(ge) end* 1621 (*v.* brycg, ende), *Brygelone* 1406 (*v.* prec., lane), a farm called *Eshold* 1675 (cf. Esholt pt. iv *infra*), *Falls* 1615 (*v.* (ge)fall 'clearing' or 'waterfall'), *Haigh farme* 1615, *le heghridyng pehyll* 13 (*v.* hēah, rydding, pightel), *Hoptongate* 1271 Font (*v.* Hopton *supra*, gata), *Howleroides* 1590 (*v.* hol[1], rod[1]), *Hulcroft* 1507 (*v.* hyll, croft), *Ymp-yorde* 1507 ('young plantation', *v.* impa 'sapling', geard), *Lilleymore* 1690 (*v.* Liley Hall *supra*, mōr), *Moreroyde* 1560, *-roids* 1643 (*v.* Mirfield Moor *supra*, rod[1] 'clearing'), *Nerve Close* 1591, *Nethirholes* 1406 (*v.* neoðera, hol[1]), *Nethermilnes* 1688, *Neweclose* 1590, *le Northwode* 13 (*v.* norð, wudu), *Nunwoode* 1541 *MinAcct*

23 (cf. Nun Brook *supra*), *bosco persone* 13, *Philiprod* 13 (*v.* rod[1]), *Ravensbridge* 1603 Stansf (probably connected with *Ravensbrook* 193 *supra* in the adjoining township), *Ratunrawe* 1406, *Rat(t)onrowe* 1595, 1607, *Rottonrawe* 1622 ('rat-infested row of houses', *v.* raton, rāw), *leridgat* 13 (possibly an error for *lidgat*, *v.* hlid-geat 'swing-gate'), *Shortwede* 1507, *Smethyroyds* 1560, *Smythie Roides* 1643 (*v.* smiððe, rod[1]), *Somerclouh* 13 (*v.* sumor, clōh 'dell'), *Stevincrofth* 13 (the ME pers.n. *Stephen*, croft), *the Stoopes* 1630 (*v.* stólpi 'post'), *Todeholleyng* 1560 (*v.* tādige 'toad', hol[1], eng), *West Mylnes* (sic) 1560 WillY, *the West mylnes* 1582, *West Milles* 1629 (*v.* west, myln), *West-riding* 1339 (*v.* west, rydding 'clearing'), *Whetclouse* 1507 (*v.* hwǣte 'wheat', clos).

xiii. Thornhill

The townships of Flockton and Shitlington (205 *infra*) remain separate civil parishes but Thornhill (210 *infra*) is now in the County Borough of Dewsbury (184 *supra*).

1. FLOCKTON (102–2414)

Flocheton(e) 1086 DB

Floc-, *Floktun(a)*, *-ton(a)* 12 Riev (*freq*, YCh 1727), 1185–95 YCh 1761, 1189, 1192 Pont, Ric 1 (1252) Ch, 1193–1211 YCh 1525, 1331 *Ass* 5, 1319 YD viii, 1323 *MinAcct* 45 *et passim* to 1536 FF, (*Ovir-*, *Over-*) 1338 YD viii, 1356 YD *et freq* to 1639 Arm, (*Nether-*, *Nethir-*) 1342, 1363, 1386 YD v *et freq* to 1639 Arm, (*Neder-*) 1477 YD viii, (*Neyther-*) 1588 LS, (*Neather-*) 1589 FF

Floketon(a), *-tun* 1145–60 YCh 1724, 1190–1204 ib 1688, 13 YD iv, vi, viii, 1201 FF, 1220, Hy 3 BM 1248–51, 1295 YD v, 1297 LS *et passim* to 1339 YD 3, (*Ouer-*, *Over-*) 13, 1308 YD viii, 1338 YD v, *Flocketon* 1194, 1298 BM

Flocktun, *-ton* 1150–70 YCh 1728, 1571 WillY, 1583 PRThl *et freq* to 1607 FF, (*Over-*, *Nether-*) 1607 FF

'Flóki's farmstead', from the ON pers.n. *Flóki* and tūn. But the earlier spellings without medial *-e-* may point to the first cl. being OE flocc 'company or troop of folk'; the sense 'flock (of animals)' is not, however, recorded before the thirteenth century (NED s.v.) and not at all in ON, and that would seem the obvious sense in such a p.n. The affixes are neoðera 'nether', uferra 'upper', but they are not now in use.

CARDWELL DELF, named from the *Cardwell* family frequent here from the seventeenth century (PRThl *freq*), *v.* (ge)delf 'pit, quarry'. COCKERMOUTH, 1817 M, doubtless a transferred name from Cocker-

mouth Cu 361.　COMMON END & LANE, cf. *Common Close* 1849 *TA*.
CROWS NEST, low down the end of a ridge, *v.* Crow Nest 186 *supra*.
CROWTREE.　FLOCKTON BECK, *Floketonbrok* 1317 YD viii, *v.* brōc,
bekkr.　FLOCKTON GATE.　FLOCKTON GREEN, formerly *Nether
Flockton*.　FLOCKTON HALL, 1849 *TA*, cf. (*le*) *Hallestedes* 1331, 1343
YD v, *Hall Dyke & Ing* 1849 *TA*, *v.* hall, stede, dīc, eng.　FLOCKTON
LANE, *Flockton-lane* 1674 PRThl, *v.* lane.　FLOCKTON MILL, (a
watermill . . . called), *Flokton mylne* 1531 YD i, *Floc(k)ton mylne* 1580
WillY, 1602 PRThl, *v.* myln.　FLOCKTON MOOR, *Flockton moore*
(*head*) 1626, 1669 PRThl, *the moreheade* 1612 ib, *v.* mōr, hēafod.
GREEN HEAD, cf. Flockton Green *supra*.　HAIGH BRIDGE & LANE,
cf. *Hague house* 1780 PRThl, from a family of *Haigh* known in the
parish from the seventeenth century (PRThl *passim*).　HARDCASTLE
LANE, named from a local family of *Hardcastle* (17 PRThl *freq*).
HILL TOP, 18 PRThl.　LANE END, 1843 O.S.　MANOR HO, 1843
O.S.　MILL BECK, *v.* Flockton Mill *supra*, bekkr.　PALACE FM &
WOOD, *Little Palace*, *Palace Wood* 1849 *TA*, *v.* palis 'a palisade'.
PAUL LANE.　PINFOLD LANE, *Pinfold Close* 1849 *TA*, *v.* pynd-fald.
SIX LANES END, 1849 *TA*.　THACKER WELL, dial. *thacker* 'thatcher',
wella.　WINDMILL HILL LANE.

FIELD-NAMES

The principal forms in (*a*) are 1849 *TA*. Spellings dated 13, 1294, 1297,
1307–1311, 1322, 1345, 1378 are YD viii, 1589–1720 *Bretton* 106–114, 1645
Arm; others dated without source are YD v.

(*a*) Archer Close, Badger, Great Bracken Hill (*v.* brakni, hyll), Bradfield,
Bradford Close, Bridge Close & Royd, Buck Pond, Bull Croft, Carr Hill &
Ing (*v.* kjarr 'marsh', eng 'meadow'), Chapel Close, Croft Reservoir (*Nether,
Over Croft* 1686), Dog Pit (*v.* dogga, pytt), East Croft, Edmund Lidgit (*v.*
hlid-geat 'swing-gate'), the Field 1720 (*Field Close* 1667, *v.* feld), Flatt
Royd, Fold Close & Croft, Frank Close, Free Royd, Garth Croft, Glebe
Croft, Goldthorp Close, Grange Moor Close (cf. *the Grainge in Flockton*
1645 Arm, *v.* grange), Grant Royd, Great Ing, Haddings (*le Hafdingges* l. 13,
le Haueding' 1322, *Hadynes* 1686, ME *hefding* 'heading', a derivative of
hēafod with -ing[1], which in e.ModE had apparently the concrete sense of
'bank or dam'; here, however, it must denote something like 'the upper
common lands' as the field is on the hillside above Flockton village just
below New Park and above a series of fields called Seven Lands, Long
Close, etc. (grid 102–238153); cf. also Haddingley 239, Heady Field 284
infra), Hanby Close, Far & Near Honley (*a close called Honley Wood* 1822
Langd 278, cf. Honley 271 *infra*, *v.* hana 'cock', lēah), House Croft, Hullage
(*Hulegghecloyth* l. 13, *Shortholeg* 1343, *v.* hulu 'a shed, hovel', ecg 'escarp-

ment', clōh 'dell', for the sense cf. Scullage *infra*), Ing Field, Kelly Close, Kiln Croft, Kiln Steads ((*le*) *Ki-*, *Kylnestede*(*s*) 13, 1305, 1335, 1345, -*steads* 1686, *v.* cyln, stede), Land Ends, Ley Close, Lime Pit Close, Little Park, Long Royd, Low Holme, Low Ing, Major Flatt, Marl Flatt, Martin Bank, Meller Hill, Mitchell, Nook Close, North End, North Field, Ox Close, Painter Ing, Peaker Croft, Pease Close, Peter Close, Pit Hill, Pit Ing, Pog Close (cf. Pog Moor i, 304 *supra*), Pond Ing, Proctor Common, Quarry Close, Round Royd, Row Croft (*Rauecroft* 1248, *Raufecrofte* 1348, cf. *the Ralfe Lands* 1689, the ME pers.n. *Ralph*, *Rauf*, croft), Scullage (*Schollegge* 13, *Scolegge* 1294, *Schallegeker* 1295, *Scholegge* l. 13, 1335, *Skoleegge*(*ker*) 1345, *Skolledge* 1677, *v.* skáli 'shed, shieling', ecg, kjarr 'marsh', cf. Hullage f.n. *supra*), Senior Moor, Seven Lands, Shoulder of Mutton, Shrugg (*v.* scrogge 'bush, brushwood'), Side Moor, South Park, Three Nooked Close, Toad Hole, Top Royd, Ullage (*v.* Hullage f.n. *supra*), Upper Park, Wall Field, Water Ing, Wheat Close, Whin Beds (*v.* hvin 'gorse', bedd), White Flatt, Wild Close, Will Croft, Wood Royd.

(*b*) *Adelwaldrode* 1305 (the OE pers.n. *Æðelwald*, rod[1] 'clearing'), *Alwayrode* l. 13 (*v.* rod[1]), *Broad Heye close* 1645 Arm, *le Caluwerod* 1307 (*v.* calu 'bald, bare', rod[1]), *Coale Pitt at Flockton* 1699 PRThl (there is an old coalpit at the west end of the township, *v.* col[1], pytt), *Cooke Croft* 1686, *Eddinggrene* l. 13, *Eddyngrode* 1378 (probably an OE pers.n. *Edding*, a derivative of the recorded *Ed*(*d*)*a*, grēne[2], rod[1]), *Edward Roydes* 1692 (the pers.n. *Edward*, rod[1]), *le Fordoles*(*feld*) l. 13, 1322, 1343, *le Sordolis* (sic for *For-*) 1308 ('the front shares of the common land', *v.* fore, dāl), *le Freredik* 1307, 1322, *le Frer'dicke* 1335 (*v.* frere 'friar', dīc), *Haukenisclif* 13 BM (*Haukems-* 13 YD vi, *v.* clif, the first el. may be an error for ME *hauker* 'one who deals with hawks'), *Hyng*(*g*)*ebrigge* 1297, 1322 (*v.* henge 'steep', brycg), *Holsyk* 1343 (*v.* hol[1], sīc), *Kirk Ing* 1677, *le Kyrkeland* 1331 (*v.* kirkja, eng, land), *Middle Flatts* 1667, *le Moycrot* (sic) 1311, *Orpitterode* l. 13 (*v.* ōra[2] 'ore', pytt, rod[1]), *le Overhall* 1391, *Pauldin Inge* 1655, *Ricroft* 1343 (*v.* rȳge, croft), *the Roods* 1589, *Nether-*, *Over Royd* 1677 (*v.* rod[1]), *Roundroyd* 1636, *le S*(*c*)*hortgrenes* 1331, 1343 (*v.* sceort, grēne[2]), *Stocke-brygge* 13, *Stokbrigfeld* 1550 WB 111 ('bridge made of logs', *v.* stocc, brycg), *le Thwychel* 1311, *Twechill* 1343 (cf. dial. *twitchel* 'a narrow passage'), *Threpwda* c. 1150 Riev ('wood in dispute', *v.* þrēap, wudu, it is possibly in this township), *le Toftes* 1331, 1335 (*v.* topt 'enclosure, curtilage').

2. SHITLINGTON, now SITLINGTON (102–2615)

Scellin-, *Schelintone* 1086 DB

Silinton(*a*) 1118–30 YCh viii, a. 1139 Pont, *Schilenton* 1202–8 Ass, *Chylington* 1316 Vill, *Schilyngton* 1359 YD iv, vi

S(*c*)*hit-*, *S*(*c*)*hyt*(*e*)*lington*(*a*), -*yng-* 1145–60 YCh 1721–4, 1155–8 ib 1752 (Pont), 13, 1287 Selby, 1269 FF, 1288 YI, 1294 YD vi, 1296 LacyComp, 1303 KF, 1307 Ch, 1324 YD iii *et passim* to 1822 Langd

Siclinton(a) 1150–70 YCh 1727–8 (Riev)

Sit-, Sytlintun, -ton(a) 12 Riev (*freq*, YCh 1722), Ric 1 (1252) Ch, *Sittlingtun* 1155–70 YCh 1753, *Sit-, Sytlington(ia)* 1190–1220 YD v, 1196 YCh viii, 13 YD i, 1208 FF, 1209 DodsN, 1243 Fees, *Sitligtona* 1190–1202 YCh viii, 13 YD v

Shitlinton Hy 2 (1230) Ch, 1155–8 YCh 1451

Schetlinton(a), *-yng-* 1155 Pont, 1440 YD vi, *Shetelyngton* 1421 Pat

Schiuelinton' 1163 P

Sutlinton 1164–81 BM

Scit-, Scyttlinton, -tuna c. 1170 Riev, 14 YD i

For other spellings, *v.* Middlestown, Netherton, Overton *infra*.

'Scyt(t)el's farmstead', *v.* -ing[4], tūn. The OE pers.n. *Scyt(t)el* is not recorded, but is assumed from such p.ns. as Shillington Bd 174, Shitlington Nb 178. The earlier spellings in *Sit-, Sil-* are due to AN influence (IPN 113). On the other hand, the recent spelling Sitlington which has no etymological significance has been adopted from motives of delicacy, as were the substitution in Littleworth i, 49 *supra*, and the early creation of the new names Middlestown, Netherton and Overton for Middle, Nether and Over Shitlington (*infra*).

MIDDLESTOWN, *Middle-, Mid(d)els(c)hitelington, -yng-* 1322 Abbr, 1324 Arm, 1687 PRThl, 1822 Langd, (*-als. Midlestowne*) 1556 Arm, FF, (*-als. Mid(d)elston*) 1565, 1589 FF, (*als. Midleston*) 1589 Arm, *Midleton* 1523 DodsN, *Myd(d)leston* 1551 WillY, 1580 PRThl, *Midellstwone* (sic) 1641 PRThl, *Midillshilton* 1659 ib, *Middles Town* 1817 M. A contracted form of Middle Shitlington; on this use of *-town* cf. Mickletown 127 *supra*.

NETHERTON, *Schitelington inferior* 13 YD xiii, 51, *Schelinton Inferior* 1234 Ebor, *Nether Shut-, Shet-, Shit(e)lington, -yng-, -tun* 1326 Ass 5d, 1328 Banco, 1366 YD vi, 1615 Arm, 1687 PRThl, (*-als. Netherton* 1616) FF, 1777 Arm, 1822 Langd, *Nederschytlyngton als. Netherton* 1529 FF, *Netherton* 1523 DodsN, 1528 YD vi, 1580 PRThl, *Nedderton* 1528 YD vi, 1541 WillY, *Neytherton* 1573 Arm. *v.* neoðera 'nether', an affix of Shitlington *supra*, and town (*v.* Middlestown *supra*).

OVERTON, *Overs(c)hit(e)lyngton* 1190 YCh 1748, 1475 YD vi, 1536 FF, (*-als. Overton*) 1589 FF, 1777 Arm, *Overton* 1496 Arm, 1523

DodsN, 1580 PRThl. *v.* uferra 'upper', an affix of Shitlington *supra*, with *town* (*v.* Middlestown *supra*).

COXLEY (BECK), *Cockesclo* 1190–1204 YCh 1688, 13 Riev, *Coxley Mill* 1794 PRThl, *Cocksleybrook* 1720 *WYEnr* 172, probably a compound of cocc² 'a cock' and clōh 'dell', but the identification of *Cockesclo* is not certain as it is described as *in territorio de Floketona* (Riev 241), that is, Flockton 203 *supra*.

HOLLINHIRST, *Holinehurst* 1206–18 YCh viii (p), *Holynhyrst, -hirst, -in-* 1294 YD vi, 1321 YD viii, 1328, 1333, 1366 YD vi, (*Nethir-*) 1486 ib, *-herste* 1416 YD viii, *Hollynhurst(e)* 1424 Rent, 1602 PRThl, *Hollinghurst* 1528 *Bretton* 24, 1543 Star, 1585 WillY, 1620 PRThl. 'Holly wood', *v.* holegn, hyrst.

MIDGLEY, *Parvam Migelheiam* 1150–70 YCh 1728, *Migelie, -laia, -ley, -lay* c. 1170 Pont, 1170–85 YCh 1722, 1196–1202 ib viii, 1241 DodsN, 1317 YD viii (p), (*Litle-*) 12 Riev, *Miggele(y), -lay* 13 YD i, 1234 Ebor, 1276 Ch *et freq* to 1474 DodsN, *Mygley* 1583 PRThl, *Mydsley* 1604 ib, *Midgley* 1657 Pick, (*Nether-, Over-*) 1822 Langd. 'Midge infested clearing', *v.* mycg, lēah, cf. Midgley iii, 132, (Otley) pt. iv, Midgeley (Goldsborough) pt. v *infra*. Insect names (some of which may have been used as nicknames) are frequent in p.ns., cf. æmette 'ant', bēo 'bee', ceafor 'beetle', emel 'caterpillar', wifel 'weevil' in EPN *passim*. But this p.n. might also be from OE micg 'liquid drainings of manure', surviving as NCy dial. *migg*; cf. also Midge Hole iii, 200 *infra*.

NEWHALL, 1542 WillY, 1601 PRThl, *Niwehall'* 1202 FF, *the Newhall* 1542 Test vi, *v.* nīwe, hall. The identity of the two older spellings is not certain.

STONECLIFF LODGE, *Stainclyff, -clif* 1200–20 YCh 1816, 13 YD vi, 'rocky bank', *v.* steinn, clif. The identity is not certain, as the spellings may possibly refer to Stancliffe (Kirkheaton) 227 *infra*. Stony Cliffe Wood *infra* is distinct.

WHITLEY, *Quitlay* 1374 YD vi (p), *Qwytteley Hall* 1454 *Grant* 61, *Whitley* 1591 PRTh, 1605 FF, *v.* hwīt, lēah, a common local p.n.

BALK LANE. BANK FM & WOOD, cf. *Banckside* 1641 WillY, *the Bank field* 1720 *WYEnr* 174, *Bank Close & Field* 1849 *TA*, named

from *Mydsley Bancke* 1601 PRThl, *v.* banke, Midgley *supra*. BIRK
WOOD, 1849 *TA*, *v.* birki, wudu. BLACKER BECK & LANE, doubtless
named from Blacker Hall in the adjacent township of Crigglestone
(102 *supra*); but the *Blacker* family was fairly common in this parish
too (16–17 PRThl *freq*). BRIGGS LANE, named from a local family
of *Briggs* (17–18 PRThl *freq*). BROAD OAK HILL. CAPHOUSE,
1582, 1633 PRThl, probably a surname *Cap(p)* (Reaney 60), hūs
THE CARRS, *The Carre* 1644 WillY, cf. also *Wmfraykerre, le Myrikerre*
1294 YD vi (from the pers.n. *Humphrey* and *miry*), *v.* kjarr
'marsh'. CHAPEL HILL, 1795 PRThl, *v.* chapel, hyll. CLAY
HOUSE BECK. COOKHILL MILL, *Cockhillmill* 1720 *WYEnr* 172,
Cocking Mill 1841 O.S., *Cockhill Croft & Mill* 1849 *TA*, *v.* cocc[1]
'hillock', hyll. DANES LANE, DEANS PLANT., *Deans, Dean Bank Top*
1849 *TA*, *v.* denu 'valley'. DIAL WOOD, 1849 *TA*, *v.* dial, wudu.
DUNLANDS, *Dunland Close* 1849 *TA*. ELM GROVE. EMROYD,
1767 *WB* 43, 1800 PRThl, *v.* rod[1], the first el. probably the fem.
pers.n. *Emma*. FURNACE HILL, *Bank-Furnice* 1708 PRThl, in
Bank Wood *supra*, where there are old ironstone pits; *v.* Smithy
Brook 212 *infra*. GULLEY WOOD. HARTLEY BANK, probably
identical with *le Hagclif* 1294 YD vi, *Haklyff Banke* (sic) 1529 YD vi,
Cliff or Hartcliffe 1623 Bretton 23, *Hagley Bank* 1720 *WYEnr* 172,
Hartley Brook 1632 SheffMan, *Harley Brook* 1771 M, *Atley Bank*
1841 O.S.; the later form is probably 'hart cliff or clearing', *v.* heorot,
clif (replaced by lēah); the first el. of the older form is doubtless hogg
'clearing'; there was a local family of *Hartley* (17 PRThl *freq*),
and its name doubtless affected the form of the older p.n. HAYNE
LANE, (*Great & Pond*) *Hayne, Little Haynes* 1849 *TA*, *v.* hegn
'enclosure'. COLD HIENDLEY, *Could Heinley* 1604 PRThl, *Cold-
hindley als. Coldhinley* 1605 FF, *Cold Heenley* 1817 M, *Cold & Burnt
Heenley* 1849 *TA*, of the same origin as Cold Hiendley i, 270 *supra*,
'hind glade', *v.* hind, lēah, with cald 'cold, bleak' as the affix, but
it may be a transferred name. LITTLE LONDON. LONGROYD FM,
Long Royd 1849 *TA*, *v.* lang, rod[1]. MUG MILL, *Mug(g) Mill* 1739
PRThl, 1771 M, 1799 Arm. NETHERFIELD HO. NEW HOUSE FM,
the new house in Middleshitlington 1657 Pick, *v.* nīwe, hūs. OLD
WHIMSEY. PERKIN WOOD, 1841 O.S., named from a local family of
Perkin (18 PRThl *freq*). PITS BECK, *Coal Pits Clough* 1841 O.S., cf
also *Pytroid* 1529 YD vi, *Pitt Royds* 1653 Bretton 75, 1740 PRThl,
the Pitt row 1720 *WYEnr* 173, named from the *Colepits, -pytes* 1606,
1616 ib, *v.* col[1], pytt. RAG HILL, 1849 *TA*, *v.* ragge 'rough stone',

hyll. ROUND WOOD, 1849 *TA*. ROYD COTTAGE, cf. *Royd Close* 1849 *TA*, *v.* rod[1] 'clearing'. SANDY LANE, 1688 PRThl, *Sandey loune, Sannde lone* 1660, 1661 ib, *Sandy Gate* 1849 *TA*, *v.* sandig, lane, gata. SHEEPCOTE LATHE. SPRING WOOD, 1849 *TA*, *v.* spring 'plantation'. STAR FM. STOCK'S MOOR, 1817 M, *Stox moor* 1740 PRThl, *v.* stocc 'stump', mōr. STONY CLIFFE BECK & WOOD, *Stoney Cliffe (Wood)* 1849 *TA*, *v.* stānig, clif and Stonecliff *supra*. THE STRANDS, *Strands* 1849 *TA*, *the Strennes* 1543 Star, *v.* strand 'shore, bank'; it refers to the low-lying land by the R. Calder. SUN WOOD, 1841 O.S. WATER LANE. WICKEN TREE HALL, *Wiggon tree Hall* 1720 *WYEnr* 175, cf. *the quicken crosse* 1613 PRThl, *v.* cwicen 'mountain ash', cros. WINDMILL COTTAGE, *Windmill Close & Croft* 1849 *TA*. WINDY BANK, *Wyndybanckehall* 1640 WB 43, *v.* wind, banke. WOOD LANE, named from *Syclington Wode* J BM, *v.* wudu. THE WYKE, *(the) Wyke* 1529 YD vi, 1849 *TA*, *Wekys* 1538 YD vi, *v.* wīc 'dairy farm'; the name now refers to meadows by the R. Calder.

FIELD-NAMES

The principal forms in (*a*) are 1849 *TA* 353. Spellings dated 1720 are *WYEnr* 172–5, 1827 *Bretton*, and others dated without source are YD vi.

(*a*) Allen Well Croft, Armine Close, Ashton Furlong, Austonley (*Halstanley* 13 YD iv, the OE pers.n. *Alh-* or *Ælfstān*, lēah), Beck Close, Birch Croft, the Bottoms 1720, Breary Royd (*Breriroda* 12 Riev, *-rode* 1296 DodsN, *v.* brērig 'briary', rod[1]), Bridle Sty (*the Bridle-stie* 1720, 'bridle path', *v.* stīg), Briggend Ing 1720 (cf. *Bryggynges* 1531, *v.* brycg, ende, eng), Broad Ing (*Brodehyngis* 1529, *Brodoyng* (sic) 1538, *v.* brād, eng), Broad lane 1720, Brook Croft & Ing 1720, Broom Bottom, Butterfield Close, Calf Croft, Cardwell Close (possibly identical with *Caldwelle Rode* 13, *v.* cald, wella), Castlegate (*-yate* 1720, *v.* castel, geat), Cattlingate Close, Chapel Syke & Well, Cherry Garth, Chopping Bill, Clay Croft & Lands (ib 1720), the Clough 1841 O.S. (*v.* clōh), Coal Pit Close (cf. *Emroyd Colepittes* 1802 PRThl, *v.* Pits Beck *supra*), Cockhouse, Cock Walshaw (cf. *Walshaw close* 1720), Colt Ing, Conney hill closes 1720 (*v.* coni 'rabbit', hyll), Constable Croft, Coplas Close, Cot Close (cf. *Coytehill* 1538, *v.* cot 'cottage', hyll), Crabtree Close, Croakwell Syke, Crook Royd (*Crooked royds* 1720, *v.* rod[1]), Dam Ing (ib 1720, *v.* dammr, eng), Devil Ing, Dick Cliffe (*Dickliffs* 1720), Dick Royd (cf. *Rykerd Rode* 1531, the pers.n. *Richard* or *Dick*, rod[1]), Dobby Croft, Dog Croft, Dyke Croft, Farnley Lee, Fryer Croft (*v.* frere, croft), Gammer Hill Butts, Gimmer Royds (dial. *gimmer* 'a young ewe'), Goose Croft (ib 1720), Goose Pit Ing, Greaves Close (*the Greves* 1543 Star, *Greaves* 1827, *v.* grǣfe 'copse'), Grimes Croft (*Grymes-, Crymyscroft* 1538, the ME pers.n. *Grim*, ON *Grímr*, croft), Hail Cotes, Hall Flatt & Yard, Hand

Royd, Hawksworth, Hay Field (*the Hay fields* 1720, *v.* hēg, feld), Holling Close (*v.* holegn), Holmes (ib 1538, *v.* holmr), Hood Bank (cf. *Hutherode* 13, the ME pers.n. *Hudde*, rod[1]), Hook Bank, Horn Close, Horse Ing, Humber, Ing Hole, the Ings 1720 (*v.* eng), Kester Close, Kiln Hill (*the Killhill* 1720, cf. *le Kylneclif* 1294, *v.* cyln, clif), Lady Balk & Croft, Laith Croft (*v.* hlaða), Langley 1720, Lawn Ing & Royd (*v.* launde 'glade'), Long Haigh 1841 O.S. (ib 1817, *v.* haga), Long Lands, Long Marsh, Long Row, Long Stones, Mare Park, Mar Land (cf. *la Marlere* 13 Selby, *v.* marle, land), Martin Croft, Mill Dam, -Hill, -Holme (cf. *molendino de Milnehuse* c. 1200 YCh 1723, *v.* myln, hūs, dammr, holmr), Nab Royd Hill (*Nab Rode* 1538, *v.* nabbi 'knoll', rod[1]), Nell Gap, New Close (ib 1538), Nussy Carr, Oakwell Close, Old Croft 1720, Old Royd 1720, Over Flatt (*Over-, Nether Flatts* 1538, *v.* flat), Ox Close (ib 1720), Paradise (*the Parradice* 1720), Penter Ing, Petterhill Close, Pighill (*v.* pightel), Pigtail (*-taile close* 1720), Pitting Royd, Priest Royds, Purl Ing, Quarry (*-close* 1720), Rein (*v.* reinn 'boundary strip'), Reynold Royd (*-royds* 1720, the ME pers.n. *Rainald*), Riddings (*v.* rydding), Robin Royd, Roger Royd, Rough Ing, Rye Garth (*v.* rȳge, garðr), Sandy Knowle, Sankers, Slater Cross, Slop, Snap Mouth (*Snapmonthes* (sic) 1531, *Snaite mouth* 1720, cf. also *le Snapheng* 1294, *v.* snap 'scanty pasture', eng, but 'Snap mouth' may be a jocular name), Sough Close (*v.* sogh 'bog'), Spink Ing, Stand Royd Greaves, Stoney Bridge, Stripe (*v.* strīp), the Stubbing (*Nether-, Over Stobbyng* 1538, *v.* stubbing), Summer Royd, Swan Dam (ib 1720, *v.* swann, dammr), Swapper, Sykes (*v.* sīc), Thomas Royd, Thrushley, Turn Hurst (*v.* trun 'round', hyrst), Tween Sykes, Great Ullis, Warren, Waumbers, Well Hill, Wheat Croft 1720, Whitley Green & Wood.

(b) *le Brodemere* 1294 (*v.* brād, mere 'pool'), *le Broderode* 1294, *-roid* 1529, *Brodrod* 1359 (*v.* brād, rod[1]), *Ellencroft* 1653 Bretton 75, *Gamelheng* 1294 (the ME pers.n. *Gamel*, ON *Gamall*, eng), *Midgley Gate* 1675 Og (*v.* Midgley *supra*, gata), *Monkes Mylne* 1287 Selby (*v.* munuc, myln), '*terra Sacsi* quam idem Sacsi habet' 1118–30 YCh viii (the ON pers.n. *Saxi*), *Turnemere* 1294 (*v.* trun 'round', mere 'pool').

3. THORNHILL (102–2518)

> *Torni(l)* 1086 DB, *Tornhill'* 1190, 1193, 1196 P, 1195 YCh 1767, l. 12 BM, 1221 YCh viii (p), 1234 Ebor, *-hull* 1232–40 YD iv, *Tornehil* 12 YD i
>
> *Thornhill, -hyll* 1196–1202 YCh viii (p), 13 DodsN, YD ii, 1204–9 YD iv, 1219 DodsN, 1246 FF, c. 1250 YD iv, 1273 YD ii, 1297 LS, 1301 Ebor *et passim* to 1822 Langd, *Þornhill* 1274 (1300) Ebor, *-hull(e)* 1238–54 AD i, 1292 YD xiii, 59, 1316 Vill
>
> *Torenhil* e. 13 YD iv, c. 1220 BM, *Thorenhil(l)* 1210–25 YCh viii (p), Hy 3 Arm (p)
>
> *Thorhil* 13 YD vi, 1200–20 YCh 1816
>
> *Thornehull* 1281 Abbr, *-hill* 1402 FA, *-hylle* 1447 YD i, *-hell* 1559 FF

Thornyl(l) 1431 YD xiii, 59, 1564 FF, *Thornell* 1522 Test v, 1534 FF, 1550 WillY

'Thorn-tree hill', *v.* þorn, hyll. The early *Torn-*, *Toren-* spellings are AN.

BRIESTFIELD, formerly BRIESTWISTLE

Brerethuisel c. 1150 Riev, *-thwisel* 1243 Fees, 1246–59 YD iv
Breretwisel(l), *-tui-*, *-twy-*, *-il(l)*, *-yl* 1193–1211 YCh 1525, 1194, 1203 BM, 1206–18 YCh viii (p), 1232–40 BM, 1246 *Ass* 22, 1340 Arm, 1402 FA, 1424 Rent, *Brerewysell* 1344 Ch
Brertwisil, *-el(l)*, *-twissel*, *-twysell* 13 YD vi, 1203 BM, Hy 3 Arm (p), 1327, 1345 DodsN
Brerdtuisil 1203 YCh 1797 (YD vi, BM)
Brettewysel 1322 YD iv, *Bretwysyll* 1434 Pat
Brestewesyll 1419 YD xii, 230
Birt(e)wissill 1451, 1458 Arm, *Birtwisell* 1509 DodsN, *Birtetwyssell* 1517 Arm
Brittwesyll 1504 Arm
Brystwyll als. Bristwysill 1536 FF, *Bristwisstle* 1616 PrHosp, *Bristwell* 1620 PRThl, *Byrstwhistill* 1521 *Grant*[2] 151
Brestwill 1546 WillY, *-well* 1561 ib, 1610 PRThl, (*-als. Breart-whistle*) 1583 FF
Breestwell 1591 WillY   *Breistewell* 1601 PRThl
Briestwisle, *-ell* 1584 WillY, 1598 SessnR, *Briestwizle* 1777 PRThl
Briestfield 1796 Arm

'Land in a river-fork overgrown with briars', *v.* brēr, twisla. The 'fork' is doubtless the ridge formed between Briestfield Beck (Smithy Brook) and Howroyd Beck, but the present village is 1½ miles from the confluence. The history of the forms is interesting and obvious from the spellings, chiefly due to metathesis of *-twisel* to *-stwill*, *-stwell*, and, with wrong analysis of the els. as *Briest-well*, the replacement of *well* by *field*. Breastfield (Burton in Lonsdale), pt. vi *infra*, may have a similar origin, as has *Breretwisel* i, 120 *supra*.

COMBS, *Cowme Smethes* 1542 TestLds, *Cowmbesmythies* 1582 *WB* 140, *Combsmithies* (a forge) 1604 *WB* 34, *Cowm(e)hill* 1641 WillY, 1691 PRThl, *Coumhill* 1681 PRThl, *Cowne-hill* 1684 ib, *y*ᵉ *Cowms* 1740 ib, *The Combes* 1815 EnclA 36; most of the spellings point to an earlier *coume* or *colm*, *culm*; it is most probably l.ME *colm* 'soot, coal-dust, slack' (cf. NED s.v.) and **hyll**. Besides the forge referred to in -*smythies* (*v.* smið ðe), there is a colliery here and the name (like Soothill 193 *supra*) may refer to the spoil from the old coal workings.

FALHOUSE [ˈfaləs]

> *Falles* 1297 LS (p), *del Falles* 1303 KF (p)
> *Falches* 14 DodsN, *Falehes* 1335 ib, *the falghes* 1424 Rent
> *Falowes* 1509 DodsN, (*the*) *Fallowes* 1534 FF, 1587 WillY, 1603 PRThl, 1654 WillS, 1657 Pick, *Whitley fallowes* 1652 PRThl, *Ouerfallowes* 1662 WB 146
> *Falhous* 1666 PRThl, *Fall-House* 1693 ib, 1822 Langd

v. **falh** 'land broken up for cultivation, ploughed land', later 'fallow land'. The later form is due to folk-etymology.

HEALEY, *les Hegh(e)leis* 1203 YCh 1797, 13 YD vi, *Heychelay* l. 13 YD v, *Heley* 1599 PRThl. 'High clearing', *v.* **hēah**, **lēah**. Healey is on the top of a ridge.

ICKLES Ho, probably of the same origin as Ickles i, 186 *supra*, *v.* **ēcels** 'land added to an estate'. An unidentified *Thickles* in Kirkheaton is some 2 miles to the west, but has no connexion (226 *infra*).

SMITHY BROOK, 1822 Langd, *Smythebrooke* 1605 PRThl, *Smythye Broke* 1613 ib, *Smethebroke* 1641 ib, *Smithe Brook* 1771 M, *v.* **smiððe**, **brōc**; the smithy (doubtless iron-smelting works) was called *Bancke Smythes* 1575 WillY, *Bancke-, Bank(e)smithies* 1593 ib, 1617 PRThl, 1639 PREm, *the Smythes* 1540 Test vi, *the Smythyes* 1614 ib. The identity of *Banksmithie* is not certain and these spellings may in fact refer to the old iron-smelting works at Furnace Hill in Shitlington 208 *supra*, which is in Bank Wood. *v.* **smiððe**, **brōc**.

THORNHILL LEES, *Thorn(e)hil(l) Leyes* 1310 YD iv, -*Lees* 1584 PRThl, 1608 YD vi, 1663 WB, -*leighes* 1586 FF, *Thornel(l)leys, -leis* 1509 DodsN, 1535 VE, 1559 FF, 1616 PrHosp, *Thorney lez* 1544 MinAcct, *Thornillease haule* 1550 WillY, *Thornylleighes* 1563 YD vi. 'Thornhill clearings', *v.* **lēah**.

LOWER WHITLEY

> *Hwitteleia* 1195–1211 YCh 1701   *Withelei* 13 YD vi
> *Wi-, Wyttelay, -ley* 1196 P, 13 DodsN, 1297 LS, -*legh* 1247 Ch

Witelay 1196 P

White-, *Whytelay*, *-ley* 1243 Fees, 1303 KF, 1316 Vill, 1351 FF, 1379 PT

Whitteley 1303 Aid, 1328 Banco

Whitlay, *-ley* 1344 Ch, 1345 DodsN *et freq* to 1587 Arm, (*Lower-*) 1822 Langd

Wytley 1369 Arm

'Bright forest-glade', *v.* hwīt, lēah, a common YW p.n. 'Lower' in relation to Upper Whitley 233 *infra*.

BLACKERHILL FM, named from the local family of *Blacker* (17 PRThl *passim*), cf. Blacker Beck 208 *supra*.   BOTTOMS FM, *the Bottoms* 1772 PRThl, *v.* botm.   BUNKERS HILL, 1817 M, a common p.n. commemorating the battle of Bunkers Hill 1775.   CARR FM, (*the*) *Carr* 1622 PRThl, 1771 M, *v.* kjarr 'marsh'.   CHAPEL LANE, cf. *Chapel Croft* 1846 *TA*.   CHURCH LANE, cf. *Church Close* 1777 PRThl.   CLEVELAND, *Cleeveland* 1792 PRThl, *v.* clif, land, but it may have been named from Cleveland YN 128; the editor of PRThl takes *Thomas Bedford Cleeveland* as a pers.n., but *Bedford* is the surname, common in the parish, and Cleeveland is his place of residence.   CLOCK ROYD. COMMON, *the Common* 1777 PRThl, ME *commun* 'common land'. CROFT HO, *Croft heads* 1634 *M*, *v.* croft 'enclosure', but possibly named from the local family of *Croft* (17 *et freq* PRThl).   THE CROSS, *yᵉ Cross* 1746 PRThl, *v.* cros; the site at the centre of the village is still marked on the 6″ O.S.; there are well known runic crosses at Thornhill, cf. YAJ, xxiii, 243–8.   CROW ROYD, 1812 PRThl, *Craw Royd* 1846 *TA*, *v.* crāwe, rod[1].   DALE GREEN, 1774 PRThl, *v.* dæl 'valley', grēne[2].   DEADMAN'S LANE.   DIMPLEDALE, 1843 O.S., *v.* dympel 'pool', dæl; it is by Smithy Brook.   EDGE END, 1713 PRThl, *v.* Thornhill Edge *infra*.   EDGE TOP, *Top of Edg* 1634 *M*, *Top of the Edge* 1795 PRThl, *v.* prcc.   FIXBY, named from Fixby iii, 35 *infra*.   FOX ROYD, *Fox roid* 1634 *M*, *the Fox Royd* 1777 PRThl, *v.* fox, rod[1] 'clearing'.   FRANK LANE.   FRECKLETON, a family of *Freckleton* (presumably from Freckleton La 150) was known here in the seventeenth century (PRThl *freq*).   GIBRALTAR, 1843 O.S.   GOAT HILL, 1766 Arm, 1776 PRThl, *v.* gāt, hyll. GOLGREAVE, *Golgrave Wood* 1846 *TA*, *v.* grǣfe 'copse'.   GREEN HILL, 1843 O.S., *le Grenehalle* 1322 YD iv, 1424 Rent, *v.* grēne[1], hall.   GROVE HO.   HALEY HILL, *Haley Green* 1846 *TA*, a local family of *Hayley* is known from the seventeenth century (PRThl).

THE HALL, *Thornhill Hall* 1626, 1705 PRThl. HATCHET HALL.
HEADFIELD, 1817 M, *Headfeild* 1642 PRThl, probably named from
le Hewed 1310 YD iv, *v.* hēafod 'a headland', here a lofty knoll round
which the Calder flows. HEBBLE MILLS, doubtless named from a
hebble or bridge over the canal (*v.* Salterhebble iii, 110 *infra*). HIGH-
FIELD, *High Fields* 1771 M. HILL TOP, 1843 O.S. HOLT LANE
HO, *Holt Lane* 1716 PRThl, *'th Hoult Lane* 1727 ib, cf. *Thomas Holt*
1698 ib, *Joseph Holt* 1716 ib, members of a local *Holt* family.
HOSTINGLEY, 1694 PRThl, *Hastingley* 1634 *M*, *v.* lēah; the first el. is
obscure, but Ritter 140 suggests late OE *hūsting* (ON *hús-þing* 'a
small assembly', *v.* þing). HOWROYD FM, *Howroyd* (*top*) 1694,
1741 PRThl, *v.* hol[1] 'hollow', rod[1]. HOYLE MILL FM, *Hooll mylle*
1557 WillY, *the hole mylne* 1613 PRThl, *the hoyle milne* 1625 ib, *v.*
hol[1] 'hollow, hole', myln. THE INGS, *Neither, Upper Ing*(*e*) 1634
M, *ye Ing, Ings* 1777, 1791 PRThl, *v.* eng 'meadow'. JUDY HAIGH
HO, *Haigh House* 1800 PRThl, the family of *Haigh* was common
locally from the sixteenth century; in PRThl there are 6 Judith
Haighs mentioned (3 of whom were married), and of these the likeliest
to have been remembered in the name of the house is Judith Haigh,
baptised 29 Jan 1739, died Nov 1799 (PRThl 272, 393); she was the
only one who seems to have spent her life here. LADY MILL, 1841
O.S. LADY WOOD, 1841 O.S., 1846 *TA*. LANE TOP, *y[e] Lane* 1696
PRThl, *v.* lane. LEES HALL, 1644 PRThl, 1817 M, *Lee Halle* 1604
Arm, *v.* Thornhill Lees *supra*, hall. LEES MOOR, 1782 PRThl, *v.*
prec., mōr. MELLOR HILL, 1843 O.S., named from the local *Mellor*
family (17 *et freq* PRThl). MILL BANK, 1843 O.S., *-Bancke* 1634 *M*,
cf. *the* (*new*) *mylne* 1610, 1613 PRThl, *ye mille Thornhill* 1711 ib,
v. myln. MITHROYD GREEN, *Myt*(*t*)*royd grene, Metheroyde grene*
1614, 1615 PRThl, *Methroide grene* 1633 ib, *Midroyd Green* 1771 M,
from ON miðr 'middle', rod[1] 'clearing'. MOOR FM, cf. *Morton*
1846 *TA*, *v.* mōr, tūn. NEW HOUSES. OUZELWELL HALL, 1843
O.S., 'thrush well', cf. Ouzelwell 137 *supra*. OVERTHORPE, *Over-*
thorp(*p*)*e* 1562 Hnt ii, 306, 1586 FF, 1616 PRThl, *et freq* to 1795 ib,
Upperthorp(*e*) 1763 ib, 1817 M, *v.* uferra 'upper', þorp 'outlying
farmstead'. PORTOBELLO, 1817 M. PRIEST ROYD, 1846 *TA*, *v.*
prēost, rod[1], cf. Priestroyd iii, 239 *infra*. PUDDING HILL, cf. *Pudding*
Poke 1846 *TA*, 'pudding bag'. LOWER & UPPER RAKES. RED HO.
SAVILE TOWN, named from the prominent *Savile* family (PRThl
passim). SCOPSLEY LANE. SHROGG WOOD, *Shrog* 1688 *WB* 178a,
v. scrogge 'a bush, brushwood'. SLAITHWAITE, named like Fixby

supra from another local place (Slaithwaite 307 *infra*).   LOWER &
UPPER SOWOOD, *Sowood* 1816 *EnclA* 20, cf. Sowood 189 *supra*.
THORNHILL EDGE, 1613 PRThl, 1771 M, *th(e) edge* 1612, 1718
PRThl, *v.* ecg, here denoting the long escarpment south of Thornhill
overlooking Howroyd Beck.   TOWN, cf. *Townend Close* 1846 *TA*.
TURNIP LANE, 1846 *TA*.   WALLIS FM, *Wallys Hall* 1586 FF, named
from the *Wallis* family (17 PRThl *freq*).   WELL GARTH HO, cf. *Well
Close* 1846 *TA*.   WILDERNESS.   WOODLEIGH.

FIELD-NAMES

The principal forms in (*a*) are 1846 *TA* 398, and those in (*b*) 1634 *M*.
Spellings dated 1203 are YD vi (YCh 1797), 1208 YD iv, 1393 *FGr* (K. 2),
1684, 1764 *Glebe*, and others dated without source are PRThl. Some f.ns. in
(*b*) may belong to Upper Whitley township (235 *infra*).

(*a*) Ash Field, Broad Ley, Brook Royd (cf. *Broke close* 1634, named from
the Bro(o)k 1743, 1763, *v.* brōc, rod[1]), Bull Croft, Calf Croft, Carwood Ing
(cf. Carr Fm *supra*, eng), Cinder Hill (*Sinder Hill* 1634, *Cyndril* 1792 *WB* 54,
v. sinder, hyll), Coal Pit Close (*Coolepitt-* 1634), Cow Close (ib 1634), Crab
Tree Close (ib 1634), Crimbles (*Crimble* 1634, *v.* crymel 'small plot'),
Cromwell, th' Dam 1770 (*v.* dammr), Dean Croft, Delly Carr, Dick Royd,
Edge End Ing (*v.* Edge End *supra*, eng), Garth Ing (*v.* garðr, eng), Gib Croft,
Gilbert Royd (ib 1777), Goit Ing (*Goite Inge* 1634, *v.* gota 'channel', eng),
the Great Flatt 1777, Great Leys (*v.* lēah), Gunson Ing 1777 (ib 1684), Haigh
Ing, High Trees, Horse Close, Hugh Ing, Kirk Field (*Kirke-* 1634), Kittle
Royd (*Keddle-, Kettleroid(e)* 1634, the ON pers.n. *Ketill*, rod[1]), Long Lands,
Longleys 1777, Long Shaw (*Laukechahke* (sic) 1208, 'long copse', *v.* lang,
sceaga), the Longshutts 1777 (dial. *shut* 'division of land'), Ludwell Field
(*-fielde* 1634, *v.* hlūd, wella), Lurking Royd, Glebe & South Mountain
(*Neyther-, Over Mounton* 1634, *Mountain* 1792 *WB* 54, *the Mountains* 1777),
North Leys, Orpine (*Orpinyate close* 1634), the Owram royd 1777, Ox Croft,
yᵉ Parsonage Fold 1777, Peck Hill, Peters Flat 1777 (ib 1684), Pitt Close,
Pitt Hills (*the Pighles* 1777, *v.* pightel 'enclosure'), Priest Croft, Quarry
Hills, Riding Close (*Middle-, Neither Riding* 1634, *the Ridings* 1777, *v.*
rydding 'clearing'), Rye Close, Simion's Croft, the Soiles 1777 (ib 1684, *v.*
sol[1] 'mud, dirty pool'), Stanwell, Starting Stoop Close, Steeple Close, Stony
Royd, Stor Hill Bank (*Storrid Bank* (sic) 1777, *v.* storð 'plantation', hyll),
Storth (*v.* prec.), Strangwell, Strong Royd, Sun Sides, Sweet Bit (ib 1634,
v. swēte, bita), Three Nook, Thrusley 1780 Arm, Toad Hole, Under Edge
Ing, the West Royds, Wharton, Wheat Royd, (Long & Little) Worton (*v.*
wyrt-tūn 'vegetable garden').

(*b*) *Barstainwelle* 1203 (possibly a scandinavianised form of OE *Beornstān*,
v. wella), *Bedforth, Brendeleis* 1208 ('burnt clearings', *v.* brende, lēah),
Brigginge (*v.* brycg, eng), *Browniroide, Buskie close, Calvecloyse* 1393 (*v.* calf,

clos), *Co(o)kbrig, Cowperro(y)de* 1404, 1405 Arm (*v.* coupare, rod[1]), *Edwin-welle* 1203 (the OE pers.n. *Éadwine,* wella), *Ellingtre flat* (*v.* ellern 'elder-tree', flat), *Estcroft* 1319 DodsN, *Fox hall, Grosmunt* 1203 (a Fr p.n. 'great hill', cf. Grosmont YN 120), *Hallowes* (*v.* halh 'nook of land'), *Harecroft* 1208, *Hobroide* (the ME pers.n. *Hobbe,* rod[1]), *Neither-, Ouer Hollyes* (*v.* holegn 'holly'), *Holmenge* 1393 (*v.* holmr, eng), *Lath Garth* ('barn yard', *v.* hlaða, garðr), *Neither-, Over Lawnde* (*v.* launde 'glade'), *Littilroyde* 1393, *yᵉ Lodge-Break* 1685, *Milhill Close, Mouseho! l, -hoole, Norcliffe Field, Oakes, Osmundfinaic* 1203 (the OE pers.n. *Ōsmund,* eik 'oak', *-fin-* is obscure), *Great & New Park(e), Pearetre flat, Pease Royde* (*v.* pise, rod[1]), *Petting Roid, Sandes, Scolefield Ing, Shepe Coate, Spines, Spine flat, Staires-foot* 1699 (*v.* stæger 'stair, steps', fōt), *Swarthing Forth* (*v.* ford), *Thornhil Brigge* 1675 Og (*v.* brycg), *Well Inge* (*v.* wella, eng), *Wheat Crofte, White Intacke* (*v.* intak).

xiv. Emley

1. LOWER & UPPER CUMBERWORTH (102–2109)

Cu'bre-, Co'breuu(o)rde 1086 DB

Cumberwrth(e), -worth(e) 1121–7 YCh 1428, 1215 ChR, 1243 Fees, 1297 LS *et passim* to 1641 Rates, (*-half(e)*)) 1552 YD viii, 1588 LS, (*Nether-, Over-*) 1606 FF, *Cumbirworth* 1379 PT

Cumbrew(o)rth 1189 Nost 4d, 1297 WCR, (*Over-*) 1581 YD viii, *-wode* (sic) 1202–24 YCh viii

Comberw(o)rth(e) Hy 3 BM, 1379 PT, 1424 YD viii, (*Nether and Over-*) 1596 PF, *Combyrworth* 1433 Hall

Combrew(o)rth 1297, 1330 WCR

'Cumbra's enclosure', *v.* worð. The first el. is the OE pers.n. *Cumbra,* which occurs also in other p.ns. like Cumberwood Wo 193, Cumberworth L. This pers.n. is ultimately from PrWelsh **Cumbroʒ* 'the Welshman' (*v.* EPN i, 119, s.v. **Cumbre**). *Half* denotes a half of the township with separate jurisdiction.

BARNCLIFF HILL, *Barncliff* 1817 M.   BIRK HO, *Byrkehouse* 1486 *Bretton* 83, *Birkhouse* 1817 M, cf. *del Byrkes* 1379 PT (p), *Byrke royd* 1550 YD viii, *v.* birki 'birch-tree'.   BROGG WOOD, *Brogs* 1843 O.S., cf. dial. *brog* 'a bushy or swampy place', *brogwood* 'brush-wood, esp. the undergrowth on which cattle feed' (EDD s.v.); these words are probably connected with dial. *brog* 'awl' (*v.* NED s.v.).   BROMLEY. BURNWOOD.   CARR HILL, *Car* 1817 M, *v.* kjarr 'marsh'.   CLIFF HILL, 1843 O.S., cf. *Boswallclyf, -well-* 1550 YD viii, *v.* clif; Boswell

is doubtless a surname.   COAL PIT LANE, cf. *Coal Pit Ing* 1842 *TA*.
COMMON END & SIDE, 1843 O.S.   CRABTREE HALL, *Crab Tree* 1843
O.S., *v*. crabbe, trēow.   CUMBERWORTH COMMON.   DEARNE
GRANGE, 1843 O.S., *v*. R. Dearne, grange.   EAST HILL, *Eastals* 1685
Glebe, *v*. ēast, halh 'nook of land'.   GREEN HOUSE NOOK, *Green
House Mill* 1843 O.S.   GREEN SIDE, 1843 O.S.   GREEN WOOD.
HEATER, cf. Little Heater iii, 170 *infra*.   JANE WELL, 1843 O.S.
KIRK STYLES, *Kirkstye* 1721 *Bretton* 82, *-Sties* 1843 O.S., *v*. kirkja, stīg
'path', replaced by *stile*.   LANE HACKINGS, 1842 *TA*, *-Hackens* 1843
O.S., *v*. lane; *Hackings* is probably a derivative of ME *hacken* 'to
hack', possibly in the later sense 'plough up soil into ridges' or the
like; it occurs elsewhere (Hacking i, 202, *Hackinge* i, 220, iii, 37, Hack-
ing(s) ii, 232, iii, 276, Hacking Croft (Menston) pt. iv *infra*).   LANE
END, 1842 *TA*.   LANE SIDE, 1843 O.S.   LEAK HALL, 1817 M, *Leyke*
1490 YD vi, (*-Hall*) 1549 ib, 1550 YD viii, *Leikhall* 1544 ib, *Leekhall*
1552 ib, *v*. lœkr 'brook, rivulet', probably an older name of Pingle
Dike, above which the hall stands; a *Sam'l Leake* was living in the
parish in 1743 PREm 159, but his surname doubtless originates in
the p.n.   LONG ROYD, 1817 M, *v*. lang, rod¹ 'clearing'.   OAKCLIFFE
HALL, *Hawcliff(e)* 1601 *Bretton* 74, 1611 Hnt ii, 251, *v*. hafoc 'hawk',
clif.   PARK DIKE & HEAD.   PINGLE DIKE, cf. *Pyghils* 1529 YD vi,
v. pightel, pingel 'enclosure'.   PONKER, 1843 O.S., possibly 'pond
marsh', *v*. ponde, kjarr.   ROW GATE.   SCHOOL GREEN.   STEPHEN
WOOD.   STOCKS.   STOVE END.   SUNSIDE HO.   TURPIN HILL.
WITHER WOOD, 1843 O.S., *Witherwoodhall* 1728 *Bretton* 82, cf. also
Witherall 1596 ib, probably ON *viðar* gen.sg. of viðr 'wood', *v*. hall,
wudu.   WOOD NOOK, 1861 *Sav*.

FIELD-NAMES

The principal forms in (*a*) are 1861 *Sav*. Spellings dated 1523 are YD vi,
1685 *Glebe*, and others dated without source are *Bretton* 72, 82–3. Some
modern f.ns. cannot be separated from those of Skelmanthorpe 223 *infra*.

(*a*) Blacker Wood, Bottom Close, Ing & Low Ing (*v*. eng), Long Close,
Marl Close.

(*b*) the *Bancke* 1699, *Birchinglie close* 1685 (*v*. bircen, lēah), *Buthroyde
Croft* 1699 (*v*. bōth, rod¹), *Healiee Closes* 1699, *Horse Close* 1699, *Kirkhouse*
1556 TestLds (*v*. kirkja, hūs), *New Wales* 1685, *Paradise* 1685, *Perwell Ing*
1685, *Rugh Close* 1699 (*v*. rūh 'rough'), *Stackwood Steele* 1685 (*v*. stigel
'stile'), *Tenterzerd* 1523 (ME *tentour* 'tenter', geard).

2. EMLEY (102–2413)

> *Amelai, -leie* 1086 DB
> *Emelei(a), -le(y), -lay(e)* 1150–70 YCh 1728 (Riev), 1190–1204 ib
>   1688, 1194, 1232–40 BM, 1237 FF, 1253 YD v, 1279–81 QW,
>   1290 YD i, 1291 Tax *et freq* to 1551 WillY
> *Emmesleia, -leg* 12 Riev, 1203 Cur
> *Emmelei(a), -le(y), -lay* 1190–1220 YD v, 13 YD i, 1238 Ebor, 1246
>   Ass 4 (p), 1253 Ch, 1276 RH, 1277–1308 WCR (*freq*), 1293
>   Ebor, 1328 YD iii, 1361 DodsN
> *Hemmeley* 1275 WCR   *Elmeley* 1842 *TA*
> *Emley, -lay* 1328 WCR, 1350 DodsN *et passim* to 1548 WillY

There may well have been an OE pers.n. *Emma*, which would have been a normal hypocoristic form of some OE pers.n. in *Eormen-* (*Eormenrēd*, etc.). There is also the recorded OE *Eama*, which is thought to enter into Emmington O 107 and is, according to Redin 63, a pet-form of some such OE pers.n. as *Eanbald, Eanbeorht*. Emley is without doubt 'Em(m)a's forest-glade or clearing', *v.* lēah. This is preferable to a derivation from OE *elm* 'elm-tree', with dissimilatory loss of *-l-* (Ekwall), since there is no trace of an early *elm* in the spellings; Elmley Wo 122, 240, which is from *elm-lēah*, shows no such loss. The *TA* form *Elmelay* merely represents a local effort to alter the name to suit an etymology (cf. Goodall 132).

BENTLEY GRANGE

> *Benet(e)le(ia), -leya* 13 YD vi, J BM, (*grangia de*) 1237 FF
> *Bentelaie, -ley* 13, 1226, 1253 YD v
> *Bentlay, -ley* 13 YD viii, 1471 YD vi, 1536 YD v, (*-Grange*) 1822
>   Langd

'Clearing overgrown with bent-grass', *v.* beonet, lēah, cf. Bentley i, 24 *supra*. It was a grange of Byland Abbey (1471 YD vi, 5), *v.* grange.

CRAWSHAW, 1643 WillY, *Croweshagh* 1208 FF, *-schaye* 1307 YD viii, *Crawesthagh* (sic for *-schagh*) 1328 WCR, *Crauschagh* 1379 PT (p), *Crowshaw* 1659 PREm. 'Crow wood', *v.* crāwe, sceaga.

EMLEY WOODHOUSE, 1760 *WB* 213a, *Wodehus* 1236, 1240 FF, (*Emlay*)*vodhouses* 1313 YD vi, *Wodhouses* 1347 YD v, (*Emlay-*) 1374 ib, *Wodhous* 1379 PT (p), (*Emlay-, -ley-*) 1472 YD v, 1578 FF, *Emley*

Wodhous 1541 WillY, 1578 FF. 'House in the wood', *v.* **wudu, hūs.**
Woodsome Lees 1676 *Bretton* 37 may preserve an older form in the
dat.pl. *wudu-hūsum.*

KIRKBY, *Kirke-*, *Kyrkeby* 13, 1290 YD i, 1294 YD viii, 1305 YD v,
1352 FF, 1379 PT *et freq* to 1605 FF, *Kirkby* 1382 DodsN, *Kirkeby
als. Kirby Graunge* 1611 FF. 'Church farm', *v.* **kirkju-bȳ**. This is an
isolated farmstead and does not mean 'village or farmstead with a
church'; it probably denotes 'farm belonging to a church', probably
'an abbey grange' (cf. Bentley Grange *supra*).

ASH LANE, cf. *Ash close* 1842 *TA*.   BAILDON DIKE & PLACE, *Beldon
Ing(s)* 1817 M, 1842 *TA*, *Bayldon Nook* ib, possibly OE **bēl** 'fire' and
dūn, denoting 'a beacon hill', but it could be a surname from Baildon
pt. iv *infra*.   BEANCROFT WELL, *Bean Croft* 1842 *TA*, *v.* **bēan, croft.**
BOOTH LANE, the family of *Booth* was common here from the seven-
teenth century (PREm *passim*).   BROOMFIELD LANE, *Broom Field*
1842 *TA*, *v.* **brōm, feld.**   BROOM HALL, 1843 O.S.   BUNKERS HILL.
BUTTS TOP, cf. *Butt Croft* 1842 *TA*, *v.* **butte** 'abutting strip'.   CARR
VILLA.   CHAPEL HO, named from *Capella* 1726 PREm.   CLOUGH
BRIDGE & DIKE, cf. *Clough Close* 1842 *TA*, *v.* **clōh** 'a dell'.   DAY-
HOLES, dial. *day-hole* 'an adit to a mine' (cf. Day Hole 189 *supra*);
there is an old colliery here.   DENTON NOOK, 1842 *TA*.   EMLEY
MOOR, 1817 M, *v.* **mōr**, cf. *Moor Ho* (*infra*).   EMLEY OLD HALL,
Old Hall 1771 M.   EMLEY PARK, 1562, 1567 WB 81, 134, *yͤ Park*
1720 PREm, *Park Hill*, *Park House* 1771 M, *v.* **park.**   EPLEY
WOOD.   FRANK LANE.   GILLCAR, *Gill-acker* 1685 *Glebe*, *Gilker*
1771 M, *v.* **æcer**, *Gill-* may be a pers.n.   GROVE HO, formerly *Rest
House* 1843 O.S.   HAG HILL, *Hag(g) Hill* 1746 *Bretton* 105, *v.* **hogg**
'clearing'.   HALLAS CHAMBERS, doubtless named from a local man,
Joseph Hallas (1787 PREm 177); for *Chambers* cf. High Chambers *infra*.
THE HEATER, cf. Little Heater iii, 170 *infra*.   HIGH CHAMBERS,
1843 O.S., ME *chambre* 'chamber', used here as elsewhere in YW,
of 'a domicile' (cf. Higgin Chamber iii, 147 *infra*).   HIGHFIELD HO,
Hickfield (sic) 1817 M.   THE HUT.   KILN LANE.   KIRKBY WOOD,
1842 *TA*, *v.* Kirkby *supra*, **wudu.**   KIRKHILL.   LADY OAK, 1843
O.S.   LOW & UPPER LANGLEY, 1843 O.S., *v.* **lang, lēah**, a common
YW p.n.   LENACRE, cf. *Coalpit Ladacre* 1842 *TA*.   LEISURE LANE,
Lezer Close & Common 1842 *TA*, *v.* **læs** (obl. *læswe*) 'meadowland'.
LEYS LANE.   LIGHTCLIFF WOOD, 1842 *TA*, 1843 O.S., 'bright

bank', *v.* leoht, clif, Lightcliffe iii, 80 *infra.* LITTLE DIKE. LONG LAWN. LOW HO, 1817 M. LOW WELL. MOOR HEAD, *Elmley Moor Head* 1771 M, cf. *ye Moresyde* 1658 PREm, *v.* Emley Moor *supra.* MOOR HO (lost), 1817 M, *Morhouses in Emley* 1562 *WB* 16, *Morehouse* 1569 WillY, *v.* prec., hūs. MOUSE HO, 1843 O.S. NINE CLOGS DIKE. OUT LANE DIKE. PARK GATE & LANE, 1843 O.S., *Park Gate, Park House* 1817 M, cf. *Parkmillne* 1648 WillS, *v.* Emley Park *supra,* geat, myln. RADLEY LANE, probably named from the *Radley* family (17–18 PREm *freq*). SHEEP COTE. SILVER INGS, 1817 M, probably 'productive meadows', *v.* seolfor, eng. SKITTERICK, 1842 *TA, v. Skitterick* ii, 168 *supra.* STRINGER HO, 1842 *TA,* named from a local family of *Stringer* (17 PREm *freq*). TAYLOR HILL, 1843 O.S., named from a local family of *Taylor* (17–18 PREm *passim*). THORNCLIFFE, *Thornelynrod le Ragged* (sic for -*clyu*-) 1313 YD vi, *Thornecliffe,* -*cley* 1645, 1657 PREm, *Thorncliff Bank* 1817 M, *v.* þorn, clif. TIPPING LANE & WELL, cf. *Tipling Lane Close* 1842 *TA,* from dial. *tipple* 'to fall, tumble' or 'to tipple, drink'. TITUS LANE. TYBURN, TYBURN HILL, *Tyburn Close & Croft* 1842 *TA,* probably from London's famous Tyburn (Mx 137). WARBURTON, *Warburton Close* 1842 *TA,* cf. *Peter Warburton,* a local man (1667 PREm 41), a surname presumably from Warburton Ch. WESTFIELD, 1843 O.S. WHITE CROSS, 1709 *WB* 48a, 1721 PREm, *Whitcross(e)* 1619 FF, *v.* hwīt, cros. WINDMILL HILL, cf. *Wind Hill Neck* 1842 *TA,* cf. Windhill i, 287 *supra* for the interchange of forms. YEW, 1771 M, *Yew Farm* 1699 *Bretton* 105, *v.* iw 'yew-tree'.

FIELD-NAMES

The principal forms in (*a*) are 1842 *TA* and modern (1935), marked *mod.*

(*a*) Allot Royd 1720 *WB* 32, 1817 M, Bark House Ing (*Barkhouse* 1720 *WB* 32, 'tan-house meadow', ME *barke* 'bark', *v.* eng), Bell Lees, Bell String Bank ('land for the maintenance of the church bell-ropes', cf. Bell Cross i, 66 *supra*), Blacker ('black marsh', *v.* blæc, kjarr, Blacker *supra*), Breary Bank (*v.* brērig 'briary'), Breckle Royd, Broad Ing *mod* (ib *TA*), Brook Croft, Broom Close, Field, Nook & Royd, Burkell, Cafit, Christe Greaves (*v.* grǣfe 'copse'), Church Croft *mod* (ib *TA*), Close before Door, Copley (cf. Copley iii, 110 *infra*), Crabtree Close, Cross Lands, Dam Ing (*v.* dammr, eng), Dina Field *mod,* Eddish Close (*v.* edisc 'enclosure'), Ellen Tree Flatt (*v.* ellern 'elder-tree'), Fog Close (*v.* fogga 'long grass'), Fowling Royd, Goose Gate, Hague Ing (*v.* haga, eng), Hall Royd, Harp Royd, Heepley Wood, High Trees *mod* (ib *TA*), Homire, Ing Bridge & Nook (*Little Ing* 1439 *Bretton* 99, *v.* eng), King Corn Clough, Knell Royd, Laith

Croft, Little Holme, Little Hirst, Long Lands, Long Shutt (dial. *shut* 'division of land'), Low Dole (*v.* dāl 'share'), Meone Field, Nab Close (*v.* nabbi 'knoll'), North Croft (cf. *Norcroft Ing* 1792 *WB* 54, *v.* norð, croft, eng), Old Royd, Peggs, Quarry, Shepherd Gap, Short Lands, Shrog (*v.* scrogge 'bush, brushwood'), Smithy Field, Smith Royd, Spice Mouth, Stone Horse Park, Stoney Royd, Storr Bank (*v.* storð 'plantation'), Swallows Bottom *mod*, Thorns (*le, the Thornes* 1313 *YD* vi, 1439 *Bretton* 99, *v.* þorn), Toad Hole, Low & Shutt Tongue, Town Knowle, Town Owler (*v.* alor 'alder-tree'), Underhill, Walker Close, Walshaw Close, Watering Close, Well Ings, West Hall 1841 O.S., Whinny Close (*v.* hvin 'gorse'), Yeldy Close.

(b) *Abbott Flatt* 1557 *Bretton* 117, *Bower* 1631 PREm (*v.* būr[1] 'cottage'), *Burnebanke* 1557 *Bretton* 117 (*v.* bruni, banke), *Emelaiebroc* l. 12 Riev (*v.* brōc), *Emlaierode* l. 12 Riev (*v.* rod[1]), *The Kistowe-Grave Close* 1684 *Glebe*, *the Milne* 1644 PREm (*v.* myln), *Shorte Royd* 1616 *Bretton* 105, *le Wro* 13 YD i, *le Wroo* 1334 YD viii (*v.* vrá 'nook of land').

3. Skelmanthorpe (102–2310)

> *Scelmer-, Scemeltorp* 1086 DB
> *Schelmertorph* 12 YD ii, *-thorp* 13 YD i
> *Skelmer(e)t', Scelmortorp* 12 YD i, *Scelmertorp* 1195 P, 13 BM
> *Scelmetorp* 1196, *Schelintorp* (sic for *-lm-*) 13 Brett, *Skelmethorp* 1486 *MinAcct* 66, 1554 WillY
> *Skelmertorp* 1243 Fees, *-thorp* 1290 Ebor, 1315 WCR, 1378 YD xiii, 51 *et freq* to 1479 Test iii
> *Skel-, Scelmarthorp(e)* 1283 YD i, 1296 WCR, l. 13 BM
> *Skelmanthorp(e)* 1316 Vill, 1535 VE *et freq* to 1596 FF
> *Skelmersthorp* 1436 YD xiii, 52
> *Shelmondthorpe* 1530 WillY, *Skelmondthorpe* 1546 Hall
> *Skelmonthorpe* 1555 WillY, 1608 PRThl
> *Skelmotheroppe* 1578 WillY

'Skelmer's outlying farmstead', *v.* þorp. There is a difficulty over the ON pers.n. *Skelmer*, which appears also in other p.ns., Skelmersdale La 122 and Skelmsergh We (*Scelmeresherhe* c. 1190 DEPN). No such name is known in OWScand, but there is a Latinised ODan *Scialmerus, Sk(i)elmerus*, which has been assumed to come from an unrecorded OScand **Skialdmar* (Nielsen 85, Björkman, ZEN 75); this Dan pers.n. is, however, now thought to be simply a variant of the common ODan *Skialm* (gen. *Skialms*) with the OScand nom. ending *-r* preserved (DaGP s.n.), as the two types *Skelm* and *Skelmerus* are alternative forms of the name of a single individual; there can be little doubt about this explanation of *Skelmerus*. Since the inflexional -*r* is not retained in the Danelaw, any connexion with ODan *Skelmerus* must be excluded. Dr Feilitzen calls attention to similar Latinised forms in OSwed charters, *Dagherus* for *Dag(r)*, *Ormerus* for *Orm(r)* and the like, where the nom. inflexional -*r* is retained, and to the fact that whilst *Skjǫld-* is known as a name theme in such ONorw pers.ns. as *Skjǫldulfr*, *Skialdvor*, it is not a theme in ODan. Further, the distribution of the English p.ns. suggests a Norw rather than a Dan provenance. *Skelmer* is most likely to be from the postulated ON *Skjaldmar* in this p.n.

GILTHWAITES, *Gulnetwayt* 1389 YD vi, 65, *Gilthwait(es)* 1771, 1817 M, *Gilfit* 1843 O.S., *v.* þveit; the first el. is obscure, but *Gulne-* might stand for *Gulue-*, possibly for the ON pers.n. *Gylfi*, which though chiefly in mythological use occurs in Norw p.ns. *Gjølstad*, *Gullerød* and possibly in OSwed p.ns. (cf. LindN 430).

THORPES, *Torp* 12 YD i, *Thorpe* 1842 *TA*, cf. also *Jakeman Thorpe*, *Little-*, *Long-*, *Senior-*, *Shackle-Thorpe* 1842 *TA*, *v.* þorp 'outlying farmstead'; these various *Thorpes* are f.ns.; *Jakeman* and *Senior* are surnames, and *Shackle* appears also in *Shackley Thorne* 1842 *TA* (cf. Shackleton iii, 201 *infra*).

BARROWSTEAD, 1842 *TA*, 'site of a barrow', *v.* beorg, stede.   BLACKER WOOD, 1842 *TA*, named from the *Blacker* family, common here from the seventeenth century (PREm *passim*), cf. Blacker i, 292 *supra*. BOGGART LANE.   BUSKER, 1771 M.   LITTLE CANNON HALL, cf. Cannon Hall i, 323 *supra*.   COMMON END.   FLEET.   GREEN SIDE. GULLY FLAT, *Gally Flat* 1843 O.S.   HIGHBRIDGE LANE, *High Bridge Mill* 1725 PREm.   HIGHFIELD HO.   HOB ROYD SHROGG, *Hob Royd* (*Wood*) 1842 *TA*, from the ME pers.n. *Hobbe* and rod[1] 'clearing', *v* scrogge 'brushwood'.   KITCHEN ROYD, 1842 *TA*.   LOWER & UPPER LANGLEY, 1842 *TA*, *Langkeleheker* 13 YD iv, *v.* lang, lēah, kjarr 'marsh'.   LIDGETT LANE, *Lidget* (*Nook & Royd*) 1842 *TA*, *v.* hlid-geat 'swing-gate'.   MARSHALL MILL, named from the family of *Marshall* (1638, 1640 PREm, 10, 14 *et freq*).   MIRY GREAVES, *Mirey Greave* 1842 *TA*, *v.* mýrr 'bog', -ig, grǣfe 'copse'.   NORTON-THORPE HALL, cf. *Thos. Norton* 1771 PREm 121, *v.* þorp.   PEASE FIELD, cf. *Pease Close* 1842 *TA*, *v.* pise 'pease'.   PICKLES LANE, *Pith Hill(s)* 1842 *TA*, *v.* pightel 'enclosure'.   PILLING HO & LANE, *Far Pilling*, *Pilling Knowle & Lane* 1842 *TA*, probably a derivative of dial. *pill* 'to bark timber, to graze land closely' (EDD).   PONKER

NOOK.   PUTTING HILL (& MILL), 1842 *TA*, *Puding Mill* 1771 M.
QUAKER GATE.   ROUND HILL.   SCHOOL HILL, *Scolehill* 1431 *WB*,
probably 'hill with a shed', *v.* skáli, hyll, but the modern form arises
from the village school being near this bank.   SCISSETT, *Sis(s)et* 1726
PREm, 1843 O.S., *Scissit Wood* 1842 *TA*; Sciss Flat and Sciss Royd
f.ns. are just across the R. Dearne in Clayton West (i, 321 *supra*), and
all probably contain the ME fem. pers.n. *Sisse* (from *Cecilia*); the
second el. may be OE (ge)set 'dwelling, fold'.   SMITHY LANE, 1842
TA, *v.* smiðõe, lane.   STROKE LANE.   THORPE DIKE & LANE, 1842
TA, *v.* Thorpes *supra*.   TINKER'S WELL, cf. *George Tinker* and other
members of this local family (1664 PREm 38, etc.).   WEST END.
WOODLANDS.   WOOL PLACE, 1842 *TA*.

FIELD-NAMES

The principal forms in (*a*), which also include some for Cumberworth
(217 *supra*), are 1842 *TA* 360.

(*a*) Balk Croft (*v.* balca 'boundary ridge'), Bintcliff Ing, Birk Royd, Booth
Acre, Bridge Royd (*Briggroyd* 1692 *Bretton* 103, *v.* brycg, rod[1]), Briery Royd,
Upper Broom, Broom Hill, Chapel Royd, Cockshott Royd (*v.* cocc-scīete 'a
place where woodcock were netted', rod[1]), Cold Staith, Crowhill, Dam
Royds (*Danroydsyke* 1523 YD vi, *v.* dammr, rod[1], sīc), Dyke Close, Elm
Croft, Fallace (possibly like Falhouse 212 *supra*, from falh 'fallow land'),
Fearnley Bank, Frith Wood (*v.* fyrhðe 'wood'), Great Ing, Green Croft,
Hanging (*the hinging* 1685 *Glebe*, probably verbal nouns from *hang* and
dial. *hing*, 'steep declivities', cf. hangende, hengjandi 'steep'), Hang Royd (*v.*
prec., rod[1], cf. the common f.n. Hanging Royd), Hatchett, Holker 1817 M
(*v.* hol[1], kjarr 'marsh'), Horse Close, House Close, Hugeley, Ing Top, Lady
Royd, Long Ing, Mousley, North Royd, Pienot Dole (dial. *pienet* 'magpie',
dāl), The Pound (*v.* pund), Randon, Rein Wood (*v.* reinn 'boundary strip'),
Rotton Butts, Shaw Croft, Slack Croft (*v.* slakki 'hollow'), South Royd,
Stone Croft, Tattershall, Thurstongs, Toad Hole, Tongue, Tumbrill,
Turner Royd, Upton Hill 1843 O.S., White Close, Wortley Royd.

(*b*) *Hyrsedene* 12 YD i (*v.* hyrse 'mare', denu 'valley').

xv. Kirkheaton

The township of Dalton has been taken into the County Borough of
Huddersfield, and the remaining townships of this parish into the Urban
District of Kirkburton (*infra* 236).

1. DALTON (6″ 246 SE) [102–1617]

Dalton(e), *-tun* 1086 DB, 1142–54 YCh 1446, 1185 Templar, 1198
Fount, 1203, 1235 DodsN, 1235 FF, 1243 Fees *et passim* to 1590 FF,

Daleton 1607 FF. 'Valley farm', *v.* dæl, tūn; it lies in the valley of Lees or Fenay Beck; the name remains as that of a township.

BRADLEY MILLS, 1843 O.S., *molendina de Bradeley* 1195–1215 YCh viii, *Bradelay* 1269 YD vi, 1331 Font; some of the spellings cited for Bradley 296 *infra* may in fact belong here; the two names seem to be independent creations, distinguished from each other by the affixes -*Mills* and *Nether-*. 'Broad glade or clearing', *v.* brād, lēah.

ARDRON HILL.   BANK END, *Bankend* 1658 WillS, *v.* Dalton Bank *infra*, ende.   BRAY'S FIELD, *Brays field*, -*Wood* 1843 O.S.   BRIERY BANK.   BRIGGATE (BRIDGE), *v.* brycg, gata 'road'.   BROWN ROYD. COLD ROYD, *Cow-royd-hill* 1822 Langd, *Cold Royd Wood* 1847 *TA*. CROSLEY LANE.   CROSS GREEN.   DALTON BANK, *Daltonebanck* 1326 WCR, *le Bank* 1331 Font, *v.* banke.   DALTON GRANGE, cf. *Dalton hall* 1581 WillY.   DALTON GREEN, 1771 M, *v.* grēne[2].   DIVES HO, 1771 M, *Dineshouse* (sic for *Diues-*) 1649 WYD, no doubt the surname *Dives* (Reaney 96).   FOX ROW.   THE GOIT, *v.* gota 'water-channel'. GREEN GARTH.   GREENHEAD.   GREEN LEA.   GRIMBLES.   THE GROVE, 1843 O.S., *v.* grāf.   GROVE PLACE, 1843 O.S., *Grove House* 1817 M.   HEBBLE BRIDGE, *v.* Salterhebble iii, 110 *infra*.   HIGH ROYD, 1720 *WB* 32, *le Heighrod* 1331 Font, *the Heeroide* 1652 *WB* 141, *v.* hēah, rod[1].   HILL TOP, *Hill Toppe* 1659 *BWr* 7, *Top of Hill* 1720 *WB* 32, *v.* hyll, topp.   JAGGER HILL, 1843 O.S.   LAVEROCK.   LEES BECK & FOLD, *the Fold* 1655 WillS, *v.* foll., bekkr, fald.   LEES HEAD, 1817 M, *Lee Head* 1771 M, *v.* lēah, hēafod.   LITTLE CARR, cf. *le Kerloyne* 1452 *WCR* 1, *v.* kjarr 'marsh', lane.   MOLD GREEN, 1771 M, *v.* molde, grēne[2].   NAB HILL, 1817 M, *Nabbs* 1663 Glebe, *v.* nabbi 'knoll'.   NETHER HALL.   NETTLETON, *Nettilton hill* 1550 Test vi, *v.* netele, tūn.   PENNY SPRING BANK.   POG FM, cf. Pog Moor i, 304 *supra*.   RAVENSHOLME.   RAVENSKNOWLE HALL, 1554 *WB* 49, *Rawensknolle* 1447 YD i, *Ravensknolle* 1481 PrHosp, 'the raven's hill', *v.* hræfn, cnoll.   RAWTHORPE (HALL), *Rawthorpe Hall* 1615 WB 6, *Rathorp Hall* 1665 Visit, *v.* þorp 'outlying farmstead'; the first el. may be rāw 'row of houses'.   ROUND WOOD, 1847 *TA*. SAND INGS.   SOUTHFIELD.   STANDIFORTH FM.   STORTHS, *v.* storð 'plantation'.   WELLHOUSE, 1771 M.   WOODLANDS, WOOD NOOK, cf. *Doltonwode* (sic) 1316 Pat, *v.* wudu.

FIELD-NAMES

(a) Ash Bridge Close 1720 *WB* 32, Battle Height 1720 ib, Green Royd 1708 *WRD* 453, le Lathcroft 1708 ib (*v.* hlaða, croft), Lockwood Wood 1847 *TA* 247, North Carr 1847 ib (*Northker* 1330 DodsN, *v.* kjarr 'marsh'), Robcroft 1708 *WRD*, Whitaker Mill 1847 *TA*.

(b) *Aspeley lane* 1567 Ramsd (*v.* æspe 'aspen', lēah), *Cloghs* 1330 DodsN (*v.* clōh 'dell'), *les Two Falladges, le Falladge dole* 1647 WYD, *le Greatannot crofte* 1647 ib (the ME fem. pers.n. *Anota*, croft), *Holeye, -lays* c. 1300, 1332 DodsN (*v.* hol¹, lēah), *the Milne* 1644 WillY (cf. *le Milneys* 1330 DodsN, *v.* myln).

2. KIRKHEATON (102–1818)

> *Heptone* (sic) 1086 DB
> *Hett*(*on*)' 12 Font
> *Hetun, Heton*(*e*) 1170–1211 YCh 1692, 1699, 1701, 1198 Fount, e. 13 BM, 13 *Lewes* 300, 1202 FF, 1208 DodsN, 1219 FF, 1241 Ebor, 1246 *Ass* 5d, 1251 Ass, 1275 WCR *et passim* to 1457 FountB, (*Kirk*(*e*)-, *Kyrk*-) l. 13 Font, 1369 YD xii, 256, 1387 Lindsay, 1433 YD x *et freq* to 1546 YChant
> *Heeton* 1307 WCR
> *Heyton* 1462 Test ii, (*Kirk-, Kyrk-*) 1488 Ipm, 1658 WillS
> *Heaton als. Kirkeheaton* 1607 FF, *Kirk*(*e*)*heaton* 1577 WillY, 1588 FF, 1616 PrHosp

'High farmstead', *v.* hēah, tūn; the village is situated on the upper slopes of a steep hill. 'Kirk' (*v.* kirkja) to distinguish it from Upper Heaton *infra* and Earlsheaton 194 and Hanging Heaton 196 *supra*; the church is frequently mentioned (as in 1244 Ebor, 1276 RH, etc.). The DB spelling *Heptone* has no doubt taken its form from Lepton which immediately precedes it in the Survey and the Recapitulation.

UPPER HEATON, *Heton* 1240 Font, (*West-*) 1265 YI, 1379 YD i, *Upparheaton* 1549 WillY, *Overheaton* 1578 ib, 1609 *WB* 86, *Westeheaton* 1588 FF. *v.* Kirkheaton *supra*; it stands nearly 150 feet higher than Kirkheaton to the north-west.

HELM, (*le*) *Helm*(*e*) 1198 Fount, 14 Font, 1391 YD i, 1457 FountB, 1540 Test vi, 1589 FF, *le, the Helme* 1331 Font, 1605 *WB* 83, *the, le Hellme* 1578 WillY, 1592 *WB* 65, *v.* helm 'shelter'; this word, which occurs several times in YW, is used in NCy dial. of 'a shed in the fields for the shelter of cattle turned out to pasture, a hovel'; in 1709 rent was paid for a *helme* at Bridge End in Rastrick (WMB 173), and in 1739 the sum of 6/8 was the charge 'for erecting a helm' at Hampsthwaite (PRHm 243).

THICKLES (lost), *Thicles* 1170–85 YCh 1792, 1185–1210 ib 1704, *Es Thichels in bosco de Heton* 1175–85 ib 1698, *Esthichels* 1195–1211 ib 1701, *Chichels* 1180–90 ib 1703, *Ticlas deversus le suh usque burganes lapidum* 1190–1210 ib 1700, *Thikles inter Gatebrigge-cloh et West-haucloh* 1195–1211 ib 1702, *Thicclis, Thideles* (sic) 1195–1211 ib 1710–11 (all from Font), *Hetonethicles* 13 Font; in the same district there is a *sichet* or stream called *Ecclesdo* which falls into *Kerder* (the R. Calder) 1170–85 YCh 1692, but this may have no connexion with *Thicles* (*v.* f.ns. *infra*). There is an Ickles Ho (212 *supra*) in the adjacent township of Thornhill and it would be tempting to identify the two. But *Thicles* is clearly in 'the wood of Heaton', a woodland area now probably represented by Tib Netherend Wood and Heaton Hill Wood, both between Woodside and Wood Lane. The other places associated with it, *burganes, Gatebrigge-cloh* and *Westhau-cloh*, have not been identified, but *v.* f.ns. *infra*; other property owned by Fountains Abbey was nearer Colne Bridge (296 *infra*) to the west of the township. The vowel -*i*- in all the spellings rules out any connexion with OE ēcels (as in Ickles 186 *supra*) and the initial *Th*- is certainly original and not due to a wrong analysis of *Esthichels* ('east *hichels*'). The name would appear to go back to an OE *þiccels, for which there is no other evidence so far. It would be a noun formation related to OE þicce[1] 'a thicket, dense undergrowth' or þicce[2] 'thick, dense', with the suffix -els (cf. EPN i, 150). Its meaning would be something like that of þicce[1] or the derivative þiccett, 'thicket, dense bushes or undergrowth', which is appropriate for a place located in woodland. *v.* Addenda.

ALLEY GREEN, cf. *Bowling Platt* 1720 WB 32. BALK LANE. BANK ROW LANE. BELLSTRING LANE, cf. Bell Cross ii, 66 *infra*. BEN-ROYD, *Benrode* 13 YD i, *the Bendroyd-, Bentroydhead* 1640, 1677 WB 125, 151, probably 'bean clearing', *v.* bēan, rod[1], but it has been confused with beonet 'bent-grass'; on *Bend-* for *Ben-* cf. Hand Bank 200, Phonol. § 46. BOG GREEN, BOG HALL, *Bog(g) Hall* 1771 M, 1822 Langd, *v.* bog 'bog, marsh'. BOYFE HALL, *Boyfall* 1721, 1746 PRMrf, *v.* boia 'boy, servant', possibly as a surname, (ge)fall 'felling of trees, clearing'. BROOMFIELD, 1720 WB 32, *Brumfeld* 13 WB 4, *v.* brōm 'broom, gorse', feld.   Carr Mount, 1843 O.S., *Great, Little Carr* 1792 *WB* 54, *v.* kjarr 'marsh'.   Cockley Hill, *Cockeslau* 13 Font, *Cockley Inge* 1652 *WB* 141, *Cockley Hill* 1752 ib 211, 'cock's hill or mound', *v.* cocc² (perhaps used as a pers.n.), hlāw; it is the name of a prominent hill.   Colne Bank, cf. *Kalnebot(h)mes, -botheme* 12, 13 Font, named from the R. Colne, *v.* botm (boðm) 'valley bottom'.   Crow Royd, 1767 *WB* 43, *Craweroide* 1594 ib 71, *Craw Royd Wood* 1720 ib 32, 'crow clearing', *v.* crāwe, rod¹.   Cuckstool, ME *cukestol* 'a cucking stool'.   Daw Knowl.   The Dene.   Gledwing, *Gleadwing* (a field) 1720 *WB* 32, 'kite wing' (*v.* gleoda), possibly so called from its shape.   The Hagg, *Haggs* 1688 *WB* 178a, *Hagg House* 1771 M, *v.* hogg, dial. *hagg* 'enclosed wood'.   Healey Green, 1600 *WB* 17, *Healie Greene* 1592 WillY, 'high clearing', *v.* hēah, lēah, grēne², cf. Healey 188 *supra*.   Heaton Fields.   Heaton Hall, 1637 WillY, 1677 *WB* 159a, *Heton halle* 1481 PrHosp, *v.* Kirkheaton *supra*, hall.   Heaton Hall Wood, *Eaton-* 1847 *TA*.   Heaton Lodge, 1843 O.S.   Heaton Moor, 1817 M, *vn' acr' sup' moram* 13 *WB* 1, *v.* mōr.   Highgate Lane, *High Gate* 1720 *WB* 32, *v.* hēah, gata.   Hobson Scrogg, *-Shrogg* 1847 *TA*, *v.* scrogge 'brushwood'.   Hodgson Fold.   Hole Bottom.   Houses Hill, *the Howzes* 1542 *WB* 36, (*the*) *Howses* 1572 WillY, 1580 *WB* 54, *v.* hūs, hyll.   Hutchin Wood, 1688 *WB* 178a, *Huchon-* 1653 ib 113, from the ME pers.n. *Huchon*, wudu.   Jidroyd, *the Juddroyd* 1803 *WB* 246, the ME pers.n. *Judde* (from *Jordan*), rod¹.   Kirkfield Cottage, *Kirkefeld* 1331 Font, *v.* kirkja, feld.   The Knowle, 1720 *WB* 32, *v.* cnoll.   Lane Side, 1843 O.S.   Long Tongue Scrog, *-shrogg* 1847 *TA*, *Long Tongue* 1720, 1792 *WB* 32, 54, *v.* lang, tunge 'tongue of land', scrogge 'brushwood'.   Low Fold, *Fold* 1771 M, *v.* fald.   Moor Top, cf. *Moor Butts* 1720 *WB* 32, *v.* mōr, butte.   North Gate.   North Hill.   North Moor, 1843 O.S., *the North-, Normore* 1652 *WB* 134, *v.* norð, mōr.   Padanaram, *Pading Narvin* 1771 M, cf. Genesis xxviii, 2, *v.* Addenda.   Royds Ho, *Great-, Neither Royd* 1720 *WB* 32, *v.* rod¹.   Shaw Cross, *Great-, Little Shaw* 1720 *WB* 32, *v.* sceaga 'copse'.   South Royd, 1843 O.S., *Suthrode* 13 Font, *le Southrode* 1331 ib, *v.* sūð, rod¹.   Stafford Hill, 1771 M, *Stafforth hill* 1688 *WB* 178a, named from a local family, *George Stafforthe* 1596 *WB* 73–4, *Lionel Stafforth* 1652 ib 132, cf. Stony Ford *infra*.   Stancliffe, cf. Stonecliff Lodge 207 *supra*.   Stoneroyd, 1720 *WB* 32, 'stony clearing', *v.* stān, rod¹.   Stony Ford, *le Stainford* (? for

Stani-) 1331 Font, (*the*) *Stony fore* 1720, 1756 *WB* 31, 212a, 'rocky ford', *v.* stānig, ford; the Stafforths mentioned in Stafford Hill *supra* may have been named from this place.   TIB NETHEREND WOOD, 1847 *TA*, *Tib-*, *Tybnetherend* 1579, 1631 *WB* 53, 1771 M, *v.* neoðera, ende; *Tib* is the ME pers.n. *Tibbe* (from *Theobald*).   WINCHAT HILL, probably from **wind-geat** 'wind-swept gap', here a small valley in the hillside facing north across the main Calder valley.   WOOD LANE.   WOODSIDE, *bosco de Heton* 1176–8 YCh 1698, l. 13 *WB* 2, *v.* wudu, sīde.

FIELD-NAMES

The principal forms in (*a*) are 1720–1756, 1767, 1792 *WB* 31–32, 43, 54, 211–12, and those marked *TA* are 1847 *TA* 247. Spellings dated c. 1180, c. 1200, c. 1210 are YCh 1692–1712, 13, 1240–1271, 1331, 1340 Font, 1804 *EnclA* 26. Others dated without source are *WB*.

(*a*) Ball Greave (*v.* ball, perhaps as a surname, grǣfe 'copse'), Barley Stors (*the barley stores* 1652, *-Storrs* 1663, *v.* bærlic, storð 'plantation'), Barr Croft (*v.* bere 'barley', croft), Borrow'd Ing ('a borrowed meadow', *v.* eng), Brow (*v.* brū), Brown Hills, Carr Shrogg *TA* (*v.* kjarr, scrogge), Clatter Collocks, Creden Holes, Croshill Syke, Crowther Slades (the surname *Crowther*, slæd 'valley'), Crow Wood 1843 O.S. (near Crow Royd *supra*), Cuckold-butts, -gap (ME *cukwald* 'a cuckold', butte, gap), Dike Royd (*v.* dic, rod[1]), Elmwood *TA*, Faugh Field (*v.* falh, feld), Fork Royd, Frier Ing, Fryer Syke (*v.* frere, eng, sīc), Goit Close (*v.* gota), Gool Field (*v.* goule 'channel'), Goose Butts (*v.* gōs, butte), Halling Sike (*v.* hall, eng, sīc), Hallot Hall 1817 M, Hall Royd (*v.* hall, rod[1]), the Harrang Croft, Heys (*v.* (ge)hæg), Hinging Bank (*v.* hangende, ON hengjandi, banke), Horse Grave (*v.* hors, grǣfe 'copse'), How Royd Bank (*v.* hol[1], rod[1]), Intack (*v.* intak), Laithe Close (*v.* hlaða 'barn'), Little Cross 1817 M, Long Ing *TA*, Lower Field 1804 *WB* (*Low Field* 1726 PRIlk), Mean Ing ('common meadow', *v.* (ge)mǣne, eng), Miry Carr, Mold Croft (*v.* molde, croft), Mountain Abbey 1843 O.S. (ib 1771 M, cf. Mountain 215 *supra*), New Field 1804 *WB*, Nooks (*v.* nōk), Norber (probably 'north hill', *v.* norð, beorg), Owler-, Owlay-, the Owda-Barrow (*Ould-a-barras* 1663 *Glebe*, possibly identical with *burganes lapidum* 1190–1210 YCh 1700 (Font), *v.* ald, probably haugr, burgæsn 'cairn, burial place'), Oulers, Oulers Ing (*v.* alor 'alder', eng), Ox Fall (*v.* oxa, (ge)fall), Picksmall (*the Picksmall* 1696, probably a jocular name for a poor field), Pighill (*v.* pightel), Plumb Tree Croft, Plump *TA*, Rails, Rams Clough (*v.* ramm, cloh), Scotland (*v.* scot 'tax', land, a common f.n.), Shitten Ing (cf. scite, eng), Shrogg *TA*, Shrog Close (*v.* scrogge), the Side Acres, Syke (*v.* sīc 'stream'), Sisbed Close, -Hill 1771 M, Lower, Upper Slade (*v.* slæd), Spring Dike, Staups (*v.* stólpi 'stoop'), Stone heap close, Tan Pit Hill, Thistle Royd, Trent H. 1771 M, Tungue (*v.* tunge), Upper Field 1804 *WB*, Waver ing (*v.* wæfre, eng, cf. *Waver* 173 *supra*), Well Royd, West Field 1804, Wheat Royd (*Quetrode* 1331, *v.* hwǣte, rod[1]), Wood Plain (*v.* wudu, plain).

(b) *Aystorth* 13 (v. storð 'plantation', *Ay-* may stand for eik 'oak'), *the Bendcrosse* 1610 (v. cros, cf. Benroyd *supra*), *Birdales* c. 1180, *Byardole land* 1610 ('town shares of common land', v. bý (gen.sg. *býjar*), dāl), *the Birkes* 1652 (v. birki), *Cisroid* 1579 (the ME fem. pers.n. *Sisse*, rod[1]), *Cliffes* 1688 (v. clif), *Dereboch't* 1240 (probably an early example of the f.n. 'dear bought'), *Ecclesdo* (*a sichet* or stream which falls into the Calder) c. 1180 (the first el. is probably Brit eclēsia (cf. Ecclesall i, 192 *supra*), but *-do* is obscure unless an error for dūn 'hill'), *Ellerbarne* l. 13 (v. elri 'alder-tree', bereærn), *Gatebriggecloh* c. 1200 (v. gata, brycg, clōh, this might well be the dell by Tib Netherend Wood and the road called Wood Lane which crosses it over a small stream, cf. *Westhau-cloh* (*infra*) and *Thickles* (*supra*)), *Gilberrode* l. 14 (the ME pers.n. *Gilbert*, rod[1]), *Gildhusecroft* c. 1250 (v. gildi-hús 'guildhouse', croft), *Gumulrod* 1331 (v. rod[1]), *Haisford* 13 (v. ford), *le Hallflat, le Hallestede* 1331 (v. Heaton Hall *supra*, flat, stede), *Hedinslaie* 13 (the ON pers.n. *Heðinn*, lēah), *Hyngande Rode* 1307 WCR, *hangandroids* 1610 (v. hangende 'steep', rod[1]), *Holdroid ferme* 1696, *le Holme de Heton* 1340 (v. holmr 'water-meadow'), *Hurrokboyum* (sic for *boþum*) 1331 (the first el. is probably connected with NCy dial. *hurrock* 'a heap of loose stones', as in Haddock Stones (Farnley) pt v *infra*, v. botm, boðm), *Kilnewelleflat* c. 1200 (v. cyln, wella, flat), *le Laghgrene* 1331 (v. lágr 'low', grēne[2]), *le Langacre* 1331 (v. lang, æcer), *le Langrod* 1331 (v. rod[1]), *Lannebrigge* 1170–85 YCh 1692, *Lauue-* 1195–1211 ib 1701 (probably for *Laune-*, v. laun 'secret, hidden', brycg), *the Ledgiard roide* 1652 (the surname *Ledgard*, rod[1]), *Leeds croftes* 1688 (v. croft), *Levencrosse* 1481 PrHosp (probably the OE pers.n. *Lēofwine*, cros), *the Mires* 1699 (v. mýrr 'bog'), *Molerode* l. 13, *Molderode* 1271, *the Mawroid* 1696 (v. molde 'earth', rod[1]), *Newrode* c. 1210 (v. nīwe, rod[1]), *the Pinfoulde* 1652 (v. pynd-fald), *Pirlwelle* 1331 (v. Purlwell 180 *supra*), *Pourod* 1331 (v. rod[1]), *Ricarderode* l. 13 (the ME pers.n. *Ric(h)ard*, rod[1]), *le Ricroft* 1331 (v. rȳge, croft), *Rierode* c. 1200 (v. rȳge, rod[1]), *le Ryssirod* e. 14 (v. risc, -ig, rod[1]), *le Rishyard* 1652 (v. risc, geard), *Smythycloy* 1271 (v. smiðöe, clōh), *le Southgrene* 1331 (v. sūð, grēne[2]), *Tempullrode* 1481 PrHosp (v. tempel, rod[1], a reference to property of the Knights Templar), *Thorne* 1331 (v. þorn), *le Toftis* 1331 (v. topt 'enclosure'), *Walthefrode* ('quas ipse Walthef tenuit') c. 1210 (ON *Valþjófr*, late OE *Wælþēof*, rod[1]), *Waltonroyd* 1609 (doubtless *Walton* as a surname, rod[1]), *le Werueldike* 13 ('circular dike', v. hwerfel, dīc), *Westhaucloh* c. 1200 (v. haugr 'mound', clōh, this was near Heaton wood and is probably the clough or dell running up from the Calder by Helm to Woodside, cf. *Thickles* and *Gatebriggecloh* f.n. *supra*), *le Westhenges* 1331 (v. west, eng), *Wherwarprode* 1333 PrHosp, *Wrythtecroft* e. 14 (ME *wright* 'wright', possibly as a surname, croft).

3. LEPTON (102–2015)

Lepton(e), *-tun(a)* 1086 DB, 1159–81 YCh 1681, e. 13 YD iv, Font, 1246 *Ass* 3, FF, 1288 YI, 1297 LS, 1303 KF, a. 1312 YD xii, 294, 1316 Vill *et passim* to 1552 WillY, (*Great(e)-*) 1621 FF, 1740 *WB* 238a. This is a compound of OE hlēp 'leap' and tūn. The exact significance is uncertain; the village is towards the top of a hillside, but there is no topographical feature of note. But the probability is that Lepton means 'farmstead on the slope of a hill'; on this use of *hlēp* (which also meant 'leaping place, jump') cf. Löfvenberg 127.

GAWTHORPE, *Goutthorp* (sic for *Gouc-*) 1297 LS (p), *Goukthorp* 1311 Font (p), *Goulkthorp* 1324 DodsN, *Gawke- Gaukethorp(e)* 1324 ib, 1379 PT, 1456 Linds, 1477 DodsN *et freq* to 1605 FF, *Gawk-*, *Gaukthorpe* 1476 Linds, 1543 FF, *Gawthorp(p)* 1597 SessnR, 1633 WillY, *-thropp* 1616 PrHosp. *v.* gaukr 'cuckoo', þorp, and Gawthorpe 102 *supra*; Cuckoo Hill *infra* is the hill above Gawthorpe.

LASCELLES HALL, *(the) Lascelhal(l)* 1434 DodsN, 1462 YD xiii, 54, *Lassel(l)hall(e)*, *-il-* 1447 YD i, 1466 Pat, 1468 WillY, 1475 YD xiii, 78, *Lacel(l)hall* 1448 *WB* 11, 1547 WillY, 1550 FF, 1584 Arm, *Lacelles Hall* 1577 Arm, *Lascelles Hall* 1577 *WB* 51, *Lasels hall* 1616 PrHosp, *Lascey Hall* 1512 DodsN, *Lassehall* 1527 FF, *v.* hall; named from the well-known family of *Lascelles* who held land in various parts of Yorkshire from the time of the Conquest (cf. DB 75n); one *Umfridus de Laceles* witnessed Kirkheaton charters in the twelfth century (YCh 1692 ff).

LITTLE LEPTON, 1496 *WB* 58, *Litle-Lepton* 1621 FF, *v.* Lepton *supra*, lytel.

ROWLEY HILL

> *Ruleia* 1175–85 YCh 1698, *-ley* c. 1225 DodsN
> *Roulaibikt* 1202 FF, *Roulay*, *-ley* 1276 RH, 1297 LS (p), 1311 Font (p), 1379 PT (p)
> *Rogheley* 1296 LacyComp (p)   *Royley* 1461 YD v
> *Rowley* 14, 1429 DodsN, 1486 YD v, 1526 *WB* 21 *et passim* to 1621 *WB* 234
> *Rulley* 1616 PrHosp

'Rough clearing', *v.* rūh, lēah, a common p.n. The spelling *Roulaibikt* probably contains OE byht 'bend, curve' (possibly in allusion to some loop in Fenay Beck at the foot of the hill).

STAGE FIELD (lost), 1847 *TA*, *(le) Stages* 1312 YD xii, 294, 1324, 1477 DodsN, 1476 Linds, *Staggefeild* 1481 PrHosp, from ME *stage* (OFr *estage*) 'a stage'; of the earlier specific uses of this word 'a scaffold for execution or exposure in the pillory' (NED s.v. from 1400) seems most appropriate.

THURGORY, *Thorgarlhaue* (sic) l. 13 *WB* 7, *Thurgrowe* 1600 *WB* 147, *Thorgrow* 1779 *WB* 7, 1847 *TA*, *Thurgary* 1720 *WB* 32, *Thurgory closes* 1803 *WB* 246. 'Thorgar's mound', *v.* haugr. The pers.n. *Thorgar* is an anglicised form of ON Þorgeirr, ODan *Thorger*, which occurs also in Thurgoland i, 314 *supra*.

ADDLE CROFT, 1771 M, probably identical with *Arkylcroft* 1476 Linds, 'Arkil's croft' from the ON pers.n. *Arnkell*, ODan *Arnketill*, common as ME *Arkil*, *v.* croft. ASHFIELD. BELMONT HO. BLAKEMAN HILL. BLOCK ROW. BOGDEN, *Bugden* 1779 *WB* 2, *v.* bog 'bog, swamp', *denu* 'valley'. BOTANY BAY, 1843 O.S., *Botany Close* 1847 *TA*, named from the penal settlement in New South Wales, a common p.n. BRACKEN HILL. BROOM GROVE, cf. *Broom Field* 1847 *TA*, *Broom Lands* 1720 *WB* 31, *v.* brōm 'broom, gorse'. BUTTER NAB. CARR HEAD, 1600 *WCR* 3d, cf. also *Carrbothom* 1547 *WB* 105, *v.* kjarr 'marsh'. CHAPEL HILL, *le Schapelclif, Chapelclif* l. 13 *WB* 7, *v.* chapel, clif, hyll. COMMON END & TOP. COPRYDING, *Cop Ridings* 1817 M, 'hill-top clearing', *v.* copp, rydding. COW HEY, 1720 *WB* 32, *v.* cū, (ge)hæg. COWMES, 1664 *WB* 316, *Caums* 1720 *WB* 32, *Combs* 1771 M, *Cawmes Mill* 1817 M, *Cowms* 1822 Langd, probably l.ME *colm* 'soot, coal dust, slack', cf. Combs 211 *supra*; it is not always clear whether the spellings belong to the latter or to this name. CROFT HO, cf. *the crofte att the dore* 1600 *WB* 147, *Croft Bottom & Head* 1847 *TA*, *v.* croft 'a croft, a small enclosure'. CUCKOO HILL, the hill above Gawthorpe *supra*. DAM HEAD, cf. *Dam Goits* 1847 *TA*, *v.* dammr, gota 'water-channel'. FENAY BRIDGE, 1843 O.S., partly in Almondbury, *v.* 258 *infra*. FIELD GATE HO, *the Field Gate* 1678 *WB* 170, *v.* feld, gata or geat. FIELD HO. FLOYD GREEN. GAWTHORPE GREEN, 1652 *WB* 309, 1771 M, *v.* Gawthorpe *supra*, grēne². GREAVE HO, 1568 *WB* 135, 1590 WillY, 1677 *WB* 317a, *Grevehous* 1428 *WB* 48, *Grave House* 1771 M, *v.* græfe 'copse', hūs. GREEN BALK. HERMITAGE. HIGHFIELD, 1752 *WB* 211. HIGHGATE LANE, 1771 M, *Hygate Lane* 1652 *WB* 275, *v.* hēah, gata. JUMBLE WOOD, *Jumble* (*wood*) 1847 *TA*, cf. Humble Jumble Row 169 *supra*. KNOTTY LANE. LANE HEAD, *Lane Head Close* 1720 *WB* 32, 1847 *TA*. LEPTON EDGE, (*the*) *Edge* 1652 *WB* 141, 1771 M, *v.* ecg, here 'a steep bank' on the east side of the township. LEPTON GREAT WOOD

& Little Wood, 1843 O.S., *Great & Little Wood* 1847 *TA*. Lepton
Thorn, 1843 O.S. Lepton Town, *v.* Town End *infra*. Lidgate,
Lydgyate 1643 WillY, *Lidget* 1779 *WB* 7, 1822 Langd, *v.* hlid-geat
'swing-gate'. Lower Hall. Low Ho, 1843 O.S. Low Moor.
Low Wood. The Nale, dial. *nale* 'an ale house' (ME *atte nale*).
Nick Green, *Nick Green Close* 1779 *WB* 7, the pers.n. *Nick*
(*Nicholas*), grēne[2]. Peace Hall. Pinfold Lane. Pond Lane.
Ratten Row, 'rat-infested row of houses', *v.* raton, rāw. Rods
Beck, *Rods Hill* 1843 O.S., (*Upper*) *Rods* 1720 *WB* 32, 1847 *TA*,
probably rod[1] 'clearing'. Spa Bottom. Spittle Royd, *v.* spitel
'hospital', rod[1]; the Hospital of St. John had property here (cf.
PrHosp) and made a gift of land to John Wood in 1528 *WB* iv, 74.
Spring Grove. Stubbings, 1847 *TA*, -*ins* 1720 *WB* 32, *v.* stubbing
'clearing'. Tandem. Thistle Hill, cf. *Thistle Field* 1847 *TA*.
Town End, *the Townend, Lepton Towne end* 1600 *WB* 147-8, cf.
Mickletown 127 *supra*. Waspnest. Woodfield, Wood Top, cf.
Wood Close 1847 *TA*. Yew Cottage, *Great & Little Yew Tree* 1847
TA, *v.* īw.

FIELD-NAMES

The principal forms in (*a*) are 1847 *TA* 247. Spellings dated 1456 are
DodsN vii, 408; all others dated without source are *WB*.

(*a*) Great & Little Balm (*Baune, Bawm Close* 1720, *Bawn Close* 1767,
either e.ModE *baune* 'bath', cf. Balne 14 *supra*, or OFr *baume* 'hollow'),
Upper Bars, Bean Close, Below Cut, Below Goit, Birkin Croft (*v.* bircen,
croft), Lower & Top Birks (*v.* birki), Blackroids 1779 (*v.* blæc, rod[1]), Blue
Royd (*Blue high roid* 1779), Brigg Close (cf. *Briggecroftys* 13, *v.* brycg, croft),
Brigg Royd (*v.* prec., rod[1]), Brow Side, Buther Close, Calm Close, Carr
Head Shrogg (*v.* Carr Head *supra*, scrogge 'brushwood'), Causeway Close,
Cheapsides 1779, Chop(p)ing Bill 1720, 1779, Clues End, Coat Close, Cock'd
Flatts, Cock'd Hat, Crooked Ing, Cross Platt, Dicken Croft (the ME pers.n.
Diccon (cf. Dickencross 110 *supra*), croft), Dounafter (*Downafter* 1779),
Dyson Close (ib 1720, the YW surname *Dyson*) Eights 1779, Great Falls
(*Fall* 1720, *Falls* 1779, *v.* (ge)fall 'clearing'), Finay Bridge Shrogg (*v.* Fenay
Bridge *supra*, scrogge 'brushwood'), Flag Cliffe (*Fleickcliffe Ing* 1779,
probably ON flaga 'flagstone', clif), Fog Close 1779 (*v.* fogga 'long grass'),
Foothill, Gillon Royd (*the Gillon royde* 1664, the surname *Gillon*, rod[1]), Gin
Close (ib 1779, the ME surn. *Gin*, cf. Reaney 136), Grooming Row, Hacking (ib
1779, cf. Lane Hackings 217 *supra*), Hallas 1779 (*Hallows* 1720, *v.* halh 'nook
of land'), Hattock Rods (*Hackett Royds* 1779, probably a surname *Hackett*,
rod[1]), Heeley Low Close, Hollin Close, Hollin Field (ib 1720, *v.* holegn
'holly'), Hustage (probably for *hūs-stedes*, *v.* hūs, stede), Isle of Man 1779,

Jacky Quarter (ib 1779), Jack Croft (*Jock(y) Croft* 1779), Judd Royd (*Jordan-rode* l. 13, the ME pers.n. *Judde* (a shortened form of *Jordan*), rod[1]), Kiln Croft (*Kilnecroftys* 13, *v.* cyln, croft), Kirkgate Close (*v.* kirkja, gata), Laith Close (*v.* hlaða 'barn'), Lakely (*The Lacliffe* 1621, *the Lakecliffs* 1664, *v.* lacu 'stream', clif), Lepton Royd 1843 O.S., Levicar (*Lefaccre* 13, l. 13, from the OE pers.n. *Lēof(a)*, æcer), Lower Holme (*v.* holmr 'water-meadow'), Low Fold, Ludge Mill 1779, Mean Close (*v.* (ge)mǣne 'common'), Mires (*v.* mýrr 'bog'), Great & Little Nab (*v.* nabbi 'hillock'), Nackitt (*Nookitt* 1779), Near Doles (*v.* dāl), Nether Shutts (dial. *shut* 'division of land'), Nook Ing, Nook oth' Lane, Old Hill, Pick Hill (ib 1792), Pinnacle (ib 1720), Poo Bank (*v.* pāwa 'peacock', banke), Quarry Field, Robin Royd Ing (ib 1720, the pers.n. *Robin*, rod[1]), Rotten Butts (ib 1720), Rowland Park, Scrogg 1779 (*v.* scrogge 'brushwood'), Shacklecroft 1779 (cf. Shackleton iii, 201 *infra*, croft), Shay Close, Bottom & Top Shays (*v.* sceaga 'copse'), Shuttle Close (*Shuttle Ing* 1720, cf. Littleworth i, 49 *supra*), Simon Croft (ib 1779, *Symondecroft* l. 13, the ME pers.n. *Simond* (OE *Sigemund*), croft), Sinkfoil Field (ModE *cinquefoil*, e.ModE *sinkfoil* the plant *Potentilla reptans*), Slade Butts 1720 (*v.* slæd 'valley', butte 'abutting strip'), Slip, South Moor, Spivey Ing 1779 (cf. *Spyvecroft* 1456, cf. Spivie Holme iii, 253 *infra*), Stone Pit Close, Swallow Close, Three Nook'd Bit, Tog Close, Tom Royd, Tout Hill 1779 (*v.* tōt-hyll 'look-out hill'), Town Ing, Trough Ing 1720, Waits, Wearing Field, Well Ing.

(*b*) *Annotcroft* 1456 (the ME fem. pers.n. *Annot*, croft), *the Byerdall Inges* 1545 ('town shares', *v.* bȳ (gen.sg. *bȳjar*), dāl, eng 'meadow'), *Brum-buttys* 13, *le Brombott'* l. 13 (*v.* brōm, butte), *le Crosclif* 13 (*v.* cros, clif), *Hytecroft* 1600, *Kilneschahynghe* 13 (*v.* cyln, sceaga 'copse', eng), *Moysey Hill* 1547, *the Newhouse* 1650, *le Northfeld* l. 13, *Sakersaerode* e. 13, *les Smithies* 1636 (*v.* smiðöe), *Wicke Green* 1677 (*v.* wīc 'dairy farm', grēne[2]), *le Wro* l. 13 (*v.* vrá 'nook of land').

4. UPPER WHITLEY (6″ 247 SW, 2016)

Witelaia, -lei, -ley 1086 DB, 13 YD vi, 1205–9 BM, (*Over-*) 1346 YD ii, *Hvitteleia* l. 12 Font, *Withe-, Wythelaya, -le(i)* e. 13 Font, 13 YD vi, c. 1203, 1220 BM, *Witthele* e. 13 BM, 1220 YD vi, *Witteley* 1298 BM, (*Vvere-*) 1246 *Ass* 3, *Whitley, Upper* 1822 Langd. *v.* Lower Whitley 212 *supra*, Whitley Beaumont *infra*. Upper Whitley was the name of the township.

ALWOLDLEY (lost), *Adwaldlaya* 13 YD vi (YCh 1816), *Adhelwoldeleia* 1200–20 YCh 1817, *Ethelwaldeleg* 1246 *Ass* 26d. 'Athelwald's glade or clearing', from the OE pers.n. *Æþelwald*, lēah, cf. Alwoodley pt. iv *infra*.

UPPER DENBY, *Denebi, -by* 1086 DB, c. 1150 Riev, 1166 P (p), 1175–1220 YCh 1808–1817, 1186–1203 BM, J Arm, 13 AD i, YD vi, viii,

1219 *Ass* 11d, 1247 Ch *et passim* to 1316 Vill, *Denby* 13 DodsN, 1253
YD v, *Overdenbye* 1614 FF, *Over Denbygh* 1615 Arm, *Upper Denby*
1822 Langd, *Demby* 1475 WillY, *Ouerdembye* 1552 YD viii. 'Village
of the Danes', *v.* Dene, bȳ, cf. Introd. 'Upper' to distinguish it from
Denby Grange *infra*.

WHITLEY BEAUMONT, *Witteley* 1271 Font, *Qwitlay* 1415 DodsN,
Qwitley 1433 ib, *Whitley hall* 1424 Rent, 1655 WillS, *Whetley Bea-
mont* 1436 DodsN, *v.* Upper Whitley *supra*. The estate belonged to
the *Beaumont* family (Lat *de Bello Monte*) from the twelfth century
(cf. *WB* ix, 1 *et passim*, and the sources cited, YAJ viii, 502 ff); the
hall was rebuilt t. Eliz by Sir Richard Beaumont.

BANK FIELD, *Bankhouse field* 1634 PRThl, *the Bankehouse feild in the
parish of Kirkheaton* 1674 ib, *v.* foll. BANK HO, *bankehouse* 1657
Pick, *v.* banke, hūs. BEN BOOTH LANE. BROWN HILL, 1846 *TA*,
Brounhill 1331 Font, *v.* brūn¹ 'brown' or brún² 'edge, brow, moor',
hyll; the name occurs several times in YW, and ON brún² is some-
times preferable topographically. CHAPEL ROW. CLOUGH GATE,
Clough Lodge 1817 M, *v.* clōh 'dell'. COAL PIT LANE. COAL PIT
SCROGG, *Coal Pit Close* 1720 WB 32, *-Shrogg* 1846 *TA*, *v.* scrogge
'brushwood'. COCKLEY WOOD, 1843 O.S., probably cocc² '(wood)-
cock', lēah, distinct from Cockley Hill 227 *supra*. CROFT SIDE, *the
Croft* 1710 *WRD* 1095, *v.* croft. CROPPER GATE, 1846 *TA*. DEER
HILL. DENBY GRANGE, *grangia de Deneby* 1331 YD v, *Denby
Graunge* 1467 Pat, *Denby Grange* 1540 MonRent *et freq* to 1822
Langd, *Nether Denbygh* 1615 Arm, *v.* Upper Denby *supra*, grange.
DUMB STEEPLE, 1817 M, 'a steeple without bells', *v.* stēpel; such
a steeple stands in a field, cf. Obelisk Grove iii, 5. FALL HO, cf.
Fall Close 1846 *TA*, *v.* (ge)fall 'clearing'. FRYER PARK WOOD,
1846 *TA*, *v.* frēre, park. GETTINGLEY, 1771 M, *Gotenley* 1687
PRThl, *Goatin(g)ley* 1725, 1728 ib, *v.* gǣten 'a kid' (a derivative of
gāt 'goat' which has influenced the form), lēah. GRANGE ASH,
(the) Grange Ash(e) 1643, 1694 PRThl, PREm, GRANGE MOOR,
Grangemo(o)re 1659 PRThl, 1660 PRThl, 1753 Arm, GRANGE WOOD,
1843 O.S., *v.* Denby Grange *supra*, æsc, mōr, wudu. GREGORY,
Gregory Place 1424 Rent 256, 1652 ib 21, *the Gregory* 1640 WB 43,
the pers.n. or surname *Gregory*, place; cf. also the nearby Gregory
Spring 199 *supra*. HALL HILL, HALL WOOD, 1843 O.S., *v.* Whitley
Beaumont *supra*. HARRY ROYD CLOUGH, 1843 O.S., *Hallroydhouse*
1610 WB 27, *Harry Rods* 1720 WB 32, the ME pers.n. *Herry*,

Harry with a pet-form *Hal*, rod[1]. HAZLE GREAVE, 1817 M, *v.*
hæsel 'hazel', græfe 'copse'. HAIGH HO, 1817 M, *Low-*, *Upp*ᵣ
Hague 1720 *WB* 32, *v.* haga 'enclosure'. THE HEIGHTS, (*the*)
Height 1677 *WB* 43, 1771 M, *v.* hēhðu 'height'. HEPPER WOOD,
1843 O.S. HIGH LEES PLANT., *High Lees* 1846 *TA*, *v.* hēah, lēah.
HILLHOUSE WOOD, cf. *Hillside* 1846 *TA*. HUNT ROYD, 1771 M,
(*the*) *Hunteroyd(e)* 1610 PRThl, 1646 PREm, *v.* hunta 'hunter', rod[1].
LILEY CLOUGH, 1843 O.S., *Lilley Clough* 1771 M, *v.* Liley Hall 200
supra. NEW HALL, *Newhale* 1428 FA, *v.* nīwe, hall. NICKERS
HILL, *Nick House Mill* 1843 O.S., from the pers.n. *Nick* (from
Nicholas), hūs. PAPER HALL, 1843 O.S. PENDLE HILL, *the Pinnell*
1710 *WRD* 1095, *Pinnill* 1720 *WB* 32, *the Pinhill* 1753 ib 106, cf.
Pinhill Top iii, 133 *infra* (from dial. *pinnel* 'clay and gravel soil').
PINION WELL. UPPER RAKES, (*the*) *Rakes* 1652, 1726 *WB* 39, 106,
cf. also (*le*) *Rakerod(e)* 13, 1331 Font, *v.* hraca, dial. *rake* 'a rough
path'. THE ROUGH. ROUND HILL WOOD. SANDS. TILE-
HOUSES, *Tile House Field* 1846 *TA*. TIMMINS SHROGG, 1846 *TA*,
v. scrogge 'brushwood'. WHITE FLATS. WHITLEY PARK, 1843
O.S., *v.* park. WHITLEY WILLOWS. WOODSIDE.

FIELD-NAMES

The principal forms in (*a*) are 1846 *TA* 247, and in (*b*) c. 1180, c. 1190,
1227 YCh 1685, 1802–12. Spellings dated 1710 are *WRD* 1095, 1720 *WB*
32, 1726 ib 104, 1753 ib 106, and others dated without source are YD vi.

(*a*) the Bank close 1710, Bell Close, Breary Close 1710, Broom close,
Brow Close, Bull Garth (*v.* bula, garðr), Burkin Banks (*v.* bircen 'birchen',
banke), Burn Tree Close, Burnt Whin (*v.* hvin 'gorse'), Calf Croft, Cherry
Royd, Clover Leys (*Claverlay* 1186 BM, *v.* clāfre 'clover', lēah), Coney
Garth (*v.* coning-erth 'warren'), Delf Close (ib 1720, *v.* (ge)delf 'quarry'),
Dog Croft, Dunkirk, Firth Ing, Goss Croft, Green Clough, Eddish &
Briery Hawkeswell (*v.* edisc, hafoc, wella), Haw Royd (ib 1720), Healey
Royd, Hob Royd, Hullage (cf. Hullage 204 *supra*), Ing Head, the Intack
1726 (*v.* intak), Little Leys (*v.* lēah), Mare Pickhill (*v.* mere[2] 'mare', pightel
'enclosure'), Myers (*v.* mýrr 'bog'), Old Walls, Pellet Croft (*Pilatecroft*
c. 1185, c. 1190, 13, *v.* pil-āte 'pill-oats', croft), Pit Royds (*Pitt Royd* 1720,
v. pytt, rod[1]), Ridings (*v.* rydding 'clearing'), Robin Royd (*Roberdroyd*,
Roberti roda 13, the pers.n. *Robin*, a pet-form of *Robert*, rod[1]), Sowood
Ing, Spring Ing, Stony Flatt, Sun Sides, Swinden Bank Lane 1753, Tan
House Lane, Three Days Work, Toad Hole, Tumble Tail (-*Tale* 1720),
Tup Acre (dial. *tup* 'a ram'), Uft Royd, Water Croft, the Well Close 1710,
Whitley Ings (*v.* eng 'meadow'), Windmill Hill (-*close* 1720), Windy Bank
1753, Wood Close.

(*b*) *Caldwellerode* c. 1210 (*v.* cald, wella, rod[1]), *Castelgata* (*v.* castel, gata), *Coterodam Alani* 13, *Kottrode* 13 (*v.* cot 'cottage', rod[1]), *Crokedelandes* 13, *Folkerode* 13 (the ON pers.n. *Folki*, rod[1]), *Heselhache* (*v.* hæsel, haga), *Holleroyde* 13, *Holrode* 1269 (*v.* hol[1], rod[1]), *Langefurlang*, *Ryerode* 13 (*v.* rȳge, rod[1]), *Scortebuttes* (*v.* sceort, butte), *Sto(c)kewelle furlanges* (*v.* stocc, wella), *Terrifordecloses* 1677 *WB* 43 (the surname *Terry*, ford), *Twychel* 13 (cf. dial. *twitchel* 'narrow lane', cf. *Twechill* 205 *supra*).

xvi. Kirkburton

Many of the old townships in the parishes of Kirkheaton, Kirkburton, Almondbury and Huddersfield, which for the most part occupy the valley of the Colne and the Holme up to the borders of Lancashire, have been re-organised to form the Urban Districts of Kirkburton, Holmfirth, Meltham, and Colne Valley and the County Borough of Huddersfield. Kirkburton Urban District includes the townships of Kirkburton, Shelley, Shepley and part of Thurstonland from this parish as well as the townships of Kirk-heaton, Lepton and Upper Whitley from Kirkheaton parish (223 *supra*). The other townships in Kirkburton parish (Cartworth, Fulstone, Hepworth, part of Thurstonland, Scholes and Wooldale) are now in Holmfirth Urban District (289 *infra*).

1. CARTWORTH (102–1407)

    Cheteruu(o)rde 1086 DB
    Karteword 1202–10 YCh viii (p), *Cartewrth* 1274–1307 WCR
      (*freq*), -*word* 1325 ib, -*worth* 1347 DodsN, 1392 *MinAcct* 88
    Carthewrthe 1286 WCR
    Cartworth 1313 WCR, 1379 PT (p) *et freq* to 1822 Langd

The first el. is probably a pers.n., since OE worð 'enclosure' is usually (but not exclusively) combined with pers.ns. Whatever the origin of the pers.n. might be in this p.n., it occurs also in Cartington Nb 40 (*Kertindon* 1233 P, *Cartyngdon* 1314 Ipm) and probably in a different form in Cratfield and Creeting Sf; Ekwall presupposes an OE pers.n. *Cræta* for the latter, and though this pers.n. is not known apart from p.ns. it would seem to be related to the hypocoristic OE *Cretta* (Redin 90). In a metathesised form this is the most likely explanation of the name, since OE cert 'rough ground' is of doubtful provenance in the north (and would have produced *Chart*-, with *Cart*- by ON influence); the cognate ON kartr is unlikely with worð.

COPTHURST, *Coppedhirst* 1307 WCR, *Coptherst* 1586 WillY, -*hirst* 1709 WMB. 'Wood of pollarded trees', *v.* copped, hyrst.

HINCHCLIFFE MILL, *Heyncheclyff* 1307 WCR, *Hingecliff* 1327 ib (p), *Hyncheclyff* 1379 PT (p), *the Hinchcliffe Croft* 1699 *YAS* 28, 12, *Hincliffe milne* 1709 WMB. 'Steep cliff', *v.* henge, clif; OE *henge* occurs only in a compound *henge-clif* glossing Lat *preruptum* 'precipitous cliff'. *Hinch-* arises through unvoicing before *-cliff*, as in Inchfield La 59.

RAMSDEN, *Rounnesdenewell* (sic for *Rommes-*) 1307 WCR, *Rommesdene* 1315 ib, *Ramesdene* 1323, 1327 ib (p) 1462, 1492 *MinAcct* 99, 02, *Rammesden(e)* 1325 WCR, 1331 *Ass* 5, 1392 *MinAcct* 88, *Romsdeyn* 1379 PT (p), *Ramsden* 1709 WMB. 'Valley of the ram', *v.* ramm, denu; it is also possible that Ramsden, like some other p.ns. in *Rams-* (Ramsbottom La 64, Ramsden Ess 168, etc.) goes back to OE hramsa 'wild garlic', or an OE pers.n. *Ramm* (cf. Ramsholme 22 *supra*). On the form *Rommes-*, *Roms-* cf. Phonol. § 4.

RIBBLEDEN, *Ryflyngdeynebrig* 1489 *WCR* 1, 1492 *MinAcct* 02. The first el. has the same origin as Rivelin (RNs.), and the name itself is the same as that sometimes found for Rivelin Side i, 226 *supra*; the el. riveling is also found in *Tackriveling*, *Rivelingdale* YN 7, *Ryuelynghow* (Lindrick) pt. v *infra*, and according to Ekwall (RN 343) it is an appellative for 'a stream' connected with OE *hrife* 'fierce', *rifelung* 'wrinkle', etc. *v.* denu 'valley'. The modern name owes its form to the name of the better-known R. Ribble; the stream, an affluent of the R. Holme, is also now called Ribble.

ARRUNDEN, 1817 M, *Arunden* 1709 WMB, *Harenden* 1771 M, *Harrunden or Arrunden* 1822 Langd; the first el. may be, as in Arundel Sx 136, OE hārhūne 'hore-hound', *v.* denu.   BANK, 1771 M, *v.* banke.   BANK BOTTOM, *le Nethirbothome* 1525 *WCR* 4, *v.* neoðera, botm (booᵐ).   BANKFIELD.   BATTY'S DAM, doubtless the surname *Battye* as in Battye Ford 198 *supra*, dammr.   BEAVER CLOUGH.   BRAY WOOD, *Bray Woods* 1709 WMB.   BROWN HILL, 1771 M, *Brounhull'* 1392 *MinAcct* 88 (p), from OE brūn 'brown' or ON brún 'brow, moor', hyll, cf. Brown Hill 234 *supra*.   CATHOLES GUTTER.   CROW HILL.   DAM HO, 1709 WMB, *v.* dammr, hūs.   DOBB, DOB DIKE, *Dob Mill* 1771 M.   DOVER, possibly another instance of Dover, from Brit dubro- (Welsh *dwfr*) 'water', but no certainty is possible without material (cf. Introd.).   DUNSLEY BANK, *Dunesleye* 1308 WCR, *Dunsley* 1709 WMB, 'Dun's clearing' from the OE pers.n. *Dun(n)*, lēah.   FOX CLOUGH.   GILL LANE.   GLEN-

THORPE. GREEN HO, *Green hous* 1709 WMB. HALL GREEN. HIGH GATE, 1843 O.S., *v.* hēah, gata. HILL HO, NETHER HILL HO, *Hillhouse* 1640 WillY, *Vpper & Nether-hillhouse* 1709 WMB, *v.* hyll, hūs. HILL TOP, 1843 O.S. HOLLIN BRIGG, 1709 WMB, *Hollynbrig* 1600 *WCR* 7d, *v.* holegn 'holly', brycg. HOLLIN HILL. HOLME STYES, *Holmesleys* (sic) 1843 O.S., *v.* holmr, stīg 'path', but more probably 'pathway to Holme' (269 *infra*). HORSEFIELD, *Horsfield Ho.* 1843 O.S. KILNHOUSE BANK, 1843 O.S., *Kylnehousebanke* 1557 WillY, *v.* cyln, hūs, banke. LAITH, *Lathe* 1771 M, *v.* hlaða 'barn'. LAMMA WELL, *Lamawells* 1709 WMB. LANE BOTTOM, cf. *Lane head* 1709 WMB. MALKIN HO, *Mawkin House* 1709 WMB, *Mokin H.* 1771 M, the ME fem. pers.n. *Malkin* (a diminutive of *Matilda*). MOORFIELD HO. MOSS EDGE, 1771 M, *Mos(s)ege* 1545, 1549 WillY, (*le*) *Mossedge* 1600 *WCR* 7d, 1709 WMB, *v.* mos 'a moss, a bog, swamp', ecg 'escarpment'. NABB, *v.* nabbi 'a knoll'. NEW GATE. OLD YEW, 1843 O.S., *v.* īw. PARK NOOK, cf. *Parkehed* 1492 *MinAcct* 02, *v.* park. ROYD HO & ING, cf. *le Roidehirst* 1492 *MinAcct* 02, *v.* rod[1] 'clearing', hyrst, eng. STONY GATE. SWAN BANK, 1843 O.S. TINKER WELL. WALTIN. WARD BANK & PLACE, *Wardplace* 1709 WMB, *Werd Place* 1771 M, doubtless the surname *Ward*, *v.* banke, place. WASHPIT, *Washpit Mill* 1843 O.S., *v.* wæsce, pytt. WATER SIDE, 1709 WMB. WEATHER HILL, *Great Wedderley* 1709 WMB, *v.* weðer 'a wether sheep', lēah or hyll. WELL HO. WEST GATE, 1843 O.S., *v.* west, gata 'road'. WHITE GATE, 1709 WMB, *Whitegate als. Whiteplate* 1657 WillS, *v.* hwīt, gata 'road', plat[1] 'a footbridge'; it is a road over the moors. WHITE GATE EDGE, 1843, *v.* prec., ecg 'edge, escarpment'. WOODHOUSE, 1587 WillY, possibly identical with *Wodhous* 1414 YD xiii, 75, 'house in the wood', *v.* wudu, hūs. WOOD NOOK & TOP.

FIELD-NAMES

The unidentified minor names in Kirkburton and Almondbury parishes cannot with certainty be allotted to the various townships, especially those from the Wakefield manorial records. The principal forms in (*a*) are 1709 WMB, and a few are modern (marked *mod*). Spellings dated 1307, 1327 are WCR, 1462, 1492 *MinAcct*, 1551, 1600 *WCR*.

(*a*) Brandow Flatts (probably 'burnt hill', *v.* brand, haugr, flat), Brearlee (*v.* brēr 'briar', lēah), Bright hill (ib 1771), Fletcher Ing (*v.* eng), Henpickel (*Henpyghell* 1551, *v.* henn 'hen', pightel 'enclosure'), Lath Croft (*v.* hlaða 'barn', croft), Modwood (cf. *Modleyne ende* 1492), Old Royde (*v.* rod[1] 'clearing'), Pickle Wood (*mod*), Pingle Wood (*mod*) (*v.* pightel, pingel 'enclosure'), Ryding (*v.* rydding 'clearing'), Walkers Bothom (*v.* botm).

(*b*) *Bentcroft* 1600 (*v.* beonet 'bent-grass', croft), *Bromehilbanke* 1462, 1492 (*v.* brōm 'broom', hyll, banke), *Carthworthmere* 1327 (for *mere* cf. Friar Mere 311 *infra*), *Ewyntreleye* 1307 (e.ModE *ewen* 'yewen, yew' (cf. īw, -en²), trēow, lēah), *Haukeshirst* 1307 (*v.* hafoc 'hawk', hyrst 'wood'), *Penson bothom* 1551 (the surname *Penson*, boōm), *Stonylegh* 1492 (*v.* stānig, lēah), *Wykeleyrode* 1307 (*v.* rod¹).

2. FULSTONE (102–1709)

Fugelestun 1086 DB, *-ton* 1298 WCR, *-is-* 1274, 1297 ib, *Fugheleston* 1306, 1307 ib, *Fogheleston* 1313, 1324 ib

Fuleston 1285 WCR   *Fulleston* 1492 *MinAcct* 02

Fouleston 1307, 1313, 1324 WCR

Foleston 1392 *MinAcct* 88

Fuston 1552 WillY

Foolstone 1709 WMB

'Fugol's farmstead', from the OE pers.n. *Fugol*, tūn.

BUTTERLEY, *Buttreley* 1274 WCR, *Butterleystiel*, *-grene* 1307 ib, *Butterlay*, *-leye* 1308 ib, 1600 *WCR* 10, *-lee* 1699 ib 10d, 1709 WMB, *Boterley* 1379 PT (p), *Buturlayeyng* 1445 *WCR* 5d. 'Clearing with rich, butter-producing pasture', *v.* butere, lēah, stigel 'stile', grēne², eng.

HADDINGLEY, *Hadingley* 1640 WillY, 1771 M, *Haddingley* 1646 WillY, (*Nether-*, *Over-*) 1709 WMB, *Haddenley* 1817 M. There are several YW p.ns. in *-ingley* which present some difficulty, as they appear only in late sources and denote very minor places; they are unlikely (except where, as in Billingley i, 94 *supra* or Headingley pt. iv *infra*, the evidence is good) to be names of any great antiquity, especially as in these more westerly parts of the Riding p.ns. formed from folk-names in *-ingas* are otherwise wanting, and lēah continued in living use until quite late. In *Castingley* 150, Gettingley 234, Hostingley 214 *supra* and in Crodingley 287 *infra*, the *-ing-* is probably spurious, in Dunningley 175 *supra* and Hardingley 249 *infra* it is a pers.n. suffix; in Whittingley 178 *supra* it is obscure. In Haddingley we may therefore have a compound of the ME *haueding* 'heading' (found in Haddings 204 *supra*) with lēah; the word would here denote something like 'headland, peak', since Haddingley Hill is a prominent hill (near the source of the Dearne).

New Mill, 1709 WMB, *Newmylle* 1462 *MinAcct* 99, *-milne(s)* 1492 ib 02, 1639 WillY, 1709 WMB, *Newemyln(e)* (*goit, -grene*) 1525 *WCR* 1d, 1587 WillY, *v.* nīwe, myln, gota 'water-channel'.

Bellgreave, *Belgrave* 1843 O.S., possibly of the same origin as or derived (as a surname) from Belgrave Ch, *v.* bēl 'beacon', grǣfe 'copse'; it is on the side of a prominent hill. Bendhill Wood. Biggin, 1709 WMB, *v.* bigging 'a building'. Briery Brow. Brown Hill. Brown's Edge, *Browns Edge Hill* 1843 O.S. Carr Gate & Carr Ho, *le Ker* 1327 WCR, *The Carr* 1709 WMB, *Gerehowes in Fulston* 1591 WillY, *v.* kjarr 'marsh', gata, hūs. Cold Hill Lane. Cold Well Hill, *Coldwell'* 1379 PT (p) *Coldewelle* 1392 *MinAcct* 88 (p), *v.* cald, wella. Croft Bottom, *the Croft* 1709 WMB, *v.* croft. Dearne Head, 1843 O.S., the source of the R. Dearne, *v.* hēafod and Haddingley *supra.* Deershaw, *Dear(e)shaw* 1637 WillY, 1709 WMB, 'deer wood', *v.* dēor 'deer, animal', sceaga. Drake Hill, *Drakeholt* 1551 *WCR* 1, 'dragon wood', *v.* draca, holt. East Field. Ebson Ho, *Ebsonhouse* 1580, 1641 WillY, *Hebson House* 1817 M, there was a *Hobsonhouse* (? rectius *Hebson-*) 1551 *WCR* 4, to which property *George* and *William Hobson* (? *Hebson*) were admitted. Fulstone Hall, *Hall* 1843 O.S. Gate Foot, 1709 WMB, 1771 M, *v.* gata 'road', fōt. Grassy Cliff. Greenhill Bank, 1843 O.S., *Grenehilloyne* 1525 *WCR* 1d, *Greenehill Banck* 1640 WillY, *v.* grēne[1], hyll, lane, banke. Grime Lane. The Gully. Hey Bottom, *Hey* 1709 WMB, *v.* (ge)hæg 'enclosure'. High Bank, 1843 O.S. High Brow. Hill End, 1817 M. Hill Top, 1771 M. Hirst Lane. Hole Bottom & Lane. Hollingreave, 1709 WMB, *Holyngreve* 1558 WillY, 'holly wood', *v.* holegn, grǣfe. Hollin Ho, 1771 M, *Hollynhowse* 1592 WillY, *Hollynghous* 1600 *WCR* 11, *v.* holegn 'holly', hūs. Holme Bottom, 1843 O.S., *v.* foll., botm. Holme Ho, 1771 M, *Holme* 1649 *YAS* 28, 2, *v.* holmr 'water-meadow'. Horn Cote, *Horn Cote*, 1843 O.S., *v.* foll., cot 'cottage'. Horn Hill, *Underhorne* 1307 WCR, *The Hurnepike, The Midle Hurne, The Hurnend* 1709 WMB, *v.* horn, here in the sense 'a projecting headland', as it denotes a narrow steep-sided ridge; *v.* also under, pīc[1] 'a pike, a hill'. Hullock, 1652 WillS, *v.* huluc 'shed, hut'. Hunger Hill, *the Hungerhills* 1699 *YAS* 28, 12, *v.* hungor, hyll. Jackson Bridge, 1843 O.S. Kaye Wood. Kirk Bridge. Lane End, *Lane ends* 1817 M. Lea Ho. Lydgate, *Lidgate* 1709 WMB, *Liget* 1771 M, *v.* hlid-geat 'swing-gate'. MARSH HO, *Marsh(banck)* 1709 WMB, *v.* mersc, banke. MARSH LANE, 1843 O.S., *v.* prec. MARSHLANDS. MAYTHORN, 1709 WMB, *(le) Mathorne* 1564 WillY, 1647 YDr, 1699 *WCR* 1, 1709 WMB, possibly e.ModE *maythern*, dial. *mathern* 'stinking camomile' (from 1578 NED s.v.), a derivative of OE *magoðe*; *may-thorn* 'hawthorn' (not recorded before 1844 (NED)). is, however, more likely. MEAR HO, 1771 M, *Mearehouse(brigge)* 1645 WillY, 1699 *WCR* 1d, the first el. is probably mere 'pool' (in the stream by which it stands). MELTHAM HO, 1571 WillY, cf. Meltham 282 *infra*, probably used as a surname. MOOR CROFT, 1709 WMB, *v.* mōr, croft. MOORLANDS, *the Moreland* 1699 *YAS* 28, 12, *Moore lands* 1709 WMB, *v.* mōr, land. MOUNT & MOUNT HILL, *Mount* 1640 WillY, 1817 M, *v.* mont 'hill, mount'. MUCKY BRIDGE. NABSCLIFFE, *Nabb(s) Cliff* 1709 WMB, cf. *Nabbe acre* 1550 YD viii, named from *Butterlaynabbe* 1308 WCR, *v.* Butterley *supra*, nabbi 'a hill, knoll'. PIKE LOW, *Picklow Hill* 1843 O.S., *v.* pīc[1] 'a pike, a peak', hlāw. PIPER WELL. POTTERS GATE. RED ROW. ROMBS CLOUGH. SCALY GATE. SCAR, *Mounts Carr* 1771 M, *Mount Scar* 1843 O.S., *v.* Mount *supra*, sker 'a rocky cliff'. SETS STONES. SHORT HORNS. SLACK BECK & MOUTH, *v.* slakki 'depression', named from Hey Slack 244 *infra*. SNOWGATE HEAD, 1651 WillY, 1699 *WCR* 12d, 1709 WMB, *Snawegatehede* 1445 *WCR* 5d, *Snawgaiteheade* 1551 *WCR* 4, *Snawgthed* (sic) 1578 WillY, 'road liable to be impeded by snow', *v.* snāw, gata; it is the main road from Holmfirth to Barnsley and Wakefield over the hills. SPRING HEAD. SPRING WOOD. STAGWOOD HILL, 1817 M, *Stackwodeker* 1307 WCR, *-wodd bancke* 1454 *WCR* 1, *-wood hill* 1709 WMB, *Stackerd Roide* 1699 *WCR* 10d; the exact meaning is not clear; ModE *stack-wood* denotes 'a faggot'; but here the p.n. may signify 'wood where wood was obtained and piled' or indeed 'wood near which ricks were kept' (cf. ON *stakkr* 'haystack', ME *stack* 'a heap, pile'). STALLEY ROYD, *Stalayroide* 1525 *WCR* 1d, *-Royds* 1709 WMB, possibly a reduced form of some p.n. from OE stæf (gen.plur. stafa) 'staff, stave' and lēah (as is Stalybridge Ch). SUDE HILL DIKE, *Sude Hill* 1843 O.S. TENTER HILL. UPPER FOLD. WALL NOOK. WESTERN FORD, *Westonfurth* 1492 *MinAcct* 02, 'ford near *Weston*, i.e. west farmstead', *v.* west, tūn, ford; it is in the west of the township. WHITELANDS LANE, *le Whitelandes* 1699 *WCR* 1d, *the Whitelands* 1699 *YAS* 28, 12, *v.* hwīt, land. WHITE LEY.

FIELD-NAMES

The principal forms in (*a*) are modern (1930, from Mr J. Hanson Green). Spellings dated 1307–1326 are WCR, 1392 *MinAcct* 88, 1445–1600 *WCR*, 1649 *YAS* Md 28, 2, 1709 WMB. The f.ns. recorded here cannot be located with certainty (cf. 238 *supra*).

(*a*) Abraham Ing, Bents (*v.* beonet 'bent-grass'), Butts Lee 1709 (*v.* butte, lēah), Coit Close (*v.* cot 'cottage'), Cold Well Ing (*Goldewellynge* 1525, *Coldall Ing* 1709, *v.* Cold Well Hill *supra*, eng 'meadow'), The Gillroyd (Inge) 1709, Great Cliffe 1709, the Greate Inge 1709, The Green, Far & Lower Intack (*v.* intak), Leys, the Little Ingewood 1709 (*v.* eng, wudu), Long Carr 1709 (*Langker* 1307, *v.* lang, kjarr 'marsh'), Long Close, Long Lands, Marshaw 1709 (*Merscawe* 1247 Ch, *Merschawe* 14 DodsN, *v.* mere 'pool', sceaga 'copse'), Matson Inge 1709, Mouspike Hill 1709 (*v.* mūs, pīc[1] 'peak', hyll), Owler Barrow (*v.* alor 'alder-tree', bearu 'wood'), the Pighel 1709 (*v.* pightel 'enclosure'), Shawcliffe 1843 O.S. (*v.* sceaga 'copse', clif), Sisters Oakes 1709, Great & Little Spirth 1853 *TA* (*v.* spyrt 'spirt, jet of liquid'), Throstle Royd, West Field, Wood Bottom.

(*b*) *Breriker* 1307 (*v.* brērig 'briary', kjarr 'marsh'), *Cuntelacheker* 1307 (*v.* læcc 'bog, stream', kjarr), *Edmundley*(*ker*) 1307 (the ME pers.n. *Edmund* (OE *Ēadmund*), lēah, kjarr), *Helwardholes* 1286 WCR, *Elwardhulles* 1326 ib (p), 1499 *WCR* 3, 1525 ib 1, *-huls* 1315 WCR (the OE pers.n. *Ælfweard* or *Æþelweard*, hol[1]), *Eweclif* 1307 ('ewe cliff', *v.* eowu, clif), *Grene Swynstyeclif* 1307 (*v.* grēne[1], swīn, stigu 'sty', clif), *Moreker* 1307 (*v.* mōr, kjarr), *Nethercrofte* 1649, *le Ouerbanke* 1649, *Paulynbothehirst* 1307 (ME *Paulin*(*us*), bōth 'booth, shed', hyrst 'wood'), *Rodland in Foleston* 1392 (*v.* rod[1] 'clearing', land), *Roghlowe-, Rolayker* 1307, *Roulayrake* 1392, *Roley* 1563 YD vi, (*v.* rūh 'rough', hlāw 'hill', kjarr), *Schepewassegrene* 1307 (*v.* scēap-wæsce 'a sheep-wash', grēne[2]), *Smythie Inge, Smythynge* 1600 (*v.* smiððe, eng), *Wygbothome* 1445 (*v.* wicg 'horse', botm), *Willestubbing* 1308 (the ME pers.n. *Will*(*e*), stubbing), *Wlfhingandleye* 1307 (*v.* wulf, perhaps as a pers.n., hangende (hengjandi) 'steep', lēah), *Wulricheleye* 1307 (the OE pers.n. *Wulfric*, lēah).

3. HEPWORTH (102–1606)

Heppeuuord 1086 DB, *Heppewrth* 1274–1308 WCR (*freq*), *-worth* 1313, 1323 ib, *Hepworthyn*' 1462, 1492 *MinAcct* 99, 02, *-worth* 1550 YD ii. In view of the *Heppe-* spellings this can hardly be OE hēope 'hip'; it is no doubt an OE pers.n. *Heppa*, which is not recorded but finds a cognate in OG *Heppo*; it could be a hypocoristic form of some such pers.n. as *Helpric*. This is the more likely, as worð 'enclosure' is most often combined with a pers.n. *v.* also Hepshaw *infra*. The Merc form *-worthyn* (*v.* worðign) is noteworthy; *v.* Introd.

BARNSIDE, *Barnedeside* 1274, 1298 WCR (p), *Barneside* 1274 ib, 1307 YD xiii, 68, 1699 *WCR* 8, 1709 WMB, *Barmeside* 1290, 1307 Ch, *Bernside* 1327 WCR (p), *Barnside-Wood* 1822 Langd. 'Burnt hill-side', *v.* berned, sīde.

BERRISTAL HEAD, *Berystalhede, -syke* 1499 *WCR* 2, *Beristall* (*campo voc*') 1600 ib 11, *Bearistall head* 1709 WMB; this appears to be a compound of OE berige 'berry' and stall 'place, stall' and would have a connotation something like that of *Bairstow* iii, 90 *infra* from OE beger 'berry' and stōw; any connexion with OE borg-stall or even *beorg-stall 'place of refuge' is phonologically improbable, but the exact significance of the compound *berige-stall* is obscure.

HEPSHAW, *Hepshamedge* (sic) 1640 WillY, *Hepshaw* 1648 YDr, (-*Edge*) 1709 WMB. This is 'Heppa's copse' from the OE pers.n. *Heppa* (probably that of the man who also gave his name to Hepworth *supra*) and sceaga.

ANCHOR HILL. BANK HO, *Banckhous* 1709 WMB, *v.* banke, hūs. BEDDING EDGE, 1709 WMB, possibly OE, ME *bedding* 'bedding', used here with the same kind of implication as in Featherbed Moss 283 *infra*. BENT HO. BIRD'S NEST, 1771 M, *v.* bridd, nest, and cf. Crow Nest 186 *supra*. BLACKSTONE EDGE, 1843 O.S., *v.* blæc, stān, ecg 'escarpment', cf. Blackstone Edge iii, 1 *infra*. BOAR CLOUGH. BROAD CARR LANE. BROCK HOLES, *Brokeholus* 1379 PT (p), *le Brok(e)holes* 1462, 1492 *MinAcct* 99, 02, *v.* brocc-hol 'badger-hole'. BUTT LANE, *le Butt over the Well* 1699 *WCR* 8, possibly e.ModE *butte* 'a butt, a barrel', but it could also be OE butt[1] 'stump, log' (used in some such way as OE stocc 'stump' is in the common Stockwell). CALF HEY. CAT CLOUGH. CHEESEGATE NAB, 1843 O.S., *v.* nabbi 'knoll'. CLAY PIT. COTE, cf. *Cotefeilde* 1600 *WCR* 11, *v.* cot 'cottage'. COWCLIFF HALL. CRIMES. CRIPPLE HOLE, 1771 M, *v.* crypel 'a burrow', hol[1] 'hole'. CROW EDGE, 1709 WMB, *v.* crāwe, ecg. DEAN DIKE & HO, *Deanehouse* 1593 WillY, *Hepworth Deane* 1709 WMB, *Dean* 1771 M, *v.* denu 'valley', dīc, hūs. DICK EDGE, *Dickedge* 1600 *WCR* 11, 1637 WillY, 1709 WMB, the pers.n. *Dick*, ecg. DOWNSHUTTS, 1843 O.S., *v.* dūne, dial. *shut* 'division of land'; the name is repeated 247, 254 *infra*. FIELDS HEAD, *Field head* 1709 WMB, *Field* 1771 M, *v.* feld. FOSTER PLACE, 1709 WMB, *Fosterplace* 1590 WillY, the surname *Foster*, place. FOX HO, 1817 M, *Foxhouses* 1709 WMB, *Foxes* 1771 M, *v.*

fox, perhaps as a surname, hūs.　GATE HEAD, *Smallegaitheade* 1551
WCR 7, *Genn-gate-head* 1647 YDr, *v.* smæl 'narrow', gata 'road',
hēafod; a local man called *Genn* is referred to in 1551 YDr i, 55.
HALL ACRE WOOD.　HAZLEHEAD.　HEY CLOUGH, *Hepworthhey*
1406 *WCR* i, *Hey* 1600 ib 11, *v.* (ge)hæg 'enclosure'.　HEY SLACK,
Heyslackes 1640 WillY, *Hay Slack*(*s*) 1709 WMB, 1771 M, *v.* prec.,
slakki 'a hollow, a depression'.　HUSKING HOLES, *Thuskinholes* 1583
WillY, 1618 FF, 1771 M, *Thuskenholes* 1588 WillY; the origin is
obscure, but it might be connected with dial. *thusking* 'large, fine'
(which is not, however, used in such contexts) or with dial. *husking*
'creeping stealthily about with bent shoulders', hence 'a clownish
fellow'; in any case initial *th-* has been regarded as the def.art.
ING ROYD.　INTAKE, 1817 M, *v.* intak.　KNOWLES, 1771 M, *venell'*
voc' Knowles Lane 1699 *WCR* 8, *v.* cnoll 'a knoll, a hillock'.　LATHAM,
1771 M.　LAW & LAW SLACK, *Law*, *Lawsike* 1709 WMB, *Law*
Slack 1843 O.S., *v.* hlāw 'hill', sīc, slakki 'depression'.　LONG
MOORS.　MARTIN'S NEST, from e.ModE *martin* 'a martin', nest,
cf. Crow Nest 186 *supra*.　MEAL HILL, 1709 WMB, possibly OE
mǣle 'multi-coloured', hyll.　MILL SHAW, *Milleshaghe* 1331 WCR
(p), *Nether Milshaw* 1588 WillY, 1699 *WCR* 11, *Milnshaw* 1709
WMB, *v.* myln, sceaga 'copse'.　MOLE CLOUGH.　MUGUP LANE.
NAB HILL, *Nabb* 1709 WMB, *v.* nabbi 'a knoll'.　UPPER & LOWER
NAB, *Upper Nab* 1843 O.S., *v.* prec.　OLD HEY CLOUGH.　OX LEE,
Hoxlegh' 1379 PT (p), *Oxlee* 1499 *WCR* 2, 1709 WMB, *v.* oxa, lēah
'clearing'.　PICKLES BRIDGE.　RIDDLE PIT, *Ridle Pit*(*t*) 1709 WMB,
Redle Pits 1771 M, e.ModE *reddle* or *riddle* (variants of *raddle*, *ruddle*)
'red ochre', pytt, probably 'pits where ochre was obtained'.　SLED
BROOK 1817 M, *Sledbrooke* 1709 WMB, *v.* slæd 'valley', brōc.
SNUG HO.　STUBBING WOOD, *Nether & Over Stubbing, the Stubbings*
Brow 1709 WMB, *v.* stubbing 'clearing'.　THE WHAMS, *v.* hvammr
'a small valley'.　LOWER & UPPER WHITLEY, *Whitley Moors* 1709
WMB, *v.* hwīt, lēah, a common YW p.n.　WICKING CLOUGH.
WOOD ROYD, *Wood Royd Hill* 1771 M, *v.* wudu, rod[1].

FIELD-NAMES

The principal forms in (*a*) are 1709 WMB. Spellings dated 1307, 1331 are
WCR, 1392, 1462, 1492 *MinAcct*, 1551, 1600, 1699 *WCR*. *v.* note on
identification of these f.ns. 238 *supra*.

(*a*) Burnedge (*v.* brende 'burnt', ecg), Fairbanck Knowl, -Knowe (*Fur-*

banke Knowles 1578 WillY, probably a surname *Fairbank*, cnoll), Far Feilds
(*le Farrefeilds* 1699, *v.* feor, feld), Hore Law ('boundary mound or hill',
v. hār[2], hlāw), Lane Head 1817 M, Over Lease in Hepworth (*Overleys* 1699,
v. uferra, lēah), Rideing Ing (*v.* rydding 'clearing', eng).

(b) *Aldebothe* 1307 (*v.* ald, bōth 'booth, shed'), *Apiltreker* 1331 (*v.*
æppel-trēow, kjarr 'marsh'), *Banks Intacks* 1699 (*v.* intak), *Bitelfelde* 1462,
Bytefeld 1492 (OE *bitela* 'beetle', feld), *Bolynbothehill* 1462 (*v.* bōth 'booth',
hyll), *Bolkyng* 1462, *Bulkyng* 1492 (*v.* bulki 'heap, hill', eng), *Brathford* 1492
(*v.* brād, ford), *Brentboth(e) Elme* 1462, 1492 ('burnt booth', *v.* brende, bōth,
elm), *Brodeyngheade* 1600 (*v.* brād, eng), *Broideland* 1492, *Burdemaseʒ* 1492,
Denerode 1307 (*v.* denu 'valley', rod[1]), *Dickcloughe* 1600 (cf. Dick Edge
supra, *v.* clōh 'dell'), *Haighfeilde* als. *Highefeild* 1600 (*v.* haga 'enclosure',
hēah, feld), *Hancockes Hill* 1600 (the surname *Hancock*, hyll), *Hep-*, *Hip-
worthmore* 1392, 1462 (*v.* mōr), *Hogyn'* 1462, 1492 (perhaps 'hog meadow',
v. hogg, eng), *le Great-*, *le Little Longlee* 1699 (*v.* lang, lēah), *le Meaning
Greene* 1699 (*v.* (ge)mǣne 'common', eng 'meadow', grēne[2]), *les two Moore
Ings* 1699 (*v.* mōr, eng), *Netil-*, *Nitilbanke* 1462, 1492 (*v.* netele 'nettle',
banke), *terr' voc' Ouermesure* 1551 ('over measure'), *le Paddocke* 1699 (*v.*
pearroc 'enclosure'), *Shirtcliffyngeside* 1600 (perhaps a surname from Shirt-
cliffe i, 167 *supra*, eng, sīde), *Skitte-*, *Skitfeld(e)* 1462, 1492 (*v.* skitr 'dung',
feld), *le Well Inge Acre* 1699 (*v.* wella, eng, æcer).

4. KIRKBURTON (102–2012)

Bertone 1086 DB   *Burgtun'* 1164–81 YCh viii
Bir-, *Byrtun*, *-ton(a)* 1091–7 to 1210 YCh viii (*freq*), 13 *Lewes*
　　300, YD iii, 1208 FF, 1229 Ebor, 1275–1330 WCR (*freq*), 1280–
　　1302 Ebor (*freq*), 1297 LS, 1314 YD iii *et passim* to 1457 DodsN,
　　(*Ki-*, *Kyrk(e)-*) 1517 ib, 1546 YChant, 1557 WillY, *Birtton* 1236–
　　58 YD ix, 394, *Birtoun* 1330 WCR
Burton(e) 1147, 1180–1202 YCh viii, (*Ki-*, *Kyrk(e)-*) 1535 VE,
　　1552 WillY, 1558 Wheat, 1580, 1605 FF, (*-Ecclesia*) 1641
　　Rates

'Farmstead near or belonging to a fortification', *v.* byrh-tūn (in
which *byrh* is the gen.sg. of burh); the early *Burg-*, *Burton* spellings
show some confusion with the more common burh-tūn. The church
of *Birton* is first mentioned in 1147 YCh viii and frequently thereafter
(*v.* kirkja).

HIGH BURTON, *Burton(e)* 1086 DB, *Birton* 1208 DodsN, *Highbyrton*,
-birton c. 1442 YD iii, 1504 Ipm, *Highburton* 1528, 1591 FF, *Hye
Burton* 1574 Wheat, *Heyburton* 1575 WillY. *v.* prec., hēah 'high,
lofty'; it stands on higher ground than Kirkburton.

RILEY, *Ri-*, *Rylay*, *-ley*, *-leg* 1202–10 YCh viii, 1246 *Ass* 29d, 1298 WCR, 1297 LS (p), 1314 YD iii *et passim* to 1621 FF, *Ryeley* 1286 WCR. 'Clearing used for growing rye', *v.* rȳge, lēah.

THORNCLIFF, *Thornotelegh* 1202 FF, *Thornetele* 1208 DodsN, FF, *Thornitelay* l. 13 *WB* 9 (p), *Thornice-*, *Thornykeley* 1275 WCR, 1297 LS, *Thorntelay* 1307 WCR, *Thornecley* 1316 YD, *Thornclay* 1517 DodsN, *Thorncliffe* 1524 *WB* 12, 1657 Pick, *Thorneclifte* 1637 WillY. 'Thorny clearing', from OE þorniht 'thorny, growing with thorns', and lēah. In the dial. *c* and *t* often interchange before *l* (as in [titl] for *tickle* or [likl] for *little*), which accounts for *Thornclay*, etc.; the later form with *-cliff* is an inversion for *-clay*, as an etymologically correct *-clif* is often reduced to *-(c)ley*.

ALLEN WOOD. BELDON BROOK, probably identical with *Baeldall* 1567 WillY, *Waldell* 1492 *MinAcct* 02, *Waldale* 1591 WillY (with *Wal-* as a misreading of *Bal-*); cf. Baildon Dike 219 *supra* (from which it is distinct), *v.* dæl 'valley'. BOX INGS. BROOKFIELD MILL. BROOM BANK & STILE. BURTON DEAN, *Burton Dene* 1803 *WB* 246, *v.* denu 'valley'. BURTON ROYD. BUSK. CAUSEWAY FOOT, *Causeyfoote* 1638 WillY, *v.* caucie 'causeway', fōt. CINDER HILL, *Cinderhills* 1842 *TA* 360, *v.* sinder, hyll. COMMON SIDE. COPLEY Ho. DAM HILL. DEAN BOTTOM, SIDE & TOP, *Dean Side* 1843 O.S., *v.* Burton Dean *supra*. DOGLEY BAR & LANE, *Dogley Lane* 1771 M, *v.* dogga 'dog', lēah. FOLLY HALL, 1843 O.S., *v.* folie. FOLLY SHROGG, *v.* scrogge 'brushwood'. HALLAS, *Hallows* 1817 M, *Old Hallas* 1843 O.S., *v.* halh 'nook of land'. HARRY BOWER. HIGH CROSS, formerly *White Cross* 1843 O.S., *v.* hwīt, cros. HIGHFIELD FM. HIGHWOOD, 1843 O.S. LAMB SPRING. LANE HEAD. LINFIT, *Linfit-Lane* 1822 Langd, doubtless 'flax clearing', *v.* līn, þveit, cf. Linthwaite 273 *infra*; for *-fit* from þveit cf. Phonol. § 49. MILL DAM. MOOR LANE. NETHERFIELD HO, *Netherfeild* 1709 WMB, *v.* neoðera, feld. NORTHFIELD HO. OAKROYD. PADDOCK, 1843 O.S., *v.* pearroc 'enclosure'. THE ROW. ROYD WOOD. SHAW LANE. SLANT GATE. SPRINGFIELD MILLS. TANYARD Ho. THORNCLIFF GREEN, 1843 O.S., *v.* Thorncliff *supra*, grēne[2]. TITHE WOOD. TURNSHAW RD.

FIELD-NAMES

Spellings dated c. 1205 are YCh viii, 13, 1314 YD iii, 1492 *MinAcct* 02, 1684, 1693, 1764 *Glebe*. On the identification cf. 238 *supra*; some recorded in Holme 270 *infra* may belong here.

(*a*) the impyard 1764 (*v*. impa 'sapling', geard), the Stewart Plats 1764 (*The Stuarplatts* 1684, -*flats* 1693, *v*. stigweard 'steward', perhaps as a surname, plat² 'a small plot of ground'), Teppy lane 1764 (*the teppylane* 1684).

(*b*) le Bothes 1314 (*v*. bōth 'booth'), *Caworthiny* 1492 (*v*. worðign), *Durildewelle*(*ker*) c. 1205, 13 (the ME fem. pers.n. *Durilda* (from ON *Þórhildr*, cf. Feilitzen 393), wella, kjarr 'marsh'), *Horsfal* c. 1205, *Horse fall Bridge* 1675 Og (*v*. hors, (ge)fall, cf. Horsefall iii, 182 *infra*), *Northkirkestall' in Burton'* 1492 ('church site', *v*. kirkja, stall, cf. Kirkstall (Headingley) pt iv *infra*), *Leake Hall* 1640 WillY, le *Maȝertre* 1314 (ME *mazere*, OFr *masere* 'a wood from which drinking cups were made, a maple', trēow), *Sissoc Rode* 1314 (probably from the ME fem. pers.n. *Sissot*, rod¹), *Thorlowe banke* 1492 (probably 'thorn hill', *v*. þorn, hlāw), *Vlfkelerode* c. 1205 (the ON pers.n. *Úlfkell*, rod¹), *Wetecroftacre* 1314 (probably hwǣte 'wheat', croft, æcer).

5. SCHOLES (102–1607)

> *Scoles* 1274–1313 WCR, 1392 *MinAcct* 88, the Scoles 1315 WCR, *le Scoles* 1327 ib, *Scolis* 1471 Brett
> (*le*) *Scholes* 1284, 1286 WCR, 1638 WillY, 1647 YDr
> (*le*) *Skoles* 1323 WCR, 1392 Brett, 1587 WillY

'The sheds or shielings', *v*. skáli.

ABINGER.   BARE BONES.   BLACK HILL.   BOSHAW, *Bawshaw*, -*shay* 1709 WMB, *Bowshaw* 1843 O.S., *v*. sceaga 'copse'.   BRADSHAW EDGE, *Bradshaw Inge* 1709 WMB, *v*. brād, sceaga 'copse' (perhaps as a surname from Bradshaw 263 *infra*), ecg, eng.   CHAPEL GATE. DAISY LEE, 1843 O.S., *Daisy Hill* 1817 M.   DEAN BRIDGE & DIKE, *Denbrig*(*ge*) 1462, 1492 *MinAcct*, cf. le Deyne Yngenooke 1600 WCR 6d, *v*. denu 'valley', brycg.   DOBROYD MILL, 1843 O.S., the ME pers.n. *Dobbe*, rod¹ 'clearing'.   DOWNSHUTTS, *Downshutt* 1843 O.S., cf. Downshutts 243 *supra*.   FLIGHT HILL, 1771 M, cf. Flight Ho iii, 67 *infra*, from l.ME *flight*, dial. *flight* 'a turf', and hyll.   GOOSE HOLE. GREEN GATE, 1843 O.S., *v*. grēne¹, gata.   HARDEN, *Hardin* 1817 M. JORDAN, 1843 O.S.   LAMBS COTE.   THE LEAS.   LEE MILLS, *Lee in Scholes* 1709 WMB, *v*. lēah.   LITTLE LAW, 1843 O.S., *v*. hlāw 'hill'. LONGLEY EDGE, 1843 O.S., *v*. lang, lēah, ecg.   MORTON WOOD,

1843 O.S. Moss Ho. New Gate. Oakscar, *Haukesker* 1307 WCR, *Hawckscarr* 1709 WMB, *v.* hafoc 'hawk', sker 'rocky bank'. Paris, 1843 O.S. Round Close, 1843 O.S. Ryefield Ho. Sandy Gate, 1709 WMB, *v.* sandig, gata. Scholes Moor, *Scholes more* 1647 YDr, *Scoles Moor* 1709 WMB, *v.* mōr. Smithfield. Snittlegate, Snittle Rd, probably from Y dial. *snittle* 'snare', *v.* gata. Spring Field. Strines, *v.* strind 'stream'. Syke Ho. Tinker Hill, 1843 O.S. Upper Ho, 1843 O.S. Wetshaw Edge, *Wet Shaw Moss* 1843 O.S., *v.* wēt 'wet', sceaga 'copse', mos 'bog'. White Abbey. White Wells. Wickleden, *Whickleden* 1699 *WCR* 10d, probably OE *cwic* 'quick-set hedge' (with *cw*- becoming *w(h)*- as in dial. [wik] for *quick* 'live', *v.* Phonol. § 39), hyll, denu 'valley'. Wild Boar Clough, 1843 O.S., *Wilberclough* 1709 WMB, 1771 M, cf. Wilber Lee 310 *infra*, *v.* clōh 'dell'; the first el. may be 'wild boar' as the modern form suggests. Wildspur Wood. Winscar Holes.

FIELD-NAMES

The principal forms in (*a*) are 1709 WMB, with a few modern ones (1930) (marked *mod*). Spellings dated 1600, 1650, 1699 are *WCR*.

(*a*) Field Ing, the Intack (*v.* intak), Milne Haigh wood (*v.* myln, haga), Moorebanck, Moor Ing (*mod*) (*v.* mōr, banke, eng), Ryecroft (*v.* rȳge, croft), Towneheade, Well Close (*mod*), Westfield Inge, Whichfield (*v.* cwice 'couch-grass', feld).

(*b*) le Barr croft 1699 (*v.* bere 'barley', croft), le Bawtree Carr 1699 (*v.* Bawtry i, 47 *supra*, kjarr 'marsh'), le Nether-, le Overbrownroid 1699 (probably the surname *Brown*, rod[1] 'clearing'), le Nether-, le Overfireroyd 1699 (*v.* rod[1]), le Gill Ing 1699 (*v.* eng), Grainrow close 1699 (*v.* grein 'fork of a river', rāw), Greenbanke 1699, Meane New Close 1699 (*v.* (ge)mǣne, 'common'), le Netherfal 1296 (*v.* neoðera, (ge)fall), le New Close Lands 1699, Scoles Banckes 1600 (*v.* banke), Scolemere 1327 WCR (*v.* Scholes *supra*, (ge)mǣre 'boundary', cf. Friar Mere 311 *infra*), Springedole 1650 (*v.* spring, dāl 'share of land'), Thomsons Close 1600, le Towneifeild leys 1699 (*v.* lēah 'clearing'), Welgrene 1492 MinAcct (*v.* wella, grēne[2]), le Wild Fore 1699 (*v.* wilde, ford).

6. Shelley (102-2011)

Scelneleie, Sciuelei 1086 DB
Shelfleie, -ley 1198 YCh viii (*Lewes* 300d) (p), 13 Font (p)
Schelflay, -ley 13 YD iii, 1275-1308 WCR (*freq*)

Seluelay, *-leia* 13 YD iii, 1201 FF, 1202–10 YCh viii, 1228 Hall
Shelvele 1254 FF (p), *Schelveley*, *-lay* Hy 3 Arm (p), a. 1290 YD
    iii (p), 1324 Arm (p), *Chelueley* 1316 Vill
Skelflay 1243 Fees   *Scheflay* 1297 LS
Schellai, *-lay*, *-ley* 1220–30 *Bodl* 102, 1314 WCR, 1359, 1381
    DodsN *et freq* to 1449 YD iii, *Scelley* p. 1290 ib
Shelley, *-lay* 1344 DodsN, 1448 Pat *et passim* to 1597 SessnR

'Glade or clearing on a shelving terrain', *v.* scelf, lēah. The village
stands on falling ground just above where it begins to slope abruptly
down to Shepley Brook. The single *Skelflay* spelling is due to ON
influence.

HEALEY, *Helay* 1359, 1481 DodsN, *Healy* 1817 M; *Heley* 1274 WCR
i, 87 (p), *Heylay* 1307 ib ii, 94 (p) may also belong here, but the
identification of spellings with any one of this common YW p.n. is
difficult (cf. Healey 180 *supra*). 'High clearing', *v.* hēah, lēah.

WOOL ROW, *Wllewro* 13 *WB* 45 (p), *Wolewra* 1266 YI, *Wlvewro* 1275
WCR, *Wolrowe* 1549 YD vi, *Woolrow* 1645 WillY. 'Wolf nook', *v.*
wulf, vrá; Woolrow iii, 4 *infra* has a different origin.

BALK LANE.   BANK END.   BARK HO, *Byrthouse* 1577 WillY, *Birk
Ho.* 1771 M.   BARNCLIFF DIKE, 1843 O.S.   BROOK BRIDGE.
BROOK HO, 1843 O.S.   CARR HO, *Car* 1817 M, *Car Gate* 1843 O.S.,
v. kjarr 'marsh'.   COPLEY HO.   DRINKER LANE.   ELDER HO.
GREEN HO, 1637 *Bretton* 50, *Grenehouse* 1639 WillY, *v.* grēne[1], hūs.
GRICE HALL & NOOK, *Grice* 1771, 1817 M, doubtless named from
the family of *Richard de Gris* 13 Goodall; although YW dial. *grice*
'steps, stairs' is possible for the p.n., it is unlikely to be the source of
the surname *Gris* (as Goodall suggests), since the ME form of that
word is *grese* (from OFr *grez*, pl. of *gré* 'step'). HARDENLEY,
Hardingley 1639 WillY, probably the surname *Harding*, lēah, cf.
Haddingley 239 *supra*.   HARTLEY BANK, 1803 *EnclA* 27, *Hardelow-
bank* 1492 *MinAcct* 02, 'hard hill' (that is, difficult to cultivate),
v. heard, hlāw, bank; the modern form has been adjusted to that of
the common p.n. Hartley.   HOLLY BANK HO.   HOP STRINES,
Hopstroyd (sic) 1771 M, *v.* hop 'small side valley', strind 'stream';
it refers to a small valley running into the main valley of Baildon
Dike in Emley.   HORSECROFT LANE, *Horscroft* 13 *WB* 45, *v.* hors,
croft.   LANE END, cf. *Lane Head* 1817 M.   LONG MOOR.   LYDGATE,
v. hlid-geat 'swing-gate'.   MOSLEY LANE.   NICHOLAS SPRING,

Nicolas Spring 1843 O.S., from the pers.n. *Nicholas*, spring 'plantation'. OAK WOOD. OX INGS, *Osanz* 1381 (16) DodsN, *Oxings* 1771 M, *Hozins* 1843 O.S.; the spelling *Osanz* could be an AN spelling of *Oxeng*, *v.* oxa, eng; ME *x* often becomes [z] in NCy dial. (cf. Phonol. § 44). PADDOCK. PEACE WOOD. PILLING TOP. RADCLIFFE WOOD. RED HILL. RENSHAW ROYD. ROUND WOOD. ROYDHOUSE, 1718 *Bretton* 70, *le Roides* 1324 YD iii, *v.* rod[1] 'clearing'. SAND HOLLOW. SHELLEY BANK, *Shelly Bank Bottom* 1843 O.S. SHELLEY HILL TOP, 1843 O.S. SHELLEY WOOD, 1843 O.S. SHELLEY WOODHOUSE, 1658 *WB* 276, *Wodehuses* 1275 *WCR*, *v.* wudu, hūs. SHROGG WELLS, *v.* scrogge 'brushwood'. STANDING HIRST, *Staning Hurst* 1817 M, *v.* hyrst 'wood'. TOWN END. WESTERLY LANE, *Westley* (sic) 13 *WB* 45, *v.* west (westerne), lēah. WINDMILL HILL. WOOD NOOK, 1843 O.S. WOODLANDS.

FIELD-NAMES

The principal forms in (*a*) are modern (1930, Mr J. Hanson Green), and 1732 *Bretton* 70. Spellings dated 13 are *WB* 45, 1381 DodsN viii, 22.

(*a*) Anour House 1817 M, Footgate Ox Close, Greenhouse Close (*v.* Green Ho *supra*), the Ing 1732, Ox Close, Sleepy Leys, Town Royd, the White Royds 1732, the Woodhead 1732.

(*b*) *Barkinlandis* 13, *Buffinlandys* 13, *Gauerhall* 1533 FF (possibly here or in the Dodworth district), *Grene Hobwode* 1381 (*v.* hob 'goblin', wudu), *Hestfled* 13 (probably for *Estfeld* 'east field'), *Middilwodeschae* 13 (*v.* middel, wudu, sceaga 'copse'), *Oldewelschae* 13 (*v.* ald, wella, sceaga), *Schellie Milne* 1425 Linds (*v.* myln), *Scidgateland* 13 (probably connected with ON skíð 'beam, skid', but *v.* skeið 'track, boundary', gata, land), *Welkars* 1381 (*v.* wella, kjarr 'marsh'), *Westwode* 1381 (*v.* west, wudu).

7. SHEPLEY (102–1809)

> *Scipelei, Seppeleie* 1086 DB, *Seppelay* 1210–35 YCh viii (p), *Sepeley* 1286 WCR   *Scepeley* a. 1218 YCh viii
> *S(c)hepelay*, -*le(y)* 13 Font (p), 1202–4 YCh viii (p), 1225 DodsN, 1236–58 YD ix, 394, 1243 Fees, 1284 Abbr, 1286 YI, 1297 LS *et passim* to 1549 YD iii
> *S(c)heplay*, -*ley* 1249 YI, 1316 Vill, 1375 FF, 1425 Linds *et freq* to 1540 Test vi
> *Sheapley* 1588 LS, 1610 FF

'Sheep clearing', *v.* scēap, lēah. Apart from the DB *Scipe-*, it will be noticed that there are no traces of the ONb scīp 'sheep' which is normal in the parallel Shipley iii, 267 *infra*.

ABBEY LANE, 1843 O.S.   CARR LANE, *Carr* 1771 M, *v.* kjarr 'marsh'. CLIFFE, *Cliff* 1817 M, *v.* clif.   CLIFFE TOP, 1843 O.S.   COAT CLOSE. CROFT NOOK, 1843 O.S., *v.* croft, nōk.   DOB ROYD, *Dobrode* 13 YD i, *Dobberode* 1307 WCR, *Dobroyd(e)* 1600 *WCR* 6d, 1709 WMB, 'Dobbe's clearing' from the ME pers.n. *Dobbe* (a pet-form of *Robert*), rod[1]; this compound is frequent in YW, esp. in f.ns.   DUNGEON WELL.   FREEZELAND, cf. Friezland 314 *infra*.   GELDER WOOD. GREEN HEAD FM.   HALL ROYD.   HEALEY HO.   HEY MOOR HO, *Hey Moor* 1771 M, *v.* (ge)hæg 'enclosure', mōr.   JENKYN HO. JOS LANE.   KID ROYD.   KNOLL, *Knowl(es)* 1771 M, 1843 O.S., *v.* cnoll 'knoll, hillock'.   LEE SIDE.   LIDGETT, *v.* hlid-geat 'swing-gate'.   LONG CLOSE.   LOW CARR FM.   NEW HALL.   NEW ROW. PIPER WELL LANE.   PIT HO.   ROUND WOOD.   ROW GATE. SHEPLEY ABBEY.   SHEPLEY CARR, 1843 O.S., *v.* kjarr 'marsh'. SHEPLEY DIKE.   SHEPLEY KNOLL.   SHEPLEY LANE HEAD, *Lane Head* 1771 M.   SHEPLEY MARSH.   SHEPLEY WOOD END, 1843 O.S., *Wood End* 1771 M.   STOCKSTILL.   STONE DIKE.   STONE WOOD, *Stones Wood* 1843 O.S.   STRETCH GATE.   STUBS WOOD, *Stubs* 1699 *YAS* 28, 12, *v.* stubb 'tree-stump'.   WEST ROYD, 1771 M, *v.* west, rod[1] 'clearing'.   WOOD END WOOD, *v.* Shepley Wood End *supra* WHINNY.   YEW TREE WOOD, 1843 O.S.

FIELD-NAMES

(a) Stubbing Top 1843 O.S.

(b) le *Rydynges* 1425 Linds (*v.* rydding 'clearing'), *Rodes* 1249 YI (*v.* rod[1] 'clearing'), *Smythe roid* 1550 YD viii (*v.* smið(ðe), rod[1]).

8. THURSTONLAND (102–1610)

Tostenland 1086 DB
Turstain(e)land(a) 1184–91 YCh vi (p), 1202–10 ib viii, *Turstein-land* 1191–1194 P (p), *Tursteinesland* 1196 P
Thurstainland(a) 13 YD vi (p), 1246 *Ass* 6d
Turstanland 1211 P (p)
Thurstanland(e) 1202 FF (p), 1243 Fees, 1250–75 YD iv, p. 1290 YD iii, 1297 LS, WCR *et passim* to 1542 Test vi

Thurstaneland 1298 Abbr
Thirwistandland 1316 Vill

'Thurstan's expanse of land', *v.* land. The pers.n. is ON Þorsteinn, ODan *Thorsten, Þursten*, later anglicised to *Thurstan* (cf. Feilitzen 390, 396).

LUMB HO, *Lumhouse* 1484 YD iii, *Lombe house* 1587 WillY, *Lumbe House* 1625 ib. *v.* lumm 'a pool', hūs; the topographical reference is uncertain, as Lumb Ho is on the side of a dell; but Clough Dike is just below and might have contained a pool.

STOCKS, *le Stokes, Stockes* 1316 DodsN, YD i, *Stokes* 1462 *MinAcct* 99, *The Stocks* 1636 WillY, *v.* stocc 'tree-stump', here denoting a place where trees have been felled and only the stumps remain.

STORTHES HALL, *Stordes* 1211 P (p), 1275 WCR (p), *(le) Storthes* p. 1290 YD iii, 1308 WCR (p), 1316 YD i, 1363 DodsN, *Stortheshall* 1580 FF, 1665 Visit, *Storeshall* 1610 PRThl, *Storries hall* 1616 PrHosp. 'The plantations', *v.* storð.

ACKROYD HO. BANK HO, *Top of Bank* 1843 O.S., *v.* banke. BANK END, 1771 M, *Bankend* 1636 *WB* 45, *v.* prec., ende. BIRKS WOOD, 1843 O.S., *v.* birki 'birch-tree'. BLACK HO, 1771 M. BLAGDENS, *Blakedon* 1318 YD i, 'black hill', *v.* blæc, dūn. BOOTHROYD WOOD, 1843 O.S., *v.* bōth, rod[1]. BROWN'S KNOLL. CARR DIKE. CLOUGH & CLOUGH DIKE, *v.* clōh 'a dell'. COLNE BANK, it does not refer to R. Colne (RNs.). CRANGLE WELL. FLASK LANE, *v.* flask 'swamp'. GRANGE, 1771 M, *v.* grange. GREEN CARRS, *Green Cars* 1843 O.S., *v.* grēne[1], kjarr 'marsh'. GREEN SIDE, 1771 M, *v.* grēne[1], sīde. HALSTEAD, *Hall(e)stedes* 1538 *MinAcct* 34, 1558 WillY 'site of a hall', *v.* hall, stede. HALSTEAD WOOD, 1843 O.S., *v.* prec., wudu. HANGING ROYD SHROGG, *Hyngandrode* 1481 PrHosp, *v.* hengjandi 'steep', rod[1] 'clearing'. HAW CLIFF. HEIGHT, 1843 O.S., *v.* hēhðu 'height'. HOLLOW GATE, *v.* hol[1], gata 'road'. ING HEAD, *v.* eng 'meadow'. LAYCOCK WOOD. MARSH HALL, *Marshall* 1606 *WB* 53, named from the family of *Henry Marshe* (1606 ib) or from *le Mersch* 1346 YD i, *v.* mersc 'marsh', hall. MOOR BOTTOM & SIDE, 1843 O.S., *v.* mōr, botm, sīde. MYERS WOOD, 1843 O.S. NORTH SPRING WOOD, 1843 O.S., formerly *Norwodd* 1538 *MinAcct*, *v.* norð, spring 'plantation', wudu. OAKS LANE, *Oaks* 1817 M. RAVENSKNOWLE, *Ravens Knowl* 1817 M, *v.* hræfn 'raven', cnoll

'knoll, hillock'. SAVILLE WOOD. SCAR END, 1843 O.S., *v.* sker
'rocky bank'. SHROGG WOOD, *v.* scrogge 'brushwood, bush'.
SMITH WOOD, 1843 O.S. STOCKSMOOR, 1843 O.S., *v.* Stocks *supra*,
mōr. SUN SIDE. THUNDER BRIDGE, 1771 M, *Founder Bridge* 1843
O.S. WELL BANK. WHITESTONES, 1843 O.S. THE WOOD.
WOOD END, 1817 M.

FIELD-NAMES

The principal forms in (*a*) are modern (1930, Mr J. Hanson Green).
Spellings dated c. 1260 are YD iv, 1538 *MinAcct* 34.

(*a*) Barn Cliffe, Black Gutter 1843 O.S., Clay Furlong, Little Hawk Cliffe
(cf. Haw Cliff *supra*), Pole, Warren House 1817 M.

(*b*) *Netherappelgarth* c. 1260 (*v.* apaldrs-garðr 'orchard'), *Atkynkarre* 1538
(the surname *Atkin*, kjarr 'marsh'), *le Berelactun* c. 1260 (*v.* bærlic 'barley',
tūn, cf. bere-tūn 'grange, demesne farm'), *Blaccliue* c. 1260 (*v.* blæc, clif),
Comerodynge 1538 (*v.* rod¹, eng), *Jonyroide(ynge)* 1538 (the pers.n. *Johnny*,
rod¹, eng), *Netherclose* 1538, *Oxpasture* 1538, *Robynroide* 1538 (the pers.n.
Robin (from *Robert*), rod¹), *Smythyplace* 1538 (*v.* smið, ðe, place), *Thorstle-
roid* 1538 (*v.* þrostle 'thrush', rod¹), *Tymberwod'* 1297 LS (*v.* timber,
wudu).

9. WOOLDALE (102–1508) [u:dl]

Uluedel 1086 DB, *Wolve-*, *Woluedal(e)* 1202–10 YCh viii, 1307
WCR, 1323 *MinAcct* 45, 1327 WCR, 1392, 1492 *MinAcct* 88, 02,
Wlvedale 1274–1323 WCR (*freq*), *Wulvedale* 1307 WCR, *Wolfdale*
1347 DodsN, *Woodall* 1580 WillY. 'Wolves' valley', *v.* wulf (gen.
plur. *wulfa*), dæl. The modern pronunciation is already reflected in
the last spelling.

HADES, *le Hadds* 1326 WCR, (*the*) *Hades* 1575 WillY, 1709 WMB, cf.
also *Hadeker* 1316 WCR, Hades Green *infra*, and the f.n. Hade Ing
infra. This appears to be dial. *hade*, a common f.n. el., which is used
in much the same way as *headland* (*v.* hēafod-land); it is without
doubt a development of ME *haved*, a dial. variant of the more usual
heved, from OE hēafod 'head', though this particular variety *hade*
appears to be restricted to p.ns. until the sixteenth century (NED s.v.
hade); other variants include *hude* and *hawde* (cf. O 448–9 s.v. *hades*).

LONGLEY, *Langeley(e)* 13 AD i, 1316 WCR, *Langlay* 1307, 1308 ib,
Longeley 1274 ib, *Longlayhirst* 1308 ib, *Longley* 1589 WillY, (*-feild*)
1600 *WCR* 3d. 'Long clearing', *v.* lang, lēah, a common YW p.n.

SHALEY, *S(c)hagh(e)lay, -ley* 1308–1331 WCR (*freq*), *Shaweley* 1323 *MinAcct* 45, *le Chaglayhous* 1407 *WCR* i, *Shaley* 1613, 1614 FF, 1647 YDr. 'Clearing by the copse', v. sceaga, lēah. The modern form comes from the common later variant *shay*.

ASH HO.   ATTORNEY'S LUMP.   BANK END & WOOD, *Banck* 1709 WMB, v. banke.   BENT, *Bents* 1771 M, v. beonet 'bent-grass'. BERRY BANKS.   BRIDGE FOLD, named from *Brigg* 1709 WMB, v. brycg, fald.   CALF CROFT WOOD, *Calfcroft* 1325 WCR, v. calf, croft. CHOPPARDS, 1817 M, *Chopards* 1647 YDr, *Chopherd* 1709 WMB. CINDER HILLS, *Syndirhilles* 1489, 1490 *WCR* i, (*les*) *Sinderhills* 1699 ib, 1709 WMB, v. sinder, hyll.   CLIFF.   CLIFF END, 1843 O.S. CLOUGH WOOD.   CORN ROYD.   COTE, cf. *Coyte-close* 1699 *WCR* i, v. cot 'cottage'.   CROSS, *Cross(e)* 1564 WillY, 1709 WMB, v. cros. CROSS GATE.   DOVER WOOD, named from Dover 237 *supra*. DOWN-SHUTTS LANE, cf. Downshutts 243 *supra*.   ELLENTREE HEAD, *Hellentreheade* 1551 *WCR* 2d, *Edentreehead* (sic) 1647 YDr, *Ellen head* 1709 WMB, *Ellintree Head* 1771 M, cf. also *les two Ellintree Doles* 1699 *WCR* 1d, v. ellern 'elder-tree', trēow, hēafod.   FOLLY, v. folie.   FORD HO.   GREAVE, *le Greaves* 1699 *WCR* 1, *Graves* 1771 M, v. græfe 'copse'.   GULLY.   HADES GREEN, *Hadegrene* 1499 *WCR* 6, v. Hades *supra*, grēne[2].   THE HEY, HEY END, HEY TOP, *Hey* 1395 WB, *le Hey yate* 1489 *WCR* i, *Hey Top* 1843 O.S., v. (ge)hæg 'enclosure', geat 'gate'.   HILL TOP.   HOLLIN HALL, *Holynhall* 1463 YD xii, 259, v. holegn 'holly', hall.   HOLMFIRTH, partly in this township, v. 289 *infra*.   HORSEGATE HILL, 1699 *WCR* 7, v. hors, gata 'road', hyll.   HUBBERTON, 1843 O.S., *Humberton* 1709 WMB.   ING HEAD, 1709 WMB, v. eng 'meadow', hēafod. JEAN WOOD HO.   KIRKROYDS, *le Kirkeroods* 1699 *WCR* 7, v. kirkja, rod[1].   LANE, LANE END.   LINSHAWS.   LITTLEWOOD, *Ly-, Little-, Littelwode* 1274–1313 WCR, (*-lane*) 1307 ib, *Litelwode* 1275 ib (p), *Littilwodlone* 1325 ib, *Litylwode* 1379 PT (p), v. lytel, wudu, lane. LONG ING, 1709 WMB, 1817 M, v. lang, eng 'meadow'.   LONG-LANDS WOOD.   LONGLEY EDGE HO.   MAY BANK.   MILL DAM. MIRY LANE.   MOREFIELD.   MOUNT.   MUCKY LANE.   MUSLIN HALL.   PADDOCK GATE, *Paddock Yate Farme* 1709 WMB, v. pearroc 'enclosure', geat 'gate'.   PELL LANE.   POG ING, v. Pog Moor i, 304 *supra*, eng.   RICH GATE.   RIDINGS, 1817 M, v. rydding 'clearing'.   ROUND ING, *Round Inge* 1709 WMB, v. rond, eng 'meadow'.   THE ROYDS, *Rodes* 1379 PT (p), *Royd* 1709 WMB, v.

rod[1] 'clearing'.   RYECROFT, 1709 WMB, *Ricroftker* 1307 WCR, *v.*
rȳge, croft, a common p.n. and f.n.   SLACK LANE.   SPRINGFIELD,
SPRING WOOD.   STAKE LANE, *Stakelaine* 1709 WMB, *v.* staca, lane,
doubtless one marked by stakes.   STAND BANK, 1771 M, *Overstand-*
bankfeild 1699 *WCR* 1, *Standbanck Hill* 1709 WMB, *v.* stand 'a
hunter's stand', or stān, banke.   STONY BANK, *Stone banck* 1709
WMB, *v.* stān(ig), banke.   SUNNY BROW.   TENTER HILL RD,
Tenter Hill 1843 O.S., ME *tentour* 'a tenter', hyll.   THONGS BRIDGE,
Thownges Brigge 1579 WillY, *Thong Br(idge)* 1771, 1817 M, named
from Netherthong 286 *infra*; the bridge crosses the R. Holme on the
township boundary, but the hamlet is in Wooldale.   THORN HO.
TOTTIES, TOTTIES HALL, *Totties* 1577 WillY, 1817 M, *Tottye's* 1647
YDr, *Tottys, -is* 1666 Visit, 1709 WMB, 1771 M, possibly an early
use of dial. *totty* in the compound *totty-grass* 'quaking grass' (used in
much the same way as beonet 'bent-grass' in the common f.n.
Bents), but it could also be a surname from ME *toty* 'tottering,
unsteady' which is the same word.   TOWN END, 1771 M, *Wooldale*
Townend 1699 *WCR* 7, *v.* tūn, ende.   UNDER BANK, 1817 M, *v.*
under, banke.   WEST FIELD.   WEST NELLY, 1843 O.S.   WICKEN,
Wickins 1817 M, *v.* cwicen 'mountain-ash' (cf. Phonol. § 39).
WINDY GAP.   WINNEY BANK, *Whinbanck* 1709 WMB, *v.* hvin
'gorse', banke.   WOODFIELD.   WOOLDALE CLIFF.

FIELD-NAMES

The principal forms in (*a*) are 1709 WMB and modern (1930) (Mr J.
Hanson Green), marked *mod*. Spellings dated 1308, 1326 are WCR, 1411–
1699 *WCR*, 1699 *YAS* Md 28, 12.

(*a*) Broomfield, Cuttel Hey (the ME surn. *Cuttel*, (ge)hæg 'enclosure'),
Dean Slack (*mod*) (*v.* denu 'valley', slakki 'depression'), Dog Stock (*mod*),
Flint Hills (*mod*), Fox Holme (*Foxholmeheade* 1600, *v.* fox, holmr), Green
Slack (*mod*) (*v.* grēne, slakki 'depression'), Green Slade (*v.* slæd 'valley'),
Hade Ing 1843 O.S. (*le Hadenge* 1411, *le Hade Inge* 1699, *Hade Ing* 1709
WMB, *v.* hēafod, Hades *supra*, eng 'meadow'), Haigh Croft, Hubberton
Ing (*mod*) (*v.* Hubberton *supra*, eng), Lathes (*v.* hlaða 'barn'), Lee banck
(*v.* lēah, banke), Litle Croft, New Lay Royd (*mod*) (*New Laith* 1709 WMB,
v. hlaða 'barn'), Parkin Ing, Pith Hill or Pig Hill (*mod*) (*v.* pightel 'en-
closure'), Priest Close, Reins (*mod*) (*v.* reinn 'boundary strip'), Rockle
Royds (*Rockley Royde* 1600, *v.* rod[1]), Round Close, Scutle Croft, Shaley Ing
(*v.* Shaley *supra*, eng), Sour Ing (*mod*) (*v.* sūr, eng), Sow (*v.* sogh 'swamp'),
Stelhouse, Nether & Over Tudehoile (probably for tādige 'toad', dial.
[tuəd], hol[1]), Upper Flatt (*mod*).

(b) *Butgapgrenes* 1308 (v. butte, gap, grēne[2]), *the Colybutts* 1699 *YAS* (v. butte 'abutting strip of land'), *Dychebrecke* 1326 (v. dīc, dial. breck 'uncultivated strip' (v. bræc[1]) or brekka 'slope'), *Dryheyhede* 1490 (v. drȳge, (ge)hæg 'enclosure', hēafod), Ellis Croft 1699 (the surname *Ellis*, croft), *le Grentrehed* 1326 (v. grēne[1], trēow, hēafod), *the Longhall steedes* 1699 *YAS* (v. lang, hall, stede, 'hall sites'), *Markehirsts* 1699 ('boundary woods', v. mearc, hyrst), *the Newlandes* 1699 *YAS*, *the Newroide*, *-rood* 1699 *YAS* (v. rod[1] 'clearing'), *Nottynghirst* 1699 (probably 'nutting wood', v. hyrst), *Over Inge* 1699 (v. eng 'meadow'), *Randallcloghe* 1499 (the pers.n. or surname *Randall* (from ME *Randolph*), clōh 'dell'), *Shalleyfurlonge* 1650 (v. Shaley supra, furlang), *the Shaws* 1699 *YAS* (v. sceaga 'copse'), *the Spirth* 1699 *YAS* (v. spyrt 'spirt, jet'), *montis voc' Toolawes* 1499 (v. twā 'two', hlāw 'mound'), *the Towne Croft* 1699 *YAS*, *Walkerbothoms* 1699 (v. walcere 'fuller', probably as a surname, botm), *Wolfedalemore* 1392 *MinAcct* 88 (v. Wooldale supra, mōr), les Woods 1699.

xvii. Almondbury

Holmfirth Urban District includes the townships of Austonley, Holme, Honley, Netherthong and Upperthong from this parish as well as the townships of Cartworth, Fulstone, Hepworth, Scholes, Wooldale and part of Thurstonland from Kirkburton parish (236 *supra*). Meltham Urban District contains Meltham township and part of South Crosland. Colne Valley Urban District includes Linthwaite and Marsden from this parish and Golcar, Scammonden and Slaithwaite from Huddersfield parish (291 *infra*). Almondbury, Lockwood and part of South Crosland are now in the County Borough of Huddersfield (295 *infra*); Farnley Tyas is a ward in Kirkburton Urban District.

1. ALMONDBURY (102–1615) [ˈɔːmbri, ˈeimbri]

   Almaneberie 1086 DB, *-bir* 1270 BM

   Almanberia, *-ber(y)* 1142–54 YCh 1446, 1250–8 YD i, 173, 1391 YD iii, 1412 YD vi, 1461 YD v, *-biri*, *-y-* 1236–58 YD ix, 393, 1274–1308 WCR (*freq*), 1287 Ebor, 1294 Ch, l. 13, 1323 YD iii *et freq* to 1428 FA, *-bir(e)* 1284 Ebor, 1297 LS, *-bury* 1275, 1316 WCR, 1304, 1313 Pat, 1316 Vill *et freq* to 1486 YD v, *Alemanbir* 1252 Skyr

   Alemaneburi c. 1154 Brett (p), *-bir* 1195–1215 YCh 1712, e. 14 Font, *-biri* 1251 Ch

   Almannesbiry 1188–1202 YCh viii, *Almanesbir'* 1235 Ebor

   Aumundebir' 1202 FF, *Almundbury* 1327 WCR, 1441 DiocV, *-bery* 1409 ib

   Almannebire 1230 Ebor

Alemannebir 1276 RH

Almandbiri 1296 LacyComp, *-bury* 1393, 1456 DodsN, 1444 Linds

Almonbiry 1323 Var, *-bery* 1439 YD iii, *-bury(e)* 1509 ib, 1548 YD v *et freq* to 1603 PRThl

Almondbury 1483 DodsN, 1487 *MinAcct* 66, 1498 HCY *et freq* to 1822 Langd, *Almondebury* 1485 Baild, *Almontbury* 1494 YD xiii 78

Aumebery 1471 WillY, *Awmbery* 1503 Test iv, 1518 FF, 1666 SelbyW

Ambry 1545 NCWills, *Ambrey* 1592 PRHfx, *Ambery* 1616 PrHosp, *-bury* 1660 SbCA

Aimbury 1787 PRBrods

The two spellings with *Alman(n)es-* suggest at least the possibility of a pers.n., which would otherwise appear (as so often in YW) mostly in an uninflected form; the late OE *Æl(l)mon*, *Ælmanus* recorded by Searle (from an older *Ælfman*) would be appropriate, as pointed out by Goodall. On the other hand the many forms with *-man(n)e-* make it likely that the medial *-e-* is significant and that would not be the case if the first el. were an uninflected pers.n. like *Ælfman*. Another suggestion, which Moorman made, is that Almondbury contains the name of the *Alemanni*, a Germanic tribe, and some evidence exists in the Greek historian Zosimus, *Historiæ Novæ*, and in Aurelius Victor, *Epitome* V, for the presence of men of this tribe in Britain during the Roman occupation. But the name Almondbury is much later than that period and it is highly improbable that a p.n. of this form would embody such a memory of Roman times, for though OE *burh* is used to describe Roman encampments (*v.* EPN i, 59) it does not normally combine with the Romano-British names of those stations, as OE *ceaster* does: Richborough K 531 (from *Rutupiæ*) is an exception, and even there it was *Reptacæstir* in OE (Bede) and *burh* is a ME replacement of *ceaster*. There is no suggestion that the *Alemanni* were an identifiable Germanic tribe in England in Anglo-Saxon times; they were a south German folk. There is much to be said therefore in favour of Ekwall's suggestion (DEPN s.n.) that the first el. is ON *al-menn* (gen.plur. *al-manna*) 'all men, the whole community, the public', used in such compounds as ON *almanna-vegr* 'a public highway', *almanna-þing* 'a public assembly'. Almondbury would denote 'a fortified place owned or maintained by the men of the village' as distinct from one owned by an individual (as in

Dewsbury 184 *supra*). The *burh* may be no more than a fortified village, but rather more than a mile from Almondbury there is an ancient encampment at Castle Hill, which is a lofty natural eminence dominating the whole neighbourhood, and Roman coins have been found here; it is likely enough that this is the *burh*, although it is so far from the site of the present village.

CASTLE HILL, *Castell hill* 1582 WillY, *v.* castel 'fortified place', hyll; the *castel* is referred to in *del Castle* 1333 *WB* 26 (p), *del Castell* 1338 YD v, *castrum de Almondbury* 1399 *WB* 5; cf. Almondbury *supra*.

FENAY, *La Fineia* 12 Font, *del Fyney* 1274, 1297 WCR (p), 1305 Cl, *Fynee* 1308 WCR (p), *le Finey* 14, 1349 DodsN, *Fenay(e), -ey* 1305 Cl, 1379 PT (p), 1393, 1456 DodsN, 1426 *Ramsd* (p), 1680 *WB* 228a, *le Feney* 1532 ib 3, *Finnie* 1698 Arm. The later forms indicate that the original vowel of the first el. was short; the name is therefore most probably a compound of OE, ON finn 'coarse grass' and ēg 'land partly surrounded by water', doubtless originally referring to the meadows between Fenay Beck and its affluent, Rushfield Dike, near Fenay Bridge. Cf. Finthorpe *infra*.

GLEDHILL HILL, *Gledehyl(le), -hill* 13 YD vi (p), 1286, 1308 WCR (p), *-hul* 1275 ib (p), *-hilles* 1492 Test iv, *Gledhill* 1379 PT (p), 1424 Baild. 'Kite hill', *v.* gleoda, hyll.

LONGLEY, *Langelei, -ley* 12 Font, e. 13 Arm, *Longele* 1370 *Ramsd*, *Longlay, -legh, -ley* 1376 ib, 1379 PT (p), 1493 DodsN *et passim* to 1624 FF, (*Over-*) 1639 SessnR. 'Long clearing', *v.* lang, lēah, a common YW p.n.

NEWSOME, *Neusu'* 13 *WB* 25, *Neusom* 1275 WCR (p), 1379 PT (p), *Newsom(e)* 1386, 1493 DodsN, 1399, 1412 *WB* 5, 40 *et passim* to 1822 Langd, *Newesom* 1472 YD xii, 298. '(At) the new houses', *v.* nīwe, hūs, -um, a common Y p.n.

LOWER THORPE, *Thorp(e)* l. 13, 1323 YD iii, 1379 PT (p) *et freq* to 1817 M, (*Upper and Lower-*) 1822 Langd, *the Thorpe* 1509 *WB* 13, *v.* þorp 'an outlying farmstead'. Upper Thorpe is now Thorpe Grange; cf. Finthorpe *infra*.

ALMONDBURY BANK, 1843 O.S., *v.* banke.   ALMONDBURY COMMON, 1843 O.S., *Almondbury Moore* 1575 SadD.   ARKENLEY LANE, *Far*

Arkenly 1850 *TA*. Ashes Common & Lane, *Ash Ho* 1771 M, *Ashes Close & Common* 1850 *TA*, v. æsc. Ashing Hirst, 1850 *TA*, *Ashen Hurst* 1843 O.S., 'ash wood', v. æscen, hyrst.

Bank End, 1843 O.S., v. Almondbury Bank *supra*. Bank Field. Bar Croft Bottom, (*le*) *Berecroft* 13, 1412 *WB* 25, 40, *Bercroft* 1432 ib 46, *Bar Croft* 1850 *TA*, 'barley enclosure', v. bere, croft. Benholmley, *Belondlaye* 1426 *Ramsd*, *Benomley* 1850 *TA*, v. lēah; the first el. may be a surname (from Byland YN 194), with dissimilation of *l* to *n*. Berry Brow, 1817 M. Birks, *Birks* (*Mill*) 1817 M, 1850 *TA*, v. birki 'birch-tree'. Blagden, 1843 O.S., probably 'black hill', v. blæc, dūn, cf. Blagdens 252 *supra*; Blagden is near the top of Taylor Hill. Blue Bell Hill. Boggarding. Bottoms, 1843 O.S., v. botm. Brickbank, 1850 *TA*. Broadfield Mills. Broad Gates, 1850 *TA*. Broken Cross, 1850 *TA*, v. brocen, cros. Bum Royd, *Burmonrode* 1399 *WB* 5, *Bormeroydeinge* 1583 *Ramsd*, *Burn Royd* 1850 *TA*, from OE, ME *burh-man* 'a burgess', rod[1] 'clearing', cf. *Burmantofts* 166 *supra*. Bunkers Hill, *Bonkers Hill* 1850 *TA*.

Caldercliffe Rd, *Caldercliffe* 1583 *Ramsd*, (*-Top*) 1850 *TA*, unlikely to be connected with R. Calder which is 5 miles away; it may be a compound of cald 'cold' and ears 'buttock, rounded hill', with clif, but the form has been affected by the r.n. Catterson, 1850 *TA*, cf. also *Catter Croft* 1850 ib. Channel Dike. Clay Hall, 1850 *TA*, v. clæg 'clay', probably as a surname. Close Hill, 1850 *TA*. Clough Hall & Ings, *Clough Ing* 1850 *TA*, v. clōh 'dell', eng 'meadow'. Coal Pit Lane, *Coalpit Close* 1850 *TA*. Cocker Lane, *Cockhill* 1850 *TA*, v. cocc[1] 'hillock', hyll. Cold Hill, *Colde Hyll* 1592 WillY, *Couldhill* 1656 WillS, *Caud Hill* 1771 M, v. cald, hyll. Crooked Tree.

Daisy Royd, *Daisy* (*Royd*) *Close* 1850 *TA*. Dam Side. Deadman Stone (lost) *Dudemanston* 1434 *WB* 47, *Dudmanstonefeilde* 1583 *Ramsd*, *Deadmanstone* 1588 WillY, 1771 M, 1850 *TA*, the ME surname *Dudeman*, stān; the modern form is an obvious analogical substitution. Dodd's Royd, *Dodsroyd* 1850 *TA*, the ME pers.n. *Dodde*, rod[1]. Do Royd, *Doe or Dow Royd* 1850 *TA*, v. dā 'doe', rod[1].

Eldon Ho.

Fair Hill. Fairlea, *Fearnlee* 1850 *TA*, v. fearn 'fern', lēah. Fenay Bridge, 1591 WillY, 1822 Langd, *Fynnay Brigg* 1532 *WB* 3, *Finney Bridge* 1817 M, v. Fenay 258 *supra*, brycg. Fenay Hall,

1822 Langd, *Finney Hall* 1817 M, *v.* prec., hall. FINTHORPE, 1822 Langd, *v.* Thorpe *supra*; the first el. is probably a reduced form of Fenay or is itself finn 'coarse grass'. FLETCHER HO, 1646 WillY, *the Flecher House* 1542 ib, ME *fleccher* 'arrow-maker', probably as a surname.

GOODHAM FIELD, *Goodham, -holme* 1850 *TA, v.* gōd² 'good', holmr. GRASS CROFT, 1850 *TA, v.* gærs, croft.

HAIGH SPRING, *Egg Spring Wood* 1843 O.S., *Haigh Intake & Spring* 1850 *TA*, the common YW surname *Haigh* (from haga 'enclosure'), *v.* intak, spring 'plantation'. HALL BOWER, 1654 WillS, *Halleboure* 1323 *MinAcct* 45, *Old Bower* 1843 O.S., *v.* hall, būr¹ 'cottage' or būr² 'storehouse'. HANGING STONE, 1850 *TA, v.* hangende 'overhanging, steep', stān. HEY, *Hay Tongue, Hey Bank* 1850 *TA, v.* (ge)hæg 'enclosure'. HIGHROYD, 1779 *EnclA* 16, *v.* hēah, rod¹. HILL SIDE, 1850 *TA*. HILL TOP, *Hill* 1592 WillY, *v.* hyll. HUDROYD, *Hood Royd* 1850 *TA*, the ME pers.n. *Hudde*, rod¹.

ING LANE, *Ing Bank & Knowls* 1850 *TA, v.* eng 'meadow', banke, cnoll 'hillock'.

JACK ROYD, 1850 *TA, Jacrode* 1399 *WB* 5, *Jekeroid* 1426 *Ramsd, Jakeraydes* (sic) 1520 YD xii, 96, from the ME pers.n. *Jakke* (a petform of *Jacob* or *James*), rod¹.

KAYE LANE, 1817 M, the surname *Kay*, lane. KIDROYD, 1850 *TA, v.* kide 'kid', rod¹. KIRK ROYD. KING'S MILLS, 1843 O.S.

LADY HO, 1843 O.S. LAITH CROFT, *v.* hlaða 'barn', croft. LANE SIDE, 1850 *TA*, cf. *Lane End* 1817 M. LONG CROFT. LONGLEY GREEN, 1850 *TA*, LONGLEY HALL, 1822 Langd, *Langley Hall* 1771 M, *v.* Longley *supra*, grēne², hall. LOWER HOUSES, 1817 M. LUMB, 1817 M, *Lumbe* 1640 WillY, *v.* lumm 'pool'. LUMB HEAD, 1850 *TA, v.* prec.

MARTIN BANK, 1850 *TA*.

NEW LAITH, *New Lathes* 1771 M, *v.* hlaða 'barn'. NEWSOME CROSS, 1843 O.S., *v.* Newsome *supra*, cros. NOOK, 1843 O.S., *v.* nōk. NORTHFIELD HO. NORTHGATE.

OAKEN BANK PLANT., *Oaking Bank* 1850 *TA, v.* ācen 'growing with oaks', banke. OAKS, *les Okes* 1323 *MinAcct* 45, 1379 PT (p), *the Oakes* Hy 8 *WB* 36, *the Ookes* 1538 Test vi, *the Okes* 1589 *YAS* 213, *v.* āc. OAKS HILL, 1850 *TA, v.* prec., hyll.

LITTLE, LOWER & UPPER PARK, *Almonbury Park* 1644 WillY, *Park* 1817 M, *Lower-, Upper Park* 1843 O.S., *v.* park. PARK GATE, 1822 Langd, *v.* prec., gata. PARKTON GROVE, 1850 *TA*. PARK

WOOD, 1850 *TA*, *v*. park, wudu. PENNY SPRING WOOD, *Penny Spring* 1843 O.S., *v*. spring 'plantation'. PRIMROSE HILL, 1843 O.S. PUMP LANE, cf. *Pump Close* 1850 *TA*.

QUARRY HILL, 1817 M, *Querrell-hill* 1624 *WB* 130, *v*. quarrelle 'quarry', hyll.

ROBIN HOOD HILL & HO, cf. Robin Hood's Bower i, 226 *supra*. RUSHFIELD DIKE & HO, *Rushfield House* 1843 O.S.

SALFORD, *Saw Fall Croft* 1850 *TA*, *v*. salh 'willow', (ge)fall 'clearing'. SHARP LANE, cf. *Sharp Royd Ing* 1850 *TA*, from the common YW surname *Sharp*, rod[1], eng. SOUTH FIELD. SPA WOOD. SQUIRREL DITCH. STILE COMMON, *Steel (Common)* 1771 M, 1843 O.S., *v*. stigel 'stile'. STIRLEY, *(Hay) Stirley* 1850 *TA*, *v*. foll. STIRLEY KNOLL, *Sterling Knowl* 1843 O.S., *Stirly Knowl* 1850 *TA*, *v*. cnoll 'hillock'. STONE PIT FM, *Stonepit Close & Hole* 1850 *TA*, *v*. stān, pytt. STONY CROSS LANE. SUN GREEN, 1850 *TA*.

TAYLOR HILL, 1843 O.S. TENTER HILL, cf. *Tenter Close* 1850 *TA*. THORPE FOLD, *Thorpe-ville* 1822 Langd, *v*. Lower Thorpe *supra*. TOWN END, *at Townende* 1426 Ramsd, *v*. tūn, ende. TUNNA-CLIFFE HILL, 1843 O.S., *Tunnercliffe-Gate* 1822 Langd, *Tunnscliffe Hill* (sic) 1850 *TA*.

WAINGATE. WATERSIDE, 1638 WillY, beside the R. Holme. WELL HEAD, cf. *Well Bank & Close* 1850 *TA*. WESTGATE. WHEAT ROYD, 1771 M, *v*. hwǣte, rod[1]. WHITEGATE RD. WHITEHEAD LANE, *Whitehead Close* 1850 *TA*. WOOD LANE.

YEW CROFT, cf. *Yew Close* 1850 *TA*.

FIELD-NAMES

The principal forms in (*a*) are 1850 *TA* 10. Spellings dated 13 are *WB*, 1323 *MinAcct* 45, 1334, 1338 YD v, 1432 *WB*, 1487 *MinAcct* 66, 1575, 1636 *WB*; others dated without source are *Ramsd*.

(*a*) Back o' th House Field, Bark House Ing, Barley Close, Bean Close, Beer Ing, Birchenley (*v*. bircen, lēah), Black Acre, Booth Nook (*v*. bōth, nōk), Botany Bay, Bowling Close, Bradley, Breery Bank (*v*. brērig, banke), Broad Ing, Broom Close, Brow End, Butt Ing, Campinot (*Campynote Crofte* 1583), Castle Fold (cf. Castle Hill *supra*, fald), Causeway Close, Chapel Croft, Church Croft, Cinder Hill (*v*. sinder, hyll), Clay Field, Cloths Croft, Cocked Hat, Cockshott (*v*. cocc-scīete 'cock-shoot'), Coit Close (*Cooteclose* 1583, *v*. cot 'cottage', clos), Cow Lane Field, Crosley Hill, Cross Lands, Crown Lands, Cruddle Churn (*cruddle* is a form of *curdle*), Day Work, Doctor Close, Dyehouse Close, Eccle Bonny, Even Royd (*v*. efen, rod[1]), Far Green, Far Syke, Field before Door, Footgate Handhill, Frying Pan,

Gallows Field, Gib Royd, Goit Field (*v.* gota, feld), Grime Ing, Grunsell, Haigh Intake, Lower Handhill, Hanging Ing (*v.* hangende 'steep', eng), Healding Bank, Heeley Close, Hey Green (*v.* Hey *supra*, grēne[2]), Hilly Sykes, Hole Bottom & Ing, Hollin Park (*v.* holegn 'holly', park), Great & Little Hollins (*Netherhollinge* 1573 WillY, *v.* holegn 'holly'), Hollin Yard, Holme Royd, Horse Close (*the Horseclose* 1589 *YAS* 213, i), Hunt Field, Hutch Close, Intake, Jocky Hall, Kiln Croft & Hole, Land o' Will, Launds (*v.* launde 'glade'), Lockwood Scarr (*v.* Lockwood 275 *infra*, sker), Long Ing, Long Tongue, May Royd, Mellor Wood, Mill Ing, Milly Sands, Mistal (dial. *mistal* 'cow-shed'), Muca Sheard, Mud Croft, Navy, Near Birks, New Mills, Nicholl Croft (*Nycollecrofte* 1583, the surname *Nichol*, croft), North Royd, Ogley, Overthwaite (*v.* þveit), Owlers (*v.* alor 'alder-tree'), Ox Close, Ox Pasture (*le Oxpastur* 1323, *v.* oxa, pasture), Park Pit, Parlour Hole, Parkin Ing Bottom, Pea Lumb, Pease Hill (*v.* pise 'pease', hyll), Pickhill (*v.* pightel 'enclosure'), Pig Tail, Pudding Hole, Randle, Lower & Middle Reyn (*v.* reinn 'boundary strip'), Rose Croft, Rough Birks, Rough Ing, Rush(y) Lee, Sal Acre (*Salaker* 1636, probably the fem. pers.n. *Sal*, æcer), Salter Hole, School Brow & Croft, Sharp Royd Ing (*Sharproydynge* 1520 YD xii, 96, *le Shorpproyde* 1636, the surname *Sharp*, rod[1], eng), Shaw Close, Short Leys, Shrogg Side (*v.* scrogge 'brushwood'), Slack Doles (*v.* slakki 'hollow, depression', dāl 'share of common land'), Slade Croft, Smithy Lane, Sour Ing, Spark Brow, Spink Acre (probably the surname *Spink*, æcer), Spring Well (*v.* spring 'well-spring'), Spring Wood (*v.* spring 'plantation'), Steep Field, Steps Mill, Stoney Lands, Stony Ridding (*Netherstonyerydinge* 1583, *v.* stānig, rydding), Stopes, Stubble, Stump Brow, Summer Field, Summer Ing, Swamp, Tanhouse Ing, Thick Hollins (*v.* þicce[2] 'dense', holegn 'holly'), Tinderley (*Tyndolay(sik)* 1334, probably OE *tyndre* 'tinder', lēah), Toad Hole (*Toodehooles* 1583, *v.* tādige 'toad', hol[1]), Tom Riding, Tongue, Town Field, Turmoil Ing, Turn Croft (*v.* trun 'round', croft), Urlburley, Warreck, Washing Close, Wasp Nest, Watering Field, Wearhill Bank, Wheat Croft, Whinny Close (*v.* hvin 'gorse'), White Croft, White Ing, William Close (cf. *William Crofte* 1583), Willow Royd, Whitacre Close, Wind End 1843 O.S., Yeldon Acre, Yokeing Bank.

(*b*) *Blackdolecarr* 1426 (*v.* blæc, dāl, kjarr), *Bride(s)croft* 1487 (*v.* bridd 'bird', probably as a surname, or brȳd 'bride', croft), *Bulecroftes* 1545 (*v.* bula, croft), *Cadeclose, -ynge* 1532 (the surname *Cade*, clos, eng 'meadow'), *Caluecroft* 13 (*v.* calf, croft), *Cawlboell* 1563 WillY, *the Combe* 1575 (*v.* cumb 'valley'), *Les Eightes* 1615 (*v.* hēhðu 'height'), *Erlerodes* 1323 (*v.* eorl, rod[1]), *Frawardhous* 1432, *Yvecroft* 1583 (the ME pers.n. *Ive, Ivo*, croft), *Leghes* 1241 FF, *La Legh'* 1323 (*v.* lēah 'clearing'), *Littillathegryme* 1583 (*v.* leið 'track', gríma[1] 'a mark', cf. Legrams Lane iii, 246 *infra*), *Littylwinter* 1583, *Maghouseyeard* 1583 (the fem. pers.n. *Mag*, hūs, geard), *Oldfe(i)ld* 1305 Cl, 1588 WillY, *Lez Ozierhoppes* 1615 (l.ME *osier* 'willow', hop 'enclosed plot of land, esp. marsh land'), *Personehaye* 1296 LacyComp (*v.* persone, (ge)hæg 'enclosure'), *the Pitrawe* 1583 (*v.* pytt, rāw), *Sykes* 1426 (*v.* sīc 'stream'), *Lestanrode* 1338 (*v.* stān, rod[1]), *Lez Wares* 1615, *Wormecliff* 1426, *castr' de Wornecliff* 1487 (*v.* wyrm 'snake, dragon', clif).

2. AUSTONLEY (102–1107)

Alstaneslei(e) 1086 DB, *Alstanley, -lay* 1274–1329 WCR (*freq*), *Alstanneley* 1313 ib, *Alstonlay* 1395 *WB, Austenley* 1588 WillY, *Austonley* 1709 WMB. 'Alstan's glade or clearing', v. lēah. The pers.n. is from OE *Ælfstān* or *Alhstān*.

BOOTH HO, *del Bothe* 1307 WCR (p), *Boythe house* 1548 Stansf, *Bothhowsse* 1569 WillY, *Booth(e)house* 1644 ib, 1656 WillS, 1709 WMB, v. bōth 'a booth, a shed', hūs.

BRADSHAW, *Bradshagh* 1411 *WCR* i, *Bradshaw(e)* 1571 WillY, 1709 WMB, *Bradsha* 1591 WillY, 'broad copse', v. brād, sceaga.

HOGLEY, *Oldehoggelay* 1308 WCR, *Hogley* 1709 WMB, *Ogley* 1817 M, 'hog clearing', v. hogg, lēah; but the first el. could be the well-evidenced ME surname *Hog* (WCR *passim*).

THE ACRES, *the Acker* 1650 *WCR* 12, v. æcer.   ALISON QUARRY, cf. *Allison Close* 1851 *TA*, from the fem. pers.n. *Alison*.   BANK END & TOP, *Bankes* 1709 WMB, *Bank Top* 1817 M, named from *Austonley bank* 1851 *TA*, v. banke.   BARTIN, 1709 WMB, *Barton Green* 1817 M, v. bere-tūn 'corn farm'.   BENT TOP, cf. *Great & Little Bents* 1851 *TA*, v. beonet 'bent-grass'.   BINGLEY WOOD, 1851 *TA*, *Near Bingley* 1851 ib, probably a surname derived from Bingley pt. iv *infra*. BOTTOMS, *Bothoms* 1709 WMB, v. botm (boðm) 'valley bottom'. BROADFIELD.   BROADHEAD EDGE, *Broad Head, Broadheads Field* 1851 *TA*, v. brād, hēafod.   BURR FM.   CARR GREEN.   CLIFF.   CLOUGH HEAD, cf. *Clough Wood* 1851 *TA*, v. clōh 'dell'.   COLD WELL, *Callwell* 1709 WMB, *Cawell* 1771 M, *Cow Well* 1817 M, *Caw-well or Call-well* 1822 Langd, v. cald, wella, the forms being due to the dial. treatment of *cald* (cf. Phonol. § 6).   CROSS GATE HEAD.   DIGLEY, 1771 M, DIGLEY MILLS, 1851 *TA*, DIGLEY ROYD, 1771 M, *Digleroyd* 1709 WMB, *Diglee-Royd* 1822 Langd, probably identical with *Dyselay* 1495 *WB*, 'ditch clearing', v. dīc, lēah, rod[1]; cf. also Diggle 311 *infra*.   EDGE END, *Edgeend* 1843 O.S., v. ecg, ende. ELLIS POND.   FIELD END, 1709 WMB, v. feld, ende.   FLUSH HO, 1771 M, *Flushouse* 1709 WMB, formally it could be ME *flush* 'pool', but the house is high up a steep hillside.   GIBRIDING LANE, *Grib Riding* (sic) 1851 *TA*, v. rydding 'clearing'.   GOODBENT END, *Goodbent Field* 1851 *TA*, named from Good Bent 290 *infra*.   GREAVES HEAD, *Greaves* 1843 O.S., v. græfe 'copse'.   GREEN ALDERS, 1843

O.S., *Green Owlers* 1851 *TA*, v. grēne[1], alor 'alder-tree'.   GREEN
GATE, 1709 WMB, *Grenegaite* 1588 WillY, v. grēne[1], gata.   GREEN
SIKES.   HART HOLES CLOUGH.   HIGH INGS, 1771 M, *Ing* 1843
O.S., v. eng 'meadow'.   HOLMBRIDGE, 1843 O.S., cf. also *Holme
Royd, Holmestall* 1851 *TA*, named from Holme 269 *infra*; Holmbridge is at the bridge which takes the Holmfirth–Holme road over
the R. Holme.   HOOBRAM HILL, *Hobbram* 1654 WillS, *Huberum hill*
1709 WMB, *Hobroom Head* 1771 M, *Hoobroom* 1822 Langd, v. hōh
'hill', brōm 'broom, gorse'.   HOOWOOD, 1709 WMB, v. prec.,
wudu.   KILN ACRE, *Kylnacre* 1306 WCR, cf. *Kiln Hill* 1851 *TA*,
v. cyln, æcer, hyll.   LOWER & UPPER KNOWL, (*Bradshaw*) *Knowle*
1709 WMB, *Over Knowles* 1771 M, *Lower Knoll* 1843 O.S., *Knowl
Wood* 1851 *TA*, v. cnoll 'knoll, hillock'.   LANE, *Lane in Austonley*
1709 WMB, v. lane.   LONG ING.   LONG WALLS.   LUMBANK,
Lomebanke 1485 WCR 1, *Lumb Bank* 1851 *TA*, v. lumm 'pool',
banke.   MILL DAM, cf. *Dam Bank* 1851 *TA*, v. dammr.   MOLLY
WELLS.   MOOR SIDE, 1817 M, v. mōr, sīde.   NETHER LANE, 1843
O.S.   NEWFIELD, 1709 WMB.   NEW HO, 1843 O.S.   NEW LAITH,
1843 O.S., v. hlaða 'barn'.   ROBERTS CLOUGH.   ROODS LANE.
RYE CLOSE LANE, *Rye Close* 1851 *TA*.   SHAW LANE.   SHAY
CLOUGH.   SPARTH BOTTOM & TOP, cf. Sparth 281 *infra*.   SPRING
GROVE.   STONEY HILL.   STUBBIN, *Stubbingker* 1307 WCR,
Stubenye (sic) 1591 WillY, *Stubing* 1709 WMB, v. stubbing 'clearing'.
TOP O' TH' HILL.   TOWN END, 1709 WMB, v. tūn, ende.   WELL
GREEN, cf. *Well Close & Intake* 1851 *TA*.   WHITE WALLS, 1709
WMB, v. hwīt, wall.   YEW TREE, 1709 WMB, *Vewtree* 1584 WillY,
v. īw, cf. The Yews i, 241 *supra*.

FIELD-NAMES

The principal forms in (*a*) are 1851 *TA* and modern (1930, Mr J. Hanson
Green, marked *mod*), and those in (*b*) are 1307 WCR. Other spellings dated
1306, 1307 are WCR, 1709 WMB.

(*a*) Andrew Croft, Ash Acre, Ashes Hill, Beaumont Croft, Bent Leys (*v.*
beonet, lēah), Berry Close, Birking Bank, Blackshaw Field, Broad Ing,
Browies Ing (*Brewis* 1771 M, probably from ME *brew-hūs* 'a brew-house'),
Charles Hey, Coit Close (*v.* cot 'cottage'), Cote Hey (*v.* prec., (ge)hæg
'enclosure'), Crosland Inge (*v.* Crosland 265 *infra*, probably as a surname,
eng), Down Shutt (dial. *shut* 'division of land'), Doxon Shaw 1709, Ellen
Inge 1709, Far Flatt, Far Greaves, Foot Ball, Frith Knowl (*v.* fyrhðe
'wood', cnoll), Gate Acre, Gild Hey, Goodside, Goose Croft, Great & Little
Hades (*v.* hēafod), Haigh Field, Hanging Royd (*v.* hangende 'steep', rod[1]),

Healdcarr (v. helde 'slope', kjarr), High Field, Hollings (v. holegn 'holly'), Hood Brow, Hook Clough, Ing Spot (v. eng, spot), Laith Croft, Lee Syke, Little Bit, Little Shaw, Long Acre, Lower Hagg, Middle Hirst (v. hyrst 'wood'), Moor Gate, Nether End, Old Cliffe, Ox Close, Peter Hey, Pig Hill (v. pightel 'enclosure'), Pikelow (ib 1843 O.S., v. pīc[1] 'pike, pointed hill', hlāw), Richards Ing, Robin Royd, Round Ing, Round Knowl, Schale Piece, Shaw Bank mod, Simon Royd (Symmerode 1306, the ME pers.n. Simme, from Simon, rod[1]), Slang (dial. slang 'a narrow strip of land between larger divisions', chiefly WMidl), Small Tail, Spout Brow mod (ib 1851, v. spoute, brū), Stone Pit, Stone Royde, Syke Ing, Tenter Bank mod, Tilth, West Field, Whart Over, Wilson Ing, Win Royd, Wood Brow, Yelke Edge 1709.

(b) Alcocrodende (the ME surname Alcok, rod[1], ende), Aleynrode (the ME pers.n. Alain, rod[1]), Bradbury Intake 1686 Bretton 71 (v. intak), Drycloghker (v. drȳge, clōh, kjarr), Emmerode 1306 (the ME pers.n. Emme, rod[1]), Fairbothem (v. fæger, botm), Fayrhirst (v. fæger, hyrst), Henribrigholme (the ME pers.n. Henry, brycg, holmr), Horssegatebank (v. hors, gata, banke), Lonehende (v. lane, ende, cf. Lane supra), Merkehirst (v. mearc 'boundary', hyrst 'wood', cf. Markehirsts 256 supra), Rodehengker (v. rod[1], eng, kjarr), Roliphirst, Wadeker (the ME pers.n. Wade, kjarr), Wilkynker (the ME pers.n. Wilkin, kjarr).

3. SOUTH CROSLAND (102–1112)

Crois-, Crosland 1086 DB, Crosland(a), -lande 1195–1215 YCh viii, 13 Font, YD xii, 237, c. 1212 Pont, 1220–30 Bodl 103, 1226, 1251 FF, 1286 WCR, 1316 Vill et passim to 1402 FA, (-fosse) 1276 RH, 1302 DodsN, 1352 YD xii, 238 et freq to 1509 WB, (Foss(e)-) 1387, 1482 WB, (South(e)-) 1577 WillY, 1588 FF, (-Roger) 1605 FF, South Crosland als. Croslandfosse 1610 Arm, Crosseland(e) a. 1230 YD iv, 1246 Ass 6d, 1308 WCR, 1328 Banco, 1341 Surv et freq to 1540 Test vi, Croslaund 1255 FF, -lond 1533 FF. 'Tract of land with a cross', v. cros, land. The DB spelling with Crois- is a substitution of OFr crois. It is further distinguished from North Crosland (infra) by the affix fosse (v. foss[1] 'ditch'), but the particular reference is obscure; the original 1″ O.S. map marks an old camp (to which foss might refer) in the north of the township. The affix -Roger doubtless refers to some former owner.

NORTH CROSLAND (lost), North Crossland c. 1240–50 Bodl 96, 1523 FF, North(e) Crosland(e) 1328 DodsN, 1504 Ipm et freq to 1822 Langd, Northcrosseland 1379 PT, 1389 DodsN, 1424 Rent, 1486 MinAcct. v. South Crosland supra. The location of North Crosland is uncertain. It may have been in Lockwood township near Crosland

Hill (275 *infra*), but Langd puts it in this township, and it may in fact have been the northern half of the township, for the southern part is described as *Sowth Crosland Half* 1588 LS 148.

ARMITAGE BRIDGE, *terra heremitagie* c. 1212 Pont, *Ermitagium* 1236–58 YD xi, 393, (*The*) *Armitage, -myt-* 14, 1462 DodsN, 1610 Arm, 1621 PRAdel, 1659 WillS, *del Ermytache* 1379 PT (p), *del Hermitege* 1429 YD i, *the Ermytaige* 1561 WillY, *Armitage Bridge* 1817 M. *v.* ermitage (OFr) 'a hermitage', brycg.

NETHERTON, *Netherton* 1495 *WB*, 1605 FF, 1633 WillY *et freq* to 1771 M, *Neatherton* 1590 FF. 'Lower hamlet', *v.* neoðera, tūn (cf. Mickletown 127 *supra*); it lies in the valley bottom below South Crosland.

ARBORARY LANE, *Horbury Lane* 1843 O.S., probably a surname from Horbury 150 *supra*.   ARMITAGE FOLD, 1771 M, *v.* Armitage Bridge *supra*, fald.   BANK END & WOOD, cf. Crosland Bank *infra*.   BUTTER NAB, (*the*) *Butternabe* 1424 Rent, 1537 *WB* 13, *-nabbe* 1601 ib 47, *Botirnable* (sic) 1462 DodsN, *Butternabsprynge* 1547 *WB* 44, 'hill with good (butter-producing) pasture', *v.* butere, nabbi.   COCKING STEPS BRIDGE.   CORN BANK.   CRAB TREE WELL.   THE CROFT.   CROSLAND BANK, *the Banke* 1652 *WB* 60, *v.* banke.   CROSLAND EDGE, *Hege* 13, 1234 DodsN, *Egge* 14 ib, *Thege* 1574 WillY, *the Edge* 1610 *WB* 48, *v.* ecg 'escarpment'.   DAFFY WOOD.   DEAN CLOUGH.   DELVES, *Delph* 1817 M, *v.* (ge)delf 'quarry'.   EDGE END, 1843 O.S., *v.* Crosland Edge *supra*.   FAR FIELDS, *Far Field* 1851 *TA*.   FIELD HEAD & HO.   GREEN GATE KNOLL, *Greengate Knowl* 1817 M, *v.* grēne[1], gata, cnoll.   HADDEN FM.   HALL HEYS WOOD, 1843 O.S., cf. Crosland Hall 275 *infra*, *v.* (ge)hæg 'enclosure'.   HAWKROYD BANK.   HEALEY HO, 1843 O.S., *Healiehey* 1652 *WB* 61, *v.* hēah, lēah, (ge)hæg.   HIGH BROW, *the Heybrowe* 1677 *WB* 90a, *High Brough* 1771 M, *v.* hēah, brū.   HILL TOP, 1771 M.   INTAKE LANE, *Upper Intake* 1851 *TA*, *v.* intak.   LOWER HALL, *Old Hall* 1843 O.S.   MAG BRIDGE, BROOK, DALE & WOOD, *Mag Lordship* 1782 EnclA 8, *Mag Wood* 1843 O.S., from the fem. pers.n. *Mag*.   MARTEN NEST.   MILL CROFT.   MOOR LANE.   NAN HOB SPRING.   NETHERFIELD.   NETHER MOOR, 1851 *TA*.   NOPPER RD.   OAK ROYD BANK.   SAND BEDS.   SCAR TOP.   SPRING HEAD WELL.   SPRING WOOD.   STEPS, *Steps Mills* 1843 O.S.   STONEPIT HILL.   STONY

BATTER. THE STUBBINGS. TOP OF CROFT. TOP OF HILL.
WALKER SYKE, 1843 O.S., from the surname *Walker* (cf. walcere),
sīc 'stream'. WELL HEADS. WHITE GATE, *Whiteyate* 1653 *WB*
67, *v.* hwīt, geat 'gate'. WHITEGATES. WHITEHEAD LANE. WOOD
END.

FIELD-NAMES

The principal forms in (*a*) are 1851 *TA* 121. Spellings dated 1286 are
WCR, 1234, 1362, 15, 1414 DodsN, and others dated without source are *WB*.

(*a*) Beaumont Croft (named from the *Beaumont* family who had property
here (*WB*), croft), Coate 1771 M (*v.* cot 'cottage'), Delve close (*v.* Delves
supra), East Field, Gate Close, Hay 1771 M (*the Heyhead* 1638 WillY, 1652,
v. (ge)hæg 'enclosure'), Long Field, Moor Field, New Field, Old Hey Wood
1843 O.S. (*v.* (ge)hæg), Pond Close, the Staups 1725 (*v.* staup 'declivity',
perhaps identical with Steps *supra*), the Turfehap 1725 (*v.* turf, hēap 'heap,
hill'), The Wash 1843 O.S. (*v.* wæsce 'washing-place'), Wheat Field, Whin
Close (*v.* hvin 'gorse').

(*b*) *Annotfeylde* 1495 (the ME fem. pers.n. *Annota*, feld), *Brierry Pighille*
1537 (*v.* brērig, pightel 'enclosure'), *Caldewenedebroc* c. 1212 Pont (as this
was a stream by which Armitage *supra* stood, it is clearly the original name of
the R. Holme, *v.* RNs.), *le Hynganderydyng* 1286 (*v.* hangende, ON *hengjandi*
'steep', rydding 'clearing'), *Hovertheschore* 1286 ('above the bank', *v.* ofer [3],
scora), *Icathenildhaw* 15, *Lyalbanke* 1495 (the surname *Lyall*, banke),
Lyttlebank 1496, *Nethercouer* 1610 Arm (ME *cover*(*t*) 'covert, thicket'),
Northend 1653, 1677, *Pyghylls* 1496 (*v.* pightel 'enclosure'), *the Sonne ende*
1620 (perhaps 'sunny end'), *Stainrigs* 1234 (*v.* steinn, hryggr), *Stokeshood*
1362, *Stockbrood* 1362 ('broad strip of land by a stump', *v.* stocc, cf. brǣdu),
Vasdynghedde 1495, *Quitker* 1414 (*v.* hwīt, kjarr 'marsh').

4. FARNLEY TYAS (102–1612)

Fereleia, Ferlei 1086 DB
Ferneleia, -lay, -ley 12 Font, 1303 KF, (*-tyes*) 1361 DodsN, (*-Tyas*)
1499 Ipm, 1505 YD xii, 249, 1599 FF, *Fernley Tyas* 1362 DodsN
Farlag' 1202 FF, *-lay* 1234 FF, *-leg*(*h*) 1236 DodsN, FF, 1240 FF,
Fareleg 1256 DodsN
Farneley(*e*), *-lay* 1267 Ch, 1297 LS, 1303 Aid, 1316 Vill, (*-Tyas*)
1322 YD iv, 1335 FF *et freq* to 1605 FF
Farnl', -lay, -ley Hy 3 BM, 1353 YD i, (*-Tyas*) 1373 DodsN, 1593
WillY

'Woodland glade or clearing overgrown with fern', *v.* fearn, lēah.
Loss of -*n*- is not uncommon with this el. (cf. Barlow, Fairburn pt. iv

infra and EPN i, 166 for other examples). The affix *Tyas* is a feudal name from the family of *le Tyeis* or *Teutonicus* who held land in this neighbourhood from the thirteenth century (YD i *freq*, 1236, 1240 FF, 1267 Ch, 1303 KF, etc.).

LONGLEY, *Longelai* 1220–30 *Bodl* 102, *Longley*, *-lay* 1353 YD i, 1391 YD iii, *Langley* 1566 PRHfx. 'Long clearing', *v.* lang, lēah.

WOODSOME HALL, *Wodehuse* 1236 DodsN, *Wodesom* 1372 FF, 1373 DodsN, 1456 Linds, 1499 Ipm, *Wodosom* 1456 DodsN, *Wodsome* 1564 Visit, *Woodsom(e)* 1605 FF, 1617 PrHosp, (*-Hall*) 1817 M. '(At) the houses in the wood', *v.* wudu, hūs, -um, cf. Wothersome pt. iv *infra*.

ANCHOR WOOD, probably ancra 'hermit', **wudu**.   ARTHUR WOOD, 1843 O.S.   BANK FOOT, cf. Farnley Bank *infra*.   BIRKS WOOD, 1843 O.S., *v.* birki 'birch-tree', **wudu**.   BURNT HILL.   BUTTS, *v.* butte 'an abutting strip'.   CARR WOOD, *v.* kjarr 'marsh'.   CLIFFE HO.   CROFTS.   EARLY CROFTS.   FARNLEY BANK, 1843 O.S., *Bank* 1771 M, *v.* banke.   FARNLEY COMMON, 1843 O.S.   FARNLEY HEY, 1843 O.S., *Hey* 1817 M, *v.* (ge)hæg 'enclosure'.   FARNLEY MOOR, 1843 O.S.   FARNLEY WOOD.   GLEN FM.   GREEN CARRS.   HEATH BANK.   HEY WOOD, *The Hey Wood* 1843 O.S., *v.* Farnley Hey *supra*, **wudu**.   HIGH FIELDS.   HUNTER NAB, 1843 O.S., *v.* huntere, nabbi.   LEIGH FIELDS.   LUD HILL, LUD HILL DIKE, *Ludwell* 1817 M, *Ludhill* 1843 O.S., 'loud spring', *v.* hlūd, **wella**, Lud Hill iii, 94 *infra*.   LUMB DIKE & ROYD, *Lumroyd* 1843 O.S., *v.* lumm 'pool', dīc, rod[1].   MILLGATE.   MOLLY CARR WOOD.   MOOR HO.   NETHERTON, 1605 FF, 'lower part of the village', *v.* neoðera, tūn, cf. Mickletown 127 *supra*.   RAW GATE.   ROAF WOOD.   ROYD HO, 1822 Langd, *Royd* 1771 M, *v.* rod[1] 'clearing'.   RUNLET END, 1817 M, ModE *runlet* 'a stream'.   SHROGG WOOD, *v.* scrogge 'bush, brushwood'.   SLATE FIELDS.   TOFT LANE.   WEST WOOD, 1843 O.S.   WHINNY WOOD.   WOODSOME LEES, 1817 M, *v.* Woodsome Hall *supra*, lēah 'clearing'.

FIELD-NAMES

The principal forms in (*a*) are 1843 *TA*.

(*a*) Broad Ing, Copy, Little Oak Plantation, Mill Croft, Far & Near Warren, Woodsome Mill.

5. HOLME (102–1006) [ɔun, ɔum]

Holne 1086 DB, 1274–1321 WCR (*freq*), 1323 *MinAcct* 45, 1591 FF
Holm(e) 1316 Vill, 1347 DodsN, 1392, 1492 *MinAcct*

'Holly-tree', *v*. holegn, cf. Yateholme, Holmfirth 289 *infra*. The
form *Holme* is due to the assimilated *Holm-* in Holmfirth.

YATEHOLME, *Holne* 1086 DB, *Yhatomgrene* 1452 *WCR* i, *Yatum* 1585
WillY, *Yateholme* 1709 WMB, *Gateham* 1771 M, (*-or Yateholme*)
1822 Langd. *v*. prec. The affix is OE geat 'a gate'.

BAILEY CAUSEWAY MOSS. BIRCHEN BANK, *Birching Bank* 1851 *TA*,
v. bircen, banke. BLACK GROUGH. BLEAKMIRES RUSHES, *Black-
mires Rushes* 1843 O.S., *v*. blæc, mýrr, risc. BOGGERY DIKE.
BRITLAND EDGE, *Bretland Edge* 1771, 1817 M, possibly 'Britons'
land', *v*. Brettas, land, ecg. BROADHURST WOOD. BURLEY BANK,
Burley Banck 1709 WMB. CAUSEWAY HOLES. CLIFF CLOSE,
Cliffe Closes 1709 WMB, *v*. clif, clos. COOK'S STUDY, 1817 M.
COW CLOSE, 1851 *TA*. CROOKED EDGE. CROSSLEYS PLANTATION.
DEAD EDGE, 1709 WMB, *the ded hegge* Hy 8 Hnt ii, 361, *v*. dēad
'dead', hecg (probably denoting a hedge that was dead). DIGLEY
WOOD, 1851 *TA*, named from Digley 263 *supra*. DON WELL, *Dun
Well* 1843 O.S., the source of the R. Don, *v*. wella. ELBOW END.
END SPRINGS. FAR NAZE END, *Naze* 1851 *TA*, *v*. næss 'headland',
or OE *nasu* 'nose'. FERN HILL. FIELD HEAD, cf. *Holme Field*
1828 *EnclA* 10. FURTHER END COTE, *Cote* 1843 O.S., *v*. cot. GILL
HEY, 1851 *TA*, *Geyllheywod* 1572 *WCR* 3, *v*. geil 'ravine', (ge)hæg
'enclosure'. GRAINS EDGE. GREAT DIKE. GREEN WOOD, 1843
O.S. GUSSET DIKE. HADES PEAT PITS. HERBAGE HILL, *Har-
bridge* 1709 WMB, *Hay Bridge Hill* 1843 O.S., *Herbage Flatts* 1851
TA, on topographical grounds probably ME (*h*)*erbage* 'herbage',
hyll. GREAT & LITTLE HEY, cf. *Hey Bottom, Heywood Croft, Little
Hey* 1851 *TA*, *v*. (ge)hæg 'enclosure'. HIGH BROW. HILL GATE
SIKE, *Heald Gate Syke* 1851 *TA*, *v*. helde 'slope', gata, sīc. HOAR
CLOUGH. HOLME BANK, *Holme Banks* 1851 *TA*, *v*. banke. HOLME
CLIFF, 1851 *TA*, *Cliffe* 1709 WMB, *v*. clif. HOLME EDGE, 1817 M,
v. ecg. HOLME MOSS, 1709 WMB, *v*. mos 'bog, swamp'. HOLME
WOODS, 1709 WMB, *Holmewode* 1462 *MinAcct* 99, (*-in Ramesdene*)
1492 ib 02, *v*. wudu. HURLING GUTTER, 1843 O.S. INGS, INGS
BRIDGE, *Ing* 1771 M, *v*. eng 'meadow'. KILN BENT, 1851 *TA*, *v*.
cyln, beonet 'bent-grass'. LAD CLOUGH. LANE, 1843 O.S., *v*.

lane.   LAUND MOSS.   LIDGATE, *Lydgate in Holme* 1709 WMB, *v.*
hlid-geat 'swing-gate'.   LIGHTENS, *Lightings* 1709 WMB, *Leighton
Brow* 1851 *TA*, possibly lēac-tūn 'garden'.   LOWER FLAT.   MEAL
MILL, 1851 *TA*, possibly OE mæl 'cross', but more probably OE
mæle 'multi-coloured', hyll, cf. Meal Hill 244 *supra*, 284, 309 *infra*.
MOULD SCAR.   NETHERLEY, 1851 *TA*, *v.* neoðera, lēah.   OLD
GATE.   RAKE DIKE & HEAD, *Rakegate* 1485 *WCR* 1, *Rack* 1709
WMB, *Rake Head* 1851 *TA*, from ME *rake* 'a rough path over a
hill' (*v.* hraca), dīc, gata, hēafod.   RAMSDEN CLOUGH, 1843 O.S.,
named from Ramsden 237 *supra*, *v.* clōh 'dell'.   REAPS MOSS &
SLACK.   THE RIDGE, RIDGE LUMB, *Ridge Top* 1851 *TA*, *v.* hrycg,
lumm 'pool'.   RIDING WOOD, cf. *Ouerrideyngehede* 1492 *MinAcct*
02, *v.* rydding 'clearing'.   RUDDLE CLOUGH, 1843 O.S., dial. *ruddle*
'red ochre', clōh.   SCHOLE CROFT, 1709 WMB, 1817 M, *v.* skáli
'shieling', croft.   SHAW BANK, *Holmeshaies* 1592 WillY, *Shawbanck*
1709 WMB, *v.* sceaga 'copse', banke.   SHOE BROAD, 1851 *TA*, 'a
narrow strip of land', *v.* scofl, brǣdu.   SNAILSDEN, *Snayls-*, *Snailsden* Hy 8 Hnt ii, 361, 1709 WMB, *v.* snægl 'snail', possibly used as a
pers.n., denu.   SNAILSDEN MOSS, 1843 O.S., *v.* mos 'swamp'.
SNAILSDEN PIKE, 1817 M, *Snealsden Pike* 1771 M, *v.* pīc[1] 'a pointed
hill'.   STATHAM, 1851 *TA*.   STONES.   SUN WOOD.   SWINER
CLOUGH & DIKE, *Swanhill Clough* 1843 O.S., *v.* swan[1], hyll.   TICKLE
SCAR.   TURF GATE.   TWIZLE CLOUGH & HOLE, *v.* twisla 'river-
fork'.   UPPER CLOSE, 1851 *TA*, *Over Close* 1709 WMB.   THE
WHAMS, *Wham* 1851 *TA*, *v.* hvammr 'small valley'.   WHEAT
CLOSE, 1817 M.   WILMER HILL, *Wildmarehill* 1456 *WCR* 1, *Wilmer-
hil(l)wode* 1462, 1492 *MinAcct*, 'wild mare hill', *v.* wilde, mere[2],
hyll.   WINDY HARBOUR.   WOOD HEY LAITH, *Wodhay* 1406 *WCR*,
Woodhay 1771 M, *Woodhay Laiths* 1817 M, *v.* wudu, (ge)hæg 'enclosure', hlaða 'barn'.

FIELD-NAMES

The principal forms in (*a*) are 1851 *TA* 214. Spellings dated 1297–1331
are WCR, 1406, 1408 *WCR*, 1462, 1492 *MinAcct* 99, 02, 1486–1650 *WCR*,
1698 (local will), 1709 WMB. The exact location of some unidentified places
is not always certain (cf. 238, 247 *supra*).

(*a*) Bennet Royd (probably the surname *Bennet*, rod[1]), Bent Croft (*v.*
beonet 'bent-grass', croft), Blagg Ing, Boothey Ley, Broad Ing (ib 1709
WMB, *Brodynghedde* 1496 *WB* 8, *-heid* 1537 ib 13, *Wakfeld Brode Ynge*
1551, *v.* brād, eng), Broadwell Wood (*Brodwelle* 1331, *Brodewell* 1709, *v.*
brād, wella), Brow Wood, Burn't Head 1709, Carr Inge 1709 (*v.* kjarr

'marsh', eng 'meadow'), Cocked Hat, Common Heys (v. (ge)hæg 'enclosure'), Corn Close, Corn Drake Holt (dial. *corn-drake* 'corn-crake or land-
rail', holt 'wood'), Corn Hey, Cote Close, Crossland Hey, Dam Close,
Dunker End (perhaps R. Don, cf. Don Well *supra*, kjarr 'marsh'), Earnshaw
Wood (cf. *Earnshaws Croft* 1698, named from the family of *John Earnshaw*
ib), Far Hills, Far Lee, Fatherland (*Fodder Lands* 1709, v. fōdor 'fodder',
land), Great Shaw, Green Syke, Haddon Brow (*Hatton* 1492, v. hǣð, dūn),
Hay Slacks Moor 1709 (v. Hey *supra*, slakki 'a hollow'), Hellen Tree Head
(v. ellern 'elder-tree'), Hishays 1709 (v. hēah, sceaga 'copse'), Far & Little
Hollings (v. holegn 'holly'), Holme Clough 1709 (v. clōh 'dell'), Hood Ing,
Hullocks (v. huluc 'shed'), Intake Green & Wood (v. intak), Kaye Edge
Bottom, Laith Close (v. hlaða 'barn'), Upper Laith Grime (v. Legrams
Lane iii, 246 *infra*), Long Paddock, Lumb Carr (v. lumm 'pool', kjarr 'marsh'),
Meadow banck 1709, Mean Croft (v. (ge)mǣne 'common', croft), Mount
Common 1709, Nab Hey (v. nabbi 'knoll', (ge)hæg), New Brick, New Hey,
Ox Field Ing, Pingle Wood (v. pingel 'enclosure'), Red Moor Ing, Round
Hill, Rye Close, Spout Close (v. spoute 'spout'), Stone Croft, Stone Pit
Hill, Stonery, Thick Hazle (*Thykhasile* 1486, *-hessils* 1499, v. þicce[2] 'dense',
hæsel 'hazel'), Thorney Ley, Three Nooks, Toad Carr, Tom Ing, Top
Syke, Trough 1771 M (v. trōg 'valley'), Twedall 1709, Tween Croft, Wart
Over (*Thwarteover* 1572, 'land lying across', v. þverr, ofer[3]), Whitcliffe 1709
(v. hwit, clif), Yoke Edge 1709.

(b) le *Blakebanck* 1308 (v. blæc, banke), *Crabbehill* 1499 (v. crabbe 'crabtree', hyll), *Dichhey* 1572 (v. dīc, (ge)hæg), *Edderley* 1527, *Gravenhay* 1462,
Grauenhey in Holme 1492 (for the first el. cf. Greno Knoll i, 246 *supra*, v.
(ge)hæg), *Highe Salowes* 1499 (v. hēah 'tall', salh 'willow'), *Hopedale* 1315
(v. hop 'small overhanging valley', dæl), *Lenchenoke* 1551 (v. hlenc 'hillside', nōk 'nook'), *Lichesechell* 1462, *Lichestell* 1492 (possibly from leoht,
hæsel, cf. Lighthazles iii, 64 *infra*), *Milnehirst* 1551 (v. myln, hyrst 'wood'),
Slackheade 1572 (v. slakki 'a hollow'), *Thormholme* (sic for *Thorni-*) 1308 (v.
þornig, holmr), *Tithefeld* 1492, the *Toft Birk* 1698, *Tofteclyve* 1297 (v. topt
'enclosure', birki, clif), *Waynwrightroide* 1408 (the surname *Wainwright*
(from OE *wægn-wyrhta* 'wagon-maker'), rod[1]), *Whatgodwille hirst* 1650
('what God wills', hyrst 'wood'), le *Wonge* 1297 (v. wang 'meadow').

6. HONLEY (102–1311)

Hanelei(a), *-lay* 1086 DB, 1243 Fees
Honeley, *-lay* 1252 Ebor, 1274 WCR (p), 1297 LS, 1482 *WB*
Honle(y), *-lay* 1274, 1298 WCR (p), 1316 Vill, 1370 YD i, 1402 FA
   et passim to 1641 Rates
Hanneley 1285, 1286 WCR
Hanley 1323 WCR, 1350, 1392, 1397 DodsN, (*als. Honley*)
   1571 FF
Hauneley 1379 PT
Hounley Half 1588 LS

'Cock clearing' (probably in the sense 'woodland glade where woodcock abounded') or possibly 'Hana's clearing' from the OE pers.n. *Hana*, *v*. hana, lēah. On the midland forms in *Hon(e)*-, cf. Phonol. § 4; *Haune-* is a misreading of *Hanne-*. *Half* refers to a half of the township.

BROCK HOLES, *Brockolenabbe* 13 YD i, *Brocholis*, *-es* 1275, 1297 WCR (p), *Brokholes* 1370 YD i (p). 'Badger holes', *v*. brocc-hol, nabbi.

MYTHOLM BRIDGE, *Mi-*, *Mythomwode* 1492 WCR, *-brigg(e)* 1492 *MinAcct* 02, 1589 WillY, *Mithambrigg* 1709 WMB. '(At) the river-mouths', *v*. (ge)mȳðe, -um, brycg; it refers to the confluence of New Mill Dike and the R. Holme. The name occurs elsewhere in YW, Mytholm iii, 135, Mytholme iii, 275, Mytholme Bridge iii, 92, and Mytholmroyd iii, 159 *infra*.

LOWER & UPPER BANKS, *Banks*, *Nichol Banks* 1843 O.S.   CLIFF WOOD, 1843 O.S., *v*. clif, wudu.   CLITHEROE (WOOD).   DEAN BROOK.   DEANHOUSE, *Danehowse* 1555 WillY, *Deanehouse* 1578 ib, *v*. denu 'valley', hūs.   EAST GATE.   ENFIELD HO.   FERN BANK. FIELD END & HO.   FISHER GREEN.   FOLLY.   GILL WOOD. GRANBY FM.   GRASS CROFT.   GREEN CLIFF.   GROVE HO.   GYNN HO, OLD GYNN, *The gynn* 1843 O.S., ME *gin* 'engine, machine'. HAGG DIKE & LEYS, LOWER, NEW & UPPER HAGG, HAGG WOOD, *Netherhog* (sic) 1546 WillY, *Hagge* 1569 ib, *Nether*, *Over hag* 1771 M, *New Hagg*, *Hagg Wood* 1843 O.S., *v*. hogg 'clearing', cf. dial. *hagg* 'a wooded enclosure, a copse'.   HAIGH LANE.   HALL ING, 1843 O.S., *v*. hall, eng 'meadow'.   HASSOCKS, 1843 O.S., *v*. hassuc 'a clump of coarse grass'.   HIGH ROYD, *Heyghrode* 1584 FF, *v*. hēah, rod[1] 'clearing'.   HOLLIN HALL & HURST, *Holling Hall* 1843 O.S., *v*. holegn 'holly', hall, hyrst 'wood'.   HOLMROYD NOOK & WOOD, 1843 O.S., *v*. holmr, rod[1], nōk.   HONLEY HEAD WOOD, 1843 O.S. HONLEY MOOR.   HONLEY OLD WOOD, 1843 O.S.   HONLEY WOOD, *Houlawood bothome* (sic) 1638 WillY, *Honley Wood Bottom* 1791 WB 22, *v*. wudu.   HOPE BANK.   INTAKE FM, *v*. intak.   KNOLL QUARRY.   LEATHER HALL.   MARSH.   MARSH PLATT, *Marsh plat* 1771 M, *v*. mersc 'marsh', plat[2] 'plot of ground'.   MIDDLEFIELD HO, *Middle Field* 1843 O.S.   MIRY LANE, *Miry Lane Bottom* 1843 O.S.   MELTHAM GATE, *v*. Meltham 282 *infra*, gata.   MOISY LANE. MOLL SPRING.   MOOR CROFT, 1741 Stanhp 102, 4 (*v*. mōr, croft). MOORFIELD HO.   MOOR PARK, 1843 O.S.   NEW DAM, cf. *the mill*

dam 1782 *EnclA* 8, *v.* dammr.   NEILEYS MILL, *Ely or Neeley* 1764
Glebe, Neeleys Farm 1843 O.S.   NEW TOWN, 1843 O.S.   NORTH
GATE.   OLDFIELD, *Oldefeld* 1296, 1307 WCR (p), *Oldfelde* 1560
WillY, *-feild* 1584 ib, *v.* ald, feld.   PARK RIDING, 1843 O.S., *v.* park,
rydding 'clearing'.   PONTEY, *Ponty House* 1843 O.S.   MIDDLE &
UPPER REINS, *v.* reinn 'boundary strip'.   RIDINGS.   RYE CROFT.
SCOT GATE.   SEVENTY ACRES, 1843 O.S.   SHAW HEAD, 1771 M, *v.*
sceaga 'copse', hēafod.   SMITHY PLACE, *Smythe place* 1553 WillY,
Smithie place 1562 ib, *Smith Place* 1771 M, *v.* smiðõe, place.   SOUTH
GATE.   SPINNER GATE.   SPRINGFIELD.   STONES WOOD.   SWINNY
KNOLL, *Swinny Knowl* 1843 O.S., *v.* cnoll 'hillock'.   THIRSTIN,
Thirsting 1843 O.S.   TIMINETS.   TOWN HEAD.   VIEW.   WATER-
FALL.   WELL HO.   WESTFIELD.   WEST GATE.   WEST HO, 1817
M.   WHEATFIELD HO.   THE WOOD.   WOOD BOTTOM, 1843 O.S.
WOOD NOOK, 1843 O.S.

FIELD-NAMES

(*a*) Broom Field (*mod*), Delph Old Wood 1782 *EnclA* 8 (*v.* (ge)delf
'quarry'), Taylor Field (*mod*).

(*b*) *Mortelbotham* 1482 *WB* (*v.* botm, perhaps this should be identified
with Mark Bottoms 287 *infra*).

7. LINTHWAITE (102–1014) [ˈlinfit]

Lindthait 1185–1202 YCh viii (p), *Lin-, Lynthwait, -thwayt(e)*,
-thweyt 1208 DodsN, FF, 1240–50 *Bodl* 96, 1318 DodsN, 1599 FF,
Linweyt 1241 FF, *Lyntwait* 1258 YI, *Lynthayt* 1284, 1308 WCR (p),
Lynwayte 1379 PT, *Linfit* 1822 Langd. 'Flax clearing', *v.* līn, þveit,
a compound which occurs several times in YW as Linthwaite, Linfit,
Linfitts, though the first el. could here be lind 'lime-tree'.

COWLERSLEY, *Colresley(e)* 1226 FF, 1286 YI (p), *Colleresley, -lay*
1277, 1308 WCR (p), *Collersley, -lay* 1362, 1389, 1504 DodsN, 1439,
1489 YD xii, 250, 304, 1504 Ipm, 1523 *WB* 17. 'Charcoal-burner's
clearing', from an unrecorded OE colere and lēah; the same first el.
appears in Coverdale (Brogden) pt. vi *infra*.

BANKWELL RD.   BARBER ROW.   BAR GATE.   BINN, cf. Binn 277
infra.   BLACKMOORFOOT, 1843 O.S., *v.* blæc, mōr, fōt.   BLACK
ROCK.   BOTTOMS, *Bottoms Wood* 1849 *TA*, *v.* botm.   BREARLEY
COTTAGE.   BROAD OAK, 1817 M, *v.* brād, āc.   BURR.   CAUSEWAY
SIDE.   CLOUGH HO, LOWER & UPPER CLOUGH, *Clough* 1843 O.S.,

cf. *Clough Field & Head* 1849 *TA*, v. clōh 'dell'.   COMMON END,
1771 M.   CROFT.   DAISY GREEN.   FIELDS HEAD, cf. *Far Field*
1849 *TA*.   FLAT HO, *Flatehowse* 1577 WillY, *Flathouse* 1638 ib, v.
flat, hūs.   FOLLY, 1849 *TA*, v. folie.   GILL ROYD.   GREEN HEAD.
GREEN HO.   GROVE HO.   GUY EDGE, 1849 *TA*, the pers.n. *Guy*,
ecg.   HAZEL GROVE, *Hazle Grove* 1817 M, v. hæsel, grāf.   HEATH,
1817 M, v. hǣð.   HEIGHT, 1771 M, *Height Hill* 1849 *TA*, v. hēhðu.
HEY, *the Hay* 1560 WillY, cf. *Hey Ing* 1849 *TA*, v. (ge)hæg 'enclosure'.   HEY GATE & KNOWL.   HEY WOOD, 1843 O.S.   HIGH
HO, *Highhouse* 1637 WillY, v. hēah, hūs.   THE HOLD, v. hald
'shelter'.   HOLE IN THE WALL.   HOLLINS GREEN, *Hollins* 1849 *TA*,
v. holegn 'holly'.   HOYLE HO, *Hoyl(e)house* 1636 WillY, 1817 M,
Hole-house 1775 Watson, v. hol[1], hūs.   IDLE HILL, 1849 *TA*, v.
īdel 'useless', hyll.   KITCHEN CLOUGH & FIELD, *Kitchen* 1849 *TA*,
probably the YW surname *Kitchen*, clōh, feld.   LAMB HEY.   LANE,
cf. *Lane Field* 1849 *TA*, v. lane.   LEES HO, *Lees Mill* 1843 O.S.,
v. lēah.   LINTHWAITE HALL, *Linfit-Hall* 1822 Langd.   LONGFIELD.
LONG WOOD, 1849 *TA*.   MILNSBRIDGE, partly in this township, v.
292 *infra*.   MORLEY LANE.   MYRTLE GROVE.   NEW GATE.   NEW
ROYD.   NORTH HO.   PARK.   PIMROYD, 1843 O.S., the surname
Pim, rod[1] 'clearing'.   ROCK.   ROYD HO, 1817 M, v. rod[1], hūs.
RYE CROFT EDGE, 1843 O.S., v. rӯge, croft, ecg.   SHAW GREEN,
1843 O.S., v. sceaga 'copse', grēne[2].   SLACKS, *Slacks Field* 1849
TA, v. slakki 'a hollow'.   SLADES, *Slade* 1771 M, v. slæd 'valley'.
SLANT GATE.   SMITHRIDING, 1849 *TA*, v. smið (probably as a
surname), rydding 'clearing'.   SPRING GROVE, *Spring Wood* 1849
TA, v. spring 'plantation'.   STOCKER HEAD, *Stock Carr*, *Stoker Field*
1849 *TA*, v. stocc 'stump', kjarr 'marsh'.   STORTH, *del Storthes*, *-is*
1329, 1353 YD i (p), *Storth Close* 1849 *TA*, v. storð 'plantation'.
TANYARD RD, cf. *Tanpit Field* 1849 *TA*.   THROSTLE GREEN.   WAIN
GATE.   WHITELEY BOTTOM.   WIGGIN CROSS, *Whickinge crosse* 1571
WillY, *Whigin Crosse* 1645 PREll, 'Viking's cross', v. víkingr, cros.
WILD BROW.   WINTER HILL.   YEW TREE LANE.

FIELD-NAMES

The principal forms in (*a*) are 1849 *TA* 262 and modern (1935) (marked
mod).

(*a*) Acre (*mod*), Appleyard Wood, Ash Field, Back Field, Back oth'
House, Ball Greave, Bents Head (v. beonet 'bent-grass'), Benty Carre (*v.*
beonet, kjarr 'marsh'), Boulder Field, Brink (v. brink), Broad Royd, Bunk

(Top), Burnt Hill, Calf Hey, Carr Ing, Coat Close, Coit Close, Common Right, Crack Hill, Cross Edge, Dam Field, Daw Royd, Dye House Croft, Edge, Ellen Tree Land (v. ellern 'elder-tree'), Elm Ing, Fancy, Far Toft, Foggett (mod), Gateing Close (v. gata, eng), Glazing Holes, Grass Hey, Greendry, Green Royd, Green Spot (v. grēne[1], spot), Hall Heigh & Royd, Hanging Royd (v. hangende 'steep', rod[1]), Headland, Heater (cf. Heater iii, 170 infra), Hill Hole, Hive Yard, Horse Croft, Hoyle Ing (v. hol[1], eng), Hut Edge, Ing Leys, Kiln Field, Laith Croft (v. hlaða 'barn'), Lamb Royd, Liquorice Hill, Lingards (v. lin 'flax', garðr, cf. Lingards 277 infra), Longlands, Marybone Ing, Middle Holme, Middle Royd, Moor Bottom, Moorcroft 1843 O.S., Near Intake (v. intak), Near Shutt (dial. shut 'division of land'), Nook Pit, Old Riding (v. rydding 'clearing'), Owlers Wood (v. alor 'alder'), Park Field (mod), Parkin Croft, Penny Field (mod), Pig Hill (v. pightel 'enclosure'), Pinnacle, Pipe, Pond Field, Reign (v. reinn 'boundary strip'), Rocher Top & Wood (v. Rocher i, 226 supra), Roger Knowl, Rough Hey, Round Ing, Rye Close, Rye Stubble (Ryestubbillnoke 1485 WCR 1, from rȳge, ME stuble 'stubble', nōk), Scar Field, Sim Royd (the pers.n. Sim (from Simon), rod[1]), Small Drink, Snock Head, Spoil Bank, Spout Ing (v. spoute, eng), Spring Croft & Ing, Steanyard, Stone Hole, Stone Pit Hole, Stone Yard, Stubble Green, Stubbing (v. stubbing 'clearing'), Such Wood, Sun Flat, Swallow Field (mod), Tenter Croft, Thorny Lee, Thorpe Ing (v. þorp, eng), Toad Hole, Tongue, Top oth' Edge, Water Spout (mod), Well Field, Wham Field, Whams (v. hvammr 'small valley'), Wheat Croft, Whin Brow (v. hvin 'gorse', brū), Wood Royd Bank, Yeld (mod).

8. LOCKWOOD (6" O.S. 260 NE 1314)

Locwode 1236–58 YD ix, 393, 1275 WCR, 1298 ib (p), 1347 YD xii, 96, Lockwode 1275 WCR, -wood 1324, 1464 DodsN et freq to 1616 FF, Lokewod(e) 1379 PT (p), 1462 YD xiii, 54, 1504 Ipm, Lokwud 1421 YD i, -wod 1504 Ipm, -wood 1523 FF. 'Wood near the enclosure', v. loc, wudu.

BARKERITE FM.   BARTON, Barton Tower 1771 M, Barton Field 1842 TA, v. bere-tūn.   BEAUMONT PARK, named from the Beaumont family who owned property here from the fifteenth century (WB).   BIRK HO.   CROSLAND HALL, Croslande hall 1551 WillY, Crossland Hall 1645 ib, v. South Crosland 265 supra, hall.   CROSLAND HILL, 1639 WillY, 1647 PREll, v. prec., hyll.   CROSLAND MOOR, 1509 WB, v. prec., mōr.   DOG HALL, cf. Doggerodes 1428 WB 6, v. dogga 'dog', rod[1], hall.   DRY CLOUGH, 1842 TA, v. drȳge, clōh 'dell'.   DUNGEON WOOD, 1771 M, woods called the Dungion 1631 WB 55, Dungeon 1660 WillS, ME dongeoun 'a dungeon'.   FELKS STILE, Felk Style 1843 O.S., v. stigel.   HEATH FIELD, Head Field 1842 TA, v. hǣð, feld.   HOB LANE.   LANE END, Lane Head 1771 M.   MOOR

END, 1817 M.   MOORLEIGH.   NAB CROFT, 1771 M, *v.* nabbi 'knoll',
croft.   NORTHFIELD, 1842 *TA*.   PARK RD.   RASHCLIFFE, 1842 *TA*,
v. clif.   ROCKFIELD.   SANDS HO.   SPINKWELL QUARRIES, cf. Spink
Well 177 *supra*.   SWAN LANE, cf. *Swan Close* 1842 *TA*.   THEWLIS
LAITH & LANE, probably from the YW surname *Theules*.   THORN-
FIELD.   THORNTON LODGE RD, *Thornton Lodge* 1822 Langd.   TOM
LANE.   WOODFIELD HO, 1843 O.S.   YEW GREEN RD, *Yew Gr.*
1771 M, *v.* īw, grēne[2].   THE YEWS, *Ewtreese* 1638 WillY, *v.* īw,
trēow.   YEWS HILL, *Yews Hill End* 1842 *TA*, *v.* prec., hyll.

FIELD-NAMES

The principal forms in (*a*) are 1842 *TA* 267.

(*a*) Alders, Back o'th Laith Field, Brierley Wood, Briery Field, Broad
Field, Broad Royd (*le Broderode* 1286 WCR, *v.* brād, rod[1] 'clearing'), Bush
Ing, Cock'd Hat, Collier, Corn Croft, Cross Close, Dead Waters, East Field,
Eddy Croft, Fleets, Footgate Field, Great Ing, Harber Royd, Horton Close,
House Croft, Ing Top, Judd Cliffe Wood, Jumble Field, Lower & Upper
Knowl, Laith Close (*v.* hlaða 'barn'), Law Field, Longroyd Bridge (*Long-
royd Brigges* 1585 WillY, *v.* lang, rod[1] 'clearing', brycg), Mark Bottom, Meg
Close, Moor Close & Field, New Field, North Royd, North Wall Field, Oat
Lands, Parkin Croft, Lower & Upper Proctor, Quarry Field, Rye Croft,
Salter Walls, Slades (*v.* slæd 'valley'), South Field, South Royd, Spa Close,
Spade Close, Stubbing, Thistle Field, Upper Park, Wall Royd, Warm Croft,
Water Field, Watering Close, Well Croft, West Field.

9. MARSDEN (102–0412)

> *Marchesden(e)* 1177–93 YCh 1517 (Font), 1274, 1277 WCR (p),
>   1349 Ch
> *Marcheden(e)* 1275 WCR (p), 1292 *MinAcct* 26, 1306 WCR, 1313
>   Pat, 1323 *MinAcct* 45, 1341 *Surv* 10, 5, 1487 *MinAcct* 66, *-done*
>   1331 YD i
> *Marchden(e)* 1323 *MinAcct* 45, WCR, 1638 BM, 1649 *MinAcct* 13
> *Mercheden* 1341 Surv
> *Mersseden'* 1379 PT   *Marshden* 1619 DodsN, 1620 Skyr
> *Marsden* 1540 Test vi, 1625 *YAS* 28, 5, 1641 Rates

Marsden clearly means 'boundary valley' and refers to its position
on the Lancashire boundary, *v.* denu. The first el. cannot, however,
be OE mearc 'boundary', as this word would neither yield the
palatalised *Marche-* which we have in Marsden nor appear with a
gen.sg. in *-es* (since it was an OE fem. ō-stem, gen.sg. *mearce*). The

first el. is therefore most probably OE *mercels* 'boundary', reduced to *Marches-* in the ME spellings, and is closely paralleled by that of Marsden La 86 (which has also spellings in *Merkeles-* as well as *Merkes-*, *Merches-*). Cf. also March Clough & Haigh *infra*. Later spellings show some confusion with *mersc* 'marsh' as is the case with Masbrough i, 189 *supra* (from OE *mearc*).

BINN, 1817 M, cf. *Binboghe* 1426 *Ramsd*, *Bean Side* 1771 M, *Binn Close & Holes* 1850 *TA*. The theme *Binn* appears in several YW p.ns., Binn 273 *supra*, Binns 289, Binns Hill iii, 126, Binn Royd iii, 54, Binns, Binns Top iii, 90 *infra*. In one or two cases we may have the YW surname *Binns* (*Binnes*, *Bynds*, etc., esp. common in Halifax from the sixteenth century, PRHfx *passim*). Mostly, however, it is from OE *binn* 'a manger, a stall', and the surname *Binns* is probably of local origin from one or another of these places.

LINGARDS WOOD

> *Lingarder* 1218 FF
> *Lin- Lyngardes* 1218 Kirkst, 1560 WillY, (*-wood*) 1426 *Ramsd*, -*gard* 1424 Rent, -*gards* 1822 Langd
> *Lin-*, *Lyngarthes* 13 Kirkst, 1297 WCR (p), 1333 Kirkst, -*garth(e)* 1296 LacyComp, 1486 *MinAcct* 66, *Linggarthes* 1593 WillY

'Flax enclosure', *v.* līn, garðr. The first spelling *Lingarder* retains the ON nom.plur. *garðar*. Lingards Cross 309 *infra* is just over the boundary in Slaithwaite township.

PULE HILL, *past' voc' le Pole* 1426 *Ramsd*, 1487 *MinAcct* 66, *Puil Hill* 1771 M, *Pule Hill* 1817 M, *v.* pōl 'a pool', hyll. There is a small pool on the hillside at Pule Bents, cf. Firth Pule *infra*. The spelling *Puil* represents the local dial. pronunciation of *pool* [puil], cf. Phonol. § 30.

STANDEDGE, *Stonegg(e)* l. 12, 13 Nost 22d, 66, *Stanegge* c. 1272 SadD, -*ege* 1468 ib, *Stone-edge* 1738 PRSad. 'Stone edge or escarpment', *v.* stān, ecg, here denoting a high ridge on the county boundary. On the modern form *Stand-* cf. Phonol. § 46.

WESSENDEN, *Questondenhede* 1426 *Ramsd*, -*sten-* 1461 *MinAcct* 09, *Questenboth* 1461 ib, *Questendenbothe* 1487 ib 66, *Whesingden* 1568 *Ramsd*. 'Valley with rock suitable for whetstones', *v.* hwet-stān, denu, bōth 'booth, shed', and on the *Qu-* spellings cf. Phonol. § 39.

ACRE HEAD. ADAM PASTURE, 1850 *TA*, cf. *Adam Ing* 1850 *TA*, the pers.n. *Adam*, eng 'meadow'. AINSLEY, *Ornsley* 1771 M, cf. Ainleys iii, 43 *infra*; *Orn-* doubtless represents *Aun-*. ASHTON BINN, 1817 M, probably *Ashton* as a surname, binn 'stall', cf. Binn *supra*.

BADGER GATE, 1843 O.S., BADGER HEY, -*Hay* 1843 O.S., from the word *badger* 'hawker', v. gata, (ge)hæg 'enclosure'. BANK BOTTOM & TOP, *Bank Top* 1817 M, v. banke. BERRY GREAVE, 1843 O.S., doubtless 'berry copse', v. berige, græfe. BINN MOOR, 1843 O.S., v. Binn *supra*, mōr. BIRKEN BANK & HOLES, BIRK MOSS, 1843 O.S., v. bircen 'birch', mos 'swamp' BLACKER EDGE, 1843 O.S. v. blæc, kjarr 'marsh', ecg, cf. Blacker i, 292 *supra*. BLACK MOSS, 1843 O.S., v. blæc, mos 'swamp'. BLAKE CLOUGH, *Black Clough* 1843 O.S., v. blæc, clōh 'dell'. BLAKE LEE. BLAKELEY, BLAKELY CLOUGH, *Blake Clough* (sic) 1843 O.S., v. blæc, lēah, clōh. BOBUS, *Bowbus Moss* 1843 O.S., v. busc. BOOTH LATHE, cf. *Booth Close, End & Head* 1850 *TA*, v. bōth 'booth, shed'. BOWSER, *Bowser Ing* 1850 *TA*, possibly the surname *Bowser*, eng 'meadow'. BRACK ROLLS. BROADRAKE GREEN. BROAD WHAM, v. hvammr 'a small valley'. BROWN HILL. BUCKSTONES, 1817 M, v. bucc 'buck', stān. BURNE MOSS. BURNT HILL, 1843 O.S., *Burn'd Hill Butts* 1850 *TA*, v. brende 'burnt', hyll, butte. BUTCHER LANE, cf. *Butcher Close* 1850 *TA*, from the surname *Butcher*. BUTTERLY, *Inn & Out Butterly* 1850 *TA*, v. butere, lēah. BUTTERLY HILL, 1843 O.S.

CAB WHAMS, v. hvammr 'a small valley'. CARR CLOUGH, *Car Clough* 1843 O.S., v. kjarr 'marsh', clōh 'dell'. CARRS. CAT HOLES, *Cat Holes Ing* 1850 *TA*, v. catt 'cat', hol[1]. CELLARS CLOUGH. CHAIN. CHAMBER. CLARK HILL, cf. *Clark Hey or Ings* 1850 *TA*, from the surname *Clark*, (ge)hæg, eng. CLOSE FLAT. CLOSE GATE BRIDGE. CLOSE MOSS, *Clowes Moss* 1817 M, v. clōh 'dell', mos 'swamp'. CLOUGH HEAD, *Clough Top* 1817 M, v. clōh. CLOUGH LEE, (*le*) *Clowley Booth* 1623, 1625 *YAS* 76 (21), 28 (5), *Cloughley* 1850 *TA*, v. clōh, lēah. CRADLES. CROW HILL, 1771 M, v. crāwe, hyll. CROWTHER LANE, cf. *Crowther Field* 1850 *TA*, from the YW surname *Crowther*.

DAN CLOUGH. THE DEAN. DINNER STONE. DIRKER (HEYS). DRY CLOUGH SIDE. DUCKPIT.

ELLEN CLOUGH.

FAIRFIELD. FAIR HILL. FIELD BOTTOM. FIRTH PULE, *Frith Pules Pasture* 1850 *TA*, v. fyrhðe 'wood', pōl 'pool', cf. Pule Hill *supra*; there are two pools on the hillside here. FOREST, 1843 O.S., *v.* forest. FORE WHAM, *v.* fore, hvammr 'a small valley'. FOUL MOSS. FOXSTONE MOSS.

GARSIDE HEY. GATE HEAD, 1771 M, *v.* gata 'road', hēafod. GILBERTS, 1843 O.S., *Gilbert Intook* 1771 M, from the surname *Gilbert, v.* intak. GOOD HILL. THE GRANGE. GREAT EDGE. GREEN HILL, *Grenelbothe* 1487 *MinAcct* 66, *v.* grēne[1], hyll, bōth 'booth, shed'. GREEN HILL CLOUGH, 1843 O.S., *v.* prec., clōh 'dell'. GREEN LAITCH, *v.* grēne[1], læcc 'stream, bog'. GREEN OWLERS, 1817 M, *Grene Oller* 1568 *Ramsd, v.* grēne[1], alor 'alder-tree'. GREY STONES, probably identical with *Graystones* 1551 *WCR, v.* græg[1], stān.

HAIGH HO. HARD END. HARD HEAD, 1843 O.S., *v.* heard, hēafod 'headland'. HARD HILL. HARROW HILL. HATTER LEE. THE HEADS, *Hades* 1850 *TA, v.* hēafod 'headland'. HEATHY LEE, cf. *Heathy Knowl* 1850 *TA, v.* hǣð, -ig, lēah, cnoll. HEMPLOW WOOD, *Hempley Bank (Wood)* 1850 *TA, v.* hænep 'hemp', lēah. THE HEY, *Hay* 1771 M, *v.* (ge)hæg 'enclosure'. HEY BRINKS, 1843 O.S. HEY COTE, HEY DIKE, 1843 O.S., HEY FOLD, HEY GREEN, *Hay Green* 1817 M, HEY HEADS, *High Edge* 1817 M, *v.* prec., brink, cot, dīc, fald, grēne[2], ecg. HIGH GATE, *High Gate Hill* 1850 *TA, v.* hēah, gata. HIGH LATHE. THE HILL, 1843 O.S., *v.* hyll. HILL TOP. HIND HILL. HOE GRAIN. HOLLINS BANK & HO, *Hollins Head & Wood* 1850 *TA, v.* holegn 'holly'. HOLME, HOLME MOOR, *Holme Moor* 1709 WMB, *Holme Green, Head & Ing* 1850 *TA, v.* holmr 'water-meadow'. HOPWOOD. HORSELEY HEAD, *le Horscloughfote* 1625 *YAS* 28, 5, *v.* hors, clōh 'dell', fōt. HUCK HILL.

ING HEAD, *Ing Head Croft* 1850 *TA,* ING LEES, 1850 *TA, v.* eng 'meadow'. INNER HEY, 1850 *TA, v.* Hey *supra.* INTAKE, INTAKE HEAD, 1843 O.S., *v.* intak.

JOPES MOSS.

KNOWL.

LADY ROYD. LAMINOT. LANE INGS, *Lane Ing Croft* 1850 *TA,* LANE SYKE, *Lane Syke Ing* 1850 *TA, v.* lane, eng 'meadow', sīc 'stream'. LAVEROCK HALL, 1843 O.S., *v.* lāwerce 'lark', hall, cf. Gawthorpe Hall 102 *supra.* LAYZING CLOUGH, cf. *Laysingbothem* 1308 WCR, probably ON leysingi 'freedman', croft, botm. LEYSING CLOUGH, 1843 O.S., *v.* prec., clōh 'dell'. LINESGREAVE HEAD, *Linesgreave* 1843 O.S., *v.* grǣfe 'copse'. LITTLE FALL, *Fall* 1850 *TA, v.* (ge)fall 'clearing'. LOADLEY CLOUGH. LONG CLOUGH,

1843 O.S., *v.* lang, clōh. LONG FOLD. LONG GRAIN, ib 1843 *TA*, *v.* lang, grein 'the fork of a river'.

MARCH CLOUGH, MARCH HAIGH, *The Haigh* 1843 O.S., MARCH HILL, 1771 M, *v.* clōh, haga 'enclosure', hyll; the first el. is probably the same as Marsden *supra*. MOUNT RD, *v.* Old Mount *infra*.

NAB END, 1843 O.S., *v.* nabbi 'hillock'. NATHANS, *Nathan Hey* 1850 *TA*, the pers.n. *Nathan*, (ge)hæg 'enclosure'. NAZE END, TOP & WOOD, *High Nase* 1764 *Glebe*, *Knayes Wood* (*Top*) 1850 *TA*, *v.* næss 'headland', or OE *nasu* 'nose'. NEARMOST GRAIN, 1843 O.S., *v.* grein 'river-fork'. NETHERLEY, 1843 O.S., *v.* neoðera, lēah. NETHER WOOD, 1623 *YAS* 76, 21, *v.* neoðera, wudu. NETTLE SPRING. NEW CLOSE, 1850 *TA*. NEW HEY, 1566 WillY, *v.* nīwe, (ge)hæg 'enclosure'. NEW HO, possibly *Newehouse* 1590 WillY, *v.* nīwe, hūs. NEW ING, *Newynge* 1499 *WCR* 2, 1625 *YAS* 28, 5, *v.* nīwe, eng 'meadow'.

OAKNER CLOUGH, 1843 O.S. OLD ASH. OLD CLOUGH. OLD-GATE CLOUGH. OLD HO, *Old House Ing* 1850 *TA*. OLD MOUNT, *Mount* 1817 M, *v.* mont 'hill'. OTTIWELLS HO, *Ottowells* (*Ing*) 1850 *TA*, probably the ME pers.n. *Otto*, wella. OWLERS, FAR OWLERS, (*Nether*) *Olers* 1771 M, *Owlers* 1817 M, *Owlers Head* 1850 *TA*, *v.* alor 'alder-tree'. OX HO, *Ox H.* 1771 M.

PARK, 1771 M, *v.* park. PETERS. PIPER HOLES, PIPERS, PIPER STONES. PLANES HO, *le*(*z*) *Playnes* 1623, 1625 *YAS*, *v.* plain 'a piece of flat meadowland'. PUDDING REAL CLOUGH. PULE BENTS & HOLES, *Pule Moss* 1843 O.S., *Pule Bents Pasture, Pule Holes* 1850 *TA*, *v.* Pule Hill 277 *supra*, beonet 'bent-grass', mos 'swamp', hol[1]. PURL CLOUGH, cf. Purlwell 180 *supra*, clōh 'dell'.

RAMS CLOUGH, 1843 O.S., *v.* hræfn 'raven' or ramm, clōh. RAVEN ROCKS. READY CARR, 1850 *TA*, *v.* hrēodig 'reedy', kjarr 'marsh'. REDBROOK, 1843 O.S. REDMIRE LEE. RIGG SHAW. ROCKLY'S SPRING. ROSE HILL. ROTCHER WOOD, cf. Rocher i, 226 *supra*. ROUGH LEE, 1817 M, *v.* rūh, lēah. ROUND HILL, 1850 *TA*. ROW GREAVES. GREAT RUSHBED, 1843 O.S., *v.* risc, bedd. RUSHY SIKE CLOUGH.

SANDHILL COTTAGES. SCAR HEAD. SCOUT, 1771 M, *v.* skúti 'overhanging rock'. SCOUT HOLES. SHAW HEYS, *Shaw Heys Moss* 1843 O.S., *v.* sceaga 'copse', (ge)hæg, mos 'swamp'. SHINY BROOK CLOUGH, 1843 O.S. SHORT GRAIN, cf. Long Grain *supra*. SHOT SCAR. SIDE ING, *Side Ing Bottom* 1850 *TA*. SIKE CLOUGH. SLADES. SMALL CLOUGH. SMATELY BANK. SMITHY HOLME.

SPARTH, 1817 M, *Sparg* 1764 *Glebe*; this el. occurs a few times in minor names in YW and Db 749; it is probably connected with Icel *sparð* 'sheep droppings' (this also may be the source of ME *spart*, a term of abuse in the Towneley Play xii, 271); cf. Taythes 68 *supra* for a similar name.   SPINKS MIRE MILL, *Spink Mire Mill* 1843 O.S., *v.* Spinks Mire 285 *infra*.   SPOUT ING, 1850 *TA*, *v.* spoute, eng. SPRING HEAD, *Spring House* 1843 O.S.   STACK END.   STANLEY Ho, *Stoneleker* 1426 *Ramsd*, -*carre* 1461 *MinAcct* 09, *v.* stān, lēah, kjarr.   STONE FOLDS.   STONEPIT LEE, *Stone Pitt Field* 1850 *TA*. STOTLEY MOSS.   STUBBING, 1850 *TA*, *v.* stubbing 'clearing'. SWELLANDS.

THIEVES CLOUGH.   TOM CLOUGH.   TONG LEE, *Townley Head* 1771 M.   TOWN GATE.   FAR & NEAR TROUGHS, *Trough(s)* 1771, 1817 M, *v.* trōg 'a valley'.

WARCOCK (HILL), *Warecock Hill* 1850 *TA*, *v.* wer-cok (describing some unidentified bird), hyll.   WARDS END.   WELL CLOSE, cf. *Well Bank & Ing* 1850 *TA*.   WHAM HEAD, cf. *Long Wham* 1843 O.S., *v.* hvammr 'a small valley'.   WHITE HASSOCK, 1771, 1817 M, *v.* hwīt, hassuc 'clump of coarse grass'.   WHITE HULL.   WHITE LEE, 1771 M, *v.* hwīt, lēah.   WHITE MOSS, 1843 O.S., *v.* hwīt, mos 'swamp'.   WHITE SIKE, *v.* sīc 'stream'.   WICKEN GRAIN, *Wicking* 1843 O.S., *v.* cwicen, dial. *whicken* 'mountain ash' (for *w*- for *cw*- cf. Phonol. § 39), grein 'river-fork'.   WICKING CLOUGH & GREEN, cf. prec.   WILLYKAY CLOUGH.   WILLMER GREEN.   WINDY BANK, 1843 O.S.   WINTER CLOUGH, 1843 O.S., *v.* winter, clōh.   THE WOOD, WOOD BOTTOM, 1850 *TA*.   WOODS, *Woods Rough* 1850 *TA*. WORLOW, *War Low* 1843 O.S., probably hār[2] 'grey' (also in the sense 'boundary'), hlāw 'mound, hill'.

FIELD-NAMES

The principal forms in (*a*) are 1850 *TA* 276. Spellings dated 1426, 1568 are *Ramsd*, 1487 *MinAcct* 66, 1623 *YAS* 76, 21, 1625 ib 28, 5, 1771 M.

(*a*) All Croft, Apple Tree Close, Beard Close, Bedding Hill, Bent Ing (*v.* beonet, eng), Black Moor Holme, Brink (*v.* brink), Broad Bottom, Broad Head, Broken Holme, Bryan Holme, Calf Close & Hey, Calf Holme, Channel Wood, Chapel Close, Clack Hey (*v.* klakkr 'hill', (ge)hæg), Coat Close (*v.* cot), Corn Bank, Croft Top, Dam Bank, Delph Hill (*v.* (ge)delf 'quarry'), Dyson Ing (the YW surname *Dyson*, eng), Even Close, Far & Near Fallow (*v.* falh), Flash Ing (*v.* flasshe 'swamp', eng), Furley Hole, Gledhill Ing, Grass Hey, Great Acre, Green Hurst (*v.* grēne[1], hyrst 'wood'), Haddon, Hatch Green 1771, Haw Walk, Hebble Close (cf. Salterhebble iii, 110 *infra*), Hole Top (ib 1771, *Hoyle Top* 1817 M, *v.* hol¹ 'a hollow', topp), Hole Wood, Hollin Tree Close, Idle Row, Kiln Croft, Laith Holme (*v.* hlaða 'barn', holmr 'water-meadow'), Lamb Croft & Slacks, Law Ing, Lees (*v.* lēah), Ley Field, Little Royd, Long Acre, Long Holme, Long Lees (*Longleybothe* 1426, 1487, *v.* lang, lēah, bōth 'booth'), Long Shutt (dial. *shut* 'a division of land'), Mark Holme, Marl Hill, Michael Field, Nether Brook, New Break, New Goit (*v.* gota 'water-channel'), New Intake (*v.* intak), Nodding Hill, Nook by Road (*Nook* 1771, *v.* nōk), Old Hey, Owl Nest (*v.* ūle, nest, cf. Crow Nest 186 *supra*), Ox Close, Patch Wood, Pellet Royd (*v.* pil-āte 'pill-oats', rod¹), Pignot Close, Pig Tail, Pinfold (*v.* pynd-fald), Pinglet, Prickle Acre, Prim, Rawnsley Foot, Rough Hey, Rush Holme (*v.* risc, holmr), Salter Hole, Shop Croft, Shrogg (*v.* scrogge 'brushwood'), Soho Holme, Stanning Stone Close ('standing stone'), Steanhold, Steem-cross (possibly contracted from *Stephencross*), Stoney Brow, Stope Hey, Tenter Croft, Three Nooks, Tilbero Close, Toad Hole 1817 M, Turf Hill (*Turuehilebank* 1487, *v.* turf, hyll, banke), Twitchell Hey (dial. *twitchel* 'a narrow passage', (ge)hæg), Upper Brook, Venus Hades, Waife Holes, Waith Holes (*v.* veiðr 'hunting, fishing', hol¹), Whin Hill Wood (*v.* hvin 'gorse'), Winnow Hill, Winter Hill.

(b) *Blenbothe* 1487 (*v.* bōth), *le Chapell ende* 1568 (named from *Marshesden chapell* 1577 Holinshed, *Mershden Chappell* 1627 DodsN, *v.* chapel), *Cleyn-legbothe* 1487 (*v.* clǣne 'clean', lēah, bōth), *Cowhey* 1625 (*v.* cū, (ge)hæg), *Eschape* 1426, *Fearnyholme* 1625 (*v.* fearnig, holmr), *Greeneleyboothe* 1426 (*v.* grēne, lēah, bōth), *Outpasture* 1623, *Shipleyboothe* 1426, *Shipleywode* (*v.* scēap, lēah, bōth, but the first el. may be a surname from Shipley iii, 267 *infra*), *Stonigate hede* 1568 (*v.* stānig, gata).

10. MELTHAM (102–0910)

Meltha' 1086 DB, *Meltham* 1255 FF, 1297 LS, 1328 YD i, 1347, 1361 DodsN *et passim* to 1588 LS, -*hame* 1583 WillY, 1608 FF, *Melteham* 13 YD i, 1388 DodsN, *Muletham* 1316 Vill, *Meltam* 1405 YD 24, 1421 YD i. Both Goodall and Ekwall base their etymologies on the 1316 spelling *Muletham*, Goodall deriving the name from a Swed dial. word *mylte* 'cloudberry' and Ekwall from an OE *mylen-geat* 'mill-gate', but the 1316 Vill spellings tend to be unreliable and neither of these suggestions will account for what are the obviously predominant and original *Melt(e)ham* forms; OE *y* does not become *e* in YW (cf. Phonol. § 33). There is an ON byname *Mjalti*, which would accord with the spellings, but it would be unusual to have a hybrid compound with OE hām 'homestead'. Moorman proposed that the first el. should be connected with OE *meltan* 'to melt, consume by fire'; we may also add YW dial. *melt* 'to prepare barley for fermentation' (cf. ON *melta* 'to make malt'); the exact form of the first el. cannot be determined, but it could be either *melt 'melting, smelting, malting' or *melta 'smelter'; there are old coal workings in this township.

HELME, 1634 WillY, *the Helme* 1421 YD i, 1547 WB, *Elm* 1771 M. *v.* helm 'a shelter, a cattle-shed'; the name occurs several times in YW.

THICK HOLLINS, 1822 Langd, *Thykholyns* 1418 *YD* 25, *Thyhholyns* 1537 FF, *Thickhollens* 1589 WillY, *-hollings* 1626 *WB* 73, 1817 M, *Thickeholling* 1640 WillY, *v.* þicce[2] 'thick, dense', holegn 'holly-tree', cf. Thick Hollins f.n. 262 Thick Hazle f.n. 271 *supra*, *Thick Hollins* iii, 47, *Thick hassalls* iii, 16 *infra*.

ASH ROYD. BANISTER EDGE, 1849 *TA*, the surname *Banister*, ecg. BANK WOOD, 1843 O.S. BELLE VUE. BELLMAN CASTLE. BENT LEY, *Benty Lee* 1849 *TA*, *v.* beonet 'bent-grass', lēah. BLACK MOOR, 1843 O.S., BLACK MOOR FOOT, 1817 M, *v.* blæc, mōr, fōt. BLUE SLATE. BOLE BENT, *Bollbents* 1849 *TA*, BOLE HOLE, *v.* bol 'rounded hill' or bola 'tree-trunk', beonet 'bent-grass', hol[1]. BRACKEN HILLS. BROADLANDS, 1849 *TA*. BROW, *The Brow* 1656 WillS, 1843 O.S., *v.* brū. BULL RING. BURNED HILL. CALF CLOSE DIKE, *Calf Close (Wood)* 1849 *TA*. CALMLANDS, 1849 *TA*. COLDERS, *Collder clough* 1547 *WB*, *Calders* 1771 M, *v.* cald, ears. COPLEY HO, cf. Meltham Cop *infra*. LOWER & UPPER COTE, *Low Cote, Cote Head* 1849 *TA*, *v.* cot 'cottage'. COWBERRY HOLES. CRADDIN HOLES, *Cradenholes* 1652 *WB* 59, *Cradding Holes* 1849 *TA*, probably from ME craþayn 'coward', dial. *cradden* 'a coward', in Scots also 'a dwarf' and then 'a daring feat, a challenge, a mischievous trick' (*v.* EDD s.v.), and hol[1]; what element of folklore lies behind this is not known, but it may correspond to such names as *Dwarfholes* Wa 32; cf. Crodingley 287 *infra*. CROFT HO, *Croft Top* 1849 *TA*, *v.* croft. DEER HILL, 1849 *TA*, *v.* dēor, hyll. DRY CLOUGH, 1843 O.S., 'dell without a stream', *v.* drȳge, clōh. DUN-NOCK RD, *Dunnock* 1849 *TA*, probably a reduced form of a p.n. containing OE dunnoc 'hedge-sparrow'. DURKER ROODS. FEATHER-BED MOSS, a name which recurs in this moorland area (306, 314 *infra*), probably a figurative description of soft boggy moor. FIELD HEAD, cf. *Field Ing* 1849 *TA*. FLAKE MOSS, *Fleak Gap & Moss* 1849 *TA*, probably dial. *flake* in one of its senses, 'a hurdle, a temporary sheep-pen, a temporary gate set up in a gap', *v.* gap, mos 'swamp'. FOX

ROYD GREEN, 1849 *TA*, *v.* fox, rod[1], grēne[2].　GILL BIRKS, 1849 *TA*, *v.* birki 'birch-tree', the first el. is probably the ME pers.n. *Gille*.　GLEDHOLT, 13 DodsN, 'kite wood', *v.* gleoda, holt, cf. Gledholt 297 *infra*.　GOIT, *v.* gota 'water-channel'.　GOLCAR BROW & HALL, *Golcar Brow & Hill* 1849 *TA*, named from Golcar 291 *infra* (probably here a surname), *v.* brū, hyll.　GRAINS ASH, 1849 *TA*, *v.* grein 'river-fork', æsc.　GREASY SLACK.　GREAVE DIKE, LOWER GREAVE, *Greave* 1843 O.S., *v.* græfe 'copse'.　GREEN BOTTOM, 1849 *TA*, *v.* grēne[1], botm.　GREEN END, *Greens End* 1849 *TA*, *v.* grēne[2], ende.　GREEN GATE LANE, *Greengate* 1849 *TA*, *v.* grēne[1], gata.　GREEN SLACK.　HALFROODS, 1849 *TA*, *v.* half, rōd[2] 'a rood, measure of land'.　HARDEN CLOUGH & HILL, *Harding* 1709 WMB, *Harden Foot* 1849 *TA*, HARDEN MOSS, 1843 O.S., *v.* hara 'hare', denu 'valley'.　HAREWOOD BRIDGE, 1849 *TA*, *v.* hara 'hare', wudu, brycg.　HASSOCKS RD.　HEADY FIELDS, possibly identical with *le Hedynges* 1421 YD i, ME *hefding* 'heading', 'headland of the common field' (cf. Haddings 204 *supra*).　HEBBLE HEAD, cf. Salterhebble iii, 110 *infra*.　HEY GREEN, 1849 *TA*, LOWER & UPPER HEY, *Lower Hay* 1771 M, *Heys* 1843 O.S., *Upper Hey Top* 1849 *TA*, *v.* (ge)hæg 'enclosure', grēne[2].　THE HEYS, 1843 O.S., *Hay, New Hay* 1771 M, *Hey Houses* 1817 M, cf. prec.　HIGH MOOR, 1849 *TA*.　HOLLOW.　HOLT HEAD.　ING HO, cf. *Ing Sike* 1849 *TA*, *v.* eng 'meadow', sīc 'stream'.　INTAKE.　KAY STONE PITS, *Kaye Stone Quarry* 1849 *TA*.　KNOWL TOP.　LAGGIN PLAT.　THE LAITH, *Laith Close & End* 1849 *TA*, *v.* hlaða 'barn'.　LANE DIKE, 1849 *TA*, *the Lane dyke* 1744 WB 77, *v.* lane, dīc.　LANE SIDE, 1817 M.　LATHE, *Lathes* 1771 M, *v.* hlaða 'barn'.　LAUND, *Laund Quarry* 1849 *TA*, *v.* launde 'glade'.　LAW COYT, *Low Cote* 1849 *TA*, *v.* cot 'cottage', the modern form represents the local dial. pronunciation.　LEGARDS SLACK, LEYGARDS LANE, named from the family of *William Ledgard* (1741 WB vii, 77), *v.* slakki 'a hollow'.　LITTLE MOSS.　MADGE KNOLL, *Madge Knowl* 1849 *TA*, MAGDALEN CLOUGH, 1843 O.S., MAGDALEN HILL, *Maggledon Top* 1849 *TA*, from the fem. pers.n. *Magdalen*, of which *Madge* here appears to be a pet-form, *v.* cnoll, clōh, hyll.　MARTEN NEST, *Martin Nest* 1849 *TA*, cf. Crow Nest 186, Martin's Nest 244 *supra*.　MEAL HILL, 1849 *TA*, *v.* mæle 'multi-coloured', hyll, cf. Meal Hill 244 *supra*.　MEAN LANE.　MELTHAM COP, 1843 O.S., *the Copp in Meltham* 1601 WB, *Cop* 1817 M, *Cop End* 1849 *TA*, *v.* copp 'a peak', denoting here a prominent peaked hill, which also gives its name to

Copley *supra*. MELTHAM EDGE, 1843 O.S., *v.* ecg 'escarpment'.
MELTHAM GRANGE & HALL. MELTHAM MOOR. MILL HEAD,
Millmoor Head 1849 *TA*, MILL MOOR, 1849 *TA*, *v.* myln, mōr.
MILLSTONE HILL. MOOR FORD HILL, 1849 *TA*. LOWER & UPPER
MOUNT. MUDDY BROOK. NEW BRIDGE, 1843 O.S. OLDFIELD
HILL. OLDHAM SPRING. OWLER BARS, 1849 *TA*, *v.* alor 'alder-
tree', barre. PAN, PANVILLE. PICKLE, 1849 *TA*, *Pighell* 1677 *WB*
76a, *the Pighill brow* 1744 ib 77, *v.* pightel 'enclosure'. POPLEY
BUTTS, 1849 *TA*, *-Coates* 1817 M, probably a surname (cf. Popeley
iii, 15), butte, cot. RAMS CLOUGH, 1699 *WCR* 1, *v.* ramm 'ram' or
hræfn 'raven', clōh. RIDGE BUSK, 1849 *TA*, *v.* hrycg, buskr
'bush'. ROCKING STONE(s). ROUGH NOOK, 1849 *TA*, *Nook* 1843
O.S., *v.* rūh, nōk. ROUND HILL. ROYD, *Royd(e)* 1654 *WB* 75a,
1744 *WB* 77, 1771 M, *v.* rod[1] 'clearing'. ROYD EDGE, 1849 *TA*, *v.*
prec., ecg 'escarpment'. RUSHY GROVE, 1849 *TA*. THE SCOPE,
1843 O.S., perhaps representing a local pronunciation of dial. *scalp*
(YW *scaup, scope*) 'a bare dry piece of stony ground, thin soil barely
covering the rock beneath' (EDD), cf. The Scalp 23, Kellingley Scalp
56 *supra*. SHOE BROADS, 1849 *TA*, 'narrow strips of land', *v.* scofl,
brǣdu. SHOOTERS NAB, *Shorter Nab* (sic) 1817 M, *v.* scēotere
'archer', nabbi 'knoll'. SLACK GREEN, 1843 O.S., *v.* slakki 'a
hollow', grēne[2]. SLADES LANE, *Slades* 1849 *TA*, *v.* slæd 'a valley'.
SLATE PITS. SNAPE CLOUGH, UPPER SNAPE, *Snape Clough & Quarry*
1849 *TA*, *v.* snæp 'boggy ground' or snap 'poor pasture'. SPARK
GREEN, 1843 O.S., *v.* spearca 'brushwood', grēne[2]. SPINKS MIRE,
1764 *Glebe*, the first el. is ME *spynke* 'finch' (or the surname *Spink*
derived from it) or dial. *spink* 'a bog-hole', *v.* mýrr 'marsh'. SPRING
HEAD, *Spring Brow & Hill* 1849 *TA*. SUNNY BANK, 1849 *TA*.
SUN ROYD, 1849 *TA*, *San Royd* (sic) 1817 M, *v.* rod[1]. SWINSEY
DIKE. TINKER LANE. TOWN GATE. WAITHE CROSS, cf. *Waith
Close* 1849 *TA*, *v.* veiðr 'hunting', cros, cf. Waife Holes 282 *supra*.
WEARLEY, *Wearley Moor* 1849 *TA*, cf. *Wear Ings* ib, *v.* wer 'weir',
lēah, eng; it is on the hillside near Meltham Dike. WENTWORTH,
1849 *TA*, probably named from Wentworth i, 120 *supra*. WEST
GATE. WEST NAB, 1817 M, *West Knab* 1771 M, *v.* west, nabbi 'a
knoll'. WET HILL. WETLANDS, 1849 *TA*, *v.* wēt 'wet', land.
WHITE HOLES. WICKEN STONES, cf. Wicken Grain 281 *supra*.
WILSHAW, 1849 *TA*. WINDY BANK. WOOD NOOK, 1771 M, *v.*
wudu, nōk.

FIELD-NAMES

The principal forms in (a) are 1849 *TA* 281. A few marked *mod* are modern (1930).

(a) Ann Heys, Back o' th' Laith, Back o' th' Mill, Birchin Ing *mod* (*Burchen Ing TA*, *v.* bircen, eng), Birmingham, Blackearth, Black Shaw (*Blakeshaws* 1764 *Glebe*, *v.* blæc, sceaga 'copse'), Bowers Lot, Briery Dole (*v.* brērig, dāl), Calf Hey, Cern Close, Clay Butts *mod*, *TA*, Clocking Lands, Dagger Close, Dam Close & Field, Dean (*v.* denu 'valley'), Dear Wood, Dud, Dud Ing, East Field, Elid's Hey, Elm Spring (*v.* elm, spring 'plantation'), Felk Cliffe, Fog Close (*v.* fogga 'long grass'), Folly Field, Garlick Hey, Gillup Royd, Gledhill Stones, Green Hey, Hanging Royd, Harp, Hives Yard, Hollin Carr (*mod*) & Close (*v.* holegn 'holly'), Holme Bottom (*v.* holmr), Honley Bridge Bottom (*Honley Bridge close* 1764 *Glebe*, *v.* Honley 271 *supra*, brycg), Leaning Close, Linthwaite Cross (*v.* Linthwaite 273 *supra*, cros), Lower Brinks, Lower Riding, Mown Hey, Murphy Lot, Near Toft *mod* (*v.* topt 'enclosure'), New Field, Newland, North Croft, Old Hey (*v.* (ge)hæg), Parlour, Peas Close & Hill (*v.* pise 'pease'), Ranald Brow & Royd, Redmary Slack, Rock Close, Rough Hey Head, Scarr Croft, Siddall Hey, Slack o' th' Moor (*v.* slakki 'a hollow'), Smithy Croft, Stamperstones, Stoney Butts, Stubble Hey, Summer Hey, Sun Croft, Sykes Ashes, Three Nooks, Toad Hole, Towns Slack, Two Brinks, Washfold Close, Well Ing, Westfield, Lower & Middle Wham (*v.* hvammr 'a small valley'), Whin Close (*v.* hvin 'gorse'), Yeoman Ing.

11. Netherthong (102–1309)

Thoying 13 YD i
Thoung 1309 WCR
Thwonges 1313 WCR, *Thwong(e)* 1323 *MinAcct* 45, 1324 WCR, 1369 FF, 1389 DodsN, 1459 Calv, 1709 WMB, (*Nether-*) 1610 *YAS* 28, 4
Thwenge 1454 DodsN   *Twyng'* 1462, 1492 *MinAcct* 99, 02
Nethyrthonge 1448 YD i, *Nether Thonge* 1658 WillS, *Nether Thongue* 1647 YDr, 1764 *Glebe*
Twhonge 1486 YD v
Nethertwonge 1578 WillY

This name and the adjacent Upperthong 288 *infra* are from OE þwang 'a thong' and then 'a narrow strip of land'; cf. Thwing YE 113 from a related þweng. Whilst the name may refer to some unidentified strip of land, it would be an unusual coincidence if it did not allude to a narrow strip of land, varying in width from 50 to 100 yards and over 2 miles long, which joins the two parts of Upperthong township; the strip, which separates Austonley and Meltham townships, extends from Wheels Brook to Heath Cottage, and, though the administrative boundary has now disappeared, it can be seen on 6″ O.S. (1904 ed.) 272 NW. A similar unusual strip used to occur at Sowerby Ramble iii, 161 *infra*.

CRODINGLEY, *Craȝanley* 13 YD i, *Croadingley* 1851 *TA*; the earlier spelling is probably a misreading of or stands for *Craþan-*; this el. would appear to be ME *craþayn* 'a craven' (*Gawayn* 1773), later *crat(h)on*, *crayon* (NED s.v.) and NCy dial. *cradden* 'a coward, a dwarf' (as in Craddin Holes 283 *supra*). The latter also has the form *crawdon* [krɔːdən] in YW, and in Scots use it has been associated with *crow-down* 'to crow or cry down'. *v.* lēah.

BROWN HILL, 1771 M, *v.* brūn, hyll. CALF HILL WOOD, *Calffall Ing* 1573 *YAS* 28, 7, *Calf Hole Lands & Wood* 1851 *TA*, *v.* calf, (ge)fall 'clearing', wudu. CARR, *Great & Long Carr, Carr Ing* 1851 *TA*, *v.* kjarr 'marsh', eng. CHILD O' TH' EDGE, *Child of the Hedge* 1851 *TA*, the name of a smaller hill standing out of the ridge of Wolfstones Height; hence *child* is here used like *calf* (as in Cow and Calf Rocks (Ilkley) pt. iv *infra*), *v.* ecg. CRIMBLES, (*le*) *Crimble* 1610 *YAS* 28, 4, 1851 *TA*, *v.* crymel 'a small piece of land'. DOCK HILL. ELM, ELMWOOD. FOLLY DAM. HAR ROYD. HOLMLEIGH, *Holme* 1709 WMB, *v.* holmr. MARK BOTTOMS, *Marke bothom* 1709 WMB, perhaps identical with *Morkelbothom* 273 *supra*, *v.* botm. MOOR GATE, 1843 O.S., *v.* mōr, gata. MOOR LANE, cf. *Moorbrooke* 1709 WMB. NEWLANDS, (*the*) *Newland* 1573 *YAS* 28, 7, 1709 WMB, *v.* nīwe, land. OAKLANDS, *the Okelandes* 1610 *YAS* 28, 4, *v.* āc, land. OUTLANE. OX LANE. ROBIN ROYD, 1851 *TA*, the pers.n. *Robin*, rod[1] 'clearing'. SANDS, *the Sandes* 1573 *YAS* 28, 7, *v.* sand. SOMERFIELD. SPRING GROVE & WOOD, cf. *Spring Bottom* 1851 *TA*, *v.* spring 'plantation'. THONGS BRIDGE, *v.* 255 *supra*. THONG MOOR, cf. Moor Gate, Moor Lane *supra*. TOWN GATE. WELL GREEN, *Wells Green* 1843 O.S., *v.* wella, grēne[2]. WELL HO 1851 *TA*. WICKINS DIKE, cf. *the Whicken Greave* 1764 Glebe, *Wiggin Greave, Wickens* (*Ing*) 1851 *TA*, *v.* Wicken Grain 281 *supra*, grǽfe 'copse', eng. WOLFSTONES, *Woolf Stones* 1771 M, *v.* wulf, stān.

FIELD-NAMES

The principal forms in (*a*) are 1851 *TA*. Spellings dated 13 are YD i, 1308 WCR, 1573 *YAS* 28, 7.

(*a*) Boggard Close, Broomy Lee, Chapel Croft, Coit Ing (*v.* cot 'cottage', eng), Crabtree Close, Crooked Hill (*the neyther Crokyd tayll* 1573, 'crooked tail of land', *v.* tægl), Crow Royd (*v.* cräwe, rod[1]), Crowther Close (the surname *Crowther*), Daisy Lee, Dod Royd (*Dogret hirst* 1573), Gill Ing, Healy Lands, Far & Near Hollins (*v.* holegn 'holly'), Lower & Upper Holt (*v.* holt 'wood'), Horse Close, Ings Ley & Wood (*v.* eng 'meadow', lēah), Kiln Acre, Laith Close, Lamb Croft, Ledgits (*v.* hlid-geat 'swing-gate'), Lighting Croft, March Croft, Millgate Wood (*v.* myln, gata), Mill Ing, Netherwood Close, Old Royd (*Olderode* 13, *v.* ald, rod[1] 'clearing'), Ox Close, Petty Royd (*Pedderroid* 1573, *v.* peddere 'pedlar', rod[1]), Pigh Hill (*v.* pightel 'enclosure'), Pistol Clough Wood, Rape Dust, Raw Cliffe Holling, Round Ing, Rye Croft, Smith Ing, Starr Royd (*v.* stǫrr 'sedge', rod[1]), Stone Pit Close, Little & Nether Stubble, Stubs, Sunny Cliffe, Tib Hey, Tom Royd, Tunnercliffe Bottom (*v.* foll., clif), Tunner Croft (*Turnurtoft* 13, *The Tunna Croft* 1764 *Glebe*, ME *tournere* 'a turner' (perhaps as a surname), topt, croft 'enclosure'), Walk Lands (cf. *Walke mylne* 1573, *v.* walc 'fulling', land, myln), Wall Lands, West Field, Wheat Ing, Lands & Royd, Whinny Reaps, Winn Close (*v.* hvin 'gorse'), Wood Wright Royd ('wood-worker's clearing', *v.* rod[1]), Yield Bank.

(*b*) *Bordeland* 1462 *MinAcct* 99, *Boreland* 1492 ib 02 (ME *bordland* 'land held by a bordar'), *the Damme Head* 1573 (*v.* dammr), *Esttwoyts* 13 (*v.* ēast, þveit), *Haygateker* 13 (*v.* (ge)hæg, gata, kjarr), *Lyncrofte* 1573 (*v.* līn 'flax', croft), *Thwonges greyve* 1575 (*v.* grǣfe 'copse').

12. UPPERTHONG (102–1208)

Thwnge 1274 WCR

Thwong(e) 1274, 1277, 1313 WCR, 1366 YD i, (*Uver-*) 1297 WCR, (*Ouer-*, *Over-*) 1315 ib, 1408, 1572 *WCR*, 1577 WillY, 1618 FF, *Overthwonges* 1314 WCR

Thoung(e) 1275, 1307, 1308 WCR, (*Hover-*) 1275 ib, *Overthownge* 1590 WillY

Overtong 1544 WillY

Thonge 1575 FF, *Overthonge* 1587 WillY

v. Netherthong 286 *supra*; for the affix, *v.* uferra 'upper'.

BURNLEE, *le* (*Ouer*)*birnedleghsike* 1489 *WCR* 1, 1492 *MinAcct* 02, *Barnleyparkehede* 1489 *WCR* 1, *Burnlee* 1638 WillY, *Burnley* 1709 WMB. 'Burnt clearing', *v.* brende (ME *berned*), lēah, sīc.

HOLMFIRTH (partly in Wooldale, Nether-, Upperthong, now the name of the urban district, *v.* 236 *supra*).

(*le*) *Holnefrith* 1274–1324 WCR (*freq*), *-frythes* 1286 ib, *-fr'* 1297 LS, 1307 WCR, *Holnfryhtes* 1313 ib, *foresta de Holne* 1274 ib *Holnesfrith* 1274 WCR

Holm(e) Frithes 1302 Pat, 1329 AD i, *-frith(e)*, *-fryth* 1304 Pat, 1379 PT, 1402 YI, 1461 Pat *et freq* to 1647 YDr, *-furthe* 1576 WillY, *-forth* 1583 ib, *-firth(e)* 1598 SessnR, 1614 FF *et passim* to 1814 *EnclA* 146

Holmesfryth' 1392 *MinAcct* 88, *-frith* 1405 Pat

Hulmefirth 1657 WillS

'The wood belonging to Holme', *v.* Holme 269 *supra*, fyrhðe. It was in the Graveship of Holme. The use of the gen.sg. in *Holnes-*, *Holmes-* should be noted (*v.* -es² in EPN i, 158). The assimilation of *-n-* to *-m-* is due to the following labio-dental *-f-*, and was extended then to Holme itself.

REAP HILL, 1709 WMB, cf. *Reproide* 1392 *MinAcct* 88; the el. *reap* appears several times in later p.ns., Reaps Wood i, 200 *supra*, Reap Hirst iii, 37, 129, Reaps ii, 309, Reaps Cross iii, 194 *infra*; formally it could be OE *rip* 'harvest, reaping' or preferably OE *reopa* 'a sheaf', used in allusion to arable corn land, but the available material is not early enough to be decisive and most of the places lie in moorland areas or denote woods; the likeliest sense is that of dial. *reap, rip* 'to gather up weeds under the harrow, to grub up wood, bushes, etc.', or ON *hrapi* 'small shrubs', but there are phonological difficulties with the latter.

WHEELS BROOK, *Queles-*, *Welesbothem* 1307 WCR, *Wheelsbrook(e)* 1709 WMB, 1817 M, *v.* hwēol 'wheel', botm, brōc; the allusion is to a valley (Hart Holes Clough) which wheels round below the farm.

LOWER BINNS, BINNS WOOD, *Binfield* 1709 WMB, *Binns Leys & Wood* 1851 *TA*, *v.* binn 'a stall', cf. Binn 277 *supra*. BIRD RIDDINGS, *Bird Riding* 1851 *TA*, the surname *Bird* or bridd 'bird', rydding 'clearing'. BIRKS HO. BLACK DIKE. BLACK GATE, *Blake Gate* 1843 O.S., *v.* blæc, gata or geat. BLACK GROUGH END, *v.* blæc, gróf 'a stream, a stream bed'. BLACK HILL, 1843 O.S. BLACK SIKE. BROAD LANE, *Broad Lane Ing* 1851 *TA*. BROAD SLADE, *v.* slæd 'valley'. BROOK WOOD, cf. *Brook West Field* 1851 *TA*. BUFT SHEEPFOLD. CROW WOOD, 1851 *TA*, *v.* crāwe, wudu. DEAD MAN'S HOLE, cf. *Little Deadman Croft* 1851 *TA*, 'hollow where

a dead man was found'.   DEAN CLOUGH & HEAD, *Deanhead* 1709
WMB, *Little Dean, Dean Slack* 1851 *TA*, cf. the nearby Deanhouse
272 *supra*, v. clōh, slakki 'hollow'.   DEAN HEAD MOSS, 1843 O.S.,
v. prec., mos 'swamp'.   DUN HILL.   ELLENTREE HEAD.   FAIR
LOANS, *v.* fæger, lane.   FERN BANK.   FORD INN, 1843 O.S., *v.*
ford.   FOX HOLES.   GOOD BENT, 1843 O.S., *v.* gōd, beonet 'bent-
grass'.   GOOD GREAVE, 1709 WMB, *v.* gōd, grǣfe 'copse'.   FAR &
NEAR GRAIN, *v.* grein 'river-fork'.   GREAT DIKE.   GREAT HILL.
GREEN, cf. *Great Green* 1851 *TA*.   GREEN LANE, *the Greyn lane* 1573
YAS 28, 7, *v.* grēne[1], lane.   HART HILL.   HART HOLES, *H(e)art*
Holes Croft & Lane 1851 *TA*, *v.* heorot, hol[1].   HEATH COTTAGE,
1843 O.S., *v.* hǣð.   HEBBLE DIKE & LANE, *Hebble Wood* 1764
Glebe, 1851 *TA*, dial. *hebble* 'bridge', cf. Salterhebble iii, 110 *infra*.
THE HEY, 1843 O.S., *Hay* 1771 M, *v.* (ge)hæg 'enclosure'.   HIGH
INGS.   HILL, 1709 WMB, *v.* hyll.   HILLOCK, 1771 M, *Hillack* 1709
WMB, *v.* hylloc.   HOLME EDGE, 1843 O.S., *v.* Holme 269 *supra*,
ecg.   HOLT.   INTAKE, *Intook* 1771 M, *v.* intak.   THE ISSUES,
ISSUE CLOUGH & HEAD.   KAYE EDGE, cf. Kaye Stone Pits 284 *supra*.
LANE.   LIP HILL, *Liphill* 1572 *WCR* 2, 1709 WMB, *Lips* 1851 *TA*,
probably OE *lippa* 'lip' in some topographical or figurative sense,
'resembling a lip', possible also in Lipwood Nb 136; these names are
unlikely to contain OE hlīep 'leap' (which is a WSax form of hlēp).
LOTTERY HALL.   MODD LANE.   NETHER HO, 1709 WMB.   NEW
CLOSE, 1771 M.   NEWLANDS, *Newland Ing* 1851 *TA*, distinct from
Newlands 287 *supra*.   PARK HEAD, *Park House* 1843 O.S.   PRICKLE-
DEN.   SHALEY BOTTOM, *Shalleys* 1709 WMB, *v.* Shaley 254 *supra*.
GREAT & LITTLE SHOOT.   SNAPE, 1575 WillY, *v.* snæp 'boggy land'
or snap 'poor pasture'.   SNAPE CLOUGH, 1843 O.S., *v.* prec., clōh
'dell'.   SNAPLEY MOSS, probably prec. with lēah 'clearing'.
SPRING HEAD.   STOPES MOOR.   TOP OF OLD BURN.   TURTON'S
EDGE, *Turton Edge* 1851 *TA*.   UNDERHILL.   UPPER BANK.
WESSENDEN HEAD, 1843 O.S., *v.* Wessenden 277 *supra*, hēafod.
WICKINS, *Nether Whickins* 1709 WMB, *Upper Wickens* 1851 *TA*, *v.*
Wicking Clough 281 *supra*.

FIELD-NAMES

The principal forms in (*a*) are 1851 *TA* 395. Spellings dated 1308 are
WCR, 1709 WMB.

(*a*) Bank Syke, Barn Royd, Bradshaw Moor, Brearley Close, Upper
Broom, Clay Butts, Clegg Bottom, Coal Gap Close, Coal Pit Gap, Coldwell

Ing, Cooper Flatt (*Cowp' Flatt* 1709 WMB, the surname *Cowper*, flat), Corn Close, Cross Croft (cf. *the Crosse* 1590 WillY, *v.* cros, croft), Crow Royd Wood, Dickroyd (*Dikrode* 1392 *MinAcct* 88, the ME pers.n. *Dikke*, rod[1]), Dog Stoke, Fearnley Wood, Flint Hill, Foal Close, Hacker Edge Top, Half Acre, Hill Top 1771 M, Hoist, Hollingwell, Hollinwood (*v.* holegn 'holly'), Horse Close, Human Field, Jennet Hoyle (*Gennit Hole* 1779, the fem. pers.n. *Jennet* (*Janet*), hol[1]), Jumble (Royd), Knowl Heights, Little Intake, Long Leys, Lydgate (*v.* hlid-geat 'swing-gate'), Matlock (Croft), Mellor Edge, Mill Dam, Mistal (dial. *mistal* 'cow-shed'), Oven Stone, Pick Hill (*v.* pightel 'enclosure'), Pike Low (*v.* pīc[1] 'pike, pointed hill', hlāw), Prickmerebanck 1709 (*Prikmer banke* 1551 *WCR*), Rough Brow, Rye Royd (*Ryeroyds* 1709, *v.* rȳge, rod[1]), Scarr Top, Scatchfield, -fold, Shoe Broad (*v.* scofl, brǣdu), Short Butts (ib 1709, *v.* butte 'abutting strip'), Simeon Wood, Slack Close (*v.* slakki 'a hollow'), Spar Doles (*Sparr doalls* 1709, *v.* spær 'spar', dāl), Stone Pit Close, Sum End, Syke Royd, Taylor Wood, Tenter Croft (ib 1709), Town End & Field, Water Close, Well Lands & Syke, Wetson, Wheat Stubble, Whorestonewood 1709 (*v.* hār 'grey, boundary', stān).

(*b*) *Admundelay* 1308 (the OE pers.n. *Ēadmund*, lēah), *Brerykerre* 1308 (*v.* brērig 'briary', kjarr 'marsh'), *Holmfurthe mylnes* 1540 Test vi (*v.* Holmfirth *supra*, myln), *Johanesrode* 1308 (the ME pers.n. *Johan* (*John*), rod[1]), *Spinkeswell* 1308 (ME spynke 'finch', wella, cf. Ouzelwell 137 *supra*), *Thoungeshirst* 1308 (*v.* Netherthong 286, hyrst 'wood'), *Wadplace* 1584 WillY.

xviii. Huddersfield

The townships in this parish have undergone an administrative re-organisation. The County Borough of Huddersfield includes the townships of Huddersfield, Lindley and Longwood from this parish together with Dalton (223 *supra*) from the parish of Kirkheaton, Almondbury (256 *supra*), part of South Crosland (265 *supra*), Farnley Tyas (267 *supra*) and Lockwood (275 *supra*) from the parish of Almondbury, and Fixby (iii, 35 *infra*) from the parish of Halifax in Morley wapentake. Colne Valley Urban District contains the townships of Golcar, Scammonden and Slaithwaite from Huddersfield parish and Linthwaite (273 *supra*) and Marsden (276 *supra*) from Almondbury parish.

1. GOLCAR (102–1016) [ˈgɔukə]

    Gudlagesarc, -argo 1086 DB, *Gouthelaghcharthes* 1272, 1308 WCR, *Guthlacharwes* 1306 ib, *Goutlackarres* 1286 YI, *Gouthlacharwes* 1306 WCR, *Gouthelakkerres* 1316 ib, *Gouthlokeres* 1428 FA

    Gu-, Goulakarres 13 YD i, *Goulayecarches* 1307 WCR, *Goulagh-carthes* 1309 ib

    Gourocarhes 1284 WCR

Govalacres 1286 DodsN

Goldecar 1337 DodsN, *Gouldeker* 1361 Arm, *-kar* 1488 ib, *Guldecar*
   1398 ib, *Goldkar(r)* 1427 ib, 1437 WB 63, *Goldkard* 1437 YD
   xii, 250

Gowlkar' 1439 YD xii, 250, *Goulkery* 1481 Test iii, *-care* 1578 FF

Goulekar 1451 Arm, *-ker* 1488 ib, *Gowlecar(r)*, *-kar* 1466 WB 64,
   1507 Arm, 1558 WillY

Golker 1504 Ipm, 1555 YD i *et freq* to 1652 WillS, *Golcar* 1534 FF,
   1558 DodsN, *Golkar(re)* 1567 ib, 1589 WillY, 1614 FF

Goolker 1608 FF

Gowker 1715 *Sav*

'Guthlac's shielings', *v.* **erg**. The first el. is an anglicised form of
the ON pers.n. *Guðleikr* or possibly *Guðlaugr*; the predominance of
earlier spellings with *-lac-*, *-lak-* etc., favours the former (cf. also
Feilitzen 278). The history of the spellings to the present contracted
form is noteworthy. On the significance of this p.n. *v.* Introd.

BOTHAM HALL, *Bothomhaull* 1464 Pat, *-hall* 1542 WillY, 1567 DodsN,
Bothamhall 1481 Test iii, *Bottom Hall* 1817 M. *v.* **botm** (with its
variant **boðm**, which is commonly found in YW), **hall**.

MILNSBRIDGE, 1577 *Tayl*, 1744 *Thn* 168, *Milnebrig* 1645 PREll,
Milnesbrigg 1651 WillS, *-bridge* 1820 EnclA 8, *Millsbridge* 1740 FGr
11, *Miln's Bridge* 1780 Arm. 'Bridge belonging to the mill', *v.* **myln**,
brycg, and on the use of the gen.sg. *v.* EPN i, 158, s.v. *-es²*.

SCARHOUSE, SCAR BOTTOM, SCAR LANE, *Skyr* 1439 YD xii, 250,
Skirhouse 1580 WillY, *Skirehowse* 1619 WB 163, *-bothome* 1586
WillY, *Skyre Lane* 1843 O.S., *Scar Field, Scaur Field* 1851 *TA*.
These places are on a steep rocky declivity, which could be aptly
described by ON **sker** 'a scar', dial. *scar* 'a rocky cliff', but the
regular forms with *Skir(e)*- cannot easily be reconciled with this,
although *sker* does once appear with the l.ME spelling *skyrre* c. 1450
(NED s.v. *scar*); on the treatment of ME *-er-* as occasional *-ir-* cf.
Phonol. § 14. The name may ultimately, however, be of similar
origin to Skier's Hall i, 112 *supra*; cf. also *lez Shyres* (Spofforth) pt. v
infra; in certain other minor names and f.ns., Skyars, *Skyres more,
Skyers supra*, we may have the surname *Skire*, but there is in most
examples the possibility of an ON **skýrr*, a mutated form of Dan
skur 'a hut' or an OE *scȳr(e)* 'hut' (*v.* Addenda).

WESTWOOD, *Westwodd(e)* 1361, 1488 Arm, (*Heighe-*) 1562 ib, (*Highe-*) 1574 WillY, *Hywestwood* 1639 WillY, *Low Westwood* 1659 WillS, *v.* **west, wudu.**

AVERS ROYD. BANK END. BLACKPOOL. BOLSTER MOOR, 1843 O.S., probably OE *bolster* 'bolster' (cf. Bolsterstone i, 257 *supra*), doubtless its use here being paralleled by Featherbed Moss 243 *supra*. BROOK HO, *Brookside* 1843 O.S., *Brook Bottom* 1851 *TA*, *v.* **brōc.** BROOMFIELD, 1851 *TA*, *v.* **brōm, feld.** BUCKLEY HALL. CARR HO, CARR TOP, cf. *Carr Bottom* 1851 *TA*, *v.* **kjarr** 'marsh'. CAUSEWAY FOOT. CLOUGH HEAD, 1771 M, *v.* **clōh** 'dell'. COPLEY BANK, 1851 *TA*, *Copley Stones* 1817 M, *v.* **copp** 'a peak', **lēah.** CRIMBLE, 1635 WillY, *Crymble* 1569 ib, *v.* **crymel** 'a small plot of ground'. DERBY LANE, cf. *South Darby Field* 1851 *TA*, doubtless from *Derby* as a surname. DIKE END. DUNKIRK, 1843 O.S. EASTWOOD HO. EUDEN EDGE. FIELD HO, cf. *Over Field* 1771 M, *Front Field* 1851 *TA*. FREEHOLD. GOLCAR EDGE. GRANGE HO. GREENROYD FM. HALL CROFT, 1851 *TA*. HALL INGS. HANGING ROYD, *Hengenderode* 12 Font, *Hyngandrode* 13 WB 2, *-royd* 1437 YD xii, 250, 'steep clearing', *v.* **hengjandi, rod**[1], a common YW p.n. HART'S HOLE. HAUGHS, *le Hay, del Hagh* 1361 Arm, *Haughe end* 1580 WillY, *v.* **haga** 'enclosure' (confused with (ge)hæg). HEAD-WALL GREEN, 1843 O.S. HEATH HO, 1771 M, *Heyth(e)howse* 1451, 1478 Arm, *Heytehouse* 1451 ib, *the Hathows* 1487 ib, *Hethehous* 1488 ib, *Heath(e)house* 1569, 1573 ib, *v.* **hǣð, hūs.** HIGH WOOD, 1851 *TA*. HILL SIDE, *Golker Hill* 1771 M. HILL TOP, 1843 O.S. HOLLIN HALL, 1771 M, *v.* **holegn** 'holly'. HOLME MILL. INTAKE, *Lower Intake* 1851 *TA*, *v.* **intak.** KILN BROW. KNOWL RD, *Knowl Field* 1820 EnclA, *v.* **cnoll** 'hillock'. LANE END, 1843 O.S. LAUNDS, 1843 O.S., *v.* **launde** 'a glade'. THE LEES, *La Lee* 1324 WCR, *Lower Leigh* 1851 *TA*, *v.* **lēah** 'clearing'. LEYMOOR, 1817 M, *v.* prec., **mōr.** MOORCROFT, *Morecroft* 12 Font, *v.* **mōr, croft.** MOOR HO, cf. *Moorfield* 1851 *TA*. NEW HO. NEW ING. NODDLE. OAKFIELD. OAKWELL. PARK HO, cf. *Park Croft* 1851 *TA*, *v.* **park.** PIKE LAW, 1851 *TA*, *v.* **pīc**[1], **hlāw.** PINFOLD LANE. RIDINGS, 1843 O.S., cf. *Upper Riding* 1851 *TA*, *v.* **rydding** 'clearing'. ROCKING STONE (HILL), *Rockingstone Hill* 1771 M, *the Rocking-stone* 1775 Watson. RYE FIELD, 1851 *TA*. SCAPEGOAT HILL, *Ship Coat Hill* 1817 M, *Scape Goat* 1851 *TA*, originally 'sheep cote', *v.* **scēap, cot, hyll.** THE SHARE, SHAREHILL, cf. *Sharode* 1361 Arm, *v.* **scearu** 'a share of land'. SIMON GREEN, 1851 *TA*. SLADES RD, *Slades Croft* 1851 *TA*, *v.* slæd 'valley'. SMALL LANE, 1851 *TA*. SPA MILL, cf. *Spaw Royd* 1851 *TA*. SPRING HEAD, cf. *Spring Field* 1851 *TA*. STONE LEIGH. SUNNY BANK. SWALLOW LANE, cf. *Swallows Croft* 1851 *TA*. TENTERS, *Tenter Croft* 1851 *TA*. THORP GREEN, possibly identical with *Thorp(e)hall* 1611 *WB* 55, 1646 WillY, *v.* þorp 'outlying farmstead'. TOWN END, *Towneheade* 1639 WillY. UPPER FIELDS, 1817 M. WALLER CLOUGH, 1851 *TA*, the surname *Waller*, clōh 'dell'. WATER HO. WATER ROYD, *Walterrode* 13 Font, the ME pers.n. *Walter*, rod[1] 'clearing'. WELLHOUSE, 1817 M, *Welhouse* 1451 Arm, 1549 WillY, *v.* wella, hūs. WHITWAM BANK, possibly from hwīt, hvammr 'small valley'. WINDOW END, 1851 *TA*. WOOD END, 1579 WillY.

FIELD-NAMES

The principal forms in (*a*) are 1851 *TA* 175 and modern (1935) marked *mod.* Spellings dated 1361 are Arm, 1820 *EnclA* 8.

(*a*) Acres Royd, The Bents *mod* (*Bents Hill TA, v.* beonet), Birks Wood, Bray Wood, Brier(y) Field, Broad Royd, Bull Close, Calf Croft, Churn Hole Gate, Clay Moor 1771 M, Cliffe Ash, Corn Croft, Cow Hey, Cow Pitts, Cromwell, Dam Field *mod*, Dibb Royd, Dolphine, Dow Riding (*Daw(e)-rydynge* 1437 YD xii, 250, 1437 *WB* 63, ME *dawe* 'jackdaw' (cf. Daw Lane 102 *supra*), rydding 'clearing'), Duke Ing, Even Field, Fall Wood (*le Fal* 13 *WB* 2, *v.* (ge)fall 'clearing'), Far Brink, Fenny Hey *mod*, Fosterd Wood, Fox Field, Gale *mod*, Goit Field (*v.* gota 'water-channel'), Goose Pond Hill, Hacking, Hazle Hey, Heap Field, Helen Ing, Hole Ing, Holes, Hollows, Horse Croft, Ingot Style (*v.* stigel 'stile'), Janny Croft, Jarvis Croft, Johnny Bank, Laith Croft & Riding (*v.* hlaða 'barn'), Lamb Hey, Longcroft *mod*, Mean Lands (*v.* (ge)mǣne 'common'), Mill Carr, New Land, Oak Ing, Old Ing, Parlour *mod*, Pig Hills (*v.* pightel 'enclosure'), Pogmire *mod* (*Pog Moor TA*, cf. Pog Moor i, 304 *supra*), Sand Bed Field, Sand Gate Foot, Schorah Field, Shaw Royd & Shrogg (*v.* sceaga 'copse', rod[1] 'clearing', scrogge 'brushwood'), Sheep Ing, Smith Hill, Spittle Bottom, Spot (*v.* spot 'piece of land'), Spout Field & Hill (*v.* spoute), Stack Garth (ON *stakk-garðr* 'stack-yard'), Steanor Wood (*v.* stæner, cf. Stennard Well 151 *supra*), Steanyard, Stone Rings (*v.* stān, hring 'stone circle'), Stubbing (*v.* stubbing), Sun Field, Swamp Field, Sweet Stripes (*v.* strīp), Tom Royd, Under Balk, Urchin Field (*Urchant Field TA*, ME *urchon* 'hedge-hog'), Walk Ing (*v.* walca 'fulling', eng 'meadow'), Well Field (ib 1820), Well Holes, Westfield *mod*, Whin Hill (*v.* hvin 'gorse'), White Goles, Wid Royd, Wilfrey.

(*b*) leʒ *Robberoyd* 1466 *WB* 64 (the ME pers.n. *Robbe*, rod[1]), *Schalyng* 1361 (probably skáling 'a hut'), *Stilbroke* 1361 (OE *stille* 'still, quiet', brōc).

2. HUDDERSFIELD (102–1416) [ˈuðəzfild]

Oderesfelt, Odresfeld 1086 DB

Huderesfeld 1114–31 DodsN, 1127 YCh 1435, 1164–81 ib 1480, 1177–93 ib 1516, 1206–18 YCh viii, 1245 *Nost* 43d, 1297 LS, 1421 Pat, *Huderisfeld* Hy 3 BM

Hudresfeld 12 YCh 1428, 1466, 1497, 1153–60 *Nost* 14, 1164–70 Font, 1215 ChR, 1274 WCR *et freq* to 1362 *Nost* 27, -*feud* l. 12 WB 1, 1208–37 *Nost* 43d, *Hudrisfeld* l. 13 ib 183

Huderefeld 1189 *Nost* 4, *Hudrefeud* a. 1211 DodsN, *Huderfeld* 1219 *Ass* 9

Hoderesfeld 1216 *Nost* 5, 1301 Ebor *et freq* to 1428 FA, -*feud* 1296 LacyComp, 1296 *MinAcct*, *Hodresfeld* 1292 *Nost* 63d, 1294 DodsN *et freq* to 1409 DiocV, *Hoderisfeld* 1286 YD iv

Huddredisfeld 1241 Pat

Huddresfeld 1248 *Nost* 10, 1451 Arm, 1488 Ipm

Hoddresfeld 1248 *Nost* 10, 1252 FF

Hodrefeud 1255 Baild, *Hodrifelde* 1286 Ebor, *Hoderfeld* 1316 Vill, 1379 PT, 1487 *MinAcct* 66, *Hudderfeld* 1428 FA

Hodersfeld 1280 Ch, 1331 *Ass* 6, 1412 *Ramsd*, 1431 YD i, *Hoddirsfeld* 1498 YD xii, 236

Huddersfe(i)ld(e) 1346 YD iv, 1525 Test vi, 1572 WillY, 1615 FF

Hudersfeld 1352, 1504 FF

Hothersfe(i)ld(e) 1540 MonRent, 1609 FF, 1634 YD i, 1637 Arm

Huthersfe(i)ld(e) 1545 NCWills, 1548 FF *et freq* to 1623 FF, -*field* 1638 SessnR, 1695 M *et freq* to 1780 PRAdd, -*fild* 1690 PRMrf

Huddersfield has a similar run of spellings for the first el. to Hothersall La 145, *Hudereshal* 1199, 1201, *Huders-, Hodersale* 1212, 1251, and for both an OE pers.n. *Hud(d)er* has been suggested; this would be a derivative of the OE pers.n. *Hŭd(a)* with an -*r* suffix (cf. Doddershall Bk 110, Wo xxiii). But in view of the single 1241 *Huddredisfeld* spelling it seems probable that in Huddersfield at least we have to deal with an OE pers.n. *Hudræd*. This name is not recorded; the theme *Hŭd-* is found but once in a dithematic pers.n. (in OE *Hudeman* BCS 1130, which Forssner 156 thinks is from OG *Hutuman*); the suffix -*ræd*, -*rēd* is common. Such a pers.n. could be reduced to *Hudres-* from an early date, and parallels to the reduction will be found in Adderstone Nb 2 (*Edredeston* 1233, *Edreston* 1234, from *Ēadrǣd*), Alfrick Wo 28 (*Alcredes-* 1204, *Alfrewike* 1275 from

Alhrǣd), Atherstone Wa 77, Lundsford Sx 456 (*Lundres-*, *Lundes-*
with a single *Lundredisford*, from an unrecorded OE *Lundrǣd*, which
presents problems very similar to those of *Hudrǣd*), etc. 'Hudræd's
piece of open country', *v.* **feld**. The spelling *-feud* is AN (*v.* IPN 113).
On the later dial. forms with *Huther-* cf. Phonol. § 41.

STREET-NAMES. Huddersfield, a town of modern growth, has few street-
names of any antiquity and those are not recorded at all early: CASTLE GATE.
CHAPEL HILL, cf. *Newchappell* 1579, 1586 WillY, *v.* **chapel**, **hyll**.   CHURCH
ST.   FOLLY HALL, 1843 O.S., *v.* **folie**, **hall**.   LOWER & UPPER HEAD
ROW, cf. The Headrow (Leeds) pt iv, *infra*. HIGH ST. KIRKGATE.
MARKET PLACE, 1721 LdsM.   NORTH GATE.   SEED HILL, 1649 *YAS* 28, 2,
'hill sown with corn', from OE *sǣd* 'seed', **hyll**.   SHIRES HILL.   THE
SHORE, SHORE HEAD.   WATER GATE.   WEST GATE.

BRADLEY, *Bradelei*(*a*), *-lie*, *-lai*, *-ley*, *-lay* 1086 DB, c. 1160–1220
YCh 1762–4 (Font), 1202 FF, 1245 *Nost* 43d, 1269 BM, 1274 WCR *et
freq* to 1343 Arm, *le Bradeleys* 13 WB 2, *Braddele*(*ia*) 13 Font, 1299
Nost 183, *Bradley*, *-lay* 1330 Font, 1442 WillY, 1472 Test iii *et freq*
to 1589 FF, (*Nether-*) 1557 *WB* 51, 1566 Arm. 'Broad forest-glade
or clearing', *v.* **brād**, **lēah**. 'Nether' to distinguish it from Bradley
Mills 224 *supra*, which is further up the Colne valley on its other
bank.

COLNE BRIDGE, *pontis illius quem* [the monks of Fountains] *fecerunt
ultra Calne inter Bradeleiam et Hetun* 1170–85 YCh 1692, *pontis ultra
Calne* 1195–1211 ib 1701, *pont' de Calna* 1219 Font 126, *Colmebridge*
1555 WillY, *Colnebridg*(*e*) 1575 ib, 1675 Og, *Cownbridge* 1799
PRHtsd. 'Bridge over the Colne', *v.* R. Colne (RNs.), **brycg**; it
connects Bradley *supra* with Kirkheaton 225 *supra*.

DEIGHTON 1843 O.S., *Dicton*(*a*) 12 Font, 1297 LS (p), *Dictunebroc*
e. 13 Font, *Dythona* 13 DodsN, *Nost* 183, *Dychton* 1284 WCR,
Dighton 1316 Vill, 1459 Test ii *et passim* to 1581 WillY, *Dygton* 1504
FF, *Dyghton als. Dyton* 1616 FF. 'Farmstead with a ditch', *v.* **dīc**,
tūn. The later form *Dighton* represents a common development of
-ct- (cf. Phonol. § 38).

EDGERTON, *Eggerton* 1311 YI, *Hegerton* 1379 PT (p), *Egerton* 1402
FA, 1436 DodsN *et freq* to 1623 FF, *Edgerton* 1512 WB 22, 1560 FF.
The first el. is the OE pers.n. *Ecgheard* or, as Ritter 146 suggests, an
unrecorded OE *Ecghere*, corresponding to OHG *Egiheri*. *v.* **tūn**, and
cf. Egerton 305 *infra* (with which it can be confused), Egerton Ch.

GLEDHOLT

> *Gledeholt(e)* 1296 LacyComp (p), 1298–1316 WCR (*freq*), 1530 WillY
> *Gledholt(e)* 1318 DodsN, 1346, 1445 YD iv, 1505 *Ramsd*, 1541 FF
> *Gleid-, Gleyd(e)holt(e)* 1400 YD iv, 1447 *Ramsd*, 1459 Test ii, 1461 DodsN, 1623 FF
> *Gleadholt* 1412 *Ramsd*

'Wood which kites frequented', *v.* gleoda, holt. On the *Gleid*-forms *v.* Phonol. § 17.

SHEPHERDS THORN, 1817 M, *Shep(p)erdthorn(e)* 1479 Brett, 1557 *WB* 51, 1589 WillY, *Shepethorn* 1481 YD iii, *v.* scēap-hirde, þorn.

WOODHOUSE HILL, *Wodehous* 1383 DodsN, *Wod(d)howse* 1552, 1575 WillY. 'House in the wood', *v.* wudu, hūs.

ALLISON DIKE.   ASH BROW, 1817 M, *v.* æsc, brū.

BALL ROYD RD.   BAY HALL, 1784 *WB* 63, *Bayhall* 1573, 1578 WillY, possibly beg 'berry' or the ME nickname *le Bay* 'brown-haired', hall.   BENTS, cf. *Little Bent, Bent Close* 1851 *TA*, *v.* beonet 'bent-grass'.   BIRKBY, 1771 M, *Birkebye* 1586 WillY, 'birch farmstead', *v.* birki, bȳ.   BLACKHOUSE BRIDGE, *Blackhouse* 1644 WillY, 1687 Arm, *v.* blæc, hūs.   BRACKEN HALL.   BRADLEY GATE, 13 YD iii, 1525 Test vi, *v.* Bradley *supra*, gata 'road'.   BRADLEY HALL, 1547 TC, *Bradlaie haule* 1550 Test vi, *v.* prec., hall.   BRADLEY LANE, 1771 M, *v.* lane.   BRADLEY PARK, 1843 O.S., *v.* park, cf. Park Fm *infra*.   BRADLEY WOOD, *Bradelay Wode* 1289 YD v, *v.* wudu.   BRAEHOLM.   BRIER HILL, 1843 O.S., *v.* brēr, hyll.

CANKER LANE.   CASSEMERE HO.   CHERRY NOOK.   CINDER FIELD HO, *Cinderfield Dyke, Cinderford* 1851 *TA*, *v.* sinder, feld, ford.   CLARE HILL, CLAREMONT.   CLAYTON DIKE.   CLOUGH HO, 1771 M, *Cloghhousse* 1519 *WB* 13, *Cloughhouse* 1554 ib 49, *Cloehouse* 1657 Pick 99, *v.* clōh 'a dell', hūs.   COWCLIFFE, *Cawckiffe* 1656 Pick 75, *v.* clif.

DAM HEAD.   DEEP DIKE.   DELVES FOLD.   DINGLE RD.   DYSON WOOD, 1843 O.S., from the YW surname *Dyson*.

FAR TOWN, 1680 *WB* 228a, *Firtowne* 1586 WillY, *v.* feor, tūn (for which cf. Mickletown 127 *supra*).   FARTOWN GREEN, 1843 O.S., *v.* prec., grēne[2].   FELL GREAVE, 1817 M, *Felgreave* 1677 Arm, -*grave* 1771 M, & FELL GROVE, adjacent farmsteads, from ON fjǫl 'a board, plank' or the surname *Fell*, *v.* grǣfe 'copse', grāf 'grove'.

FIELDHOUSE, 1843 O.S., *Feldehaus* 1571 WillY, *v.* feld, hūs.   FLASH
HO, 1771 M, *Flosh(e) house* 1542 *WB* 43, 1637 WillY, *v.* flasshe
'swamp' (which often appears as *flosshe*), hūs.

GLEN FIELD & LEA.   THE GOIT, *Goit Close* 1851 *TA, v.* gota 'a
water-channel'.   GRANGE FM, *Bradeley Grange* 1421 Pat, *v.* Bradley
supra, grange.   GREENHEAD PARK, *Greneheade* 1581 WillY, *-hed* 1616
FF, *Greenehead* 1651 WillS, 1675 WYD, 'green headland', *v.* grēne[1],
hēafod (in the sense 'hill').   GREENHOUSE RD, *Grenehouse* 1565,
1585, 1592 WillY, *Green House* 1698 Arm, *v.* grēne[1], hūs.

HALL WOOD, 1843 O.S.   HEADLANDS.   HEATON FOLD, *Heton*
13 Font, 'high farmstead', *v.* hēah, tūn, a common YW p.n.; *v.*
fald 'fold, enclosure'.   HEBBLE BECK & BRIDGE, dial. *hebble*
'bridge', *v.* Salterhebble iii, 110 *infra*.   HIGHFIELD.   HIGH PARK,
1843 O.S.   HILLHOUSE, 1784 PRHtsd, *v.* hyll, hūs.   HOLME
MILLS, possibly identical with *Higholme* 1581 WillY, *v.* holmr
'water-meadow'.   HUDDERSFIELD BRIDGE, *Huthersfelde Briddge* 1638
Stansf, *v.* brycg.

INTAKE BANK, *Intack* 1771 M, *-head* 1822 Langd, *v.* intak.

LAMB COTE, 1843 O.S., *Lambecoyte* 1568 WillY, *Lamb Coat* 1817
M, *v.* lamb, cot 'shed'.   LEE HEAD, 1771 M, *v.* lēah 'clearing'.
LONG HILL.   LONGROYD LANE, doubtless leading to *Long Rodbryg*
1533 FF, 'the Bridge called *longroidebridg* betwene the Towneships
of Huddersfeild and Quarmebie' 1597 SessnR, *Longroyd Bridge* 1547
WB, -brigge 1609 FF, 'long clearing', *v.* lang, rod[1], brycg.   LONG-
WOOD HO, 1817 M, *v.* Longwood 302 *infra*, hūs.   LUNNCLOUGH
HALL.

MARSH, 1644 WillY, 1817 M, *v.* mersc.   MARSH FOLD.   MILL
BECK, MILL GATE, cf. *Mill Close & Pasture* 1851 *TA, v.* myln.
MOLE HILL, cf. Mole's Head 303 *infra*.

NETHEROYD HILL.   NEW HO, 1771 M, *Newhouse* 1631 *WB* 55,
1638 WillY *et freq* to 1756 *WB* 212b, *v.* nīwe, hūs.   NORTH BANK,
1851 *TA*.   NORWOOD RD.

OAKLANDS.   OAKS HO, *del Okes* 1277 WCR (p), *Oaks Ing* 1851
TA, v. āc.   OLD LANE.   OXLEY.

PADDOCK, 1771 M, *Parock* 1576 WillY, *Parrockfoot als. Paddock-
foot* 1766 Arm, *Paddock Foot* 1817 M, *v.* pearroc 'a small enclosure';
paddock is a late variant of this, usually not found before the sixteenth
century; *v.* fōt.   PADDOCK BROW, *Paddock Head* 1843 O.S., *v.* prec.
PARK FM & HILL, cf. *Parkefoote* 1584 WillY, *Far & High Park* 1851
TA, named from Bradley Park *supra*.   PEACE PIT.

RED DOLES, *Reddoor* (sic) 1843 O.S., *v.* dāl 'share of the common land'; the first el. may be rēad 'red'. RIDDINGS, *Far, Near, North Riding(s)* 1851 *TA*, *v.* rydding 'clearing'. ROYDS, 1817 M, *v.* rod[1] 'clearing'.

SCALE HILL. SCREAMER WOOD, 1843 O.S. SHEEPRIDGE, 1843 O.S., *Shepridge* 1557 *WB* 51, *v.* scēap, hrycg. SLANT GATE. SPINKFIELD RD. SPRING WOOD, 1817 M, *v.* spring 'plantation'. STEEP LANE. STONE PIT HILL. STORTH, 1771 M, *v.* storð 'plantation'. SUNNY BANK, 1817 M. SUN WOODHOUSE, *Sun Ho* 1771 M, 'sunny house', cf. Woodhouse *supra*, *Sun Ridings, Sun Royd Ing* 1851 *TA*.

THORN BANK. THORNLEIGH, *Thornyley* 1284 YD i, *v.* þornig 'growing with thorns', lēah.

UPPER LAITHE, *Upper Laith* 1843 O.S., *v.* hlaða 'barn'.

WEST HILL. WHEAT HOUSE RD. WHITACRE LODGE (lost), 1843 O.S., if not from the YW surname *Whitaker*, possibly identical with *Wythacris, Whithacres* 13 YD vi, *Whitacre* 1292 *MinAcct* 26, *v.* hwīt 'white', æcer. WIGGAN LANE. WILLOW LANE. WOOD FIELD, 1851 *TA*. WOODSIDE, 1771 M.

FIELD-NAMES

The principal forms in (*a*) are 1851 *TA* 226 and include some for Lindley and Longwood townships. Spellings dated 12, e. 13, c. 1210 are Font, 13 *WB* 2, 1250, l. 13 *Nost* 43d, 183, c. 1297, 1333, 1436 DodsN vii, 275–280, 1542 *Ramsd*, 1578 *WB* 53, 1585, 1588 WillY.

(*a*) Beck Ing, Berry Close, Lower & Upper Birks (*v.* birki 'birch'), Black Pit Ing, Bottoms, Break Ing, Bridge Royd, (Flat & Hanging) Broad Oak, Broom, Bunkers Hill, Carr Wood (*v.* kjarr 'marsh'), Causeway Close (*v.* caucie), Coal Pit Close, Cow Hey, Cropper Row 1817 M, Cuckolds Clough 1843 O.S., Dog Bolts, Four Days Work, Frith Wood (*Firth Wood* 1843 O.S., *v.* fyrhðe 'wood'), Great Carr (*v.* kjarr), Hall Green, Hanging Lawn (*v.* hangende 'steep', launde 'glade'), Hellewell Syke (*v.* hǣlig, wella, sīc, cf. Holywell Green iii, 50 *infra*), Honey Hall Ing, Horse Bent Close (*v.* beonet 'bent-grass'), Howel Hole, John Royd, Lad Greave (*Lad Greave Wood* 1843 O.S., *v.* ladda, grǣfe 'copse'), Laith Croft (*v.* hlaða 'barn'), Leaning Bank & Brow, Leighton Close (*v.* lēac-tūn 'herb-garden'), Little Ing (*v.* eng 'meadow'), Long Croft, Long Lawns (*v.* launde 'glade'), Maple Tree Riding, Master Royd, Ned Stubbing (*v.* stubbing 'clearing'), New Drop 1843 (cf. Little Drop iii, 151 *infra*), New Ing, North Leys (*v.* lēah), Old Royd (*v.* ald, rod[1] 'clearing'), Owler Close & Ing (*v.* alor 'alder-tree'), Ox Bottoms, Ox Hey, Pail Close, Peas Croft, Pellett Royd Wood (*Pilaterode* e. 13, c. 1210, *v.* pil-āte 'pill-oats', rod[1]), Pit Hills (*v.* pightel 'enclosure'), Pond Close, Rails Ing, Ransley Ing, Rawnsley Field, Rock Hey, Rows,

Saddle Row, Sandgate 1817 M, Saville Ing (from the surname *Savile*, eng), Smithy Croft, Sour Ing, Stock Hey (*v.* stocc 'stump', (ge)hæg 'enclosure'), Tenter Field (ME *tentour* 'a tenter'), Throstle Nest (*v.* þrostle, nest, cf. Crow Nest 186 *supra*), Tongue, Two Days Work, Wallet, Well Bent & Royd (*v.* wella, beonet, rod[1]), West End, West Ings, White Bent, White Leys, Windy Hill, Wood Croft, Wood Smithies.

(b) *Actona, Actunebroc, -sic* e. 13, c. 1210 (*v.* āc, tūn, brōc, sīc), *Aspencloch* c. 1210 (*v.* æspen, clōh 'dell'), *Bernolfcrof* e. 13 (the OE pers.n. *Beornwulf*, croft), *Butts* c. 1297 (*v.* butte 'an abutting strip'), *Calnclif* e. 13 (*v.* R. Colne (RNs.), clif), *Chamberlayn-Pythil* c. 1297 (ME *chamberleyne*, probably as a surname, *pightel* 'enclosure'), *Chisliaker* 13 (probably a ME adj. *chisli* 'gravelly' formed from cisel 'gravel', æcer), *Clayepit* 1588 WillY, *the Clay-pitt* 1604 Arm (*v.* clǣg, pytt), *Cokewell Clough* 1533 Stanhp 102, 4, *Flatt* c. 1297 (*v.* flat), *Gilleclogh, -cloh* e. 13, c. 1210 (the ME fem. pers.n. *Gille*, clōh 'dell'), *Hayforth* 1250 (*v.* hēg, ford), *Halche* 13 (*v.* halh 'nook of land'), *Hardhirst* 13 (*v.* heard, hyrst), *Hethihalgh, Hechihalch* e. 13 ('heathy nook', *v.* hǣð, -ig, halh), *Hytheland* 13, (*le*) *Holleclowe* 13 DodsN, (*v.* hol[1], clōh 'dell'), *le Hustede* 13 (*v.* hūs, stede, cf. Husteads 315 *infra*), *plac' voc' Kapel-chat* 13 (*v.* capel[1] 'chapel'), *Kirkethauet* c. 1297 (*v.* kirkja, þveit), *Lurteburne* c. 1210 (*v.* lorte 'mud', burna 'stream'), *Midelcroft* 12, *Milnetoft* 1333 (*v.* myln, topt 'enclosure'), *le Owtshott* 1542 (*v.* ūt, dial. *shut, shot* 'a division of land'), *Pikiresford'* 1202 FF (the OE pers.n. *Pīcer*, as in Pixham Wo 225, Pickering YN 85, and ford), *Raynaldker* 13 (the ME pers.n. *Rainald* (cf. Feilitzen 346), kjarr 'marsh'), *roda Ricardi* 13 ('Richard's clearing', *v.* rod[1]), *Rissilacum* c. 1210 (a Latinised p.n., *v.* risc, -ig, lacu 'stream'), *Sykehouse* 1542 (*v.* sīc 'stream', hūs), *Snowden* 1436 (*v.* snāw 'snow', denu 'valley', if not an error for dūn 'hill'), *Stainhou* e. 13 ('stone mound', *v.* steinn, haugr; it is at a boundary), *Stenerode* 1202 FF ('stony clearing', *v.* steinn or stǣnen, rod[1]), *Stone Delves* 1578, *Stonesdelfe* 1585 ('stone quarries', *v.* stān, (ge)delf), *Sunniuesic* e. 13 (the ON fem. pers.n. *Sunnifa* (cf. Feilitzen 378), sīc 'stream'), *Thynnes* 1547 TC, *Thorrethrod* 13 (from the ON pers.n. *Þorrøðr*, rod[1]), *Walwrdlandes* 12, *Wlfcroft(sik'*) c. 1250, *Wolvecroft* c. 1297 (the OE pers.n. *Wulf*, ON *Úlfr*, croft).

3. LINDLEY (102–1118)

    Lillai(a) 1086 DB, *Lillay* 12 Font
    Lin-, Lynlay, -ley(e) e. 13 Font, 1275, 1297 WCR, 1284 AD ii,
      l. 13 Font, 1316 DodsN *et freq* to 1400 YD iii, (*South-*) 1421 YD
      vi, (*Nether-*) 1656 PREll
    Lynnelay, -ley 1260 Font, 1313–1324 WCR (*freq*)
    Lyndelay 1343 YD iii
    Lindley 1822 Langd

'Flax clearing', *v.* līn, lēah. The assimilation of -*nl*- to -*ll*- in the spellings *Lillai* is fairly common (cf. Phonol. § 52). 'South' to dis-tinguish it from Old Lindley iii, 50 *infra*.

HAUGHS, *Hagh* 1198 Fount, *Haghebroc, Haye* 13 Font, *le Haghe in Lynnelay* 1260 ib, *del Haye* 1379 PT (p). *v.* haga 'enclosure'.

QUARMBY

> *Cornebi, Cornelbi* 1086 DB
> *Querneby* 1219 *Ass* 9, 1236–58 YD ix, 394 (p), 1274–1316 WCR
>   (*freq*), l. 13 *Nost* 44, 1297 LS *et freq* to 1428 FA, *-be* 1331 YD i,
>   *Qwerneby(e)* 14 YD vi, 1386 YD i, *Quermeby* 1243 Fees
> *Quernby* 1383, 1384 DodsN, 1393 YD iii *et freq* to 1509 DodsN,
>   *Qwernby* 1447 YD i
> *Whern(e)by* 1451 Arm, 1487 YD iii, 1498 YD xii, 236, 1506
>   DodsN
> *Wharn(e)by* 1462 YD xiii, 54, 1506 DodsN, *Warneby* 1592 FF
> *Whermby* 1487 YD iii, 1542 FF
> *Wharm(e)be* 1488 WB 65, *-by* 1492 Arm, 1533 FF, 1545 LS
> *Whornby* 1498 YD xii, 304
> *Quarmby(e), -bie* 1519 Arm, 1555 YD i, 1587, 1614 FF
> *Quermbye* 1604 FF, 1636 *YAS* 72, 25

'Farmstead with a mill', *v.* kvern, bȳ. On initial *Wh-* for *Qu-* cf. Phonol. § 39. The change to *Quarm-* has a common assimilation of *-n-* to *-m-* before the labial *-b-*. On the DB spelling *Corne-*, cf. EPN i, 122 s.v. *cweorn*.

ACRE HO & MILLS, *Acre Mill* 1843 O.S., *v.* æcer.   BANNEY ROYD. BIRCHENCLIFFE, *-clife* 1707 PREll, *Birkesaheclif* 13 WB 2, *Bircham-Cliffe* 1822 Langd, originally 'birch wood bank', *v.* bircen, sceaga, clif.   BRIARCOURT.   BURFITTS RD, *Burthwayt* 1436 DodsN, 'storehouse clearing', *v.* búr², þveit, cf. Bouthwaite (Fountains Earth) pt. v *infra*.   CLIFFE FM, *Cliffe* 1362 DodsN, *v.* clif.   CLOUGH WELL.   COTE ROYD.   COWRAKES, 1843 O.S., *Cor Heights* (sic) 1817 M, *v.* cū, hraca 'a rough path'.   CROSLAND RD, *Crosland Lane* 1843 O.S.   DAISY LEA.   DEER'S CROFT, *Dearscroft* 1579 WillY, from the surname *Dear* (ME *dere* 'dear'), croft.   FIELD HEAD & TOP.   GATEHOUSE, *Yatehouse* 1588 WillY, *v.* geat 'gate', hūs. GATESGARTH.   THE GRANGE.   GREEN LEA.   GREEN STILE. HAIGH CROSS, 1843 O.S., *v.* the nearby Haigh Ho. 303 *infra*.   THE HEIGHT, 1843 O.S., *v.* hēhðu.   HILL TOP, 1672 PREll.   HOLLIN CARR, *v.* holegn 'holly', kjarr 'marsh'.   THE HOLLY.   INGLEWOOD.   LANGLEY TERRACE.   LAUND, *Laund End* 1843 O.S., *v.* launde 'forest-glade'.   LIDGET ST.   LINDLEY MOOR, 1843 O.S.,

Linley-moor 1775 Watson, *v.* mōr.   Low Hills.   Marsh Ho, 1843
O.S., cf. *Copers Marsh, Marsh Cross* 1771 M, *v.* mersc.   Middle
Wood.   Moor Land, cf. Lindley Moor *supra*.   Nab End.   North-
field.   Norwood.   Oakes, *Oaks* 1817 M, *v.* āc.   Oak Wood,
1851 *TA* 226.   Peat Ponds Fm.   Plover Well.   The Portlands.
Potovens Rd, cf. Potovens 158 *supra*.   Prince Royd.   Raw
Nook, *Nook* 1817 M, *v.* nōk.   Rein Wood, *Reins* 1851 *TA*, *v.* reinn
'boundary strip'.   Royd.   Royds Hall, *Roidshall* 1640 WillY, *v.*
rod[1] 'clearing', hall, now partly in Longwood 304 *infra*.   Salendine
Nook, 1817 M, *Salondynenoke* 1572 Arm, *Salonden* 1583 WillY,
Salladine 1771 M, from ME *celydoine*, e.ModE *sal-, selandine* 'celan-
dine', nōk.   Springfield.   Stoneleigh.   Sunny Bank, 1843
O.S.   Tanyard.   Trough, *Stone Trough* 1817 M, *v.* trōg 'a
trough'.   Warren Ho, 1843 O.S., *Warren* 1851 *TA*, *v.* wareine
'warren'.   Weather Hill, *Wether Head* 1843 O.S., *v.* weðer 'a
wether sheep'.   Yew Tree.

FIELD-NAMES

Some modern f.ns. are included in Huddersfield 299 *supra*.

(*a*) Newhouse Fold 1843 O.S.

(*b*) *Crikeleʒ* 1488 WB 65 (possibly PrWelsh **crüg* (*v.* cruc[1]) 'a hill' with
OE hyll, cf. Crigglestone 101 *supra*), *Herthehows* 1487 Arm (probably OE
heorð (cf. Brightside i, 209) 'hearth', *v.* hūs), *Lynleybank* 1331 WCR (*v.*
banke), *Thorntonland* 1498 YD xii, 236.

4. Longwood (102–1016)

Langewode 1202 FF, *Langwode* 1306, 1383 DodsN, *-wood* 1573
WillY, *Long(e)wod(e)* 1542 FF, 1563 YD vi, *-wood* 1587, 1608 FF.
'The long wood', *v.* lang, wudu. The village lies on a long narrow
strip of the township (1 mile long, 300 yds wide) below Longwood
Edge and separating Golcar and Lindley.

Ball Royd, *Balrodebroke* 1361 Arm, *-royd(e)* 1479 ib, 1551 WillY,
-roid 1526 ib, *Balderoide* 1548 Stansf, 1590 FF. The place stands
down the rounded end of the ridge which forms Longwood Edge,
and the name could doubtless be a compound of OE ball 'a ball, a
rounded hill' and rod[1]; but the first el. may be the ME surname
Ball(e).

HAIGH HO, *Netherhaigh* 1455 DodsN, *Haighehous* 1592 WillY, *Haigh Howse* 1635 ib, *Ha(i)ghous(e)* 1645, 1656 PREll, *-House* 1817 M, *v.* haga 'enclosure', hūs.

MOLE'S HEAD, *Mallesheved* 1275, 1277 WCR (p), *-head* 1579 Arm, *Mallsheved* 1286 WCR (p), *Malsehedde* 1479 Arm, *Malshead* 1570 WillY, *Maul(e)s-, Mawleshead* 1633 *WB* 177, 1636 *YAS* 76, 25, 1647 WillY, *Mouls Head* 1817 M, from the ME fem. pers.n. *Malle* (a pet form of *Matilda* or *Mary*), and hēafod, here used of a steep declivity.

NETTLETON HILL, *Nettelton* 1284–1315 WCR (*freq*) (p), *Netelton* 14 YD vi, *Nettleton* 14 DodsN, *Nettilton* 1313 WCR (p), *Nettylton Hill* 1563 YD vi, *Netlonhill* 1658 WillS, *Flat & Hanging Nettleton Hall* 1851 *TA* 226. 'Farmstead overgrown with nettles', *v.* netele, tūn, cf. *Netteltonstall* iii, 171 *infra*; for the affixes *v.* flat 'level', hangende 'steep'.

OUTLANE, *le Outelone* 1326 WCR, *Owteland* (sic) 1590 WillY, *Outlane* 1593 PREll, 1642 WillY, 'the public road called *the Outlane*' 1775 Watson, *v.* ūt, lāne; it is on the Roman road which here forms the wapentake boundary.

SLACK, *del Slac* 1274 WCR (p), *Slack(e)* 1548 FF, 1576 WillY, 1620 FF. *v.* slakki 'a depression in a hillside', here the small valley where Longwood Brook rises. Slack is well-known as the supposed site of the Roman station of *Cambodunum* (AntIt); it lies close to the Roman road from Manchester to the R. Calder (cf. Roads) and Roman coins and tiles have been found in the immediate vicinity. The distances *Calcaria* (Tadcaster) to *Cambodunum* 20 miles, *Cambodunum* to *Mamucium* (Manchester) 18 miles in AntIt are a rough approximation (direct distances are 29 miles and 19 miles). *Cambodunum* itself has been equated with Bede's *in Campodono* (OE Bede *Donafeld*), where, near the royal seat, under Edwin king of Northumbria the first church was built after the Conversion, soon to be destroyed by the pagan Mercians (Bede ii, 14). A similarity in name is the only evidence for the supposed identity. Cf. Introd.

BANKHOUSE, *(le) Bankehous(e)* 1498 YD xii, 236, 1525 Test vi, *Banckhouse* 1589 WillY, *v.* banke, hūs. BULL GREEN. BUTTERWORTH HILL, 1843 O.S., *v.* butere, worð, cf. Butterworth iii, 54 *infra*. CHATHAM. CLAY WOOD BANK. CLIFF END. CLOUGH BOTTOM, 1646

WillY, *v.* clōh 'dell', botm.   COAL PIT LANE.   COTE.   CROFT
TOP, *the Croft* 1775 Watson, *v.* croft.   DELPH HILL.   DODICE
GREEN.   DODLEE, 1643 PREll, 1771 M, the ME pers.n. *Dodde*,
lēah.   ELDON.   FIELD HO.   GREEN EDGE.   GREEN HILL.   HALL
EDGE FM.   HARROW CLOUGH.   HEATH HILL.   HIRST, 1650
WillY, *Hyrste* 1557 ib, *v.* hyrst 'wood'.   HOLMES GATE.   HOLM-
FIELD.   INTAKE.   KEW HILL.   LAMB HALL.   LEECHES, *Laches*
1817 M, *v.* læcc 'stream, swamp'.   LONGWOOD EDGE, 1771 M, *v.*
ecg 'escarpment'.   MOUNT, 1843 O.S.   PARK.   PENDLE HILL.
PETTY ROYD, 1843 O.S.   PIGHILL WOOD, cf. *Pingel* 1608 YD vi, *v.*
pingel 'small enclosure'.   RAKESTRAWS, *Rake Straw* 1771 M.
ROUND INGS, *Roundings* 1771 M, *v.* rond, eng 'meadow'.   ROYDS
HEAD, *Roilsehead* 1646 WillY, *Royles Head* 1817 M, probably the ME
pers.n. *Rolle* (cf. Royles Head iii, 125), hēafod; the name has changed
under the influence of the nearby Royds Hall (302 *supra*).   SCAR
TOP.   SHAW, 1650 WillY, *Shay* 1817 M, *v.* sceaga 'copse'.   SNOW
LEE, 1647 WillY, probably the surname *Snow*, lēah.   SPARK HALL.
SPRING HILL, 1843 O.S.   STAFFORD MILLS.   STANDING STONE.
STOOPS, 1817 M, *v.* stolpi 'a post'.   TENTER.   THORN HILL.
WELL FIELD.   WHIN GATE.   WHOLESTONE HILL *&* MOOR, *Hole-*
stone Moor 1843 O.S.   WINTER HILL, 1771 M, *v.* winter, hyll.

FIELD-NAMES

Some modern f.ns. may be amongst those of Huddersfield 299 *supra*.

(*a*) Crool 1817 M.

(*b*) *Littelwod(lone)* 1326 WCR.

5. SCAMMONDEN (102–0415)

    Sc-, *Skambandene* 1275, 1277, 1323 WCR, *Schambandene* 1286,
      1323 ib
    Skambaynden' 1277 WCR, 1301 Ebor
    Scambenedene 1284 AD iii
    Scammendene 1316 WCR
    Scamanden(e) 1323 *MinAcct* 45, 1324 WCR, 1487 YD iii, 1640 WillY
    Scamedene 1327 WCR
    Scamenden 1431 YD i
    Scamonden 1525 Test vi *et freq* to 1621 FF, *Skam-* 1547 FF
    Scammonden 1581 WillY, 1627 DodsN, 1699 *WCR* i

'Skammbein's valley', *v.* denu. The first el. is an ON byname *Skamm-bein* 'short leg', which is not recorded independently but which occurs in the Icel p.n. *Scambeinstaþir* (Lind BN) and a f.n. *Scambaynkeld* (N. Deighton) pt v *infra*; it is parallel to such bynames as *Skammfótr* 'short foot', *Skammhals* 'short neck', etc. The spelling *Scamban-* is partly anglicised.

DEANHEAD, *Deyneheade* 1574, 1590 FF, *Denehead* 1587 FF, *Deane-head* 1588 WillY, 1615 YD v, *le Deanhead* 1615 ib, *Deanhead* 1621 FF. 'Head of the valley', *v.* denu, hēafod.

EGERTON, *Eggerton* 1495 YD xiii, 46, *Egerton* 1587 WillY, 1709 WMB, *Edgerton* 1771 M. 'Ecgheard's or Ecghere's farmstead', *v.* Edgerton 296 *supra*.

ACRE HEAD, 1851 *TA*, *v.* æcer, hēafod.   BANK, *the Banks* 1709 WMB, *v.* banke.   BROAD LEE, 1699 *WCR* 1, *Brode Lee* 1709 WMB, *v.* brād, lēah.   CAMP HILL.   CARR HO, CARR TOP, *Carr Leys* 1851 *TA*, *v.* kjarr 'marsh'.   THE CARRS.   CAUSEWAY GREEN.   CHAPEL HILL, 1851 *TA*.   COW GATE HILL, 1709 WMB, *v.* cū, gata, hyll.   CRAGGS.   CROFT HOUSE (MOSS), 1843 O.S., *Crofthous(e)* 1577 WillY, 1709 WMB, *v.* croft, hūs, mos 'swamp'.   CROWTHER LATHE.   CRULT MOOR, *Crutt Hill* 1851 *TA* possibly dial. *crut* 'a dwarf'.   DEANHEAD CLOUGH, 1843 O.S., *v.* Deanhead *supra*, clōh 'dell'.   DEAN HEAD MOOR, 1843 O.S., *v.* prec., mōr.   DELPH HILL, *Delf Hill* 1843 O.S., *v.* (ge)delf 'quarry'.   DOE HOLES.   THE FOREST.   GREAT FIELD HEAD, 1843 O.S.   GREEN FIELD LODGE, 1843 O.S.   GREEN HOLES.   GREEN SLACKS, *Green Slack* 1851 *TA*, *v.* grene[1], slakki 'a hollow'.   HAN HEAD, 1591 WillY, 1648 PREll, 1709 WMB, *v.* hana 'a cock', hēafod.   HARDENBY, 1843 O.S., near the foll., *v.* bȳ.   HARD END.   HEAD GATE, 1771 M, *v.* hēafod (here the 'head' of Deanhead *supra*), gata.   HEAD GREEN, cf. *Head Field* 1771 M, *v.* prec., grēne[2].   HEY CROFT, *Hay Croft(s)* 1709 WMB, 1817 M, *High Croft* 1771 M, *v.* hēg, croft.   HEY LATHE, *Hey* 1817 M, *Hey Laith* 1851 *TA*, *v.* (ge)hæg 'enclosure', hlaða 'barn'.   HEY WOOD, 1851 *TA*, *v.* prec.   HIND HILL, 1851 *TA*, *v.* hind 'a hind', hyll.   HOLE BOTTOM, 1851 *TA*, *v.* hol[1], botm.   HOLLIN HEY, 1843 O.S., *v.* holegn 'holly', (ge)hæg.   HUDSON CROFT, *Hudsons Croft* 1771 M, the surname *Hudson*, croft.   INTAKE, *Intake Mill* 1851 *TA*, *v.* intak.   JACOB'S WELL.   THE KNOWL.   LANE SIDE, 1771 M.   LEY FIELDS, *Leyfield* 1709 WMB, *v.* lǣge 'fallow' feld.   LOW

PLATT, 1843 O.S., *v.* plat[2] 'a small plot of ground'.   THE MOOR-
LANDS, cf. *Scammonden Moor* 1814 *EnclA* 146, *Moor Field* 1851 *TA*.
MOSELDEN HEIGHT, *v.* Moselden iii, 72 *infra*.   THE MOSSES.   NEST,
1851 *TA*, *v.* nest.   NEW HEY, 1817 M, *v.* nīwe, (ge)hæg.   NEW HO,
1851 *TA*.   O'COT 1851 *TA*, *v.* cot 'cottage'.   OLD HO, 1771 M,
Oldhouse 1536 HAS 50, 15.   OWLET HOWL (sic for HALL), *Owlet
Hall* 1851 *TA*, cf. Gawthorpe Hall 102 *supra*.   PINFOLD LANE, *Pin
Fold Field* 1851 *TA*, *v.* pynd-fald.   POLE HILL & MOOR, *Pole*
(*Chapel*) 1817 M, *v.* pāl 'a pole', hyll.   REDGATE LANE.   ROE
HILL, *the Roe Hill* 1787 *HAS* 50, 17, *v.* rā 'roebuck', hyll, cf. Hind
Hill *supra*.   RYEFIELD, 1851 *TA*.   SCAR, *Scarr* 1709 WMB, *v.*
sker 'a scar, a rocky bank'.   SHAW CLOUGH & LAITH, cf. *Shaws*
1851 *TA*, *v.* sceaga 'copse', clōh, hlaða.   SLEDGE GATE, cf. Sledgate
Lane 310 *infra*.   SOUTH STRINES CLOUGH, *v.* strind 'a stream'.
SPRING GROVE, 1843 O.S., *v.* spring 'plantation'.   SPRING ROYD,
1851 *TA*, *v.* prec., rod[1].   SPRUTMAN CLOUGH.   STALPES, *Stoop*
1843 O.S., *v.* stólpi 'a post, a stake'.   STILES HO, *Steelhous* 1709
WMB, *v.* stigel 'stile', hūs.   STUBBING CLOUGH.   TOP OF HILL,
1843 O.S.   TURNER HO, 1817 M, *Turners H.* 1771 M, the surname
Turner, hūs.   WALL NOOK, 1817 M, *v.* wall, nōk.   WEST CARR,
West Car 1771 M, *v.* west, kjarr 'marsh'.   WHITE LEE, *Whitelees*
1709 WMB, *v.* hwīt, lēah.   WOOD EDGE & FM, cf. *Wood Field &
Head* 1851 *TA*.   WOODHOUSE.   WORMALD.   YEWS, *Euse* 1709
WMB, *v.* īw 'yew-tree'.

FIELD-NAMES

The principal forms in (*a*) are 1851 *TA* 346. Spellings dated 1331 are
WCR, 1653, 1787, 1796 HAS 50, 15–17, 1699 *WCR* 1, 2. Some modern f.ns.
may belong to Slaithwaite 310 *infra*.

(*a*) Abb Ing, Bay Croft, Berry Mill, Bilesmire Close 1764 *Glebe*, Birks
Hill (*v.* birki), Bottoms (*v.* botm), Brig Field, Brook Ing, Bullstones 1843
O.S., Calf Croft & Hey, Carper Ing, Clay Ho, Coal Pit Ing, Cold Ass 1771
M (*v.* cald, ears), Cow Leys, Crossley Bank, Denton Clough, Eaves (*Eaves
tenement* 1796, *v.* efes 'edge, border'), Elmer Lee, Far Ing, Feather Bed
(cf. Featherbed Moss 283 *supra*), Foot Ball Field, Frith Ing (*v.* fyrhðe, eng),
Great Brink, Hazle Hirst (*v.* hæsel, hyrst), Hive Yard, Hollin Wood (*v.*
holegn 'holly'), the Inger Brook 1787, Kiln Croft, Lighthazles (*v.* leoht,
hæsel, cf. Lighthazles iii, 64 *infra*), Long Bank (*le Longbanke* 1699, *v.* lang,
banke), Mare Bank, Meanwood Field (*v.* (ge)mæne 'common', wudu), Mill
Hill (*the Mill Hill* 1709 WMB), New Field, Owlers Ing (*v.* alor 'alder', eng),
Penny Holme, Plash (*v.* plæsc 'pool'), Rotcher Bottom (cf. Rocher i, 226

supra), Rough Hirst, Rough Knowl, the Scrogg 1787 (*v*. scrogge), Slacks (*v*. slakki), Smithy Hole (ib 1796, *v*. smiðð, hol¹), South Ing, Spa Ing, Spang, Spout Hill (*v*. spoute), Sprite Platt, Sprun, Stannerings (possibly for 'stone rings'), Stoney Royd, Tenter Croft, Toad Hole Ing, Tommy Lees (cf. *Tommyheyes* 1653, *v*. (ge)hæg, lēah), Tor End 1817 M (*v*. torr 'rock'), Walker Edge, Well Hollins (*v*. wella, holegn), West Ing, West Knowl.

(b) *Coldcotes* 1331 (*v*. cald, cot 'cottage'), *Ingesbrooke* 1699 (*v*. eng, brōc), *Moorfield* 1653, *le Ordhille* 1331 (*v*. ord 'a point, projecting ridge', hyll), *Swift Inge* 1653, *Thornheywood* 1699 (*v*. þorn, (ge)hæg).

6. SLAITHWAITE (102–0813) [ˈslauwit]

Sladweit, -wait 1178, 1192, 1193 P (p)

Slathwait, -thweyt 1191 P (p), 1235 ChR, 1236 Kirkl 465, 1256 DodsN, 1286 WCR, *Slathwat* 1499 Ipm

Slahthuait 1213–27 YAJ xxxviii, 357

Sclagtwayt 1277 WCR (p)

Slayisthayt 1285 WCR   *Slaitwait* 1297 LS

Slaghwaite 1306 DodsN, *Slaghthayt* 1307 WCR (p), -*thwayt(e)* 1373 FF, 1402 FA, -*thewayte* 1402 Pat, -*twat* 1488 WB 65, -*wayte* 1539 WillY, *Slaghwitt* 1652 PREll

Slaghethwayte 1307 DodsN, *Slagheweate* 1588 WillY

Slaughwayte 1360 DodsN, *Slaughthwayte* 1593 WillY, -*twait* 1656 Pick, -*thwaite* 1814 *EnclA* 146

Slaxthwayt 1379 PT

Slakwayth 1410 Pat, -*with* 1543 WillY, -*thwaytt* 1540 MonRent, -*thwaite* 1543 *MinAcct* 23

Slayghwayte Halfe 1588 LS, *Slaighwaite* 1641 Rates

Slawghethwaite als. Slawghewaite 1591 FF, *Slawghwaite als. Slawhethwaite als. Slawhewaite* 1605 FF

Slaughit 1665 Visit, *Slaythwayte* 1627 DodsN, *Slawitt* 1750 TaxS

Ekwall (DEPN s.n.) has suggested that the first el. of this difficult name is OE slāh 'a sloe', and most spellings can be accounted for by it; but certain spellings in *Sclag-, Slak-* as well as those in *Slai-, Slaigh-* could hardly be explained by *slāh*. The first el. is therefore probably ON *slag* 'a blow', as -*g* would be affricatised as in Maunby YN 274 (hence *Slagh-*, etc.), and eventually form a diphthong (as in *Slaug-*); in *Slak-* the -*g*- was occasionally unvoiced to -*k*- by assimilation to the following -*þ*-, and the *Slay(gh)*- spellings for *Slaugh-* exhibit the same variation as Haigh and Haugh from OE *haga* or Shay and Shaw from *sceaga* (cf. Phonol. § 3). In many of the spellings, -þ- has been lost after the fricative -gh-, as it has in the late spellings *Slaughit*, *Slawitt*, the source of the modern dial. pronunciation ['ˈslauwit]. The meaning of ON *slag* is 'blow, stroke, skirmish', which Goodall accepts for the p.n. Lindkvist 122, however, thought it might mean 'mowing', since related words have that sense, ON *slá* 'to strike, to mow', *slátta* 'mowing, a hay-field'; Rygh (NG iii, 130, iv, 78) suggests similar meanings for *slag* in such Norw p.ns. as *Slagsvold*. In SvON (*Älvsborgs län* i, 100, xii, 165), Swed *slag* is thought to mean 'place where timber is cast down', and this or a closely related meaning might well be the one required here, since ON *þveit* 'a clearing, a meadow', has itself the root meaning of 'something cut down'. Hence 'clearing where timber was felled'.

ACRE BOTTOM, cf. Acre Head 305 *supra*.   AINLEY PLACE, 1817 M, *Audley Place* (sic) 1633 WillY, probably a surname derived from Ainleys iii, 43 *infra*, place.

BADGER GATE CLOUGH, probably e.ModE *ba(d)ger* 'a badger, a hawker', gata.   BAILEY SLACKS.   BANK GATE.   BANK NOOK, 1843 O.S., *v.* banke, nōk.   BAR HO.   BARRETT, 1817 M, BARRETT CLOUGH, 1843 O.S., the surname *Barrett*, clōh.   BENT ING, *v.* beonet, eng.   BENTS, 'the fields called *the Bents*' 1775 Watson, *Lower Bents* 1851 *TA*, *v.* beonet 'bent-grass'.   BIRKS, *Burks* 1843 O.S., *v.* birki 'birch'.   BLACK COP.   BLACK HEATH.   BLAKE CLOUGH, 1843 O.S.   BLAKE STONES.   BOOTH, *Boothe* 1585 WillY, *v.* bōth 'a booth, shed'.   BOOTH HEY & NAZE.   BRADLEY BROOK, 1771 M, *v.* brād, lēah, brōc, distinct from Bradley 296 and Bradley Mills 224 *supra*.   BRADSHAW, 1771 M, *Brasha* 1817 M, *v.* 'broad copse', *v.* brād sceaga.   BROADFIELD.   BROOK SIDE, 1771 M.   BUNKERS HILL.   BURNT PLATTS, *Burn Plats* 1817 M, 'burnt plots of ground', *v.* brende, plat².

CARR LANE.   CARTERS.   CARTGATE HEAD & FOOT, 1843 O.S., *v.* cræt, gata.   CASTLE, 1771 M, *Castell* 1590 WillY, *v.* castel, probably here 'residence'.   CAUSEWAY (FOOT).   CLARK HEY.   CLOUGH HO, 1843 O.S., *v.* clōh 'dell', hūs.   COCKLEY COTE.   COCK RING.   COP, COP HILL, *Copt Hall* (sic) 1771 M, *Cop Hill* 1817 M, *v.* copp, copped, hyll.   CROW TREES.   CUPWITH HILL, 1843 O.S., *Cupwith* 1817 M.

DEEP GATE.   DEER HILL.   DELVES, *Delfs* 1817 M, *v.* (ge)delf 'quarry'.   DOWRY.   DROP CLOUGH, 1843 O.S., cf. Little Drop iii, 151 *infra*.

EARNSHAW FOLD, *Earnshaw Ing* 1851 *TA*, the surname *Earnshaw*, fald, eng.   EDGE.   ELMS HILL.

FOLLINGWORTH, *Folingworth* 1771 M, cf. Fallingworth iii, 54 *infra*. FOLLY.   FOXSTONE EDGE.

GOAT HILL, 1843 O.S.   GOSLING GREEN.   GREEN BOTTOM. GREEN LANE, 1843 O.S.   GREEN SLADE, *v.* grēne[1], slæd 'valley'.

HAW COTE, *Halcote* 1637 WillY, 'cottage near the hall', *v.* hall, cot.   HEATH.   HEY END & LEYS.   HEYROYD.   HEYS.   HIGH-FIELD, 1817 M.   HILL TOP, 1771 M.   HOLLINS, 1843 O.S., *v.* holegn 'holly'.   HOLLY WELL, 1843 O.S., *v.* hālig, wella.   LOWER & UPPER HOLME, 1843 O.S., *v.* holmr 'water-meadow'.   HOLT, HOLT LAITH, *Laith* 1843 O.S., HOLT HEAD, 1771 M, *v.* holt 'wood', hlaða 'barn'.   HOWGATE WOOD.

ING HEAD, 1771 M, *v.* eng 'meadow'.   INTAKE LANE.

KRIVES LANE.

LAUND, *Lawn* 1797 PRHtsd, *v.* launde 'a glade'.   LINGARDS CROSS, *Lingarth* 1709 YDr, *v.* the nearby Lingards 277 *supra*. LONGLANDS.

MANSERGH HO, possibly a surname derived from Mansergh We. MEAL HILL, *Mele hill* 1488 *WB* 65, 'multi-coloured hill', *v.* mǣle, hyll, cf. Meal Hill 244 *supra*.   MEAN HEY, cf. *Mean Barn & Platt* 1851 *TA*, *v.* (ge)mǣne 'common', (ge)hæg, platt[2] 'plot of land'. MERRY DALE, 1817 M, *v.* myrig, dæl.   MOOR FIELD, *Moorfields* 1817 M, MOOR GATE, 1817 M, MOOR SIDE EDGE, formerly *Slaith-waite Moss* 1843 O.S., *v.* mōr, mos 'swamp'.   MOSS, *v.* prec.

NAB.   NAZE, *Upper Nase* 1851 *TA*, *v.* næss 'headland' or OE *nasu* 'nose'.   NETHER END.   NEW CLOSE, 1843 O.S.   NEWGATE.

OAK.   ONELY HO.   OWLER CLOUGH.   OWLERS WOOD, (*Nether*) *Olers* 1822 Langd, *v.* alor 'alder-tree'.

PADDOCK.   PARK GATE, 1843 O.S.   PICKLE TOP, 1843 O.S., *Pickle Hole* 1851 *TA*, *v.* pightel 'enclosure'.   PLAT MILL.   POLE GATE, cf. Pole Hill 306 *supra*.   POTTERS.

REAPS (HILL), 1817 M, *Rapes* 1771 M, *v.* Reap Hill 289 *supra*. ROCK WOOD.   ROTCHER, 1843 O.S., *v.* Rocher i, 226 *supra*.   ROUGH HEY, 1843 O.S., *v.* rūh, (ge)hæg.   ROW, 1843 O.S., *v.* rāw 'row of houses'.   RYE LOAF.

SALLY BANK.   SCOTLAND.   SCOUT WOOD, *v.* skúti 'projecting rock'.   SHAW CARR & FIELDS, *Shaw* 1771, *Shay* 1817 M, *v.* sceaga 'copse'.   SHRED.   SHROGG(S), *v.* scrogge 'brushwood'.   SLACKS, *Slack* 1843 O.S., *v.* slakki 'a hollow'.   SLAITHWAITE HALL, 1843

O.S., *Slaighwaite Hall* 1590 WillY.   SLAITHWAITE MOOR, formerly *Slaithwaite Common* 1843 O.S.   SLATE PITS.   SLEDGATE LANE, probably a road suitable for the use of a sled, cf. Sledge Gate 306 *supra* for a similar name.   STONES LAITH.

THORN.   THORPES.   TIDING FIELD, 1843 O.S., probably *tithing* 'tithe'.   TOM PITTS.   TYAS LANE.

WARING BOTTOM.   WATERSIDE.   WENTWORTH.   WEST END, 1843 O.S.   WEST GATE.   WHAM, *v.* hvammr 'valley'.   WHITE REAPS, cf. Reaps *supra*.   WILBER LEE, 1843 O.S., *Wildborleghe* 1326 WCR (p), *Wilborley* 1551 WillY, 'wild-boar clearing', *v.* wilde, bār, lēah.   WINDY BANK.   WOOD BOTTOM, NOOK & TOP.   WOOL CLOUGH.   WOOL ROYD, *Wolleroyde* 1577 WillY, *v.* wulf 'wolf' or wulle 'wool', rod[1] 'clearing'.   WORTLEY KNOWL.   WORTS HILL, 1843 O.S.

FIELD-NAMES

The principal forms in (*a*) are 1851 *TA* 364; a few modern f.ns. may be amongst those of Scammonden 306 *supra*.

(*a*) Dam Bank, Fieldholm 1771 M, Great Croft, The Hurst 1843 O.S. (*v.* hyrst), Far & Near Ing, Mill Dam, Sparth 1817 M (*Spark* 1771 M, *v.* Sparth 281 *supra*), Steam Hill, West Top 1771 M.

(*b*) Crimblebrooke 1618 *WB* 162 (*v.* crymel 'a small piece of ground', brōc).

xix. Rochdale

Rochdale is in Lancashire (La 54), and the townships of Saddleworth and Springhead, now united as Saddleworth Urban District, are in the Tame valley in the western watershed of the Pennines (cf. SadD 465). Saddleworth was formerly divided into four quarters or hamlets called *meres*: Friar Mere, Lord's Mere, Quick Mere and Shaw Mere (Langd).

1. SADDLEWORTH (102–0106)

Sadelwrth l. 12, e. 13 *Nost* 22d, 66, -*word* c. 1230, c. 1280 Whalley, -*worth* c. 1230 ib, 1316 Vill, 1331 FF, 1379 PT, -*wurth* 1254 Pat (p)

Sadelesworth 1303 Abbr

Sadleworth(e) 1425 DodsN, 1559 YD xiii, 49

Sadilworth 1487 WCR 1, *Saddilworth(e)*, -*yl*- 1541 *MinAcct* 23, 1586 FF

Saddleworth 1572 WB 67

Saddelworth 1605 FF

The first el. is OE sadol 'saddle', used to describe a feature resembling a saddle in shape or appearance such as a ridge, but the exact application is not clear; cf. OE *sadolhongra* BCS 1282, *Sadel-howe* (Tadcaster East) pt iv *infra*; *v.* worð 'enclosure'.

CASTLESHAW, *Castylshaw* 1544 SadD, *Castleshaw*(*e*) 1581 FF, 1657 WillS. 'Copse near the fort', *v.* castel, sceaga. The name refers to a Roman fort, traces of which have been found near the Roman road from Manchester to *Cambodunum* (cf. Slack 303 *supra*).

DELPH, NEW DELPH, *Delf*(*e*) 1544 SadD, 1581, 1617 FF, 1656 WillS, 1635 PRSad, (*-in Friermere*) 1733 YDr, (*New*) *Delph* 1817 M, 1822 Langd. *v.* (ge)delf 'quarry'.

DENSHAW, 1635 WillY, 1722 PRSad, *Deanshaw* 1771 M, 1822 Langd. 'Copse in the valley', *v.* denu, sceaga.

DIGGLE, *Diggel* l. 12 *Nost* 22d, *Dighil*(*l*) e. 13 ib 66, 1468 SadD, *Dighull* c. 1272 SadD, *Dikele* 1249 Pat (p), *Deghall* 1638 BM, *Diggle* 1822 Langd. Probably 'ditch hill', *v.* dīc, hyll, with the not uncommon voicing of intervocalic *-k-* (cf. Phonol. § 37); cf. Digley 263 *supra*.

FRIAR MERE, 1468 Sad, *Frear Me*(*e*)*re* 1582 SadD, 1771 M, *Friermere* 1733 YDr, *-Meer* 1817 M, *v.* frere 'friar', (ge)mǣre 'boundary'. The Black Friars are said to have had a house near Delph. This was one of the quarters or *meres* of Saddleworth township, and *mere* represents an extension of meaning of OE (ge)mǣre; it is used of the other quarters of Saddleworth and occasionally elsewhere, as in *Thurlestone Meare* i, 344 *supra*.

HARROP DALE, *Haropp*(*e*) e. 13 *Nost* 65d, 1308, 1314 WCR (p), *Harrop* 1274 ib (p). 'Rock valley', *v.* hær, hop, but such names are ambiguous, as the first el. could be hara 'hare'.

HILBRIGHTHOPE (lost), *Hildebrighope* 1279 QW, *Hilbdebrighthope* c. 1293 SadD, *Ildbrictorp* (sic for *-op*) 1297 LS, *Hillbrigthorpe* 1310 SadD, *Hildebrithorpe* 1456 SadD, *Hilbright & Hope* 1535 VE. 'Hildebeorht's valley', from the OE pers.n. *Hildebeorht* and hop, but some forms have substituted þorp 'outlying farmstead'.

HOLLY GROVE, *Holyngreue* c. 1272 SadD, *Holingref* 1297 LS (p), *Hollin Grove* 1771 M, 1822 Langd, *Hollingreave* 1723 PRSad. 'Holly copse', *v.* holegn, grǣfe (replaced by grāf 'grove').

LORD'S MERE, 1822 Langd, -*Meer* 1817 M. 'The lord's boundary', *v.* (ge)mǣre and Friar Mere *supra*; it was one of the quarters of Saddleworth.

QUICK, *Thoac, Tohac* 1086 DB, *Quik(e)*, *Quyk(e)* 1199 (1232) Ch, 1316 Vill, 1329, 1369 FF *et passim* to 1385 *Ass* 5, *Qwyke* c. 1272 SadD, *la Quyk* 1297 LS, *Quwic* 1219 *Ass* 7, *Qwyk* 1379 PT, 1545 LS, *Quyck(e)*, *Quick(e)* 1388, 1440 DodsN, 1562 FF, 1587 *Dep et passim* to 1771 M, (-*Mere*) 1822 Langd, *Whicke* 1431 DodsN, (*le*) *Whyke* 1425 ib, 1533 AD v, *Wyke als. Whykke* 1557 FF. *v.* cwic 'a quickset hedge' (first recorded in 1456 NED s.v. *quick*). On the forms with *W(h)*- cf. Phonol. § 39. Quick was one of the quarters or *meres* of Saddleworth (*v.* Friar Mere *supra*).

SADDLEWORTH FIRTH (lost), *Sadelworthfrith(e)*, -*fryth* 1316 WCR, 1323 *MinAcct* 45, 1331 FF, *Sadle-* 1431, 1440 DodsN, 1597 FF, *Sad(d)il-* 1553 AD v, 1592 FF. *v.* fyrhðe 'wood'.

SHAW HALL, SHAW MERE, *Schag'* 1379 PT (p), *le Shagh* 1388 SadD, *Shaw Hall* 1771 M, *Shaw Mere* 1822 Langd, 1843 O.S., *v.* sceaga 'copse'. This was one of the quarters or *meres* of Saddleworth, cf. Friar Mere *supra*.

ACKER, *Acre* 1746 PRSad, *v.* æcer.   ADAM'S CROSS, 1843 O.S. ALDERMAN'S HILL, *Aldermans* 1817 M, cf. Alderman's Head i, 332 *supra*.   ALPHIN, 1843 O.S., *Alphenstone* 1468 SadD, *Alfin Hill* 1817 M, probably OE *elfen* (Merc *ælfen*) adj. from elf 'fairy', stān, hyll. ARMIT RD.   ASHWAY GAP & HEY, 1843 O.S., *Ashway Moss* 1810 *EnclA* 65.

    BADGER EDGE & SLACK, 1843 O.S.   BAKESTONE DELPH, *Bake-stone-Delf* 1822 Langd, -*Quarry* 1843 O.S., *v.* bæc-stān, (ge)delf 'quarry'.   BALLGROVE, *Ballgreave* 1612 *WB* 68, *Boegreave* 1657 WillS, *Balgrave* 1658 ib, *Bow-greave* 1738 PRSad, *v.* ball 'a rounded hill', grǣfe 'copse'.   BANK CLOUGH & GAP.   BELL YARD.   BENT, *Lower Bent*, 1843 O.S., *v.* beonet 'bent-grass'.   BENTCLIFFE. BENTLEYS.   BESWICK, 1843 O.S.   BILL O' JACKS, *Bills o' Jacks* 1843 O.S., an older and common form of patronymic in YW; a gravestone in the churchyard commemorates *Bill o' Jacks an' Tom o' Bill's*, i.e. William Bradbury and Thomas his son, both horribly murdered April 2, 1832 (SadD ii, 564).   BINN GREEN.   BIRCHEN CLOUGH, 1843 O.S., *v.* bircen, clōh.   BIRCHES, 1727 PRSad, *Birch*

H. 1771 M.   BIRCH SCAR.   BIRD GRAIN.   BLACK CHEW HEAD, *Blackchew-hede* 1468 SadD, 'black valley head', *v.* blæc, cēo, hēafod, cf. Chew Brook *infra*.   BLEA GREEN.   BLEAK HEY NOOK, *Blake Hey Nook*, 1817 M, *v.* blæc, (ge)hæg, nōk.   BLINDSTONES MOSS, 1843 O.S.   BOARD HILL.   BOARSHURST, 1726 PRSad, *Boar Hurst* 1771 M, *v.* bār 'boar', hyrst 'wood'.   BOGGART STONES, *Boggart o' th' Moss* 1843 O.S.   BOOTHSTEAD, *Booth Ste(a)ds* 1730 PRSad, 1771 M, *Booth* 1843 O.S., *v.* bōth 'shed', stede.   BOWK HO, 1729 PRSad, *Bouk H.* 1771 M.   BRIARFIELD.   BRIMMY CROFT, 1733 PRSad, *Brimy Croft* 1771 M.   BROAD GREAVE HILL.   BROADHEAD, 1730 PRSad, *v.* brād, hēafod 'headland'.   BROADHEAD MOSS & NODDLE, 1843 O.S., *v.* prec., mos 'bog', dial. *noddle* 'head'.   BROAD MEADOW, 1747 PRSad.   BROAD STONES, *Brodeston* l. 12, e. 13 *Nost* 22d, 66, c. 1272 SadD, *v.* brād, stān.   BROADSTONE HILL, 1843 O.S., *v.* prec.   BROCKLEY MOOR.   BROW, 1726 PRSad, *v.* brū.   BROWN HILL, 1843 O.S.   BRUN, 1724 PRSad, probably ON brún 'a moor' or bruni 'place cleared by burning'.   BRUN MOOR, *v.* prec.   BURN-EDGE, *Brun-edge* 1725 PRSad, *Brown Edge* 1771 M, *Burntedge* 1817 M, *v.* brende 'burnt', or bruni (cf. Brun *supra*), ecg.   BUTTS LANE.

CALF HEY, 1740 PRSad, *Calf Hay* 1771 M, *v.* calf, (ge)hæg. CARR, *Car* 1736 PRSad, CARRCOTE, 1723 PRSad, *Carr Coit* 1771 M, *v.* kjarr 'marsh', cot 'cottage'.   CARTSHEAD.   CASTLE HILL, 1745 PRSad, *v.* Castleshaw *supra*.   CAUSEWAY SETT, 1726 PRSad, *Causey-side* 1822 Langd, *v.* caucie, sīde.   CHARNEL HOLES, *Charnel Rocks* 1843 O.S.   CHERRY CLOUGH, 1750 PRSad.   CHEW BROOK, 1843 O.S., *v.* cēo 'valley', brōc, cf. Black Chew Head *supra*.   CHEW HILLS, *Chew* 1843 O.S., *v.* prec.   CHURCH BANK, cf. *Church Moor* 1771 M.   CLOUGH HO, *Clough* 1726 PRSad, *v.* clōh.   COAL CLOUGH.   COLT HILL, *Cole-hill* 1739 PRSad, *Coat Hill* 1771 M. COTE INTAKE.   COTEMANS, *Coteman's* 1749 PRSad.   COURT MILL, *Court* 1843 O.S.   COWARDS.   CRANE KNOLL.   CRAWSHAW HEY, *Crawshagh* 1388 DodsN, *Crowshawe* 1640 SadD, *v.* crāwe 'crow', sceaga 'copse'.   CRIB, 1739 PRSad, OE *crib* 'a crib', later 'a hovel'.   CRITCHLEY COTTAGE.   CROMPTON KNOLL, named from Crompton (La 52).   CROOK GATE.   CROSS, 1726 PRSad, *v.* cros.

DACRES HALL.   DALE, 1732 PRSad, *v.* dæl.   DEAN HEAD & ROCKS, 1843 O.S., *Dean-head* 1736 PRSad, *v.* denu 'valley', hēafod. DELPH GREAVE, *Delph-Greaves* 1735 PRSad, *Delf Grove* 1771 M, *v.* Delph 311 *supra*, græfe 'copse'.   DELPH SLACK, 1747 PRSad, *v.* prec., slakki 'a hollow'.   DEN QUARRIES, *Den* 1379 PT (p), 1735

PRSad, *v.* denn 'a den, lair'. DENSHAW MOOR, 1809 *EnclA* 4, *v.* Denshaw *supra*, mōr. DICK HILL. DIGGLE BROOK, 1843 O.S., DIGGLE EDGE, *Diglee Edge* 1771 M, *v.* Diggle *supra*, brōc, ecg. DIGGLE LEE, *Diglee* 1724 PRSad, *v.* prec., lēah. DISH STONE, 1843 O.S. DOB CROSS, *Dobcrosse* 1662 PRSad, the ME pers.n. *Dobbe*, cros. DODLE, *Dowdle-croft* 1733 PRSad, *Dodle-croft* 1739 ib, cf. dial. *doddle* 'a pollard tree'. DOLEFIELD. DOVE STONE WOOD, 1771 M, *v.* dūfe, stān, wudu. DOWRY GREEN, 1724 PRSad, *Dowry* 1771 M, *Dorey* 1843 O.S., cf. Dowry iii, 67 *infra*. DOWRY CASTLE HILL, *Dorey Castle* 1843 O.S. DRY BRIDGE. DRY CLOUGH. DRY CROFT. DUNGE BOOTH, 1764 *Glebe*, *Dundge booth* 1724 PRSad, *v.* dung 'dungeon, underground room', bōth 'booth, shed'.

EDGE END & HILL.

FAIRBANKS, *ffairbanks* 1722 PRSad, *v.* fæger, banke. FAIR SPRINGS. FEATHERBED MOSS, 1843 O.S., *v.* Featherbed Moss 283 *supra*. FERNHILL. FERN LEE, 1741 PRSad, *Fernelee* 1379 PT (p), *v.* fearn, lēah. FERNTHORPE HALL. FERNY HOLES. FIELD HO. FOULRAKES, 1749 PRSad, *v.* fūl, hraca 'rough path'. FOX STONE, 1843 O.S. FRENCHES, 1843 O.S., *French's* 1724 PRSad, *French-Mill* 1732 ib. FRIAR NAZE & WOOD, cf. Friar Mere *supra*. FRIEZLAND. FUR LANE, *Fur-lane* 1725 PRSad.

GARNERS, 1737 PRSad, cf. *Garner Holly* 1843 O.S., from the surname *Garner*. GATE HEAD, 1658 WillS, *v.* gata, hēafod. GOLBURN CLOUGH, *Gold-*, *Gowburn-clough* 1748–9 PRSad. GRAINS, 1724 PRSad, *v.* grein 'river-fork'. GRANGE, 1544 SadD, 1730 PRSad, *Castleshawe Graunge* 1617 FF, *v.* grange. GRANGE HEY, 1843 O.S., *v.* prec., (ge)hæg. GRASSCROFT, 1728 PRSad, *v.* gærs, croft. GREAT GRUFF, *v.* grōf 'stream-bed'. GREAVE. GREAVES, 1843 O.S., *v.* græfe 'copse'. GREEN ASH. GREEN BROW. GREENFIELD, 1642 WillY, *Grenefeld* 1323 *MinAcct* 45, *v.* grēne[1], feld. GREENFIELD BROOK, 1843 O.S. GREEN GRAIN. GREENMANS. GREEN OAK FM. GROVE HO, cf. *Grove-mill* 1750 PRSad.

HAIGH GUTTER. HALLS, *Hall's* 1731 PRSad. HANSON HO, *hanson hous* 1719 PRSad. HARROP COTE, HARROP EDGE, 1750 PRSad, HARROP GREEN, *v.* Harrop Dale *supra*, cot, ecg, grēne[2]. HAW CLOUGH. HAWK YARD, 1843 O.S., *Hauekeserd* l. 12 *Nost* 22d, *Haukeserd* e. 13 ib 66, *Hawkeyeard* 1613 *WB* 69, from the OE pers.n. *Hafoc*, geard. HAWTHORPE HALL. HAY BOTTOMS. HEARTH HILL FM. HEATHFIELDS, 1724 PRSad, *v.* hǣð, feld. HEIGHTS, 1843 O.S., *v.* hēhðu. HEZZLEGREAVE (local), *Hasilgref* 1297 LS,

v. hæsel, grǣfe 'copse'. HEY, 1725 PRSad, *Hay* 1771 M, *v.*
(ge)hæg. HEY BARN, 1734 PRSad. HEYS, 1722 PRSad, *Hawes*
1771 M, *v.* haga 'enclosure'. HIGH GROVE HO, 1843 O.S. HIGH
STILE. THE HILL, *Hill* 1379 PT (p). HILL END, 1747 PRSad.
HILLS FM, *Hills* 1746 PRSad. HILL TOP, *Hill-topp* 1733 PRSad.
HIND HILL, 1843 O.S., *v.* hind 'hind', hyll. HOAR CLOUGH, 1843
O.S., *v.* hār 'grey', clōh 'dell'. HOLDEN, *Holden's* 1739 PRSad.
HOLLIN BANK, *Holling-bank* 1743 PRSad, *Allen Bank* 1817 M, *Banks*
1843 O.S. HOLLIN BROWN KNOLL, *-Low* 1843 O.S. HOLLIN
HALL, 1735 PRSad, *v.* holegn 'holly'. HOLLIN HEYS. HOLLINS,
1728 PRSad, *v.* holegn 'holly'. HOLME CLOUGH, 1843 O.S., *Holme-*
clogh-hede 1468 SadD, *v.* holmr, clōh. HOREST FM. HOWELS HEAD,
Hawelshede 1468 SadD, *Owl's Head Hill* 1843 O.S. HULL BROOK,
1843 O.S. HUNTERS HILL, *Hunter-hill* 1744 PRSad. HUSTEADS,
1822 Langd, *Housesteads* 1737 PRSad, *v.* hūs, stede.

INTAKE, *Intack* 1737 PRSad, *v.* intak.

JUNCTION, 1817 M.

KILN GREEN. KINDERS, 1771 M, *Kindar's* 1727 PRSad, KINDER
STONES. KNARR, *Knar* 1724 PRSad, *v.* cnearr 'a rugged rock'.
KNOLL, 1736 PRSad, KNOLL TOP, 1729 ib, *Knowle Top* 1771 M, *v.*
cnoll 'hillock'. KNOTT HILL, 1544 SadD, *Cnothill* l. 12, e. 13 *Nost*
22d, 66, *Cnouthull* c. 1272 SadD, *Quotil* (sic) 1297 LS (p), *Knothill*
1617 FF, *Knotty Lane* 1771 M, *v.* knútr 'a rocky hill'. KNOWL,
1731 PRSad, *v.* cnoll.

LACEBY. LADCASTLE, 1728 PRSad, *v.* ladda, castel. LADDOW
MOSS, *Ladder Moss* 1843 O.S., *v.* ladda, haugr, mos 'swamp'.
LADHILL, *v.* prec. LAMB KNOLL. LANE HEAD, 1723 PRSad.
LARK HILL, 1843 O.S. LEE CROSS, 1732 PRSad, *Lee Croft* 1771
M, *v.* lēah, cros. LIFTREY DIKE. LINFITTS, 1817 M, LINTHWAITE,
Linthwaite(s) 1728, 1732 PRSad, *v.* līn, þveit, cf. Linthwaite 273
supra. LOAD CLOUGH. LONG CLOUGH, 1843 O.S., *v.* lang, clōh
'dell'. LONG RIDGE, 1843 O.S. LOW GATE LANE, 1843 O.S.
LUMB HOLE BROOK. LURDEN.

MANNS, *Man's* 1732 PRSad. MANTLEY (GATE), *Mantelawe* 1468
SadD, *Mantle Yate* 1771 M, *v.* hlāw 'hill'. MARLED EARTH,
Marledearthhead 1650 WillS, *v.* marlede, eorðe. MARSH, *March*
1843 O.S., *v.* mersc. MARSHLANDS, *Mescheland* (sic) 1379 PT (p),
Marshland 1843 O.S., *v.* mersc, land. MARTIN HO. MERE
CLOUGH, 1468 SadD, *v.* (ge)mǣre 'boundary', clōh 'dell'. MIDDLE
EDGE MOSS, 1810 *EnclA*, *v.* ecg, mos 'swamp'. MILL CROFT, 1843

O.S., *v.* myln, croft.　Moor Croft, 1735 PRSad, *v.* mōr, croft.
Moor Dale.　Moor Gate, 1843 O.S., *Moor-yate* 1728 PRSad,
Moor Lane, *Moor* 1771 M, *v.* mōr, geat.　Mountain Fm.　Mow
Walls Lane, *Mow-wall* 1738 PRSad.　Mytholme Bridge, prob-
ably as Mytholm Bridge 272 *supra*.

Nab End.　The Nook.　Noon Sun (Hill), *Noon Sun* 1741
PRSad, probably 'the house below the hill over which the noonday
sun appeared'.　North Clough, *Northclogh-hede* 1468 SadD, *v.*
norð, clōh.　North End.　Northern Rotcher, *v.* Rocher i, 226
supra.　Nut Bottom.

Oaken Hill & Lee, *Oaken-hill* 1750 PRSad, *Oaken Hill Lee* 1843
O.S., *v.* ācen, hyll.　Oak Hole.　Oaklands.　Old Hey, 1817
M, *v.* (ge)hæg 'enclosure'.　Old Horse Head Pile, 1843 O.S.
Oven Stones.　Ox Hey, 1843 O.S., *v.* oxa, (ge)hæg.　Ox Rake,
v. oxa, hraca 'track'.

Pennyworth, 1843 O.S.　Pickhill Brook.　Pike Ho.　Pilling Brook.　Pinfold, 1662 PRSad, *v.* pynd-fald.　Pingle Mill,
v. pingel 'enclosure'.　Platt Hill, *Platte* 1379 PT (p), *Platt Lane*
1743 PRSad, *Plot Hill* 1771 M, *v.* plat² 'plot of ground'.　Pob
Green, 1725 PRSad.　Pots & Pans, 1843 O.S., druidical stones.
Pottery Hill.　Priest Clough.

Rag Stone, *Wragstone* 1843 O.S.　Rams Clough, 1739 PRSad,
v. hræfn 'raven' or ramm 'ram', clōh.　Rapes (Hill), *The Reaps*
1843 O.S., *v.* Reap Hill 289 *supra*.　Raven Stones, 1843 O.S., *v.*
hræfn 'raven', stān.　Readycon Dean, *Redokindenhede* 1468 SadD,
Radycon Dean 1843 O.S., *v.* rēad 'red', ācen 'oaken', denu.　Reaps,
1843 O.S., *v.* Rapes *supra*.　Ridge, 1843 O.S., *v.* hrycg.　Rimmon
Pit Clough, 1843 O.S., *Rimmon Pit* 1468 SadD.　Rocher Moss,
v. Rocher i 226 *supra*, mos 'swamp'.　Rough Hey.　Rough Knarr,
cf. Knarr *supra*.　Round Hill, 1726 PRSad.　Royle Clough,
Rie-holes 1747 PRSad, *v.* rȳge, hol¹.　Running Hill, 1722 PRSad.
Rush Slack.　Rye Fields.　Rye Top, 1741 PRSad, *Royd Top*
1771 M, *v.* rȳge, topp.

Saddleworth Fold, 1725 PRSad, *Fold* 1843 O.S., *v.* fald.　Sail
Bark Rocks, *Seal Bark Rocks* 1843 O.S., probably 'willow bark
rocks', *v.* salh.　Salterhebble, 'salters' bridge', cf. Salterhebble iii,
110 *infra*; the road from south Lancashire to the Ryburn valley
crosses Hull Brook here, and was doubtless the old salters' way from
Cheshire.　Sandbed, 1817 M, *Sandybed-yate* 1726 PRSad.　Scout,
1843 O.S., *v.* skúti 'overhanging rock'.　Settstones Lane.　Sett-

LING WELL. SHAW GATE & ROCHER, *v.* Shaw Hall *supra.* SHAWS, 1843 O.S., *v.* sceaga 'copse'. SHEPHERDS GREEN, 1843 O.S. SHERBROOK, 1843 O.S., *v.* scīr[2] 'bright', brōc. SHIP FM, *Ship* 1843 O.S. SLACK (GATE & HEAD), 1771 M, *Slackyate* 1725 PRSad, *v.* slakki 'a hollow', geat. SLADES (BARN), 1817 M, *v.* slæd 'valley'. SLATE PIT MOSS, 1843 O.S., *v.* slate, pytt, mos 'swamp'. SOUTH CLOUGH, *Southclogh-hede* 1468 SadD, *v.* sūð, clōh. SPA CLOUGH. SPRING FIELD. SPRING HEAD, 1843 O.S. SPRING HILL. STABLE CLOUGH, *Stabilicloh* l. 12, e. 13 *Nost* 22d, 66, *Stabliclogh* c. 1272 SadD, ME *stable* 'stable, stall', clōh 'dell'. STAINS. STANDING STONES. LOWER & UPPER STONES, *Stones* 1730 PRSad, *Lower Stones* 1843 O.S. STUBBING. SUGAR LOAF. SUMMER HILL. SUNFIELD, 1734 PRSad, 'sunny field'. SWAINSCROFT FM, *Swaynscroft* 1544 SadD, *Swinescroft* 1643 WillY, probably the ME pers.n. *Swain* (ON *Sveinn*), croft.

TAME CROFT, 1738 PRSad, *v.* foll. NEW & OLD TAME, 1729, 1732 PRSad, 1771 M, named from R. Tame (RNs.). TAME WATER, 1723 PRSad, *v.* prec., wæter. TANG, *Fang* (sic) 1843 O.S., probably from OE þwang 'thong, strip of land' (as in Netherthong 286 *supra*), with dial. *f*- for *th*-. THE THORNS, *Thorns* 1726 PRSad, *v.* þorn. THURSTON CLOUGH, 1736 PRSad, probably the ME pers.n. *Thurston* (ON *Þorsteinn*), clōh. THURSTONS, *Thurstones* 1734 PRSad, *Thurstlands* 1771 M, *Thorstones* 1843 O.S., probably connected with prec. TUNSTEAD, *Tunsted* 1658 WillS, 1724 PRSad, 'farmstead', *v.* tūn-stede. TURNER HILL. TURNEY BANK, *Turnilbanke* 1426 *Ramsd*, *Turnelbanke* 1461 *MinAcct* 09, 'round hill bank', *v.* trūn, hyll, banke.

UPPER MILL, 1730 PRSad. UPPERWOOD HO, *Up[r] Wood House* 1843 O.S., *Wood-house* 1722 PRSad.

WADE HILL, 1771 M. WAIN STONES, 1843 O.S., *v.* wægn, stān. WALL HILL, *Wall(e)hill* 1624 WB 70, 1646 WillY, *v.* wall 'wall', hyll. WARLOW PIKE, 1843 O.S., *Harelowe* 1468 SadD, *v.* hār 'grey, boundary', hlāw 'mound, hill', pīc[1] 'pointed hill'. WARMSEY CLOUGH. WARROCK HILL, 1843 O.S., *Warrack-hill* 1728 PRSad, possibly connected with dial. *warrick* 'to chain down' (as timber on a wagon) or the ME surname *Warrock* (Reaney 343). WARTH MILLS, *v.* varða 'a cairn'. WATER CLOUGH. WATERS, 1722 PRSad, *Water (Coit)* 1771 M, *v.* wæter, cot 'cottage'. WATERSIDE, 1749 PRSad. WEAKEY, 1843 O.S., *Wakey* 1817 M. WELL HEAD, 1740 PRSad. WELLIHOLE, 1724 PRSad, *Holi Hole* 1817 M. WHAM,

1843 O.S., *v.* hvammr 'small valley'. WHAMS, 1749 PRSad, *v.* prec. WHARMTON, *Warmton* 1817 M, 1843 O.S., *Wharntonbrow* 1724 PRSad, *v.* cweorn 'mill', tūn, cf. Quarmby 301 *supra*. WHITE BROOK, *Wytibroke* e. 13 *Nost* 66, *Whitebrok* c. 1272 SadD, *v.* hwīt 'white', brōc. WHITE GATE. WHITE HO. WHITE LEE, 1656 WillS, *v.* hwīt, lēah. WIBSEY. WICKEN CLOUGH, 1843 O.S., cf. Wicking Clough 281 *supra*. WICKENS, 1725 PRSad, *v.* prec. WILD-CAT LOW, 1843 O.S., *v.* hlāw 'hill'. WILDERNESS, 1843 O.S. WIMBERRY STONES, 1843 O.S. WOOD, 1723 PRSad, *v.* wudu. WOODBROW, 1738 PRSad. WOODMANS, *Woodman's* 1724 PRSad. WOOLLEYS. WOOLROAD, 1725 PRSad.

YARNS HILL, probably earn 'eagle', hyll. YEOMAN HEY. YEW TREE, 1726 PRSad.

FIELD-NAMES

Spellings dated without source are SadD. Springhead f.ns. are included here.

(*a*) Barn 1736 PRSad, Bed 1771 M, Brook-Bottom 1822 Langd, Chapel Heights 1822 Langd, Chicken Clough Moss 1810 *EnclA* 65, Coit 1771 M (*v.* cot), Fould 1817 M (*v.* fald), Green 1734 PRSad, Groan 1771 M, Hob-hole 1738 PRSad (*v.* hob 'goblin', hol[1]), Midge Grove 1771 M, Ormsrake 1791 Sad (*Ormesrake* 1468, from the ON pers.n. *Ormr*, hraca 'rough path'), Ridding 1843 O.S. (*v.* rydding), Rocking-Stone 1822 Langd, Rocks of Greenfield 1822 ib, Woodwardhill 1792 PRSad (ib 1468, ME *wodeward* 'forester').

(*b*) *Ashenbenthe* 1544 (*v.* æscen, beonet 'place growing with bent-grass'), *Coldegrefehyll* 1468 (*v.* cald, grǣfe 'copse'), *Cumbroch, -brok* l. 12, e. 13 *Nost* 22d, 66, *Combesbrok* c. 1272 (*v.* cumb 'valley', brōc), *Rowtandlode* 1468 (OE *hrūtand* 'roaring', (ge)lād 'stream'), *Swinistker* e. 13 *Nost* 65d ('pig-sty marsh', *v.* swīn, stigu, kjarr), *Wessherroide* 1487 WCR 1 (ME *wasshere* 'washer (of sheep)', rod[1]).

2. SPRINGHEAD (101–9604)

Springhead 1825 PRSad, apparently a modern name.

ASHES LANE, *Ashes* 1747 PRSad, *v.* æsc. ASHFIELD HO. AUSTER-LANDS, 1771 M, *Osterlands* 1722 PRSad, probably from eowestre 'sheep-fold', land. BACK O' TH' LOW, *Back o'th Lowe* 1732 PRSad, *v.* hlāw. BAR STACKS. BLACK LEACH, *v.* blæc, læcc 'stream, bog'. BLUNDER HALL. BROWN HILL, 1744 PRSad, *v.* brūn, hyll. BUTT FM. CABIN, 1724 PRSad. CARRHOUSE FM, *Carr-house* 1738 PRSad, *v.* kjarr 'marsh', hūs. CLAYTONS, 1740 PRSad. CLOUGH

HEAD.   COOKCROFT.   COLD HO.   COVER HILL, 1722 PRSad. CRAWSHAW BENT, *Crowshaw Bent* 1737 PRSad, 1771 M, 'crow copse', *v.* crāwe, sceaga, beonet 'bent-grass'.   DEN HILL, *v.* Den Quarries 313 *supra*.   DOCTOR HO, *Doctor-house* 1726 PRSad, *Doctors Houses* 1817 M, cf. 'Old Doctor Buckley's wife buried here' 1728 PRSad, 358 (the wife of James Buckley, apothecary of Oldham La). EARNSHAW HEAD, 1732 PRSad, cf. *John Earnshaw* 1716 ib 16. GREEN LEACH, 1817 M, *v.* grēne[1], læcc 'stream, bog'.   GROTTON, 1379 PT (p), 1607 FF, 1662 PRSad, *Groton* 1531 SadD, possibly OE *grota* 'particle of sand' or groten 'gravelly, sandy', tūn.   GROTTON HEAD, 1748 PRSad, *v.* prec.   HARBOUR HILL, *v.* here-beorg 'shelter'.   HERDS LOW.   HIGH LEE.   HIGH MOOR, 1594 SadD, 1725 PRSad.   INTAKE.   KNOWSLEY.   LANE, 1817 M.   LOAD HILL, 1734 PRSad, *v.* lād 'water-course', hyll.   LOAD HILL PLATTING, 1745 PRSad, *Plotting* 1771 M, dial. *platting* 'a small footbridge' as in Miles Platting La (Ekwall, PN -ing 25).   LOWBROOK.   LYDGATE, 1817 M, *Lydiate* 1729 PRSad, *v.* hlid-geat 'swing-gate'.   MASON ROW.   NEW HOUSES, 1722 PRSad.   NEW ROYD, *New Road Head* 1771 M, *v.* nīwe, rod[1].   THE PASTURES, *Pastures* 1748 Sad, *v.* pasture.   QUICK EDGE FM, *Quick(e)-edge* 1594 SadD, 1722 PRSad, named from Quick Edge (La), cf. Quick 312 *supra*, from which it is, however, distinct.   RED HO.   ROEBUCK LOW, 1729 PRSad, *v.* hlāw 'hill'.   ROUND HILL.   SCOUT HEAD, 1736 PRSad, *v.* skúti 'overhanging rock'.   SHELDERSLOW, 1531 SadD, 1725 PRSad, *Skelderslow* 1822 Langd, from ON skjaldari 'shield-maker' (perhaps as a surname), hlāw 'hill, mound'.   STONE BREAKS, 1724 PRSad, probably stān and bræc[1], dial. *breck* 'uncultivated strip' or brekka 'slope'.   STRINES, 1722 PRSad, *Strinds* 1662 ib, *v.* strind 'stream'.   THORNLEE, 1740 PRSad, *Thorneley* 1662 ib, *v.* þorn, lēah.   HIGHER & LOWER THORPS, *Thorp's* 1738 PRSad, *v.* þorp 'outlying farmstead'.   WALKERS, *Walker's* 1738 PRSad.   WARM HOLE.   WHITE GATES.   WINDY HARBOUR, *v.* wind, -ig, here-beorg 'shelter, lodging'.   WOOD BROOK, 1722 PRSad.

INDEX OF TOWNSHIPS IN PART II

Ackton, 85
Ackworth, 93
Adlingfleet, 2
Airmyn, 13
Almondbury, 256
Altofts, 119
Ardsley East and West, 174
Askern, 44
Austonley, 263

Badsworth, 96
Balne, 14
Batley, 179
Beal, 55
Bramwith, Kirk, 29
Bretton, West, 99
Burghwallis, 35

Campsall, 45
Carleton, 71
Cartworth, 236
Castleford, 69
Cridling Stubbs, 61
Crigglestone, 101
Crofton, 113
Crosland, South, 265
Cumberworth, 216

Dalton, 223
Darrington, 63
Dewsbury, 184

Eastoft, 4
Eggborough, 57
Elmsall, North, 36
Elmsall, South, 39
Emley, 218

Farnley Tyas, 267
Featherstone, 86
Fenwick, 47
Flockton, 203
Fockerby, 5
Fryston, Ferry, 65
Fulstone, 239

Golcar, 291
Goole, 16

Goole Fields, 16
Gowdall, 17

Haldenby, 6
Hardwick, East, 72
Hardwick, West, 88
Heck, 18
Hensall, 19
Hepworth, 242
Hessle, 89
Holme, 269
Honley, 271
Hook, 20
Horbury, 150
Houghton, Glass, 70
Huddersfield, 295
Huntwick, 90

Kellington, 59
Kirkburton, 245
Kirkby, South, 40
Kirkhamgate, 154
Kirkheaton, 225
Knottingley, 73

Lepton, 229
Lindley, 300
Linthwaite, 273
Lockwood, 275
Lofthouse, 136
Longwood, 302
Lupset, 155

Marsden, 276
Meltham, 282
Methley, 125
Middleton, 139
Mirfield, 197
Morley, 182
Moss, 48

Netherthong, 286
Newland, 121
Normanton, 121
Norton, 49

Ossett, 188
Oulton, 141

Ousefleet, 7
Outwood, 156
Owston, 31

Pollington, 21
Pontefract, 75
Pontefract Park, 83
Purston Jaglin, 87

Ravensthorpe, 192
Rawcliffe, 22
Reedness, 9
Rothwell, 143

Saddleworth, 310
Sandal Magna, 107
Scammonden, 304
Scholes, 247
Sharlston, 114
Shelley, 248
Shepley, 250
Shitlington, 205
Skelbrooke, 43
Skellow, 34
Skelmanthorpe, 221
Slaithwaite, 307
Smeaton, Kirk, 51
Smeaton, Little, 52
Snaith, 25

Snydale, 122
Soothill, Nether, 193
Soothill, Upper, 196
Springhead, 318
Stanley, 159
Stapleton, 65
Stubbs, Hamphall, 43
Stubbs, Walden, 53
Sutton, 50
Swinefleet, 10

Tanshelf, 83
Thornhill, 210
Thorpe Audlin, 97
Thorpe on the Hill, 149
Thurstonland, 251

Upperthong, 288
Upton, 98

Wakefield, 163
Walton, 112
Warmfield, 117
Whitgift, 11
Whitley, 60
Whitley, Upper, 233
Whitwood, 124
Womersley, 54
Wooldale, 253